AMERICAN TRINITY

JEFFERSON, CUSTER, AND THE SPIRIT OF THE WEST

INTO THE WEST

AMERICAN TRINITY

JEFFERSON, CUSTER, AND THE SPIRIT OF THE WEST

LARRY LEN PETERSON
Recipient of the 2016 C. M. Russell Heritage Award

Other Books by Larry Len Peterson:

Charles M. Russell, Legacy: Printed and Published Works of Montana's Cowboy Artist
    (Helena and Great Falls, MT, 1999)
A Most Desperate Situation: Frontier Adventures of a Young Scout 1858-1864, Walter Cooper
    (Helena, MT, 2000, 2001)
Philip R. Goodwin: America's Sporting and Wildlife Artist
    (Hayden, ID, 2001; Missoula, MT, 2007)
The Call of the Mountains: The Artists of Glacier National Park
    (Tucson, AZ, 2002)
L. A. Huffman: Photographer of the American West
    (Tucson, AZ, 2003; Missoula, MT, 2005 and 2013)
Charles M. Russell: Printed Rarities from Private Collections
    (Missoula, MT, 2008)
Halfway to Midnight
    (Missoula, MT, 2011)
Charles M. Russell: Photographing the Legend, A Biography in Words and Pictures
    (Norman, OK; Tulsa, OK; Great Falls, MT, 2014)
John Fery: Artist of Glacier National Park and the American West
    (Hayden, ID, 2015)

Front Dust Jacket Cover: *Seeking the White Man's Book*, 1912, oil, 36" x 24", Edgar S. Paxson (1852-1919).
Frontispiece, ii: *Into The West*, 1913, pen & ink, 17" x 13", Charles M. Russell (1864-1926).
Back Dust Jacket Cover: *Cheyenne Chief Two Moon on Custer's Hill: 25th Anniversary of the Battle*, 1901, hand-colored photograph, 10" x 14", L.A. Huffman (1854-1931).
Above courtesy of the Big Sky Collection, Larry and LeAnne Peterson.
Front End Sheet: *Buffalo Grazing The Big Open North Montana 1880*.
Back End Sheet: *Sioux Chief Spotted Eagle's Hostile Camp, Tongue River, Mont. Dec. 1879*.
Both End Sheets, hand-colored photomurals, 3' x 5', L.A. Huffman (1854-1931), courtesy of Bev and Gene Allen.

Peterson, Larry Len, author
American Trinity, Jefferson, Custer, & the Spirit of the West
Print ISBN 978-1-59152-188-4
epub ISBN 978-1-59152-205-8
mobi ISBN 978-1-59152-206-5
Copyright 2017 by Larry Len Peterson

Library of Congress Cataloging-in-Publication Data

Names: Peterson, Larry Len, author.
Title: American trinity: Jefferson, Custer & the spirit of the West
  / by Larry Len Peterson.
Other titles: American trinity: Jefferson, Custer and the spirit of the West
Description: Helena, Montana : Sweetgrass Books, 2017. | Includes
  bibliographical references and index.
Identifiers: LCCN 2017004162 | ISBN 9781591521884 (hardcover : alkaline paper)
Subjects: LCSH: Indians of North America--West (U.S.)--History. | Indians,
  Treatment of--West (U.S.)--History. | Jefferson, Thomas,
  1743-1826--Political and social views. | Jefferson, Thomas,
  1743-1826--Relations with Indians. | Custer, George A. (George Armstrong),
  1839-1876--Political and social views. | Custer, George A. (George
  Armstrong), 1839-1876--Relations with Indians. | Manifest Destiny. |
  Imperialism--Religious aspects--Christianity--History. | West
  (U.S.)--Discovery and exploration. | West (U.S.)--Race relations--History.
Classification: LCC E78.W5 P47 2017 | DDC 978.004/97--dc23
LC record available at https://lccn.loc.gov/2017004162

All rights reserved. No part of this publication may be reproduced, stored in a retrieval system, or transmitted, in any form or by any means, electronic, mechanical, photocopying, recording, or otherwise—except as permitted under Section 107 or 108 of the United States Copyright Act—without the prior written permission of Larry Len Peterson. To request permission to reproduce selections from this book, write to Sweetgrass Books, PO Box 5630, Helena, MT 59604

sweetgrassbooks
an imprint of Farcountry Press

Produced by Sweetgrass Books
PO Box 5630; Helena, MT 59604

Produced in the United States of America.

Printed in Canada.

*Dedicated to the Great Plains,
Home to the Spirit of the West*

All royalties from the sale of this book will be donated to the Montana Historical Society to provide travel scholarships for reservation schools to bring students to Helena to visit the Society under the direction of Kirby Lambert, Outreach and Interpretation Program Manager

Thus, it seems that generals win battles; politicians run countries; scientists discover truths; artists create genres; inventors make breakthroughs; teachers shape minds; philosophers change minds; priests teach morality; businessmen lead businesses; conspirators cause crisis; gods make morality.
—MATT RIDLEY, *THE EVOLUTION OF EVERYTHING*

Table of Contents

Preface and Acknowledgments ... ix
Introduction ... xvii

Part I *The Searchers: Finding Each Other*

CHAPTER ONE: *Out of Africa: Origin of the Races* ... 3

CHAPTER TWO: *When the West Belonged to God: Discovering the New World Before Columbus* ... 17

CHAPTER THREE: *Lost Souls in Revelry: Collision of Races* ... 31

CHAPTER FOUR: *Create Humanity and Conquer Nature: The British Invasion* ... 47

CHAPTER FIVE: *American Exodus: Survival on the Plains* ... 63

CHAPTER SIX: *The Blind Healing the Blind: White Medicine Men* ... 79

CHAPTER SEVEN: *Weapons of Mass Destruction: Infectious Disease* ... 99

Part II *The Mystery: Clash of Spirits*

CHAPTER EIGHT: *The World is Not Enough: Cultural Literacy for Religion* ... 127

CHAPTER NINE: *The Spirit of the West: Native American Religion and Its Chroniclers* ... 139

CHAPTER TEN: *Smoking to the Spirit of the Buffalo: Plains Indian Ceremonies and Rituals* ... 167

CHAPTER ELEVEN: *The Language of God: Indian Myths, Legends, and Their Chroniclers* ... 191

CHAPTER TWELVE: *The Way: Historical Christianity to the Dark Ages* ... 221

CHAPTER THIRTEEN: *The Faith of Our Fathers: Religion in America* ... 245

Part III *Thomas Jefferson: Winning the West*

CHAPTER FOURTEEN: *A Revolution: The Enlightenment, Scientific Revolution, and the Romantic Movement* ... 271

CHAPTER FIFTEEN: *All Men are Created Equal: Thomas Jefferson and His Legacy* ... 291

CHAPTER SIXTEEN: *Father of the American West: Thomas Jefferson and the Corps of Discovery* ... 313

CHAPTER SEVENTEEN: *Father of the Removal Policy: Thomas Jefferson and the Doctrine of Discovery* ... 331

CHAPTER EIGHTEEN: *Manifest Destiny: If God is for Us, Then Who Could Ever Stop Us?* ... 349

CHAPTER NINETEEN: *Cleansing the West: Religion, Guns, and Romance* ... 371

CHAPTER TWENTY: *The Descent of Man: Scientific Racism* ... 401

CHAPTER TWENTY-ONE: *Survival of the Fittest: Charles Darwin Explains Evolution* ... 419

Part IV *The Golden Rule, or the Golden-Ruled? Custer: The Son of the American West*

CHAPTER TWENTY-TWO: *The Better Angels of Our Nature: Custer and the Fight to Make the Union Whole* ... 443

CHAPTER TWENTY-THREE: *A Civil War Legend Unleashed: Custer Revealed* ... 471

CHAPTER TWENTY-FOUR: *American Idols: Grant and Custer After the Civil War* ... 489

CHAPTER TWENTY-FIVE: *Son of the American West: Custer, O Fallen Star* ... 511

CHAPTER TWENTY-SIX: *The Children of Manifest Destiny and Shifting Shadows: Education to Kill the Indian* ... 547

CHAPTER TWENTY-SEVEN: *Lamentations of the Fall: Genocide, Ethnic Cleansing, and Post-Traumatic Stress Disorder* ... 581

Notes ... 601
Bibliography ... 647
Index ... 679

Preface & Acknowledgments

No one cares how much you know, until they know how much you care.
—THEODORE ROOSEVELT

We were back trailing on the old frontier on June 25, 2001—the 125th anniversary of the Battle of the Little Bighorn. It was a grand day. My history-loving friend Jim Bennett and I were heading north on the highway from Sheridan, Wyoming, where we were attending the Little Big Horn Associates annual meeting. At the entrance to the Little Bighorn Battlefield National Monument, the ranger handed us commemorative brochures that featured my 1901 L. A. Huffman photograph of Two Moon at the 25th anniversary (see back dust jacket cover). I purchased a *True West* commemorative magazine and a copy of *Lakota Noon* that Gregory F. Michno personally autographed. Next, my other historian heroes graciously signed my commemorative envelope: Brian W. Dippie, Jerome A. Greene, Paul L. Hedren, Paul Andrew Hutton, Neil C. Magnum, and Robert M. Utley. Together, they are my "Magnificent Seven." An added bonus was visiting with one of the great editors and nicest persons of the West, Chuck Rankin of the University of Oklahoma Press. Will Rogers—part Cherokee and a 100-percent American—said, "A man only learns by two things, one is reading, and the other is associating with smarter people." Reading forces you to imagine, question, and reflect. I had done the reading, and on that memorable day I had the good fortune to hang out with smarter people.

Brice C. Custer—George was his great uncle—signed my Michno book, as did George A. Custer IV, Brice's nephew. That was followed by exploring the battlefield with the superintendent, and for the first time I felt like I grasped what had unfolded on that legendary day. As the sun marched west, a hundred mounted Indians thundered up Custer Hill whooping all the way—a heart-thumping moment in time. It was a bittersweet experience.

I have been haunted by the question: who were we and who are we as Americans and a nation? I believe a nation is defined by the people who create its history, and they are remembered by the authors who write their biographies. Reflecting on that era and all its symbolic meaning, I've wrestled with explanations to make sense of why the Indian's way of life was destroyed and what authority justified it. That question awakes afresh every time I pass by a painting that hangs in the entrance to our home. It is Edgar S. Paxson's 1912 oil masterwork *Seeking the White Man's Book,* a painting inspired by the story of Montana Indians in the 1830s trekking all the way to St. Louis to bring Christianity back to their homeland (see front dust jacket cover). Was this just a legend or was it true? Why would Native Americans who were already deeply religious want to embrace Christianity? What role did Christianity play in our attitudes toward people of color? Was the painting just another twentieth-century racist attempt at minimizing the white man's destruction of the Indian's way of life? Was it historical airbrushing? I've looked for answers for many years now.

For me, Graceland is not Memphis, Tennessee. It is the Great Plains. This perception has always been about the land and the sky. In *Wolf Willow* (1962), Wallace Stegner said, "The drama of this landscape is in the sky, pouring with light and always moving. The earth is passive. And yet the beauty I am struck by, both as present fact and as revived memory, is a fusion; this sky would not be so spectacular without this earth to change and glow and darken under it." Well said Mr. Stegner. Similarly, Ivan Doig, in *This House of Sky: Landscapes of a Western Mind* (1978), also understood what we Montana natives appreciate when he said, "I glance higher for some hint of the weather, and the square of air broadens and broadens to become the blue expanse over the Montana rangeland, so vast and vaulting that it rears, from the foundation-line of the plains horizon, to form the walls and roof of all life's experience that my younger self could imagine, a single great house of sky."

In many ways, humans are defined by place. The town of Plentywood, Montana, hugs the Canadian and North Dakota borders close to the Medicine Line and Fort Union. Our garden was wheat, and the river that ran through it was the Missouri. The land was scattered with self-reliant German and Scandinavian farmers and ranchers. The weather was harsh—a fact every American seems to know. Biting cold whipped across the scalloped snow underneath the breadth of a fresh prairie sky without pause.

It was always winter but seemed never Christmas. Brief in appearance, the summer brought blowing soil and blistering heat. At times, the town looked more like a setting from a dust bowl museum. Even so, homes might be far apart but good neighbors were not far away.

The countryside around my hometown provided childhood fantasy. Prairie sweetgrass sprinkled with prickly pears painted the badlands, which provided the foundation for long-abandoned Indian tipi rings—circular rock formations that, in a different world, held the Indians' dwellings in place—that ignited my imagination of a passing way of life. Sitting Bull himself trudged through this land before his final days were confined to the reservation. Unfortunately, our county was named after Phil Sheridan, who said, "The only good Indians I ever saw were dead," which later morphed into the infamous observation that, "The only good Indian is a dead one." I believe that, until you spend a dozen winters on the Northern Plains, you have really no appreciation for what hardships Native Americans endured. I greatly admire their grit. A summer outing just won't cut it.

Next door was the Fort Peck Indian Reservation where new battles were fought in my youth on the athletic field and in the gym. All we knew about Indian history came from the cowboy and Indian movies of the 1950s and 1960s, a genre based on shaky facts, lies, myths, and legends. The reservation was close but a world apart. But my interest in Native American history has never waned.

I began this project a number of years ago. Hundreds of books and articles strewn all over my library were abandoned at times as I completed biographies on Charles M. Russell, L. A. Huffman, John Fery, and a novel, *Halfway to Midnight,* dedicated to my hometown for its 100th anniversary. Americans need to read stories to understand what makes us Americans. We should appreciate the printed word. Stories galvanize us into one nation. However, our country is not defined by publications on history, philosophy, science, medicine, religion, or ethnicity, but about the ideas that flow out of them—lots of ideas.

We write to understand, and I hope we read for the same reason. When that happens, the writer and the reader share a connection. They see the same truth. I needed to write about this vast subject to understand. But writing about this topic was not a natural act. Charles Darwin observed, "Man has an instinctive tendency to speak, as we see in the babble of our young children, whereas no child has an instinctive tendency to bake, brew, and write." Why should I care so much about Native American history, their stories? Because the narrative affected my land, challenged my understanding of Western history, and reflected core truths about human values—especially American ones—and answered some of the questions.

Our way of understanding the world must constantly be scrutinized for hidden cultural biases. For me, there was no defined premise as when a scientist conducts an experiment to test a theory to which he's already committed. In past years, as a scientific and medical researcher, I've been down that road many times. But here, as a writer, I didn't start with any prior convictions about what authority or who specifically to blame for the racist treatment of Native Americans, and I believe I've been reasonably objective as far as one can be. Culture always influences our historical filters. My goal was not about painting a black door black or painting a white door black but about capturing portraits over time of a door of many colors. I only looked so far ahead because the story was very far from planned in the exact sense. At times, I felt like a frontiersman searching in strange and unknown territory. This is a big book because the story is big and can't be condensed, and it's too important to me to be ignored. And if it makes even a small contribution, that seemed to be worth the effort. You can be the judge.

One book more than any other inspired this publication. It is the landmark *The Vanishing American: White Attitudes & U.S. Indian Policy* (1982) by my dear friend, emeritus history professor at the University of Victoria, Dr. Brian W. Dippie. It is my favorite idea book on the American West. At the time of its publication, the *Canadian Review of American Studies* called the *Vanishing American*, "The best study of American cultural attitudes regarding the Indian produced to date. Written in a clear and enjoyable style." It still is. While Dr. Dippie presented white attitudes and policies toward Indians, *American Trinity* attempts to explain why and how they came about. He has also written landmark books on Custer, Charles M. Russell, Frederic Remington, and George Catlin, among others. Our paths met many years ago because of our mutual love for Montana's most famous citizen, the incomparable western painter, Charles M. Russell. In one evening of conversation with Dr. Dippie, a lifetime of knowledge and friendship was gained.

As I began the journey, I discovered what an important role philosophy played in racism. It came in the form of idealism, realism, the philosophy of the Enlightenment, the Doctrine of Discovery, Manifest Destiny, and social Darwinism, among others. Fortunately, for several decades I was under the tutelage of Dr. Harold "Skip" Grover, Jr. who received his Ph.D. in public administration with a special emphasis in organization and management theory from George Washington University. His B.A. was a double major in history and political science, and his masters was in international relations and policy. Skip is a deep thinker, an idea man, and as Eleanor Roosevelt commented, great minds talk about ideas. The kinds of books he fed me were challenging and provocative, as were our lengthy conversations.

If there was one revelation in researching this book, it was how important religion was in turning history again and again in certain directions. ISIS has made that clear to an ever increasingly secular West that is in denial of that truth. For centuries, the brilliant were polymaths—European Renaissance men who knew and appreciated much about many different disciplines. Whether it was science, medicine, philosophy, or the arts, I was surprised to discover that the brightest often were ordained in the Christian ministry, which led to both good and bad outcomes.

Religion is a topic that evokes strong emotion. Most authors avoid it unless they are Christian writers, even though science, medicine, philosophy, and religion are often interconnected—many times unknowingly. In *God is Red: A Native View of Religion* (1972), Vine Deloria, Jr. presented a brilliant essay comparing Native American religious views to Christianity. It is a must read for anyone who wants to understand the history of the American West. It inspired me to dig deeply into Christian and Indian religions. I felt comfortable writing about science and medicine, less so about philosophy, but religion was challenging.

A few years back, a lifelong friend of mine declared that religion was the source of all evil, and he didn't think Jesus ever existed. In his reasoning, Jesus was just a myth—the opiate of society as Karl Marx said. Really? Hitler, Stalin, and Mao weren't religious men and were responsible for the death of over 100 million humans in the twentieth century. And there is historical documentation that Jesus indeed walked this Earth.

Opposed to my friend's opinion are some of my other friends who are devoted evangelical Christians. Thus, over the last fifteen years, I have searched for the historical Jesus and the truth about Christianity—not man's interpretation of it. Coming to my aid were three people who have mentored me in many invaluable ways.

One of the finest and wisest attorneys in Oregon, Don Carter is a devoted Christian who currently serves on the board of directors at George Fox University in Newberg, Oregon, and he is also on their academic advisory board. In the past, he served as seminary board chairman and chairman of the board at Rolling Hills Community Church in Tualatin, Oregon. *Forbes* ranks George Fox among the top ten "Best Religiously Affiliated Colleges" in the nation. Don's gracious wife, Faith, is past director of the global outreach program at Rolling Hills Community Church, one of the largest churches on the West Coast. Knowing my interest in learning more about devotional, historical, and theological Christianity, she provided me with a vast number of academic textbooks from her course work completed several years ago at George Fox, where she received a master's of art in ministry leadership. My insightful wife, LeAnne, studied with me and also provided invaluable insights on Christianity. The four of us have spent many hours exploring faith and religion.

My friend and retired Federal Administrative Law Judge Riley Atkins has been very supportive of this project and introduced me to a colleague and friend of his, Robert J. Miller, who wrote the brilliant 2006 book *Native America, Discovered and Conquered: Thomas Jefferson, Lewis & Clark, and Manifest Destiny*, on the Doctrine of Discovery. He is an enrolled citizen of the Eastern Shawnee Tribe of Oklahoma. Currently, he is a professor at the Sandra Day O'Connor College of Law at Arizona State University where he teaches a number of Indian law classes and civil procedure. I appreciate his support, and the informative conversations I have had with him.

After studying dozens of books on Custer—Son of the American West—over the years, I concluded that he is intriguing not only because he is America's failed representative out West, but also because, to some, he symbolizes America's racist views toward Native Americans. Right during the time I was working on Part IV and Custer, in October 2015, T. J. Stiles published *Custer's Trials: A Life on the Frontier of a New America*. It was reassuring that Stiles came to conclusions similar to mine. His book went on to win the Pulitzer Prize in history. It is the finest biography I have read in many years, and it came along just at the right time for me. It is a must read.

American Trinity includes more than 1,600 endnotes and a bibliography with hundreds of entries—over 170 published in the last three years alone—but I want to highlight some of them that I haven't mentioned for high praise and to urge you to read them. The authors are mostly contemporary, and their scholarship has been very helpful to me on this project:

Part I: Jared Diamond, *Guns, Germs, and Steel;* Charles C. Mann, *1491;* Roger L. Nichols, *American Indians in U.S. History;* Colin G. Calloway, *One Vast Winter Count;* Edwin Gaustad and Leigh Schmidt, *The Religious History of America;* Robert F. Berkhofer, Jr., *The White Man's Indian;* Peter Nabokov, *Native American Testimony;* Rodney Stark, *How the West Won;* Elizabeth A. Fenn, *Encounters at the Heart of the World;* and Paul Kelton, *Cherokee Medicine, Colonial Germs.*

Part II: Nassim Nicholas Taleb, *The Black Swan;* Francis S. Collins, *The Language of God;* Richard Twiss, *One Church, Many Tribes;* Thomas E. Mails, *The Mystic Warriors of the Plains;* Vine Deloria, Jr., *God is Red;* Randy S. Woodley, *Shalom and the Community of Creation;* Robert M. Utley, *The Lance and The Shield;* Bart D. Ehrman, *Did Jesus Exist?;* Roger E. Olson, *The Story of Christian Theology;* Nancy Pearcey, *Total Truth;* Stephen Prothero, *American Jesus;* and Jon Meacham, *American Gospel.*

Part III: Jon Meacham, *Thomas Jefferson;* Harry R. Rubenstein and Barbara Clark Smith, *The Jefferson Bible;* Stephen E. Ambrose, *Undaunted Courage;* James P. Ronda, *Lewis and Clark Among the Indians;* Amy S. Greenberg, *Manifest Destiny and American Territorial Expansion;* Dan Flores, *American Serengeti* and *Visions of the Big Sky;* and Keith Thomson, *Private Doubt, Public Dilemma.*

Part IV: Geoffrey Ward, Ric Burns, and Ken Burns, *The Civil War;* Doris Kearns Goodwin, *Team of Rivals;* H. W. Brands, *The Man Who Saved the Union;* Stephen E. Ambrose, *Crazy Horse and Custer;* Paul Andrew Hutton, *The Apache Wars* and *Phil Sheridan and His Army;* Jerome A. Greene, *American Carnage;* Gary Clayton Anderson, *Ethnic Cleansing and the Indian;* Ward Churchill, *Kill the Indian, Save the Man;* David Wallace Adams, *Education for Extinction;* and Peter Cozzens, *The Earth is Weeping.*

Others who have answered my call include: Gene Allen, Dr. Robert Amon, Jennifer Bottomly-O'Looney, Duane Braaten, Gus Chambers, Jim Combs, Rodric Coslet, Dr. Michael D. Duchemin, Steven A. Eckhart, Jack Gladstone, Molly Holz, John Howard, Kirby Lambert, David Mihalic, Tom Minckler, John Murphy, Doug Nelson, Tom Petrie, Trevor Rees-Jones, Tom Nygard, Lorne Render, Steven Schmidt, Neil Snyder, Dave Solberg, Dr. Rick Stewart, Curtis Tierney, Emily Wilson, Bruce Wittenberg, and Paul Zalis. Thanks also to Bob Drummond, Mike Overby, Stu Johnson, and Peter Stremmel at the Coeur d'Alene Art Auction for their support of many of my book publications. Stuart Rosebrook at *True West* magazine is much appreciated for his passion and promotion of books on the American West. Special thanks to noted western author Candy Moulton, dedicated executive director of the Western Writers of America and their outstanding *Roundup* magazine. Also, my admiration goes out to Richard Edwards, Director of the Center for Great Plains Studies at the University of Nebraska-Lincoln. He grew up near me across the border in Stanley, North Dakota. His deeply personal memoir, *Natives of a Dry Place: Stories of Dakota before the Oil Boom,* is dear to my heart, and I appreciate the signed copy he sent me. Special thanks to everyone associated with the Buffalo Bill Center of the West, Gilcrease Museum, Montana Historical Society, Charles M. Russell Museum, and the National Cowboy and Western Heritage Museum.

It was important that this publication was a product of the Great Plains. Sweetgrass Books, an imprint of Farcountry Press, in Helena, Montana, did an outstanding job. I would like to thank Kathy Springmeyer, director of publications, for her truly professional handling of this project, attention to detail, and exemplary communication skills. Also, much appreciation to the talented senior editor and polymath Will Harmon who made this a much better read in many ways. Will became not only an editor but a mentor. Designer Shirley Machonis made my vision of how the book should look come to stunning reality. I would like to thank Ann Seifert for her stellar proofreading job. Much gratitude to another team member, Judy Staigmiller, for producing a very informative index. Friesen Printers in Manitoba on the Canadian prairies manufactured this publication and my last two art books—all three high-quality products.

Love to my daughter Haley and her husband James Hostetler, daughter Lara and her husband Pat Fuchs, and sisters Linda Zuber and Cathy Hensel. Thanks to my constant companions, Vizsla dogs Beau and Abby, along with horses Big Sky and Sunny out in the pasture. Most importantly, thanks again and love to my wife LeAnne, who understands my obsession and passion for the American West. There is no cure.

In the end, we all seek the American Dream where we are architects of our own history. That should be available to all. History echoes the past that lives with us today. We cannot change history, but we must attempt to hear the echoes and do the right thing in the future. Who were we and who are we as Americans and a nation? I want to know. The Spirit of the West dwells within those who care.

Dr. Larry Len Peterson
Spirit of Winter Ranch
Sisters, Oregon
Winter, 2016

Introduction

American Trinity is for everyone who loves the American West and wants to know more about the good, the bad, and the ugly. It's about individuals and their lives, hopes, religions, ideas, and failings. America is perpetually changing, a constantly evolving experiment in progress. That is fortunate, but we need to be reminded about our entire past—the good and bad—to inform the process and keep it alive. Ossification is the first step on the road to extinction for great ideas and regretted pasts. This story unfolds in a time when the world was lit only by fire. Its goal is not to solve the problem of racism, but to state the problem correctly so we are hopefully guided in the future by the better angels of our nature.[1]

The past of the American West is key to its magic and its tragedy. In 1843, when John James Audubon traveled up the Missouri River toward Fort Union on the steam vessel *Omega,* the Great Plains vibrated with life.[2] The sheer aggregation of nature's people was inspiring. Little did the famous animal painter know that he was on the cusp of a holocaust. From 1820 to 1920, the largest human destruction of animal life in history was unfolding. One of the wonders of the world was being reduced to a blank slate. By the 1880s, pronghorns and wild horses would be the only large animals left. The Great Plains was a slaughterhouse. After the Civil War, 20,000 game hunters shot 10 million bison alone. In the 1920s, 3 million wild horses were sent to dog food factories in the Midwest and ended up in metal cans on grocery store shelves. The march to civilization was truly a meat grinder.[3]

Native Americans fared no better, as their halcyon days of freedom and hope were over. Their population, estimated in the millions before the arrival of Europeans in 1492, plummeted to less than 250,000 by 1900. Infectious diseases—mainly smallpox—brought by the Europeans killed up to ninety percent of many of the tribes. Audubon saw this firsthand with a Mandan couple at a village along the Missouri River. After the death of their only child to smallpox, the grieving parents wanted to die also. Aububon wrote, "In an instant he shot her dead, reloaded his gun, put the muzzle in his mouth, touched the trigger, and fell back dead."[4] Those who survived were pocked with grotesque scars, a perpetual nightmarish reminder of friends and family lost. The destruction of the bison herds further physically and emotionally weakened the tribes.

But most importantly, the loss of hope crushed Native Americans. The crucial component of hope is the capacity of the individual to act independently and make his or her own choices. Hopeful people don't just have a wish or goal, they have a strategy to achieve it and motivation to succeed. Hope is the belief that the future will be better than the present and that you can be empowered. It is feeling that what is wanted can be obtained. The white man systematically cleansed the four components of hope from the Indian: the senses of trust, empowerment, survival, and spirituality. Hope has an eye to the future. Hunger, terrorism, and disease steal hope. There was no future for Native Americans.[5]

It is the moral choices that haunt and disturb. Those special human behaviors unleashed when some people are placed in charge of others in a realm like the American West without real law and accountability. The so-called Indian Wars were about the consolidation of power and later about the relocation of those who survived to reservations. Was it genocide or merely ethnic cleansing? Pulitzer Prize–winning author Wallace Stegner said, "No one who ever studied Western history can cling to the belief that the Nazis invented genocide."[6] Others have disagreed with that statement. Ken Burns said that history is not about battles, but about dignity, humanity, human freedom, and the future. The key to Burns' successful PBS documentaries is that he always tries to answer the question, "Who are we as American people?" That question is also at the heart of *American Trinity*.[7]

Anti-Indian sentiments were always only obliquely about them. They were victims but not the cause. The Indian was a symbol, not a real person. The politics of hate and racism that was directed toward them was also experienced in prior centuries by Jews, Islamic people, enslaved Africans, Christians, and others. But politics alone can't change cultural attitudes. Hatred and racism, when taken into the public domain, are singularly difficult to justify, which is why Europeans and Americans have always sought vindication from the highest sources of authority in their cultures. In the Middle Ages, it was religion supplemented later by the philosophy of the Enlightenment. In nineteenth-century Europe and America, religion and philosophy were joined by science and medicine to support Manifest Destiny, scientific racism, and social Darwinism—the misguided doctrine that in human history, as in nature, the strong survived by eliminating the weak.

At their best, science and technology feed us; medicine heals us; religion nourishes our souls; and philosophy enlightens us. They provide us with our identity and ideals as a nation, with the implied question, "Who are we?" underlying all sorts of heated debates. Ideals, however, are often hard to maintain and implement. Why? Perhaps it is because the political opportunist almost always lacks the courage of his or her convictions. Like Jefferson and so many other leaders who struggled with abolition and the fate of Native Americans, that was not necessarily because they lacked convictions. It was often because their convictions were almost always subordinated to the needs of ambition and ingratiation. That said, former Secretary of State Henry Kissinger, a strong proponent of realist policies, believed national actions molded by "moral impulses and crusading ideals"[8] were likely to be dangerous. "The most fundamental problem of politics," he wrote in his Harvard doctoral dissertation over sixty years ago, "is not the control of wickedness but the limitation of righteousness."[9]

What makes one race rise and another fall? In **Part I, *The Searchers: Finding Each Other,*** we discover that we are all African Americans. Around 100,000 years ago, modern humans began migrating out of Africa—the origin of our species—to undiscovered lands. Some headed north to Europe and others trekked east where, starting around 40,000 BCE, they eventually crossed the Bering Land Bridge to call the New World their home. Along the way, both groups diverged into many different races that acquired unique religions, cultures, weapons, DNA, germs, and skin color. The first wave of humans to the New World would arrive in Alaska from Siberia as hunter-gatherers; the second wave from western Europe would arrive as conquerors determined to colonize; and the third wave would arrive on slave boats from Africa where it all began.[10]

Until 11,000 years ago, at the end of the latest period of continental glaciation, most humans lived in small bands because they were nomadic hunter-gatherers. There was little to no religion based on the support of a ruler. As the Paleo-Indians migrated south into southern Alberta and beyond, they were amazed to discover towering mastodons, armored rhinos, dire wolves, saber-toothed cats, and ten-foot-long armadillos. Familiar animals today were super-sized—beavers the size of couches and turtles weighing a ton or more. By about 9000 BCE, however, they had all disappeared. Before the Pleistocene Epoch (2.6 million to 11,700 years ago), there were three species of horses and at least two camels that vanished long before man entered the Americas. Today's North American big-game hunters may be surprised to learn that moose, brown bear, and caribou also migrated from Asia and are not native to North America. With the extinction of many mammals during the last glacial period, bison flourished unrivaled and could be found in great quantities from Georgia to Colorado and from the Northwest to Lake Erie. But it was the grasslands of the Great Plains where the bison herds expanded the most.[11]

Around 1500, precipitation on the Great Plains increased dramatically and so did the bison population. The improved hunting prospects also caused a dramatic rise in Indian populations. The early Spanish explorers had no idea they were entering a land inhabited by Indians who had lived in great cities and were sophisticated farmers. No single religious institution, no single sacred book, no unified priesthood or common creed, and no core group of rituals could be found in the lives of Native American people.

There were three major periods of conflict between the whites and Indians of North America. The first lasted from the arrival of the Spaniards in 1492 until they reconquered the Pueblo Indians in New Mexico in 1692. By the 1820s, Spain was forced to abandon her colonies. The second conflict among the English, the French, and a large number of Native American peoples east of the Mississippi started with the Virginia uprising in 1622 and ended after the War of 1812. The final conflict took place between the newly formed United States and the Indians in a series of wars that started in the 1790s and symbolically ended in 1890 at the massacre at Wounded Knee in South Dakota.[12]

One of the cornerstones of perceived European exceptionalism was Western medicine. Physicians in ancient times were mystics, and in the first 200 years of America, many were elevated to gods. They became part of the elite as the Age of Enlightenment and the Scientific Revolution unfolded. Physicians who saw themselves as Renaissance men held divinity degrees and dabbled in the arts and sciences. Confident in their craft, in the nineteenth century many of the healers were leaders in supporting the crusade for scientific racism that attempted to explain the inferiority of slaves and Indians. That progressed to eugenics—a set of beliefs placed into practice whose goal was improving the genetic quality of the human population—which was embraced by the Nazis in the twentieth century with a devastating outcome.

Physicians were frustrated by the mass human destruction from infectious diseases. From the time of first contact of Native Americans with Europeans, recurrent smallpox epidemics killed millions. Eventually, in

1796 Edward Jenner in rural England would produce a vaccine for smallpox from a cowpox virus, but it came too late.[13] Native Americans' deaths from these diseases provided a sign to Christians that they were God's chosen ones. No one knew at the time that deadly bacteria and viruses even existed. That was in the future.

As seen in Part I, European Christians forced their religion on Native Americans, but the reverse never occurred. In **Part II, *The Mystery: Clash of Spirits,*** one of the cornerstones of racism, religion, is examined by comparing Native American religion with the white man's Christianity. They were literally worlds apart. Christianity gave citizens an idea of history having a direction toward hope and salvation for all who could be reached. Their leaders founded many of the private universities, and missionaries spread the good word to the hinterlands. Was Christianity superior to other religions? Does God take sides? Religion can inspire the most noble, compassionate actions, but it can also lead to destructive and violent outcomes. We have seen that one of the greatest sources of peace and one of the greatest sources of conflict among people is religion. It becomes particularly dangerous when it focuses on the drawing and defending of boundaries.

Many tribes shared religious traditions, but they also had their own unique vision on life. Native Americans accept the mystery of faith. Christians attempt to make sense of theirs. Since Indians were seen as heathens, their rich spiritual lives were either totally ignored or devalued. As Manifest Destiny swept westward, the Indian was expected to welcome Christianity and abandon his own religion. Spiritual tensions between the two groups are as old as their first encounters in the New World.

Indian ceremonies have an underlying theme of gratitude expressed by human beings on behalf of all forms of life. Native Americans understood that one of the reasons they were placed on Earth was to restore harmony in practical ways. Their ceremonies required not only symbolic acts but also practical restitution and restoration. The most quintessential Indian ritual for those tribes living west of the Missouri River on the Great Plains was the Sun Dance, which gained popularity in the early 1800s and was derived from the ancient ceremonies of many different tribes.

At least since the time modern humans left Africa they have communicated their beliefs through a number of modalities, including paintings, carvings, dances, and sounds. However, the most important method of expression is through oral histories. These myths and legends have been transmitted from one generation to the next by selected tribal historians. These historians were often trained at an early age by their elders to perpetuate these myths and legends. At the core of the Indians' way of life was their spiritual beliefs that were often demonstrated through ceremonies and rituals. Everything in nature had its own spirit, and the spirits in nature were considered stronger than human power.

By contrast, the white man came with his Bible, the best-selling, most read, most translated, and most revered book in the history of Western civilization. European and American cultures highly prized the written word. It was considered the highest form of civilized thinking. Famed Boston pastor Cotton Mather viewed Indians as corrupt copies of the Jews or representatives of the degeneracy of Satan. As English colonists and later Americans confiscated Indian lands, they relied on their Christianity and words from the Bible to justify their actions. The American Eden was for white Christians and not heathen Native Americans with their disgusting beliefs and ceremonies.

The moral principle of treating others as one would like to be treated oneself—the Golden Rule—is found in most human cultures and religions. It is a unifying principle. James, Jesus' brother, called it the Royal Rule. If there is one common thread among almost all religions, it is that rule. It is often claimed as a Christian doctrine, but that is not totally accurate. In ancient Egypt around 2000 BCE, an Egyptian goddess in *The Story of The Eloquent Peasant* was perhaps the earliest to command the Golden Rule.

After exploring religion, we arrive at other important sources of authority to justify racism in Western culture. In **Part III** *Thomas Jefferson: Winning the West,* Jefferson is profiled as a man of the Enlightenment. He considered Sir Francis Bacon, John Locke, and Sir Isaac Newton—men of the Enlightenment—as the three greatest men who had ever lived, having laid the foundation of his generation's understanding of the physical and moral sciences. At a dinner party, Jefferson pointed this out, explaining to John Hamilton, "I told him they were my trinity of the three greatest men the world had ever produced, naming them."[14]

The Enlightenment laid the intellectual groundwork for societies in Europe and the New World that was often paved with the blood of "progress." Westerners believed that they possessed a mastery over the natural world—Indians being part of it—that set them apart from their ancestors and everyone else. Knowledge armed white Christians with a freedom and power they believed no other creature possessed.

As a man of the Enlightenment, Jefferson's God was the God of nature. His ideal dream for the West was nature's people—the Indians—abandoning their way of life as hunter-gatherers and picking up the plow, reading the Bible, and sharing the bountiful land with their Eastern brothers. Stephen Prothero, chair of the Department of Religion at Boston University, wrote in *American Jesus*, "Jefferson's legacy in American religion is at least as long as it is in American politics. More than anyone else, Jefferson was responsible for setting the ground rules for religious practice in the United States."[15]

When Thomas Jefferson wrote in the Declaration of Independence that "All men are created equal," he may have believed that only white men were equal or that the African Americans and Indians had yet to achieve that possible status, but hoped someday they would. Jefferson's vision was for an America composed of a large web of white families. Not part of these families, enslaved blacks ideally would be shipped back to Africa and Indians pushed farther west.

As the nineteenth century unfolded, the American West of the Louisiana Purchase found its "Father" in President Jefferson. He sent his representatives, Lewis and Clark and their Corps of Discovery, up the Missouri in search of a passage to the Pacific Ocean. For the Indians, a perfect storm was brewing. The elitists viewed Indians as mentally inferior, on par with the ape. Men of the Enlightenment saw God in nature but had no time for Indian myths and legends. Enlightenment philosophy also had no tolerance for Native American or Christian miracles—those events beyond human power, self-achievement, or explanation.

Could there have been any better tool for prying the land away from Native Americans than the Doctrine of Discovery? It was a philosophy based on a 1,000-year-old belief promulgated by Catholic Church leaders that God granted them the world. This was translated by Protestant American leaders into the right to control the lands owned by natives. Jefferson was the architect of the Indian removal policy and exercised America's Discovery authority to remove them west of their homelands.[16]

Although Manifest Destiny was not used to define American expansion to the Pacific Ocean until 1845, it was clearly in place after the Revolutionary War. The phrase was not a new idea but grew out of the principles and legal elements of the Doctrine of Discovery. Expansionism heated up during the 1820s and was fueled by the Second Great Awakening, which reminded and convinced American Protestants that God wanted them to spread the word of his salvation. Every human from sea to shining sea needed to be spiritually converted to Christianity, and this would usher in a millennium of peace on Earth. The barbaric Indians were not the only challenge. There was a vivid strain of anti-Catholicism in the movement. Romanticism inspired America to look to the great Western frontier for its identity.

Manifest Destiny was American predestination. Minds were overflowing with the wealth that the West represented. By 1800, almost a million settlers were living in the area between the Mississippi River and the Appalachians. Americans believed that the West had the potential of Eden regained and that Eden was to be populated by white settlers at the expense of the indigenous people. Some, like Abraham Lincoln and Ulysses S. Grant, would eventually question that premise. But before the Civil War, America guided by Manifest Destiny gobbled up Florida, Texas, the Southwest, California, and Oregon as the major controversy was whether a new state would be a free state or a slave state.

Ethnocentric judgment, an evaluation of one peoples' qualities by another people, is as old as ancient times. As a social doctrine, racism was an invention of Europeans in modern times as they became colonial powers. For racists, physical characteristics are an indicator of moral and mental qualities that allows grouping into either inferior or superior races.

Scientific racism, manifested most dismally in exaggerated claims about the capacity of so-called science to explain—or explain away—human intelligence and nature, was perhaps the most serious intellectual disease of the nineteenth century. Its destructive force toward Native Americans was almost as devastating as smallpox. It involved some of the post-Renaissance's most profound thinkers, as well as an extraordinary cast of charismatic figures, not a few of them charlatans and rogues. They were all driven by ambition to confirm white supremacy, but attempts to do so rested heavily on analogies and wishful thinking. Science without direction from a moral compass leads to tragic results. You cannot reason someone out of something they have not been reasoned into.

Social Darwinism championed survival of the fittest, who no doubt were white, and the white man was greedy. The Indians—what was left of them after disease, starvation, and death at the hands of soldiers—were placed in barren gulags called reservations. After a century of broken promises and broken treaties, the final indignation would be the white man chipping away at the Indians' landholdings.

Charles Darwin, a pioneering geologist as well as the greatest of all biologists of his time, in his *Origin of Species* (1859) and other writings, would inspire social Darwinism—a modern name—which argued that the strong should see their wealth and power increase while the weak should see their wealth and power decrease. Of course, this gave further support to white Americans that the American West belonged to them. No scientist in the history of Western civilization had a greater impact on how different races viewed each other. Even though fundamentalist Christians were irate with him over destroying the creation story of Adam and Eve, Darwin became the symbol of the power of scientific racism, which led to eugenics and is still felt today.

To understand white attitudes toward Native Americans in the second half of the nineteenth century is to understand Darwinism and scientific racism. Theodore Roosevelt's views toward the West were a combination of his lifelong support for Darwinism and Manifest Destiny. He idolized Darwin. Roosevelt lived for a time in Dakota Territory, where he ranched and hunted. Later, as president, the wilderness warrior would set aside several hundred million acres in the West to be enjoyed by the public.

Why is George Armstrong Custer a legend—loved and hated? In **Part IV** *The Golden Rule, or the Golden-Ruled? Custer: The Son of the American West,* his story begins at the time of the Civil War, a horrific contest where we learn about American values. Victory served to bolster Northerners' attitudes of Manifest Destiny, scientific racism, and social Darwinism. It was the proving grounds for Union military leaders whose next task was winning the West. The Civil War and the Indian Wars were a two-part play with many of the same actors starring in both tragedies, packed with underlying tones of conflict over religion and property rights. At the center of both were men of color who had little say about the outcome.

Before he entered the West, Custer, the boy general, was one of the stars of the Civil War. Fame and success were his constant companions during the bloody battles as he honed his skills as a professional killer. He became a cultural icon and wore flashy garb as he won battles in the face of others dying. Custer was brave, lucky, and a real professional in combat where he led well-timed charges.

For many in the North, the war was about reuniting the country and not about emancipation. That was true for Custer and his mentor and idol, General George McClellan, an egotistical racist who had little regard for Lincoln or Grant. The carnage of war hardened many soldiers who served under Grant, such as Custer, William T. Sherman, and Phil Sheridan—all from Ohio—and they would play major roles in the Indian Wars.

The core issue facing the United States in regard to Native Americans was how to use incredible power with self-restraint. General Custer had fought the good fight in the Civil War. He learned that the closest person to God on Earth is a general. The nation was one again, but far from whole. Northerners, Southerners, and freed African Americans all agreed that the Indians needed to be defeated.

The next fight would not be the good fight. From the end of the Civil War to the end of his life in 1876, Custer as a person would fragment and slowly self-destruct. Managing was not his strong point, and that deficiency would lead to lethal consequences. Both Marcus A. Reno and Frederick W. Benteen were problem officers, and Custer's inability to maintain good relationships with them would have dire consequences. Before he was killed, Custer hadn't notched a significant win in years.

Custer, a Darwin disciple, felt a visceral fascination with the natural world. For Custer, wilderness was heaven to his romantic notions. Wilderness in its simplest form allows other creatures their rights on this planet and the opportunity to experience the survival of the fittest. It is the proving grounds for determining who is the fittest. Custer knew that it is in the little things and in the lonely places that we prove ourselves capable of the big things. Every time he attacked "hostile" Indians and every time Theodore Roosevelt killed a trophy animal, they were reaffirming Charles Darwin's survival of the fittest and their own superiority. One of the reasons Custer and the Battle of the Little Bighorn are still in the conscience of the average American citizen is that they are powerful symbols of the shortcomings of humanity. Custer searched for pleasure, profit, and popularity. He failed, and America is fascinated with legends that fall. Custer was the "Son of the American West." No one is the same size as Western history, no one is that big. But Custer comes close. Victories are celebrated and defeats are studied. Most often we learn more from losing than from winning, and there is a lot to learn from Custer's life about nineteenth-century America.

Michael O'Keefe in 2012 published an 899-page, two-volume compilation of nonfiction books, pamphlets, novels, and periodicals titled *Custer, the Seventh Cavalry, and the Little Big Horn*. At the time of publication, there were 345 novels in print. Many more have been published since then. The best stories are about legends, and legends are often born out of tragedy. Why are there so many publications on Custer? As the newspaper editor in John Ford's 1962 film, *The Man Who Shot Liberty Valence*, said, "This is the West, sir. When the legend becomes fact, print the legend."[17]

T. J. Stiles, author of the Pulitzer Prize–winning *Custer's Trials*, wrote, "Certain people and events achieve iconic status. More than just famous, they speak to Americans about who they are as a people and a nation. Truths about them, and arguments about them, are truths and arguments about ourselves. Over the decades, Custer has served as a symbol of American notions of heroism and individualism, and fears of hubris. And, of course, he himself has become a battleground in the debate over the conquest and dispossession of American Indians. He has been treated as a convenient stand-in for large historical developments and high-level policy decisions—as has the Little Bighorn."[18]

The forced relocation of Indians in the West, away from major urban populations in the East, that had dominated American policy since the 1820s would eventually change. In 1887, with most of the conflicts in the West over, American policy moved to assimilation. However, that did not mean that racism vanished. Increasingly, there was the notion that the Indians could be educated and assimilated in American society. The mind was not fully formed at birth but a tabula rasa written on by experience and reflections upon experience. There was hope for the heathen. That hope came in the form of off-reservation Indian schools toward the end of the nineteenth century.

In a strange way, Lieutenant Richard Henry Pratt's face, scared and dimpled from smallpox as a child, was a comforting sight for the bewildered and sad Indian children shuffling onto the grounds of the Carlisle Indian School in Pennsylvania. His scars were a bittersweet reminder of many of their family and friends back home in the West. Pratt believed the Indians' inferiority was because they grew up in a different culture that could be effectively erased with education. He championed ethnic cleansing and Christian conversion, and coined the saying, "Kill the Indian in him and save the man."[19] He said that the Indian was born a blank slate who could grow to possess a civilized language, purpose-driven life, and good habits. In the end, his off-reservation Indian schools were deemed a failure.

Noted historian David McCullough, recipient of two Pulitzer Prizes and two National Book Awards, wrote in *Brave Companions: Portraits in History* about the essence of history, "It is a shame that history is ever made dry and tedious, or offered as a chronicle almost exclusively of politics, war, and social issues, when, of course, it is the full sweep of human experiences: politics, war, and social issues to be sure , but also music, science, religion, medicine, the way things are made, new ideas, high attainment in every field, money, the weather, love, loss, endless ambiguities and paradoxes and small towns you never heard of. History is a spacious realm. There should be no walls. . . . What history is chiefly about is life, and while there are indeed great, often unfathomable forces in history before which even the most exceptional of individuals seem insignificant, the wonder is how often events turn on a single personality, or the quality of character."[20]

The *American Trinity* story is older and bigger than the American West. It is the story of the grand sweep of human experiences and their eventual influence on white racist attitudes toward Native Americans. History is important. When there is no knowledge of the past, there cannot be a vision of the future. Events did turn on the lives of famous Americans like Thomas Jefferson and George Armstrong Custer—two strange companions—as their interpretation of truths motivated them in winning the West. This is part of our Western heritage, this is *American Trinity*.

Part I

The Searchers: Finding Each Other

CHAPTER ONE

Out of Africa: Origin of the Races

God, who is not limited in space or time, created the universe and established natural laws that govern it. Seeking to populate this otherwise sterile universe with living creatures, God chose the elegant mechanism of evolution to create microbes, plants, and animals of all sorts. Most remarkably, God intentionally chose the same mechanism to give rise to special creatures who would have intelligence, a knowledge of right and wrong, free will, and a desire to seek fellowship with Him. He also knew these creatures would ultimately choose to disobey the Moral Law.
—FRANCIS S. COLLINS, M.D., PH.D.—DIRECTOR OF THE NATIONAL HUMAN GENOME RESEARCH INSTITUTE AND DIRECTOR OF THE NATIONAL INSTITUTES OF HEALTH—IS THE RECIPIENT OF THE PRESIDENTIAL HONOR OF FREEDOM AND THE NATIONAL MEDAL OF SCIENCE.

Good friend, for Jesus' sake forebeare to digg the dust enclosed heare; Bleste be the man that spares thes stones, And curst be he that moves my bones.
—WILLIAM SHAKESPEARE, WORDS WRITTEN BY HIM AS THEY APPEAR ON HIS TOMBSTONE (1616) IN THE HOLY TRINITY CHURCH, STRATFORD-ON-AVON, WARWICKSHIRE, ENGLAND

Kennewick Man

In July 1996, two college students stumbled across a human skull while wading in the shallow waters of the Columbia River near Kennewick, Washington. Townsfolk first thought that the skull might have belonged to a homicide victim, but after the almost complete skeleton was examined, it became evident that it was over 8,500 years old.

That skeleton became known as the famed Kennewick Man or, as the Indians called it, the Ancient One. While it is one of the oldest and most important remains ever found in North America, it is also one of the most controversial. Native American leaders demanded the remains be handed over to them for an appropriate ritual burial. Indians believe that bodies that go to the ground need to stay there. Their spiritual journey is interrupted if exhumed.

Before they could obtain the remains, a group of scientists filed a lawsuit claiming that the Kennewick Man could not be proven to be Native American. In fact, they speculated that he was European because of his long and narrow skull. Native Americans in general have short craniums and broad cheeks. These findings for a while led to theories that at least some of the Indians' ancestors came across the Atlantic from Europe. But his face had the appearance of those seen in Polynesia and northern Japan, where the skulls are relatively long and narrow.

The Kennewick Man was approximately five feet, seven inches tall, died at age forty, and possessed a stronger right arm than the left one. He appeared to be a spear thrower. Forensic examination also showed that in the past he had a spear point in his right leg and five broken ribs—perhaps he had been kicked. Because of high carbon levels detected in his bones, it was postulated that he was a salmon and seal eater.

In 2008, an intact skeleton of a female named Eva of Naharon who died in her twenties was found in a submerged cave in the Yucatán Peninsula and had a similar appearance to the Kennewick Man. Her clan were hunter-gatherers who lived on animals of the forest, and when she died they buried her a quarter of a mile deep in a cave. That site had spiritual significance as it symbolized the underworld. Since then, the caves were submerged as sea levels rose at the end of the last glacial period.

Radiocarbon dating determined that she was 13,600 years old and stood four feet, seven inches tall. Hers are the oldest bones found in the Americas and make her older than the Clovis people. The caves were used only to bury the dead, and a ceremony was performed by shamans.[1]

Little did Lewis and Clark know when they entered the Columbia River that it was home to several tribes that roamed from British Columbia down the Pacific coastline and as far east as Nevada and Wyoming. Hunting kept them on the move, searching for food sources throughout the year. After the salmon spawned on the Columbia, clogging the river, some tribal families moved on to abundant hunting grounds while others made the fishing villages along the Columbia their social center of life.

Their way of life continued relatively unchanged until Franklin Roosevelt's New Deal legislation generated funds to build Bonneville Dam in 1933. The Warm Springs, Yakama, Umatilla, and Nez Perce tribes were relegated to only five sites along the Columbia where they could fish once Bonneville and other dams flooded out their fishing settlements. Thousands of years of an economic and spiritual way of life were wiped out.[2]

The controversy over the origins of the Kennewick Man was settled by science. A twenty-first-century research tool is proving in many instances to be as important as radiocarbon dating. The recent availability of low-cost, high-throughput DNA sequencing, which is being used to study ancient DNA extracted from bodies and bones at archaeological sites, is revealing a tremendous amount of new information. Before these advances, reading DNA required the laborious amplification of short segments, one at a time. By 2008, companies such as 454 Life Sciences, a Roche Company, in Branford, Connecticut, and the San Diego-based Illumina started marketing machines that could read millions of DNA samples in parallel.

Ancient DNA is revealing not only who mated with whom and when but which genes were then promoted by Darwin's natural selection in the resulting offspring to improve their chances of survival. It has already transformed our ability to see just how the genes of human beings, their domestic animals, and their diseases have changed over thousands or tens of thousands of years. From analysis, it turns out that in the prehistory of our species, almost all were invaders and usurpers.

In 2005, after eight years of legal battles, scientists led by Douglas W. Owsley, division head of physical anthropology at the Smithsonian Institution, won access to study the bones of Kennewick Man. The controversy over who had the rights to his remains continued for years but was settled in June 2015 when Danish scientists published an analysis of DNA obtained from his skeleton. Eske Willerslev, a geneticist at the University of Copenhagen and lead author of the study published in *Nature*, stated, "It's very clear that Kennewick Man is most closely related to contemporary Native Americans. In my view it's bone-solid."[3] They also compared his genome with living New World people as well as the Clovis-period, 12,600-year-old skeleton found by a construction crew in 1968 near Wilsall, Montana, known as Anzick-1 or the Anzick child.[4] From these results, it's clear that the first humans migrated to the New World in several waves that spread distinct branches to South America, northern North America, and the Arctic.

The odd-shaped skull of Kennewick Man puzzled many because it did not look like that of a living Native American. Dr. Willerslev called on Dr. Christoph Zollikofer and Dr. Marcia Ponce de León, experts on skull shapes at the University of Zürich, department of anthropology, to help solve the puzzle. They showed that living Native Americans have a wide range of head shapes, and the skull of the Kennewick Man would lie within a range that was considered normal.[5]

Scientists collected saliva samples from members of the Colville Tribe in eastern Washington. Among all the samples from Native Americans in the study, the Kennewick Man's DNA was the closest match to the Colville DNA. The study would seem to conclude that there are two major branches of Native Americans. One branch, including Kennewick Man and the Colville Tribe, spread out across the northern region of the New World and eventually gave rise to the Ojibwe and Athabaskan tribes. The Anzick child from Montana appears to be from a separate branch of Native Americans who spread down into Central and South America.

Analysis of his remains is consistent with the Beringia hypothesis of early Amerindians emigrating from Siberia. It's possible that these two branches split before they migrated to the New World. Those two migrations were followed about 4,000 years ago by at least two more waves of people across the Arctic. The Paleo-Eskimos became extinct centuries ago, while the other gave rise to today's Inuit peoples. However, as we shall see, many migration theories have been entertained.[6]

Darwinian Evolution

So how did the ancestors of the legendary Sitting Bull and Crazy Horse come to call the Great Plains their home? It is a mythical story of hope and survival. Their blood lines trace back to the earliest migration of humans to America in a time and land much different than today. They most likely came across the Bering Land Bridge, which was created by a dramatic drop in sea levels during the last glacial period of the Pleistocene, which began to wane about 11,700 years ago. When massive ice sheets covered large parts of North America and Europe, shallow areas of the sea floor were exposed.

With the discovery of radioactivity and the natural decay of certain chemical isotopes, scientists have been able to date with precision almost every type of rock and fossilized plant and animal. The three radioactive chemical elements that transform into stable elements that are most useful for inorganic dating are uranium to lead, potassium to argon, and strontium to rubidium. This tool has dated the Earth to around 4.55 billion years with about a one percent error rate. For the first 500 million years, the Earth was not conducive to life. Asteroids and meteorites constantly bombarded the surface, and in one instance tore the moon loose from the Earth. Asteroids also bombarded the Earth with its known deposits of gold, and 300 million years ago an asteroid blasted the Appalachian Mountains and formed what would be known as the Cumberland Gap—the gateway west for settlers seeking the American Dream.[7]

About 650 million years into Earth's existence, different types of microbial life appeared. Although the organisms were single celled, they most likely carried DNA and were self-replicating. In the late 1940s, a chemist and atomic energy scientist named Willard Libby deduced that carbon-14 could be used to date organic matter. Radiocarbon 14 is always being created by cosmic rays bombarding atmospheric nitrogen. When it combines with oxygen, radioactive carbon dioxide is formed. During photosynthesis, plants take up carbon dioxide and release oxygen. Radioactive carbon dioxide is ingested by animals when they eat plants, but when a plant or animal dies, there is no more radioactive uptake. At that point, radioactive decay begins. Using this method, dating accuracy diminishes when the organism is more than 50,000 years old, so the dates for fossilized organic matter are expressed in ranges that widen with the increasing age of the material.

How life began on Earth has been a hotly debated topic for several millennia. Religion and science have been at odds over it for centuries.[8] In most species, evolution takes a long time. One way of comprehending how little time humans have been on Earth was presented in 2006 by Francis Collins, head of the National Institutes of Health, in *The Language of God:*

> A major part of the problem in accepting the theory of evolution is that it requires one to grasp the significance of extremely long periods of time involved in the process. Such intervals are unimaginably beyond individual experience. One way to reduce the eons of history into a more comprehensible form is to imagine what would happen if the 3.5 billion years of the earth's existence, from initial formation to today, were instead compressed into a twenty-four-hour day. If the earth was formed at 12:01 A.M., then life would appear at about 3:30 A.M. After a long day of slow progression to multi-cellular organisms, the Cambrian explosion would finally occur at about 9 P.M. Later that evening, dinosaurs would roam the earth. Their extinction

would occur at 11:40 P.M., at which time the mammals would begin to expand.

The diversions of branches leading to chimps and humans would occur with only one minute and seventeen seconds remaining in the day, and anatomically modern humans would appear with just three seconds left. The life of a middle-aged human on earth today would occupy only the last millisecond (one-thousandth of a second). It is not surprising that many of us have a great deal of difficulty contemplating evolutionary time.[9]

It is more than a little sobering, but the majority of organisms that have ever lived on Earth have disappeared without a trace. Most will never be discovered because fossil formation takes just the right environment for it to occur. Resin may trap a fly or a tar pit a dinosaur, but in most cases animals and plants just decay back to dust and disappear from discovery forever.

With that in mind, the first discovered fossils of invertebrates appeared around 550 million years ago. This period in history is known as the "Cambrian explosion."[10] It should be cautioned at this point not to become too concerned over specific dates. Anyone who has followed science on the origins of life knows that new discoveries and analytical tools can quickly change our knowledge and perception of life. Another caveat is that 550 million years ago just may have been the time when conditions for fossil formation were optimal. It's possible that invertebrates may have been around millions of years earlier. Time will tell—maybe.

Terrestrial plants first appeared around 400 million years ago, originating from their aquatic relatives. Thirty million years later, animals followed them onto land. The most notable extinction occurred at the end of the Permian period around 252 million years ago when almost ninety percent of known species died. This led to the age of reptiles.[11]

About 230 million years ago, the prehistoric superstar took the stage—the dinosaur. Thirty million years later a single landmass, Pangea, broke apart, and parts of the Americas and Europe were formed. This explains why fossils of some animal and plant species can be found across different continents. Flora and fauna from each continent subsequently developed separately. They were so unique to each landmass that Columbus said about the New World, "all the trees were as different from ours as day from night, and so the fruits, the herbage, the rocks, and all things." Around 135 million years ago, Earth witnessed another massive set of volcanic eruptions as South America split away from Africa.[12]

The dinosaur's dominant reign came to an abrupt end 65 million years ago when a large asteroid collided with Earth in the area of the Yucatán Peninsula. Ash filled the atmosphere, leading to catastrophic climate change and the end of the great beasts.[13]

Humans

Various scientific studies of human origin point to eastern Africa in present-day Ethiopia as the likely spot. The process began approximately 7 million years ago. At that time, African apes separated into several populations. One evolved into the modern gorilla, another into two modern chimps, and around 2.5 million years ago archaic humans appeared. A number of different archaic human species developed. Different species of primates would interbreed over the last 2 million years.

Fossil records indicate that our ancestors stood upright by 4 million years ago. The spread to southern Asia occurred around 1 million BCE and to Europe about 500,000 BCE. Early humans were crafting sharpened stone knives more than a million years ago. All humans fed themselves only by hunting wild animals and gathering wild plants in a manner similar to some of the Plains Indians as recently as the nineteenth century.[14]

The world held half a dozen species of humans. Modern *Homo sapiens* came into existence about 200,000 years ago, with successive generations sporting increasingly larger craniums. For tens of thousands of years, modern humans and archaic humans shared Africa, and DNA evidence shows that there was interbreeding.

In 1967 in the Omo Valley in Ethiopia—which is dry now but then was full of lush vegetation—Omo 1 was discovered. He is the oldest and most complete skeleton yet discovered. Argon dating of the soil layer he was discovered in dates to 195,000 years ago. He weighed 160 pounds and was as tall as modern Africans. As expected, he was a hunter-gatherer who used stone tools and had an intellect similar to ours. The humans in this area migrated all over the African continent.[15]

Anthropologists tell us that humans developed languages tens of thousands of years ago. Yuval Noah Harari traces the trajectory of our species into a succession of three revolutions: cognitive revolution (when we got smart), agricultural revolution (when we got nature to do what we wanted), and scientific revolution (when we got dangerously powerful).[16]

At first, *Homo sapiens* existed in insignificant foraging bands, but around 70,000 to 100,000 years ago, during a "cognitive revolution," our ancestors moved out of Africa. Boats, battle axes, and beautiful art eventually appeared. By 60,000 years ago, our ancestors used bone sewing needles to stitch together animal furs for clothing, and later on they were weaving plant fibers together to make fabrics. Around 30,000 years ago, they were documenting the phases of the moon. By 9,000 years ago, they were using flint-tipped dentistry drills and brewing (and drinking) alcohol.[17] Genetic mutations may have caused rewiring of the brain that allowed a new type of language characterized by group cooperation. These events most likely occurred over great geographic and temporal distances. The oldest *Homo sapiens* remains in Europe were found in Romania and date to 40,000 years ago. In the Rhone Valley in southern France, researchers have discovered 50,000-year-old flint arrowheads—the oldest in the continent.[18]

Neanderthals did not interbreed with modern humans in Africa. They lived in Europe. Around 55,000 years ago, an exceptionally cold period drove the Neanderthals south to the Middle East (near present-day Israel), where they interbred with modern humans leaving Africa. Their offspring then spread to Europe, Asia, and eventually to the New World. Today, we 7 billion humans are hybrids. Within a blink of evolutionary time, interbreeding and genetic mutations led to variations in physical appearance, including skin color; "black" became red, yellow, and white. This fact makes racism even more offensive and absurd.[19]

The history of our understanding of the Neanderthal represents our ever-changing knowledge of the human past. In the summer of 1856, a group of German miners working in a cave unearthed pieces of what appeared to be a very old human skeleton. The skull differed dramatically from modern human skulls. It appeared to be tens of thousands of years old, suggesting this hominid would have been present long before modern humans arrived in Europe. Hermann Schaaffhausen, an anatomist, proposed that they were from a prehistoric race of human-like savages. With Darwin's *On the Origin of Species* published in 1859, the Neanderthal was seen as a missing link between apes and human beings. It was believed that these primitive brutes would not have possessed moral or religious thought. We now know that the scientists were wrong.[20]

Recent evidence has shown that Neanderthals painted pictures, dressed themselves up with shells and feathers, created pigments including ochre, buried their dead, and had the capacity for speech—all behaviors once thought unique to modern humans. DNA studies suggest that Neanderthals and modern humans diverged from a common ancestor in Africa about 350,000 to 400,000 years ago. Between 300,000 and 200,000 years ago, Neanderthals moved out of Africa and into parts of the Middle East, western Asia, and Europe. By around 40,000 years ago, Neanderthals and modern humans in Europe were coexisting in some parts of the continent and continued to do so until as late as 24,000 years ago—a remarkably long time for such strikingly similar predators.[21]

Like modern humans, Neanderthals used fire and cooked meat and vegetables, made tools, and possibly even played musical instruments. Physically, they had larger brains and sharper vision than we do, were stronger, and were better at adapting to cold temperatures. Probably in order to make more efficient use of vitamin D from less sunlight at higher latitudes, some had pale skin—which allowed light to penetrate the skin where the vitamin is formed—and blonde or red hair.

Mysteriously, about 42,000 years ago the Neanderthal civilization experienced a steep decline along with many large animals that they had shared the continent with for some 200,000 years. What happened? Several scenarios have been proposed. The first is the Campanian Ignimbrite eruption, a huge volcanic eruption near Naples, Italy, around 40,000 BCE, which caused a volcanic winter during an already cold ice age. The Neanderthals gathered on the Iberian Peninsula where they eventually died out. Another factor was the smarter and more resourceful modern humans who dominated the habitat and food chain.[22]

Of note is that there is a small amount, up to five percent, of Neanderthal DNA found in modern Europeans and other non-Africans. This suggests that when African immigrants overwhelmed the Neanderthal populations of Europe and western Asia some 40,000 to 30,000 years ago, they interbred with them to some small extent, thus anticipating the scenarios of admixture described by studies of later waves of migration.[23]

Recently, a team of Oxford archaeologists have added additional information. They used newer carbon dating to determine that the Neanderthals may have become extinct before the volcanic eruption. The presence of modern humans in Europe was a competitive stressor along with climate change. In addition, the humans brought infectious diseases with them that the Neanderthals were not immune to. Humans, it turns out, are the most invasive species that ever lived. Whenever we moved into new environments, we have always caused a special devastation on the invaded world—faunal and other ecological collapse soon follows. A similar scenario would play out when the European invaders to the Americas caused the collapse of native Indian populations, in part from infectious diseases—especially smallpox—that they carried with them from their homeland.

Modern human invaders from Africa transmitted tapeworm,

tuberculosis, stomach ulcers, and several types of herpes according to research published in the *American Journal of Physical Anthropology*.[24] Charlotte Houldcroft from the University of Cambridge's Division of Biological Anthropology wrote, "For the Neanderthal population of Eurasia, adapted to the geographical environment, exposure to new pathogens carried out of Africa may have been catastrophic." The spread of infectious disease was slower than when the Europeans arrived in the New World because only small groups of some fifteen to twenty were affected at one time. Regarding Neanderthal extinction, Houldcroft added, "I don't think any single factor was solely responsible, and we may never know which theory is correct. . . ."[25]

One of the most common themes of recent research on ancient DNA is that the mixing of native and immigrant populations happened much more often than previously suspected. This new research allows us to identify the many different elements of that complex history. The familiar textbook notion that for most of human existence, people native to one region developed in isolation from those native to a different region, no longer makes sense. One of the cornerstones of scientific racism in nineteenth-century America was polygenism—the belief that Native Americans originated in the New World and whites in Europe. For racists, polygenism made whites superior in every way.

It is now apparent through the study of ancient DNA that mass migrations occurred repeatedly, overwhelming natives while conserving some of their genes. The first farmers of central Europe could not have been descended solely from their hunter-gatherer forerunners just 4,500 years ago. Long after the arrival of farming in Europe from the near East—a transition that had largely displaced the genes of the indigenous hunter-gatherers—another massive migration into the heartland of Europe from its eastern periphery occurred. People from the steppes northeast of the Black Sea swamped the European genomes with their DNA, and that relatively new pool of DNA is still ubiquitous among Europeans today. The present-day inhabitants of many places in the world are rarely related in a simple manner to the more ancient peoples of the same region. In short, no natives are purebreds.[26]

When *Homo sapiens* left Africa and went to Asia, they mated with another archaic human, *Homo erectus*, who went extinct some 30,000 years ago. *Homo erectus* (meaning "upright man") is another species that lived through most of the Pleistocene, dating as far back as 1.9 million years ago. Besides Africa, *Homo erectus* also inhabited India, China, and Java.[27] They were probably the first hominid to live in a hunter-gatherer society, most likely in small band societies. They were also the first to hunt in coordinated groups, use complex tools, and care for the ill.[28]

Jeff Rose of the Ronin Institute studied the eastern routes out of Africa taken by humans. In 2010 his team excavated areas on the arid Arabian Peninsula where they found evidence of Africans present almost 100,000 years ago. Back then, the area was not desert but was filled with lush vegetation maintained by a wet climate. The people used rivers to advance east through India and on to Asia. Many of the largest rivers in the world are in Asia. These waterways are still important today, and ninety percent of the world's population lives within ten miles of a river.[29]

Around 63,000 years ago in Southeast Asia, there were bands of modern humans who were hunter-gatherers from Africa. They used caves as shelters mainly to protect them from the monsoon rains and not as homes (because the caves were home to many poisonous snakes). The oldest modern human remains in Asia are found in a number of caves in Laos. It's challenging to discover fossils in Asia because they tend to deteriorate in the humid climate. However, in limestone caves in southern China, a mandible—102,000 years old—was found that is either from a *Homo sapiens* or *Homo erectus*.[30]

Another important extinct species of note is *Homo sapiens ssp. Denisova*. In March 2010, Dr. Svante Pääbo—best known for his discovery that up to five percent of Neanderthal DNA is found in modern Europeans and other non-Africans—was working in the area of Denisova Cave in the mountains of western Siberia when he found a 50,000-year-old finger bone of a juvenile female. The area had also been inhabited by Neanderthals and modern humans. The Denisovans lived mainly from Siberia to Southeast Asia and also interbred with modern humans and Neanderthals. Up to six percent of the DNA of aboriginal Australians is derived from Denisovans.[31] Like many other archaic humans, Denisovans had a wide range of habitats, and their DNA has been discovered as far away as Spain, where researchers previously believed Neanderthals were the only inhabitants. They apparently shared the same living quarters in caves where interbreeding occurred. Almost seventeen percent of Neanderthal DNA in that area is from the Denisovan genome.[32] In 2013, a femur around 400,000 years old, also discovered in Spain, was found to be closer to Denisovan mitochondrial DNA than that of the Neanderthal. Analysis of genomes of modern humans show that they mated with at least two groups of ancient humans: the Neanderthals and the Denisovans.[33]

In another anthropological twist, most modern Europeans have certain

DNA sequences that are similar to those of some American Indians but different from those of most Asians, including natives of Siberia. Eske Willerslev's research group at the University of Copenhagen read the genomes of two pieces of human remains found near Lake Baikal, Siberia; one lived 24,000 years ago, the other 17,000. Both had genes similar to modern Europeans and modern American Indians but distinct from modern Siberians or other East Asians. Published in *Nature* in 2014, these results imply a population of hunter-gatherers who lived in Northern Eurasia during the last ice age. They partly gave rise to the ancestors of the first Americans in East Asia and to Europeans before they themselves died out in Siberia. They were replaced by immigrants from elsewhere in Asia. As this example demonstrates, once again, one of the common themes of research on ancient DNA is that the mixing of native and immigrant populations happened much more frequently than previously suspected.[34]

Archaic Genes

What archaic genes passed to modern humans? Rasmus Nielsen and Emilia Huerta-Sanchez, both of the University of California, Berkeley, when working in Tibet found that the gene that decreases hemoglobin at high altitude is the same as the one found in *Homo sapiens ssp. Denisova*. In the thin air of the Tibetan plateau, the local people can survive only because of specially evolved versions of a gene called EPAS1. Tibetans can increase oxygen transport to their body under low oxygen levels much more efficiently than humans who don't possess the special EPAS1. The researchers found this version of the DNA sequence of EPAS1 in the ancient genetic material of the Denisovans. Mating with Denisovans seems to have enabled the subsequent population to survive at high elevations in Tibet. The gene also increases athletic performance.[35]

While around one to five percent of the DNA of all modern humans' genome—other than those living in Africa—is from the Neanderthal DNA, that specific DNA differs from person to person, so there's a total of twenty percent Neanderthal DNA floating around in modern humans. One of the most important findings is that up to ninety percent of human leukocyte antigen (HLA) genes are from Neanderthals—another example of hybridization that made us stronger and tougher. HLA is the locus of genes that encode for proteins on the surface of cells responsible for regulation of the immune system in humans. The group of genes resides on chromosome six. The proteins encoded by HLAs help in fighting infections, rejecting foreign proteins as in transplant rejection, and as a defense against cancer.

We gained more variety of HLA by interbreeding in a relatively short amount of time, as opposed to waiting for a gene mutation in the evolutionary process. Thus, we acquired immunity relatively quickly.[36] However, all is not positive. Some HLA types that are inherited can lead to a host of autoimmune diseases, including type 1 diabetes, gluten-sensitive enteropathy, systemic lupus erythematosus, and Sjogren's syndrome, to name a few.[37]

Scientists have only scratched the surface of how interbreeding with archaic humans led to what we know as modern humans today. The fact that skin color is a product of interbreeding has profound implications. The color of our skin—from black to white—is determined by the number of melanosomes in our melanocytes. Certainly, interbreeding and gene mutations played a significant role in this process.

That the color of our skin would be the basis for racism over thousands of years demonstrates the power of tradition, culture, science, and religion. Those factors will be examined in more detail in the forthcoming chapters. Each played its part in enabling one human race to feel superior to another even though the basis of skin color was probably determined tens of thousands of years ago before any "modern" civilizations. For those objecting to marriages between humans based on different colors of skin, they're a little late. It's been going on for tens of thousands of years.

As populations massed in Western Europe and Eastern Asia, the New World awaited invasion by a diverse group of modern humans. Ancient humans probably never saw the New World, but some of their unique DNA would. So would Old World germs like the unseen traveler, smallpox, that would devastate almost everyone it encountered in its relentless journey through time and space. The first wave of humans would arrive in Alaska from Siberia as hunter-gatherers; the second wave from Western Europe would arrive as conquerors determined to colonize; and the third wave would arrive on slave boats from Africa, where we all began.

CHAPTER TWO

When the West Belonged to God: Discovering the New World Before Columbus

... The Western Hemisphere before 1492. It was, in the current view, a thriving, stunningly diverse place, a tumult of languages, trade, and culture, a region where tens of millions of people loved and hated and worshipped as people do everywhere. Much of this world vanished after Columbus, swept away by disease and subjugation. So thorough was the erasure that within a few generations neither conqueror nor conquered knew that this world had existed.
—CHARLES C. MANN, *1491*

When asked by an anthropologist what the Indian called America before the white man came, an Indian said simply, 'Ours'.
—VINE DELORIA, JR.

Recent genetic research shows Amerindians in the Bering Strait region of Alaska have the strongest DNA relations with the indigenous populations of Siberia. DNA analysis, in combination with linguistic, archaeological, and anthropologic research, has given us a better understanding of how humans migrated to the Americas. If there is one constant in the study of the migration and settlement of the Americas, however, it is that times and dates of events are perpetually changing as new sites and information are analyzed. Present research should be thought of as a general—and emerging—template to our understanding of this subject.[1]

Bering Land Bridge

Most scientists believe that the Paleo-Indians' first major settlements in America took place during the late Pleistocene, but the exact times have been subject to change as new data becomes available. The Great Plains of the late Pleistocene supported African-like animals: lions, mammoths, cheetah-like cats, saber-toothed cats, giant ground sloths, long-horned bison, short-face bears, hyenas, giant dire wolves, camels, and horses.[2]

The Pleistocene lasted from 2.5 million to 11,700 years ago. The largest human migration to the Americas probably took place around 13,000 to 16,500 years ago.[3] The settlement of the Americas was made possible by a temporary land bridge connecting Siberia and Alaska called the Bering Land Bridge. Ice sheets formed that covered most of North America and Europe, causing the sea level to drop dramatically. This exposed a fifty-five-mile reach of what had been shallow ocean floor between present-day Siberia and Alaska. During this period, Asian hunters could have followed game across the bridge into Alaska. As the climate warmed, much of the ice melted, sea level rose, and the people were trapped in the Americas.

Some of the newest migration models divide the movement into two general chronologies. The short chronology theory pegs the movement beyond Alaska into the Americas as no earlier than 15,000 to 17,000 years ago. The theory contends there were a number of waves of migration.[4] The newer, long chronology theory states that the first group of people entered the Americas around 21,000 to 40,000 years ago.[5] That would explain certain archaeological findings in Central and South America. That migration was then followed by a secondary wave beginning around 15,000 years ago.[6]

As Paleo-Indians migrated south into southern Alberta and beyond, they were amazed to find towering mastodons, armored rhinos, great wolves, saber-toothed cats, and ten-foot-long armadillos. Familiar animals today were super-sized—beavers the size of couches and one-ton-plus turtles. However, by around 9000 BCE these animals had disappeared. Before the Pleistocene, there were three species of horses and at least two camels that disappeared long before humans entered the Americas. Today's big-game hunters may be surprised to learn that moose, brown bear, and caribou also migrated from Asia and are not native to North America.[7]

Human Civilizations

Until 11,000 years ago, most humans lived in small bands (not unlike gorillas and chimpanzees). These small bands were pre-literate, nomadic hunter-gatherers, with members all from one family. Leadership was informal, there was no division of labor, and no religion based on the support of a ruler.[8]

As human bands began to farm and settle in one location, tribes developed. Tribes had hundreds of individuals rather than dozens. Overall, this society differed little from bands other than living in villages. As outsiders came to live in the villages, the need for formalized conflict resolution grew. Thus, chiefdom societies arose characterized by thousands of humans living in multiple villages. A typical chiefdom was twenty square miles of land and was composed of a number of villages each with a population of 350 to 650 people, making a total aggregate population of 2,800 to 5,400 individuals.[9] A chief ruled over a rudimentary bureaucracy and used religion to justify his rule. Slaves were first used to work the farms.[10]

How did a chief maintain his power? He tended to form military groups that had weapons while the rest of the general population did not. Also, as politicians do today, the chief tried to keep the masses happy by some wealth redistribution as long as it didn't affect the chief's wealth. By maintaining a police force, he curbed public disorder and violence, which also pleased the masses.

More importantly, as we will explore in more detail when we discuss religion, a chief tried to gain public support by using religion to justify his position. Bands and tribes had supernatural beliefs but weren't used to answering to a central authority, accepting wealth redistribution to the chief and his family and friends, or maintaining peace between unrelated individuals.

Chiefdoms formed ideologies—precursors to organized religion—which justified the chief's position. His beliefs were carried to the masses either through a charismatic person who was a political leader and priest or just a priest whose preaching provided spiritual justification for his ruler. The priest would justify wealth being transferred to the chief. Just as important, the priest had to convince the masses to live peacefully together and, if there was conflict, to not settle problems by violence. When achieved, a kinship of sorts developed between the strangers who made up a village. The priest also emphasized the importance of self-sacrifice to the point even of going to war and dying to support their chief.

The oldest complete law code in the world, the 2,000-year-old code of Hammurabi, was the fruit of war and conquest. After conquering all of southern Mesopotamia, the Babylonian Hammurabi, who ruled for forty-two years, self-consciously styled himself as the "King of Justice." Instead of embarking on a mass slaughter of his defeated subjects, he set about uniting his empire under a single set of laws. A steel carving completed 1754 BCE, now in the Louvre, lists the code's 282 laws—with scaled punishments—and declares that Hammurabi was sent by Babylon's patron deity, Marduk, to rule over men to bring about the well-being of the oppressed.[11] Using spiritual justification to control the masses would become a common theme used by European colonial powers centuries later.

New World Migration Patterns

One of the most important and famous archaeological sites ever discovered is in New Mexico. Findings there have given support for migration down the Bering Land Bridge. Clovis people are considered to be the ancestors of most American Indians. The Clovis culture was named after stone tools—especially ivory and bone spear points—found at several sites in New Mexico in the 1920s and 1930s.

In 1929, Ridgley Whiteman discovered the Clovis Man site in eastern New Mexico. Scientific results from the area were reported on November 25, 1932, in an issue of *Science News*. Eventually, radiocarbon testing showed the remains to be about 13,000 years old.[12]

By the 1930s, more Clovis sites were found in eastern North America that gave further credence that the Clovis culture was the first widespread culture in the New World. It appeared that hunters spread rapidly across North America, reaching the Atlantic coast of Nova Scotia in Canada and Virginia as early as 8500 BCE.[13]

However, newer archaeological sites revealing earlier inhabitants in Virginia, Oregon, Washington, South Carolina, Pennsylvania, and Texas, among other locales, have challenged this assumption.[14] In addition, in 1997 archaeologists working in Chile found artifacts more than 30,000 years old, suggesting human migration to South America occurred much earlier than the Clovis culture. These findings would support the theory of a long migration over the Bering Land Bridge. A few researchers also postulate that some human migration occurred early on from Asia by boat.[15]

Recent genetic findings show that Clovis people are direct ancestors of about eighty percent of all Indian populations in North and South America. The remaining twenty percent represent later migrations of Paleo-Indians.[16] The assumption that the Clovis people migrated across the Bering Land Bridge is supported by the analysis of the remains of the Anzick child unearthed in Montana and the Kennewick Man found in Washington state.

The migration to Alaska across the land bridge was not the most challenging journey south. It was the travel from Alaska to the rest of North

America that posed more daunting obstacles. A Pacific coastal route was open for land travel before 23,000 years ago and again after 15,000 years ago. The summer periods were warm enough to support vegetation and animals for food as the migration progressed. Language analysis pegs the movement of tribes along the eastern slope of the Rocky Mountains and eastward across the Great Plains to the Atlantic seaboard by at least 13,000 to 10,000 years ago.[17]

Progression of Civilization

Archaeological time periods in the Americas differ from those attributed to Old World history learned in our high school classes. Old World history is divided into Paleolithic, Mesolithic, Neolithic, Chalcolithic, and Bronze Age. The periods in America have been defined as the Paleo-Indian or Lithic stage—this includes the big-game hunters of the Clovis and Folsom cultures (before 8000 BCE); Archaic stage—subsistence on nuts, seeds, and shellfish cultures (8000 BCE to 1000 BCE); Formative stage—characterized by formation of permanent villages, ceremonies using pottery, weaving, and food production (1000 BCE to 500 CE); Classic stage—origins of metallurgy, urbanism, and ceremonial centers with theocracy mainly in Mesoamerica and Peru (500 CE to 1200 CE); and Post-Classic stage—complex urbanism and militarism as seen in the Aztec and late Mayan cultures (1200 CE onward).[18] Since 1958, when these classifications were first published, they have been further refined by more local classifications as more historical information has become available.

The Agricultural Revolution, or Neolithic Revolution, evolved around 12,000 years ago in the Fertile Crescent of southwest Asia—today's Iraq, Kuwait, Iran, Turkey, Syria, Jordan, Israel, Palestine, and Lebanon. Since there is early evidence in the region for writing and the formation of state-level societies, it has been nicknamed "The Cradle of Civilization."[19]

About 10,000 years ago, humans transitioned from hunting and gathering (although for many centuries hunting intensified as game diminished) to farming, which allowed larger populations to live together for the first time in one place. It also gave rise to communicable diseases that could spread rapidly in denser populations. Over the next 5,000 years, the cultivation of domestic plants occurred in China, South America, and Mesoamerica (an area extending from central Mexico south to northern Costa Rica), the Andes, and the southeastern United States.[20] While 10,000 years ago Indians in Mesoamerica and Peru were discovering agriculture and forming small villages, New England had few inhabitants due to persistent ice sheets.[21]

The invention of farming occurred in Europe about 8,500 years ago and caused a rapid evolutionary shift in the genes of Europeans as they adapted to new diets, new pathogens, and new social structures. It also was the period when Europeans' skin changed from dark to light through genetic mutations. Some of this can be inferred from the study of modern DNA, but ancient DNA can catch it in the act. One gene that changed rapidly was the mutation for lactase persistence—that is, the ability to continue digesting lactose (the sugar in milk) after infancy. Normally, mammals don't need to digest lactose as adults, and the necessary lactase gene switches off when a baby is weaned from its mother. This changed for human beings, however, when dairy farming introduced milk into the adult diet. A gene mutation that prevented lactase from switching off spread in Europeans fairly late, around 4,300 years ago, probably long after dairy farming was invented, but it gave its possessors a significant advantage. They derived nutrition from drinking milk and suffered less indigestion than their rivals.[22]

Two genes that affected skin color were also subject to rapid evolutionary selection as early farmers tried to subsist on grain-rich, vitamin D–poor diets in northern areas with low levels of sunlight. Very few foods naturally contain vitamin D. Low levels can result in impaired bone mineralization and bone damage—like rickets. Sunlight helps the skin to convert a form of cholesterol into a form of vitamin D. The shift to pale skin—which produces vitamin D more efficiently than darker skin—among northern Europeans after the advent of farming appears to have proceeded rapidly, pointing to some of the strongest selection pressures ever recorded in human genetics. Ironically, one of the earliest forms of racism was based on skin color.[23]

After 9500 BCE, during the Archaic Era, climate moderated in North America and the ice sheets gradually melted. That led to the extinction of a number of large mammals—including mammoths, sloths, and camels—forcing humans to look elsewhere for reliable food sources. Bison were one of the larger animals that survived. The human search for big game led to migration from the drought-stricken Great Basin—a 400,000-square-mile area between the Rocky Mountains and the Sierra Nevada—into the Rockies and across the continent until they reached the Atlantic Ocean.

This way of life may have lasted in Montana and Wyoming for the next 5,000 years and even longer to around 1300 CE in the southern Rockies. Native American farmers of the Great Plains grew their crops in the low-lying river valleys. It wasn't until the nineteenth century that Europeans using animal-drawn plows tilled the tough sod of the upland areas.

Most Indians lived in small family groups or bands. They ventured out only about 100 miles from home for hunting, fishing, and gathering wild plants. Tools were made out of stone, bone, or wood. As researchers uncovered their habitat, they named the sites after the types of spear points that were used. Sites such as Clovis, Sandia, Folsom, or Cascade each had its unique tools.[24]

While bows and arrows were present in Africa, northern Europe, and Asia by 9000 BCE, their appearance in the North American Arctic occurred later. Some estimates are as late as 6000 BCE.[25] This hunting method gradually made its progression southward: 200 CE in the southern plains of Saskatchewan and Alberta; 500 to 600 CE in the southern plains of Texas; 500 CE in California (present in petroglyph hunting scenes in the Coso Range); and 575 to 700 CE in the American Southwest.[26]

The increased efficiency of the bow and arrow didn't preclude the hunters still treating slain animals with respect. They acknowledged the fact that every animal possessed its own spiritual powers. Dancing to prepare themselves and their prey before hunting, the Indians also butchered the animals in a special ritual that would not anger the animal spirits.[27]

American Buffalo

The bow and arrow emerged as one method to kill their prized prey. As many of North America's ice age mammals became extinct, the bison flourished unrivaled and could be found in great quantities from Georgia to Durango (Mexico) to Great Slave Lake in Canada and southeastern Washington state to Lake Erie. But it was the grasslands of the Great Plains where the bison herds expanded the most. In dry periods, the short grasses of the western Plains retained enough moisture to provide not only food but water.[28] The grasses of the northwestern Plains were especially high in nutrition. In addition, longer and warmer seasons allowed for longer mating seasons.[29]

The species name for the American bison is *Bison bison,* often popularly called buffalo. There are two kinds: the plains and the larger, darker wood bison. They were known to the Spanish explorers as *cibola, bisonte,* or *armente.* Lakota called them *tatanka.* The bison is the largest of North American land animals. A bull might grow to six feet, six inches tall at the shoulder and weigh 2,000 pounds, whereas the cows are shorter and may weigh half that. Mating season is in the summer months, and a cow gives birth to only one calf. Average life ranges from twenty to forty years. They can run up to thirty-five miles per hour and sustain that speed for thirty minutes. Perhaps the Lakota are most closely associated with this symbol of the American West, and they call themselves *Pte Taoyate,* or the "People Who Belong to the Buffalo."[30]

Before the arrival of the modern horse in the Americas, common methods of hunting bison included driving startled herds over cliffs or so-called buffalo jumps, or herding them into pens. Early on, the Plains' people hunted on foot and used dogs pulling travois to haul the meat back to camp. With the introduction of Spanish horses, Native Americans hunted the massive herds on horseback, using arrows and fourteen-foot-long lances to kill bison. They could kill up to 300 bison in a ten-minute hunt. Their meat, hides, bones, sinew, and horns were all used. Nothing went to waste. Unfortunately, this source of food was erratic and unpredictable as the herds roamed the vast, open prairies.

There was no more resilient large animal on the Great Plains than the bison. A great number of large mammals disappeared during the Pleistocene, but not the king of the Plains. But the bison still had its challenges. The Great Drought (8,500 to 4,730 years ago) saw the disappearance of the animal and humans on the Southern Plains. Two more arid periods followed: the Scandic Drought (300 to 900 CE) and the Pacific Drought (1250 to 1525).[31]

As Spanish explorers like Coronado in the 1530s explored the Plains, the Little Ice Age was beginning, which allowed herd expansions as plentiful rains nourished high-nutrient grasses like buffalo grass and grama grasses. In *American Serengeti,* Dan Flores estimates there were around 25 million bison at their peak, but the first half of the nineteenth century brought drier and warmer conditions. The peak of the drought occurred between 1858 and 1866, signaling the end of the Little Ice Age.[32]

Just at the time the great herds were stressed by a food and water shortage, white settlers in the 1840s and 1850s traveling the Overland Trails to Oregon and California brought rinderpest, anthrax, and bovine tuberculosis that infected the bison and decimated their numbers. Conditions worsened as rapidly expanding wild horse populations competed for grazing lands. White and Native American hide hunters killed large numbers of bison, and by the time of the Civil War only 10 to 12 million bison remained. By the 1880s, thousands of professional hunters had decreased the population to a few hundred animals.[33] Other large game animals that roamed much of the West were also killed in great numbers; populations of elk, sheep, pronghorns, grizzlies, wild horses, and wolves all declined.[34]

Domestic Life

It was the ability to grow maize that transformed the early life of humans. Maize yields more grain per acre than any other cereal. *Corn* is the term used in the United States and parts of Europe for sweet, yellow, uniform kernels. Early Indian maize, however, was a type of "corn" that was multicolored and eaten after drying and grinding.[35] The earliest known maize in the Americas was from the Tehuacan Valley in Mexico and has been dated to around 5500 BCE by radiocarbon dating and 3500 BCE by newer, mass spectrophotometric analysis.[36] Since domesticated corn does not disperse seed and reproduce without human husbandry, it took many centuries for Mexican corn, along with beans and squash, to reach the American Southwest, and many more centuries for it to appear in the Northern Plains and the Northeast. Northeastern corn also had to be frost resistant, a mutation that required time, and it first appeared sometime before 900 CE.[37]

Archaeological digs reveal that people living around 3000 BCE had taken up pottery, cultivated grains and squash, and fished. Inland bands hunted deer and elk. Humans over the centuries adapted their lives to the locale in which they lived. Home became very important to their social and spiritual identity.[38] During this period in Mesoamerica, corn, beans, and squash had been domesticated, as had the turkey. In eastern North America, sunflowers were domesticated, but there were no domesticated animals other than dogs.[39] This is in stark contrast to the rest of the world where sheep, goats, pigs, and cows had been domesticated by 6000 BCE. By about 4000 BCE horses were domesticated in Ukraine. Around 500 years later, llamas and alpacas in the Andes were domesticated. By 2500 BCE, the camel had also been domesticated in Central Asia and Arabia.[40]

In 1200 BCE, the "Golden Era" in North America arose. Planting and harvesting became even more important to many groups from coast to coast. The use of fire to improve desired vegetation became commonplace. In the Pacific Northwest, brushes and grasses were burned and replaced by camas and bracken. Likewise, in the Midwest and East, forests were burned to make way for farm land, berry bushes, and shrubs. On the prairies, fire steered bison into traps.[41]

Several centuries later, the landscape had dramatically changed across North America. Large societies supported by sophisticated agriculture were thriving from coast to coast. In the desert Southwest between 1000 BCE and 1000 CE, three distinct cultures developed. In southern Arizona was the Hohokam culture that featured irrigated fields of corn, beans, pumpkins, and squash. They traded with natives of California who visited their towns. However, by 1400 CE their culture disintegrated from drought and overpopulation. In central Arizona, the Mogollon culture developed. They were noted farmers and pottery makers. Their society also faded from drought, overpopulation, and Apache raids.[42]

By 700 CE, Ancestral Puebloans settled in Arizona, New Mexico, and Colorado. They hunted, farmed, and were noted basket-makers. For centuries they lived in impressive villages noted for their adobe and stone buildings. But by 1300 CE they too disappeared.[43]

Further east in the Mississippi Valley, the Woodland culture developed in the later Archaic Era. The best-known settlement was Poverty Point, Louisiana, where by 1400 BCE people built large mounds as high as seventy-five feet and encompassing miles of land. The mounds were used for homes, ceremonies, public business, play, and burial sites. Other Woodland cultures developed north of Louisiana in Ohio, Kentucky, and West Virginia.[44]

About 100 BCE, the Hopewell culture arose in Illinois. Over centuries, benefitted by a warming trend and a lull in widespread wars, hundreds of Hopewell villages dotted the country from the East to the edge of the Great Plains and down to the Gulf of Mexico. Trading among villages was commonplace. The Hopewell culture also spread due to religious fervor and was known for its elaborate funeral rites, which often took place on top of earthen mounds. The mound making was all done by human labor because no animals large enough for the task had yet been domesticated.[45]

Hopewell ceremonies included spiritual trances aided by tobacco that sent the people's souls to the spirit worlds. Eventually, shamans appeared who became gatekeepers to the Indians' spiritual life. Even more, shamans acquired healing lore, developed religion for the masses to follow, communicated with gods, and directed where mounds should be built. They most likely influenced the later Cahokia society.[46]

As in Mesoamerica, corn was the most important crop grown. Yet people needed to supplement their corn diet because, by itself, corn is deficient in niacin (vitamin B3). A diet lacking in niacin will lead to pellagra, known by its four Ds: dermatitis, dementia, diarrhea, and death. In fact, pellagra was common as late as the early twentieth century in the American South and in Europe where corn became a dietary mainstay. Foods that are rich in tryptophan—which the body can convert to niacin—include fish, poultry, and red meats.[47]

However, as the weather cooled around 350 CE, the northern villages declined. Five hundred years later, a warming trend allowed a new society to flourish, the Mississippian culture, characterized by maize cultivation. These people were probably descendants of the earlier Hopewell people. The Mississippian culture remained intact until the appearance of Europeans centuries later.[48]

The city of Cahokia near the Mississippi River and across from present-day St. Louis, Missouri, was the center of the new culture. It peaked at about the time of the Norman invasion of England and the Crusades. The Cahokia culture was fully established by 950 CE and was populated by descendants of the Hopewell. With fertile soil and plentiful water, the population exploded. The city was the largest urban area north of Mexico, with an estimated 30,000 people spread over a five-mile radius. There were really no other urban centers that could be called cities north of the Rio Grande. The city's skyline was dominated by Monk's Mound, a 100-foot-tall earthen structure built over hundreds of years. The city was the religious, economic, and political center for villages over half the continent. Hundreds of villages with characteristic mounds were present from southern Canada to the Gulf of Mexico and from the Plains east to the Atlantic Ocean.[49]

In the thirteenth century, a devastating earthquake destroyed the city and caused the entire western side of Monk's Mound to collapse. Floods were common, and by 1350 the population had fled. It would be the last large Indian community to exist north of Mexico. By the time the French—who named it—arrived in the seventeenth century, the inhabitants had scattered.[50]

Out on the Great Plains, the changing climates also led to adaptation. From 300 to 700 CE, strong, drying, westerly winds produced warmer temperatures. Four hundred years later, tropical Pacific rains allowed prairie grass to flourish, but once again drought and colder conditions followed from 1250 to 1525 CE. By the sixteenth century, the prairie grasses were retreating, causing population shifts as hunters and farmers looked for better opportunities.[51]

By 1000 CE on the Northern Plains, people were growing corn in the river valleys and hunting bison. On the Great Bend of the Missouri River, the Hidatsa, Mandan, and Arikara built communities on corn cultivation. Many thought "Mother Corn" had led them into the fertile valley and then turned herself into seed to initiate the first crops. Producing corn—planting, cultivating, and harvesting—was the total responsibility of the women.[52]

Indians at the Time of Columbus

The ancestors of many of the modern American Indian tribes had found their home by 1500 CE. They would be occupying the same locales right up until the first Europeans arrived. Early desert cultures of the Southwest disseminated and were known as Puebloans who occupied northern Arizona and New Mexico and the deserts of southern Arizona. The Apache from the north migrated to that region around the same time, but the Ute and Navajo came later, just before the Spanish invaded.[53]

Around 1500 CE, Plains cultures were in place that would eventually produce the Blackfeet, Arapaho, Cheyenne, Comanche, and Sioux tribes. They were nomadic groups that chased bison all over the Plains. Hunts were all on foot because they did not have horses until the Spanish introduced them. Eventually, these tribes were joined by other groups—like the Lakota Sioux—who were dislocated from prior homes north and west of Lake Superior in Canada.[54]

Along the Missouri, Platte, and Kansas Rivers, east of the Plains, the Wichita and Kansa (Kaw) people combined farming in the fertile valleys with seasonal bison hunting. North of them, the Pawnee of Nebraska and the Arikara of South Dakota shared a similar lifestyle. Major trading posts on the upper Missouri valley were found in Mandan and Arikara villages. Plains hunters would arrive with hides, meat, and horns and exchange them for locally grown food crops.[55]

In what would become the eastern United States, three cultures developed—in the South, Muskogean; the Atlantic coast, Algonquin; and in New York, Georgia, and Tennessee, the Iroquoian. Farming and hunting were important to these groups, as was fishing in rivers, lakes, and the Atlantic Ocean. When food was scarce, the Iroquois raided other groups and sometimes fought all-out wars. Each group had its own language and religion, which intensified the rivalries and also led to conflict.[56] By 1500 CE, there were as many as 600 distinct groups numbering into the millions of people. The exact number is controversial. Most groups were not in organized tribes though they might have shared a similar culture.[57]

Around 1500 CE, the precipitation on the Great Plains increased dramatically and so did the bison population. The improvement in hunting prospects caused a dramatic rise in the Indian populations that practiced more regular communal bison hunts. Some have suggested that the bison population once stood at 75 million, but more recent reports place it at 30 million. We will probably never know for sure exactly how many there really were. Either way, one bison—around 900 pounds—provided a small group of Indians a steady supply of meat for several weeks. It was a welcome source of nutrition and calories since many of the plants the people ate were low in protein.[58]

As their religion developed, medicine men and women performed rituals and songs that were intended to spiritually draw bison to the jumps and to ensure a successful hunt. More than 100 jump sites have been identified, with the most famous one—Head Smashed In—located in southern Alberta. The site featured a sixty-foot cliff and was used for more than 5,000 years, right up until the nineteenth century. As with most jumps, there was a nearby grazing area of grass that attracted the bison. More than 100,000 bison died there over the centuries. It could take days to get the herd in position to run over the jump. Eventually, after the Spanish arrived with horses, hunting bison on horseback with lances and bows and arrows became an important means of killing the giant beasts. Indians made use of every part of the bison except the grunt and mumbles.[59]

It should be remembered that many of the Indian groups had no writing. Much of what we know about them comes from the journals of the first Europeans to encounter them. At the time of Columbus (1492), the largest Indian populations lived south of the Rio Grande. They were not nomadic, but lived in some of the largest cities in the world. The majority lived on farms and fished.[60] In 1491, the Inka[61] of Peru had created the largest empire in the world. They were bigger than the Ming Dynasty in China, Ivan the Great's Russia, the Ottoman Empire, the Aztec Empire, and bigger by far than any European nation. It was also the shortest lived—100 years—being destroyed by the Spanish in the sixteenth century.[62]

Based on sheer numbers, North America was more notable for its animals than its people. Naturalist Ernest Thompson Seton once described North America as home to 60 million bison, 30 to 40 million pronghorn, 10 million elk, 10 million mule deer, and 2 million mountain sheep. While his estimates may be on the high side, the point is that the land teemed with large mammals that found the environment quite to their liking. It was a time when nature ruled, and the West belonged to God.[63]

Why was there a lack of progress in farming in the Western Hemisphere? The most likely explanation is the absence of large, domesticated mammals, chiefly cattle, sheep, horses, donkeys, camels, and water buffalo. As Jared Diamond wrote, "The Americas had only one species of big domestic mammal, the llama/alpaca, confined to a small area of the Andes and the adjacent Peruvian coast. . . . [But] the llama never bore a rider, never pulled a cart or plow, and never served as a power source or vehicle of warfare."[64]

The early Spanish explorers had no idea that they were entering a land inhabited by Indians who had lived in great cities and were, despite the lack of domesticated livestock, sophisticated farmers. Neither the Europeans nor the Indians knew that they had come from common ancestors who began to leave Africa around 100,000 years ago in search of a better life. Both groups had found a better life, but the Europeans weren't satisfied. They wanted more. They wanted what the Indians had, and in time they would succeed in their quest, but at a tragic cost to the natives. Religion, science, medicine, and philosophy would convince white men that they were entitled to rule the world.

CHAPTER THREE

Lost Souls in Revelry: Collision of Races

The love of possessions is the disease among them.
—SITTING BULL

The notion that Indians and Frenchmen shared a special affinity has a long history. While Indian peoples were resisting Spanish conquistadors in the South, Indians in the Great Lakes and the Mississippi Valley were smoking the calumet with French explorers. While English colonists invaded Indian lands and put bounties on Indian scalps, French traders exchanged merchandise for furs, married into Indian societies, and fathered Indian children.
—COLIN G. CALLOWAY, *ONE VAST WINTER COUNT*

For most of us, harkening back to our grade school history classes, the first encounter of the English with Native Americans took place at the first Thanksgiving in the fall of 1621. In the American consciousness, the Pilgrims exemplify the extraordinary imagination and belief, fortitude and courage, shown by colonists across early America.

The festivities involved fifty English men and women and ninety Native Americans. Only a year earlier the colonists had arrived on a leaky wine ship, the *Mayflower*, and undertook the building of a hillside settlement overlooking the ocean, living in a few wooden huts and a stockade. Their first winter was miserable, and half of their number perished from malnutrition and disease. Having brought inadequate supplies from England, they struggled to farm the land and relied heavily on their Indian hosts for expertise in food.

The Pilgrims celebrated for three days, and Edward Winslow Witt, who buried his wife the previous spring, commented, "Our harvest being gotten in, our governor sent four men on fowling so that we might after special manner rejoice together after we had gathered the fruits of our labor."[1] Over the years, the story has been heavily mythologized. What we do know is that English colonists—350,000 of them arriving in the seventeenth century—while diverse, were also very English. They clung to their old identities and tried to preserve them. In this they failed and instead a new national character was born possessing the primary traits that are still visible in Americans today. They also failed in preserving good relationships with the Native Americans who helped them survive in the early years. As Europeans secured a foothold in the New World, they became more belligerent to those who welcomed them to America. They flowed around and passed Native Americans like a tide cutting off an island from the shore.

No single religious institution, no single sacred book, no unified priesthood or common creed, no core group of rituals can be found in the model patterns of the lives of Native American peoples early on. It was only centuries into colonization that a pan-Indian identity emerged and, likewise, that intertribal religious movements such as the Native American church, with its peyote-based ritual observance, came into being.[2]

Anti-Indian sentiments were always only obliquely about the Native American. They were victims but not the cause. The politics of hate that was directed toward the Indians was also experienced in prior centuries by Jews, Muslims, sub-Saharan Africans, other Christians, and their fellow travelers in a seemingly endless list of new mutations that continues even today.

The more familiar driving thrust of the assault on Jews was similarly felt by the Indians. In the Middle Ages, Jews were hated for their religion. In fact, they were even blamed for causing the plague by poisoning the wells. That also was the starting point for colonial Europeans' focus on the heathen Indians—a religious ethnic cleansing. In the nineteenth century, Jews were hated for their race as were the Indians.[3]

The legitimization of anti-Indian feelings in the New World changed over time. Hatred and racism, when taken into the public domain, are singularly difficult to justify, which is why Europeans and Americans have always sought vindication from the highest source of authority in their culture. In the Middle Ages it was religion, supplemented later by the philosophy of the Enlightenment. In nineteenth-century Europe and America, it was science and medicine. German anti-Semitism and America's hatred of Native Americans was based on scientific racism (the so-called scientific study of race), Manifest Destiny, and social Darwinism—the doctrine that in human history, as in nature, the strong survive by eliminating the weak. Historically, humans have repeatedly failed to show tolerance for differences among people, which is the essential foundation of a free society.

By the time of Columbus, humans had spread over the entire Western Hemisphere. Agriculture was practiced in two-thirds of the present-day United States, with many areas of the Southwest terraced and irrigated. Mounds by the thousands and maize fields dotted the Midwest and Southeast. The forests along the Eastern seaboard had been thinned to allow for farms, and the Pacific Northwest's streams were filled with salmon nets. In all regions, fire was used to burn fields, brush, and trees.[4]

From that time on, agricultural products that were native to one land were adapted to another, transported by European ships. Central America became home to African bananas and coffee, and Africa proved fertile land for maize from Mesoamerica. The main food for many parts of Europe became maize. Mesoamerican peppers and tomatoes found their way to Thailand and Italy, while Andean potatoes became a staple in Ireland. Apples native to the Middle East appeared all over the Americas. This symbiotic relationship has been called the Columbian Exchange.[5]

Unfortunately, fruits and vegetables were not the only things traded. European diseases wiped out large numbers of natives throughout the Americas. In the early sixteenth century, Hernando de Soto's expedition to the Southeast noted large numbers of people but not a single bison. That all changed as infections killed entire villages. One hundred years later, La Salle, who canoed down the Mississippi, saw no evidence of any humans. What they did find were great herds of bison that had greatly expanded due in part to the lack of hunters and a trend toward increased precipitation. Elk showed up in large numbers around the Yellowstone area about 500 years ago. Natives of the coasts were also decimated, which allowed clams and mussels to thrive. The beautiful wilderness that European writers loved to describe was artificially created by human destruction brought on by communicable diseases.[6]

European Invaders Land in America

As early as the tenth century, Norsemen from Iceland, some led by Leif Erikson, stayed for a time in New England or Nova Scotia, which they called Vinland. Others followed, but their few encampments never developed into permanent settlements.

By the late fifteenth century, two developments prompted the discovery of new lands outside of Europe. There was a large merchant class that sought foreign trade in spices, dyestuffs, and textiles from India and the Far East. It was theorized that sailing west of Europe would lead to a shorter route than sailing around Africa and the dangerous Cape of Good Hope to reach these lucrative trade markets. With a new type of vessel, the caravel, which was faster and more seaworthy, the Portuguese took the lead in maritime exploration. They were encouraged by Prince Henry the Navigator and eventually discovered the Azores. In 1488, Bartholomew Dias passed the Cape of Good Hope (which he called the Cape of Storms), and ten years later Vasco da Gama followed and reached India.

Another development in this period was the rise of kings that led to organized states with the power and resources to sponsor explorations. During the fifteenth century, Portugal led the way. Soon it would have a rival in Spain, which would be the first to find America and the first to find a use for it.

In 1492, after wresting Granada from the Moors, Spain under the direction of Queen Isabella and her husband Ferdinand II paid for three ships led by Christopher Columbus, who intended to discover a passage to the Orient by sailing west. Columbus earlier had sent a proposal for his voyage to a committee of Catholic churchmen for approval. At that time, essentially all doctors, lawyers, astronomers, or cartographers held ecclesiastical titles. The expedition was an affair of state but clearly also of church. The most loyal Roman Catholic nation in Europe at the time, Spain took seriously its responsibility to the pope and to maintaining the purity of its faith.

Columbus shared the religious vision of Catholic mission even as he shared the conviction that God ruled human history. A regular communicant, given to daily prayer as well as the study of religious writings, the mariner interpreted his expedition in scriptural terms. "God made me," he declared, "the messenger of the new heaven and the new earth of which he spoke in the Apocalypse of St. John, after having spoken of it through the mouth of Isaiah; and he showed me the spot where to find it." Later he wrote, "Following the light of the sun, we left the Old World."[7]

He gave all glory to God, and in 1493 he wrote that his success was not of his doings, "but to the holy Christian faith, and to the piety and religion of our Sovereigns." He added, let all "give thanks to our Lord and Savior Jesus Christ, who has granted us so great a victory in such prosperity. Let processions be made and sacred feasts be held, and the temples be adorned with festive boughs. Let Christ rejoice on earth, as he rejoices in heaven in the prospect of the salvation of the souls of so many nations hitherto lost." It was a new chapter in salvation history, and it was directed at Native Americans.[8]

At this time, iron was used for tools in all complex Eurasian societies. That was not the case in the Americas, where stone, wood, and bone were still the principal materials for tools in all societies. The Europeans carried with them swords, lances, daggers, small firearms, and battle armor and helmets made of steel to protect themselves. The Native Americans' clubs, axes, and bows and arrows proved no match to the invaders.

Columbus carried a letter addressed to the Emperor of China, which he never had the opportunity to deliver, but he did find America at the island of San Salvador on October 12, 1492. He also explored the other Bahamas and Cuba. By March 1493, he was back in Spain. Columbus never did find China or Japan, but he did find gold in the new world. The goal was always to find a shorter passage to China and the Orient, and even after Ferdinand Magellan sailed around the tip of South America (1519-1522), for the next two centuries explorers probed the American rivers in search of the Pacific.

When Columbus came ashore in 1492 in the Bahamas, North America was not a wilderness with a few scattered natives living like animals off the land. By some conservative estimates, there were between 2 million and 10 million people. There were at least 300 distinct cultures—some estimate as many as 600—and over 200 different languages. In North America, most of the population was concentrated along the coastal areas of what is now California, with the Southwest having the second major concentration of Indians. The Europeans called groups of Indians "tribes," which tended to trivialize their complex civilizations. The Indians had a variety of political organizations. Some were hunters, while some were farmers, and there were numerous different religious beliefs.[9]

A large number of Indians were traders, and by the time of Columbus seashells from the East Coast could be found hundreds of miles inland. Precious stones from the Far West could be found on the East Coast, while mica from the Appalachians was traded for copper from the Great Lakes area.

The New World and Old World were much different. European countries were characterized by centralized governments, authoritarian religious groups, well-defined class structure, books (especially the Bible), scientific inventions, and technology. Conversely, the Indians were regionally fragmented.

There were the Five Nations of the Iroquois Confederacy in New York, the confederation led by the Powhatan in Virginia, and the chiefdoms in the Southeast. These organizations were the exception, as most groups in North America operated as individual villages with a council of respected elders. The Indians revered nature more than scientific or technological progress. History was mainly understood through oral presentations. The earth, sun, moon, plants, and animals all had spiritual powers. This concept was absolutely foreign to the Europeans, who saw these ideas as heretical. Nature to the white man was to be conquered, and its fruits to be developed for human consumption. God deemed them His chosen people. They were the second Israelites.[10]

As late as 1500, less than twenty percent of the world's land area was marked off into states run by bureaucrats and governed by laws—just the opposite of today. Those societies that developed a centralized government and organized religion the earliest turned out to dominate the modern world. This fact, along with germs, writing, and technology, led the Europeans to dominate the New World Indians.[11]

Each Indian tribe was as culturally different as the various countries in Europe, but unlike Catholic Europe, each had distinct religions and mythologies with their own stories of creation and the afterlife. Throughout North America, the tribes related stories of the coming of the white man. It's possible that the word had traveled throughout the New World after the landing of the earliest European explorers.

In 1833, Black Hawk in his autobiography recalled his great-grandfather's dream of the coming of the whites. His great-grandfather was born around what would become Montréal. The white visitor may have been the Frenchman Samuel de Champlain, who established a trading post there in 1611. The explorer stated that he was the son of the King of France and the Great Spirit directed him to come to the area where he would meet a nation of people who had never seen a white man. He declared that they should be his children, and he should be their father.[12]

Many natives thought that the newcomers might be supernatural deities. Columbus reported that the natives thought he and his men had come from heaven until some of the natives held the Spaniards' heads underwater until they drowned. This made them suspicious that they were not actually gods. Conversely, the European's stereotype of the Indian ranged from noble savage and pleasant Thanksgiving visitor to bloodthirsty barbarian who stood in the way of civilizing an untamed wilderness.

The first impression of the lifestyle of Indians came from Columbus in a widely published letter in 1493:

It is true that, after they have been reassured and have lost this fear, they are so guileless and so generous with all that they possess, that no one would believe it who has not seen it. They refuse nothing that they possess, if it be asked of them, on the contrary, they invite anyone to share it and display as much love as if they would give their hearts. They are content with whatever trifle of whatever kind that may be given to them, whether it be of value or valueless....

They do not hold any creed nor are they idolaters; but they all believe that power and good are in the heavens and were very firmly convinced that I, with these ships and men, came from the heavens, and in this belief they everywhere received me after they had mastered their fear. This belief is not the result of ignorance, for they are, on the contrary, of very acute intelligence and they are men who navigate all those seas, so that it is amazing how good an account they give of everything. It is because they have never seen people clothed or ships of such a kind....

In all these islands, I saw no great diversity in the parents of the people or in their manners and language. On the contrary, they all understand one another, which is a very curious thing....

In all these islands, it seems to me that all men are content with one woman, and to their chief or king they give as many as twenty. It appears to me that the women work more than do the men. I have not been able to learn if they hold private property; it seemed to me to be that all took a share in whatever anyone had, especially of eatable things.[13]

A publication even more widespread was Amerigo Vespucci's *Mundas Novus,* published about 1504-1505. As Europeans perceived that they would have future confrontations with the Indians, reports were less positive and more devaluing:

They have no cloth either of wool, linen or cotton, since they need it not; neither do they have goods of their own, but all things are held in common. They live together without king, without government, and each is his own master. They marry as many wives as they please; and son cohabits with mother, brother with sister, male cousin with female, and any man with the first woman he meets. They dissolve their marriages as often as they please, and observe no sort of law with respect to them. Beyond the fact that they have no church, no religion and are not idolaters, what more can I say? They live according to nature, and may be called Epicureans rather than Stoics. There are no merchants among their number, nor is there barter. The nations wage war upon one another without art or order. The elders by means of certain harangues of theirs bend the youths to their will and inflame them to wars in which they cruelly kill one another, and those whom they bring home captive from war they preserve, not to spare their lives, but that they may be slain for food; for they eat one another, the victors, the vanquished, and among other kinds of meat human flesh is a common article of diet with them. . . .[14]

The interaction of whites and Indians over the centuries has been analyzed in a variety of ways. Naturally, historians in textbooks and nonfiction organize the information usually in a linear manner describing people, dates, policies, movements, and institutions over decades and centuries—who, what, when, and where. On the other hand, anthologies present a common theme of the conflicting values that characterized the white settlement of the American West.

Most avoid in-depth discussions on the important impact religious differences played in American history—how and why. The cultures never seemed to understand each other completely. In general, the Europeans tended to trivialize the Indians' religious beliefs, customs, and love for the land. The Indians believed God was in all objects, while the Europeans believed the Indians would not be civilized without knowing their Christian God.

The three main European powers interacted with the Indians in their own unique ways. The French seemed to get along with the Indians the best, while the Spanish considered the Native Americans to be both pagan and inferior. The English felt superior and thought of the Indians as savages and devil worshipers who stood in the way of developing an English-speaking colonial world in North America. Synonyms for Indians included savage, infidel, heathen, and barbarian. The terms were associated with lack of civility and Christianity.

Battles and Spoils

There were three major periods of conflict between the whites and Indians of North America. The first lasted from the arrival of the Spaniards until they reconquered the Pueblo Indians in New Mexico in 1692. By the 1820s, Spain was forced to abandon its colonies. The second conflict among the

English, the French, and a large number of Native American peoples east of the Mississippi started with the Virginia uprising in 1622 and ended after the War of 1812. The final conflict took place between the newly formed United States in a series of wars that started in the 1790s and symbolically ended in 1890 at the massacre at Wounded Knee in South Dakota.[15]

Even the most charismatic Indian leaders could not cobble together a multi-tribal military force to oppose the Europeans. Neither unexpected ambushes nor more organized military assaults could stem the onslaught from Europe. The Europeans overwhelmed the Indians with their military force and destroyed village after village with their hidden weapon—infectious diseases.

In 1494, the Treaty of Tordesillas divided the New World by a line drawn north and south, 370 leagues west of the Cape Verde Islands. Under the treaty, Spain claimed all lands west of this line, while Portugal claimed all lands to the East. Any lands already ruled by a "Christian king" would not be colonized. Spaniards soon were swarming over the Caribbean islands and onto the mainlands of North and South America. The natives were no match for these invaders who were better armed and unscrupulous. Gold was the invaders' goal, and wherever the Spaniards traveled they killed or enslaved the natives. Overworked and bedeviled by disease, the natives soon were few in number, and this prompted the Spaniards to purchase African black slaves from the Portuguese. This began an involuntary migration that ultimately carried nearly 10 million Africans to the New World.

The conquistadors overwhelmed whole countries. Hernando Cortés, with only 1,500 men, conquered all of Mexico (1519-1521), and Francisco Pizarro with even fewer men conquered Peru (1531-1535). They ransacked palaces and shipped gold and silver back to Spain. It was a stunning defeat for the natives whose population was even greater than the 9 million citizens of sixteenth-century Spain. There were six major Spanish expeditions: Juan Ponce de León (1521), Lucas Vazquez de Ayllón (1526), Panfilo de Narváez (1528), Hernando de Soto (1539-1543), Tristan de Luna (1559-1561), and Juan Pardo (1566-1568); and one French: Jean Ribault (1562-1564).[16] Many Spanish victories over the natives were aided by repeated smallpox outbreaks that decimated the populations—1531, 1532, 1538, 1545-1548, 1550, 1559-1560, 1563-1564, 1576-1580, 1587, and 1595.[17]

The Indians were enslaved and used to mine the great deposits of silver ore that were discovered in both Mexico and Peru. They also were used to supply labor for Spanish ranches and farms. Over the next century, the Spanish depleted their labor force through overwork and disease, and the

Mexican population of natives declined from perhaps as many as 25 million to just a few million. Comparable declines were seen in Peru.

The slave trade can be traced back to ancient Egypt where black Africans enslaved and sold other black Africans. As historian John Thornton notes, slavery was intrinsic to "many if not all pre-colonial African societies."[18] Thus, by the time of the Spanish invasion, the exportation of black slaves had been going on for several thousand years. In the last few centuries, the slaves were sent mainly to Islamic societies.[19]

Slavery was widespread in pre-Columbian North America, where at least thirty-nine societies had slaves, according to the Standard Cross-Cultural Files. It was apparently quite brutal among the Northwest Indians. Later, in 1838 when the Cherokee were forced to leave their homeland in Georgia to resettle in the Oklahoma territory—the famous Trail of Tears—they took their black slaves with them.[20]

The first shipment of slaves from Africa occurred in 1510, and the last shipment ended when Cuba abolished the slave trade in 1868. Almost 15 million slaves were transported from Africa, but only 9.5 million survived the trip to the New World. Historian Philip Curtin has determined that of those who survived the trip, around 400,000 went to North America, 3.6 million to Brazil, 1.6 million to Spanish colonies, and the remaining 3.8 million to British, French, Dutch, and Danish colonies in the Caribbean.[21]

The Catholic Church took the lead in outlawing slavery in Europe, and Thomas Aquinas produced the definitive anti-slavery position in the thirteenth century. In 1435, Pope Eugene IV threatened excommunication for those who were attempting to enslave the indigenous population of the Canary Islands. Around a century later, in 1537 Pope Paul III issued three major pronouncements against slavery directed toward preventing enslavement of Indians and Africans in the New World. Their actions are not well remembered today because the popes had little power in this era in Spain and Portugal, and also because so many Catholics involved in New World slavery just ignored their demands. Interestingly, the death rate for slaves was substantially higher in English colonies than in those held by the French and Spanish.[22]

Europeans Explore North America

Their first ventures into the lands north of Mexico were not productive for the Spaniards and were characterized by violence. Ponce de León explored the shores of Florida in 1513. He was almost immediately attacked by the Calusa tribe. The conflict continued for years, and in 1521 a Calusa arrow mortally wounded the explorer as he and his men were driven back to Cuba.[23]

In 1539, Hernando de Soto with an army of 600 men, an interpreter, and hundreds of horses, mules, pigs, and dogs landed at Tampa Bay. Over the four years that they explored the western side of the peninsula, the conquistadors looted, murdered, raped, and enslaved Indians. Eventually, they made their way to Mexico with little to show for their ventures.[24]

Later, from 1540 to 1542, Vázquez de Coronado circled through present-day Arizona, New Mexico, Texas, Oklahoma, and Kansas. He also had little to show for his efforts. Finally, in 1565, a permanent fort was established at St. Augustine, Florida, which acted as the base to send missionaries as far north as South Carolina and eventually to Chesapeake Bay. By the end of the sixteenth century, the Spanish had spread as far west as New Mexico and Arizona where missions and military posts were built close together. They taught the Indians Christianity along with techniques of farming and handicrafts. During the 1600s and 1700s, they established missionaries in Texas, and during the eighteenth century in California.

By 1635 there were more than forty Spanish missions in Florida alone. They lasted for about 100 years until British soldiers destroyed them and sold thousands of Indian converts into slavery. The most long-lived missions were in the Southwest. By 1633 there were over 60,000 Zuni, Hopi, and Pueblo Indians baptized in over ninety chapels that were scattered throughout seven missionary districts. The first Spanish mission in California was established on July 16, 1769, near San Diego.[25]

Most of the colonists viewed the Indians as vicious barbarians. Some, however, took the opposite approach and saw them as noble savages. They reasoned that the Indians were passive people who were recipients of whatever happened in their lives—much like animals. In the 1530s, Bartholomew Las Casas, a Dominican missionary, described them as noble savages and believed they had been waiting for thousands of years for Christian instruction.[26] The most noted proponent of the noble savage doctrine was the French philosopher Jean-Jacques Rousseau (1712-1778), who glorified humans in the state of nature. Yet as historian Rodney Stark points out, nature was not immune to killing. "Warfare was chronic everywhere in the New World," he wrote.[27]

Las Casas became known as "Defender of the Indians" for railing against his countrymen because of their cruel treatment of native peoples. "In God's name," he cried, "we must consider whether our tortures and murders of

Indians do not surpass every imaginable cruelty and injustice!" He asked, "Whether it could be worse to give the Indians into the charge of the devils of hell than to the Christians of the Indies."[28]

Another controversial topic is the representation of Native Americans living in close harmony with nature and with deep reverence for the Earth. Environmental archaeologist Karl Butzer contends that "the empirical evidence . . . contradicts the romantic notion that the Native Americans had some auspicious recipe to use the land without leaving a manifest and sometimes ugly imprint upon it."[29] Native Americans would disagree.

Throughout the West, Europeans planted crosses on Indian sacred grounds and attempted to transform a wilderness where Satan lived into an area that God blessed, where European civilization could prosper. The Indians were seen as dangerous and deceptive in a beautiful Eden that needed to be claimed by Christians. To the Spanish, fighting infidels was nothing new because they had spent more than seven centuries driving out non-Christians in Europe. If they could rid themselves of the scourge of Islam, they reasoned, then they certainly could do the same to the Indian religions in the New World.

Under Spanish laws, the conquistadors were required to read to Indians they encountered the Requerimiento, a 1513 document drafted by theologians at the request of the King of Spain. Indian people understood neither its language nor its concepts. The Spanish demanded the Indians to acknowledge the Christian church as supreme and accept the pope and the king and queen of Spain as lords over their lands. If they accepted, they could keep their land—a promise usually not kept—but if they refused, the Spaniards threatened to take their entire families and place them in slavery. The Spaniards rationalized that the blame was placed on the Indians since they had given them fair warning about the consequences.[30]

In general, most Indians initially were not totally opposed to the good news the Christians delivered to them. The Indians believed that this new religion would not negate their religion, and perhaps they could both be worshipped. In reality, in some ways religion was much more important to many of the Indians than to their European counterparts, and the natives were curious about this new medicine man, the son of God. They were courteous as the priests preached Christianity even though they didn't understand a word they were saying. At the same time, they feared the Europeans. People who were so convicted in their beliefs must have powerful spirits. However receptive the Indians were, they were not about to give up their traditional religions.

Spaniards, much more than the English or French, emphasized making new colonies that would worship the pope. Especially in South America, it was important not only to Christianize the natives but also to educate them. Universities in Peru and Mexico were founded hundreds of years before Harvard.

Cortés urged the establishment of Franciscan missions, believing that the natives had to be spiritually converted. As one might expect, the subjugation by the Spanish of Indians south of the Rio Grande did not go without resistance and fighting. Military forts were built nearby. The Catholic monks believed that the native Mexican church was a false church that was controlled by the devil. They spread the word of the pope and admonished the Mexicans for worshiping idols and demons that infuriated the Christian God. They let the native Mexicans know that the reason they had been dominated by the Spanish was because they were worshiping the wrong God and made them pledge allegiance to the Christian God.

Over time, the conversion of Native Americans to Christianity failed. Surprised and disappointed, the Franciscans thought they would be dealing with natives who were simple, pliable, and childlike, but instead they found highly intelligent people with their own intellectual and spiritual understanding of faith.

Cortés's legacy is bleak. When he landed in central Mexico, there were possibly as many as 25 million natives, but after his arrival, the population of the region collapsed from war and disease. By 1620 when the Pilgrims landed in Massachusetts, there were only 730,000 Mexicans left, and the original native population didn't recover until the 1960s. "We, Christians, have destroyed so many kingdoms," Pedro Ciesa de Leon said, "for wherever the Spaniards have passed, conquering and discovering, it is as though a fire had gone, destroying everything in its path."[31] The only reason the Spanish cared about the decrease in the native population was because they needed the natives for slaves. This led to the importation of slaves from Africa.

Friendly French

The tribes of Florida were the first in North America to face Spaniards, and within a generation the French also arrived. In 1524, the French under King Francis I sent Florentine navigator Giovanni da Verrazano to the New World, and he explored the Atlantic coast from North Carolina to Nova Scotia. Ten years later, the king sent Jacques Cartier, who sailed the

St. Lawrence River as far as the first rapids before turning back. Cartier avoided the brutality exhibited by de Soto and his army.

In 1513, Ponce de León sailed out of Puerto Rico through the Bahamas and made his way to Florida on Easter Sunday. The next year, Spain's King Ferdinand appointed him governor of what they thought to be an island. The king urged the new governor to lead the native population "by all the means you may be able to devise . . . into the knowledge of Our Catholic faith, that they may come to a knowledge thereof and become Christians and be saved."[32] Over the next few decades, Indian fishermen along the Atlantic Coast traded with the French.

In time, ports in France, England, Portugal, and Spain saw their fishermen in the spring heading in their boats for the Grand Banks where they could fish for cod. By the 1580s, there was a brisk exchange between the groups in furs, tools, weapons, clothing, and jewelry. This mutually beneficial exchange continued into the early 1600s when Samuel de Champlain established a small village around 1608 that eventually became Québec—the same year that the Spanish established Santa Fe. Until then, the only European settlement north of Mexico was St. Augustine.[33]

The Jesuits—founded in 1540 by Ignatius Loyola, who became one of the most rigorous missionary instruments of the Catholic Counter-Reformation—had their base in Québec. They were active in exploring, mapping, translating, and reporting on Algonquin and Iroquois tribal life. While they worked hard at converting the Indians to Christianity, with mixed results, Jesuits were far less insistent that Indians ceased being Indians before they became Christians. They presented the Huron with wampum belts and told them it would smooth the transition to Christian paradise.

Throughout New France, many Indians accepted the Catholic faith, relocated to French mission villages, attended mass, and wore crosses, and some became devout Catholics. The Huron, however, tolerated the Black Robes only because they wanted to trade with them. Most resented the missionaries' intrusion into their rituals and ceremonies.[34]

By 1670 the French explorers had reached Lake Superior. Indians in the Great Lakes region and the Mississippi Valley worked alongside the French, who were interested in trading with them, especially for hides. Beaver pelts became the most important trade item with the Indians. Frenchmen gave gifts and worked hard to cultivate relationships with Indian leaders so they could do business with them. At the same time, French explorers, traders, and priests continued to explore the waterways of North America in search of a passage to China.

While the French were peaceful and cooperative with them, the Huron showed little interest in becoming French Catholics. Undaunted, the Jesuits worked diligently among the northern tribes. They learned the native languages and customs. They believed that the Indians could become Christians without losing some of their native customs. Everywhere the Jesuits went they built chapels and erected wooden crosses in Indian villages and proclaimed God's presence. Throughout New France many Indians accepted the Catholic faith and became French citizens. The women were especially fond of the new religion because it gave them increased social status.

To achieve acceptance, French missionaries attempted to find similarities between native religions and their own. They also made concessions to Indian practices. After three years of working with the Indians, the Jesuits could count only 100 Huron Christians. The Jesuits lacked the military support that the Spanish often gave their missionaries. Complicating matters was a smallpox outbreak from 1639 to 1640 that enraged the natives against the Jesuits. The Huron noted that the Jesuits did not become sick and feared they were sorcerers who needed to be killed. The missionaries, as had the Spanish, countered, stating that if the Indians would have been devout Christians, they would have been spared from the disease.

The Indians who became Christians were rewarded with French citizenship and trade advantages. Indian Christians paid less for many trade items and were permitted to own guns, unlike those who didn't convert. This put the Huron at a disadvantage with their enemies such as the Iroquois, who obtained their guns from the Dutch and English who didn't require them to become Christians.

Unfortunately, all did not remain tranquil. In 1609, the Five Nations of the Iroquois Confederacy in western New York and the French became hated enemies after Champlain and his men helped the Huron attack and defeat a Mohawk group. For much of the seventeenth century, Indian tribes viewed the French either as trading and military partners or as competitors and enemies.

French efforts in the Mississippi Valley left a significant imprint on the interior of the North American continent. In 1669, Jesuit Jacques Marquette arrived at a mission in Wisconsin and from there explored the upper Mississippi River. Marquette spoke six Indian languages, which proved beneficial when he journeyed in 1673 down the Mississippi River with Louis Jolliet. Together they were looking for a route to the great western sea and on to Asia, but instead followed a river that drained into the

Gulf of Mexico. France now laid claim from the mouth of the St. Lawrence River in the north to the mouth of the Mississippi in the south.

Later, in 1682, René-Robert Cavelier, Sieur de La Salle completed the exploration of the Mississippi River south to the broad delta that flowed into the Gulf of Mexico. Mobile, Alabama, was the oldest French town on the Gulf Coast, founded in 1702 as a fort. New Orleans became the major center for French missionary activity and the political capital for all of the Louisiana Territory when it was founded in 1718.

French dominance did not last. In 1763, the French government suppressed the Society of Jesus (Jesuits) because the order had become too powerful and wealthy. The royal family and the wider Catholic Church were jealous of its status. Later, the pope abolished the Society of Jesus everywhere, although it was restored in 1814. New France's development stalled and never really recovered. Without the Jesuits, the Catholic influence dwindled.

In the early seventeenth century, the Swedes and Dutch joined the French in setting up permanent trading posts in America. In 1609, Henry Hudson, an Englishman working for a Dutch company, planted trading posts on the Delaware and Connecticut Rivers. The Swedes also developed posts on the Delaware River from 1638 until the Dutch seized them in 1655. By the early 1620s, the Dutch West India Company brought settlers to the Hudson River Valley. Dutch farmers were looking for land, which led to fighting with the English. Starting in the 1640s, the two groups fought each other until the English ousted the Dutch two decades later.

European invaders had left their mark before the colonization of North America by England. Precious metals and other bounty flowed to Europe as disease killed off native populations. The Spanish and French failed to find an inland passage to the Pacific and also failed to completely convert the native masses to Christianity. The English invaders came next. Unlike their predecessors, they planned to stay and make the New World their home. Little did the natives understand that their problems had just begun. Nelson Mandela said, "To deny people their human rights is to challenge their very humanity." Colonial Europe created their own humanity with little regard for the rights of people of color as they conquered nature.

CHAPTER FOUR

Create Humanity and Conquer Nature: The British Invasion

We shall be as a city upon a hill, the eyes of all people are upon us.
—PURITAN JOHN WINTHROP, FUTURE GOVERNOR OF THE
MASSACHUSETTS BAY COLONY ABOARD THE SHIP *ARBELIA*
BEFORE ARRIVING IN AMERICA

Savages we call them, because their manners differ from ours, which we think the perfection of civility; they think the same of theirs.
—BENJAMIN FRANKLIN

While the Spanish and French along with other Europeans posed a significant threat to the Indians' way of life, it was the British colonists who arrived in the late sixteenth century that proved to be the greatest and most lasting menace. They came to America with the intention of settling the land in numbers large enough to drive the Indians as far west as necessary. Like the Spanish, the English were no strangers to war and conquering other peoples. First, they conquered the Scots, and then they invaded Ireland. The unification of England, Wales, Scotland, and Ireland into Great Britain formed perhaps the most formidable colonial power in history. Historian Francis Parkman a century and a half ago concluded, "Spanish civilization crushed the Indian; English civilization scorned and neglected him; French civilization embraced and cherished him."[1]

There were a variety of motives that inspired the English to cross the Atlantic. The English settlers included pious Pilgrims, greedy gold hunters, ambitious London investors, spiritual seekers, and conservative Puritans who were intent on building a city of God on a hill in the middle of a fallen world. A nation's ideology is a contest of ideas.

Italian John Cabot (Giovanni Caboto, 1450-1500) was sent to America in 1497 by King Henry VII to explore the area off eastern Canada. Since Cabot did not find a passage to the Orient, the king thought this newly discovered land was a barrier to his goals. But it would be his son King Henry VIII (1491-1547) and his granddaughter Queen Elizabeth I (1533-1603) who would finish exploring the New World. During that period, England changed from being a Catholic country to a Protestant one.

Francis Drake (1540-1596), knighted by Queen Elizabeth I in 1581, explored the continent but also had a thriving business in piracy. He looted a number of Spanish ships, at the same time enforcing, like Columbus, regular religious services aboard his ships. Drake believed that any blow against Catholic Spain was a blow on behalf of England and the Anglican Church. The defeat in 1588 of the Spanish Armada by the English destroyed Spanish naval supremacy and hampered their clamp on the New World. For the Protestant English, it also affirmed that God was on their side.

Henry VIII was originally a strong supporter of the Catholic Church and denounced the Reformation led by Martin Luther. But soon his loyalties would change. At the time, the Catholic Church owned about one fourth of England and collected a yearly income of more than £320,000 from the rent of land owned by monasteries. In 1509, Henry married Catherine of Aragon, daughter of Ferdinand and Isabella, but in twenty years of marriage she bore him no son who lived. Desperately in need of an heir, in 1529 he asked the pope for a divorce, which was denied. Henry defied him and went ahead and married Anne Boleyn, eventually making himself head of the English Church. In 1539, he confiscated the monastic lands.

Henry's new wife bore him a daughter, Elizabeth, who became Queen in 1558 and ruled for forty-four years in a time when the Enlightenment triumphed on land and sea. As England became a powerful nation, it turned its eyes to building a North American colony. Sir Walter Raleigh (1552-1618) became a favorite of Queen Elizabeth, who supplied him with essentially everything he wanted. Raleigh asked for a charter to found a colony in the New World, and it was granted.

Oxford-trained Protestant clergyman Richard Hakluyt the Younger (1552-1616) worked closely with Walter Raleigh, and in 1584 presented Queen Elizabeth *A Discourse on Western Planting*. The book outlined what would become England's distinctive approach to the New World: settlements and towns as opposed to trading posts and forts. Missionaries would have the opportunity to learn the language and customs of the natives, and then they could "distill into their purged minds the lively liquor of the gospel."[2] Hakluyt believed that Indians would remain heathen as long as they did not hear the true gospel, and they wouldn't hear it unless missionaries came to them.

In 1584, Raleigh sent out a force to explore the land and eventually founded Virginia in honor of Elizabeth the Virgin Queen. However, many of the settlers in the area were killed by hostile Indians, and by the end of the sixteenth century, England was still without a colony in North America. Next, Raleigh turned his attentions to South America.

King James I (1566-1625) succeeded Elizabeth, and in 1604 he immediately ended the ongoing war with the Spanish. In 1606, a number of English entrepreneurs—who developed joint stock companies in which participants profited or suffered in proportion to the number of shares they purchased—petitioned King James to establish colonies in America. The joint stock company became the principal instrument of England's overseas expansion. There were two groups, one from London and one from Plymouth, England. The two companies incorporated and formed the Virginia Company of Plymouth, which operated in the northern part of the continent, and the Virginia Company of London, which operated in the southern part.

The Plymouth group sent exploratory expeditions in 1606-1607 and founded a colony on the rocky coast of Maine. It survived only one winter. Another colony that set up in Virginia fared better, and thousands of young, mostly male apprentices poured into the tobacco fields to toil alongside growing numbers of enslaved Africans. A similar pattern developed in the Chesapeake colony in Maryland.

On Thursday, April 10, 1606, James I issued the First Charter of Virginia to the Virginia Company of London. He spoke of high expectations with "so noble work" that would carry to the New World the "Christian religion to such people as yet live in darkness and miserable ignorance of the true knowledge and worship of God. . . ." His lofty, idealistic words were soon followed by passions of the flesh. The company was to take possession of "all the lands, woods, soil, grounds, havens, ports, rivers, mines, minerals, marshes, waters, fishing, commodities. . . ." His covetous desires went on for three paragraphs, followed by what the king considered the grand prize, to "dig, mine, and search for all manner of mines of gold, silver, and copper." It turns out that of the 3,805 words in the Charter, only 98 were about God.[3]

The Virginia Company was directed to convert Native Americans to Christianity, which was "the most pious and noble end of this plantation." Scholar and Jesuit historian Francis Paul Prucha zeroed in on the goal of the English. He wrote, "The great distinguishing feature of English relations with Indian groups was replacement of the Indians on the land by whites, not conversion and assimilation of the Indians into European colonial society."[4]

In 1606, the Virginia Company of London sent a hundred men and four boys crammed aboard three small ships that sailed up a river they called the James, eventually landing on a peninsula they named Jamestown, a quasi-military outpost. Captain John Smith (1580-1631), its leader and savior, described the location as one of "pleasant plain hills and fertile valleys, one prettily crossing another . . . a plain wilderness as God first made it." John Rolfe noted that settlers saw themselves as "a peculiar people, marked and chosen by the finger of God, to possess the land, for undoubtedly He is with us."[5] A colony was established, but it was not Eden. Appalling conditions—hostile natives, polluted water, and rampant disease—were made worse by infighting and political chaos.

The colonists were unable to grow enough food, and by the winter of 1609 they faced starvation. They ate vermin, leather, and even the starch from their collars. "Nothing was spared to maintain life," colonist George Percy recalled and added that men "can do those things which seem incredible, as to dig up dead corpses out of graves and eat them."[6] Nine out of ten died. Fortunately, John Rolfe developed a new strain of sweet tobacco, and within a year there were wooden vending machines for tobacco in London ale houses. Virginia was in business.

For Alexander Whitaker, a minister in Henrico, Virginia, the natives needed to be converted to Christianity. He wrote in his *Goode News from Virginia* in 1613:

> Let the miserable condition of these naked slaves of the divell move you to compassion toward them. They acknowledge that there is a great good God, but know him not, having the eyes of their understanding as yet blinded: wherefore they serve the divell for feare, aftermost base manner, sacrificing sometimes (as I have heere heard) their own Children to him. . . . Their priests . . . are no other but such as our English witches are. They live naked in bodie, as if their shame of their sinne deserve no covering: Their names are as naked as their body: they esteem it a virtue to lie, deceive and steal as their master the divell teacheth to them.[7]

As would become a common pattern for centuries, colonists always needed more land, but also felt a need to bring Christianity to the Indians. John Rolfe married an Indian princess named Pocahontas, and in 1614 she converted to Christianity, which delighted the Virginia Company. Rolfe took pains to emphasize that his courtship came not from "carnal affection" but from his concern "for the good of this plantation, for the honor of our country, for the glory of God, for my own salvation, and for converting to the true knowledge of God and Jesus Christ an unbelieving creature: namely Pocahontas."[8]

The union brought ethnic peace for a while and made for good propaganda back in England. The Indians accepted muskets, powder, and lead in return for listening to the missionaries. Pocahontas was renamed Rebecca Rolfe and was a hit at the Royal Court in London.

However, Pocahontas, still in her early twenties, died as she prepared to return home, probably from tuberculosis. Rolfe was killed five years later in the Indian resistance. Her death had destabilized relationships with the natives, and after Nemattanew, a charismatic Indian shaman, was murdered by some colonists, the Powhatan Confederacy killed 347 colonists—a third of all the English people in America—in what came to be known as the Massacre of 1622. Even the missionaries who had come to spread the gospel hardened their hearts. Virginia governor Francis Wyatt proclaimed, "Our first work is expulsion of the savages. It is definitely better to have no heathen among us, who at best were but as thorns in our sides, then to be at peace in league with them."[9] Attitudes changed quickly.

Captain John Smith, just twenty-seven years old, rose to a leadership position, but the post of governor of the Virginia Colony went to a nobleman, Lord De La Warr. With government in place, an advertising campaign was launched to attract English people to buy stock in the London Company and move to the New World. A great migration lasted until 1640, with as many as 50,000 Englishmen leaving for Virginia, Maryland, Bermuda, and the West Indian islands. Twenty thousand settled in the northern part of Virginia, which was now called New England—named by John Smith.

Along with Smith came the Puritans. Their religious beliefs were formed by John Calvin, who believed that God was omnipotent and good and men were evil and that they were either predestined to go to heaven or to hell. Puritans were described as prudish, cruel, fanatic, and superstitious. Other religious groups also migrated to the New World, and while they relied on the Bible, each formed a different opinion on how God wanted the church to be run. Two principal groups of Puritans were the Congregationalists and the Presbyterians. Both groups were dissatisfied with the Church of England, which they felt was a corrupt institution in need of reforming. Most Congregationalists were not separatists, and they preferred to stay within the Church of England.

In his book *The White Man's Indian,* Robert F. Berkhofer, Jr. explained how Europeans and Americans understood Native Americans:

> Whether describing physical appearance or character, manners or morality, economy or dress, housing or sexual habits, government or religion, Whites overwhelmingly measured the Indian as a general category against those beliefs, values, or institutions they most cherished in themselves at the time. For this reason, many commentators on the history of white Indian imagery see Europeans and Americans as using counterimages of themselves to describe Indians and the counterimages of Indians to describe themselves. Such a negative reference group could be used to define White identity or to prove White superiority over the worst fears of their own depravity. If the Puritans, for example, could project their own sins upon people they called savages, then the extermination of the Indian became a cleansing of those sins from their own midst as well as the destruction of a feared enemy.[10]

The Pilgrims

Six hundred miles to the north, Plymouth had been established. Settlers had learned from colonists there, and from the disasters at Jamestown, the importance of building colonies on firm foundations of family, authority, law, trade, and a division of labor. Jamestown had underestimated the importance of women, whose work was invaluable and who allowed a colony to grow.

In 1620, the group that settled New England at Plymouth was separatist and frowned upon by the English government. The Pilgrims were united by the religious community that they had formed in Leiden, Holland. The rest, who came from all over England, had little in common. One hundred and two persons boarded the *Mayflower* bound for Virginia. When they made landfall at Cape Cod, they decided to stay.

The first passenger ashore was a nine-year-old girl, who later remembered a land "very uneven, abounding in small hollows in swamps, and covered with blueberry and other bushes." The migrants, ravaged by scurvy, sought shelter in burrows that they dug into the riverbank, where they sustained themselves on fish and dried peas.[11]

In late December 1620, they began a settlement they named Plymouth after the English port from which they had embarked. They came to be known as Pilgrims, and their first governor was John Carver. After he died, they chose in 1621 William Bradford (1590-1657), who was reelected a number of times until his death. Bradford, even before he got off the *Mayflower,* had predetermined beliefs about the Indians. He called them "savage people, who are cruel, barbarous and most treacherous."[12]

In 1628, Congregational Puritans bought part ownership in the New England Company and founded the Massachusetts Bay Company. They elected John Winthrop (1587-1649) of Groton Manor, Suffolk, as governor. Winthrop justified taking land from the Indians and argued that land "which is common to all is proper to none. This Savage people ruleth over many lands without title or property; for they enclose no ground, neither have they cattle to maintain it, but remove their dwellings as they have occasion. Why may not Christians have liberty to go and dwell amongst [the Indians] in their wastelands and woods?"[13]

Later, in the 1780s, American Hugh Henry Brackenridge wrote that Indian land claims were meaningless and absurd, arguing, "I would think the man a fool and unjust who would exclude me from drinking the waters of the Mississippi River because he had first seen it. He would be equally so who would exclude me from settling in the country west of the Ohio, because in chasing a buffalo he had been first over it."[14] This reflected the changing attitude about the Indian from noble savage to enemy and unreasonable champion of unreasonable claims. The Indian either needed to be silenced, moved, or assimilated, and if not, then slain. That belief became the basis for government policy for generations.

Winthrop explained to the colonists his vision of a city on a hill ruled by the principles of God. He believed God loved everybody equally but did not intend them to play equal roles in society. He strived to make a society that adhered to religiously inspired authority without democratic self-rule. In time, however, the Pilgrims did not adopt his ideals. Instead, they created the democratic New England town meeting, which was more similar to the way the Indians ruled themselves.

Besides problems with the Indians, Winthrop was challenged by dissidents like Anne Hutchinson (1591-1643), a devoted Puritan, who came to the colony in 1634 with her husband and eleven children. Much of her popularity arose around her belief in the doctrine of salvation by faith, not works. She was seen as rejecting the power of the clergy and religious authority. Eventually, she was placed on trial and banished to Rhode Island. Four years later, she moved from there to what is now the Bronx in New York. In September 1643, she and her family were killed by Indians. Upon hearing this, Winthrop felt empowered and believed they had been murdered because "these people have cast-off ordinances and churches" and needed to pay the price.[15]

In 1630, the Puritans began their Massachusetts Bay Colony, founding the city of Boston. Thousands of Puritans arrived in Massachusetts during the following decade, which placed extreme pressure on the natives' way of life. The new immigrants transformed the Massachusetts Bay Company from a trading business into a commonwealth. The Puritans of New England allowed only church members to vote and levied taxes to pay ministers' salaries. However, unlike in England, they did not want their clergy to take part in government, and the ministers had little authority in their own church.

The Puritans were driven by not only their faith but also their greed for land. Any Indian action to stop them from acquiring land was seen as an act of the devil. This led to war, and in May 1637 John Mason led a militia composed of whites and Indians against the largest Pequot village on the Mystic River. The village was burned and destroyed and the Indians slaughtered. One appalled Puritan said, "It was a fearful sight to see them frying in the fire . . . and horrible was the stinck & sente thereof." But more common was the sentiment of Captain John Underhill, who was questioned back in England about killing Indian women and children. He simply replied, "We had sufficient light from the word of God for our proceedings." One Puritan minister announced that God himself had subdued the Pequots.[16]

The Puritans put pressure on the Indians to move into "praying towns" where they could be taught to be good Christians. Indian shamans were seen as devils and demeaned by the whites. John Elliot modeled these communities after the Old Testament accounts, and strict Puritan rules prohibiting drunkenness, polygamy, Sabbath breaking, and other activities were implemented.

Colonist Daniel Goodkin wrote that the Pilgrims had been chosen to create a quiet and peaceful settlement. The Indians, however, thought differently. They believed that they were superior to the Englishman. Pilgrim writers did concede that the Indian parents were more loving to their children than were the English ones. The rigid Europeans viewed child rearing as moving straight from childhood (around seven years old) to adulthood where they were sent off to work. In contrast, Indian parents regarded the years before puberty as a time of leisure and playful development. They kept their children close to the family until they were married.[17]

Even though Winthrop's group were not separatists, Roger Williams (1603-1683), who arrived in 1631, was. Williams was very charismatic and soon befriended Winthrop. He believed the state should not be involved in religious matters and was so inflammatory toward those in power in New England that he moved to Rhode Island. The Rhode Islanders did not confine voting to church members or collect taxes to support the clergy.

In 1620, George Calvert, Lord Baltimore (1579-1631), purchased rights in southeastern Newfoundland from another nobleman. He was Catholic and eventually formed the colony of Maryland in honor of the Queen and Charles I. In time, more Puritans came to the colony than there were Catholics, and in 1649 the Maryland Toleration Act was passed, securing freedom of worship for all Christians whether Protestant or Catholic. By the middle of the seventeenth century, England had formed a number of colonies where farming—especially tobacco—and fishing were common. In effect, England controlled the continent.

The Narragansett Indians did find a supporter in Roger Williams, who spoke on their behalf and demanded their religious freedom and land rights. But more commonly, Protestant leaders like Boston's Puritan preacher Cotton Mather considered the Indians agents of Satan. Satan was cleansed from Native American boys and girls with soap and water, hard work, and learning the importance of personal sacrifice and economic independence. Indians believed in sharing their wealth, which was frowned on by Christian leaders. In the Puritan's mind, greed was a cornerstone of civilization, and the Indians weren't selfish enough.[18]

While many Europeans immigrated for religious freedom and to escape oppressive rule, the colonies were still a place where lower-class whites were oppressed. Resisting white rule, the Indians took pride in their independence, and the colonists were enraged that they were not able to control them. In frustration, one Jesuit commented that the Indian barbarians had the law of wild asses and were born to live and die with liberty without any control. The Indian culture was one of sharing the wealth, and they were shocked at how the Europeans divided themselves into upper and lower class. The Indians felt that no man was superior to any other man.[19]

The Indian and European ways of life were polar opposites and demonstrated enormous differences in values and practices, religion, the conduct of family and social life, concepts of property ownership and land use, and traditional attitudes toward work and leisure. Despite white communities shunning half breeds, they were welcome in the Indian villages. The Indians viewed the whites as barbarians as much as whites viewed Indians as barbarians.

A Delaware tribesman explained to Benjamin Franklin, "If a white man in traveling through our country enters one of our cabins, we all treat him as I treat you. We dry him if he is wet, we warm him if he is cold. . . . But if I go into a white man's house in Albany and ask for victuals and drink, they say, 'Get out.' . . . You see they have not learned those little good things we need no meeting to be instructed in because our mothers taught them to us when we were children."[20]

The struggle between Indians and the English was no better demonstrated than in the conflicts between Protestant missionaries and the Indians who cherished their own religion. Missionaries were generally insensitive to tribal traditions and routinely violated tribal integrity. They closely linked Christianity with progress in Western civilization. Indians were forced to learn Christian practices of prayer or scripture reading and adopt European dress. Cultural transformation was the goal.

Even so, missionaries often acted as cultural buffers who moderated the effect of the white man on natives. In his travels across New Jersey and Pennsylvania, Quaker John Woolman worried about the English depleting the Indians' game. He sought to spend "some time with the Indians, that I might feel and understand their life and the spirit they live in."[21]

Missionaries provided information back to an inquisitive Europe on what the natives were like. The Jesuits produced seventy-three published volumes of accounts of their travels and labors in New France from 1610 to 1791. The general theme of these accounts was that they regarded Indians as heathens but fit for conversion. This was summed up by an early clergyman who declared, "The Israelites had a commandment from God to dwell in Canaan; we have leave to dwell in Virginia. They were commanded to kill the heathen; we are forbidden to kill them, but are commanded to convert them."[22] Despite being insensitive to the Indians' own religion, it was an improvement over many parishioners who regarded Indians as subhuman and subject to extermination or enslavement.

Besides religion, English immigrants, like the Spanish and French, brought with them infectious diseases that decimated Indian populations. Both Indians and Europeans believed that infectious diseases were the will of celestial powers and that supernatural forces played important roles in their day-to-day life. Both understood that these unseen forces could be good or evil. For example, Governor Bradford attributed diseases that killed

Indians to the hand of God who favored the Pilgrims. In his reasoning, the natives were removed so that the Pilgrims' colonies could expand. It was very common for colonists to establish villages on the prior sites of Indian lands—typically, choice locations—where they had died from disease.[23] For the Indians not killed in the 1616 smallpox epidemic, another hit in 1633 that killed a third to half of the remaining Indians in New England. The Pilgrims believed that it was the will of God that the natives showed little resistance to diseases, even though they knew smallpox had killed millions in Europe.[24]

As Indians died from disease, Puritans felt an urgency to educate those who survived so they could be saved. They felt that any reasonable human who could read the Bible would want to undergo conversion. Twenty Indian boys had their tuition paid for to enter Harvard. In 1658, Harvard went as far as establishing an Indian college, ultimately unsuccessful. Later, other attempts were made at educating Indian children. It was believed that if the Indians knew the English language there would be fewer disputes, and they would be more easily converted to Christianity.[25]

In 1693, the charter for the College of William and Mary in Virginia made provisions to also educate Indians. The charter stated that the Church in Virginia might be provided "with the seminary of ministers of the gospel," so that "the Christian religion may be propagated amongst the Western Indians, to the glory of Almighty God."[26]

Fearing that the English were going to make slaves of their children, the parents and tribal leaders refused to send them to the college when it opened in 1700. (Native resistance would be repeated in the late nineteenth century when Indian children were forced to attend off-reservation schools.) Not discouraged, in 1723 the college erected Brafferton Hall on the campus to house Indian boys. The Indian leaders saw the white man's education as making their children absolutely good for nothing. Quaker missionaries also attempted to educate the Indian children, with little success. Nonetheless, in 1756 the Congregational minister Eleazar Wheelock founded Moor's Indian Charity School in Connecticut. Eventually the school was moved to New Hampshire where in 1769 it merged with a Latin school also started by Wheelock to become Dartmouth College.[27]

The Indian populations in Massachusetts were not only diminished by disease but also by continued warfare. In 1675, a conflict now called King Philip's War was waged between Indians in Rhode Island and Massachusetts against the English. Farms and entire villages were destroyed, and hundreds of colonists were injured, captured, or killed.

In February 1676, Mary Rowlandson, a minister's wife at Lancaster, Massachusetts, was seized during an Indian raid and endured three months of privation in freezing conditions. She ate "filthy trash" with her captors, whom she called "barbarous creatures." Her trauma enraged the Puritans.[28]

An army of 1,000 Englishmen attacked the Narragansett and their Mohawk allies. The colonial militiamen killed the Indian leader, Metacomet, and cut his head off. Their barbaric trophy was placed on top of the town gate where it served as a reminder to the Indians not to mess with Englishmen.[29] The authorities sold more than 1,000 Indians into slavery—including the chief's wife and children. Most were shipped to the Caribbean and some ended up in North Africa. Those not sold into slavery by the English became slaves after intertribal conflicts. The victorious Indians sold their Indian captives into slavery to the English in exchange for guns, pots, and axes.[30]

The liberties that many immigrants felt were being abused at home in England by royal disregard for the rights of freeborn Englishmen ended up being defended in America through the bondage of others—both indentured servants and slaves—and the subjugation and removal of Native Americans. And for all their inward-looking community spirit, the fortunes of many New England communities depended on continued expansion. The Puritan idea of a "sufficiency"—having enough land to be comfortable—was compromised by commercial greed and voracious land grabs.

Battles Among Europeans

European powers encouraged trading with different Indian tribes for guns and horses. This led to rivalries between different tribes who then became even more dependent on European traders to supply them with ammunition. In return, the Europeans obtained animal hides and Indian slaves who were used as laborers in gold and silver mines in northeastern Mexico, New France, and the Caribbean. When shortages in Indian slaves occurred, slaves from Africa were shipped into North America.[31]

In the eighteenth century, the English gained international power under the leadership of Prime Minister William Pitt. His plan was to reduce France's influence and power in the New World by keeping the French bogged down in wars in Europe. The English also tried to break the close ties that the Indians had with the French.

In 1689, King William's War began when the King of France refused to recognize William of Orange of the Netherlands as the new King of

England. The war had a profound and lasting effect on the Indians in America. It lasted for eight years and forced tribal people into choosing sides. Shortly after it ended, another war broke out in 1702, Queen Anne's War. The French and Spanish joined forces against the English. Tribal leaders often took the side of the colonial power that would aid them in fighting their own Indian rivals.[32] In addition to the Indians killing each other, smallpox hit the southeast in the 1690s. Slave activities propelled the virus across a vast geographic expanse.[33]

The wars took a toll on Indian and French commerce. But in 1711, with the preliminary terms of the Treaty of Utrecht worked out between the French and the British, the French with renewed vigor began active trading with the Indians and searching for the Western Sea—the Pacific. In 1718, the French had a number of trading houses near the shores of Lake Superior along with forts and missions in Illinois country. By the 1730s, French explorers were working their way through the parklands and out onto the Canadian plains, which prompted several tribes to move westward. The European explorers brought with them a number of infectious diseases. Lethal cases of smallpox and bacterial infections struck the Northern Plains in 1717. On average, epidemics struck the region every 5.7 years between 1714 and 1919.[34]

Conflict was reignited when the French and Indian War broke out in 1755. It began in western Pennsylvania where the British and French vied for control of the forks of the Ohio River region around Pittsburgh. This was a strategic area for controlling trade in the upper Ohio River Valley. The European powers would make agreements with the Indians to gain their support in these wars, but then would never come through with their promises.[35]

Eventually, in February 1763, Britain, France, and Spain signed the Peace of Paris. France relinquished all its territories east of the Mississippi—except New Orleans—to the British, and they guaranteed unrestricted navigation of the Mississippi River by the British. France transferred Louisiana west of the Mississippi to Spain. Eventually, Spain transferred the Louisiana Territory back to France.

The English authorities assured the Indians that they had no interest in obtaining their lands from them. Even so, the Indians were not accepting of the Englishmen in the place of the French who had been ousted from their lands. But there was no peace for England because now they faced American colonists who wanted their independence.[36]

The Paris agreement had left the Indians at the mercy of the English who they perceived as the biggest threat to their way of life. In Ottawa, tribal leader Pontiac described the English as people "who have come to trouble your country," and he ordered the Indians to "drive them out, make war on them!" This would allow the spirits to help the Indians regain the land they had lost over the prior generations. The conflict came to be known as Pontiac's Rebellion (1763-1766). A number of forts were attacked by war parties and fell to the Indians. Only Detroit and Pittsburgh remained in English control. But the rebellion was crushed, and the British and their colonial allies controlled the area once again.[37]

The War of Independence

The American War of Independence was seen by the Indians as a war between the colonies and the British to determine who would control their lands. The Indians had little to celebrate when the colonies gained their independence. Indian villages along the Mississippi and Missouri were courted by the British, Americans, and Spanish to support their interests. Indian confederations like the Iroquois split, with some supporting the Americans while others supported the British. After the War of Independence was over, the United States claimed Indian lands as far west as the Mississippi by right of conquest. The 1783 Treaty of Paris ended the war between the British and the United States but gave no protection to the Indians who had fought with the British. Pioneers heading west were angry at the natives who had supported their enemy and were not hesitant to use brutal force against them.

The secretary of war in the Washington administration, Henry Knox, attempted to keep white trespassers out of Indian lands, but frontiersmen ignored him. Knox stated that Indians, "being the prior occupants, possess the right of the soil." Their land, he said, "cannot be taken from them unless by their free consent." He did add a disclaimer, saying that it could be taken from them if it was a "just war."[38]

Knox did succeed in making treaties with the Creek, the Cherokee, and the Ohio tribes, establishing permanent boundaries between the Indians and whites. The Intercourse Act of 1790, the brainchild of Knox, included white Indian agents living among the various tribes. Their purpose was to keep the peace between the Indians and white settlers and traders.[39]

As the 1790s progressed, vast regions of land in eastern Ohio, Kentucky, and Tennessee were made available to settlers. Federal government control weakened, and settlers seized lands from Indians claiming "Settler Sovereignty," a form of local government law independent from federal rules.

The new American government treated the Indians as dangerous and defeated enemies. Some of the Indian leaders tried to protect themselves through multi-tribal confederacies to negotiate with the Americans, but gained little to show for their efforts. The Indians saw the new nation not as a shining city on the hill but a country composed of whiskey peddlers, land grabbers, and leaders who did not keep their promises.

Initially, Indian leaders tried to negotiate with individual states, but Congress passed the Northwest Ordinance of 1787 to make it clear that the Indians had to negotiate with the United States. The ordinance stated that the United States would deal with the Indians with utmost good faith. It reassured the Indians that their land would not be confiscated except for just and lawful wars authorized by Congress. Ominously, the ordinance presented a plan for national expansion into Indian-controlled lands.

Four years earlier, Thomas Jefferson's plan of government for the western territory divided the trans-Appalachian West into sixteen states. Eventually Michigan, Ohio, Indiana, Illinois, and Wisconsin entered the Union as states from the Northwest Territory. Later, states west of the Mississippi were admitted but typically only after they went through a territorial stage that was stipulated in the ordinance.[40]

In 1790, the Indian Trade and Intercourse Act reaffirmed that the federal government controlled Indian affairs and only licensed traders were permitted to operate in Indian country. Indian lands could not be transferred without Congressional approval. But many states resented the federal control and made their own treaties with the Indians. They looked the other way when squatters and land speculators grabbed western lands from the natives. Those who resisted were either removed from the area or killed.[41]

In 1793, Spain went to war with France, which lessened the attention and resources that could be spent on the Southwest. Three years later, Spain went to war with England, depleting its resources even further. The results of the wars prompted Spain in 1800 to return the Louisiana Territory to France. The treaty was signed on October 1, 1800, at King Charles IV's Royal Palace in San Ildefonso, Segovia, and the transfer went into effect one year later.

Napoleon Bonaparte envisioned the acquisition of the Louisiana Territory as an effective tool to prevent the United States from expanding westward. But France's ownership of the area would last only three years after Bonaparte grew tired of slave revolts in Haiti and infectious diseases killing his soldiers and slaves.

President Thomas Jefferson was concerned that the French might close the port of New Orleans to U.S. merchant traffic. Spain had done so in 1794. With that in mind, he contacted his representatives in France, James Monroe and Robert Livingston, and asked them to inquire with French officials about the possibility of buying New Orleans. In 1803, the French not only offered New Orleans but the entire Louisiana Territory. Within weeks, the Louisiana Purchase was consummated, and the United States had doubled its size.

Most modern accounts stressed greed and racism as the basis for expansion by Europe and the United States. But author Rodney Stark presented the positive side:

> Granted, both were significant factors, but so too were idealism and charity, especially on the part of Christian missionaries, who often were at least as concerned to educate and modernize foreign lands as to convert the world to Christ. For example, by 1910 British and American overseas mission organizations had established eighty-six colleges and universities, 522 teachers colleges (often referred to as normal schools), and thousands of elementary schools in Asia and Africa. Nor were missionaries the only idealists involved. The earliest British military intrusions into Africa were devoted mainly to stamping out the slave trade.[42]

The primary means of cultural transmission was colonialism. An estimated total of 600,000 people came from Britain to America between 1640 and 1760. The thirteen colonies had 1.6 million residents by 1760. In 1800, Europeans controlled thirty-five percent of the land surface of the globe. By 1878, that figure had risen to sixty-seven percent. On the eve of World War I in 1914, Europeans dominated eighty-four percent of the world's land area. The British Empire alone ruled about twenty-five percent of the Earth's inhabitants.[43]

Thus, Christian whites believed history had a meaningful direction—a belief that unfortunately led humankind to commit horrific crimes against those of differing ethnicity and skin color. Ironically, from colonialism through imperialism, incessant wars were launched to promote democracy and human rights. As author John Gray wrote, "The most barbarous forms of violence have been promoted as means to a higher civilization."[44]

CHAPTER FIVE

American Exodus: Survival on the Plains

The Lakota culture was hardly a generation old at the time of Sitting Bull's birth. Only around the beginning of the nineteenth century were the Lakotas fully transformed from pedestrians to mounted nomads.
—ROBERT UTLEY, *THE LANCE AND THE SHIELD: THE LIFE AND TIMES OF SITTING BULL*

The Sioux used to keep winter counts, picture writings on buffalo skin, which told our people's story from year to year. Well, the whole country is one vast winter count. You can't walk a mile without coming on some family's sacred vision hill, to an ancient sun dance circle, an old battleground, a place where something worth remembering happened.
—MARY CROW DOG, *LAKOTA WOMAN*

American historians have used the Exodus story to symbolize a number of events in U.S. history: the American Revolution, the Civil War, and the Civil Rights Movement in the 1960s. In the book of Exodus, a suffering group of Israelites forced by their Egyptian captors to be slaves are delivered to the Promised Land by Moses after crossing the Red Sea.

Soon after colonists declared independence from Great Britain, Benjamin Franklin, Thomas Jefferson, and John Adams proposed a design for the national seal. The scene was the Egyptian pharaoh and his troops charging through a divided Red Sea pursuing their Israelite slaves. The motto for the design was, "Rebellion to Tyrants is Obedience to God." Their design never was accepted by the Continental Congress, but from the beginning of our country the exodus has represented success against a much stronger enemy. It has also been manipulated to justify oppressing the weaker. In the sixteenth century, a Spanish Franciscan monk characterized Hernando Cortés as a modern-day Moses sent by God to liberate the heathen Indians and bring them to Jesus. Countless missionaries sought the same goal.

For centuries, Native Americans were confronted again and again with no good alternative except fleeing from their white oppressors. Imagine the despair when tribes broke apart and some members fled to the West while others remained to take a last stand.

Exodus is founded on hope—hope of a better tomorrow. The basic economic problem all societies face is scarcity. Whites had unlimited wants but limited resources. They wanted the Indians' resources and were willing to do almost anything to obtain them. Hope finally vanished for Native Americans in the last half of the nineteenth century as exodus no longer was an option.

Early on, when the French established colonies, they were mainly accepting of the Indians and had no problem with intermarriage as long as the expectation was fulfilled that the Indians would become Christians. The Indians were accepted as French nationals who could live in France whenever they wished, and their mixed-breed offspring would be accepted as citizens. The French much more than the Spanish or British sought Indians' acceptance of their political authority.

Unlike the Spanish, who read documents to the Indians proclaiming their land for Spain, the French worked diligently at having the Indians participate in their colonial governance. In June 1671, with four Jesuit fathers in attendance, representatives of New France at Sault Ste. Marie announced to representatives from fourteen Indian nations that the King of France, Louis XIV, was taking possession of the Mississippi Valley. When the French discovered a river, they operated on the assumption that all the territories that were drained by the river came under French rule.

The area encompassed territories from Montréal as far as the Gulf of Mexico. They informed representatives from the Indian nations that they were now dependent on the king and subject to his laws and his customs. While the French attempted to be more inclusive than the Spanish, the Indians still only had a vague idea of what the terms meant. The Indians who believed God was in all of nature, including the land, had no concept that humans could proclaim that they controlled their sacred lands.[1]

In time, the Spanish, French, and English forced Eastern tribes to the

West. In turn, the Eastern natives competed with long-established Plains tribes for resources. Each of the Plains tribes had a comparatively well-defined country that they had learned by heart. Every ridge and valley was intimately known. Every shallow rut affording safety and retreat, every waterhole, no matter how hidden in rocks or prairie, was indelibly marked in their mind. The golden age of the Plains Indian tribes lasted from 1752 to 1875.

Some of these tribes were descendants of farmers and hunters who had lived on the Great Plains for centuries, while some were descendants of nations who had been forced onto the Plains by the great Eastern tribes, who had themselves been pushed westward by white colonization.

An Arapaho explained the dilemma faced by the Plains Indians:

The white men were not going to disappear; the buffalo would not return; our relatives and friends and heroes of old times would not come back to earth. We must go ahead on the new road we had taken.

Then, more than ever, we needed to carry out our old religious ceremonies, and more than ever the Government was determined to make us discontinue them. The old people were despondent and the young and better educated were confused. It was then that our chief Left Hand went to Agent Stouch to give him a better understanding of our plight. Left Hand, an orator and a leader in all things, made him see that our Man-Above and his God were the same, and that we differed only in the way we worshipped. "Our way," he said, "has come down to us through many generations, and is the only way we know. Among white people there are many ways of worshiping, and many kinds of belief about God. They are all tolerated, but our way is not tolerated. Our children go to school and learn your way and will worship as they are taught. But many of us are old, and cannot change our ways. When we die, our way of worship will end. We are so sure that our God and your God are the same that we do not try to take our children away from you; we know your way is good, but we do not understand it. We want you to teach our children your way and let us follow our own. We invite you to come and visit our ceremonies, and to see that they are ancient and reverent and containing nothing harmful."[2]

His hopes for reconciliation between the Indian and the white man would not come to fruition. For centuries after the white man first set foot in North America, there was a general relocation and decline of Indian populations. Centuries of endurance inspired by hope were in time replaced by anger, indifference, and anxiety about an uncertain future.

Most of the peoples of the Plains followed a similar pattern of life. Their dress and habits were quite similar, as were their spiritual views. Before 1700, however, relatively little is known about most of the nomadic Northern Plains Indians except from legends and myths. Perhaps one of the best understood is their migration patterns from 1500 to 1800.[3]

In his landmark book *One Vast Winter Count: The Native American West before Lewis and Clark,* author and historian Colin G. Calloway explained the complexity of Indian life in the West, writing, "In this book, the American West is not a canvas for a single national narrative; it is a series of Indian homelands. It is also a series of frontiers, zones of interaction that formed, overlapped, and re-formed around those homelands as Indian communities moved, mingled, and adjusted to new environments, other Indians, and eventually, Europeans. Each community existed at the center of the kaleidoscopic world and had to hold its place as surrounding pieces rearranged themselves in response to outside influences and internal pressures."[4]

Space Travelers

In 1783, the main Indian tribes in the original colonies from north to south were the Abenaki, Iroquois, Delaware, Powhatan, Cherokee, and Creek. In the U.S. western territories, the main tribes from north to south were the Chippewa, Ottawa, Potawatomi, Miami, Illinois, Shawnee, Chickasaw, and Choctaw. In the distant past, near Mackinac Island in northern Michigan, three great Anishinaabe peoples split: Ojibwe (or Chippewa) headed north, Potawatomi went south, and the Odawa (Ottawa) remained.[5] The Seminole lived in Spanish Florida, and the Algonquin and Huron called British eastern Canada their home.[6]

The Algonquin were probably the largest group of linguistically related tribes in North America and were scattered from the Atlantic to the Rocky Mountains as whites forced them west. Sister Algonquian languages included the Ottawa, Cree, Cheyenne, Arapaho, Ojibway, Illinois, Miami, Kickapoo, Blackfoot, and Shawnee. Other tongues were the Siouan, Shoshonean, Caddoan, and Iroquoian.[7]

The Promised Land of the Plains Indians

Pre-contact trade in the West was vibrant, and the trade villages active at that time reveal which tribes settled into a less nomadic life. As other tribes were forced to relocate from the East, the trade villages became like centralized shopping centers providing goods for tribes living hundreds of miles away. Major primary trade centers were the Mandan and Hidatsa villages in North Dakota, Arikara villages in South Dakota, Pueblo villages in New Mexico, and The Dalles in Oregon. Secondary permanent trade centers were the Pawnee villages in Nebraska, Wichita villages in Kansas, and Caddo villages in Texas. Primary seasonal trade centers were the Shoshone Rendezvous in Wyoming and Kettle Falls Rendezvous in Washington.[8]

The Blackfoot were three closely allied Algonquian tribes—the Blackfeet, the Blood, and the Piegan. The tribes were among the most ancient inhabitants of the Great Plains. They originally lived in eastern Canada, and some broke off and relocated to the Plains. The Piegan were trading furs for whiskey with the Hudson's Bay Company long before Meriwether Lewis encountered them in 1806. Another Blackfoot tribe, the Blackfeet, ended up in northwestern Montana and Idaho fighting the Kootenai and Shoshone along the way. Since they tended to kill any white men who entered their territory, they were greatly feared. The Blackfoot tribes lived in tipis and hunted bison like other Plains Indians. They were preceded there by the Flathead and Nez Perce.[9]

Another Algonquian tribe was the Cree. Some were known as forest dwellers, while others became Plains Cree and were bison hunters. They eventually settled mainly in Canada, but today some are sharing reservations with other tribes in North Dakota. They were one of the first to encounter the French Jesuits in 1640 and eventually were devastated by a smallpox epidemic in 1776. The Cree fought many battles against the Sioux, but in 1870 were defeated by the Blackfeet. They survived mainly on hunting, fishing, and trapping.

The Ojibwe now live on a number of reservations mainly in Minnesota but were an Algonquian tribe who were forced from eastern Canada and eventually ended up in North Dakota. They often were allied with the French and traded with them, swapping beaver plews and other pelts for firearms, which they used when they encountered the Sioux to the west. By 1851, white settlers had forced them west of the Mississippi.

Before the Blackfoot, the Gros Ventre and the Arapaho were roaming east of the Montana Rockies in search of bison. The Hidatsa were village farmers along the Missouri River in what is now North Dakota. North of them were the villages of the Mandan and the Arikara. South of them were the stationary Pawnee and the Ponca.

By the 1650s, the Huron were forced to the west end of Lake Superior where they confronted the Sioux. The Sioux were easy prey for the Huron since they did not have guns. Nonetheless, the Sioux, who numbered perhaps as many as 38,000, were a dominant force in the upper Mississippi watershed. The name Sioux was the white man's term.

Eventually, the nomadic Sioux obtained firearms from French traders. In 1641, Indians around Sault Ste. Marie told the Jesuits that the Sioux west of the area had never seen Europeans or heard of their Christian God. The first written account of the Sioux was recorded by Pierre-Esprit Radisson in 1661 when he met them and called them the "nation of beef." The Sioux were hoping to obtain guns from Radisson to defend themselves against the Cree who roamed vast areas of land and who Radisson called "the best huntsman of all America." The Cree were not the only tribe that the Sioux battled.[10]

The Eastern Sioux were known as the Dakota and the Western Sioux were known as the Lakota. The Lakota (also known as Teton) originally occupied the land between the upper Mississippi and Red River Valleys but made a slow progression westward toward the Great Plains as they were pressured by the presence of white civilization. The Lakota—the largest tribe of linguistically associated bodies—left Minnesota for South Dakota. By 1776, the Lakota controlled the lush Black Hills region. The seven tribes that composed the Lakota were the Hunkpapa, Oglala, Minneconjou, Brule, Ooenunpa or Two Kettles, Itazipico or No Bows, and Blackfeet (not the Algonquian Blackfoot of Montana). The Lakota would become known as the finest bison hunters of the Plains and included famous warriors like Red Cloud, Sitting Bull, and Crazy Horse. They were a nomadic tribe that lived in tipis and moved by dog travois and later horse travois.[11]

The other two subcultures of the Sioux were the Eastern Dakota and Western Dakota. The Eastern Dakota today live in the eastern Dakotas, Minnesota, and Iowa. The Western Dakota were also known as the Yankton and settled along the Missouri. The Assiniboine separated from the Western Dakota before the 1640s. The Assiniboine started in Minnesota and made their way west through southern Canada and into northern Montana. Many now reside on the Fort Peck Indian Reservation in northeastern Montana. The Yankton and Arikara traveled west from the woodlands of northwestern Wisconsin through Minnesota to North and South Dakota.

The Sioux became feared raiders on villages on the Northern Plains, and one of their favorite targets was the Mandan. As Pierre-Antoine Tabeau explained, "The Sioux, always wandering, left little to capture for the enemy, who often knew not where to find them." Historian Gary Clayton Anderson added that the Eastern Sioux "were well armed by 1700 and a match for all aggressors."[12]

As would so many of the Plains Indians, the Sioux moved between the woodlands and plains depending on the time of year. They fished; harvested wild rice, berries, nuts, and roots; and hunted bison, deer, elk, antelope, and bear. They would trade many of these items for corn from other Indians who lived on the Missouri and Wisconsin Rivers. With the influx of Sioux, the Gros Ventre migrated north from South Dakota through North Dakota to eastern Montana. The Sioux frequently battled the Blackfeet, Crow, and Shoshone for control of territory.[13]

The Northern Cheyenne lived in North Dakota until they were pressured by other tribes to relocate and migrated through South Dakota and eventually to Nebraska, Kansas, Colorado, and Oklahoma. The Apache, some who made their home in Colorado, were pushed southward into Texas and New Mexico. Comanche dominated the Southern Plains.

The Cheyenne were a Plains tribe who originally were forced west from the Great Lakes region about 300 years ago. The name is derived from the French *chien* ("dog") since they had a ritual of dog eating. They were an Algonquian Plains tribe who lived in tipis, hunted bison, and were great horsemen. They frequently fought with the Sioux, one of their prime enemies. After the Battle of the Little Bighorn, the malaria-infested Cheyenne were forced to live in Indian Territory, now Oklahoma. Under the leadership of Dull Knife and Little Wolf, some fled to their old hunting grounds and eventually settled on the Lame Deer Reservation in southeastern Montana. They are known as the Northern Cheyenne, and those who remained behind in Oklahoma are called Southern Cheyenne.

The Northern Arapaho, Northern Cheyenne, and Lakota for a time shared religion and culture while they lived in close proximity. The Northern Arapaho eventually migrated from South Dakota to Colorado, and the powerful Shoshone relocated from northeastern Nevada to Idaho and Wyoming. The Shoshone became bitter enemies of those who lived in the villages of the Plains. "Woe to those who crossed their path," wrote one explorer in 1742.[14]

The Crow were another Plains bison hunting tribe that split from the Hidatsa tribe during the second half of the eighteenth century. They were further divided into the River and Mountain Crow. Before the whites, the Crow were corn planters, and the women practiced pottery. By the time of their first encounters with the whites, they were nomadic hunters. They were quite successful and became the largest of all tribes. The Crow were one of the most adaptive tribes to the white man and became scouts for the U.S. military. Most notable were the Crow scouts in Custer's command. They were perhaps the only Indian tribe that lamented Custer's defeat and were rewarded with perhaps one of the better allotments of land for their Crow Reservation in southeastern Montana.

The Osage originally had their villages in Kansas, Missouri, and Illinois and were Plains Indians of the Siouan language group. They were known for their divided labor, with some taking up the making of moccasins, others pipes, and yet others arrowheads. They were eventually relocated to Indian Territory.

In close proximity to the Osage were the Pawnee, part of the Caddoan family, who were a federation of tribes living near the Platte River in what now is Nebraska. They lived in earth lodges, planted corn, and seasonally hunted bison. Like the Crow, the Pawnee served as U.S. Army scouts during the Indian Plains Wars, but, unlike the Crow, they were rewarded in 1876 by the U.S. government with removal to Oklahoma.

In time, the Omaha, Kiowa, and Ponca moved from eastern Nebraska to western Nebraska, and some moved northward into South Dakota. Constant conflict among all these tribes had been the norm for generations, but that changed when they fought a new enemy. After the 1851 Fort Laramie Treaty, the Sioux and whites battled each other for the first time.

Awaiting the displaced tribes from the East were the ancient Mandan. The Mandan's ancestors in South Dakota can be traced as far back as around 1000 CE. Apparently, they were attracted to that area due to a climate shift from 900 to 1250 CE to warmer and wetter conditions. There was another climate shift around 1250, with a subsequent drastic reduction in rain on the Plains. One of the first recorded dust bowls occurred there. Many would follow.[15]

The Numakaki, the name the Mandan called themselves until the 1830s, numbered at the time of Columbus more than 12,000 living on the Northern Plains. Around 1400 the Mandan's ancestors migrated from the south and east and ended up on a fifty-mile stretch along the Missouri River between the mouths of the Knife and Cannonball Rivers. Their religious life included the Okipa ceremony and elaborate rituals performed every summer. The ancestors of the Hidatsa arrived sometime after that to the upper Missouri River.

The Mandan were a full-fledged society who had extensive commercial trading and agricultural skills and were widely known as very hospitable people. Their way of life has been well documented since the time of Lewis and Clark. A number of explorers traveling up the Missouri River interacted with them.

Like so many other tribes, the Mandan were destroyed by smallpox. They also were attacked by other Indian tribes on horseback who actively raided their villages. Eventually, steamboats from St. Louis brought their own problems. Norwegian rats arrived in 1825 on U.S. Army keelboats and ate the Mandan's corn. Whooping cough and cholera also reduced their numbers. By 1838, there were only 300 Mandan, and their society was in a state of collapse and near extinction.[16]

The Prime Measure of Wealth: The Plains Horse

Another nomad of the Plains was the horse. Its reappearance was one of the few positive outcomes of contact with whites. The domestication of the horse by the Plains Indians revolutionized their life. The mobility to hunt animals far from their villages and trading centers like the Mandan villages transformed their lives from constantly being on the move to a more stationary existence. As Elizabeth A. Fenn in *Encounters at the Heart of the World* wrote, "But horses did not alter the basics of the Mandan existence as they did for itinerant peoples like the Sioux, Crow, Arapaho, Blackfeet, and Assiniboine. By the second half of the eighteenth century, the Mandan had simply, and profitably, added horses to the marketable goods they bartered with others."[17]

The horse had been in the New World for 45 million years, but disappeared about 13,000 years ago. At Polecat Bench Butte in Wyoming, there is a 56-million-year-old site where fossils of the earliest horse relatives have been discovered, as well as those of the first real primates. The earliest horses—known as dawn horses—were small and had not yet lost all their toes except the large central one that is now the hoof. Both humans and horses are highly social animals with intricate networks of friendships and alliances. Among humans, horses have an ambiguous status: part pampered and beloved pet, part feral beast, and part domestic helper.[18]

Since the time of Columbus, horses had made a steady migration north from Mexico with the Spanish colonists and conquistadors. The southwestern Apache, Navajo, and Ute were becoming excellent riders by the mid-seventeenth century. A hundred years later, mustangs could be found in the southern parts of Alberta and Saskatchewan.[19]

The mobility of the Plains Indians was almost completely reliant on the horse, which became one of the most important items that Cortés and his conquistadors brought in 1519 to the New World, along with their guns and germs. The first Iberian horses were seen in the Southwest, while guns penetrated the Plains from the northeast and east. Indian survival on the Plains was in large part dependent on whether they had horses and guns, both of which gave them an advantage against their enemies.[20]

By the mid-1550s, there were tens of thousands of horses in Mexico. Many made their way to the American West where they became central to the ranching tradition of herding livestock from horseback and the Indian tradition of hunting bison from horseback. The Pueblo Revolt of 1680 that drove the Spanish out of New Mexico also led to trading horses to other tribes.[21]

In 1682, La Salle reported that the Apache and Pawnee had horses. The horse spread throughout North America almost as fast as smallpox did. Comanche and Ute traded horses to the Shoshone. Thereafter, the Shoshone traded them to the Crow and also to the Salish and Nez Perce in the plateau region who then traded them to the Blackfeet. The Blackfeet and Gros Ventre traded them to the Assiniboine. Other herds were released in Texas and California when the Spanish abandoned their missions.[22]

Hudson's Bay Company traders noticed horses with Spanish brands owned by the Cree and Assiniboine in the 1750s. In the villages of the Mandan, Hidatsa, and Arikara, horses were obtained from the Crow, Kiowa, Arapaho, and Cheyenne, among others. The Lakota then purchased horses at the Arikara villages and traded them to their Dakota relatives. Horses were a status symbol, designating wealth and power. The addition of horses to Indian communities greatly increased their mobility; before the horse, they were limited to using dog travois to help them move their possessions.[23]

With the introduction of the horse in the middle of the Little Ice Age, 1552 to 1850, Plains Indians hunted bison from horseback. The bison were just recovering from three centuries of dry, warm weather that had decreased the grasses on the Great Plains and the size of the herds. The increase in bison numbers allowed Indian populations (at least those who survived European diseases) to prosper. Some agricultural societies in which women had played dominant roles were transformed into hunter societies where women lost much of their status. In the sixteenth century, Spanish explorers reported that the Indians were hunting bison, living in skin tipis, and traveling great distances as nomads to hunt the bison herds.[24]

The Blackfeet were known as the most formidable power on the Northern Plains in no small part because they mastered the equestrian warrior-hunter culture. They obtained guns and ammunition from the Hudson's Bay Company soon after it was chartered in 1670.[25] Their enemy, the Crow, did not obtain horses until around 1725 when they brought them back from the Green River in Wyoming. The Crow attributed spiritual power to the horses, and it was considered good horse medicine to own many horses. They sang special songs about horses and held ceremonies and dances honoring them.[26]

Home on the Range

One of the most anticipated events of a young Indian boy's life was when he received a colt and horse gear. It was the boy's job to take care of the colt, and eventually he was also expected to take care of his parents' horses. The Indian boys learned how to ride the horses at a fast gallop for hours, and a horse that was exhausted by its white rider would travel another twenty miles for an Indian.

At the time of the arrival of Columbus, the cultural differences between Europeans and Native Americans were no more evident than in the area of child rearing. That fact, whether unknown or ignored, would wreck havoc later when the U.S. government in the nineteenth century forced Indian children to attend off-reservation schools like the Carlisle Indian Industrial School in Pennsylvania to be assimilated into American society. It was a process that could only be judged as a failure.

As Robert Utley wrote in his classic book *The Lance and The Shield: The Life and Times of Sitting Bull*, "Like all Sioux parents, Sitting Bull and Her-Holy-Door doted on their children. 'A child is the greatest gift from Wakan Tanka, the Great Mystery,' a tribesman explained years later, sent 'in response to many devout prayers, sacrifices, and promises.'"[27] Children were the tribe's future, and the parents doted on them. For Native Americans, love's purpose was not to shape their children's destiny but to help their children shape their own destiny. They believed in respectful teaching, and physical punishment was not part of discipline.

In the nineteenth century, many Native Americans on the Great Plains—like their Pleistocene ancestors—lived as hunter-gatherers. They were nomadic and moved from one environment to another, relying on each new generation to create and modify its own environment. One way the Indians evolved to deal with the variability was by nurturing a vast range of children with different temperaments and abilities. This ensured that some in each new generation would have the coping skills to address the unpredictable and unforeseeable environments they would face. The childhood of native children provided a period of endless possibility, exploration, learning, and imagination. In contrast, the minds of white children were channeled by "parenting" to be adaptable to only one unique environment and expertise. That could be lethal in the American West.[28]

In Indian culture, the care and responsibility of the infant was the mother's role, and she was often assisted by the grandmother and other relatives. She owned the lodge and all possessions in it. It was not uncommon for boys to run naked through the village until the age of seven. Europeans found this repulsive, and it bolstered their opinion that they were dealing with savages and heathens.

Unlike Europeans, the Indian parents did not discipline their small children. In contrast, they were coddled and spoiled. If older boys proved unruly, they might be frightened by an owl, medicine man, or the threat of white men coming to harm them. Young children were never whipped or handled roughly but greatly loved for who they were. From early childhood, the Lakota—and many other tribes—taught them four virtues: bravery, generosity, fortitude, and wisdom.[29]

Boys were expected to learn about those things that would make them productive members of their tribe. Spirituality, pride, and respect for elders were ingrained into the children by their parents. Oral histories were taught to them so they would have pride in their ancestry. Usually at age four or five, a boy's father would present his son with a bow and arrow and begin instruction on how to use them.

Play between the sexes was common and encouraged by the parents. It usually revolved around miniature tipis, travois, and weapons, preparing them for adulthood. Around eleven years of age, the sexes were separated and more mature training began. Boys were coached to take long runs and to learn how to fast while staying awake for extended periods of time. For those who wanted to be a warrior, showing cowardice was unacceptable.

Motivational ceremonies were held for the boys to prepare them for adulthood. One was the Blackfoot Medicine Lodge Ceremony where the boys in the village would watch the warriors count their coup. One by one, each warrior would stand up holding a bundle of small sticks. As each stick in the bundle was shown to the boys, the warrior relayed the brave deed associated with it. The idea was to create enthusiasm among the boys to someday become warriors.

Like other tribes, the Mandan and Hidatsa had age-based societies for all males and females over the age of twelve. Membership to a society denoted a responsible and worthy citizen of the tribe. Names of some of the societies were Magpies, Stone Hammers, Gun, and River. One of the most prestigious for childbearing women was the Goose Society, and for postmenopausal women it was the White Buffalo Crows Society. For men who wanted to police the village, it was the Black Mouths.[30]

In the early teenage years, a youth might be invited to join a Warrior Society. In the ensuing year or two, he might steal an enemy's horse, count coup, or take a scalp. Author Frank Bird Linderman described counting coup:

> To count coup a warrior had to strike an armed and fighting enemy with his coup-stick, quirt, or bow before otherwise harming him, or take his weapons while he was yet alive, or strike the first enemy falling in battle, no matter who killed him, or strike the enemy's breastworks while under fire, or steal a horse tied to a lodge in an enemy's camp, etc. The first named was the most honorable, and to strike such a coup a warrior would often display great bravery. An eagle's feather worn in the hair was a mark of distinction and told the world that the wearer had counted coup.[31]

By nineteen, the young brave was participating in his first Sun Dance, and a year later he could be leading a small war party. Being named a chief might come as early as age twenty-five. Such status might last only a little more than five years, and then his fighting days would came to a close. If fortunate, by that time he would have many war honors and horses. Success also involved having multiple tipis with one or more wives—each one having a number of children.

In 1932, Frank Bird Linderman published *Red Mother*, a compilation of interviews with the Crow woman Pretty-Shield. She described her marriage to Goes-Ahead:

> "Tell me of your marriage, about your man," I suggested.
>
> Her face lighted. "Ahhh, I was sixteen when my man, Goes-ahead, took me. I have already told you that my father had promised me to Goes-ahead, when I was thirteen. When I became sixteen years old my father kept his promise."
>
> "Did you fall in love with him before he took you?" I asked.
>
> "No, no," she smiled. "I had not often spoken to him until he took me. Then I fell in love with him, because he loved me and was always kind. Young women did not then fall in love, and get married to please themselves, as they now do. They listened to their fathers, married the men selected for them, and this, I believe, is the best

way. There was no deformed children born in those days," she said, thoughtfully. "And men and women were happier, too, I feel sure," she added, with a challenge in her words. "A man could not take a woman from his own clan, no matter how much you might wish to have her. He had to marry a woman belonging to another clan, and then all their children belong to their mother's clan. This law kept our blood strong."[32]

After the age of thirty-five, Indian men focused on hunting and defending the village against attack by other tribes or the white man. Spiritual meditation was extremely important at this period of his life and was part of becoming a wise and recognized elder. The cycle would repeat itself as he would encourage young boys to follow his life's path. The sacred path would eventually be completed, and he would become like a child again to return to the Father who gave him birth.

Many tribes of the Northern Plains loved sports. In 1832, while observing village life among the Mandan, George Catlin wrote, "I have this day been a spectator of games and plays until I am fatigued with looking on." Upon further visiting, he concluded that sports and gambling were an obsession to the Missouri River dwellers. There were games involving bows and arrows and others resembling hacky sack. Many tribes were known for their exciting foot races, which showcased the great athletic ability of Indians. Fur trader Alexander Henry described the almost-daily sport, writing, "This violent exercise [is] performed on the hottest days," and noted that he was impressed at how swift they were.[33]

Indians and whites held opposite attitudes toward land. The Indians believed they were custodians of the land and viewed with disdain the whites' clearing of forests, over-cultivating the ground, slaughtering wild animals in massive quantities, and mining gold and silver. Europeans saw the land as a possession, and they strived to obtain it through private ownership. The Indians had the custom of sharing the land in common with their fellow Indians. Robert Utley wrote, "Generosity reflected a true appreciation of the tribe's values. People were what counted, not property. Mere possession of property conferred no prestige, indeed could be viewed as disgraceful. The prestige came from giving away the property. An elaborate system of gift-giving, among individuals, families, bands, and even tribes, afforded constant opportunity for the practice of this virtue." As one Lakota observed, "A man must take pity on orphans, the crippled and the old. If you have more than one of anything, you should give it away to help those persons." This imperative applied to the prime measure of wealth, the horse, and the prime staple of diet, the bison, as well as to all other possessions.[34]

Before the Louisiana Purchase and the influx of Americans from the East, Plains tribes in some instances battled each other for survival and at other times traded with each other for goods. Some Indians who had been displaced out West by whites understood their power and greed. Other tribes who had little contact with Americans felt somewhat insulated from influences of the newly formed country. Few understood the determination of Americans to make the West their own.

Thomas Jefferson, the Father of the American West, represented white attitudes in his own era. His vision was one of white American families living on the land all the way to the Pacific Ocean. Soon, tribal traditions, beliefs, and religions in place for centuries on the Plains would be challenged by Manifest Destiny. Plains Indians would suffer the consequences of the white man's religion, philosophy, science, medicine, and germs.

CHAPTER SIX

The Blind Healing the Blind: White Medicine Men

I swear by Apollo the physician, and Aesculapius the surgeon, likewise Hygeia and Panacea, and call all the gods and goddesses to witness, that I will observe and keep this underwritten oath, to the utmost of my power and judgment.
—ORIGINAL VERSION OF THE HIPPOCRATIC OATH

Let's consider medicine (that sister of philosophy), which only started saving lives less than a century ago (I am generous), and to a lesser extent than initially advertised in the popular literature, as the drops in mortality seem to arise much more from awareness of sanitation and the (random) discovery of antibiotics rather than from therapeutic contributions. Doctors, driven by the beastly illusion of control, spent a long time killing patients, not considering that "doing nothing" could be a valid option (it was "nihilistic")—and research compiled by Spyros Makridakis shows that they still do to some extent, particularly in the overdiagnoses of some diseases. . . . I have also in the past speculated that religion saves lives by taking the patient away from the doctor.
—NASSIM NICHOLAS TALEB, THE BLACK SWAN

As Native Americans searched for a better way of life for their families and sometimes just to survive, Western civilization searched for answers to the diseases that were increasingly killing their loved ones—many illnesses converged on them because of high-density living in Europe's urban areas.
Racism is predicated on superiority. One of the cornerstones of

perceived exceptionalism is Western medicine. Physicians became part of society's elite as the Age of Enlightenment and the Scientific Revolution unfolded. Physicians who saw themselves as Renaissance men held divinity degrees and dabbled in the sciences. In the nineteenth century, many of the healers embraced the crusade for scientific racism that attempted to explain the inferiority of slaves and Indians. Whites were superior, and men of color were inferior and unable to know what was best for them. However, noted physician and co-founder of Johns Hopkins Hospital William Osler (1849-1919) warned that medicine is "a science of uncertainty and an art of probability."[1]

In the early twentieth century, many physicians also supported eugenics, which aimed to improve a country's genetic stock by forced sterilization of "unfit" groups. These groups included those with mental and physical impairments, Jews, and perceived inferior races. Francis Galton, a half-cousin of Charles Darwin, coined the term *eugenics* in 1883, one year after his famous relative died. Even though Darwin did not support eugenics, by the early twentieth century it was practiced around the world by governments and institutions.[2]

Few of us today appreciate that the sophistication of Western medicine until recently was only questionably better than that practiced by the Indian medicine man or shaman. In 1890, when Frederick Jackson Turner declared "the frontier has gone," Western medicine had very little to brag about. The understanding of germs was in its infancy, and there were no antibiotics to treat communicable and infectious diseases. Nationwide vaccinations were in the future, as was the effective treatment of heart disease, cancer, and diabetes.

The average life expectancy of an American male in 1850 at birth was thirty-eight, at age five was fifty-five, and at age forty was sixty-six; in 1900 at birth was forty-eight, at age five was fifty-eight, and at age forty was sixty-six; and in 2000 at birth was seventy-four, at age five was seventy-four, and at age forty was seventy-eight. These statistics show that in 1850, a large number of children died before age five. If a male survived childhood diseases and made it to age five, he could add another seventeen years to his life expectancy. By 1900, better sanitation and the reduction of infant deaths dramatically increased life expectancy at birth by ten years. Over the last 150 years, if a male was alive at age forty, his life expectancy surprisingly increased only by twelve years. By 2000, immunizations were credited for almost totally eliminating infant deaths, but advances in the treatment of heart disease—mainly by control of high blood pressure, diet, exercise, and cholesterol blood levels with statins—and cancer increased life expectancy by only four years. Preventative medicine saves lives.[3]

However, a disturbing trend is now surfacing. The life expectancy of whites dropped from 78.9 in 2013 to 78.8 years in 2014 due to drug overdoses, liver disease, and suicide. Life expectancy in 2014 of Hispanics was 81.8 years, Blacks was 75.2 years, and Native Americans was 73.7 years.[4] Medical errors in 2016 were the third leading cause of death behind heart disease and cancer in the U.S.[5]

Before the twentieth century, prominent physicians in Europe and America often did more harm than good. Hand holding and comforting the inflicted was the only therapy for most illnesses. Today, treatment often trumps empathy. That fact is lamented by most. Raymond Barfield, MD, professor in the schools of both medicine and divinity at Duke University in Durham, North Carolina, expressed what many today believe: "As a physician I am granted an almost priest-like authority, and I can use that authority to translate the patient's experience into biological language. But that's a sadly diminished way to respond to a stunning human drama. It's not just for the sake of the patients that we need to rethink this—it's for the doctors too."[6] For him, theology is the key to understanding the mystery.

Undaunted Courage

At the beginning of the nineteenth century, brave Americans headed west into the great unknown, and the New World would never be the same. Thomas Jefferson, the Father of the American West, sent Lewis and Clark and their Corps of Discovery to explore the new Louisiana Purchase. Across the ocean, the Spanish king also sent a team west by boat. The memory of the doctor and the orphans on board the ship has faded into historical obscurity, but in many ways what they accomplished would rival the achievements of the famous Lewis and Clark.

In 1798, the English physician Edward Jenner (1749-1823) introduced a vaccination procedure for smallpox, one of the most deadly infectious diseases in history. It was the major killer of Native Americans for centuries. With the vaccine, the world took a giant leap ahead toward modern medicine. It couldn't have come soon enough. Wave after wave of smallpox was killing humans worldwide with no indication of any relief. In the early 1700s, the famed French writer and philosopher Voltaire estimated that sixty percent of the population of England had contracted smallpox at one time or another, and twenty percent of the total population had died from it. In the sixteenth century, after the Spanish conquistadors invaded the New World, smallpox spread rapidly as it devastated the Indian populations who had no immunity to the European virus.

Back in Spain—the country that initially introduced smallpox to the Americas—the first relatively large-scale international healthcare expedition in history was about to unfold just five years after Jenner announced his technique for vaccination. The demand for smallpox vaccine, a live cowpox virus, was rapidly increasing around the world. Small amounts had already reached North America. But the question was how to get larger quantities across the ocean—a trip that could take weeks—while it was still viable? A Spanish doctor, Francisco Javier de Balmis (1753-1819), had an idea. He called on a group of orphaned boys to save the world.

Dr. Balmis knew that the cowpox virus could be transmitted from one person to another by taking the pus from an infected person and introducing the pus containing the virus into a scratch on an uninfected person's skin. But shipping one person infected with cowpox across the Atlantic to the New World would not work. The problem was that by the time the infected person arrived, his immune system would have cleared the active pustules, and there would be no virus to inoculate uninfected humans.

With the support of King Charles IV of Spain, whose daughter had almost died from smallpox, Balmis would hatch his scheme. A bunch of unexposed orphans were needed to join the trip. Along the way, pus from the initial boy infected with cowpox would be introduced to a second, and then from the second to a third, and so on, with some redundancies built in to account for unforeseen problems. This would result in a succession of carriers that would produce surviving live cowpox virus upon arrival in the New World.

On November 30, 1803, the doctor set sail on the *Maria Pita* with twenty-two orphaned boys—ages eight to ten years old—along with a deputy surgeon, two assistants, two first-aid practitioners, three nurses, and the rectoress of the orphanage.

The successful mission that continued for seven years took the vaccine to the Canary Islands, Colombia, Ecuador, Peru, Mexico, the Philippines, and China.[7] It eventually reached overland to North America. Edward Jenner himself wrote, "I don't imagine the annals of history furnish an example of philanthropy so noble, so extensive as this."[8] It took nearly 200 years more, but vaccines eventually made it around the world, and as of 1977 smallpox had been eradicated.

It seems fitting that Spain, credited for bringing smallpox to the New World, would also be instrumental in ultimately halting the disease. The development of the vaccine by Jenner was perhaps the greatest medical advancement to date. His vaccination would be an inspiration to Frenchman Louis Pasteur (1822-1895), who created the first vaccine for rabies and anthrax decades later. Pasteur is probably best known for his invention of the technique of treating milk and wine to stop bacterial contamination called pasteurization. He is known as the "father of microbiology," and is credited with convincing most of Europe that the germ theory promoted by Francesco Redi in the seventeenth century was true. It would be left to German physician and microbiologist Robert Koch (1843-1910) at the end of the nineteenth century to play an important role in identifying the specific causative agents of tuberculosis, cholera, and anthrax—diseases that caused much devastation to the Indian populations.

While bacteria were identified as the culprits in many diseases, modern treatment would take years longer. Antibacterial chemotherapy agents, commonly known as antibiotics, began in 1907 with the discovery of arsphenamine, an arsenic-based compound, for the treatment of syphilis. In 1933, the first systemically active antibiotic, sulfur-based prontosil, was discovered in the Bayer Laboratories in Germany.

But it would be the discovery of penicillin by Scottish biologist, pharmacologist, and botanist Sir Alexander Fleming (1881-1955) that would be arguably the greatest antibiotic discovery of all time. In 1928, he accidentally discovered the antibiotic substance penicillin G from the mold *Penicillium notatum* (today classified as *Penicillium chrysogenum*). He later stated, "When I woke up just after dawn on September 28, 1928, I certainly didn't plan to revolutionise all medicine by discovering the world's first antibiotic, or bacteria killer, but I suppose that was exactly what I did."[9] The mass production of the antibiotic did not occur until after the bombing of Pearl Harbor in 1941. Margaret Hutchinson, a resourceful chemical engineer, developed a fermentation method to produce large quantities of the lifesaving drug. By D-Day in 1944, there was enough antibiotic to treat all the wounded in the Allied Forces.

Until Jenner's breakthrough, in many ways Western medicine and Native American medicine were not much different. Each were part faith, part power of suggestion, part hope, and part luck; medicine was definitely an art and not a science. Both groups relied on herbal medicines available from local plants without much else to offer their patients. Yet the elite touted their Western medicine as another example of their racial superiority over Native Americans. Perception is everything.

Indian medicine men and shamans (priests) worked closely together, as we will see later. That was not the case for physicians and priests. There has always been a palpable tension between the Christian clergy and the medical profession. In time, friars were discarded in favor of the physician, and the sick entered the hospital and not the church for healing. Physical ailments were treated by a doctor and not a spiritual leader. Some of the finest schools in Europe, however, required that their men of science also had a divinity degree.

The drop in mortality rate in the urban areas of Europe arose more from the awareness of sanitation. The best medicine anyone—European or Indian—could practice was to avoid communities where communicable diseases circulated. If exposure did occur, simple nursing care was offered to the ill, along with quarantine to prevent the spread of disease. Children were the most vulnerable. Calm was encouraged so that basic social services such as gathering food, water, and firewood could continue uninterrupted.[10]

Hippocrates (460-370 BCE) and Galen (129-200 CE): The Fathers of Western Medicine

The history of Western medicine in many ways can be summed up as the blind leading the blind. It's yet another story of man's premature belief that he has things figured out. That will never happen, but it does inspire hope and confidence, and, just as often, arrogance and hubris.

Hippocrates of Kos born in Greece is considered one of the most outstanding figures in the history of medicine. In fact, he is often referred to as the "Father of Western Medicine."[11] While his work is often credited with establishing medicine as a profession, many of his teachings have proven to be wrong.

Before Hippocrates, diseases were believed to be caused by gods and evil spirits. He suggested that they were caused by natural events and assured his followers that when they got sick they were not being punished by the gods. He helped separate the discipline of medicine from religion, although as we shall see the split has never been completed. Many of his convictions we now know were based on incorrect anatomy and physiology because the Greeks did not believe in the dissection of humans. Therapy for the sick often included fasting and the consumption of apple cider vinegar. He once said that "to eat when you are sick, is to feed your sickness." We know now that good nutrition is vital to recovery.[12]

Observation and documentation were very important to Hippocrates. He categorized diseases as acute, chronic, endemic and epidemic, relapse, convalescence, and exacerbation.[13]

Writing and documenting in books his thoughts and observations—which were eventually adopted by all Western physicians—was one of the main differences between Western medicine and Indian medicine. We have a rich legacy of the written word in medicine, while Indian medicine was handed down from generation to generation by word of mouth and included myths and legends.

The next great physician was another Greek, Galen, who was born in 129 CE and eventually settled in Rome. He was influential in the development of anatomy, physiology, pathology, pharmacology, and neurology.[14]

The underlying principle of most medieval medicine was Galen's theory—inspired by Hippocrates—of humors, a theory that dominated all Western medicines until the nineteenth century. The theory stated that within every individual there were four humors, or principal fluids—black bile, yellow bile, phlegm, and blood. These were produced by various organs in the body, and they had to be in balance for a person to remain healthy. The balance of humors in humans could be achieved by diet, medicines, and by bloodletting—using either leeches or knives.

Healing included both physical and spiritual therapeutics, such as the right herbs, a suitable diet, clean bedding, and the knowledge that care was always at hand. Other procedures used to help patients included mass, prayers, relics of saints, and music.[15] The Romans invented numerous surgical instruments such as forceps, scalpel, cautery, cross-bladed scissors, and surgical needles. Galen was noted to be an accomplished surgeon who performed procedures on brains and eyes.[16]

Galen may have been the first famous physician to attempt to treat smallpox. In Rome he had become the physician to royalty, and in 166 CE when an epidemic struck, he was called on. Close to half the population perished, and the ancient world never recovered from the results of the disease. His medical efforts bore little fruit.

After 400 CE, the study and practice of medicine in the Western Empire went into deep decline as the Dark Ages progressed. Most of the writings of Galen and Hippocrates were lost to the West. Eventually, the first medical schools were opened in southern Italy. Around the twelfth century, there were also medical schools built in France and England.[17]

Paracelsus (1493-1541)

A number of notable physicians practiced after the famous voyage of Columbus to America. Paracelsus was a Swiss German Renaissance physician, botanist, chemist, astrologer, and general occultist. He founded the discipline of toxicology. Paracelsus used observations of nature instead of looking to ancient texts for his medical practice. He is also credited for naming zinc and noted for discovering that some diseases are rooted in psychological conditions.[18]

At the age of sixteen, he started studying medicine at the University of Basel and eventually received his doctorate degree from the University of Ferrara. At that time, he was also a practicing astrologer—which was used to cure diseases—as were many of the university-trained physicians working in Europe.

Paracelsus pioneered the use of chemicals and minerals in medicine and also was responsible for the creation of laudanum (tincture of opium), which became a mainstay of treatment for pain, cough, and a number of diseases until the nineteenth century. Like other physicians, he criticized apothecary practices that were often not applied in a dosage-correct manner. He was a contemporary of the famed Copernicus, Leonardo da Vinci, and Martin Luther. His openly defiant acts against medical authorities were compared to Martin Luther's defiance of the Catholic Church. He said, "I leave it to Luther to defend what he says, and I will be responsible for what I say. That which you wish to Luther, you wish also to me: you wish us both in the fire."[19]

Paracelsus was one of the first physicians who thought his profession needed a solid knowledge in the natural sciences, especially chemistry. He believed physicians should have academic training. At the time, surgeons were not academically trained and were instead associated with barbers and butchers in the same guild.

Rejecting the theory of humors championed for centuries by Hippocrates and Galen, Paracelsus incorrectly believed that sulfur, mercury, and salt contained the poisons contributing to all diseases. He concluded that the three also defined the human identity. Sulfur embodied the soul; salt represented the body; and mercury epitomized the spirit. By understanding the chemical nature of the three, a physician could discover the means of curing disease.[20]

Paracelsus believed humans must ward off the influence of evil spirits with morality and a healthy lifestyle. From his belief in astrology, he concluded that diseases were caused by poisons brought here from the stars, and he believed in the curative powers of alpine mineral springs.[21]

The dominant medical treatments in his time were specific diets to help cleanse the putrefied juices in the body, in combination with purging and bloodletting to restore balance in the body. Doctors at the time thought that infection was a natural part of the healing process. Nonetheless, he advocated for cleanliness as well as regulation of diet. He maintained that syphilis could be treated by carefully measured doses of mercury, which proved to be effective although it carried a number of debilitating side effects.[22]

Michel de Nostredame (1503-1566)

Michel de Nostredame or Nostradamus, born eleven years after Columbus arrived in America, was a famous French apothecary, seer, and physician. At the age of fifteen, he entered the University of Avignon, but a year into his studies the university closed because of the plague. Starting in 1521, he then spent eight years researching herbal remedies. That was followed by entering the University of Montpellier to study for a doctorate in medicine, but he was expelled after it was revealed that he had been an apothecary (archaic for pharmacist), which was considered a manual trade and carried an immediate expulsion according to the university statutes. Apothecaries, in a turf war, had been slandering doctors to gain business. Undaunted, he continued his work as an apothecary and developed a famous and popular "rose pill" that supposedly protected against the plague, but it was total placebo.[23]

By 1545, he was fighting a major outbreak of the plague in a number of French cities. It became clear to him that poor sanitation made the plague worse. With little success as a doctor, Nostradamus moved toward the occult. However, he did write two books on medical sciences, including a description of the methods he used to treat the plague, such as bloodletting. None of his treatments were very beneficial. Nostradamus also published his predictions on disease outcome based on astrology.[24]

His *Les Propheties* (1555) was a sensation when it was first published and continues to be popular, rarely being out of print. This collection of prophesies supposedly predicted future world events, but today most academic authorities remain skeptical. He is yet another example of a renowned physician who in reality was more of a showman than a genuine healer.[25]

English Physicians Lead the Way

William Harvey (1578-1657) was a noted English physician and the first to describe in complete detail the systemic circulation properties of blood. He graduated as a doctor of medicine at the age of twenty-four from the University of Padua. He then returned to England were he obtained another doctor of medicine degree from the University of Cambridge. Subsequently, Harvey accepted a position at St. Bartholomew's Hospital where he stayed for most of the rest of his career. He became the physician to King James I in 1618 and Lord Chancellor Bacon.

To Harvey, the work of studying the heart was tedious; he said, "I found the task truly arduous . . . that I was almost tempted to think . . . that the movement of the heart was only to be comprehended by God. . . ."[26] Harvey went on to prove how the blood circulated in a circle by means of countless experiments initially done on fish and other animals.

Relatively unknown today, Thomas Browne was born in London in 1605. After earning an undergraduate degree at Oxford, he studied medicine in Europe in a period of revolutionary medical discoveries—highlighted by the chemical-based medicines of Paracelsus and by Harvey's celebrated research on the mechanics of blood circulation. He eventually settled in Norwich, England, where he practiced medicine and grew a pharmacological garden.

Browne's fame sprang not from scientific discoveries but from words—the most enduring of these is *Religio Medici* (1642)—or *The Religion of a Doctor*—a subtle defense of Christianity. He is credited in the *Oxford English Dictionary* for the coinage of nearly 800 words, including hallucination, indoctrination, locomotion, insecurity, zoology, computer, veterinarian, and electricity. His mind was equally divided among science, medicine, religion, literature, and history. Browne, a polymath, epitomized the close link that these disciplines had and have. He proved that the Scientific Revolution was not made only by abstract thinkers like Newton but also by curiosity seekers and amateur experimentalists. Unlike Newton and Jefferson—products of the Enlightenment—Browne did not reject miracles or understand revelations as a series of noble myths. Nor did he do the reverse and banish religion from the realm of rationality. Science, like all other forms of reason, was for him the most powerful proof that the created universe was more than brute matter. For some, Thomas Browne has been portrayed as a curious naturalist and not as Thomas Browne the Christian spiritual writer. Browne himself might have rebuked this imbalance by quoting himself: "We carry within us the wonders we seek without us."[27]

During the later period of the Renaissance came an increase in experimental investigation, particular in the field of dissection and body examination. This advanced our knowledge of human anatomy. During the Age of Enlightenment in the eighteenth century, science was held in high esteem, and physicians upgraded their social status by becoming more scientific. Previously, the health field was crowded with self-trained barbers, surgeons, apothecaries, midwives, drug peddlers, and charlatans. Across Europe, medical schools relied primarily on lectures and readings in the first years of school, and then in the final year students would have limited clinical experience by trailing the professor through the hospital wards. Laboratory work was uncommon, and dissections were rarely done because of legal restrictions on cadavers.[28]

Even though a certain tension remained between religious leaders and physicians in America and Europe, during the 1700s Jesuit missionaries with medical training brought information on the latest advances in medicine to the Royal Court in China.[29] Christian medical missionaries from the London Missionary Society, the Methodist Church of Britain, and the Presbyterian Church in the United States are also credited with bringing Western medicine to many parts of the world.[30]

John Hunter (1728-1793), a Scottish surgeon, would become one of the most distinguished scientists and surgeons of the century. He was a friend, teacher, and collaborator with Edward Jenner. After a career in the army, Hunter was elected as a fellow of the Royal Society in 1767 and became the leading authority on venereal diseases. He believed erroneously that gonorrhea and syphilis were caused by a single pathogen. By 1776, he was appointed surgeon to King George III. Ten years later, he was chosen to be surgeon general by Prime Minister William Pitt. Over his lifetime, Hunter built up a collection of over 13,000 specimens of separate organ systems, from the simplest plants and animals to humans. Today, he is regarded as the "Father of modern scientific surgery."[31]

From 1776 up until 1832, medical leaders still treated patients on the basis of the centuries-old concept of the four humors. Overactive humors were treated by bloodletting, purging with mercury compounds, and inducing vomiting with tartar emetics. Older physicians became mentors to medical students who learned their trade through apprenticeships. Only the wealthiest students could attend medical school in prestigious institutions like those found in Edinburgh.[32]

The best-known brain-body interaction in medicine is the placebo effect—the more drastic the placebo, the greater the response. Capsules are better than pills, injections superior to capsules, and placebo surgeries are best of all. The favored remedies of the nineteenth century, such as toxic doses of mercury and copious bloodletting by lancet and leach, were especially ferocious placebos, abetted by the plausibility and charisma of their practitioners.[33]

Rising opposition to the idea of treating humors mounted from the 1830s until after the American Civil War. In an 1860 address to the Massachusetts Medical Society, Oliver Wendell Holmes, Sr. (1809-1894) expressed his concern over earlier medical treatments in the nineteenth century, saying, "I firmly believe that if most of the pharmacopeia were sunk to the bottom of the sea, it would be all the better for mankind and all the worse for the fishes."[34] He discovered, as is typical in medicine, that change was slow.

While additional therapies were added, such as quinine, alcohol, iron compounds, and cod liver oil, few really had any medical efficacy. Greater advances were found in the area of diagnostic instruments. Bacteria and microorganisms were first observed with a microscope by Antonie van Leeuwenhoek in 1676, initiating the scientific field of microbiology.[35] In the 1820s, the stethoscope came into common use, and in the 1830s the compound microscope was used to examine body fluids. By the 1850s, the ophthalmoscope and laryngoscope were developed, as was the hypodermic syringe. In the 1870s, thermometers were used to monitor fevers.[36]

Diagnostics improved, while efficacious treatments lagged. This led to all sorts of quackery. For example, in Sonoma, California, during the 1880s, faith healer Emily Preston claimed to heal illness with a medieval form of therapy called blister treatment. Bandages were soaked in caustic chemicals and wrapped around the patient's body, causing the skin to blister and supposedly release disease. While lucrative for Preston and other quacks, the patients left with the hope of improvement. Yet the only improvement was perhaps in their mental attitude through the power of suggestion.[37]

During the nineteenth century, among the more important advancements were the use of anesthesia and the development of both antiseptic and aseptic operating theaters.[38] Before the advent of anesthesia, surgeons attempted to complete their surgeries as quickly as possible to minimize patient suffering. Surgeries were usually restricted to amputations. The use of ether in the 1840s changed this. It was followed by the addition of nitrous oxide and chloroform for anesthesia. Patients were under anesthesia for short periods of time, usually less than thirty minutes.[39]

Medical advances were one of the few positives derived from war. With the advent of anesthesia, more surgeries were performed, which enhanced the surgeon's proficiency, but this led to more post-operative infections. General anesthetics were used over 80,000 times during the Civil War, with chloroform the most common. Out West during the Plains Indian Wars from 1865 to 1876, general anesthesia was used over 1,200 times. After the Civil War, the term *normal* replaced *natural* to describe a person in good health. Patients' health began being monitored for temperature, respiratory rate, and pulse. Urine analysis also became commonplace.[40]

In the 1860s, John Lister, who studied the work of Louis Pasteur, developed antiseptic techniques for wounds. Until then, most physicians thought infections were caused by bad air. In 1862, Lister used carbolic acid spray to sterilize instruments, wounds, and surgical sites, which markedly reduced the incidence of gangrene. His groundbreaking work led to modern antiseptic operating theaters within a few decades.[41]

During much of the nineteenth century in America, including the Civil War, there were no antibiotics. Instead, surgeons prescribed coffee, whiskey, and quinine. Illnesses were treated in the 1860s with over 871 different substances—silver nitrate to stop bleeding, magnesium sulfate as a laxative, opium for an analgesic and antidiarrheal, and strychnine for an antispasmodic, among others. Botanicals—herbs—made up sixty-seven percent of all treatments.[42]

Herbalism, The Treatment of Choice for Centuries

Well into the nineteenth century, the most effective treatments employed by Indian medicine men and Western physicians came from plants. Many ancient cultures, including the Egyptians and Greeks, used selected molds, plant materials, and extracts to treat infections and for other medicinal purposes.[43]

Herbalism, the use of plants as healing agents, has been used by generations of people throughout the world.[44] The use of medicinal plants dates back tens of thousands of years. The first written evidence of herbal remedies is over 5,000 years old. They were commonly used in Egypt and Greece hundreds of years before Christ was born. Native Americans medicinally used more than 2,500 of the approximately 20,000 plant species that were native to North America. An argument could be made that medicine men and Indian shamans were probably some of the most expert herbalists in history.[45]

There are four approaches to the use of plants as medicines. The *magical/shamanic* approach is present in almost all societies with the exception of cultures influenced by Western-style industrialization. The practitioners are regarded as endowed with gifts or powers that allow them to use herbs in a way that is hidden from the average person, and the herbs are said to affect the spirit or soul of the person. This was very important in the Native American culture.

The *energetic* approach includes traditional Chinese medicine where herbs are regarded as having actions in terms of their energies and affecting energies of the body. The practitioner has extensive training but need not possess supernatural powers.

The *functional dynamic* approach was used by early practitioners where herbs had a functional action that was not necessarily linked to a physical compound but rather to a physiological function.

The *chemical* approach of modern practitioners explains herbal actions in terms of their chemical constituents. Secondary metabolites work together synergistically. This approach is common today in the Western world.[46]

Herbalists tend to use extracts from parts of the plants, such as the roots or leaves, but don't isolate particular phytochemicals.[47] This was certainly true for Native American medicine. Europeans introduced many herbal plants to the New World. Some of the plants used for medicinal purposes and their origins were detailed in an exhibit of The New York Botanical Garden titled *Wild Medicine: Healing Plants Around the World*, held from May 18 to September 8, 2015. A partial list follows:

- Willow bark has been used for thousands of years to treat aches, pains, fevers, and flu-like symptoms. The chemical closely related to aspirin occurs naturally in willow bark. The active ingredient was first discovered in 1828. Since it brought on an increased risk of stomach upset and ulcers, in 1899 the Bayer Company in Germany altered salicylic acid to create acetylsalicylic acid, which is safer for the stomach. Its origin is in Europe and Asia.
- The foxglove leaf contains powerful active chemicals that are used to treat heart disease. In 1775, the English physician and botanist William Withering used foxglove infusions as a treatment for dropsy, a swelling of the legs due to fluid retention now known as edema, often associated with congestive heart failure. Foxglove contains digitalis and is found throughout Europe.
- The opium poppy fruit, among the first plants cultivated in China, has traditionally been used to treat pain, headaches, asthma, and diarrhea. When the plant's main active ingredient, morphine, was isolated in 1803, it was lauded as one of the greatest medicinal discoveries in history. Its origin is in southwestern Asia.
- The belladonna berry leaf and root contain atropine, which was isolated in 1833 by German Friedlieb Ferdinand Runge. In Renaissance Italy, women dropped juice from the berries into their eyes to make them dilate. One story claims that this is how the plant received its common name, which translates to beautiful woman. Origins are Europe, North Africa, and western Asia.
- Pacific yew bark contains the active chemical ingredient paclitaxel, which

is now used to fight cancer—especially breast cancer. Native Americans viewed yew as the chief of trees. They used its wood to manufacture bows, and the trees served as a symbol of battle. Traditional medicinal uses of Pacific yew by the Indians included inducing sweating and improving lung health. The origin is the West Coast of North America.
- Jaborandi—which means "slobber weed"—was named by the people of the Amazon. A chemical in the leaf causes salivation and sweating and has been used for medicinal purposes for centuries. Today, the active chemical, pilocarpine, is used to treat severe dry mouth in the elderly, chemotherapy patients, and those suffering from Sjogren's syndrome. It is the active ingredient in FDA-approved medicines for glaucoma. Jaborandi is native to Brazil.
- The ephedra stem has been used as a medicinal plant since prehistory and has been found in burial sites in Iraq dating back 60,000 years. It was an important treatment in Chinese medicine. It helps alleviate the symptoms of asthma, allergies, coughs, and colds. Today, it is used in a number of decongestants. It can cause a similar effect as adrenaline in the body, which raises heart rate and blood pressure.
- The cacao seed is the source of chocolate. Chocolate has been prized for its healing qualities and its great taste for centuries. It has its origins in Mexico and South America.
- Tea leaf products are used topically to relieve certain skin disorders, since it has antibacterial and anti-inflammatory qualities. Its origin is China.
- Rosy periwinkle leaf is the source of the powerful anti-cancer chemicals vincristine and vinblastine. It has played a role in traditional medicine for centuries in India and China where it has been used as a drink to treat diabetes, toothache, indigestion, and constipation. Not until the last few decades were its anti-cancer properties discovered. Its origin is Madagascar.
- The ginseng root is the best known of the immune system boosters. The main chemicals in ginseng lower blood sugar, fortify the immune system, and stimulate the cardiovascular and nervous systems to improve physical and mental well-being. The Chinese traditionally used the plant to treat general weakness and to improve attention and endurance. The origin is China and Korea.
- Cinchona bark was used to make tonic water, and from that it was recognized as a medical treatment. One of the active chemicals found in the bark is quinine. The bark has been in high demand since at least the seventeenth century when the first Europeans in the Americas learned

from the Indians of its healing powers. It was traditionally used to treat fevers, including those caused by malaria. Quinine is the source of antimalarial medications. Its origin is Central and South America. During the seventeenth century, Jesuits in Peru had discovered the effectiveness of cinchona bark for treating malaria. Their claims were rejected by most European physicians who for many years used alternative and ineffective treatments. It wasn't until the 1830s that clinical tests by French Army doctors demonstrated quinine's effectiveness. By 1881, 20 million pounds of cinchona bark were being exported from Latin America. Access to a successful treatment for malaria made possible the colonization of sub-Saharan Africa by whites.[48]

- The inside of the aloe leaf is used to treat burns and to help reduce pain and speed healing for cuts and other minor skin irritations. Mexicans used it to soothe burns, and some Puerto Ricans used it to ease flu symptoms. Its origin is Africa.
- Citrus fruits are notably rich in vitamin C, which has powerful antioxidant properties. They are found mainly in tropical areas.
- Nearly every part of the coconut food from the coconut palm is used medicinally. Coconut water calms the stomach and is a diuretic, and also has antimicrobial properties. Its origin is Central and South America and other tropical areas in Africa, Asia, and Australia.
- Saw palmetto fruit is today one of the ten best-selling herbal remedies in the United States. The active chemicals are used in herbal therapies for symptoms of an enlarged prostate. Its origin is southeastern United States.

In addition to medicinal purposes, many of the plants had vitamins and minerals that were ingested simply for maintaining good health.[49]

There is still much to learn in the world of science and medicine. Similar to the early cartographers of the New World, neuroscientists are mapping the human mind. German neurologist Korbinian Brodmann (1868-1918) published the first such map in 1909 at about the time Theodore Roosevelt was heading to Africa on a safari. In July 2016, a team from Washington University in St. Louis published a report in *Nature* pinpointing 180 distinct areas in the cerebral cortex—more than half of them were previously unknown. Lead author Matthew Glasser noted, "The cerebral cortex underlies most of human cognition, providing such functions as speech production and understanding, ability to use tools, ability to make decisions, et cetera. Indeed, it is responsible for the stuff that makes us human, and the cortex has expanded dramatically in humans relative to our closest living relatives, the apes." The researchers said they understand the specific function of some areas, but they were still only scratching the surface on understanding what all the areas did. The blind still are leading the blind—the mystery continues. That's a good thing.[50]

Infectious Disease and Statistics

Along with military warfare and slavery, the Indian populations in the New World were dramatically decreased by infectious diseases like cholera, measles, tuberculosis, whooping cough, typhus, typhoid fever, and influenza. However, the major culprit was smallpox. In the heavily populated areas in central Mexico and some of the islands in the Caribbean, up to seventy-five percent of the native populations died from epidemic diseases during the first several generations after the Spanish arrived.[51]

Worldwide epidemics have been common throughout history. Some of the more noted include the Plague of Justinian, 541-750 CE, which reportedly killed half of Europe's population. It was caused by the bacteria *Yersinia pestis*, which also caused the Black Death of 1347-1352 when approximately 25 million Europeans died over five years. In the fourteenth century, the plague reduced worldwide population from 450 million to 350 million people.[52]

While smallpox devastated the New World after the arrival of Columbus, it also killed an estimated 60 million Europeans during the eighteenth century. Thirty percent of those infected died, including eighty percent of the children under the age of five. For those who survived, thirty percent were blind. It was indeed rare to find a smallpox survivor who didn't have disfiguring depressed scars on their face. To add to the misery, in the 1800s tuberculosis killed an estimated one in four adults in Europe.[53] Still, European invaders to the New World proclaimed that native deaths from European infections were a sign that their Christian God wanted the colonists to rule over and own the natives' land.

The first influenza epidemic in Europe occurred between 1556 and 1560, carrying with it a mortality rate of twenty percent. This soon spread to the New World where it wreaked further havoc on the Indian populations. The most noted outbreak of influenza occurred during the pandemic of 1918 when the so-called Spanish flu killed an estimated 25 to 50 million people, about two percent of the world's population. Troops returning home from Europe after World War I proved to be effective vectors in spreading the infection. Even today, influenza kills around 500,000 humans worldwide each year.[54]

Number Games

Infection and death rates from germs from the time Columbus arrived to the 1800s are notoriously unreliable. When researchers survey a number of different historical accounts, they often get different results. David Henige illustrated in *Numbers from Nowhere: The American Indian Contact Population Debate* the use and abuse of data in this debate. He explained that the extrapolation of numbers is totally subjective.[55]

One has to be skeptical regarding numbers, percentages, statistics, and the interpretation of them, especially prior to 1900. It's easy to be misled by data. A number has a way of ending an argument. What can you say to it? There's no nuance, no room for interpretation—it is what it is. Unfortunately, numbers turn out to be a lot like words: powerful and illuminating, but capable of being deployed to bad or manipulative ends—or just unintended erroneous conclusions.[56]

Reporting bison counts, population numbers on Native Americans, the percentage of people infected with a disease, and the percentages who die from the disease has to be assessed in perspective. Counts were notoriously not very accurate. It's amazing the variation in the estimated number of bison that roamed the West before the white man. Was it 10 million or 100 million? There's absolutely no way to tell. Because it could take weeks or months to travel from the Midwest to the Pacific Ocean, how could anybody be so presumptuous as to think they could accurately document a dynamic mass of animals like the bison? Equally, why would anyone accept these numbers as being accurate? The same is true for accurately determining how many Indians in the West died of smallpox. The mortality rate for Indians was likely higher than was seen in Europe because Native Americans had no prior exposure and little to no immunity to smallpox. Sometimes, placing exact numbers on a subject subtly denotes knowledge and expertise, while in reality it can be very misleading, and even be a form of propaganda.

Census taking, especially before the late 1800s, was very unreliable and in some cases nonexistent for the Indian populations of the United States. Imagine trying to ride a horse around isolated areas of the country and collect data. It was hard enough in the cities back East and almost next to impossible on the western borders of the country. Out West where many Indian tribes still led the life of nomadic hunter-gatherers, there was no specific locale they called home.

The federal census in 1790 showed the U.S. population to be 3,929,214. From the eighteenth through the middle of the twentieth century, enumerators traveled from house to house to take the census. A printed population schedule was first developed and used for the 1830 census. In 1850, the census identified people who were white, black, or mulatto (mixed blood)—and rarely identified Indians. There was no census in Indian Country (most of the Midwest). In 1860, there was a census of Indian Territory (Oklahoma), but no Indians were included. This showed either the challenges that arose from trying to count humans in remote areas or the lack of care about how many Indians there actually were. Finally, in 1900 there was a census in Indian Territory that included the Indians.[57]

It's obvious that the first census taking was another example of art and not science. Paul Kelton points this out in *Cherokee Medicine, Colonial Germs*. In 1824, Cherokee leaders undertook a census of their people and determined the count was 17,283. It was the first census in over 100 years. In 1721, the British had determined there were 10,379 Cherokee men, women, and children.

In the hundred years between the two counts, six smallpox outbreaks had afflicted the Cherokee in southern Appalachia. Those trying to minimize the effect of smallpox on the Indians could conclude that the death rate wasn't that severe since almost 7,000 more Indians were alive after the outbreaks than before, albeit almost 100 years later.

But the first outbreak of smallpox is really unknown and could have been killing the Cherokee well before the first census. No one knows the Cherokee count before the first outbreak. In addition, the British relied on "knowledgeable traders," whatever that means, to take the census. They were probably motivated more by finishing it and getting paid than by providing an accurate count for which there was no incentive. Kelton rightfully concludes, "Perhaps more research will help answer some of these questions, but for now the numbers leave one unsatisfied in interpreting the indigenous experience with colonialism's most dreaded germ."[58]

With that in mind, let's continue, and step further into muddy waters. As has been noted, population figures for Native Americans before the Spanish arrived for the first time in the New World have varied widely. At the beginning of the twentieth century, pre-Columbian population estimates were around 10 million, but 100 years later some historians placed it at over 100 million.[59] In North America, pre-Columbian population estimates in 1900 ranged from a low of 2 million to a high of 18 million, and everywhere in between.[60]

Formulas to determine population numbers sometimes are generated with an agenda in mind. The higher the pre-Columbian count, the larger impact Europeans had as the cause of the reduction in native populations. Some claim these are rooted in a bias against Western civilization and/or Christianity.

On the other hand, low estimates tend to lessen the white impact on Indian life in the New World. Under this scenario, the "Vanishing American" theme was just in the imagination of reformers, and the impact of racism on Indian populations was muted. Historian Francis Jennings argued, "Scholarly wisdom long held that Indians were so inferior in mind and works that they could not possibly have created or sustained large populations."[61]

Brian Dippie wrote in his landmark publication, *The Vanishing American,* "Where Indian population is concerned, exact figures have always been elusive. Their continuing imprecision allows us to regard Indian population counts for what they are: subjective estimates reflecting the desire to be (or not to be) considered Indian, as well as white assumptions about what an Indian is and what his ultimate destiny will be."[62] The numbers game changes with changing attitudes toward Native Americans.

Historians are excellent at describing wars, strategies, leaders, soldiers, heroes, and battle sites. However, much less time has been spent on appreciating the death, pain, and suffering that the Indians experienced as infectious diseases from Europe ravished their bodies and, more than any other factor, destroyed their communities and civilizations. Details of their deaths and battle wounds can cause nightmares. But dying in battle would have been welcome compared to contracting smallpox or watching your wife, children, and friends die from the dreaded diseases. The Indians were crushed mentally, socially, and physically from infectious diseases introduced by the Europeans, but from the ashes of physical death and disability, their faith in an afterlife strengthened, while many colonists who sought material possessions at any cost, at times lost their passion for Christianity as they embraced the Enlightenment's world of science and technology.

Infectious diseases are more than just numbers of infections and death rates. They are about real human suffering and loss of hope. In the next chapter we will take a closer look at the unseen evil that brought havoc to the new world. It led to an urgency by some Americans to "kill the Indian to save the man."

CHAPTER SEVEN

Weapons of Mass Destruction: Infectious Disease

Variola [smallpox] was a virus of empire. It made winners and losers, at once serving the conquerors in determining whom they would be.
—ELIZABETH FENN, POX AMERICANA

The grimmest examples of germs' role in history come from the European conquest of the Americas that began with Columbus's voyage of 1492. Numerous as were the Native American victims of the murderous Spanish Conquistadores, they were far outnumbered by the victims of murderous Spanish microbes.
—JARED DIAMOND, GUNS, GERMS, AND STEEL

Life is the cumulative effect of a handful of significant shocks. For Native Americans their shocks arrived in many forms. None was greater than infectious diseases. Early on after the arrival of the Spanish in North America, the devastation from disease was noted. Diseases are more than numbers. They affect real people who have signs and symptoms and also loss of hope. Disease kills indiscriminately.

In May 1539, Hernando de Soto and his private army landed near Tampa Bay, Florida. He was a leader in the slave trade and helped to fund the conquest of the Inka. Throughout Florida, his army killed countless Indians, and the ones they didn't kill, they raped, tortured, and enslaved.

Unknowingly, perhaps the worst problem that De Soto left behind in Florida were his pigs that traveled with his army. While exploring the

American South for four years, he reported a bountiful number of people but very few bison or other big game. The pigs were as important to the conquistadors as their military forces since they were a major supply of meat. However, close contact between domesticated animals and humans perpetuated many infectious diseases.

For example, bird influenza led to human influenza, cow rinderpest led to measles, and a cow virus led to human smallpox. Indians differed from their European counterparts in that they did not live in close contact with many animals. Thus, they didn't contract diseases from them and acquired no immunity. They domesticated only the dog, turkey, llama, alpaca, duck, and guinea pig. The pigs that were left behind in Florida quickly migrated to other areas and transmitted anthrax, brucellosis, leptospirosis, trichinosis, and tuberculosis not only to Indians but also to deer and turkeys. Everywhere the infected animals traveled, they exposed Indian villages with devastating results.[1]

A century later, the French explorer La Salle canoed down the Mississippi and saw sites of former villages and cities with very few humans around compared to what De Soto had reported. The Caddoan population had plummeted from an estimated 200,000 to about 8,500, a drop in population of almost ninety percent. One theory has it that with the Indian populations decimated, the bison prospered. The same held true for elk that were seen in large herds. West coast Indian populations also collapsed, which led to an explosion of fish, clams, and mussels. The kill rate was dramatic.[2]

In comparison, the infamous bubonic plague or "black death" caused by the bacillus *Yersinia pestis* that afflicted Europe from 1347 to 1351 killed about a third of its victims. The bubonic plague arrived by steamship on many American rivers in the nineteenth century. Fleas carry the bacteria to humans when they bite them. When the bacterium infects the flea, it causes a starvation state in the insect that increases its need for blood. That leads to increased biting and further spread of disease. The fleas rode the backs of rats throughout Europe in the fourteenth century and then infected people living in densely populated urban areas with poor sanitation. It was also seen in urban areas in colonial North America. Franciscan priests commented in 1617 that "great plagues [pestes] and contagious sickness" struck the mission at St. Augustine, founded in 1565 by the Spanish. Half the converts reportedly died. Forty years later, a smallpox epidemic hit the same colony for the first time.[3]

By the 1690s, smallpox spread throughout the Southeast. One English colonist commented, "The whole country is full of trouble & sickness, tis smallpox which has been mortal to all sorts of the inhabitants & especially the Indians who tis said to have swept away a whole neighboring nation, all to 5 or 6 which ran away and left their dead unburied, lying upon the ground for the vultures to devour."[4]

It's not difficult to understand why early historians depicted Indians as nomadic—they didn't know that almost all of the villages had been destroyed by European diseases. Besides not having immunity to the infectious diseases as the Europeans did, the natives possessed immune systems that were more susceptible to diseases due to their limited gene pool. For example, ninety percent of Native Americans have type O blood, whereas Europeans are more evenly split between type O and type A. On the positive side, in 1491, Native Americans were apparently free of cystic fibrosis, Huntington's chorea, newborn anemia, schizophrenia, asthma, and possibly juvenile diabetes, all of which plagued European populations. For these diseases, a limited gene pool was beneficial to the Indians.[5]

Smallpox epidemics would later hit again before and after the Revolutionary War. George Washington inoculated his army against smallpox at Valley Forge during the winter of 1778. His subsequent victory is credited, in part, to this instance of foresight because the British troops were infected, which led to a marked decrease in their fighting force. In 1780, smallpox spread into most of western North America, killing nine out of ten victims. The Great Plains and the Rocky Mountain Indians—including the Mandan, Sioux, Crow, Blackfoot, Cheyenne, and Shoshone—were all infected with smallpox. The Sioux and Cheyenne who were in close proximity to roads and wagon train trails were hit hard. The Shoshone transmitted the disease down the Columbia River and into the Pacific Northwest. Not only were the Indians killed in large numbers, but all of their organizations and societies were decimated. Confused, abandoned by their gods, beset by foreigners and their diseases, the Indians lost their resistance to death.

The collapse of the Indian populations had the opposite effect on game animals. They thrived with fewer human predators. Likewise, large forests proliferated since there were fewer Indians who either cut the woods down or burned them to, in some instances, make way for agriculture. By 1800, the American West was filled with woodlands that were not present 200 years earlier.

Neither Europeans nor the Indians had an accurate concept of how infectious diseases were transmitted. The Europeans eventually came to the erroneous conclusion that tuberculosis, a bacterial infection, was a genetically inherited disease, and some thought it might just be due to unclean environments. Both groups at one time or another believed that it was a manifestation of the will of God that the people became sick. Evil manifested itself in illness. That belief had been in vogue since Galen's era. This proved beneficial to Christian missionaries who used the threat of death from disease as a reason to convert. Little did the two groups know that they were trading diseases. Trade goods were not the only thing exchanged across the ocean.

Besides the diseases brought by Europeans, the African slave trade introduced others like malaria and yellow fever into the New World. Malaria has a mortality rate of around ten percent and usually occurs in areas of stagnant water. In turn, the Europeans took back with them syphilis, which spread rapidly throughout Europe and beyond.[6]

Epidemics had a major influence on trading practices and new alliances. In the 1630s, wherever the Jesuit missionaries traveled they brought not only the word of God with them but also diseases like smallpox with subsequent devastation. At times, the Indians blamed the black robes for it, and they became very bitter toward the priests. Indian shamans, who saw the Jesuits as competition, believed the priests were witches. When the Jesuit priests objected to the Indians torturing their Indian captives, the chiefs ordered holes burned in the hands and feet of their captives to mock the crucifixion story.[7]

Alfred Crosby coined the term "virgin soil epidemic" and defined it as epidemics "in which the populations at risk have had no previous contact with the diseases that strike them and are therefore immunologically almost defenseless."[8] Many civilizations outside of the Americas lived in close contact with their domesticated animals. Thus, many scientists believe cattle are the most likely source of measles, tuberculosis, and smallpox. Flu and whooping cough can be traced to pigs, and malaria to birds.[9]

Smallpox

Of all of these diseases, smallpox has been documented most extensively because of its ability to spread quickly from the European colonists to Indians, who then spread it to their fellow Indians with devastating results. Smallpox had a high rate of mortality and morbidity.

One of the great medical achievements of the twentieth century was eradicating smallpox. The last naturally occurring case was diagnosed on October 26, 1977. Before its demise, smallpox killed countless millions of people around the world in addition to the Indian populations of the New World.

Smallpox is an ancient disease, perhaps originating at the time humans started tending flocks of animals around 6,000 years ago. Pharaoh Ramses V (d 1145 BCE) had evidence of smallpox on his mummified body, although that hasn't been verified. Some believe he had measles. There is no clear description of smallpox in either the Old or New Testaments of the Bible or the literature of the Greeks or Romans.

Earlier sources concluded that smallpox had its origin in West Africa in animals like camels, while other data suggested its appearance occurred much earlier in rodents.[10] The latest research places its origin from cattle around 6,000 years ago.[11] Perhaps a chance mutation let the virus jump from animals to humans. Human smallpox presents only in humans and most likely did not exist in the Americas when humans first arrived there. By the time of the arrival of Columbus to the New World, the virus had caused major epidemics in Europe, Asia, and Africa. Many of the conquistador invaders were immune to smallpox since they had recovered from prior infections, while other Spaniards who were infected spread it to the Indian populations.[12]

A synonym for smallpox is variola. Some writers allege that the term *variola* had its origins in the Latin *varus,* meaning a papule, pimple, or tubercle. Other writers, however, believe it was derived from the word *varius,* which means spotted or variegated. The Saxon equivalent, *pocca,* meaning a bag or pouch, has given rise to the English word pock. Syphilis, which was transported from the New World to Europe soon after 1492, caused some confusion with nomenclature, so it became necessary to prefix the adjective, small, to the term *pock* or *pox,* in order to distinguish it from the great pox, syphilis—which became known simply as the pox.

Arab armies spread the smallpox virus from Africa into southwestern Europe during the sixth century. In 910, the Persian physician Rhazes documented the first description of symptoms of smallpox and measles in his classic work *A Treatise on Smallpox and Measles.* It was further spread to northern Europe during the Crusades (1096 to 1291). By the time of Columbus, smallpox was well established across most of Europe. Royalty were not immune, and in 1562 twenty-nine-year-old Queen Elizabeth I of England survived a smallpox attack but was left with permanent disfiguring facial scars and baldness.

The smallpox virus made its first appearance in the New World on the Caribbean island of Hispaniola in 1509, carried there by slave ships from Africa and then onto the mainland when the Spanish invaded Central Mexico in 1520. Following the conquest of Mexico by Spanish conquistador Hernando Cortés, who took the reigning Aztec emperor Montezuma hostage, some 3.5 million Aztec Indians died of the newly introduced disease. The devastation from smallpox helped the Spanish conquer the Aztecs and Inkas. One of Cortés' men reflected on their victory over the Aztecs, "When the Christians were exhausted from war God saw fit to send the Indians smallpox, and there was a great pestilence . . . we soldiers could scarcely get about the streets because of the Indians who were sick from hunger, pestilence and smallpox."[13]

In 1633, the settlers at Plymouth, Massachusetts, were responsible for a severe outbreak of smallpox in the Indian population with a death rate approaching ninety percent. A year later, governor John Winthrop stated, "But for the natives in these parts, God hath so pursued them as for 300 miles space the greatest part of them are swept away by the smallpox which still continues among them. So as God hath thereby cleared our title to this place."[14]

In the 1690s, as smallpox swept through the South, English colonists believed God was on their side as disease cleared the pathway for the settlement of the Carolinas. Governor John Archdale echoed most colonists' belief that they had not brought disease on the Indians, but God had, thus absolving them of any responsibility. In his divine wisdom, the governor proclaimed, "The Hand of God was eminently seen in thinning the Indians to make room for the English. . . . But again, yet at other times pleased Almighty God to send unusual sickness among them, as smallpox . . . to lessen their numbers."[15]

While the Spanish government struggled with domestic and foreign problems, the Spanish missions proliferated. The first Spanish missions arose in Baja California in 1697. They were started by the Jesuits, but in 1767 the King of Spain transferred the missions to the Franciscan order. By that time, a number of missions had been founded throughout California. Missionaries led the way in defending natives against exploitation by government officials. In the mid-1700s, the Jesuits attempted to protect the Indians in Latin America from European efforts to enslave them. The Portuguese and Spanish colonial officials banished the Jesuits for interfering.[16]

The missionaries had little regard or time to understand Indian beliefs or culture. The friars segregated unmarried men and women and forced Catholic moral codes on them while requiring unreasonable labor. Those who didn't work hard enough were whipped, branded, and placed in solitary confinement. They were basically treated as docile and submissive animals. Indians saw the missionaries as sexually aggressive toward their women and stealing their land and property. Grouping the Indians in confined areas led to epidemics—in 1769 measles and in 1781 smallpox—devastating the missions. Many Indians committed suicide, while others left the missions and headed to the mountains where they spread the diseases even further.

The smallpox epidemic of 1779 to 1783 was the most extensive to date. In Mexico City where it started, 18,000 people died between September and December 1779. Infection traveled south to Guatemala and into South America. At the same time, it was carried north by travelers, and by 1780 it was infecting individuals in New Orleans, San Antonio, Santa Fe, Philadelphia, Charleston, and other Eastern cities. The Pueblo and Apache were easy victims. By 1781, the disease traveled to the Northern Plains, infecting the Assiniboine, Cree, and Mandan. Historian Theodore Binnema described it as "an immeasurable catastrophe," and at no prior time had "so large a portion of the population of the plains faced such a calamity. Never have so many communities simultaneously faced such a multitude of challenges."[17]

Prior to 1780, the Mandan, Hidatsa, and Arikara in their large villages on the Great Bend numbered 24,000. When smallpox hit, eighty percent of the population was killed. By the time of the Lewis and Clark Expedition, there were only about 2,000 Arikara, 1,200 Mandan, and 2,700 Hidatsa. The Crow who visited the villages also contracted the disease, and the number of their lodges was reduced from 2,000 to less than 300.

Likewise, the tribes in western Montana, Idaho, Washington, and Oregon were also hit hard. The Kootenai fled to the mountains, never to return to the Plains. Like the white man, the Indians had no concept of infectious disease. They believed one man couldn't transmit the disease to another man any more than a wounded man could give his wound to another man. Everywhere Lewis and Clark explored, they saw badly scarred men, women, and children and remnants of abandoned villages for thousands of miles. Smallpox particularly was deadly to children. Ninety percent of the people who died of smallpox in eighteenth-century Britain were children. They were also especially prone to being pockmarked.[18]

In many ways it was smallpox that cleared the West of Indians so the white man could claim their lands. The winning of the West was not just about courageous pioneers triumphant over nature, but also about a deadly virus and its ability to cause infectious genocide. The myth of Lewis and Clark exploring a pristine wilderness was far from true. The land had been the home of Indians and animals for many centuries before they arrived. They saw only a snapshot in time.

It would not be until 1832 that the United States established a smallpox vaccination program for Native Americans. Almost twenty years earlier, the Vaccine Act of 1813 made cowpox vaccine available to the white American public. In 1824, the Cherokee took part in early efforts to eradicate smallpox and some were vaccinated.[19]

A new smallpox epidemic in 1837 once again decimated the Indian populations. This time it was carried by the steamboat *St. Pete's* as it paddled its way up the Missouri River from Council Bluffs to Fort Union. The Omaha and Pawnee were exposed to the virus at Council Bluffs. At Fort Kiowa in present-day South Dakota, bands of the Yankton and Santee Sioux fell ill and died in great numbers. Further north at Fort Clark, Hidatsa, Mandan, and Arikara also crossed the virus's deadly path. Finally, at Fort Union, the Assiniboine, Plains Cree, Blackfeet, Piegan, and Blood fell in great numbers. Some estimates ranged from 10,000 to 15,000 deaths. The commissioner of Indian Affairs placed even a higher number at 17,200 Mandan, Hidatsa, Arikara, Assiniboine, and Blackfeet who had "sunk under the smallpox." Joshua Pilcher, then a U.S. Indian agent, called the upper Missouri country "one great graveyard."[20]

Lack of recent exposure was one reason that the Mandan were hit the hardest. Another reason was that they had not been inoculated to prevent smallpox. In 1827, Catlin was on the steamship *Yellow Stone* with two physicians who had a federal mandate to vaccinate Native Americans against smallpox. Many of the nations downstream from the Arikara were successfully treated by physicians. Thousands of Omaha, Sioux, and Pawnee were vaccinated, and by 1833 more than 17,000 had been vaccinated nationwide.[21]

However, those on the upper Missouri River and beyond—Mandan, Hidatsa, Crow, Blackfeet, Assiniboine, and Cree—were not inoculated. Toward the winter of 1832, time ran out for physicians to continue their inoculation work. The next year they asked for permission from the commissioner of Indian Affairs to administer vaccine to the northern tribes but were turned down. Those untreated tribes were considered to be nonproductive and not important enough to receive the inoculations.[22] Secretary of War Lewis Cass wrote Indian agent John Dougherty on May 9, 1832, "Under any circumstances, no effort will be made to send a Surgeon higher up the Missouri then the Mandans, and I think not higher than the Arikaras."[23] He concluded that after a decline in population from so many smallpox breakouts and a fading fur trade, the Indian barbarians of the Northern Plains were economically and politically unimportant. Cass commented that they were "far beyond the operation of any causes, primary or secondary, which can be traced to civilised man."[24]

The consequences of the government's refusal to inoculate the Indians on the Northern Plains would turn out to be devastating in the years to come. Estimates of the percentages of smallpox deaths after the breakout in the late 1830s placed the Arikara at thirty-three percent, the Hidatsa at fifty percent, and the Mandan at a stunning ninety percent over the next ten years. The government seemed little concerned.[25]

There are many notable cases of smallpox in American history. The famous and affluent were as susceptible to smallpox as were the poor. Those infected included Lakota Chief Sitting Bull, George Washington, Thomas Jefferson's wife, Andrew Jackson, and Abraham Lincoln. In 1758, Jonathan Edwards, the famous theologian, died following an inoculation of live smallpox virus to prevent the full-blown disease.

In an interview with ethnographer and historian Frank Bird Linderman, Crow Indian Pretty-Shield related her personal experience with the dreaded disease:

"My father was very old when he died, old," she said, "that his skin was cracking a little."

"Did the Lacota kill your father?"

"No. Smallpox killed him, more than 100 others, in one moon," she said. "I had it myself. A wise-one named Sharp-shin healed me. I believe that, if he had been asked, he might have saved others.

"This bad-sickness came to us from the Shoshones. We were in our winter camp when it came. We did not know what sickness it was. We did not scatter, as we ought to have done, and the bad-sickness got into every lodge before we knew its power. My people became terrified and died. I was not yet 17 years old, just married. Tst, tst, tst, my heart was on the ground with many others.

"Until the bad-sickness came to our world my people were scarcely ever sick. War and accidents took many lives. We were used to these, expecting to have to meet them any day, but the bad-sickness was new, and terrible. I will not try to tell you how awful it was. When a woman sees whole families wiped out, even whole clans, and cannot help, cannot even hope, her heart falls down and she wishes that she could die. I am going to leave this now. I do not like to think about it."[26]

For John James Audubon (1785-1851), his voyage up the Missouri on the steam vessel *Omega* presented a picture of the Mandan in stark contrast to George Catlin's 1832 glowing report. Audubon arrived after a devastating smallpox outbreak (1837) and reported how different his experience was. "Ah, Mr. Catlin, I am now sorry to see and to read your accounts of the Indians you saw—how very different they must have been from any that

I have seen."²⁷ While he shot a number of animals at his next stop at Fort Union that he would use in his three-volume *The Viviparous Quadrupeds of North America* (1845 and 1848), Audubon later lamented the slaughter on the Great Plains: "What a terrible destruction of life, as it were for nothing, or next to it. . . . The prairies are literally covered with the skulls of the victims. . . . This cannot last; even now there is a perceptible difference in the size of the herds, and before many years the Buffalo, like the Great Auk, will have disappeared; surely this should not be permitted."²⁸ But it was, and the great animal herds joined the fate of the Indians in myth and legend adding to the "The Spirit of the West."

One of the major controversies today is whether smallpox was mainly responsible for the reduction of Indian populations or whether it was the actions of the white invaders. Those who champion smallpox as the main culprit have been criticized for attempting to minimize the objectionable actions of the white man. Epidemiologists say that smallpox killed up to forty percent of its victims in modern times, but is this accurate for Indians living during the colonial period? Virgin soil theorists believe as high as ninety percent died. The answer probably lies somewhere in between.²⁹

Alfred Crosby stated in *Ecological Imperialism,* "It was their germs, not these imperialists themselves, for all of their brutality and callousness, that were chiefly responsible for sweeping aside indigenes and opening the [Americas] to demographic takeover."³⁰ Jared Diamond, in his Pulitzer Prize–winning *Guns, Germs, and Steel: The Fates of Human Societies,* supported that conclusion and wrote, "As for the most advanced native societies of North America . . . their destruction was accomplished largely by germs alone, introduced by early European explorers and advancing ahead of them."³¹ Likewise, Charles Mann, in *1491: New Revelations of the Americas before Columbus,* winner of the National Academy of Science's Keck Award, supported the claims that native "societies were destroyed by weapons their opponents could not control and did not even know they had."³²

However, Paul Kelton, in his book *Cherokee Medicine, Colonial Germs,* warned not to minimize colonial violence by hiding it under the umbrella of unfettered biological infection. He made the point that "scholars have overlooked how colonialism's violence set the stage for these supposedly unintended biological events, curtailed the abilities of Natives to protect themselves from infection, exacerbated mortality, and impeded recovery."³³

The most successful infectious agents are the ones that don't kill their host too quickly. The longer the host lives, the greater chance of spread to many individuals. The longer the incubation period—the time between onset of infection and symptoms—the better it is for the virus to spread undetected among humans. Smallpox was the perfect killer.[34]

The Life of Smallpox

Perhaps relating the experience of contracting smallpox—or as doctors say, the clinical course—may help the reader to greater appreciate the nightmare germ and empathize with the victims. In general, the period of incubation of smallpox is between ten and fourteen days. The onset is sudden and violent. A chill is followed by a rapid rise of temperature with a fever approaching 104 degrees. Nausea and vomiting occur with great frequency. An excruciating headache continues until the skin erupts. Convulsions are very common in children, and at times there may be coma. General aches and pains are complained of—especially back pain.

The skin eruption usually appears on the third day following the chill, manifesting itself first upon the face, and then rapidly appearing on the scalp, neck, ears, forearms, and hands. Within twenty-four hours the entire body is involved. The rash spreads for three or four days. The eruption begins as small, flat red spots or macules. The color is at first pinkish red, later assuming a deeper tinge. By the fifth day of the eruption, small blisters are noted. Blisters change from clear to yellowish pustules that eventually rupture and dry and then form yellowish or brownish crusts. Schamberg, one of the most famous dermatologists in the early twentieth century, counted over 40,000 pustules on one patient. The eruptions are often accompanied by delirium with hallucinations and delusions. This has led some to commit suicide and homicide.[35]

Approximately three to four weeks pass before the crusts detach and fall off. Those scabs can cling to nonhuman material like clothing and bedding, which can lead to inadvertent infection by caregivers. It could also have led to the possibility of intentional infection by whites to Indians.

This makes the entire duration of the disease about five or six weeks. Almost always, it is accompanied by severe itching that can range from slight annoyance to endurable distress. Many of the lesions may become secondarily infected with staph and strep bacteria that increase the chance of deep skin scars—pockmarks. Scratching the lesions spreads the bacterial infection, leading to more scarring. Humans cannot tolerate itch. Scratching causes pain, which is actually more tolerable.

The portal of entry for the virus is the mucous membranes of the upper respiratory tract, where it then spreads to the blood, causing a transient viremia.

The severity of the infection is roughly correlated with the severity of the skin and mucosal eruption. Death is usually attributable to pulmonary complications.

Another more insidious method of spreading is through clothing. Under the right conditions, virus-containing skin scabs and desiccated droplets can remain viable for up to two years. Thus, clothing such as a buffalo robe that had dormant virus could inflict the next wearer with smallpox.[36]

For Christian missionaries, smallpox converted some Indians who had lost faith in their medicine men and shamans. Anthropologist Calvin Martin concluded that the shamans were "powerless to amend the shattered universe." Their patients viewed the shaman's "ability to control and otherwise influence the supernatural realm, dysfunctional—because his magic and other traditional cures were now ineffective." In time, they probably lost confidence in the Christian doctors since they provided perhaps even less effective treatment than their Indian counterparts.[37]

Cherokee historian William McLoughlin also believed European infections undermined the Indians' confidence in their healers, writing, "The remedies tried by their medicine men often simply hastened the death of the victims," and "This failure of their doctors/priests tended to erode faith in them and their rituals. . . . Tribal animosity against the priest resulted in what seems to have been a repudiation of them and their methods, perhaps even their assassination."[38]

In his 1775 book *The History of the American Indians,* English trader and author James Adair described the 1738-1739 epidemic among the Cherokee, providing one of the best accounts of how indigenous practitioners responded to smallpox. He had a very dim view of how the Cherokee treated their smallpox patients. He condemned the Indian practitioners for having the patients "lie out of doors, day and night, with their breast frequently open to the night dews, to cool the fever; they were likewise afraid that the deceased would otherwise pollute the house, and by that means, procure all their deaths." He erroneously thought they should have applied warm compresses.[39] Yet, over 100 years later, Western medicine was similarly treating tuberculosis by isolating patients in tuberculosis hospitals in the Rocky Mountains and using outside sleeping porches even in winter at subzero temperatures. Today, we know that isolation units are critical in preventing spread of disease.[40]

A poignant question is, did whites spread smallpox on purpose by using smallpox tainted clothing? In 1763, with the Indians attacking Fort Pitt during Pontiac's War, General Jeffrey Amherst asked Colonel Henry

Bouquet, "Could it not be contrived to send the smallpox among those disaffected tribes of the Indians? We must, on this occasion, use every stratagem in our power to reduce them."[41] Bouquet had access to infected clothing and wrote, "I will try to inoculate the Indians by means of blankets that may fall in their hands."[42] Commander Amherst added, "You will do well to try to inoculate the Indians by means of blankets as well as to try every other method, that can serve to extirpate this execrable race."[43]

There are very few recorded cases of direct orders occurring because officials probably avoided written documentation that could get them in trouble later. Elizabeth Fenn has commented that "actual incidents may have occurred more frequently than scholars have previously acknowledged."[44]

Millions of Native Americans died after the introduction of smallpox in the New World, and their civilizations were changed so dramatically that their populations have never recovered. More than war, more than broken promises and treaties, more than social Darwinism, or eugenics, smallpox has burned into the moral memory of generations of Indians a distrust in the white man that may never be forgotten.

The Smallpox Vaccination Story[45]

Variolation is the immunization of susceptible individuals with material containing live virus taken from smallpox lesions. Some of the death, pain, and suffering from smallpox could have been prevented in the Indian population if more had been inoculated through variolation as had been done around the world for centuries. Inoculation involved obtaining powdered smallpox scabs and then scratching the material into the skin or placing it in the nasal passages. When successful, lasting immunity was attained. However, inoculation was risky—up to two percent of those inoculated died. Still, this mortality rate was much lower than of those who were infected naturally in epidemic areas. Variolation against smallpox was initiated in China as early as the tenth century, and the practice eventually spread to Persia, Turkey, Greece, Arabia, and North Africa. By the early eighteenth century, variolation was also practiced in Britain.[46]

One of the most colorful and important champions of this form of immunization against smallpox was Reverend Cotton Mather, a Congregational minister at North Church in Boston and author of 444 published works. He was the son of Reverend Increase Mather, president of Harvard College. Cotton Mather is best known for being a symbol of the intolerant and harsh Puritan clergyman. His successes in science made him the first native-born

American in 1713 to become a fellow of the Royal Society. He was elected even though, like most people of the time, he and his father believed in witches. He introduced variolation in Boston in 1721 and was met with widespread disapproval. Bostonians were outraged with him after he had variolated his own son who nearly died from the procedure. Their opposition was centered on the familiar theme that variolation was a deliberate infection with a serious disease of healthy persons and was considered a serious offense against God and mankind. It's ironic that a pious man of God introduced the immunization procedure, not a physician. Nevertheless, variolation was widely practiced both before and during the Revolutionary War.[47]

A smallpox outbreak started in April 1721 after the British naval frigate, *Seahorse*, returned to Boston with an infected crew. The educated resisted inoculation as advocated by Mather. His stature had diminished greatly in the prior thirty years since he famously condemned the Salem "witches." A sequence of tragedies included losing his wife and ten of his children to accidents and epidemics. Arguments and scandals with the religious community had marginalized his influence in Boston.

Weakening his position further were the physicians of the Enlightenment Age in Europe, who regarded inoculation as a misplaced superstition. William Douglas, the only M.D. in Boston, considered it lethal folly. Even so, Mather called on surgeon Zabdiel Boylston to inoculate two family slaves and his son.

At first, the local Boston paper, *New England Courant,* owned by James and his son Benjamin Franklin, condemned Mather, but that all changed as the smallpox epidemic spread. By October 1721 a quarter of the population was infected and more than 200 were dead. Fourteen percent died while only a little over two percent of those inoculated succumbed. In time, King George had his daughter inoculated, and Benjamin Franklin became a leading advocate of the procedure.[48]

In 1796 Edward Jenner, a doctor in Berkeley, Gloucestershire, rural England, inoculated a patient with the virus from a cowpox lesion, which successfully provided immunity to smallpox. He named the material that was used for inoculation, vaccine, from the root word *vacca,* which is Latin for cow.

Jenner was born in 1749 in Berkeley near Bristol in southwestern England. He was the last child of Reverend Stephen Jenner, the Vicar of Berkeley. In 1757, when a smallpox epidemic broke out, eight-year-old Jenner was variolated and almost died from the procedure. At age thirteen, he began an apprenticeship to become a physician. After completion at age twenty-four, he opted to return to Berkeley and become a country doctor.

In 1770, a dairy maid first introduced him to the fact that cowpox protected humans against smallpox. This was well known among the regional farmers, and it serves as yet another example of how primitive "modern" medicine was at the time. The cowpox vaccination procedure was eloquently delineated in Jenner's 1801 publication *The Origin of the Vaccine Inoculation*.

Well-known London physician Dr. Matthew Baillie (1761-1823) suggested to the British Parliament that Jenner should be given a cash grant for his scientific work, which he proclaimed was "the most important discovery ever made in medicine."[49] Later, when Pasteur developed his anthrax vaccine in 1881, he adopted the term *vaccination* as a tribute to Jenner for his protective inoculation. No credit was attributed to the dairy maid.

The Jennerian vaccination was introduced in 1800 to France, Russia, India, the Mediterranean, and later, under the patronage of the Catholic Church, in Naples and Palermo. Quaker Dr. Benjamin Waterhouse (1754-1846) is credited with popularizing vaccination in the United States. Since he was an objector to war in the early part of 1775, he escaped to Britain where he studied medicine; he subsequently received his medical degree in Holland. He returned to America in 1782 and was regarded as the best-educated physician in the country. One year later, he was appointed to the newly founded chair of Theory and Practice of Physics at the new Harvard Medical School. He spent the next thirty years in that position. He learned of Jenner's work in 1799 and made a presentation at Harvard to the American Academy of Arts and Sciences. He received a supply of live vaccine in June 1800 from England and started his vaccination program, which included several of his own children.[50]

One year later, Waterhouse wrote to President Thomas Jefferson and requested him to sponsor the distribution of the vaccine to the Southern states. The president agreed, and he had his family and some 200 people at his home, Monticello, also vaccinated. (When Jefferson was twenty-three years old he had been variolated.[51]) Cherokee leaders who were visiting Jefferson eventually carried some of the vaccine and instructions on how to use it back to their people. *Gentlemen's Magazine* opined, "It is a pleasing reflection that these untutored savages have spread it throughout their country, and that they are eminently expert in the practice of the new inoculation."[52]

In reality, it was the Protestant missionaries who brought the vaccine to them and gave them instructions on how to administer it to others. Even so, natives remained faithful to their own religious and healing beliefs. Often ministers found themselves practicing medicine and condemning Indian practitioners while at the same time promoting Christianity.

"I am much gratified at the good sense manifested by the Cherokee Indians," Edward Jenner commented in 1802. "Who would have thought that vaccination would already have found its way into the wilds of America?"[53] It was the Indians of the Ohio Valley and Great Lakes, who had also visited Jefferson, who were the first to be vaccinated. They arrived in December 1801 in Washington, D.C., and Jefferson told their leader, Little Turtle, that the "Great Spirit had lately made a precious donation to the enlightened white men over the great water, first to a single person, and from him to another on this side of the waters, and then explained to him the history of the cow or kinepock as a gift from heaven to preserve them from the smallpox, and even to banish it from earth."[54]

In 1813, Congress appointed a federal vaccine agent for the preservation of the genuine vaccine material and its distribution to all U.S. citizens. However, Indians were not U.S. citizens and most never received the vaccine. The vaccine was supplied throughout the United States postage free to both civilians and the military under the direction of Dr. James Smith of Baltimore, a student of Dr. Benjamin Rush (1746-1813), at the University of Pennsylvania. Smith established a private foundation, the International Vaccine Institute. Unfortunately, the Senate did not approve Smith's request for a federal charter. By the 1820s, the institute's funds were exhausted, and Smith's goal of establishing a national vaccination center in the United States was not realized. It would not be until the 1940s that the elimination of smallpox was achieved in most countries of Europe and North America. Large epidemics continued in India where more than 1 million cases were reported in 1944.

In 1999, the United Nations estimated that the Earth's population in the beginning of the sixteenth century was about 500 million. In 1966, one researcher estimated the Indian population in 1491 was between 90 and 112 million people. He concluded that at the time Columbus sailed to America, more people were living in the New World than in Europe. By the first third of the seventeenth century, diseases had killed 80 to 100 million Indians. These statistics have since been challenged as far too high by many academic researchers. Conversely, many Indian activists see this as a ploy. They contend that the fewer Indians in America, the more it looks like it was an empty land. In their view, that makes the white man appear less guilty for stealing it.[55]

As recently as 1967, the World Health Organization estimated that 15 million people contracted smallpox and 2 million died that year. After vaccination campaigns throughout the nineteenth and twentieth centuries, the World Health Organization certified the eradication of smallpox in 1979. Dr. Donald A. Henderson (1928-2016) led the global battle to eradicate smallpox. Three years earlier, routine smallpox vaccination of U.S. hospital employees had been discontinued. Side effects from the vaccination were greater than the chance of catching the disease.[56]

Tuberculosis

Unfortunately, another deadly infectious disease that has not been eradicated is tuberculosis *(Mycobacterium tuberculosis)*. Until its treatment in the 1950s by antibiotics, almost every family in American history had a relative who was afflicted with the dreaded disease.

Tuberculosis (also known as TB) is usually acquired by the inhalation into the lungs of mycobacteria. Most of those infected have no symptoms, but one in ten can progress to active disease, which, left untreated, can kill almost half. It is estimated that about seventy percent of symptomatic cases in the United States represent activation of latent childhood infections.[57]

There are a number of factors that determine the likelihood of active disease and influence its severity. Childhood and old age are periods of increased vulnerability. There is convincing evidence that some people may be genetically predisposed to the disease. Blacks and Indians appear more susceptible than whites. By far, the most typical cause of death from tuberculosis is involvement of the lungs. The other common organs to be involved are the meninges, the kidneys, and the fallopian tubes.

With tissue destruction from the bacteria, those infected may experience temperature elevations—usually most marked in the mid-afternoon—along with night sweats, weakness, fatigue, and the loss of appetite and weight. Typically, the lungs are the primary site of attack, which produces a cough, production of purulent sputum, coughing up blood, and shortness of breath.

It is an old disease. Egyptian mummies dating to 3000 BCE have evidence of tuberculosis. Johann L. Schönlein (1793-1864) named the disease tuberculosis in 1839. Other names are consumption and phthisis—a Greek word for consumption. Hippocrates identified the infection as the most common and widespread disease of his time.[58]

Low-cost, high-throughput DNA sequencing has not only been helpful in tracking our ancestors but also in discovering the source of disease. Tuberculosis found in America today is consistent with a genetic strain of the disease brought by European settlers. But there is a twist. In Peru, a 1,000-year-old mummy was found to have symptoms consistent with tuberculosis. How could this happen 500 years before Europeans arrived?

In 2014, Johannes Krause of the Max Planck Institute for the Science of Human History in Jena, Germany, wrote in the journal *Nature* that all human strains of tuberculosis share a common ancestor in Africa from about 6,000 years ago. Dr. Krause suggested that the TB DNA in the Peru mummy most closely resembled the DNA of TB in seals, which resembles that of TB in goats in Africa, which resembles that of the earliest strains found in African people. It's possible that Africans gave tuberculosis to their goats, which in turn gave it to seals, which then crossed the Atlantic and gave it to Native Americans. The mystery continues.[59]

Other than smallpox, the most deadly threat to the Indian was *Mycobacterium tuberculosis,* the bacteria that causes tuberculosis. Its clinical course varied much differently than smallpox in that it could cause death relatively soon after infection, or take debilitating years to finally kill its host, or be relatively innocuous. Susceptibility varied greatly, so someone could be carrying the germ without knowing it for years and then spread it to new victims. It was the perfect storm.

After 1050, in the Mississippian Period, larger Indian populations aggregated as maize supported village life. Traders spread the disease far into the frontier. This led to an increase in tuberculosis. Infection rates rose dramatically after the arrival of Columbus when Indians came in contact with European strains of the bacteria. Matters worsened with deteriorating living conditions among the tribes when Spanish conquistadors took Indians as slaves and natives gathered in cramped conditions at missions. Poor nutrition and overwork made them especially susceptible to diseases like tuberculosis.

Over the years, tuberculosis became an increasingly serious health problem. In 1800, one in seven humans died of TB. In 1887, a report showed the death rate on Nevada Indian reservations at 45 per 1,000, but on the New York reservations the rate was an astounding 625 per 1,000. The higher death rates east of the Mississippi were attributed to an increased exposure to whites.[60]

The sanatorium cure was the brainchild of Hermann Brehmer, a Silesian botany student who suffered from tuberculosis. After traveling to the Himalayan Mountains, he returned home cured and was inspired to study medicine. In 1854, he titled his doctoral dissertation *Tuberculosis is Curable,* which shocked an incredulous medical community. That same year he opened an institution at Görbersdorf to treat tuberculosis patients that emphasized good nutrition and cold air therapy on sleeping porches. Thus, the blueprint for the sanatorium was developed and used well into the twentieth century. By 1900, 1 in 171 Americans were confined to a sanatorium.

In 1865, a French doctor showed that tuberculosis could be transmitted from humans to cattle and from cattle to rabbits. But it wasn't until March 1882 that Robert Koch in Germany identified tuberculosis as being caused by a bacterium that was closely related to the germ that caused leprosy. After Koch's report, it took many years before skeptical physicians believed that tuberculosis was indeed an infectious disease. He received the Nobel Prize in 1905 for his discovery.[61]

In 1900, tuberculosis was the leading cause of death in the United States, accounting for approximately 200 deaths per 100,000 population. Since antibiotics were not available to treat the disease until after World War II, many remedies were attempted. Those included nutritious diets, fresh air, and exercise. Patients were treated orally with cod liver oil, iodide, and iron, all with little relief. Arsenious acid, pyrogallic acid, choroid of zinc, and nitrate of silver were used topically for skin lesions.

In 1940, Selman A. Waksman (1888-1973) and his team at Rutgers University in New Jersey isolated actinomycin, which successfully killed the tuberculosis bacteria but was too toxic for humans and animals. Subsequently, streptomycin proved effective with fewer side effects. Drug resistance followed, which prompted the introduction of p-aminosalicylic acid (1949), isoniazid (1952), pyrazinamide (1954), and rifampicin (1963), among others. Tuberculosis is usually treated with a combination of three or four antibiotics at the same time for many months.

An estimated twenty-five percent of the entire North American West was settled by health seekers, largely those with tuberculosis. Areas such as Montana, Idaho, Arizona, New Mexico, California, and Colorado attracted a large number of consumptives who were drawn to the supposedly curative mountain air. Western cities like Colorado Springs, Pasadena, and Tucson got their start in great part as popular places to find the cure. In 1900, so many consumptives flooded California that the state board of health attempted to ban tuberculars from entering the state.[62]

Today, the World Health Organization estimates that 9 million people contract tuberculosis every year, and an estimated 2 to 3 million people die from it.[63]

Cholera

Cholera *(Vibrio cholera)* is another bacterial infection that proved debilitating to Indians and whites. It attacks the intestinal lining, causing severe diarrhea, vomiting, and muscle cramps. Dehydration often follows, leading to death if not treated. It spreads mainly through water and food contaminated with human feces from poor sanitation.

The name cholera is from the Greek word for bile, and the disease most likely had its origins in the Indian subcontinent in Asia. In 1817, it was spread by trade routes to Russia and then on to Europe and North America. A second pandemic of cholera occurred from 1829 to 1851 worldwide and killed hundreds of thousands of people. In America, it reached New York first in 1832—probably from Irish immigrants arriving from Europe—and then by 1834 spread across to the Pacific Coast. President James Polk died from it.

In 1848, steamboat traffic up the rivers of the central part of the United States brought the disease to the Indians. It spread throughout the Mississippi River system, killing over 4,500 people in St. Louis and over 3,000 in New Orleans. It then spread along the California, Mormon, and Oregon Trails, killing 6,000 to 12,000 people on their way to the California gold rush from 1849 to 1855. The Pawnee, who once numbered 25,000, lost half their population to cholera between 1840 and 1850, owing to contact with westbound settlers taking the Platte River Trail. By the end of the century, their numbers had dropped to a few hundred.[64]

In total, approximately 150,000 Americans and Indians died between 1832 and 1849 from cholera. A number of other pandemics followed, including one in the 1870s that killed thousands. In 1873, it spread from New Orleans along the Mississippi River and to ports on its tributaries. By the time of the Wounded Knee Massacre in 1890, another 50,000 Indians had died.

Unraveling the mystery of the cause of cholera is another example of how recent our understanding of infectious diseases really is and the impact that good sanitation has on eradicating disease. One of the biggest challenges of high-density urban living is what to do with all the human and animal wastes. Five generations ago, there were no sewers beneath city streets and sidewalks, but at times these same pathways were covered in several feet of horse and human excrement. In major cities in the United States, communicable diseases were a constant factor in day-to-day life. This was the case in Chicago, for example, and in 1868, just a few years after the end of the Civil War, the entire city was raised—by the use of thousands of jackscrews—to install a sewer system that drained into Lake Michigan.

Besides the challenge of tons of sewage in city streets, citizens also had to deal with polluted air from coal fireplaces and tainted drinking water. Every time a drink of water was taken, sickness or death could be the outcome. In London between 1831 and 1860, cholera killed thousands of people.

But what was the cause of cholera? No one knew. A Sherlockian solved the puzzle. His name was John Snow (1813-1858), an English physician who would become famous for his leadership in the adoption of anesthesia—he used ether and chloroform to enable patients to undergo surgical and obstetric procedures without pain—and medical hygiene. His groundbreaking work in tracing the source of an 1854 cholera outbreak in Soho, London, led to basic changes in the water and waste systems of London and eventually cities around the world. The eradication of cholera in urban areas in America led to a reduction of the disease in Indian communities.

At the time of the Soho cholera outbreak, standard medical understanding of the cause of many diseases was thought to be bad air. Germ theory was still in the future. Earlier, Snow had spent time with English miners who had developed cholera. Because he had breathed the same air as they had, Snow discounted the airborne theory of transmission. He focused on filthy water instead; Snow was ready to put his theory to the test. By talking to local residents, he determined that the outbreak occurred around a public water pump on Broad Street. He later used a dot map to identify where the cluster of cholera cases coincided with close proximity to that pump. Further investigation showed that the water company was taking water from sewage-polluted sections of the Thames and delivering it to some homes and the water pump.

Later, researchers discovered that an old cesspool of fecal material was leaking into the public well. Snow noted that one group didn't contract cholera—the employees at a local brewery who drank beer instead of water with their meals. His investigation is considered the seminal event in the creation of the science of epidemiology.[65]

While cholera is little known in the United States today, in 2010 the disease infected 3 to 5 million people worldwide and caused close to 100,000 deaths. As with many diseases, children are the most susceptible. Today a vaccine is available.

Typhus

Another infection of note that reached the Native American populations is typhus, a bacterial disease caused by the *Rickettsia* bacteria. It is transmitted to humans by parasites such as lice, fleas, and ticks. It mainly was a problem of poor sanitation found more commonly in urban areas or military camps.

Symptoms include back pain, delirium, high fever, joint pain, severe headaches, muscle pains, and rashes. Almost ninety-five percent of all cases have a rash that appears typically around the fourth or fifth day after exposure. The rash—usually flat, red spots—first appears on the abdomen. Some spots may have blood in them.

The first reported case was in 1489 when the Spanish invaded Moorish Granada. While 3,000 men were killed in warfare, 17,000 died of typhus. A number of epidemics followed throughout Europe from the sixteenth to the nineteenth century. In the mid-seventeenth century, typhus killed ten percent of the total German population. Typhus epidemics broke out in the United States in 1837 in Philadelphia and in 1843 in New Hampshire. Subsequently, it spread out West to the Indian populations, but caused a mere fraction of the deaths that smallpox did.[66]

Typhoid Fever

Typhoid fever—not to be confused with typhus—is caused by the *Salmonella typhi* bacteria. One to four weeks after exposure—which made it a convenient passenger on trans-Atlantic trips—there is an onset of fever, weakness, abdominal pain, constipation, and headaches. However, some people can carry the bacteria for up to three months, and a small percentage, around two to five percent, can become permanent carriers. At one week, rounded, more or less circumscribed, rose-colored spots that are slightly elevated appear on the skin. Symptoms can last months if not treated. Risk factors include poor sanitation and poverty—common conditions among Indian populations. The infection can proceed to intestinal hemorrhage, septicemia, inflammation of the brain and heart, and eventual death.

Typhoid fever was described in 400 BCE in Athens. Some believe that the English colony of Jamestown, Virginia, died out because of a typhoid outbreak. It did kill more than 6,000 settlers and countless Indians between 1607 and 1624. Later, during the Civil War, almost 82,000 Union soldiers alone died from typhoid. In February 1862, eleven-year-old Willie Lincoln, Abraham Lincoln's third and favorite son, also died from the dreaded disease. In 2013, there were 161,000 deaths and worldwide approximately 22 million illnesses.[67]

One of the most important events in American history for reducing not only typhoid deaths but other waterborne communicable diseases was chlorination of the public water supply. In the United States, this was first achieved in 1908 in Jersey City, New Jersey, thanks to the tireless efforts of John L. Leal (1858-1914), a physician and water treatment expert. After graduating from Columbia College of Physicians and Surgeons in 1884, Leal opened a practice in Paterson, New Jersey, and eventually was named city physician in 1886. In 1891, he was appointed as health inspector and was responsible for the construction of a network of sewers to remove domestic and industrial waste from the city. One of his many publications described the cause of waterborne typhoid fever outbreaks in Paterson.[68]

In 1899, Leal was hired as a sanitary advisor to the East Jersey Water Company. Complaints to the private water company—and eventually a lawsuit—by Jersey City officials that the water was not "pure and wholesome" led Leal to find a solution. From his background in bacteriology, he knew that chlorine killed bacteria. Leal had also read reports from England where in 1897 high concentrations of chlorine were used to disinfect a reservoir and pipelines in Maidstone.

In June 1908, Leal hired a sanitary engineer, George Fuller, to construct a chlorination plant to disinfect the water supply for Jersey City. It proved successful in removing pathogens from the drinking water. Leal's model for chlorination of public water led to plummeting numbers of typhoid fever deaths and other waterborne diseases. By 1914, more than 21 million people were drinking chlorinated water around the United States. Four years later, more than 1,000 North American cities where 33 million people lived were drinking water disinfected with chlorine.[69]

Whooping Cough

By 1806, whooping cough had traveled as far north as the Mandan and Hidatsa villages in North Dakota. Fur trader Charles McKenzie described the bacterial infection *(Bordetella pertusis)* as a "violent cough" or a "hooping cough."[70] Alexander Henry visited the villages that same year and wrote that the epidemic had spread even beyond the upper Missouri to "the Red and Assiniboine Rivers and even to Fort des Prairies [near present-day Edmonton, Alberta] and several other parts of the Northwest."[71] In 1813-1814 and again in 1819, yet more outbreaks spread across the Northern Plains. Having the condition was especially detrimental to those who were hunters when they tried to quietly sneak up on their prey.

Whooping cough or pertussis (also known as the hundred day cough) is a highly contagious bacterial disease with initial symptoms similar to those of the common cold: a runny nose, fever, and mild cough. Its common name comes from the high-pitched gasp or whoop that occurs when an infected person inhales after a coughing fit.[72]

The period of time between infection and the onset of symptoms is usually seven to ten days. Coughing and sneezing spreads the airborne disease. Patients are infectious to others from the start of symptoms until about three weeks into the coughing fits. Infants are most likely to develop complications, which include pneumonia, encephalopathy, seizures, and death.

There was no vaccine during the nineteenth century. In 1942, during World War II, American scientists combined the whole-cell pertussis vaccine with diphtheria and tetanus toxoids to generate the first DPT vaccine.[73] Even so, worldwide whooping cough still affects 48.5 million people yearly. In 2013, there were 61,000 deaths worldwide from whooping cough. It is still one of the leading causes of vaccine-preventable deaths. Pertussis currently is the only vaccine-preventable disease that is associated with increasing deaths in the United States. This is due in part because some parents refuse to have their children inoculated over concerns of the side effects from vaccination.[74]

Measles

Almost ninety percent of Indians who were exposed to measles contracted the viral disease, which was spread by coughing and sneezing through the air. The initial symptoms usually start ten to twelve days after exposure and last seven to ten days. They include fever to 104 degrees Fahrenheit, hacking cough, runny nose, and red eyes. Koplik spots—small white spots inside the mouth—are seen two to three days after the symptoms begin. Then red, flat spots appear on the skin, first on the head and then spreading down to cover most of the body several days after the initial symptoms. In total, most typical cases last about three weeks. More serious complications occur in almost thirty percent of the cases and include diarrhea, blindness, inflammation of the brain, and pneumonia. Fatalities were seen more commonly in those Indian populations that were malnourished.[75]

In 1529, a measles' outbreak carried by a black slave in Cuba killed two thirds of the natives who had previously survived smallpox. Two years later, measles was responsible for the deaths of half the population of Honduras, and it eventually ravaged the natives of Mexico, Central America, and the Inka civilization. From 1855 to 2005, measles infections have been estimated to have killed about 200 million people worldwide. This great scourge of mankind was best described by the British historian Lord Thomas B. Macaulay as "the most terrible of all the ministers of death."[76] As late as 2011, the World Health Organization estimated that 158,000 deaths were caused by measles despite the efforts of worldwide vaccination.[77]

Syphilis

Unwittingly, the Indians got a modicum of revenge. The sexually transmitted disease syphilis *(Treponema pallidum)* traveled from the New World to the Old World. It is a chronic, systemic, infectious disease caused by a spirochete bacterium usually spread through sexual intercourse. There are a number of clinical varieties. The clinical course has been divided into primary, secondary, and tertiary syphilis.

The skin lesions of primary syphilis have a pinkish-red hue that in time becomes a more brownish or yellowish red color. About three weeks after exposure, a chancre—a single painless ulceration on the genitals—occurs in about forty percent of the cases. Most acute symptoms resolve after three to six weeks, but up to twenty-five percent of those infected present with a recurrence of secondary symptoms—a rash again, fever, sore throat, and weight loss. Many don't recall the initial chancre. Tertiary syphilis may occur from three to fifteen years after the initial infection and can involve the skin (gummas), nerves, and heart. Cardiac involvement can lead to aortic aneurysms. About thirty to sixty percent of those exposed to syphilis will get the disease.

Syphilis was present in the New World before the arrival of the Spanish. Christopher Columbus and his men brought syphilis back to Europe. His crew joined the army of Charles VIII of France, and around 1494 or 1495 in Naples, Italy, an outbreak took place when the French army invaded. Subsequently, it spread rapidly throughout Europe. It was known as the great pox.

A complete description of clinical syphilis was given in 1530 by an Italian pathologist, Girolamo Fracastoro (aka Hieronymus Fracastorius), in a poem titled "Syphilis sive morbus Gallicus," in which a mythical shepherd named Syphilus was afflicted with a sexually transmitted disease as punishment for blasphemy to the Sun God. Jean Fernel in the sixteenth century called the same disease *lues venereal.*[78]

There is evidence from infectious disease specialists that syphilis has changed over the course of recorded history. A pandemic of syphilis occurring at the end of the fifteenth century was associated with severe and often fatal systemic manifestations. Skin lesions were frequently extensive, destructive, and disfiguring. Syphilis of such severity is rarely seen in the twentieth century. At the end of the fifteenth century, mercury was introduced for its treatment, giving rise to the saying, "One night with Venus, a lifetime with Mercury." Later, inorganic arsenic, guaiac wood, and sulfur baths were also used with some success. The causative agent wasn't identified until 1905.[79]

Today, even though penicillin is an effective treatment, there are about 12 million infected individuals globally, and the disease still causes over 100,000 deaths a year. Untreated, the mortality rate ranges from eight to fifty-eight percent.

As with the HIV, SARS, Ebola, and Zika viruses, along with MRSA (Methicillin-resistant *Staphylococcus aureus*), the potential for an emerging infectious disease to wreak havoc on the world remains a real possibility. As Sonia Shah wrote in *Pandemic: Tracking Contagions, from Cholera to Ebola and Beyond,* more than 300 infectious diseases have been detected in new areas during the last fifty years. Almost ninety percent of epidemiologists predict that one will emerge to cause a worldwide deadly pandemic sometime in the next two generations.

According to the World Health Organization, over 8 million humans still die from infectious diseases each year. Germ resistance to antibiotics is an ongoing problem, as is the appearance of new infectious agents. As was the case with the Europeans bringing disease to Native Americans, many still worry about the spread of germs by a mobile society. Author of *The Black Swan,* professor and businessman-trader Nassim Nicholas Taleb in 2010 warned, "I am not saying that we need to stop globalization and prevent travel. We just need to be aware of the side effects, the tradeoffs—and few people are. I see the risks of a very strange acute virus spreading throughout the planet."[80]

There were many more diseases introduced by Europeans that afflicted Native Americans. All had deleterious consequences on their populations.[81] By far, smallpox killed the most. Their deaths from disease provided further support to Christians that they were God's chosen ones. Another cornerstone of racism is the belief in religious superiority. Was Christianity superior to other religions including Native American religions? Does God take sides? Those are questions that are as pertinent today as they were to past generations. That's where one of the great mysteries of life rests.

Part II

The Mystery: Clash of Spirits

CHAPTER EIGHT

The World is Not Enough: Cultural Literacy for Religion

[Miss Watson] went on and told me [Huck Finn] all about the good place [heaven]. She said all a body would have to do there was go around all day with a harp and sing, forever and ever. So I didn't think much of it. But I never said so. I asked her if she reckoned Tom Sawyer would go there, and she said not by a considerable sight. I was glad about that, because I wanted him and me to go together.
—MARK TWAIN, THE ADVENTURES OF HUCKLEBERRY FINN

All men need the gods.

—HOMER

Viewed sociologically, religion is a set of beliefs and practices focused on the sacred or supernatural, through which life experiences of groups and individuals are given meaning and direction.
—MICHAEL O. EMERSON AND CHRISTIAN SMITH, DIVIDED BY FAITH: EVANGELICAL RELIGION AND THE PROBLEM OF RACE IN AMERICA

In August 1941, no one was certain that triumph over the Nazis was inevitable when Franklin Delano Roosevelt met with his friend Winston Churchill on the deck of the HMS *Prince of Wales* off Newfoundland.[1] The United States had not yet entered the war, and it was Churchill's goal to entice them to. Freedom and democracy were retreating in the face of authoritarianism across Eurasia. Austria, Bulgaria, Estonia, Germany, Greece, Hungary, Italy, Latvia, Lithuania, Poland, Portugal, Romania, and Spain all had turned to autocracy on their own without needing to be occupied.²

Churchill well knew that the bond between the United States and the rest of the English-speaking world rested on more than similar parliamentary systems, and that the most important of all cultural affinities was Christianity—a notion that seems more foreign today as each year passes.³

Over the years, American and British exceptionalism traditionally had been held to reside in a series of values and institutions: personal liberty, jury trials, uncensored newspapers, regular elections, habeas corpus, open competition, and religious pluralism. The arrogance of our time is to assume that these ideals are somehow the natural condition of an advanced society, or conversely in the case of religion, for example, an archaic society.

In the 1800s, Alexis de Tocqueville (1805-1859) was a witness to American exceptionalism and wrote about it in his *Democracy in America.* Like Native Americans, he was struck by the lack of cohesiveness of the extended family and by the opposite emphasis on individualism. The Frenchman wondered at the stubborn elevation of private property over raison d'état and of personal freedom over collective need—positions foreign to Native Americans.

That Sunday morning in 1941 aboard the *Prince of Wales,* a service was held "under the big guns" after British and American crewmen were paraded jointly on the decks. The prime minister himself picked the readings and hymns, which included "For Those in Peril on the Sea," also known as "Eternal Father Strong to Save," "Onward Christian Soldiers," and "O God, Our Help in Ages Past"—and everyone on board sang. The crew listened as the chaplain read from Joshua 1 in the language of the King James Bible, revered in both nations: "As I was with Moses, so I will be with thee; I will not fail thee, nor forsake thee. Be strong and of good courage." Churchill was thrilled, "The same language, the same hymns and, more or less, the same ideals."⁴

With the Allied victory in 1945, the following decade blossomed into the 1950s era of Christian nationalism. Abraham Vereide, a Methodist pastor in Seattle, organized prayer meetings for politicians that grew into the National Prayer Breakfast at which presidents speak today, but not always pray. House Democrat Louis C. Rabaut, a Roman Catholic from Detroit, sponsored a successful bill, passed in 1954, to include "Under God" in the Pledge of Allegiance. "In God We Trust" was added to our paper currency.

Of any evangelical pastor, it was Billy Graham—the man who George H. W. Bush dubbed "America's pastor"—who played a key role in the "invention" of a Christian America.⁵ President Dwight D. Eisenhower confided in

Graham that he believed he had been "elected . . . to help lead this country spiritually." In his inaugural speech, he took his oath for "Almighty God" and insisted that Americans "who are free must proclaim anew our faith." Becoming the first president to be baptized while in office, Eisenhower two weeks later was the honored guest at the first National Prayer Breakfast. Christian nationalism, as it had dominated Native Americans a century earlier, was ready to fight moral permissiveness at home and a godless communism abroad.[6]

Christian nationalism, as did so many other institutions, unraveled during and after the Vietnam War. America was disillusioned. Richard Nixon was seen as the stereotypical Christian hypocrite after Watergate. On his 1969 inauguration day, Nixon held a service that included clergy from five different faiths, and the swearing-in ceremonies had five additional clergymen. In his address, he urged that "to a crisis of the spirit" the nation needed "an answer of the spirit." He not only participated in the National Prayer Breakfast but also sponsored regular Sunday morning worship services at the White House. Nixon's anti-Semitic rants recorded on White House tapes further eroded his status.[7]

Fast-forward to today where the closing of Europe's churches reflects the rapid weakening of faith there, a phenomenon that is painful to both worshipers and others who see religion as a unifying factor in a disparate society.[8] The Church of England closes about twenty churches a year, and the Roman Catholic Church in Germany has shut about 515 churches in the past decade. So far the United States has avoided a similar wave of church closings because American Christians remain more religiously observant than Europeans.[9] However, religious researchers say there are a declining number of American churchgoers, which suggests the country could face the same problem in coming years. Will there be a new awakening? Time will tell. From 2000 to 2010, the number of actual churchgoers in the United States fell three percent. Scott Thumma, professor of the sociology of religion at Connecticut's Hartford Seminary, says America's churchgoing population is graying. Unless the trends change, he says, "Within another thirty years the situation in the U.S. will be at least as bad as what is currently evident in Europe."[10] The Christian share of the U.S. population is declining, while the number of U.S. adults who do not identify with any organized religion is growing, according to an extensive new survey by the Pew Research Center.[11]

Christianity still dominates American religious identity at seventy percent, but the number of Christians dropped by eight percent from 2007 to

2014. The percentage of people not affiliated with a religion has increased over that period. There are more religiously unaffiliated Americans than Catholics or mainline Protestants. The unaffiliated now amount to twenty-five percent of all Christians, compared to twenty-one percent for Catholics and fifteen percent for Protestants.

In 2007, twenty-five percent of millennials did not affiliate with a religion, but seven years later that figure had risen to thirty-four percent, with no indication that they will become more religious as they get older. There's also a continuing religious disaffiliation among older people. It's easy to conclude that the share of people who say religion is important to them is declining. The religiously unaffiliated are not just growing, but as they grow, they are becoming more secular.[12]

While religious affiliation is declining in the United States, the Pew survey shows that only about 2.4 percent of Americans identify themselves as atheists.[13] Those who aren't going to church are simply disaffected and indifferent, and many are uneducated about religious doctrine. They have no biblical literacy and embrace the postmodern notion that good behavior is relative and that being judgmental is the big problem in life and religion.[14]

Religion can inspire the most noble, compassionate actions, but can also lead to the most destructive, violent actions because it makes ultimate claims. Danger arises when people give absolute, uncritical obedience and commitment to religious text, doctrinal leaders, or institutions. Absolute certainty and good-versus-evil dualism can be appealing because it radically simplifies the world and provides a sense of purpose, empowerment, and belonging to someone who might feel disempowered, hopeless, and lost.[15]

We have seen that one of the greatest sources of peace, and one of the greatest sources of conflict among people, is religion. Religion becomes dangerous when it focuses on the drawing and defending of boundaries that tend to divide the world into us versus them. Division and strife are the results. Religion then becomes another cornerstone of racism.

The First Awakening before the Revolutionary War was a religious revival that unified individuals and the masses behind a common cause. That was followed by the Second Awakening that gave impetus to Manifest Destiny as Americans headed westward in search of a better life. Good white Christians were entitled by their God to kill Indians and take their land.

Religion still matters. The religious wars in the Middle East and radical Islamic terrorism will be occupying much of America's attention and resources in the foreseeable future. To devalue the importance of religion in America's past is to miss an important factor in how whites approached dealing with enslaved African Americans and Native Americans. Yet today, historical nonfiction that deals with Native Americans written by white authors often focuses on battles, massacres, disease, statistics, and weapons. In contrast, Native American authors are more interested in their religion, god, and the mystery.

Religious differences between Native Americans and their European invaders, and later, Americans, played an important role in destroying the ethnicity of our indigenous people—perhaps even more so than science, medicine, and western philosophy. How and why did Christianity become so important in the history of Western civilization? Why were Christians so adamant about sending out missionaries to convert the "heathen" Indians? Was religion one of the main reasons Europeans believed that their culture was superior to that of the Indian? These questions are at the core of understanding why the white man had to "kill the Indian"—his ethnicity—to "save the man" spiritually. It also justified physically killing Native Americans to save the land for whites.

Why should we study religious traditions? As the ancestors of Native Americans migrated across Asia toward the Bering Strait, they did more than exchange technology and breed with the locals. They acquired religious beliefs from a number of different groups and left behind some of their own. Another reason is to better understand why Native Americans were so resistant to accepting Christianity forced on them by missionaries and in some cases the U.S. government.

Religions Revealed

Gods cannot be invented. Like living beings they grow and die. They grow when the situation is ripe for them, and they die when the situation changes.[16]

Religion is as old as humans. Neanderthals and early modern humans practiced burial rituals with religious elements. There is a 100,000-year-old human skeleton in an Israeli cave that is stained with red ochre and surrounded by religious elements.

Religious ideas are some of the most extreme examples of good and evil in human history. Religious motivations can lead to selfless sacrifice, profound love, social justice movements, and awe-inspiring beauty, as well as bigotry, close-mindedness, and mass murder. As they often do, tragedy and devastation have had a major impact on theology.

What is religion? Many scholars believe that the root word of religion comes from the Latin *ligare,* which means connecting or binding. That's where ligament comes from. There is no one single feature that all religions must possess. World religions include (approximate time of origin): Hinduism (3000 BCE), Judaism (1800 BCE), Confucianism (551 BCE), Buddhism (500 BCE), Daoism (300 BCE), Christianity (mid-first century CE), Shinto (500 CE), Islam (570 CE), and East Asian shamanism (late Stone Age).

Faith in future progress became fundamental to Western Christianity and a core principle of the major colonial powers. This was in contrast to Muslims' commitment to the idea of decline. The Palestinian historian Tarif Khalidi has interpreted passages by Muslim scholars to "suggest a universe running down, an imminent end to man and all his works."[17] The Islamist conception of the universe and its resulting opposition to reason, science, and philosophical inquiry have had a profound impact down to the present day. Likewise, while the Chinese were known as great inventors and innovators, such progress was abandoned or even outlawed in China because of Confucian opposition to change on the grounds that the past was greatly superior.[18]

According to the latest statistics, over half the world's population believes in one God—monotheism. Another belief system is pantheism, which is a belief that God is identical with the universe or that the natural world is itself divine—as seen in Native American religion. There are other traditions, such as Zen Buddhism, that do not feature God, gods, or supernatural beings. Such traditions emphasize uncovering the spiritual possibilities within ourselves. Some religions see God as a parent, some as a ruler lord or judge, and in some traditions God is seen as having animal or human-animal hybrid forms. In other cases, including Native American religions, the natural elements themselves—the sun, stars, fire, plants, and animals—are themselves seen as deities.

Hinduism is considered by some scholars to be the oldest living major religion in the world. There are nearly 1 billion Hindus, which makes it the world's third-largest religion after Christianity and Islam. Most Hindus are found in South Asia. Hindus have many gods and they can be good or evil. Gandhi believed in selfless action. He wrote, "I was not built for academic writings. Action is my domain. What I understand, according to my lights, to be my duty . . . I do. All my action is actuated by the spirit of service."[19]

Buddhism claims to offer something all of us dearly want—a way out of suffering. Buddhism is a tradition of tremendous diversity in many forms. One element that is shared by all Buddhists is a connection with the historic Buddha born sometime in the sixth or fifth century

BCE. His teachings were passed down orally for centuries before they were written down.

Buddhism denies a permanent, unchanging self. Buddha taught that our mental suffering is self-created. The discontent we experience is created by our clinging, which can be ended by waking up to the right perspective, living a moral life, and practicing meditation. Buddhism today is a religion of hundreds of millions of people who live in virtually every region of the world. All are committed to five precepts: not harming, not stealing, not lying, no sexual impropriety, and no intoxicants that cause heedlessness.[20]

Chinese religion and cosmology includes **Confucianism** and **Daoism.** Throughout history, most Chinese believed in a host of supernatural beings, and these can generally be arranged into three categories: gods, ghosts, and common ancestors. In general, ancestors are seen as helping the living family members and serving as the family representative in the spirit realm. The final type of supernatural being is the ghost. While gods and ancestors are generally honored and worshipped, ghosts must be appreciated and held at bay. Offerings are made to ghosts so they will leave you alone. In many cases, ghosts are deceased humans who were not cared for by the living. In China, the relationship between family members does not end when one of them dies, it just changes. Native American religion has components of some of these beliefs.

Confucius was born in 551 BCE in China. He lived during a time of great chaos and looked for answers in history. Reverence for the past is an essential feature of Confucian thought. Confucius emphasized learning and studying rather than introspection and intuition. There has been a revival of Confucianism in recent years. Like Native American religion, Confucianism counters American individualism and fosters a greater sense of family and community. Confucianism sees the sacred in everyday lives. Tradition, culture, education, the arts, and human relationships—and above all family—are worthy of our reverence.[21]

Daoism means way or path. While Confucians emphasize acquiring knowledge and following tradition and rituals, Daoists advocate returning to a more natural state. To achieve this, people have to rid themselves of the learned, ritualized way of acting and the overall artifice that they have internalized from their cultures. It means no striving activity and no activity driven by goal-oriented, conscious, intentional planning. It can be thought of as effortless action. It means acting in such a way that is natural to who you are. The ultimate goal is to live in harmony, much like the goal of Native Americans' spirituality.

Daoist priests act as mediators with the spirit world to confer blessings on the community. Some of their activities include music and dancing, rituals of purification and repentance, protection of the community, and the spiritual endeavor of thinking and seeing of the gods.[22]

Shamanism is one of the world's oldest and most widespread forms of religion. Not only in the Native American community but throughout the world, religious specialists helped mediate the relationship between humans and spirits in very different ways. Known as shamans, these men and women often altered their state of consciousness and traveled to other realms to serve the community.

Today, there are shamans still practicing in virtually every part of the world. The term *shaman* comes from Siberia, meaning a person who is moved or raised. Shamans were important among many nomadic hunting and gathering communities, where they performed many functions: healer, medium, priest, diviner, sorcerer, and sage. To accomplish their jobs, shamans entered altered states of consciousness and made contact with gods or spirits.

Shamans use a range of different techniques to enter the altered states: dancing, drumming, fasting, and ingesting consciousness-expanding substances such as peyote, psilocybin, and mushrooms. There are two general methods to become a shaman. The first is hereditary. The other is being chosen by the spirits. Many shamans perform ritual animal sacrifice. The shaman offers gratitude to the animal for its sacrifice, and the animal is usually consumed after the ritual. The shamans wear colorful clothing and use a great deal of implements when acting as a vehicle for the spirits, including flags, fans, and bells.[23]

Islam is the second-largest religious tradition in the world. It has 1.5 billion followers, and the largest Muslim majority country in the world is Indonesia. A Muslim is one who is a follower, while Islam refers to the religion. Mohammed was born in 570 CE in Mecca on the Arabian Peninsula. Much of the Arabian Peninsula was peopled by nomadic tribes that traveled in camel caravans. There was no unifying ideology that brought all the tribes together, but there were frequent raids, and the people lived by a code of revenge and honor where an offense had to be avenged. The religion at that time was largely polytheistic, and various deities were associated with natural forces, localities, and tribes.

At age forty, Mohammed was visited by the angel Gabriel, and an illiterate Mohammed was now miraculously literate. By the time of Mohammed's death in 632 CE, nearly all of Arabia followed Islam. The Qur'an emphasizes that Mohammed, like all prophets, is just a human being and must not be worshipped. All worship must be directed to God alone. The Qur'an has 114 chapters, and it emphasizes that God can forgive anything if a person genuinely repents and seeks mercy.

Another important point is that the God of Islam is the same God worshipped by Jews and Christians. Muslims believe that the earlier prophets—including Adam, Abraham, Moses, John the Baptist, and Jesus—were prophets of God. Those prophets who brought with them a scripture—Moses, Jesus, and Mohammed—are considered messengers of God. Judaism and Islam share a common ancestor, Abraham. The Jews go through his son Isaac, and the Muslims go through his son Ishmael. Muslims believe Jesus was born of a virgin birth, healed and performed miracles, and will return at the end times. However, they do not believe he is divine or the son in the Holy Trinity.

The rise of the Islamic Ottoman Empire at the end of the thirteenth century eventually led to expansion in the fifteenth and sixteenth century into Europe, Asia, and Africa. At its height, the empire created the most advanced culture in the world. From the eighth to the thirteenth century, Baghdad became a center of culture, scholarship, and science. Muslim Spain was described as a culture where there was extensive cooperation among Muslims, Jews, and Christians.

The true meaning of Islamic jihad is to live in accordance to God's wishes. The word means struggle or effort. There is an Islamic just war doctrine with many limitations on how warfare can be conducted. Among them, warfare must be defensive and must not involve targeting civilians, women, or children. The Qur'an states, "Fight those in the way of God who fight you, but do not be aggressive; God does not like aggressors. . . . If they desist then cease to be hostile." Of course, any religion can be interpreted to justify evil behavior.[24]

After Mohammed's death in 632 CE, Islam split into Sunni and Shia communities. The split was and remains not just about Mohammed's successor but about the nature of leadership itself. The schism eventually led to eighty-five percent of Muslims being Sunni, residing mainly in Saudi Arabia, Turkey, Pakistan, India, and Indonesia—all, in general, recent U.S. allies. Iran and Iraq are countries populated with large numbers of Shiites.[25]

In the eighteenth and nineteenth centuries, almost every part of the Muslim world was colonized by European powers. Africa was no exception, and scholars estimate that up to twenty percent of African slaves brought to America were Muslim. Today, around twenty-five to thirty percent of all American Muslims are African Americans.[26]

Much like African American slaves and Native Americans, Muslims felt disempowered and humiliated by the Christian colonial aggressors. The range of responses to colonization was grouped into three categories. One argument stated that the decline in the Muslim world was due to straying from the straight path of Islam. This could be solved by returning to true Islam and rejecting the West. Conversely, a second response was to imitate the West. Modernization would be accomplished through secularization and westernization. A third alternative was to take the middle ground and modernize, but retain Islamic traditions. Variations on all these responses were repeated by Native Americans in the nineteenth century in the United States as the government wavered between segregating the Indians in the West during the early part of the century and assimilating them by means of government schools.

Many who are critical of religion point to the past and the numerous wars started in the name of God. How could godly men take slaves and destroy Native American culture? Dr. Francis Collins addressed this distressing question in his book *The Language of God,* writing, "The Beatitudes spoken by Christ in the Sermon on the Mount were ignored as the Christian church carried out violent Crusades in the Middle Ages and pursued a series of Inquisitions afterward. While in the Mecca phase of his life, Muhammad never used violence in responding to persecutors, Islamic jihads commenced in the Medina phase and extended over centuries, even to present-day violent attacks such as the September 11, 2001, creating the unfortunate impression that Islam is necessarily violent."[27]

Where there is good in religion, there is also evil. But religion doesn't have the market on evil cornered. In *The Black Swan,* Nassim Nicholas Taleb pointed out the hypocrisy of secularism, writing, "I am most often irritated by those who attack the bishop but somehow fall for the securities analyst—those who exercise their skepticism against religion but not against economists, social scientists, and phony statisticians. . . . These people will tell you that religion was horrible for mankind by counting deaths from the Inquisition and various religious wars."[28]

The Golden Rule or the Ethic of Reciprocity

The moral principle of treating others as one would like to be treated oneself—the Golden Rule—is found in most human cultures and religions. It is a unifying principle. James, Jesus's brother, called it the Royal Rule. While it may be somewhat subjective, it perhaps is the best code humans have to live by. It is one of the primary laws because it rules and encompasses all of the other laws of the Christian Kingdom. Matthew 22:39 states that the second greatest commandment is, "You shall love your neighbor as yourself." Romans 13:8-10, written by Paul, exhorting to love one's neighbors, states, "Owe no one anything, except to love each other, for the one who loves another has fulfilled the law. For the commandments, 'You shall not commit adultery, You shall not steal, You shall not covet,' and any other commandment, are summed up in this word: 'You shall love your neighbor as yourself.' Love does no wrong to a neighbor; therefore love is fulfilling the law."

If there is one common thread among almost all religions, it the Golden Rule. It is often claimed as a Christian doctrine, but that is not totally accurate. In ancient Egypt around 2000 BCE, an ancient Egyptian goddess in *The Story of The Eloquent Peasant* was perhaps the earliest to command the Golden Rule. In Leviticus 19:18 in the Old Testament is written, "You shall not take vengeance or bear a grudge against your kinsfolk. Love your neighbor as yourself: I am the Lord."

The philosophical schools in ancient China—Taoism and Confucianism—address the Golden Rule. In 500 BCE, Confucius taught, "Never impose on others what you would not choose for yourself." In ancient India, tradition as far back as 800 BCE stated, "Hence, keeping these in mind, by self-control and making dharma [right conduct] your main focus, treat others as you treat yourself." In 400 BCE, the Greek philosopher Isocrates stated, "Do not do to others that which angers you when they do it to you."

In Matthew 7:12, Jesus taught, "Do to others what you want them to do to you. This is the meaning of the law of Moses and the teaching of the profits." In Luke 6:31, he taught, "Do to others what you want them to do to you."

Mohammed taught, "None of you truly believes until he wishes for his brother what he wishes for himself."

Hinduism teaches, "One should never do that to another which one regards as interest to one's own self." This, in brief, is the role of dharma. Other behavior is due to selfish desires.

One of the cornerstones of Buddha's principles of ethics in the sixth century taught, "Hurt not others in ways that you yourself would find hurtful."

President Lincoln stated during the Civil War that if he could find a church that lived by the Golden Rule he would join it. He never attended a church.

Ignorance and disrespect of religion has led to tragic results, especially in the case of Native Americans. What follows in Part Two is an overview of the religions of Native Americans and Christians. They can be compared and contrasted with each other and other world religions, and then it is up to the reader to draw personal conclusions.

CHAPTER NINE

The Spirit of the West: Native American Religion and Its Chroniclers

The white men tried to make the Indian white men also. It would be as reasonable and just to try to make the Indians skin white as to try make him act and think like a white man. But the white man has taken our territory and destroyed our game so we must eat the white man's food or die.
—RED CLOUD'S ABDICATION SPEECH, JULY 4, 1903

To Indians practicing the very principle of religious freedom that the white people celebrated, the government's reasoning made no sense. If whites could choose among all the mutations of Protestantism and Catholicism, so the Indian should have the same right to choose between them or, if they wanted, the Ghost Dance religion that drew on Christian principles.
—ROBERT M. UTLEY, *THE LANCE AND THE SHIELD: THE LIFE AND TIMES OF SITTING BULL*

And your young men shall see visions, and your old men shall dream dreams.
—ACTS 2:17

Author Richard Twiss, a member of the Rosebud Lakota Sioux tribe, in his book *One Church, Many Tribes* wrote, "Religion is often defined as man's searching for God; true Christian faith is God's searching for and finding man. Religion is a striving to please God, fearful of failure and condemnation; faith is God's pleasing man, filling us with His love and acceptance."[1]

The next three chapters present an introduction to Native American religions, myths, legends, ceremonies, and rituals, demonstrating just how different their culture was from the whites who wanted to change the natives' world to their world. Many tribes shared traditions, but they also had their own unique vision on life. It's no wonder that in most instances the transformation never came to fruition. Chroniclers—mainly of Northern Plains' life—are also profiled. American racism is no more evident than in the ethnic cleansing of Native American religion attempted by white Americans as they swept westward guided by Manifest Destiny.

Some aspects of Native American religions have been lost, but the silence of God doesn't indicate the absence of God. Native Americans accept the mystery of faith. Christians attempt to make sense of theirs. Since for many Europeans Indians were heathens, the natives' rich spiritual lives were either totally ignored or devalued. But spirit is the intellect of the soul, and there is no better place to find it than in the faith of Native Americans. All native cultures have a supernatural orientation—the idea of a native atheist would be an oxymoron.

As Manifest Destiny swept westward, the Indians were expected to welcome Christianity and abandon their own religions. Some were accepting of Christianity but did not want to give up their own beliefs. And of course, it never entered the white man's mind that he should accept any part of the Indians' religion. Spiritual tensions between the two groups are as old as their first encounters in the New World.

In 1930, in his epic *American,* on the life of Crow Chief Plenty Coups, Montana author Frank Bird Linderman explained the challenges Christians faced in understanding the God of the Crow:

> Ah-badt-dadt-deah literally translated means The-one-who-made-all-things. I have sometimes thought that it is more nearly a term than a name, and that to the Crow the name of his God is unpronounceable, as with some of the ancient peoples. However, the Indian—certainly any that I know—will scarcely ever speak the name of his God aloud; and if you pronounce it in his presence you will feel his reverence. There will be instant silence, and the Indian's attitude will have changed. His God is All, Everywhere; and this is the reason why, in

crossing a stream, he will sometimes give the water a bit of fat meat or some little finery. This is not to propitiate evil spirits who live in the water, but it is an offering to the All-high so that the Indian may pass safely through an element that he recognizes is not naturally his own. But if you speak of E-sac-ca-wata (Old-man-coyote), or Napi, or Nu-lach-kin-nah (Old man), a powerful character to whom the Almighty entrusted much of the work of creation, every old Indian will smile. The Indians hold him in no reverence and are ready to laugh at the mention of his name, since it was he who made the seeming mistakes in nature, not the Almighty who commissioned him. This, to me, is a delicious touch, for thus, in his few fault-findings with created things like the elements that sometimes torture, the Indian cannot blaspheme against his God, for whom he holds the deepest reverence. Here, too, I believe is proof that the Indian of this section certainly is a monotheist.[2]

Much of what we know about Indian religion is from oral histories passed down through generations and then relayed to further generations of ethnographers who interviewed Indians over several centuries. Both oral histories relayed in the early Christian church and in Native American gatherings in the form of liturgies, myths, and songs were often associated with a ceremony to emphasize the importance of the message.

Yet there are other sources. The Wind River Mountains, the Bighorn Basin, and the Pryor Mountains, along with the more well-known regions of the Southwest—New Mexico's Petroglyph National Monument and Utah's Great Gallery—possess a treasure trove of pictographs (images painted on stone) and petroglyphs (images etched in stone) that hold supernatural and religious meaning to Indians. The white man who dismisses these as just art is totally missing the point.[3]

Mnemonic pictographs for centuries were used to record winter counts, which were a form of a calendar record that marked each passing year. Instead of stone, they were traced on bison hides. Indians understood that visual images were often better remembered than words.

Over the last thirty years, archaeologists have come to the conclusion that much of the rock imagery was produced by shamans who were the tribal priests. Their intent was to relate to their tribal members and future generations what they had experienced—sometimes visions of an afterlife—through their special supernatural relationship with their Gods. The sites subsequently became important for spiritual and religious ceremonies.

Near life-size Dinwoody petroglyph images created by Shoshonean shamans in the Bighorn Basin at the Legend Rock site or in the Thermopolis area near the Wind River Range in Wyoming reveal human figures with the clawed feet of birds and sometimes wings with their arms posed in a classic shaman position—raised and held wide. These fascinating images are believed to have been first created over 6,800 years ago and continued until the early twentieth century.

Another tradition of shield figures was left by a group other than the shamans. Some are wheel- or circle-shaped images—often painted—portraying shield-bearing foot soldiers believed to be honoring a military tradition. Others show horses and firearms; these may have been recorded after vision quests by non-priest individuals or they may relate mythical stories. While we have gained much information from these rock images, by far most of what we know about Indian religion is derived from the oral tradition.[4]

Native American Traditions and Its Chroniclers

Indians believed that they came to know the same God as the Christian by divine providence, but natives knew him in an abstract way, which left the natives to much wondering and superstition. The spiritual life was full of mystery. In contrast, the Christian gained knowledge through reading the Bible and a spiritual connection through Christ, enabling him to know the specific will of God in those things in which He had made His will known. We in Western civilization are taught to think with logic, first developed by the Greeks. This logic says, for instance, that contradictions are impossible. Hebrew and Native American minds assume that contradictions and paradoxes do exist, so they have no trouble holding seemingly contradictory truths and tensions. Western minds resist paradoxes, so we try to reason them out logically. Our debates about predestination and free will are prime examples of this effort. The Jews and Indians knew that God was supreme, so that everything that happened must be at least indirectly caused by him. For Indians these paradoxes are called mysteries.

Unfortunately, his interpretations often gave the white man what he felt was a right to impose his will—which often had nothing to do with the message of Jesus—on the Indian. Christian missionaries either did not recognize this or believed that the Bible instructed them to bring the good news to the Indian, and that good news—or word—was the only word the Indian should embrace.

George Catlin

Although many today remember George Catlin (1796-1872) as a painter, he was also one of the first to document the Indian's life in the West as one of the finest writers on the subject. Catlin was a champion of his native friends:

> I find that the principal cause why we underrate and despise the savage, is generally because we do not understand him; and the reason why we are ignorant of him and his modes, is that we do not stop to investigate—the world has been too much in the habit of looking upon him as altogether inferior—as a beast, a brute; and unworthy of more than a passing notice. If they stop long enough to form an acquaintance, it is but to take advantage of his ignorance and credulities—to rob him of the wealth and resources of his country—to make him drunk with whiskey, and visit him with abuses which in his ignorance he never thought of. By this method his first visitors entirely overlook and never understand the meaning of his thousand interesting and characteristic customs; and at the same time, by changing his native modes and habits of life, blot them out from view of the inquiring world for ever.[5]

George Catlin traveled to the American West five times during the 1830s, and was one of the first white men to paint the Plains Indians in their native homes. Early in life, he had a brief career as a lawyer, and following that he produced two major collections of paintings of American Indians. He also published a series of books chronicling his adventures among the native peoples of North, Central, and South America.

His first travels west started from St. Louis—which became his base of operation for the five trips he took between 1830 and 1838. He visited over fifty tribes in that six-year period. In 1831, he accompanied General William Clark on a diplomatic mission up the Mississippi River. In 1838, he made his longest voyage, from St. Louis to Fort Union, a trading post on the Missouri River near present-day Fairview, Montana, on the Montana-Dakota border. On that trip, he visited eighteen tribes, including the Pawnee, Omaha, and Ponca in the south and the Mandan, Cheyenne, Crow, Assiniboine, and Blackfeet to the north. His paintings of everyday life, including hunting scenes, inspired later Western painters such as the legendary Charles M. Russell.[6]

During his trip, Catlin admired the Indian's generosity and sense of fairness. He wrote, "I love the people who are honest without laws, who have no jails and no poorhouses. I love the people who keep the Commandments without ever having read them or heard them preached, who never take the name of God in vain, and who are free from religious animosities."[7]

Upon returning from the West in 1838, he assembled his paintings and artifacts and went on a national public lecture tour, presenting his experiences with the American Indians. Later, he approached the U.S. government to purchase his paintings, but the government declined. Not discouraged, in 1839 Catlin took his traveling show on a tour of European capitals. Charles Baudelaire, a French critic, opined that in Catlin's paintings, "he has brought back alive the proud and free characters of these chiefs, both their nobility and manliness."[8]

In 1841, Catlin authored books in two volumes on the manners, customs, and condition of the North American Indians, which included around 300 engravings. That was followed in 1844 by Catlin's *North American Indian Portfolio,* which included twenty-five plates. His publications are unparalleled in providing a historical glimpse at the spiritual and everyday life of Native Americans.

However, those days of notoriety faded as time passed, and by 1852 he was forced to sell the original Indian gallery of 607 paintings due to personal debts. Thereafter, for the next five years he traveled through South and Central America and later explored the Far West again.

Now part of the Smithsonian's American Art Museum's collection, Catlin's first collection of Indian portraits painted in the 1830s has nearly completely survived. His Indian artifacts ended up in the Department of Ethnology at the National Museum of Natural History.[9]

Dr. James R. Walker

Perhaps the finest autobiographical account of Oglala religion and fundamentals of Oglala mythology—especially the Sun Dance—was recorded by Dr. James R. Walker (1849-1926). He spent eighteen years in South Dakota as agency physician on the Pine Ridge Reservation, the home of the Oglala Sioux. From 1896 until 1914, he collected material on every aspect of Lakota life. As he provided the reservation with medical care and became a trusted friend, the doctor developed a keen interest in the traditional ways of the Lakota. They instructed him on every aspect of traditional religion, and as George Sword commented, "The Gods of the Oglala would be more pleased if the holy men told of them so that they might be kept in remembrance and all the world might know of them."[10]

Along with Sword and Little Wound—the head chief of the Oglala—other important leaders were American Horse, Red Cloud, Bad Wound, and numerous shamans. Walker's goal was to record Lakota religion as it was before the white man arrived with his message of Christianity. In 1917, he published a monograph titled *The Sun Dance and Other Ceremonies of the Ogalala Division of the Teton Dakota*. It has become one of the classic works on understanding the traditional Lakota way of life. Eventually, Indiana native Maurice Frink collected the papers of Walker, which became the basis of *Lakota Belief and Ritual*.[11] Frink would serve as executive director of the Colorado Historical Society from 1954 to 1962. In 1913, after graduating from high school, Frink visited Walker for the summer at Pine Ridge in order to learn about Indians firsthand.

James Riley Walker was born on March 4, 1849, in a log cabin in Illinois. After lying about his age, fourteen-year-old Walker enlisted as a private in the Union Army. He eventually graduated from Northwestern University medical school in 1873. Thereafter, he ventured north to a Chippewa reservation in northern Minnesota before an epidemic of smallpox broke out in the winter of 1882-1883. Of the 190 people exposed to the disease, 84 contracted it and 72 died. In 1906, President Theodore Roosevelt decorated Walker for heroism in preventing the spread of the disease.

After arriving at the Pine Ridge Reservation, Walker was inspired to learn the ways of the traditional holy men. He believed that if he understood their religion he could be a more effective physician. Early on, one of the first challenges was trying to convince the Indians that tuberculosis was not caused by a worm that ate away the lung. The Indian medicine man perpetuated this misconception by pretending to take a worm out of the patient's chest.

Wisely, Walker did not embarrass the medicine man in front of his people. He privately showed the medicine man that the sputum contained bacteria. His main treatment modality of the disease was based on cleanliness, protection and nourishment of the body, and an abundance of fresh air and sunshine.

Walker wrote that, in the Indian world, communicating with mysterious spirits is available to every person from the great chiefs down to the common warrior. One of the ways this was achieved was through prayer:

In the life of the Indian there was only one inevitable duty—the duty of prayer, the daily recognition of the Unseen and Eternal. His daily devotions were more necessary to him than daily food. He wakes at daybreak, puts on his moccasins, and steps down to the water's edge. Here he throws handfuls of clear, cold water into his face, or plunges in bodily. After the bath, he stands erect before the advancing dawn, facing the sun as it dances upon the horizon, and offers his unspoken orison. His mate may precede or follow him in his devotions, but never accompanies him. Each soul must meet the morning sun, the new sweet earth, and the Great Silence alone![12]

When you arise in the morning, give thanks for the morning light. Give thanks for your life and strength. Give thanks for your food and give thanks for the joy of living. And if perchance you see no reason for giving thanks, rest assured the fault is in yourself.[13]

Walker recorded Red Cloud, who perhaps best summarized the beliefs of his people in his July 4, 1903, abdication speech:

As a child I was taught the Supernatural Powers *(Taku Wakan)* were powerful and could do strange things; that I should placate them and win their favor; that they could help me or harm me; that they could be good friends or harmful enemies. I was taught that the Sun *(Wi)* was a Great Mystery *(Wakan Tanka)*, that he was the Supreme Mystery *(Iyotan Wakantu)*, and that he was our grandfather *(Tunkansila)*, and my people addressed him as Father *(Ate)*. This was taught me by the wise men *(wicasa ksapa)* and the shamans *(wicasa wakan)*. They taught me that I could gain their favor by being kind to my people and brave before my enemies; by telling the truth and living straight; by fighting for my people and their hunting grounds. . . .

These things were taught before the Sun Dance. The Lakotas believe them and they lived so as to win the favor of the Supernatural Powers *(Taku Wakan)*. The shamans could heal the sick with the help of the Good Mysteries *(Wakan Waste)* and by driving away the Evil Mysteries *(Wakan Sica)*. Two Legs (the mythical bear) taught the Lakotas what medicines were good.

When the Lakotas believe these things they lived happy and they died satisfied. What more than this can that which the white man offers us give?

Taku Shanskan is familiar with my spirit *(nagi)* and when I die I will go with him. Then I will be with my forefathers. If this is not the heaven of the white man, I shall be satisfied. *Wi* is my father. Though *Wakan Tanka* of the white man has overcome him. But I shall remain true to him.

Shadows are long and dark before me. I shall soon lie down to rise no more. While my spirit is with my body the smoke of my breath shall be towards the sun for he knows all things and knows that I am still true to him.[14]

Walter McClintock

Another noted ethnographer was Walter McClintock (1870-1949), who was born in 1870 in Pittsburgh, Pennsylvania. His education at the private Shadyside Academy, which his father helped found, was followed by graduation from Yale in 1891. Five years later, President Grover Cleveland selected a group of conservation-minded individuals to travel to northwestern Montana for the purpose of establishing a national policy on land preservation. Included were Gifford Pinchot, chief of the U.S. Forest Service; forester Henry S. Graves, who later became the dean of the school of forestry; and McClintock.

Billy Jackson, who was one-quarter Blackfeet, and Jack Monroe led the group. Afterward, McClintock returned with Jackson to the annual Sun Dance ceremony gathering. There he met Chiefs White Calf, Running Crane, Little Plume, and Little Dog—all traditional Blackfeet leaders. After the Sun Dance, he returned to Jackson's home in East Glacier and stayed until autumn, often visiting his new friends at the nearby Blackfeet camps. Such experiences forever changed McClintock's life. He became so well respected that the Blackfeet ceremonially adopted him, and Chief White Calf later bestowed on him an Indian name, stating, "This is the white weasel, one of the sacred animals in our beaver bundle. We name you 'A-pe-ech-ken' (white-weasel-moccasin), because your color is light and your eyes are blue. We pray this name may bring you long life and good luck."[15] Their friendship was mutually beneficial. White Calf understood that McClintock would help him in dealing with the white man. Through copious notes and photographs, McClintock was able to document a vanishing way of life.

In 1907, Theodore Roosevelt warmly welcomed McClintock to the East Room of the White House, where he was introduced to cabinet members, Supreme Court justices, and diplomats from around the world.

McClintock's books on the Blackfeet left an enduring legacy. *The Old North Trail, or Life, Legends and Religions of the Blackfeet Indians,* published in 1910, is a landmark study into the center of the Blackfeet world. Its 539 pages explored their ceremonial customs and spiritual beliefs, McClintock's adoption into the tribe, and current issues facing the Blackfeet. He expressed optimism regarding assimilation when he wrote, "Under the passing of the old conditions and the coming in of the new policy, the younger generation of Blackfeet is already responding, and manifesting a capacity for improvement. They are becoming the owners of real estate, and are developing thrift and an ability to provide for the future."[16] He noted that the younger generations' marked advance toward civilization was due to being educated and trained to work in industry. As many whites believed at that time, the older Indian generation had fixed habits of hereditary savagery, which made them unable to work in the white man's world.

The Old North Trail contains dozens of photographs taken by the author and eight full-color illustrations skillfully painted by McClintock. In addition, the first index contains sheet music to nine songs. The final page of the book consists of a fold-out map showing "The country of the Blackfeet Indians." McClintock wrote, "The Blackfeet are firm believers in the supernatural and in the control of human affairs by both good and evil powers and the invisible world. He believed bad luck is punishment by the evil power because of violation of the laws of the medicines. He is a slave to a constant dread of evil power and evil spirits are ready to pursue and punish him."[17] McClintock, although sympathetic to the Indians' plight, still viewed their religion as inferior, writing, "Without the medium of a divine revelation, through which the Christian races receive knowledge of the true God, and with only their senses and reason, and the light of nature to guide them, the Blackfeet evolved a very reasonable form of pagan religion in their Sun-worship. . . ."[18]

Although Christian missionaries and the U.S. government through federally funded schools had attempted to assimilate Native Americans for decades, their attempts fell short. Still, in 1910 McClintock remained optimistic about spiritual conversion of his Indian friends. He wrote, "The whole question of lifting up the Indian is one of economical, educational, and moral difficulty to both state and church. They are together responsible for its solution, the work of each supplementing the other. Christian missions among the Blackfeet have not yet made equal progress with the government. Nevertheless, the virility of the Blackfeet character, and the robustness of their physical manhood, under the old conditions of barbarism, give assurance of what should be forthcoming under Christianity, rightly applied. The Blackfeet stock is endowed with as favorable qualities for grafting upon it the fruits of our Christian civilization, as was the Anglo-Saxon before its conversion to Christianity."[19]

Other books from McClintock on the Blackfeet followed: *Old Indian Trails, The Tragedy of the Blackfeet, Blackfoot Tepee, The Beaver Bundle, Dances of the Blackfeet, The Warrior Societies, Hand-Painted Tepees,* and *Picture Writing.* For his outstanding efforts, the U.S. Geological Survey named the first peak along the Continental Divide north of Cut Bank Pass as Mount McClintock.

While his residence remained in Pittsburgh, McClintock traveled each summer during the 1930s and 1940s to Glacier National Park. During the winter months, he was busy lecturing at both Yale and the Southwest Museum in Los Angeles. He authored several leaflets on American anthropology published by the Southwest Museum. In addition to his extensive writings on the Blackfeet, McClintock's collection of photographs depicting Blackfeet life is now stored in the two institutions and is regarded as one of the most comprehensive records of any Indian people. In the Southwest Museum's anthropology leaflet #8 published in 1937, McClintock reflected, "Forty years ago, when the old generation of primitive Blackfoot Indians was still alive, I had unusual opportunity for study and observation by living in their camps. With horses of my own, and Indian tepee and camp equipment, I took care of myself and was independent. Always had cameras and notebooks, and made records of everything as I went along. I was introduced into the innermost circles of the tribe and became intimately associated with her Life. . . . In the spring of 1896, when I first went among them, their country was still in its natural beauty and richness, before devastation by our white civilization."[20]

John G. Neihardt and Black Elk

Black Elk, like most Indians, felt his religion was superior to Christianity because he saw a lack of spirituality in the white man's world—"for want of which the world is becoming impoverished, in spite of its material wealth." Supporting his words were the wise teachings of several tribes:

> Any man who is attached to the senses and to the things of this world is one who lives in ignorance and is being consumed by the snakes which represent his own passions.
>
> Our father has made his will known to us here on this Earth, and we must always do that which he wishes if we want to walk the sacred path.

There can never be peace between nations until there is first known that true peace which is within the souls of men. This comes when men realize their oneness with the universe and all its Powers, and when they know that the Great Spirit is at its center, that all things are his works, and that this center is really everywhere, it is within each of us. He watches over and sustains all life. His breath gives life; it is from him and to him that all generations come and go.

Every step we take upon mother Earth should be done in a sacred manner; each step should be a prayer. The power of the pure and good soul is planted as a seed, and will grow in man's heart is he walks in a holy manner. The Spirit is anxious to aid all who seek him with a pure heart.

We are two-legged as the birds are because the birds leave the world with their wings, and we one day leave it in the spirit. This is one of the things we learned from the holy birds.

The breath of the Spirit is seen in the corn, since when the wind blows, the pollen falls from the tassel onto the silk surface surrounding the ear, through which the fruit becomes mature and fertile.

We should all remember how merciful God is in providing our wants, and in the same manner provide them for children, especially those who are without parents.

The old men tell us that everything they see changes a little during a man's natural lifetime, and that when change comes to any created thing it must accept it, that it cannot fight, but must change.

Our people were wise. They never neglected the young or failed to keep before them deeds done by illustrious men of the tribe. Our teachers were willing and thorough. All were quick to praise excellence without speaking a word that might break the spirit of a boy who might be less capable than others. The boy who failed at any lesson only received more lessons in care, until he was as far as he could go.

A man should rely on his own resources; the one who trains himself is ready for any emergency.

The youth who thinks first of himself and forgets the old will never prosper, nothing will go straight for him.

A man who is not industrious will always have to borrow from others, and will never have things of his own. He will be envious and tempted to steal. He will be unhappy. The energetic man is happy and pleasant to speak with; he is remembered and visited on his deathbed. But no one mourns for the lazy man.

A thrifty woman has a good tipi; all her tools are the best, so is her clothing.[21]

John G. Neihardt (1881-1973), an amateur historian and ethnographer, recorded for posterity one of the great spiritual classics of the Northern Plains, *Black Elk Speaks,* published in 1932. Neihardt was born in 1881 in Illinois and spent most of his adult life in Nebraska, where in 1921 he became the state's poet laureate.

Early on, he traveled down the Missouri River in an open boat from Fort Benton, Montana, to Sioux City, Iowa, and generated a travelogue titled *The River and I*. That experience led him to more extensive travel in the West and research for his large poetry project: a collection of five epic poems to represent the time span from the arrival of the fur traders on the Plains to the end of the Ghost Dance movement at the 1890 Wounded Knee Massacre. The poems were eventually compiled and published as *A Cycle of the West*. Research for the publication included interviewing many cavalry men and Lakota who had participated in the 1876 Battle of the Little Bighorn.

Neihardt researched the Ghost Dance movement, and in the summer of 1930 contacted an Oglala holy man named Black Elk (1863-1950) who at age thirteen had survived the Battle of the Little Bighorn. Black Elk was among the Indians who had attacked Reno from the southern end of the village.[22]

Later, as a young warrior, Black Elk survived the Wounded Knee Massacre. Neihardt and Black Elk would become close friends. Black Elk, a distant relative of Crazy Horse, gave Neihardt a Sioux name meaning "flaming rainbow," after a prominent image in one of his visions.[23]

In the spring of 1931, Neihardt spent two weeks interviewing Black Elk, the Lakota medicine man, on the Pine Ridge Reservation in South Dakota. The conversations began early after breakfast and often continued long after dark. Ben, Black Elk's son, interpreted for them, and Neihardt's daughter, Enid, acted as stenographer. Neihardt edited the transcripts of the conversations into *Black Elk Speaks.*

As Black Elk spoke, he filled his sacred pipe with the bark of the red willow. There were four ribbons hanging down from the stem of the pipe that represented the four quarters of the universe: the black ribbon represented the West and his descendants; the white ribbon for the North, which was the home of the great white cleansing wind; the red ribbon for the East, which brought the light and where the Morning Star lived to give men wisdom; and the yellow for the South where the power for summer resided.

He recollected a Sun Dance that he attended next to a river where there was a big feast and a big dance. He remembered seeing painted holy men with strips of rawhide tied into their flesh and then fastened to the top of a tree. The men would dance to the drums weighing on the rawhide strips as long as they could stand the pain or until their flesh tore loose.

Black Elk Speaks is both the recounting of a great religious vision imparted on Black Elk when he was a young man, and it is the story of his people's attempts to stem the flood of the white man—sometimes by war and sometimes by spiritual means. He possessed great spiritual abilities and experienced visions that enabled him to enter battle without fear and to also heal others. He was viewed by many to be the only surviving Oglala to understand the religious foundation of his people, but some Lakota and critics say that the book isn't totally representative of their beliefs.

Neihardt later served as professor of poetry at the University of Nebraska and as a literary editor in St. Louis, Missouri. He was a poet in residence and lecturer at the University of Missouri in Columbia from 1948 on. He died in Columbia in 1973. Some of his publications include the *Divine Enchantment*, 1900; *The River and I*, 1910; *The Song of Indian Wars*, 1925; and *Indian Tales and Others*, 1926.[24]

Circle of Harmony

From ethnographers like Catlin, Grinnell, Linderman, McClintock, and Neihardt, a better understanding of Indian religion has been gained. While Christianity and other world religions can be defined as what their followers believe in, trying to characterize the various Indian religions can be challenging. The diverse Indian religions do have a great deal in common, but using the term *religion* to define Indian spiritual beliefs is limiting. In fact, the word *religion* does not appear in any of the hundreds of languages and thousands of dialects spoken in North America. The very use of *religion* suggests that life is divided into the spiritual realm and a secular realm. This is not the case for the many aspects of Indian life. In fact, it would be unfathomable to think of their spiritual world in those terms.

For Indians, all senses bring a connection to the spirit world—there is nothing that can be seen, smelled, or touched, living or inanimate, that does not have a spirit. Their spiritual and ordinary lives are as interconnected as two strands of DNA that form a double helix. As John Lame

Deer, a Miniconjou Sioux, stated, "We Indians live in a world of symbols where the spiritual and the commonplace are one. To you, symbols are just words, spoken or written in a book. To us, they are a part of nature, part of ourselves—the earth, the sun, the wind and the rain, stones, trees, animals, even little insects like ants and grasshoppers. We try to understand them not with the head but with the heart, and we need no more than a hint to give us the meaning."[25]

Ethnographers noted that Indians had dreams and visions that served as messages or instructions that any faithful follower could expect to receive as a gift from unseen powers. The path of the ordinary person's life was illuminated by dreams. They served as a guidebook for the living, and each day they provided guidance. The dream in the Indian world was as real as the sun, the moon, and the bison.

It was not easy for the white man to understand the Indians' belief system. Everything about the Plains Indians centered on their spiritual beliefs, and all they undertook began with and was thereafter influenced by that single fact—child rearing, crafts, community relationships, warfare, philosophy, and storytelling, among others. They never built churches or composed a book of sacred writings like the Bible. They had no prayer books, hymnals, holy days, or Sabbath. Yet all they owned in every act of their lives was bound with their "religion."

Long before the American Indians settled on the Plains, their Asian ancestors' world was filled with spirits, myths, and legends. As tribes developed throughout the New World, each shaped its own spiritual worldview. For some, the birds carried messages to the gods, while rivers sang to some, and the rocks talked to others. Unlike Europe, where there were state religions, America was brimming with almost as many religions as there were Indian peoples.

The Christian world is filled with good and evil, but the Indian world is viewed in terms of balance and imbalance, harmony and disharmony. For the Plains Indian who lived in a harsh environment, it was beneficial to have tribal members who placed a premium on harmony, unselfishness, and forgiveness. Greed, at least as it is understood in materialistic terms today, was seldom present on the Plains. Next to a fine war record, charity was the basis for achieving and maintaining a high standing in the tribal community.

Just as evangelical Christians have struggled with a balance between spiritual emotion and knowledge, so have the Indians. For the Indian, good fortune came to those who acquired sacred knowledge. While the white man's knowledge often came from books, the Indian's knowledge came from supernatural forces that had helped him hunt well, farm well, raise children well, and fight well. As we will see in a later chapter, Gnostics in the early Christian church also believed that sacred knowledge was important in understanding their God.

Creation

Both Native American religions and Christianity have in common the role of the Creator, but besides that there are many differences. Indians spend little time concerned about the beginning and end of time. They have no desire to have a personal relationship with the Creator in the same manner as Christians did with Jesus.[26]

Different tribes had different names for their Creator that guided them and that they identified with: for the Crow it was Old Man Coyote and First Maker; for the Blackfeet it was Napi or Old Man; for the Sioux it was the Great Spirit or Mystery; and for the Arapaho it was the Man-Above. Many felt He dwelt in the sun and that its radiance and warmth came from Him.[27]

Religious systems included a number of minor deities: Above Person, Ground Person, and Underwater Person. The Above Person was the most important because he brought rain, while the Underwater Person brought wind. The Sioux had a total of sixteen gods in four ranking orders. They all were a personal manifestation of one supreme being who was Wakan Tanka, the Great Mystery.

Indian tribes had sacred sites that were known by oral tradition. For example, the Sioux, Cheyenne, and Arapaho had traditions of sacred locations in and near the Black Hills in South Dakota and the Bear's Lodge (Devils Tower) in Wyoming. Like Christianity, Native Americans such as the Pawnee and Arikara believed the earliest people emerged from the darkness into a lighted world. They said they came from the stars. For the Pueblo, they were led into the light by Mother Corn.[28]

The Mandan have a legend about their ancestors climbing up a vine rope from the underground to the surface of the Earth. That site was on the western bank of the Mississippi at its mouth near present-day New Orleans. They then headed up the Mississippi River and eventually the Missouri River to their present-day location in North Dakota.[29]

According to Kiowa author and Pulitzer Prize–winner N. Scott Momaday, born in 1934, "The Kiowas came one by one into the world through a hollow log. There were many more than now, but not all of them got out. There was a woman whose body was swollen up with child, and she got stuck in the log. After that, no one could get through, and that is why the Kiowas are a small tribe in number. . . . They called themselves Kwada, 'coming out.'"[30]

Anthropologist George A. Dorsey described the Wichita's story of creation that when the Earth was created it was composed of land and water that eventually separated. Darkness was everywhere. Man Never Known on Earth was the only human living, and he created all living things. He explained, "After the man and the woman were made they dreamed that things were made for them and when they woke they had the things of which they had dreamed."[31]

The Blackfeet legends related that the bison had emerged from the Earth, and if they were not treated right, they might return there. It was Old Man who armed the ancient Blackfeet with bow and arrows that were used to kill the bison. He taught his people the power of dreams. "Whatever these animals tell you to do you must do, you must obey them, as they appear to you in your sleep," he instructed. "Be guided by them. If anybody wants help, if you are alone and traveling, and cry aloud for help, your prayer will be answered. It may be either Eagles, perhaps the Buffalo, or by the Bears. Whatever animal answers your prayer, you must listen to him."[32]

The Earth with all its natural flora and fauna was viewed by the Indian with a sense of mystery. Everything that existed had a soul and every soul was interconnected. Indians believed that if they could maintain harmony among themselves and the natural world, then they could avoid imbalances that could lead to misfortunes such as sickness or accidents. For many Indian people the way to keep harmony with the animals they killed was to feed themselves and to pray to the animal's soul. It was their belief that the animal had intentionally given up its life so that it could benefit them, and they begged for forgiveness to the spirit of the animal.

A recurring theme was Mother Earth as a life host—the symbiotic relationship between human beings and animals, and animals as teachers. The plots were unpredictable but commonly included humor. A Navajo man clarified the use of humor, saying, "They are not funny stories. Many things about the story are funny, but the story is not funny. If my children hear the stories, they will grow up to be good people; if they do not hear them, they will turn out bad."[33]

In direct contrast to Genesis in the Bible where God created Adam in his own image and gave him dominion over all other creatures, Indian legends made humans no more important than any other living thing or inanimate object. In Indian rituals and stories, death is not seen as a mystery but as part of nature's normal cycle, and all creatures must pass through this part of the cycle to complete the circle of life. Jenny Leading Cloud of the Rosebud Indian Reservation explained, "We Indians think of the earth and the whole universe as a never ending circle, and in the circle, man is just another animal. The buffalo and the coyotes are our brothers; the birds, are cousins. We end our prayers with the words, all my relations—and that includes everything that grows, crawls, runs, creeps, hops, and flies."[34]

The Land

The American West is a collection of Indian homelands. Those lands were more important than time or recalling history. In the 1930s, anthropologist Ruth Underhill noted that Native Americans didn't think of themselves as possessing the land, "it is the land that possesses the people."[35] Lakota Luther Standing Bear in the 1930s said, "People in the northern Great Plains know that narrative about landscape is as necessary to their survival as water."[36]

It's not difficult to understand why Curley, a Crow Indian chief, in 1912 refused to sell any more of his land to the federal government as it attempted to decrease the holdings of Indians on the reservations. He commented:

> The soil you see is not ordinary soil—it is the dust of the blood, the flesh, and the bones of her ancestors. We fought and bled and died to keep other Indians from taking it, and we fought and bled and died helping the Whites.
>
> You will have to dig down through the surface before you can find nature's earth, as the upper portion is Crow.
>
> The land as it is, is my blood and my dead; it is consecrated; and I do not want to give up any portion of it.[37]

Often the metaphor of marriage was used to explain the deep love and devotion that Native Americans had for their land. They found themselves inseparable from it and studied every hill, spring, and tree on it. Chief Seattle explained this intimacy:

> Every part of this soil is sacred in the estimation of my people. Every hillside, every valley, every plain and grove, has been hallowed by some sad or happy event in days long vanished. Even the rocks, which seem to be dumb and dead as they swelter in the sun along the silent shore, thrill with memories of stirring events connected with

the lives of my people, and the very dust upon which you now stand responds more lovingly to their footsteps than yours, because it is rich with the blood of our ancestors, and our bare feet are conscious of the sympathetic touch.[38]

Land was equally important in the Bible where it was seen to be blessed, cursed, and redeemed. The issue of land was a central theme throughout the Scriptures as seen in the garden, the promised land, the exiles, and the return to the promised land. It's clear that land was sacred in God's eyes: "Cursed is anyone who moves their neighbor's boundary stone." (Deut. 27:17a).[39]

One reason many young native people have found it difficult to succeed off the reservation is their strong connection to home. They possess a strong sense of belonging to the greater community. When an Indian converted to Christianity and rejected his traditional tribal religion, he appeared to the community as rejecting them. It made it very challenging for native individuals to stand against familial pressure and thus make a unilateral decision for Christ.

Society

Besides vision cults, many tribes developed animal clans or societies that occasionally transcended tribal lines. The clan could be made up of unrelated families, although they were considered members of the same guiding spirit, or totem—from the Ojibwa term *odem*—which signified the mystic bond between the spirit, the place, and the people. Even though they were not blood related, members of the same clan were forbidden to intermarry, even if they were from different tribes. Certain traits characterized a clan. For instance, among the Cheyenne, those who joined the clan called the Mouse People were thought to be very attentive to things in their immediate vicinity but blind to the big picture of life. Even if members of the tribe did not belong to a specific animal clan, they often forged special relationships with animal spirits that determined their role in society. Many of the animals had some form of wisdom or craft. They were not gods, but they did have power.[40]

Mary Standing Soldier achieved almost legendary status for healing her people who were injured in battles against the U.S. cavalry during the nineteenth century. The Cheyenne woman carried the claws of a wild bear that she had fought off single-handedly as a girl. When helping those in need on the battlefield, she reputedly growled like the bear as she removed bullets from wounded warriors and gave them the strength to carry on. One of her descendants reportedly said that when she got older, she took on the appearance of the bear, developing hair all over her body.[41]

Out of time

Up until the end of the Dark Ages in Europe, the average citizen, especially in rural areas, had only a vague concept of time. That all changed with the invention of the clock. Likewise, before the arrival of Europeans who were obsessed with time—past, present, and future—Native Americans lived an integrated spirituality that connected every moment between the past and present. Heaven, earth, and hell were all to be experienced both now and later, but they enjoyed the present and didn't worry about the future. Likewise, the Christian God also lives out of time and can see past, present, and future at once. In 1917, Redbird Smith, chief of the Keetoowah Nighthawk, who is credited for reviving Cherokee religion and tradition, said this about the future: "This religion does not teach me to concern myself of the life that shall be after this, but it does teach me to be concerned with what my everyday life should be. The Fires kept burning are merely the greater Fire, the greater Light, the Great Spirit. I realize now as never before it is not only for the Cherokees but for all mankind."[42]

The native person's priority was what they were doing right now. They had a circular view of time, as opposed to the Western's linear one. For the Westerner, time is like a flat line and moves from one end to the other. Time is separated into the past, present, and future. But to Native Americans, everything is eternally connected because time is a continuous, unbroken circle. In the nineteenth century, white men didn't wear wristwatches but carried pocket watches. Some Plains Indians said, "White man carries his God in his pocket," because he never did anything without consulting it.[43]

The circle in Native American religion is a symbol for understanding harmony and their relationship to everything else. Canadian Cree theologian Stan McKay explained it this way: "There are many teachings in the aboriginal North American nations that use the symbol of the circle. It is the symbol for the inclusive caring community, where individuals are respected and interdependence is recognized. In the wider perspective it symbolizes the natural order of creation in which human beings are part of the whole circle of life. Aboriginal spiritual teachers speak of the reestablishment of the balance between human beings and the whole of creation, as a mending of the hoop."[44]

The hoop or circle that symbolizes life is found in nearly all Native American tribes. It's a powerful representation of the earth, life, seasons, and cycles of maturity, among others. Having been found in some of the most ancient petroglyphs, the circle was the template for the Sun Dance, pow wow, Native American church, and Ghost Dance.

Gift Giving

One of the hallmarks of Native American societies was the sense of hospitality. Friends and relatives constantly visited each other, and no one went away from a visit hungry. Anthropologist Carl Starkloff noted, "On reading the various accounts and monographs by explorers and anthropologists, what strikes one is the almost universal hospitality shown by Indian tribes, especially to their White visitors. It is quite remarkable as described in David Bushnell's writings about explorers and missionaries among the Siouan, Algonquian, and Caddoan tribes west of the Mississippi. . . ."[45] Even though the land was considered the tribes' sacred inheritance, before the middle of the nineteenth century they shared it with white settlers who they regarded as special guests.

Throughout North America, it is a cultural norm for Native Americans to have "giveaways." In the Northwest it is called a potlatch. The items may have personal value or not and might include horses, rifles, blankets, baskets, money, or other gifts. Sometimes even sacred items such as drums or eagle feathers are gifted. In contrast to modern American society, the gifts are given by the person who is being honored and not to them.[46]

In general, Indians were not materialistic and therefore gathering wealth was not important. For example, the Cherokee understood "sufficient" to be enough, while for the white man, "more" was the goal. Indians gained respect by redistributing their wealth and not by hoarding it.[47]

U.S. Senator Henry Dawes—famous, or infamous, for the reservation Allotment Act of 1887—did not take to heart what Jesus said in Matthew 6:24, "No one can serve two masters," in regard to the love of Jesus and the love of money. After touring Indian Territory in 1887, Dawes described the problem of the Cherokee: "The head chief told us that there was not a family in the whole nation that had not a home of its own. There is not a pauper in that nation, and the nation does not owe a dollar. It built its own capital . . . and built its schools and hospitals. Yet the defect of the system was apparent. They have got as far as they can go, because they hold their land in common. . . . There is no selfishness, which is at the bottom of civilization. Until these people will consent to give up their lands, and divide them among their citizens so that each can own the land he cultivates, they will not make much progress."[48]

Senator Dawes' values of individualism, materialism, and selfishness that represented America at the time were not those of Native Americans. In fact, the Indians emphasized not collecting too many material possessions so as to avoid becoming greedy. They felt that it was demonstrating ingratitude toward their Creator when they took more than they needed. They believed this freed them from worry and brought harmony to their world.

Death and Afterlife

In the Indians' mind, animals never died, and they treated their spirits with upmost respect, believing that someday their prey would return to provide food, clothing, and other necessities as they had done previously—another example of completing the circle of life. As an Iglulingmiut hunter of the Far North explained, "The greatest peril of life lies in the fact that human food consists entirely of souls. All the creatures that we have to kill and eat, all those that we have to strike down and destroy to make clothes for ourselves, have souls, souls that do not perish with the body. The spiritual duty of the hunter was to appease those souls lest they should revenge themselves on us for taking away their bodies."[49]

The afterlife was as important to the Indian as all the ceremonies he undertook while living. Like Christians, they believed in the immortality of the soul. Some dreams led to the understanding of divisions of the afterlife into different ghost countries. However, the view of the world of the dead differed widely among tribes. While some viewed it as a wonderful place, a happy hunting ground, others, like the Blackfeet and Gros Ventre, imagined it as a darker place of ghostly shadows living an existence full of melancholy. In an interview with Frank Linderman, Plenty Coups, chief of the Crow, expressed his opinion on life after death, saying, "I am old and am living in an unnatural life. I know that I am standing on the brink of the life that nobody knows about, and I am anxious to go to my Father, Ah-badt-dadt-deah, to live again as men were intended to live, even on this world."[50]

Since their God was eternal, He had no beginning and no end. Thus mankind was provided with a never-ending life after death. Most Indians believed that when a man died, his soul left the body after his last breath unless the person had been hanged. Thus they feared the justice often imparted by the white man who often made a public spectacle of lynching "deserving" individuals.

All Indians who died not scalped and not strangled went immediately to heaven with the same personality and emotions they had on Earth. Their physical abnormalities that they had in this life remained with them into eternity. Like the Christian God, their God and His world in the afterlife lived out of time. Thus they remained at the age they were when they entered eternity. If they died quickly by wound or disease, the maladies did not remain with them in the afterlife. Since they wanted to avoid their enemies—especially the white man—every warrior attempted to reduce the likelihood of running into them in the afterlife by scalping as many as possible on Earth. Their ghosts then had to live on ground level.

For a warrior killed in battle but not mutilated further, his soul had no sign of the wound that actually killed him. However, the soul after death was disfigured by every mutilation inflicted on the body before death. This explains the rationale behind shooting arrows into an unscalped body. It tormented an enemy for eternity.

The white man had a hard time reconciling the Indians' belief that the afterlife was a happy place with their need at the same time of seeking revenge on their enemies. Colonel Richard Dodge concluded, "His belief as to the effect on the soul of certain previous conditions of life and death are, according to his ideas, solidly founded on reason. His belief in the perfect happiness of his Paradise is purely a matter of faith."[51]

Indians had no hell for sinners. Since there was no punishment for misdeeds by children, they grew up in an environment of love that was free from fear of punishment or condemnation from their parents or spiritual leaders. Luther Standing Bear, a Sioux born in 1868, wrote:

> The Indian loved to worship. From birth to death, he revered his surroundings. He considered himself born in the luxurious lap of Mother Earth, and no place was to him humble. There was nothing between him and the Big Holy (Wakan Tanka). The contact was immediate and personal, and the blessings of Wakan Tanka flowed over the Indian like rain showered from the sky. Wakan Tanka was not aloof, apart, and ever-seeking to quell evil forces. He did not punish the animals and the birds, and likewise, he did not punish man. He was not a punishing god. For there was never a question as to the supremacy of an evil power over and above the power of Good. There was but one ruling power, and that was Good.[52]

Vine Deloria, Jr. (1933-2005) was a leading Native American scholar whose writings and teachings are perhaps some of the finest in comparing Native American and Christian religions. He authored many acclaimed books on evolution and creationism, including *Red Earth White Lies, Spirit and Reason,* and *Custer Died for Your Sins. God is Red* is perhaps the finest work on native religious views, and *Time* magazine appropriately named Deloria as one of the greatest religious thinkers of the twentieth century.[53]

As noted by Deloria, Indian tribal religions had an absence of the fear of death. Many Indians simply saw the next life as a continuation of the present existence, and that the souls of some people remained in various places where they had died or suffered traumatic events. Indians visiting the Sand Creek location, where the Cheyenne were massacred by Colonel Chivington and his troops, said that they could hear the cries of the women and children who were still living at the site.[54]

Indians believed that, when they died, their bodies turned to dust, which nourished the plants and animals that fed the next generation of people. With their ancestors still spiritually alive in the land, they were fearful that the whites would not honor their ancestors in the appropriate manner. This was a fundamental reason why Indians resisted the white man's invasion of their tribal lands. Young Chief Joseph, the famed Nez Perce leader, recalled the words of his dying father: "My son, my body is returning to my mother earth, and my spirit is going very soon to see the Great Spirit Chief. When I am gone, think of your country. You are the chief of these people. They look to you to guide them. Always remember that your father never sold his country. You must stop your ears whenever you are asked to sign a treaty selling your home. A few more years and the white men will be all around you. They have their eyes on this land. My son, never forget my dying words. This country holds your father's body. Never sell the bones of your father and your mother."[55]

While Christians focused on a personal, individual relationship with Jesus, Indians much more emphasized the integrity of tribal existence in the present, so there was no fear of death. Many tribal religions had death songs, which allowed white men to better understand their view. The song was sung as a man faced death and often taunted his enemies. Most often the song was a statement by the individual to summarize his life on Earth. Any emphasis on the individual was in the context of placing importance on his life as a tribal member. There was no confession of sins or remorse for failures. It was a goal of Indian religion to actually produce people who had no fear of death. The core concern was for the integrity of the communal life, which minimized a sense of personal identity.

In general, there was no overwhelming fixation on the afterlife, and most believed that it would be just a continuation of their experience they had on Earth. Chief Seattle remarked that death is merely a changing of worlds. Many of the tribes employed various means of burial, with almost all of them aiming at the return of the body to earth.[56]

In 1815, Big Elk, an Omaha chief, spoke at the death of Black Buffalo, a fellow Omaha, where he counseled his fellow chiefs, "Do not grieve. Misfortunes will happen to the wisest and best of men. Death will come, and always out of season. It is the command of the Great Spirit, and all nations and people must obey. What is past and cannot be prevented should not be grieved for. . . . Misfortunes do not flourish particularly in our path. They grow everywhere."[57]

The Indians understood that the spirit never died because there is no beginning or end to a circle or spirit.

A Collision of Religions

At first, Native Americans wanted to believe and make friends with the white people and accept their new religion. However, the whites seemed unable to communicate effectively their culture that was so foreign to the Indians. Brule Chief Spotted Tail encouraged his people to accept Christianity, but soon he became disillusioned with its contradictions:

> I am bothered what to believe. Some years ago, a good man, as I think, came to us. He talked me out of all my old faith. And after a while, thinking that he must know more of these matters than an ignorant Indian, I joined his church and became a Methodist. After a while he went away. Another man came and talked and I became a Baptist; then another came and talked and I became a Presbyterian. Now another one has come and wants me to be an Episcopalian. What do you think of it?
>
> All these people tell different stories, and each wants me to believe that his special way is the only way to be good and save my soul. I have about made up my mind that either they all lie, or that they don't know any more about it than I did at first. I've always believed in the Great Spirit, and worshiped him in my own way. These people don't seem to want to change my belief in the Great Spirit, but to

change my way of talking to him. White men have education and books, and ought to know what to do, but hardly any two of them agree on what should be done.[58]

In Indian religion, there is no personal relationship between a deity and the individual. Instead, it is a covenant between the community and a particular God. Ceremonies of the community are the chief characteristic of their religious activity. They are very interdependent on each other. Harvey Cox noted in his book *The Secular City* that "tribal man is hardly a personal 'self' in our modern sense of the word. He does not so much live in a tribe; the tribe lives in him. He is the tribe's subjective expression."[59]

Joining a tribal religion by agreeing to its doctrines is impossible. Indians are not concerned about what an outsider believes. There is no separate religious standard of behavior outside the requirements of ceremonies. As Deloria stated, "The customs of the tribe and the religious responsibilities to the group are practically identical, and the existence of two sets of values side-by-side is unthinkable."[60]

Chief Joseph commented on why he had banned missionaries from their lands. "They will teach us to quarrel about God," he said, "as Catholics and Protestants do on the Nez Perce reservation [in Idaho] and other places. We do not want to do that. We may quarrel with men sometimes about things on earth, but we'd never quarrel about the Great Spirit. We do not want to learn that."[61]

Another prominent Indian spokesman who expressed his frustration over bickering Christians was Red Jacket, the great Seneca orator. He observed, "We say there is but one way to worship and serve the Great Spirit. If there is but one religion, why do you white people differ so much about it? Why not all agree, as you can all read the book?"[62] He pointed out that whether Indian or white, religion was handed down by father to son. His religion taught to love each other and to get along. Quarreling about religion never occurred because religion was a private matter between the Great Spirit and each man. That was quite a contrast to Christianity, where religious wars had taken place in Europe and Asia for centuries. Among Indians, religious wars were avoided because of the recognition that other tribes had special powers and medicines given to them that precluded an exclusive franchise being issued to any one group of people.

In comparing Native American religious reality with modern Euro-American religious reality, a number of differences are apparent. For Native Americans, truth comes by appreciating how others have lived. This is achieved primarily through stories and examples that demonstrate how one should live. Truth is closely related to experience. Words are most powerful when spoken rather than written. The verbal story tries to relate truths, as do ceremonies and traditions. No one questions these truths because explaining them tends to weaken their power and makes the words less believable. In contrast, Christians understand truth by learning what others have believed through doctrines and laws. Learning them teaches one how to live, and thus truth may be unrelated to experience. Words are most powerful when written, and stories are for illustration.[63]

In the nineteenth century, it became clear to the U.S. government and the American people that the Indian tribes could not be broken politically until they had been destroyed religiously. The best way to destroy their religion was to ban their ceremonies on the reservations, which were controlled by missionaries and political patronage appointees. This led to a steady decline in the influence of traditional leaders and also in the religious solidarity of the people. We will look next at Native American rituals and ceremonies. Destroying the physical and spiritual food of a race is the most effective method of ethnic cleansing.

CHAPTER TEN

Smoking to the Spirit of the Buffalo: Plains Indian Ceremonies and Rituals

The purpose of our ceremonies is not entertainment, but attainment. The attainment of the Balanced Life. Our dramas, our songs, and our dances are not performed for fun as they might be in the white man's world; they are more than that; they are the very essence of our lives.
—A TEWA INDIAN

The Okipa ceremony includes all parts of the creation. Women play a significant role, because women are a part of the creation story. Man is no better than woman, and woman is not better than man. We are equal in the creation of the Great Spirit.
—CEDRIC RED FEATHER, MANDAN

Indian ceremonies have an underlying theme of gratitude expressed by human beings on behalf of all forms of life. As Vine Deloria Jr. noted, "They act to complete and renew the entire and complete cycle of life, ultimately including the whole cosmos present in its specific realizations, so that in the last analysis one might describe ceremonials as the cosmos becoming thankfully aware of itself."[1]

A pipe or a pair of moccasins that may appear trivial or mundane to a non-Indian's eyes, may have enormous spiritual significance to an Indian. A carving or a painting that the white observer considers ornamental art may be part of a sacred process. A dance that might be viewed as purely recreational could have a profound spiritual meaning.

Native Americans understood that one of the reasons they were placed on Earth was to restore harmony in practical ways. Their ceremonies required not only symbolic acts but also practical restitution and restoration. One example of the ways this was achieved was through the ancient Cherokee Propitiation and Cementation Ceremony that occurred each fall. Anyone with a grievance against another tribal member was required to participate in the ceremony.

With a fire blazing, a holy man said prayers during the ceremony. Family and friends on each side of the dispute would face each other and give an account of their grievances. They all would then go to the fire and pray for the strength to forgive. The two would then remove their clothes and exchange them. Thereafter, they spoke words of forgiveness and vowed never to bring the issue up again. A pipe was passed back and forth between all those who participated. They concluded the ceremony by exchanging gifts, and they prepared a great feast for the entire community.[2]

The Sun Dance

The quintessential Indian ritual for those tribes living west of the Missouri River was the Sun Dance, which gained popularity in the early 1800s and was derived from the ancient ceremonies of many different tribes. Almost every Indian ethnographer noted in great detail the different aspects of the ceremony. By the summer of 1910, Dr. James Walker on the Pine Ridge Reservation in South Dakota was starting to write his monograph on the Sun Dance. He augmented his written word with twenty-five songs recorded on phonographic cylinders.[3]

One of Walker's biggest supporters, Clark Wissler, an anthropologist from the American Museum of Natural History, had suggested that the young doctor focus his studies on the Sun Dance and other ceremonies. On February 14, 1911, Wissler cautioned Walker about documenting an overly ideal description of the Sun Dance:

> There can be little doubt that the Sun Dance was the one great unifying ceremony of the Plains Indians toward which all other ceremonial activities converged. . . . In the statement of procedure you are entirely dependent on your informants and should endeavor to render the statements of Indians with fidelity. When there are important disagreements, it may be well to give each side a place in your

narrative. Thus, a student will feel that he is himself weighing the evidence rather than simply taking your word for it. . . .

The result in the end will be a complete interpretation: yours and those of your informants. You are right in that mythology furnishes the best basis for such interpretations, it being to these practices what the Bible is to those of the Christian religion. In our work it is of the utmost importance to reflect the most intelligent Indian interpretations. The investigator owes us his last word as the case appears to his practised vision.[4]

Wissler's cautionary note should be taken into account for anyone who reads a description of the Sun Dance or other ceremonies and testimonials. As might be expected, every author gives his or her particular take. Walker was very much a man of his time and believed that the Lakota were one of the last groups of primitive humans in America. Many whites still believed in the stereotype of the noble savage in which human culture and society became understood as a triumph of the strong over the weak and the more developed over the most primitive—social Darwinism.

Walker explained the importance of ceremonies that were governed by the shamans: "The Oglalas were very religious, but not at all pious. They did not worship any thing. By sacrifices and ceremonies they propitiated their Gods to secure their aid, or placated them to appease their anger. . . . One or more of the Oglala Gods is ever present, therefore it behooves an Oglala to avoid offense by conduct in accord with the ceremonies prescribed by the shamans."[5]

Little Wound, chief of the Oglala, explained further:

The Oglalas have many dances and they are all ceremonies and must be done according to the form adopted by the shamans. . . . They have dances for war and for peace; for victory and defeat; for chase and for ripe fruits; for enjoyment and for mourning; for going away and for returning; for warriors and for all the people; for the societies and for individuals; for men and for women; for widows and for maidens; for shamans. . . . The sacred dances are the Dance for the Dead, the Scalp Dance, the Holy Dance, and the Sun Dance. . . . Each dance has it's songs so that when the songs are heard, it may be known what dance is danced. The music of the songs is different for each dance. . . . The Sun Dance has twenty-four songs, four of these must be sung each time the Sun Dance is danced. . . .[6]

The emergence of the Sun Dance coincided with the acquisition of the horse from the Spanish in what is now New Mexico, which led to the Golden Age of the Plains Indians, who survived by the unpredictable means of hunting on horseback and gathering on foot. The horse allowed a better means to hunt bison in the summer. The ceremony was practiced by the Arapaho, Arikara, Assiniboine, Cheyenne, Crow, Gros Ventre, Hidatsa, Sioux, Plains Cree, Plains Ojibwa, Sarsi, Omaha, Ponca, Ute, Shoshone, Kiowa, and the three Blackfoot tribes, among others. As with most tribal matters, the Sun Dance varied somewhat among tribes, but for all of them it was the ultimate ceremony for sacrifice and thanksgiving.

Vast tribal assemblies came together in late spring or early summer for the hunt, and the Sun Dance was the prominent ceremony. It was held at the part of the month when the moon was full because they believed the eternal light of the Creator was shining down upon the whole world. They wore their finest clothing and rode their best horses. Friendship and kindness was in everyone's heart. Some believe it was so named from gazing at the sun while dancing during the ritual. Very common among the Sioux, Cheyenne, and Arapaho, the Sun Dance was not centered around worshipping the sun, but affirming the unity of the tribe and its close relationship with supernatural powers that had brought forth plenty in the past. By respecting these powers, a bison hunter could expect success.

The holy men Little Wound, American Horse, and Lone Star collectively explained:

> The Sun Dance is the greatest ceremony of the Oglalas. It is a sacred ceremony in which all the people have a part. It must be done in a ceremonial camp. It must be conducted by a shaman who knows all the customs of the people. He must know all the secret things of the shamans. . . .
>
> The ceremony of the Sun Dance is in four parts. One part for the dancer and the people to prepare for the dance; one part to gather at the place for the dance; one part for the camp and the ceremonies before the dance; the last part for the Sun Dance. . . .
>
> If one wishes to become a shaman of the highest order, he should dance the Sun Dance suspended from the pole so that his feet will not touch the ground . . . if one has scars on his breast or his back that show that he has danced the Sun Dance, no Oglala will doubt his word. He is eligible for leadership of the war party or for

chieftainship. . . . The ceremony of the Sun Dance may embrace all the ceremonies of any kind that are relative to the Gods. . . .[7]

Almost every tribe shared the basics of the Sun Dance. An affluent member sponsored the building of a large camp and the feasts associated with the gathering. Besides that expense, the patron also was committed to long periods of fasting and praying. Often, but not always, the patron was someone who had recently lost a loved one and wanted to make sacrifices in the memory of that person. The Crow commonly performed the dance as a way of gaining revenge against another tribe who had killed a close relative.[8]

Long before the ceremony, word was spread throughout the area of the time and location of the festivities. A special Sun Dance bundle was in the care of the shaman who organized the event. He conducted the entire impressive ritual. The shaman and the patron spent weeks prior to the ceremony sharing the sponsor's personal spiritual struggles and working out practical details of the celebrations.

Lasting more than eight days, the ceremony started with the building of the special camp, which usually took about four days. A center pole, the Sun Pole, was the focal point of the camp, and an extensive ritual accompanied its raising. Some were chosen to find a suitable tree, which was treated like an enemy, and after one was chosen, the entire camp rode out to count coup on the tree—striking it as a wooden enemy warrior. The top of the tree was left forked after it was cut down and the bark stripped so that ceremonial objects such as a bison skull or medicine objects could be hung from it during the ceremony. The Sioux always used the cottonwood tree because they considered it sacred. When there was a light breeze, the voice of the cottonwood tree could be heard offering prayers for the men and for all things to the Great Spirit. As soon as the tree had been cut, all involved began a fast that continued until the ceremony was over, usually three to four days later. The circular camp was ringed by tipis, and after the pole was raised in the center, the dance could begin.

Before the Sun Dance, the great warriors gave a public dramatization of their military exploits. The young braves then entered the lodge—purified and painted in special ways by their sponsors. Then the whoop of the dance and the beat of the drums rang out as participants danced in place, gazing toward the sun or the sacred medicine bundle at the top of the pole. Several days of dancing exhausted some, and they collapsed. They were dragged into the shade where they received powerful visions.

Some individuals submitted themselves to self-torture as a way of gaining sympathy from the spirits and as a demonstration of thanksgiving for their good fortune. The skin of their chest was pierced with a knife and two wooden skewers inserted through their skin. Lines of bison hide hanging from the top of the Sun Pole were then tied to the skewers. Next, participants flung themselves backward with enough force to free themselves. The Ute, Shoshone, Arapaho, and Kiowa dancers did not participate in physical torture in their Sun Dance.

The costumes were fairly standardized, with wreaths of sage placed on the head. Tied to each wrist was a special eagle whistle, and a skirt of painted hide reached from the waist to the ankles. Stunning quill feathers were often worn on the back of the dancer's head. The noise made by the eagle bone whistles was believed to be heard by the Spirit, and each was painted with red, green, blue, and yellow dots and lines that symbolized the outstanding perception of the eagle.

Toward the end of the Sun Dance, time was reserved for those who wished to make public gifts to the poor or to reward someone for kindness. Occasionally, the chiefs presented new names to men who had excelled in battle, and new chiefs were selected to replace those who had either been killed in battle or were too old to continue their role.

After the conclusion of the Sun Dance, sacred objects were wrapped up and taken home by their keepers until the next ceremony in a year. However, the lodge and all the sacred bundle offerings were left behind for the weather to dispose of over the forthcoming months.

Eventually, the U.S. government banned the ceremony between 1904 and 1935—a milder form has been permitted since then. Indians felt the white man misunderstood the intent of the Sun Dance, which to them was a religious right. Sioux John Lame Deer explained, "Many white men think of it as an initiation into manhood, or a way to prove one's courage, but that is wrong. The Sun Dance is a prayer and sacrifice." Black Elk expressed the spiritual importance of the torture, saying, "As we thus break loose, it is as if we were being freed from the bonds of the flesh." A better term for the Sun Dance might be a *dance in the sun*.[9]

The inspiration for the Sun Dance may very well be the Mandan Okipa ceremony, which had been undertaken for centuries before 1800. One scholar called it "without question, the most elaborate, complex, and symbolic ceremony performed on the Northern Plains."[10] According to Pulitzer Prize winner, Elizabeth A. Fenn, "So compelling was the Okipa that it may well have shaped the development of the famed Sun Dance among other

Plains peoples." She continued, "Scholars have yet to determine the precise connections between the Okipa and the various iterations of the Sun Dance as performed by Plains tribes, but most acknowledged the deep resonance between some aspects of the events. The most obvious similarities are the intense physical suffering that forms a part of both ceremonies. The extent of this personal sacrifice—usually piercing and suspension from the flesh of the chest—varies from one Sun Dance to the next, and some peoples did not include it."[11]

The Okipa is a fine example of the importance of ceremonies to the Plains Indians. They acted like an anchor—much like most religious traditions—in a life that was full of change and identity crisis.

The Power of Storytelling and Animals

The Old Testament of the Bible dates creation to around 6000 BCE. Through modern scientific measurements, we know that is not the case. Indian creation legends don't put a time on creation, and it's uncertain how long these stories have been around. They do share some similarities with those from Siberia, which would make them at least tens of thousands of years old. As migration occurred from Alaska southward throughout the Americas, individual tribes created their own specific tales. So from the northeastern forest dwellers came versions of stories with arctic hare and wolf; from the farmers of the southern tribes came legends of corn maidens and sacred mountains; and from the Pacific and Atlantic coastal tribes came stories of aquatic animals, seabirds, and ocean monsters. A special time to tell these stories was around a warm fire on a cold winter night. The next chapter will provide a glimpse of Indian myths and legends.

The stories were made even more special when they were preceded by special rites. For example, before starting his stories, a Cheyenne medicine man would smooth the ground and pass his hands over his body with brushing motions. In other cultures, listeners were expected to present gifts to the narrator. The group would hear stories of the workings of supernatural powers and the spirits of clever animals—ravens, coyotes, raccoons, foxes, beavers, blue jays, and spiders—who spoke the language of the people. Sometimes animals were friends and helpers, sometimes troublemakers, and other times a combination of the two. The most frequently mentioned animal was the coyote, universally respected across western North America for its remarkable cunning and supreme ability to adapt to all different environments—on the prairie, in the woodland, in the mountains, and in the desert. In his book *Coyote America,* Dan Flores chronicled the history and spirituality of this highly successful survivor that is today living in every state except Hawaii.

In dealing with day-to-day real life, Indians appealed to animals common to the area in which they lived. For the person who understood and respected the power of every animal from the tiny butterfly to the massive bison, special powers or medicines could be received by them. Some warriors painted their bodies with butterfly symbols intended to invoke the insect's power to dodge arrows and bullets from their enemies.

Rituals were also important during a hunt. Before attacking bison, Omaha hunters would make three ceremonial stops. Right before or after killing the animal, it was customary to speak or sing words of respect to it. The hunter was relaying to the animal's spirit that the killing was done out of need and not out of greed. In addition, after the first animal of the hunting season was killed, villages held special ceremonies with the intent of convincing the soul of the animal not to speak unkindly about the hunters to the rest of the animal spirits so as not to discourage them from coming.

Often the placating of spiritual powers began with an animal-calling ceremony prior to the hunt. Before bison hunting season, the Plains Indians sang songs and displayed fetishes such as stones shaped like bison heads to entice the animals into their hunting grounds. The Mandan staged extravagant and exhaustive bison-calling dances. In 1832, George Catlin witnessed and described one of these ceremonies in a Mandan village along the upper Missouri River:

> The chief issues his order to his runners or criers, who proclaim it through the village—and in a few minutes the dance begins. About 10 or 15 Mandans at a time join in the dance, each one with the skin of the buffalo's head (or mask) with the horns on, placed over his head, and in his hand his favorite bow or lance. Lookers-on stand ready with masks on their heads, and weapons in hand, to take the place of each one as he becomes fatigued and jumps out of the ring. During this time of general excitement, spies or 'lookers' are kept on the Hills in the neighborhood of the village, who, when they discover buffalo in sight, give the appropriate signal, by 'throwing their robes,' which is instantly seen in the village and understood by the whole tribe. At this joyful intelligence, there is a shout of thanks to the Great Spirit.[12]

Besides being hunters, certain tribes, especially those that lived near rivers, supplemented their diets by farming. They also developed ceremonies to show their appreciation for a bountiful harvest. Some of these ceremonies lasted a number of days and were accompanied by fasting and dietary restrictions. Songs and dances gave praise to the spirits of the harvest. They believed this would ensure harmony with nature and continued sun and rain at the appropriate times so that the seeds could sprout and thrive.

Others painted their faces with marks resembling bear claw scratches to bestow special strengths and wisdom when entering battle. The bear was believed to be invulnerable to other animals, giving it the power to fend off most of the bullets and arrows shot at it. Many tribes, including the Sioux and Chippewa, believed that bear power could cure illness, and medicine men would often dress as a bear when trying to heal the sick. The bear was sacred, but provoking its spirit could lead to harm. Apache hunters avoided killing bears or even touching their carcasses because of the bad luck it could bring them.

The wolf symbolized craft in war. Indian scouts wore wolf skins while they were on a war party, and in Indian sign language the gesture for a scout was the sign for the wolf. The animal was highly respected and was regarded as a reliable ally. The wolf sometimes even talked, explaining where the enemy was lurking.

Birds were also sacred animals, believed to carry prayers to the sky spirits and return from them with blessings of power and instruction on how to live an earthly life. Thus, the bird was a symbol of the soul and intermediary to the gods. No bird was more revered than the eagle. Wearing eagle feathers into battle was believed by the Plains warriors to bring blessings from the eagle in the form of endurance, quickness, ferocity, and sharpness of sight.

In some Indian tribes, the killing of eagles was outlawed because they were revered as masters of the air. This led to difficulty acquiring eagle feathers for headdresses and other uses. Legend has it that an Iroquois warrior obtained eagle feathers by lying down in a trench and covering himself with brush. Another warrior would place bait on top of him so the eagle would be attracted. When the eagle swooped down for the bait, the hiding warrior would grab the revered bird and pluck several feathers. Eagles flew high in the sky where the air was pure and the Great Spirit lived. Those on the earth who wanted to communicate with the Great Spirit often called on the eagle spirit to be their messenger.

Hawks, owls, ravens, and magpies also exemplified courage and wisdom. The birds interacted with people, telling them of future events, leading them to game, advising them of danger, and recommending courses of action. Various parts of birds often found their way into medicine bundles.

The animal that was closest to the Great Spirit on the Plains was the bison. The Plains Indian obtained food, clothing, shelter, and tools from the bison and prayed directly to it in thanks for all that it provided for them. The bison was seen as another intermediary between the Indian and the Great Spirit.

In a Sioux legend, their sacred peace pipe was given to them as a gift from White Buffalo Calf Woman, and after she taught them how to use it, she transformed herself into a white bison calf. All life, spiritual and material, was symbolically contained within the bison. The Blackfeet called the bison *Ni-ai,* which meant "my shelter and my protection." The Kiowa people of the Southern Plains sacrificed a bison calf to honor the power of the sun. Parts of the calf were then used for healing ceremonies and also worship.[13]

An animal's spirit contained so much power that Indians would decorate their tools and weapons with the fetish, a war emblem of that power. The Crow and Blackfoot covered their arrows with rattlesnake skins, which gave them the ability to strike with the swiftness of a rattlesnake. Great Plains hunters braided bison hair ropes around their necks to communicate with the spirit of their prey and secure the bison's cooperation in the hunt.

Medicine Bundles

Critical to the spiritual life of the Great Plains Indian was a collection of spiritually charged items known as a medicine bundle. Each bundle contained a number of charms such as beads, stones, dried herbs, claws, teeth, or other parts of animals that were wrapped in a pouch made from the skin of the creature with whom the bundle's owner had established a special relationship. The special relationship was often realized by the owner during a vision or dream. A young man who had a vision of a bison would construct his bundle out of bison skin. In Crow tradition, if a warrior dreamed of the moon, he had to include an owl skin in his bundle because the owl was considered the moon's representative. Likewise, if he dreamed of water, he included the skin of an otter—leader of the water animals. There were certain taboos related to the bundles. For instance, the owner of a beaver bundle could not show fear of water, the beaver's favorite environment.

Plenty Coups described the medicine bundle:

A medicine bundle contains the medicine or talisman of its possessor. Often the skin and the stuffed head of an animal as large as a wolf is used. Sometimes, however, the bundles are small, containing the skin, claws, teeth, or heads of lesser creatures, depending wholly upon what animal or bird offered "help" to the dreamer. The medicine bundle is of first importance, the possessor believing implicitly that the superlative power of the animal or bird that offered aid in his dream is always at hand and at his service when he is in need. The contents of these bundles are secret and sacred to the Indian.[14]

Ethnologist William Wildschut concluded that it was impossible to classify the many different Crow Indian bundles on either similar contents or functions. He did divide them into the following meaningful categories:

1. Sun Dance Bundles. These were the only individually owned bundles employed in a ceremony in which the entire tribe participated and were considered the principal war medicine bundle of the Crow—although they were seldom taken on war parties.
2. War Medicine Bundles. These accompanied the Indians during warfare and horse stealing. There were many varieties because they contained the material representations of the original maker's vision.
3. Shields. These were painted and decorated and were viewed as important or as medicines. Some have even had the power to predict the outcome of a raid or battle.
4. Skull Medicine Bundles. These featured the human skull as the principal article and were used for many purposes. They were often buried with their owners.
5. Rock Medicine Bundles. These contained sacred rocks that were used as war medicines.
6. Medicine Pipe Bundles. These contained pipe stems or stems and bowls. They were used either in the Medicine Pipe Ceremony or by the leaders on war expeditions.
7. Love Medicine Bundles. These contained sacred objects that have the power to attract members of the opposite sex.
8. Witchcraft Bundles. With great secrecy and rarely used, witchcraft or revenge bundles were created with the intent to harm personal enemies of their owners.
9. Healing Medicine Bundles. These contained the articles that were used in healing by the medicine man.

10. Hunting Medicine Bundles. These were created to bring success in hunting for bison and other animals.[15]

While sacred, the bundles—like many other rites and ceremonies—were bought and sold among individuals. The purchase of a bundle was expensive and involved the transfer of knowledge, including songs, stories, and traditions.

Vision Quests

Many young Indian men and some Indian women—some as early as age nine—went on vision quests, seeking the animal spirit that would become their lifelong helper. Going for a vision was responding to the Great Spirit who was calling them to reflection and service just as God called Abraham and blessed him and ordered that he might be a blessing to others (Genesis 12:1-3). Away from the village and alone in nature, the seeker would fast, use other forms of deprivation, and pray for guidance and instruction from the spirits. Usually the area of the vision-seeking was on a hill or mountainside so as to be closer to the One Above—the more rugged and mysterious the country, the better. These visions provided the all-powerful medicine believed necessary by every young man before going to war.

Those Indians who connected with the same animal during their vision quest often organized into cults with special rituals and responsibilities. There were an array of different cults that were dedicated to a diverse group of animals, including wolves, bison, bear, deer, mountain sheep, dogs, rabbits, and horses.

The religious life of most Indians centered around the vision quest, which demonstrated an amazing direct faith where each individual established a personal link with the spirit world. The exception was found in the agricultural South and Southwest where the individual experience was secondary to the complex ceremonial group traditions. There was an underlying current of supernatural force in every Indian's life that became clear through visions. As a Teton Sioux explained, "It is the general belief of the Indians that after man dies, his spirit is somewhere on the earth or in the sky, we do not know exactly where, but we believe that his spirit still lives. So it is with Wakan Tanka. We believe that he is everywhere, yet he is to us as the spirits of our friends whose voices we cannot hear."[16]

Historian Robert M. Utley in *The Lance and The Shield: The Life and Times of Sitting Bull* wrote about dreams and vision quests, noting,

"*Wichasha Wakan* were dreamers—men who had experienced dreams with sacred content or who had attained visions of powerful spiritual meaning. Not all dreamers were holy men, but all holy men were dreamers. One function of holy men was to help people interpret dreams, for they imposed obligations as binding as a personal vow, and to ignore their intent was to invite personal calamity."[17] Spontaneous dreams gave meaning to ceremonies, rituals, and cults. Vision quests came with much effort and had to be sought.

Often the preparations for a vision quest began years before puberty. Children as young as seven or eight were denied food for a day so they could become accustomed to fasting. As they grew older, the days of fasting would increase in preparation for their vision quest. Their fathers and grandfathers would give them instructions about what to expect on their spiritual journey.

Sweat lodges were an important part of the experience and were used for physical and spiritual purification before leaving on a vision quest. The entrance usually faced east toward the rising sun. There was a sacred path between the lodge and a fire where rocks were heated and then carried into the lodge to produce steam. The sweat lodges were usually airtight, made by covering a circular frame of bent wood with hides or blankets. They were also used before other important ceremonies, including those before raids or hunting expeditions, as therapy for ailments, or just to relax.

The vision quest generally lasted four days—a sacred number for many Indians—but it could be cut shorter if the vision was achieved. If four days passed and the vision was not received, sometimes there was self-mutilation, including cutting off a finger as an offering and the hope that the spirits would take pity on the seeker.

Arriving in various forms, the visions provided spiritual authority that was permanently ingrained in the dreamer's mind. Whatever was seen became an emblem for life whose likeness was often painted on rattles, horses, and the seeker's body. Crazy Horse painted lightning on his face and patterns of hailstones on his body. Objects seen in the vision made their way into the Indian's medicine bundle and onto shields that were believed capable of bearing protection from the gods.

During the nineteenth century, whites viewed Indian visions and dreams as irrational and unbelievable. The men of the Enlightenment dismissed vision quests and dreams much like they did miracles, because scientific laws could not explain them. But in Western civilization, dreams created literary masterpieces. Dreams have been considered divine ever since Jacob in the book of Genesis dreamed of a ladder that connected heaven and earth. In

1678, John Bunyan said that *Pilgrims Progress* had come to him while he was sleeping. Authors of the romantic era embraced dreaming. In 1797, *Kubla Khan* came to Samuel Taylor Coleridge in a dream possibly brought on by two grains of opium taken to check dysentery. When he awoke, there were several hundred lines already composed in his head. On June 16, 1816, Mary Shelley and her husband were staying with other guests of Lord Byron at his home on Lake Geneva, Switzerland. Frankenstein came to her in a dream. Robert Louis Stevenson's 1885 nightmare in which he woke up screaming was the basis for his famed work, *The Strange Case of Dr. Jekyll and Mr. Hyde.*

Native Americans' power and inspiration were not found solely in vision quests and group ceremonies such as the Sun Dance but also in personal dreams. In 1873, nine-year-old Black Elk, an Oglala, was riding along the Little Bighorn River when he collapsed from a mysterious disease that left him unconscious for twelve days. He dreamed of two cloud-borne men who called him up into the heavens. This dream transformed his life, and eventually Black Elk would become a great holy man, which he attributed to the great beauty and harmony that he saw in the universe in his dream. It gave him the power to heal sickness and end strife.[18]

Shamans, Medicine Men, and Medicines

As with other religions, the religions of the American Indians featured specific individuals in their villages who were dedicated to learning the knowledge of spiritual powers. The French trappers in Canada—who were the first Europeans to observe these individuals—noted that healing was also one of their functions, labeling them *medecins* (doctors). This is how the term *medicine man* originated. The bear medicine was the most sought after, because bear medicine men could treat all ordinary diseases, and only they were allowed to treat those who were wounded.[19]

There were also priests or shamans—a word originally associated with Siberian healers. Little did the Europeans know at that time that the Indians' ancestors came from Asia. As with Christians, the medicine man struggled to keep a balance between the material world challenges and those of the spiritual world. With the blessings of the medicine man, the hunter and farmer, along with the sick, were filled with hope and the expectation of success.

Usually male but occasionally a postmenopausal woman, the medicine man was responsible for handing down the stories, legends, and history of the people. Verbal communication was important because little was written down. Luther Standing Bear called it the "library of our people." There were no sharp distinctions in their stories between mortals and immortals, animals and humans, past and present, and space and time.[20]

The attraction to the spirit world was stronger for some than for others. Those who went on multiple vision quests sometimes could become medicine men or shamans. Often these terms are used interchangeably, but the medicine man—doctor—usually stressed the healing role, while the shaman—priest—emphasized more mystical powers. Robert M. Utley described Sitting Bull as "a holy man and not a medicine man although he had mastered healing with roots and herbs. White Bull declared that he was a doctor and carried roots for healing, but medicine was not his main gift."[21]

It was expected of these men to use whatever gift they had received to benefit the community. They were not only healers but also were prophesiers of the future, casters of love spells, communicators with the spirits of the deceased, and controllers of the weather. George Bird Grinnell explained:

> It is generally believed that, among the Indians of North America, the priests and the shamans, "medicine men," or doctors, are the same. This is not the case with the Pawnees. Among them the priestly office was entirely distinct from that of the doctor, and has nothing in common with it. The priest was in a sense the medium of communication with Ti-ra-wa; he prayed to the deity more efficaciously than could a common person, acted, in fact, as an intercessor; he knew the secrets of the sacred bundles, and when he asked anything good for the tribe, or for an individual, it was likely to be granted. His education in the power given him from above brought him into especially close relationship with Ti-ra-wa, who seemed to watch over him and to listen to him when he interceded for the tribe. He was an intermediary between Ti-ra-wa and the people, and held the relation to the Pawnees and their deity not unlike that occupied by Moses to Jehovah and the Israelites.
>
> The office of the "medicine man" shaman, or doctor, had to do only with sickness or injury. He was the healer. Disease was caused by bad spirits and it was the doctor's part to drive off these evil influences.[22]

The Cherokee believed disease came from growing out of harmony with the animals, not giving thanks for the gift of food that they had been given. In the first few decades after the American Revolution, Indian medicine men grasped pathology just as well as white doctors. That is, neither knew much. Indians believed harmony was broken between human beings, the

Creator, and the animals through ingratitude. For every disease spread to humans by animals, there was a plant that could cure it. It was important to kill only animals that were going to be eaten.

The medicine man asked not only about the symptoms but also about dreams, feelings, and strains, and relationships that had occurred prior to illness in that person's life. Medicine given to the patient was always associated with prayer.[23]

In *Shalom and the Community of Creation: An Indigenous Vision*, author Randy S. Woodley described his own recollection of the Cherokee story of how disease—probably smallpox—came into the world:

> Every traditional Cherokee knows that it is considered polite to thank the Creator and the animal when it furnishes its own life so people may eat and sustain their lives. It was said that during this "era of ingratitude" the Cherokees even began to kill that which they were not going to eat. These were evil days indeed!
>
> As a result of these abuses, the animals held council, in order to protect themselves from the evil that had come upon the once grateful Cherokee. After much debate, the animals decided to bring diseases upon the Cherokee people. The Cherokees began getting sick and dying from these diseases. After many Cherokees had died they pleaded with the animals, "Please, we will become grateful and kill only that which we will eat." But the animals would not recant.
>
> All the same time, the plants were watching all of these things. They watched as the Cherokee children got sick, and even died. The plants decided to hold a council. In the council they agreed to provide medicine for the Cherokee. Each night, as the Cherokees would sleep, the plants would come to them in their dreams and show them how to use the plants to heal the diseases that the animals had brought upon them.
>
> The Cherokees recovered and agreed to kill only what they absolutely needed. They also agreed to say a prayer of thanks to any animal that they killed, and to any plant that would be harvested for food or medicine. The Creator was happy with the Cherokees once again because harmony was restored among all that he had created.[24]

Treatment for illness often began with the individual appealing to his personal medicine bundle or finding healing in the sweat lodge. As George Sword explained, "The white people call it a sweat lodge. The Lakotas do not understand it so. The Lakota think of it as a lodge to make the body strong and pure. . . . He may do this to cure himself when he is sick or he may do it to make himself feel strong. He should always do it when he is about to do some important ceremony so that he will be clean inside before the Wakan beings."[25]

If that failed, a doctor (herbalist) was requested. If the doctor produced no results, a priest or holy man (shaman) came to help. Both used the power of placebo or suggestion. With the encouragement of the medicine man, the sick were filled with hope and the expectation of success.

As a medical doctor who was obviously biased toward Western medical treatments, James Walker explained his impression of the medicine man:

> These medicine men had material medicines of actual medicinal qualities and some that were not so effective. Their ministrations were most effective by suggestion. I learned the twelve ritual songs that may be incanted either aloud or in whispers while treating a patient. Their method of procedure is to first smoke the pipe while gazing at the patient; then to blow smoke from the pipe into the nostril cavities of the buffalo skull to arouse the favor of the Buffalo God, deity of the Buffalo medicine men; then to prepare the medicine to be administered, incanting while doing so a song describing the effect that the medicine will cause; then to administer the medicine by portions, singing while each portion is administered a song that suggests progressive relief and rattling the medicine rattle to frighten away the cause of the illness; and finally to sing a song of triumph declaring the disease conquered. The entire process is psychological and very successful because of its power of suggestion.[26]

Besides being used for ceremonies and sustenance, plants were extensively used by herbalists as treatments. This paralleled the independent use of plants in Europe that were used for an array of medicinal purposes. The medicine man probably did less harm than many white doctors who treated a number of maladies with bloodletting and toxic heavy metals.

In one survey of Indian herbal medicines, 68 laxatives, 88 cold remedies, and 113 plants for reducing fever were listed. In addition, 41 plants were recommended for nervous ailments and more than 100 relieved an upset stomach.[27]

To alleviate pain from a toothache, crushed leaves of the tulip tree were applied to the patient's face. For burns, pine bark was boiled and applied as a salve. For infants suffering from colic and gas pains, catnip tea was administered. Sassafras was a cure-all administered for everything from scurvy to spring fever. All medicinal plants were considered gifts from their gods.

The remedies were passed on from one healer to the next generation of healers and were closely guarded secrets. Cures were attained only with the cooperation of the spirit world, and medications were thought to become more potent with prayer. The healers were considered to have special abilities to communicate with the plant spirits. When the herbalist was deciding the best plant medicine to use for a sick patient, he would pray to the supreme power for assistance in healing.[28]

Much of the knowledge of the different kinds of medicinal plants was received by the herbal doctor in dreams or visions. The doctor never forgot to leave offerings in the hole where he dug up his herbs, which he then covered up. Shrewdly, the doctors often tracked sick animals and discovered from them the plants they had eaten when they were sick. One of the most helpful animals to follow was the bear, because it had good claws for digging herbs. A prominent Sioux medicine man said that bears even told him which herbs to use and that a badger gave him advice on the remedies for sick children. His principal remedy was the yarrow plant, which was used for an appetite aid, headaches, heart ailments, and stomach problems.

For fractures, he used splints and hide wrappings. Another Sioux doctor used a bear claw to scratch the patient's arm, drawing blood, and then he rubbed the herbs into the wound so there would be faster absorption of the medicine. Transdermal delivery of medications—used only in more recent decades by physicians—has revolutionized the delivery of many modern medicines.[29]

In his book *The Old North Trail,* Walter McClintock mentioned thirty-four herbs used by the Blackfeet in treating a dozen different diseases including colds, snow blindness, eye diseases, and stomach troubles, plus snake and rabid dog bites.[30]

During the early 1800s, European doctors trivialized the Indian medicine man, but their repertoire wasn't much better. Western medicine was still quite primitive, and both groups relied heavily on the power of suggestion and faith. They too relied heavily on herbal treatments. George Catlin was impressed with the Plains medicine man, stating, "Many of them acquire great skill in the medicinal world, and gain much celebrity in their nation."[31]

Failing to cure the patient, the doctor left and the shaman—often dressed in extravagant costumes—came to the patient's aid. As George Sword explained, "The holy man is the most potent in treating the sick. He can speak with the Great Mystery and they will help him. He does not treat the sick with medicines. He has a ceremonial bag. It is called *wopiye* in Lakota. This does not have medicines in it. It has a mystery in it and this mystery makes the bag very potent. It has all the potency of the mystery. The holy man invokes his ceremonial bundle or bag. It may be like a bag or it may be like a bundle. Or it may be anything that is revealed to him in a vision."[32]

Secretive, the shaman usually did not allow the white man to observe his rituals. Their services came at a cost, and they were often paid in horses, blankets, and other valuables to secure the services of a shaman. Shamans impressed their clients by performing magical tricks or making themselves disappear or having themselves bound up like Houdini and then miraculously escaping. The Crow shamans would impress large crowds by producing food or employing tricks that would make their audience collapse. Much like the Puritan ministers who abhorred the flamboyant sermons by evangelicals, other shamans disapproved of these public displays, commenting, "In our forefather's day, the shamans were solitary men, but now they are all priests or doctors, whether prophets or conjurers producing games, or clever merchants selling their skills for pay." Another shaman—who echoed the beliefs of the Desert Fathers in the Bible who isolated themselves for prayer—opposed public displays and declared, "True wisdom is only to be found far away from people, out in the great solitude, and it is not found in play but only through suffering. Solitude and suffering open the human mind, and therefore a shaman seeks his wisdom there."[33]

The treatment a shaman might administer depended on the health condition he was treating. Obvious problems like broken bones or snakebites were treated in a commonsense approach with herbs or other medicines, but internal problems with no obvious cause were attributed to supernatural imbalances. The breaking of taboos, hostile sorcerers, and unfulfilled dreams were believed to lead to physical maladies.

Unlike herbal cures, treatment for mysterious diseases entailed much ritual where the shaman used psychic powers to see what was wrong with the patient. Long before researchers discovered illnesses could be caused from microscopic germs, many Indians believed that disease was caused by small, inanimate pathogens like a tiny ball of fluff, a rock, or a feather hidden in the patient's body. It was the shaman's role to find the pathogen and remove it. After praying and fasting, a Sioux shaman entered the sick person's tipi carrying objects of power that might include a pipe, a drum, herbs, deer hooves, a rawhide rattle, or a bone whistle. Chanting and beating his drum, the healer sang songs appealing to the healing powers of Wakan Tanka.

Physical touch was important for healing. The shaman would stroke the patient's body with his hand or a feather and blow pipe smoke over the affected area of the body. Power of suggestion was important, and he would boastfully let the patient know of his past successes and healing other sick individuals. Reputation was everything.

The final part of the healing process took place when the shaman would apply his lips over the inflicted body part and attempt to suck out the pathogen up through the skin. Magically, he would then extract a small stone, plant, or stick from his mouth, which demonstrated the patient was now cured. Researcher Robert Lowie commented, "Hence the physician tried to extract it, usually by suction, exhibiting to the patient and his relatives the splinter, thorn, or whatever had supposedly cause the problem."[34] If the patient remained sick, the shaman then blamed the disease on a hostile medicine man or on a pathogen that was just too powerful for him to cure.

In most cases, the shaman was held blameless for unsuccessful treatments. That was certainly true of the passive Mandan with their deep faith. They summarized deadly infections like smallpox—against which the shaman proved ineffective—as "unfortunate," and they understood "the impotency of their rites . . . on the grounds that, when the original ceremonies were introduced to the tribe, the sacred beings made no promise of immunity to the white man's diseases."[35] As might be expected, with the arrival of Christian missionaries visiting the Indian villages, the undermining of the traditional healing powers of the medicine man and the shaman increased.

Father Nicholas Point detested the celebrity status attained by the Indian medicine men and shamans, probably because it was an additional hindrance in converting the Indian to Christianity. He said that the treatments were applied in a manner "best calculated to degrade human nature." Frustrated, he gave a detailed description of the process:

> If, for example, the medicinal power was attributed to a bear claw, and deemed applicable to the treatment of a given wound, the medicine man hurled himself upon the poor patient as a bear upon his prey, imitating as closely as possible the roaring in the fury of the animal. If he was called upon to cure an internal malady, he sucked vigorously at what was thought to be the spot on the surface of the body directly above the internal malady. Then, like a man holding the malady in his mouth, he retired with violent gyrations, or vomited what he claimed was the malady he had just sucked from his patient. If this medicine was that of a wolf, the medicine man, to

give thanks to his will for a cure so marvelous, but so perilous to him, began to howl like a wolf.[36]

With healing powers came extraordinary prestige and influence not only among the shaman's own people but also other tribes. In time, priests moved beyond healing and into the realm of prophecy. Some foretold the arrival of visitors, the coming of storms, and the approach of enemies. Perhaps the best example is the story of the creation of the Ghost Dance. A prophetic movement was started in 1869 by a Paiute medicine man named Wodziwob. He preached that, with the completion of the Union Pacific transcontinental railroad, a train would bring their ancestors back from the dead. That would be a sign of a reversal in the fortunes of the Indians who were being subjugated by the white man.

He revived the Round Dance, which symbolically repeated the sun's journey across the sky. But his fame came to an end when no train appeared and instead a severe drought struck the region. Over the next two decades, more settlers made conditions even worse. Bison were killed off, and the white man's diseases destroyed more and more villages.

There was renewed hope in a new shaman and fellow tribesman of Wodziwob named Wovoka, who lived in western Nevada. Earlier in life, he had worked for a Presbyterian rancher who introduced him to Christianity and gave him the name of Jack Wilson. The new shaman, while ill during an eclipse of the sun on January 1, 1889, had a vision and recalled, "When the sun died, I went up to heaven and saw God and all the people who had died a long time ago. God told me to come back and tell my people they must be good and love one another, not fight, or steal, or lie. He gave me this dance to give my people." The ritual he promoted was supposed to raise people from the dead and thus was given the name the Ghost Dance.[37]

His message was similar to the apocalyptic teachings by Jesus that the end times were imminent. Wovoka warned that the world was soon coming to an end and would be destroyed by a great flood. A new world would then be inhabited by the spirits of Indians both dead and alive. Their new world would be like their old world before the white man. He instructed his followers to prepare for the great day by living correctly and gathering for the Ghost Dance.

He was called the new Christ, and his word spread through Indian communities throughout the West. Participants formed a great circle and moved clockwise in the direction of the sun with slow, shuffling steps around a central fire. Special Ghost Dance songs were sung as they danced, with some collapsing in a trance. After awakening, they told of visions and composed new songs for the Ghost Dance.

Initially peaceful, the revival turned warlike on the Great Plains. Hunger and hardship, along with the government coercing them into selling their land, infuriated the Indians. In 1890 at Wounded Knee, soldiers from the U.S. 7th Cavalry Regiment, Custer's old unit, attempted to disarm a group of Sioux at a Ghost Dance, but events turned violent, which led to the slaughter of up to 300 Indians, many of them women and children. The tragedy ended the Ghost Dance ceremony, but Wovoka continued to have faithful followers until he died in 1932.[38]

Smoking to the Spirit

A common substance used in rituals was tobacco, one of the most sacred of all plants. Pipe smoking became an effective way of communicating with the spirit world and other people. No hunting or raiding party, no harvesting or planting, no healing, and no wooing was initiated without offering tobacco to the spirits.

Long before Columbus set foot in America, tobacco was widespread in the Americas. Most believed it had its origins in South America and traveled through Mexico and the American desert all the way to Hudson Bay and eastward to the Atlantic Ocean. In areas where it couldn't be grown because of the climate, tobacco was traded for. Woodland tribes in the Great Lakes region believed that tobacco gave them something to offer to not only the Great Spirit but also to the moon, the sun, thunder, and water.

The Crow of Montana held tobacco in such high regard that tobacco societies sprang up within the tribe. They devoted themselves to cultivating a special species of the plant for exclusive use in their own rituals and believed that good luck came to them just by growing the plant. The good fortune was not exclusive just to the tobacco societies but to all the members of the tribe as well.

In 1738, when Pierre La Vérendrye visited the Mandan, he was presented with "Indian corn in the ear and a roll of their tobacco."[39] He was not impressed with the tobacco taste and commented that it "was not very good." Most Europeans agreed with his assessment, and trader Alexander Henry added, "I find the flowers a very poor substitute for our own Tobacco being only a mere nauseous insipid weed."[40] The Indians felt the same way toward the European's tobacco, commenting that it was too strong.

In their wisdom, Indians understood the dangers of chronic tobacco smoking. Young men tended to avoid it because, as Buffalo Bird Woman explained, her people knew "that smoking would injure their lungs and make them short winded so that they would be poor runners." She added, "A young man who smoked a great deal, if chased by enemies, could not run to escape from them, and so got killed. For this reason all the young men of my tribe were taught that they should not smoke."[41] Social smoking was undertaken only by men who were too old to go to war.

George Sword explained the importance of the tobacco pipe:

The pipe was first given to the Lakotas by their God. The spirit of the God is in the smoke from the pipe. The pipe that was given by the God is kept by a keeper. The keeper was appointed by the shamans. When the keeper dies, his kinspeople keep it. Usually this is his oldest son. This is the ceremonial pipe of all the Lakotas. . . .

When a pipe is smoked in this manner, the spirit that is in the smoke goes with it into the mouth and body and then it comes out and goes upward. When this spirit is in the body, it soothes the spirit of the smoker. When it goes upward, it soothes the God. So the God and the spirit are as friends.[42]

Ancestral pipes served as models for new pipes. Many were beautifully decorated by master craftsmen. The stems were often made of wood or reed and were adorned with feathers, beads, and other symbolic ornaments particular to a pipe's purpose. The Pawnee painted their pipes used for war ceremonies red and adorned them with male eagle feathers. A peace pipe was painted blue and decorated with female eagle feathers.

Soapstone, a mineral that is waterlogged underground and easily worked after mining before it dries hard, was used for the pipe bowls. While the bowl shape and stem decorations varied among tribes, the one feature that remained constant was that the two were always separate.

The calumet was the decorated stem and has been commonly referred to as the peace pipe. Its use was implemented in ceremonies for outsiders who were visiting, and it was a friendly gesture that offered peace. The custom dated to at least 1300 and was used among the Caddoan-speaking Pawnee. In time, they passed it on to the Arikara who then passed it on to the Mandan.[43]

Besides tobacco, other plant products were burned in ceremonies. In many Plains tribal traditions, their purification and prayer ceremonies often involved smudging. Sage, sweetgrass, or cedar was lit with fire and allowed to smolder and smoke. Then the participant fanned the smoke over himself or others or into the air with his hand or a feather. It is believed that the smoke did two things: it had the power to cleanse and purify, and it took prayers and carried them up into heaven to the Creator.[44]

Today, many Native Americans believe that their dire current social, economic, and spiritual condition is a result of failing to continue ancestral rituals and ceremonies. Spiritual power is viewed as helping them survive in a modern world where they don't fit in. A significant movement among natives is to restore many of the traditional ceremonies, especially the Sun Dance.[45]

CHAPTER ELEVEN

The Language of God: Indian Myths, Legends, and Their Chroniclers

Through these Indian legends from ancient times you can listen to the voices of the North American Indians. Never would they have opened their hearts to strangers in the past! Here, together, we are fortunate to hear an echo of these voices of the winds.
—MARGOT EDMONDS AND ELLA E. CLARK,
VOICES OF THE WINDS: NATIVE AMERICAN LEGENDS

Legends as well as cultures overlap and influence each other, not only when people of different tribes live in adjacent territory, but even when they encounter each other through migration or trade over long distances.... Yet with all the regional images and variations, a common theme binds these tales together—a universal concern with fundamental issues about the world in which humans live.
—RICHARD ERDOES AND ALFONSO ORTIZ,
AMERICAN INDIAN MYTHS AND LEGENDS

At least since the time modern humans left Africa, they have communicated their beliefs through a number of modalities, including paintings, carvings, dances, and sounds. But the most important method of expression is through oral histories. These myths and legends have been transmitted from one generation to the next through selected tribal historians. These historians are often trained at an early age by their elders to perpetuate these myths and legends. Often the storytelling was reserved for the cold seasons when people would gather around warming fires.

At the core of the Indians' way of life was their spiritual beliefs, which were often demonstrated through ceremonies or rituals. Everything in nature had its own spirit, including mountains, trees, waters, the earth, sky, animals, birds, and man. The spirits in nature were considered stronger than human power.

Oral histories included tales of human and world creation; tales of the sun, moon, and stars; monsters and monster slayers; counting coup; war and the warrior code; tales of love and lust; trickster tales; stories of animals and other people; ghosts and the spirit world; visions of the end; and many more.

Even though facts are important, the greater goal is to convey truth through stories whether they are fiction or nonfiction. The highest purpose of storytelling is to articulate a society's value system. Mythology is the ultimate expression of a group of people's values—the good and bad ways to live their lives. The operative components of myth are the legends that comprise it. Myth defines the universal experience, and it also supplies those grand themes that writers want to use. Stories both true and imagined will tell readers what we were, are, and want to be. It is true that facts provide ingredients for history. History inspires legend, and common legends, when compiled, constitute myth. But because people's perceptions of the facts are shaped by their experience of the world and the expectations of their fellow human beings, what they describe as factual has been filtered by their worldview, that is, their mythology. Because of this circle, truth can be told through legend and explained by myth.[1]

George Bird Grinnell

Although there were innumerable ethnographers and chroniclers who came West to record a passing way of life, one of the most important to follow Catlin years later was George Bird Grinnell (1849-1938), a polymath—a scientist, hunter, explorer, naturalist, entrepreneur, editor, and author. Most importantly, he is considered one of the most influential conservationists in North American history.

Born in Brooklyn, New York, Grinnell, when he was seven years old, moved with his family to Audubon Park, an estate of wild land belonging to the widow of the famous naturalist John James Audubon. "Grandma"

Audubon ran a small school in her home that Grinnell and his siblings attended. He was later to attribute much of his interest in hunting and natural history to her influence. It was there that Grinnell spent days reading Audubon's accounts of his 1843 journey to the Yellowstone country in what is now eastern Montana and Audubon's disgust at the slaughter of bison he witnessed along the way. Until he married at age fifty-three, Grinnell returned from many excursions in an untamed West to the moneyed comfort, familiar surroundings, and rich store of memories of his family's home in Audubon Park.[2]

Coming from a wealthy family, Grinnell completed his undergraduate work at Yale, and in 1870 accompanied Othniel C. Marsh, a renowned paleontologist, on a fossil collecting expedition. During his six months of travel, the young man found himself irresistibly drawn to everything the West had to offer, including Native Americans. Two years later, he joined a large group of Pawnee Indians gathered on a bison hunt. In one article in *Forest and Stream* titled "What We May Learn from the Indians," he described how they protected the game on which they survived by practicing proven methods of conservation and hunting.

Grinnell returned to the Black Hills in 1874 to catalog birds and mammals of the region for Colonel William Ludlow, chief engineer for the Department of Dakota Territory. While on the trip, he met Lieutenant Colonel George Armstrong Custer, and also became friends with the famous scout "Lonesome" Charley Reynolds as he tried to defend gold seekers from the Sioux.

Impressed by his efforts, Ludlow asked Grinnell to join an expedition through Montana Territory the following year, focusing on the country around Yellowstone National Park. Grinnell was shocked when he witnessed the senseless slaughter of wildlife and stated so in his official report to Ludlow. Due to his growing reputation as a sportsman who enjoyed hunting but loathed the wanton killing of wildlife, Grinnell was hired by *Forest and Stream* as its natural history editor in the spring of 1876. For ten dollars a week, he wrote book reviews and several pages of copy while still working on his doctorate in osteology and vertebrate paleontology at Yale. If that wasn't enough, he also assisted Professor Marsh at the Peabody Museum in New Haven, Connecticut. Bound by his commitments, Grinnell was forced to turn down an invitation to accompany the troops on what was to be Custer's fateful campaign against the Sioux in Montana Territory in 1876. Years later, Grinnell recalled, "Had I gone with Custer I should have in all probability been mixed up in the Custer battle, for I should have been either with Custer's command, or with that of Reno, and would have been right on the ground when the Seventh Cavalry was wiped out. Very likely I should have been with Reno's command as Charley Reynolds and I were close friends and commonly rode together."[3]

By 1880, Grinnell owned almost a third of *Forest and Stream* and became its president and editor. Eventually, Grinnell crossed paths with Theodore Roosevelt, and they became two of the founders of the Boone and Crockett Club. Limited to 100 members, the Boone and Crockett Club was established in 1887. Its members shared an enthusiasm for big-game hunting while loathing the disastrous effects both market hunters and settlers had on the indigenous wildlife populations. From its inception, Grinnell remained the group's most influential member.

Grinnell's interest in northwest Montana was piqued after reading James Willard Schultz's (1859-1947) poignant description in a *Forest and Stream* article titled, "To Chief Mountain." In 1885, the two explored the region that would in 1910 become Glacier National Park.

In 1889, Grinnell wrote his first book on Indian life, *Pawnee Hero Stories and Folk-Tales: With Notes on the Origin, Customs, and Character of the Pawnee People.* It received critical and popular acclaim. Encouraged by the public's acceptance of his work on Native Americans, Grinnell urged his friend Schultz to write a book on the Blackfeet. Though Schultz had written an article, "Life Among the Blackfeet," for *Forest and Stream,* he preferred someone else to write the first major book about these people. Schultz sincerely believed Grinnell should be the author and provided him with insightful notes.

Nonetheless, Schultz, encouraged by Grinnell, went on to become a noted author of such classics as *My Life as an Indian* (1907), *Sinopah* (1913), *The Indian Boy* (1913), *Blackfeet Tales of Glacier National Park* (1916), *Plumed Snake Medicine* (1924), and *Signposts of Adventure* (1926). In addition to the thirty-seven books published in his lifetime, four other manuscripts were published posthumously by the University of Oklahoma Press. Schultz brought to the American public compelling narratives of the Blackfeet, written with the compassion and understanding that could only come from his own experience living with them.[4]

Published in 1892 by Charles Scribner's Sons, *Blackfoot Lodge Tales: The Story of a Prairie People* by Grinnell, stands as one of the most remarkable works ever published on the native people of Montana. Grinnell wrote:

I give the Blackfoot stories as they have been told to me by the Indians themselves, not elaborating nor adding to them. In all cases except one they were written down as they fell from the lips of the storyteller. . . . These are Indian stories, pictures of Indian life drawn by Indian artists, and showing this life from the Indian's point of view. . . .[5]

The most shameful chapter of American history is that in which is recorded the account of her dealings with the Indians. The story of our government's intercourse with this raises an unbroken narrative of injustice, fraud, and robbery. Our people have disregarded honesty and truth whenever they have come in contact with the Indian, and he has had no rights because he has never had the power to enforce any. . . .[6]

Americans are a conscientious people, yet they take no interest in these frauds. They have the Anglo-Saxon spirit of fair play, which sympathizes with weakness, yet no protest is made against the oppression which the Indian suffers. They are generous; a famine in Ireland, Japan, or Russia arouses the sympathy and calls forth the bounty of the nation, yet they have no heed to the distress of the Indians, who are in the very midst of them. They do not realize that Indians are human beings like themselves.

For this state of things there must be a reason, and this reason is to be found, I believe, in the fact that practically no one has any personal knowledge of the Indian race. . . .[7]

The Indian is a man, not very different from his white brother, except that he is undeveloped. In his natural state he is kind and affectionate in his family, is hospitable, honest and straightforward with his fellows—a true friend. If you are his guest, the best he has is at your disposal; if the camp is starving, you will still have set before you your share of what food there may be in the lodge. For his friend he will die, if need be. He is glad to perform acts of kindness for those he likes. While traveling in the heat of summer over long, waterless stretches of prairie, I had an Indian, who saw me suffering from thirst, leave me, without mentioning his errand, and ride thirty miles to fetch me a canteen of cool water.

The Indian is intensely religious. No people pray more earnestly nor more frequently. This is especially true of all Indians of the plains. The Indian has a mind and feelings of a child with the stature of a man; and if this is clearly understood and considered, will readily account for much of the bad that we hear about them, and for many of the civil traits which are commonly attributed to him. Civilized and educated, the Indian of the better class is not less intelligent than the average white man, and has every capacity for becoming a good citizen.[8]

The stories in the book were divided into four parts: "Stories of Adventure," "Stories of Ancient Times," "Stories of Old Man," and "The Story of the Three Tribes." Below are two stories from the book.

The Race

Once Old Man was traveling around, when he heard some very queer singing. He had never heard anything like this before, and looked all around to see who it was. At last he saw it was the cottontail rabbits, singing and making medicine. They had built a fire, and got a lot of hot ashes, and they would lie down in these ashes and sing while one covered them up. They would stay there only a short time though, for the ashes were very hot.

"Little Brothers," said Old Man, "that is very wonderful, how you lie in those ashes and coals without burning. I wish you would teach me how to do it."

"Come on, Old Man," said the rabbits, "we will show you how to do it. You must sing our song, and only stay in the ashes a short time." So Old Man began to sing, and he lay down, and they covered him with coals and ashes, and they did not burn him at all.

"That is very nice," he said. "You have powerful medicine. Now I want to know it all, so you lie down and let me cover you up."

So the rabbits all lay down in the ashes, the Old Man covered them up, and then he put the whole fire over them. One old rabbit got up, and Old Man was about to put her back when she said, "Pity me, my children are about to be born."

"All right," replied Old Man. "I will let you go, so there will be some rabbits; but I will roast these nicely and have a feast." And he put more wood on the fire. When the rabbits were cooked, he cut some red willow brush and laid them on it to cool. The grease soaked into these branches, so, even today if you hold red willow over a fire, you will see the grease on the bark. You can see, too, that ever since, the rabbits have a burned place on their backs, where the old one that got away was singed.

Old Man sat down, and was waiting for the rabbits to cool a little, when a coyote came along, limping very badly. "Pity me, Old Man," he said, "you have lots of cooked rabbit; give me one of them."

"Go away," exclaimed Old Man. "If you are too lazy to get your food, I will not help you."

"My leg is broken," said the coyote. "I can't catch anything, and I am starving. Just give me half a rabbit."

"I don't care if you die," replied Old Man. "I worked hard to cook all these rabbits, and I will not give any away. But I will tell you what we will do. We will run a race to that butte, way out there, and if you beat me you can have a rabbit."

"All right," said the coyote. So they started. Old Man ran very fast, and the coyote limped along behind, but close to him, until they got near to the butte. Then the coyote turned around and ran back very fast, for he was not lame at all. It took Old Man a long time to go back, and just before he got to the fire, the coyote swallowed the last rabbit, and trotted off over the prairie.[9]

The Fast Runners

Once, long ago, the antelope and the deer met on the prairie. At this time both of them had galls and both dew claws. They began to talk together, and each was telling the other what he could do. Each one told how fast he could run, and before long they were disputing as to which could run faster. Neither would allow that the other could beat him, so they agreed that they would have a race to decide which was a swifter, and they bet their galls on the race. When they ran, the antelope proved the faster runner, and beat the deer and took his gall.

Then the deer said: "Yes, you have beat me on the prairie, but that is not where I live. I only go out there sometimes to feed, or when I am traveling around. We ought to have another race in the timber. That is my home, and there I can run faster than you can."

The antelope felt very big because he had beaten the deer in the race, and he thought wherever they might be, he could run faster than the deer. So he agreed to race in the timber, and on this race they bet their dew claws.

They ran through the thick timber, among the brush and over fallen logs, and this time the antelope ran slowly, because he was not used to this kind of traveling, and the deer easily beat him, and took his dew claws.

Since then the deer has had no gall, and the antelope no dew claws.[10]

The following Cheyenne legend transcribed by Grinnell was published by Scribner's that same year.

How the Buffalo Hunt Began

The buffalo formerly ate man. The magpie and the hawk were on the side of the people, for neither ate the other or the people. These two birds flew away from a council between animals and men. They determined that a race would be held, the winners to eat the losers.

The course was long, around a mountain. The swiftest buffalo was a cow called Neika, "Swift head." She believed she would win and entered the race. On the other hand, the people were afraid because of the long distance. They were trying to get medicine to prevent fatigue.

All the birds and animals painted themselves for the race, and since that time they have all been brightly colored. Even the water turtle put red paint around his eyes. The magpie painted himself white on head, shoulders, and tail. At last all were ready for the race, and stood in a row for the start.

They ran and ran, making some loud noises in place of singing to help themselves to run faster. All small birds, turtles, rabbits, coyotes, wolves, flies, ants, insects, and snakes were soon left far behind. When they approached the mountain the buffalo-cow was ahead; then came the magpie, hawk, and the people; the rest were strung out along the way. The dust rose so quickly that nothing could be seen.

All around the mountain the buffalo-cow led the race, but the two birds knew they could win, and merely kept up with her until they neared the finish line, which was back to the starting place. Then both birds whooshed by her and won the race for man. As they flew the course, they had seen fallen animals and birds all over the place, who had run themselves to death, turning the ground and rocks red from the blood.

The buffalo then told their young to hide from the people, who were going out to hunt them; and also told them to take some human flesh with them for the last time. Young buffaloes did this, and stuck that meat in front of their chests, beneath the throat. Therefore, the people do not eat that part of the buffalo, saying it is part human flesh.

From that day forward the Cheyennes began to hunt buffalo. Since all the friendly animals and birds were on the people's side, they are not eaten by people, but they do wear and use their beautiful feathers for ornaments.

Another version adds that when coyote, who was on the side of the buffalo, finished the race, the magpie, who beat even the hawk, said to coyote, "We will not eat you, but only use your skin."[11]

Grinnell explained that the chief God of the Blackfeet and their Creator was Napi Old Man. The people were created by Old Man. One account was that he married a female dog and their progeny were the first people. He was also involved in the origins of death. Old Man originally made people with very strong bodies. But that changed when a child fell ill and the Old Man took the woman to a nearby river. Old Man picked up a dry buffalo chip and a stone. He told the woman to pick which one she wanted him to throw in the water, and if it floated the child would live and her people would live forever. If it sank, then her child would die and all people would die when their time came. The woman stood still a long time looking at the stone and the buffalo chip. At last she told him to throw the stone. He told the woman to go home to her dead child. Thus, on account of a foolish woman, all humans die. This Indian legend mirrors the fall of Adam and Eve in the Garden of Eden heralding man's loss of immortality.

The Blackfeet do not especially believe that their future life is an unhappy one, but they don't expect any promise of something special either. They don't have any fear of death because when their time comes, they accept their fate with no regret and are at peace.[12]

In discussing Old Man, Grinnell described his character as complex and containing a mixture of opposite attributes. In oral tradition, he was spoken of respectfully, and he was powerful and very wise but at times so helpless that he asked assistance from animals. Sometimes, Old Man could sympathize with people and other times he would play malicious tricks on them that were devilish. He was an odd combination of strength and weakness, wisdom and folly, and childishness and malice. Old Man was also known to the Cree, Chippewa, and Algonquin. He had eternal life, and before he departed, he told his Indian people that he would take care of them and some day return—reminiscent of Jesus' comments to his disciples at the Last Supper.

In 1911, Grinnell sold *Forest and Stream* to focus on studying and writing about Native American culture. His prolific book-writing career included such classics as *Blackfeet Indian Stories* (1913), *The Fighting Cheyenne* (1915), *The Cheyenne Indians* (1923), *When Buffalo Ran* (1923), and *By Cheyenne Campfires* (1926). Understanding the importance of his younger readers appreciating the West's history, myths, and legends, Grinnell wrote *Jack Among the Indians, Jack in the Rockies,* and *Jack, the Young Cowboy.*

His writings proved inspirational for other great authors like James Willard Schultz, Walter McClintock, and Frank Bird Linderman. Grinnell's sincere empathy for the plight of all American Indians was in direct opposition to the popular doctrine of Manifest Destiny and social Darwinism where nature and nature's people were but minor irritants to the spread of progress.

Frank Bird Linderman

One of famed artist Charles M. Russell's (1864-1926) closest friends, Frank Bird Linderman (1869-1938), was born in Cleveland, Ohio, and arrived in the Flathead Valley in northwestern Montana in 1885. For seven years, he made a living as a trapper and guide in the Flathead and Swan Valleys before becoming an assayer at the Curlew Mine in Victor, south of Missoula. In 1893, he married Minnie Jan Johns of Missoula, and they settled in Sheridan, Montana, where Frank ran an assay office. Six years later, he purchased the *Sheridan Chinook* newspaper and his writing career began.

Linderman had political ambitions and was elected in 1903 and 1905 as a representative from Madison County to the Montana legislature. After being appointed assistant secretary of state in 1905, he moved to Helena, where he resided for the next twelve years. During these years, he became friends with many of the local native leaders, including Rocky Boy of the Chippewa and Little Bear. The Chippewa and Cree were summarily left out of the reservation process and became squatters on any open land they could find. In 1908, Linderman met with an influential group of Montanans—including Senator Paris Gibson; William Bole, editor of the *Great Falls Tribune;* and Charlie Russell—who gathered to advocate the idea of creating a reservation for these wandering people. Writing almost 500 letters and telegrams over a ten-year period, Linderman used his political influence in an attempt to persuade the legislature to aid his cause.

To support Linderman's efforts, on January 10, 1909, Charlie Russell appeared in a *Great Falls Tribune* editorial for money to help the Cree and Chippewa survive the winter, telling a reporter, "It doesn't look good for the people of Montana if they will sit still and see a lot of women and children starve to death in this kind of weather. Lots of people seem to think that Indians are not human beings at all and have no feelings. These kind of people would be the first to yell for help if their grub pile was running short and they didn't have enough clothes to keep out the cold, and yet because Rocky Boy and his bunch are Indian, they are perfectly willing to let them die of hunger and cold without lifting a hand."[13] In 1916, the success of Linderman's tireless campaign culminated with the creation of the Rocky Boy Indian Reservation near Havre, Montana.[14]

Linderman had always been intrigued with Indian culture, and now, partly inspired by the successful writings of George Bird Grinnell, he became totally immersed in their legends, customs, and beliefs. In September 1915, Charles Scribner's Sons released Linderman's *Indian Why Stories,* a collection of Blackfeet, Chippewa, and Cree legends retold by War Eagle, a mythical storyteller modeled after Chippewa leader Chief Penneto. Dedicated to his friends George Bird Grinnell and Charlie Russell, *Indian Why Stories* was illustrated by Russell. With delightful stories like "Why the Chipmunks Back is Striped," "How the Ducks Got Their Fine Feathers," and "How the Otter Skin Became Great Medicine," the book was warmly received by the public and widely popular with children.

War Eagle described the main character: "Napi, Old Man, is very old indeed. He made this world, and all that is on it. . . . He was a busy worker, but a great liar and thief. . . . It was Old Man who taught the beaver all his cunning. It was Old Man who told the bear to go to sleep when the snow grew deep in winter. . . . There was no other man or woman then, and he was chief of all the animal people and the bird people."[15]

At the end of *Indian Why Stories,* Grace Stone Coates profiled Linderman:

> The first Indian he ever talked to was Red-Horn, a renowned Flathead. Linderman's account of their meeting, the inception of a lifelong friendship, is moving and beautiful. The boy didn't know a Flathead from a Kootenai. . . .
>
> Linderman's Blackfeet name is Iron-tooth. The Crows call him

Sign-talker. The old Kootenais named him Bird-singer and the early Crees and Chippewas called him Sings-like-a-bird. His name is one to conjure with among the Crees and Chippewas. They called themselves Linderman Indians, because—wrung by their pitiful homelessness—he was instrumental in wrestling from a dilatory and indifferent government the Rocky Boy (Stone Child's) Reservation near Havre, Montana.[16]

As Frank Bird Linderman stated in his preface to *Indian Why Stories:*

There is a wide difference between folklore of the so-called Old World and that of America. Transmitted orally through countless generations, the folk stories of our ancestors show many evidences of distortion and a change in material particulars; but the Indian seems to have been too fond of nature and too proud of tradition to have forgotten or change the teachings of his forefathers. Childlike in simplicity, beginning with creation itself, and reaching to the whys and wherefores of nature's moods and eccentricities, these tales impress me as being well worth saving.

The Indian has always been a lover of nature and a close observer of her many moods. The habits of the birds and animals, the voices of the winds and waters, the flickering of the shadows, and the mystic radiance of the moonlight—all appealed to him. . . . And the stories were handed down from father to son, with little variation, through countless generations, until the white man slaughtered the buffalo, took to himself the open country, and left the red man little better than a beggar. But the tribal storyteller has passed, and only here and there is to be found a patriarch who loves the legends of other days.

Old-man, or Napa, as he is called by the tribes of Blackfeet, is the strangest character in Indian folk-lore. Sometimes he appears as a God or Creator, and again as a fool, a thief, or a clown. But to the Indian, Napa is not the deity; he occupies a somewhat subordinate position, possessing many attributes which have sometimes caused him to be confounded with Manitou, himself. In all of this there is a curious echo of the teachings of the ancient Aryans, whose belief it was that this earth was not the direct handiwork of the Almighty, but of a mere member of a hierarchy of subordinate gods. The Indian possesses the highest veneration for the Great God, who has become familiar to the readers of Indian literature as Manitou. . . .

I propose to tell what I know of these legends, keeping as near as possible to the Indian style of storytelling, and using only tales told me by the older men of the Blackfeet, Chippewa, and Cree tribes.[17]

A story from *Indian Why Stories:*

How the Ducks Got Their Fine Feathers

Another night had come, and I made my way toward War Eagle's Lodge. In the bright moonlight the dead leaves of the quaking aspen fluttered down whenever the wind shook the trees; and over the village great flocks of ducks and geese and swans passed in a never-ending procession, calling to each other in strange tones as they sped away toward the waters that never freeze.

In the Lodge War Eagle waited for his grandchildren, and when they had entered, happily, he laid aside his pipe and said:

"The Duck-people are traveling tonight just as they have done since the world was young. They are going away from winter because they cannot make a living when ice covers the rivers.

"You have seen the Duck-people often. You have noticed that they wear fine clothes but you do not know how they got them; so I will tell you tonight.

"It was in the fall when leaves are yellow that it happened, and long, long ago. The Duck-people had gathered to go away, just as they are doing now. The buck-deer was coming down the high ridges to visit friends in the lowlands along the streams as they have always done. On a lake Old-man saw the Duck-people getting ready to go away, and at that time they all looked alike; that is, they all wore the same colored clothes. The loons and the geese and ducks were there and playing in the sunlight. The loons were laughing loudly and the diving was fast and merry to see. On the hill where Old-man stood there was a great deal of moss, and he began to tear it from the ground and roll it into a great ball. When he had gathered all he needed he shouldered the load and started for the shore of the lake, staggering under the weight of the great burden. Finally the Duck-people saw him coming with his load of moss and began to swim away from the shore.

"'Wait, my brothers!' he called, 'I have a big load here, and I am going to give you people a dance. Come and help me get things ready.'

"'Don't you do it,' said the gray goose to the others; 'that's Old-man and he's up to something bad, I am sure.'

"So the loon called to Old-man and said they wouldn't help him at all.

"Right near the water Old-man dropped his ball of moss and cut twenty long poles. With the poles he built a lodge which he covered with the moss, leaving a doorway facing the lake. Inside the lodge he built a fire and when it grew bright he cried;

"'Say, brothers, why should you treat me this way when I am here to give you a big dance? Come into the Lodge,' but they wouldn't do that. Finally Old-man began to sing a song in the duck-talk, and keep time with his drum. The Duck-people liked the music, and swam a little nearer to the shore, watching for trouble all the time, but Old-man sang so sweetly that pretty soon they waddled up to the lodge and went inside. The loon stopped near the door, for he believed that what the gray goose had said was true, and that Old-man was up to some mischief. The gray goose, too, was careful to stay close to the door but the ducks reached all about the fire. Politely, Old-man passed the pipe, and they all smoked with him because it is wrong not to smoke in a person's lodge if the pipe is offered, and the Duck-people knew that.

"'Well,' said Old-man, 'this is going to be the Blind-dance, but you will have to be painted first.

"'Brother Mallard, name the colors—tell how you want me to paint you.'

"'Well,' replied the mallard drake, 'paint my head green, and put a white circle around my throat, like a necklace. Besides that, I want a brown breast and yellow legs; but I don't want my wife painted that way.'

"Old-man painted him just as he asked, and his wife, too. Then the teal and the wood duck (it took a long time to paint the wood duck) and the spoonbill and the blue-bill and the canvas back and the goose and the brant and the loon—all chose their paint. Old-man painted them all just as they wanted him to, and kept singing all the time. They looked very pretty in the firelight, for it was night before the painting was done.

"'Now,' said Old-man, 'as this is the Blind-dance, when I beat upon my drum you must all shut your eyes tight and circle around the fire as I sing. Everyone that peeks will have sore eyes forever.'

"Then the Duck-people shut their eyes and Old-man began to sing: 'Now you come, ducks, now you come—tum-tum, tum; tum-tum, tum.'

"Around the fire they came with their eyes still shut, and as fast as they reached Old-man, the rascal would seize them, and wring their necks. Ho! Things were going fine for Old-man, but the loon peeked a little, and saw what was going on; several others heard the fluttering and opened their eyes, too. The loon cried out, 'He's killing us—let us fly,' and they did that. There was a great squawking and quacking and fluttering as the Duck-people escaped from the lodge. Ho! but Old-man was angry, and he kicked the back of the loon-duck, and that is why his feet turn from his body when he walks or tries to stand. Yes, that is why he is a cripple to-day.

"And all of the Duck-people that peeked that night at the dance still have sore eyes—just as Old-man told them they would have. Of course they hurt and smart no more but they stay red to pay for peeking, and always will. You have seen the mallard and the rest of the Duck-people. You can see that the colors Old-man painted so long ago are still bright and handsome, and they will stay that way forever and ever. Ho!"[18]

In the foreword to *Indian Old-Man Stories* (1920), Linderman expanded on Indian religion, myth, and legend:

It is a mistake to declare that the sun is a god of the Indian, or that Old-man and the sun are one and the same character. Nothing can be farther from the truth. The god is Manitou, and He is All—Everything—Nature; while the sun is referenced by all the tribes that I know only as the greatest manifestation of the deity, whose name is seldom mentioned.

Old-man, or Napi, created the world and its inhabitants. His mistakes and weaknesses are freely discussed, and the laugh accompanies tales of his doing; but mention Manitou and silence falls upon the merrymakers. Reverential awe replaces gaiety, and you will feel that you are guilty of intended sacrilege.[19]

. . . .

He [the Indian] believes in a future life and does not exclude from his heaven other created beings. He does not dare to decide who are fit for his paradise, but leaves that to his God. Because he believes that in a future life there will be happiness and comfort (and in the Indian's life on earth there was hardship and hunger) he has supposed that his dog and his pony will share in that life, and contribute to his welfare as they did in his life on earth. Old Indians have told me that there was no devil "until the black robes wrought him," and so I take it that in the pure beliefs of the Redman there was no such thing as Satan. I have been told by aged Indians that all men, save suicides, go to heaven, eventually, that all men are punished here for their ill deeds.[20]

. . . .

I have asked old Indians "what becomes of all the animals that have been slain since the world began?" and I've had them face the South and move the hands in a circle, as the sun goes, leading me to believe that "nothing is destroyed," was the answer intended. The Indian is intensely religious and profoundly superstitious; but the reasons for some of his most solemn ceremonies have been lost. Even the words of ancient songs are lost, and he uses words he cannot define, he has told me.

It is a mistake to declare that the Indian does this or that. Tribes differ materially in customs, and while I have been led to believe that, fundamentally, their religion is much the same, they do not agree in all particulars. But, unlike ourselves, they declare each man to be right in his own beliefs, and would have him hold fast to them without intruding their own.[21]

The dust jacket to *Indian Old-Man Stories* published by Charles Scribner's Sons gave tribute to the great author: "Maker of the foremost collections of Indian tribal legends, has known and lived among the Indian peoples of the North and West during the period of more than forty years. He has been an accepted and trusted member of their tribes, has listened countless times to their interpretive stories told around the lodge-fire. These he has set down in his famous volume of 'Why Stories,' in a form to appeal to every young person."

Linderman went on to publish numerous classic books on Indian subjects: *Indian Old-Man Stories* (1920), *How It Came About Stories* (1921), *Kootenai Why Stories* (1926), *Old-Man Coyote Stories* (1931), and *Red Mother* (1932).

In 1930, the John Day Company published Linderman's *American: The Life Story of a Great Indian, Plenty-Coups of the Crows*. Linderman had interviewed Chief Plenty Coups on the Crow Reservation through an interpreter. *American* was one of the most powerful and revealing books ever written on the Plains Indians. Plenty Coups gave Linderman the name Sign Talker and proudly stated in the book, "I am glad I have told you these things, Sign Talker. You felt my heart and I feel yours. I know you will tell only what I have said, that your writings will be straight like your tongue, and I sign your paper with my thumb so that your people and mine will know I told you things I have written down."[22]

For the twenty-fifth anniversary of Glacier National Park, Linderman was chosen by the Great Northern Railway to write text for a book introducing the magnificent Blackfeet portraits by Winold Reiss. Linderman wrote:

> Blackfeet! No tribal name appears oftener in the history of the Northwestern Plains; no other is so indelibly written into the meager records of the early fur trade of the upper Missouri River, and none ever inspired more dread in white plainsman. . . .
>
> The tribes of the Blackfeet nation, the Pecunnies (Piegan), Bloods, and Blackfeet, are one people. . . . Nobody can tell their numbers when they came out of the North. Old Pecunnie warriors have told me that their tribe once counted 750 lodges, probably less than 4,000 people; and we know that, of the three tribes of the Blackfeet nation, the Pecunnie was the most numerous.[23]

Perhaps Linderman's greatest book was *American: The Life Story of a Great Indian*. Plenty Coups, chief of the Crow nation and a visionary leader, was born in the summer of 1848 near Billings, Montana. Under his leadership, he allied the Crow with the white man during the Indian wars because the Sioux and the Cheyenne were the traditional enemies of the Crow. In addition, as a young man he had experienced a vision quest that revealed to him that non-native American people would ultimately take control of his homeland in Montana. Thus he believed that cooperation with the white man would benefit his people much more than opposition. He embraced the importance of a white man's education, famously stating, "Education is your greatest weapon. With education you are the white man's equal, without education you are his victim and so shall remain all of your lives. Study, learn, help one another always. Remember there is only poverty and misery in idleness and dreams—but in work there is self-respect and independence."[24]

In Linderman's interview, the old chief recalled as a young child moving camp frequently, which he considered great fun. His earliest remembrance was playing and singing. He recalled his teachers being his grandfathers, fathers, and uncles. "All were quick to praise excellence without speaking a word that might break the spirit of a boy who might be less capable than others. The boy who failed at any lesson got only more lessons, more care, until he was as far as he could go."[25] The earliest task was learning to run and then to swim.

An excerpt from *American:*

One morning after I was eight years old we were called together by my grandfather. He had killed a grizzly bear the day before, and when we gathered near him I saw that he held the grizzly's heart in his hand. We all knew well what was expected of us, since every Crow warrior has eaten some of the heart of a grizzly bear, so that he may truthfully say, 'I have the heart of a grizzly!' I say this, even to this day, when there is trouble to face, and the words help me to keep my head. They clear my mind, make me suddenly calm.

Most tribes of the plains practice this custom. . . . Therefore, to eat of the raw heart of the grizzly bear is to obtain self-mastery, the greatest of human attributes. I knew an old warrior who told me that he had once eaten a small portion of a human heart, the heart of an especially brave enemy, and that he had seen this done more than once when he was a young man. He was not a Crow, however.[26]

Although historically important, Linderman's books had limited commercial success in his lifetime, prompting him to lament, "The critics all praise my books, but the public won't buy them." Frank Bird Linderman would be pleased to know that many of his books are still in print today and are enjoyed by Western history enthusiasts around the world.[27]

Examples of Other Native American Legends from the Northern Plains

Voices of the Winds by Margot Edmonds and Ella E. Clark presented 130 Native American legends. Many were told to the authors by elder storytellers and tribal authors. In their introduction, they wrote, "You will discover here through Indian oral histories how tribal traditions and cultures have been preserved from generation to generation from their earliest beginnings in Alaska during the last Ice Age."[28] What follows are a few examples of some of the more brief legends:

An Address to Mother Corn (Arikara)

In these religious ceremonies, corn was honored and referred to in the endearing and also the highly respectable title of "Mother Corn." At a certain time in the ritual, one of the leaders of the tribe made an address to Mother Corn in the following words, or in words with similar effect.

"In ancient time the Great Spirit Above sent Mother Corn to our people to be their friend and helper, to give them support and health and strength. She has walked with our people on the long and difficult path that they have traveled from the faraway past, and now she marches with us toward the future.

"In the dim, distant past days, Mother Corn gave food to our ancestors. As she gave it to them, she now gives it to us. And as she was faithful and bountiful to our forefathers and to us, so will she be faithful and bountiful to our children. Now and all time to come, she will give to us the blessings for which we have prayed.

"Mother Corn leads us as she led our fathers and our mothers down through the ages. The path of Mother Corn lies ahead, and we walk with her, day by day. We go forward with hope and confidence in the future, just as our ancestors did during all the past ages. When the lonely prairie stretched wide and fearful before us, we were doubtful and afraid. But Mother Corn strengthened and encouraged us.

"Now Mother Corn's return makes our hearts glad. Give thanks! Give thanks to Mother Corn! She brings us a blessing. She brings us peace and plenty. She comes from the Great Spirit of the above, who has brought us good things."

Throughout the address and the elaborate ceremony that preceded and followed it, a stock of corn stood before the altar, representing the spirit of Mother Corn.

About sunset, the staff of corn was dressed like a woman and carried at the head of a religious procession to the brink of the nearby river. White people call it the Missouri River; the Arikaras always called it the Mysterious Waters. With reverence, they placed the stock in the water so that it might float along as a symbol of their affection for Mother Corn.[29]

Origin of the Prairie Rose (Dakota-Sioux)

Long, long ago, when the world was young and people had not come out yet, no flowers bloomed on the prairie. Only grasses and dull, greenish gray shrubs grew there. Earth felt very sad because her robe lacked brightness and beauty.

"I have many beautiful flowers in my heart," Earth said to herself. "I wish they were on my robe. Blue flowers like the clear sky in fair weather, white flowers like the snow of winter, brilliant yellow ones like the sun at midday, pink ones like the dawn of a spring day—all these are in my heart. I am sad when I look on my dull robe, all gray and brown."

A sweet little pink flower heard Earth's sad talking. "Do not be sad, Mother Earth. I will go upon your robe and beautify it."

So the little pink flower came up from the heart of the Earth Mother to beautify the prairies. But when the Wind Demon saw her, he growled, "I will not have that pretty flower on my playground."

He rushed at her, shouting and roaring, and blew out her life. But her spirit returned to the heart of Mother Earth.

When other flowers gained courage to go forth, one after another, Wind Demon killed them also. And their spirits returned to the heart of Mother Earth.

At last Prairie Rose offered to go. "Yes, sweet child," said Earth Mother, "I will let you go. You are so lovely and your breath so fragrant that surely the Wind Demon will be charmed by you. Surely he will let you stay on the prairie."

So Prairie Rose made the long journey up through the dark ground and came out on the drab prairie. As she went, Mother Earth said in her heart, "Oh, I hope that Wind Demon will let her live."

When Wind Demon saw her, he rushed toward her, shouting: "She is pretty, but I will not allow her on my playground. I will blow out her life."

So he rushed on, roaring and drawing his breath and strong gusts. As he came closer, he caught the fragrance of Prairie Rose.

"Oh—how sweet!" He said to himself. "I do not have it in my heart to blow out the life of such a beautiful maiden with so sweet a breath. She must stay here with me. I must make my voice gentle, I must sing sweet songs. I must not frighten her away with my awful noise."

So Wind Demon changed. He became quiet. He sent gentle breezes over the prairie grasses. He whispered and hummed little songs of gladness. He was no longer a demon.

Then other flowers came up from the heart of the Earth Mother, up through the dark ground. They made her robe, the prairie, bright and joyous. Even Wind came to love the blossoms growing among the grasses of the prairie. And so the robe of Mother Earth became beautiful because of the loveliness, the sweetness, and the courage of the Prairie Rose.

Sometimes Wind forgets his gentle songs and becomes loud and noisy. But his loudness does not last long. And he does not harm a person whose robe is the color of Prairie Rose.[30]

The Legend of Standing Rock (Dakota-Sioux)

Years ago, a man from the Dakota-Sioux tribe married a girl from the Arikara tribe. After they had one child, the man brought another wife to their home. The first wife pouted because she was jealous. When time came for their people to break camp, she refused to move from her place. After their tent was taken down, she sat there, on the ground, with her baby on her back. Her husband and the rest of their people moved on.

At noon, her husband stopped the line of people and said to his two brothers, "Go back to your sister-in-law. Tell her to come on. We will wait for you here. But hurry! I fear that she may become desperate and kill herself."

The two rode off and in the evening arrived at their camping place. The woman still sat on the ground. The elder brother said to her, "Sister-in-law, we have come to get you. The camp is waiting for you. Get up and join us."

When she did not answer, brother-in-law put out his hand and touched her lightly on her head. She had turned into stone!

The two brothers lashed their ponies and rode back to camp. They told their story, but were not believed. "She has killed herself," said her husband, "and my brothers will not tell me."

The whole village broke camp and returned to the place where they had left the woman. There she sat, a block of stone in the form of a woman. Her husband's people were very excited. They chose a pony, a handsome one, made a new travois, and placed the stone in its carrying net. Pony and travois were beautifully painted and then decorated with streamers of various colors. The stone was considered holy, and was given a place of honor in the center of the camp.

Whenever the people moved and made a new camp, the stone and travois were taken with them. For years the stone woman traveled with that group. It stands today in front of the Standing Rock Indian Agency in South Dakota.[31]

Origin of the Sioux Peace Pipe (Dakota-Sioux)

Long, long ago, two young and handsome Sioux were chosen by their band to find out where the buffalo were. While the men were riding in the buffalo country, they saw someone in the distance walking toward them.

As always they were on the watch for an enemy. So they hid in some bushes and waited. At last the figure came up the slope. To their surprise, the figure walking toward them was a woman.

When she came closer, she stopped and looked at them. They knew that she could see them, even in their hiding place. On her left arm she carried what looked like a stick and a bundle of sagebrush. Her face was beautiful.

One of the men said, "She is more beautiful than anyone I have ever seen. I want her for my wife."

But the other man replied, "How dare you have such a thought? She is wondrously beautiful and holy—far above ordinary people."

Though still at a distance, the woman heard them talking. She laid down her bundle and spoke to them. "Come. What is it you wish?"

The man who had spoken first went up to her and laid his hands on her as if to claim her. At once, from somewhere above, there came a whirlwind. Then there came a mist, which hid the man and the woman. When the mist cleared, the other man saw the woman with the bundle again on her arm. But his friend was a pile of bones at her feet.

The man stood silent in wonder and awe. Then the beautiful woman spoke to him. "I am on a journey to your people. Among them is a good man whose name is Bull Walking Upright. I am coming to see him especially.

"Go on ahead of me and tell your people that I am on my way. Ask them to move camp and to pitch their tents in a circle. Ask them to leave an opening in the circle, facing the north. In the center of the circle, make a large teepee, also facing the north. There I will meet the Bull Walking Upright and his people."

The man saw to it that all her directions were followed. When she reached the camp, she moved the sagebrush from the gift she was carrying. The gift was a small pipe made of red stone. On it was carved the tiny outline of a buffalo calf.

The pipe she gave to Bull Walking Upright, and then she taught him the prayers he should pray to the Strong One Above. "When you pray to the Strong One Above, you must use this pipe in the ceremony. When you are hungry, unwrap the pipe and lay it bare in the air. Then the buffalo will come where the men can easily hunt and kill them. So the children, the men, and the women will have food and be happy."

The beautiful woman also told him how the people should behave in order to live peacefully together. She taught them the prayers they should say when praying to their Mother Earth. She told him how they should decorate themselves for ceremonies.

"The earth," she said, "is your mother. So, for special ceremonies, you will decorate yourselves as your mother does—in black and red, and brown and white. These are the colors of the buffalo also.

"Above all else, remember that this is a peace pipe that I have given you. You will smoke it before all ceremonies. You will smoke it before making treaties. It will bring peaceful thoughts into your minds. If you will use it when you pray to the Strong One Above and to Mother Earth, you will be sure to receive the blessings that you ask."

When the woman had completed her message, she turned and slowly walked away. All the people watched her in awe. Outside the opening of the circle, she stopped for an instant and then lay down on the ground. She rose again in the form of a black buffalo cow. Again she lay down, and then arose in the form of a red buffalo cow. A third time she lay down, and arose as a brown buffalo cow. The fourth and last time she had the form of a spotlessly white buffalo cow. Then she walked toward the north into the distance and finally disappeared over a far-off hill.

Bull Walking Upright kept the peace pipe carefully wrapped most of the time. Every little while he called all his people together, untied the bundle, and repeated the lessons he had been taught by the beautiful woman. And he used it in prayers and other ceremonies until he was more than one hundred years old.

When he became feeble, he held a great feast. There he gave the pipe and the lessons to Sunrise, a worthy man. In a similar way the pipe was passed down from generation to generation. "As long as the pipe is used," the beautiful woman had said, "Your people will live and will be happy. As soon as it is forgotten, the people will perish."[32]

How Medicine Man Resurrected Buffalo (Arapaho)

At one time an Arapaho Medicine Man named Black-Robe wanted very much to be able to make magic because his people were very hungry. How could he lure the buffaloes back to the Arapaho hunting grounds? Buffalo meat was their principal food.

Black-Robe decided to ask Cedar-Tree for his help. "Go west and hunt buffalo for our people. Try very hard to find at least one buffalo."

Cedar-Tree hunted hard as he was asked to do. After a long time, he saw some black objects at a distance. "Could they be buffaloes?" He wondered.

Encouraged, he walked faster, but as he drew closer he was less sure the black objects were buffaloes. Suddenly, he saw the black things fly toward the sky. By then, Cedar-Tree seemed certain the objects were oversized ravens.

Disappointed, he returned to his village, reporting to Black-Robe what he had seen. The medicine man scolded him for not believing that what he had seen were buffaloes.

"If you had only believed strong enough, the buffaloes would not have changed to ravens," said Black-Robe.

By now the Arapahos were desperately hungry. One woman on the verge of starving made soup from the soles of her moccasins. Next day her uncle, Trying-Bear, set out early to hunt for anything edible. He had no weapons. Fortunately, on the way he met Black-Robe, who loaned him a bow and some arrows.

"Tomorrow morning, I will come to your tent to learn of your success," said Black-Robe." You must even try to find the dried buffalo, if not a live one."

After hunting a long time to the northwest, Trying-Bear finally found a dried buffalo. He ran home swiftly to tell his people. Black-Robe painted his white pony black and wrapped up a black buffalo robe about himself. He stuck his lucky eagle feather in his hair, mounted his black pony, and took off in a rush to find the dried buffalo.

"Follow me, Trying-Bear," Black-Robe called.

Because he wanted to see what Black-Robe would do with the dried buffalo, Trying-Bear followed rapidly. Medicine Man arrived about midday at the place of the dead Buffalo. He dismounted, took aim with his magic eagle feather, and threw it straight at the carcass. Immediately, a live buffalo jumped to his feet!

Black-Robe turned and saw Trying-Bear. "Shoot it!" commanded Medicine Man. Trying-Bear shot it dead.

"Let's skin it and carry everything edible back to our people," said Black-Robe.

A feast of thanksgiving and rejoicing followed. Black-Robe had saved his people from starvation. Araphoes still love to tell the story of how their Medicine Man resurrected the dead buffalo with his magic eagle-feather-medicine![33]

The Buffalo Rock (Blackfeet)

There was once a very poor woman, the second wife of a Blackfeet. Her buffalo robe was old and full of holes; her buffalo moccasins were worn and ripped. She and her people were camped not far from a cliff that would be a good place for a buffalo drive. They were very much in need of a buffalo, for they were not only ragged but starving.

One day while this poor woman was gathering wood, she heard a voice singing. Looking around, she found that the song was coming from a buffalo rock [a fossil shell]. It sang, "Take me. Take me. I have great power."

So the woman took the buffalo rock. When she returned to her lodge, she said to her husband, "Call the men and have them sing to bring the buffalo."

"Are you in earnest?" her husband asked.

"Yes, I am," the woman replied. "Call the men, and also get a small piece of the back of a buffalo from the Bear Medicine man. Ask some of the men to bring the four rattles they use."

The husband did as his wife directed. Then she showed him how to arrange the inside of the lodge in the kind of square box with some sagebrush and buffalo chips. Though it was the custom for the first wife to sit next to her husband, the man directed his second wife to put on the dress of the other woman and to sit beside him. When everything was ready, the men who had been summoned sat down in the lodge beside the woman and her husband. Then the buffalo rock began to sing, "The buffalo will all drift back. The buffalo will all drift back."

Hearing this song, the woman asked one of the young men to go outside and put a great many buffalo chips in line. "After you have them in place, wave at them with a buffalo robe four times, and shout at them in a sing song. At the fourth time, all the buffalo chips will turn into buffaloes and go over the cliff."

The young man followed her directions, and the chips became buffaloes. At the same time, the woman led the people in the lodge in the singing of songs. One song was about the buffalo that would lead the others in the drive. While the people were chanting it, a cow took the lead and all the herd followed her. They plunged over the cliff and were killed.

Then the woman sang,

> More than a hundred buffalo
> Have fallen over the cliff.
> I have made them fall.
> And the man above the earth hears me singing.
> More than a hundred buffalo
> Have fallen over the cliff.

And so the people learned that the rock was very powerful. Ever since that time, they have taken care of the buffalo rock and have prayed to it.[34]

Origin of the Sweat Lodge (Piegan)

A girl of great beauty, the Chief's daughter, was worshipped by many young handsome men of the Piegan tribe. But she would not have any one of them for her husband.

One young tribesman was very poor in his face marked with an ugly scar [from smallpox]. Although he saw rich and handsome men of his tribe rejected by the Chief's daughter, he decided to find out if she would have him for her husband. When she laughed at him for even asking, he ran away toward the south in shame.

After traveling several days, he dropped to the ground, weary and hungry, and fell asleep. From the heavens, Morning-Star looked down and pitied the young unfortunate youth, knowing his trouble.

To Sun and Moon, his parents, Morning-Star said, "There is a poor young man lying on the ground with no one to help him. I want to go after him for a companion."

"Go and get him," said his parents.

Morning-Star carried the young man, Scarface, into the sky. Sun said, "Do not bring him into my lodge yet, for he smells ill. Build four sweat lodges."

When this was done, Sun led Scarface into the first sweat lodge. He asked Morning-Star to bring a hot coal on a forked stick. Sun then broke off a bit of sweetgrass and placed it upon the hot coal. As incense arose Sun began to sing, "Old Man is coming in with his body; it is sacred," repeating it four times.

Sun passed his hands back and forth through the smoke and rubbed them over the face, left arm, and side of Scarface. Sun repeated the ceremony on the boy's right side, purifying him and removing the odors of earthly people.

Sun took Scarface into the other three sweat lodges, performing the same healing ceremony. The body of Scarface changed color and he shone like a yellow light.

Using a soft feather, Sun brushed it over the youth's face, magically wiping away the scar. With a final touch to the young man's long, yellow hair, Sun caused him to look exactly like Morning-Star. The two young men were led by Sun into his own lodge and placed side by side in the position of honor.

"Old Woman," called the father. "Which is your son?"

Moon pointed to Scarface, "That one is our son."

"You do not know your own child," answered Sun.

"He is not our son. We will call him Mistaken-for Morning-Star," as all laughed heartily at the mistake.

The two boys were together constantly and became close companions. One day, they were on an adventure when Morning-Star pointed out some large birds with very long, sharp beaks.

"Foster-Brother, I warn you not to go near those dangerous creatures," said Morning-Star. "They killed my other brothers with their beaks."

Suddenly the birds chased the two boys. Morning-Star fled toward his home, but Foster-Brother stopped, picking up a club and one by one struck the birds dead.

Upon reaching home, Morning-Star excitedly reported to his father what had happened. Sun made a victory song honoring the young hero. In gratitude for saving Morning-Star's life, Sun gave him the forked stick for lifting hot embers and a braided sweetgrass to make incense. These sacred elements necessary for making the sweat lodge ceremony were a gift of trust.

"And this my sweat lodge I give to you," said the Sun. Mistaken-for-Morning-Star observed very carefully how it was constructed, in his mind preparing himself to one day return to earth.

When Scarface did arrive at his tribal village, all of his people gathered to see the handsome young man in their midst. At first, they did not recognize him as Scarface.

"I have been in the sky," he told them. "Behold me, Morning-Star looks just like this. The Sun gave me these things used in the sweat lodge healing ceremony. That is how I lost my ugly scar."

Scarface explained how the forked stick and sweetgrass were used. Then he set to work showing his people how to make the sweat lodge. This is how the first medicine sweat lodge was built upon the earth by the Piegan tribe.

Now that Scarface was so very handsome and brought such a great blessing of healing to his tribe, the Chief's beautiful daughter became his wife.

In remembrance of Sun's gift to Scarface and his tribe, the Piegans always make the sweat lodge healing ceremony an important part of their annual Sun Dance Celebration.[35]

A final story from *American Indian Myths and Legends:*

Coyote and the Origin of Death (Caddo)

In the beginning of this world, there was no such thing as death. Everybody continued to live until there were so many people that the earth had no room for any more. The chiefs held a council to determine what to do. One man rose and said he thought it would be a good plan to have the people die and be gone for a little while, and then return.

As soon as he sat down, Coyote jumped up and said he thought people ought to die forever. He pointed out that this world is not large enough to hold all of the people, and that if the people who died came back to life, there would not be food enough for all.

All the other men objected. They said that they did not want their friends and relatives to die and be gone forever, for then they would grieve and worry and there would be no happiness in the world. Everyone except Coyote decided to have people die and be gone for a little while, and then come back to life again.

The medicine men built a large grass house facing the east. When they had completed it, they called the men of the tribe together and told them that people who died would be restored to life in the medicine house. The chief medicine man explained that they would sing a song calling the spirit of the dead to the grass house. When the spirit came, they would restore it to life. All the people were glad, because they were anxious for the dead to come and live with them again.

When the first man died, the medicine men assembled in the grass house and sang. In about ten days a whirlwind blew from the west and circled about the grass house. Coyote saw it, and as the wind was about to enter the house, he closed the door. The spirit of the whirlwind, finding the door closed, whirled by. In this way Coyote made death eternal, and from that time on, people grieved over their death and were unhappy.

Now whenever anyone sees a whirlwind or hears the wind whistle, he says: "Someone is wandering about." Ever since Coyote closed the door, the spirits of the dead have wandered over the earth trying to find someplace to go, until at last they discovered the road to the spirit land.

Coyote ran away and never came back, and when he saw what he had done, he was afraid. Ever after that, he has run from one place to another, always looking back first over one shoulder and then over the other to see if anyone is pursuing him. And ever since then he has been starving, for no one will give him anything to eat.[36]

In *American Indian Myths and Legends,* authors Richard Erdoes and Alfonso Ortiz concluded, "In the end, however, these legends are not told merely for enjoyment, or for education, or for amusement: they are believed. They are emblems of a living religion, giving concrete form to a set of beliefs and traditions that link people living today to ancestors from centuries and millennia past. As Bronislaw Malinowski said, 'Myth in its living, primitive form is not merely a story told but a reality lived.'"[37]

By late in the nineteenth century, George Bird Grinnell wrote that if the Indian was understood better by the American public and could be educated, then assimilation could be accomplished. In 1879, Richard Henry Pratt opened an off-reservation school in Carlisle, Pennsylvania, that initially produced encouraging results. Many other schools built in the West followed.

Grinnell was in the vanguard of ethnographers who would attempt to educate the public in the ways of the Indian through publications in periodicals and books. He may not have appreciated the depth of racism in an America that cared little for lesser humans. The rich Native American religions, rituals, and ceremonies were relegated to the trash heap by a Christian nation that saw that the only hope for the heathen savages was conversion and assimilation. Education was a way of leading Indians out of their primitive state, but many Americans believed they would never attain the level of a white person.

Today, it is ironic that America is seeing a decline in religion and church adherence. Numerous seekers now find spirituality in nature and are disillusioned with many of the Christian denominations, which are viewed as hypocritical and intolerant. Manifest Destiny seems as distant and passing as the Native American way of life. Secularization is currently in vogue. But there was a time when Western civilization and its greatest leaders were driven and guided by Christianity. The next two chapters will examine who some say is the most important man who ever lived and the religion he inspired.

CHAPTER TWELVE

The Way: Historical Christianity to the Dark Ages

Jesus is by all accounts the most significant person in the history of Western Civilization. But he was not the most significant person in his own day. Quite to the contrary, he appears to have been almost a complete unknown.
—BART D. EHRMAN, AUTHOR AND PROFESSOR OF
RELIGIOUS STUDIES AT THE UNIVERSITY OF NORTH CAROLINA

The further the spiritual evolution of mankind advances, the more certain it seems to me that the path to genuine religiosity does not lie through the fear of life, and the fear of death, and blind faith, but through striving after rational knowledge. In this sense I believe that the priest must become a teacher if he wishes to do justice to his lofty educational mission.
—ALBERT EINSTEIN

I pray that the eyes of your heart may be enlightened.
—EPHESIANS 1:18

The Bible is the best-selling, most read, most translated, and highly revered book in the history of Western civilization. European and American cultures highly prize the written word. It is considered the highest form of civilized thinking. We ask: what does the law say, what does the Constitution say, what does the Bible say?

Bible classes in seminary are usually taught to students from essentially an academic, historical perspective unlike what they've heard at church or Sunday school. This approach, taught in both Protestant and now Catholic mainline seminaries, is what is called the "historical-critical" method. It is in direct opposition to the "devotional" approach to the Bible one learns in church where the emphasis is on what the Bible has to say—especially personally or about society.[1] The following is a brief story about early, historical Christianity so that we can better understand the Christians' attitudes toward Native Americans and their religions, and the havoc it created.

Dawn

At the beginning of recorded history, people lived lives of misery and were exploited by tyrannical empires that covered huge areas. The first empires arose in Mesopotamia more than 6,000 years ago, and they were followed by Egyptian, Chinese, Persian, and Indian empires. Western civilization began in Greece. The Greeks excelled in warfare, democracy, literacy, the arts, and technology. And more importantly, they provided lasting achievements in the area of speculative philosophy and formal logic. The Greeks referred to writing as "the mother of memory."[2]

Plato (428-348 BCE) and Aristotle (384-322 BCE) are the two most influential figures in Western philosophy. Consistent with Native American beliefs, Plato said that everything both animate and inanimate is inhabited by a soul. It was a soul that caused the sun to move, and it was the human soul that was capable of thought, such as philosophy. Souls came first and were immortal. He believed God was remote and impersonal and took no part in day-to-day life.[3]

The early classical thinkers emphasized the rational order of the universe, which was later to become an important inspiration for the development of modern science. Plato had by far the greatest impact on Christian thinkers through the Middle Ages.[4] He identified the sources of chaos and evil as some part of God's creation. In contrast to the Greeks, the Bible presented the material world as originally good because it was created by God.[5]

Ancient religions were almost never interested in true beliefs. Pagan religions—those that were polytheistic and neither Jewish nor Christian—were not characterized by creeds that had to be recited, beliefs that had to be affirmed, or scriptures that conveyed divine truth. Ancient religions didn't require you to believe one thing or another. They were more focused on what you did, that is, proper practices such as sacrifices to the gods and set prayers. With the worship of many gods, there was not the emphasis on one religion being right and the others being wrong. Another difference from today is that ancient polytheistic religions were not overly focused on the afterlife.

In contrast, Christians conveyed to others that it did matter what you believed and that believing the "correct" things could make you right while believing "incorrect" things could make you wrong—sending you to hell. Christians believed that only they held the truth about God, about Christ, about salvation, and about eternal life. Christianity was an exclusivist religion—a fact that would not bode well for Native Americans.[6]

Christian theology had a direct influence in the way Westerners viewed the nature of the world. Plato and Aristotle were highly influential in its development. They wrote about a mediator between their gods and the common human. The Greeks developed the idea of the immortality of the soul. St. Augustine and St. Thomas Aquinas, two of the major theologians of Christian history, throughout their lives sought to reconcile Greek philosophy with Christian ideas.

Bookish Judaism

Books played almost no role in the polytheistic religions of the ancient Western world. Emphasis was instead placed on honoring the gods through ritual acts of sacrifice—reminiscent of Native American ceremonies like the Sun Dance. In contrast, Judaism stressed its ancestral traditions, customs, and laws, which were recorded in books. Jews throughout the Roman Empire understood that God had given direction to his chosen ones through the writings of Moses, referred to as the Torah, which means guidance or law. The Torah consisted of five books: Genesis, Exodus, Leviticus, Numbers, and Deuteronomy.[7]

One major theme in the Torah is God's activity in history, from a linear, single beginning and moving toward an end time. Jews and Christians relying on the Old Testament believed the world was 6,000 years old. In contrast, Native Americans believe in the circle of life. Another theme was the covenant, the agreement between God and his people. Genesis, the first book of the Torah, is concerned primarily with three origins: of the universe, of humanity, and of the children of Israel—the descendants of Abraham, Isaac, and Jacob. Abraham is considered the patriarch of all three monotheistic religions: Judaism, Christianity, and Islam. Abraham was promised by God that he would be the father of many nations, including one through his son with Sarah, Isaac—the Jews; and one through his son with Hagar, Ishmael—the Arabs.

Another theme in the Old Testament is the sacred value of creation and the harmony that humans should have with all living things—similar to Native Americans' belief. A fine example of this is found in Job 12:7-10:

> For ask now the animals, and they will teach you; ask the birds of the air, and they will tell you; or speak to the earth, and it will teach you; and the fish of the sea will declare to you. Who [is so blind as] not to recognize all in these that it is God's hand which does it? In His hand is the life of every living thing and the breath of all mankind.

Even though today this passage seems quite strange and not relevant, its theme was very much embraced by ancient people throughout the world. Another passage, from Ecclesiastes 3:18-20, would make proponents of social Darwinism and survival of the fittest cringe:

> I also said to myself, "As for humans, God tests them so that they may see that they are like the animals. Surely the fate of human beings is like that of the animals; the same fate awaits them both: As one dies, so dies the other. All have the same breath; humans have no advantage over animals. Everything is meaningless, all go to the same place; all come from dust, and to dust all return."

Jews have lived in almost every part of the world, but they have typically managed to avoid being assimilated into the locally dominant cultures, in much the same manner as Native Americans. In some cases, Jews were able to flourish, such as in Poland in the Middle Ages. A pattern that repeats itself countless times is one where Jews were all too often violently attacked. In fifteenth-century Poland, ruthless campaigns were conducted against Jews. Later in that same century, in Spain, Jews were forcibly expelled after Christian rulers replaced Muslims. Anti-Semitism was pervasive throughout Europe in the Middle Ages, and Jews were exiled from many countries.

The fear of false gods was enshrined in the Ten Commandments in the Jewish Old Testament: Thou shalt not make unto thee any graven image, or any likeness of anything that is in heaven above, or that is in the earth beneath, or that is in the water under the earth. Extreme aniconism—the religious prohibition against images of living creatures that are religious figures—thus has deep roots in Judaism and may be a reason that the Jews traditionally were people of words, not images. There is no centuries-long tradition of Jewish religious art analogous to that of Christianity. That changed in the twentieth century when Jewish painters, sculptors, and photographers made important contributions to the visual record of the century.[8]

Jesus Christ, An Unknown Legend in His Time

Israel was controlled by a number of powers: first by the Babylonians, then the Persians, then the Greeks, then the Egyptians, then the Syrians, and then the Romans. Jesus was born under Roman rule. When Jesus of Nazareth was born, all of Palestine was ruled by a client king named Herod. When Jesus died, the northern part of Israel, Galilee, was ruled by one of Herod's sons, but Judea in the south was ruled by a Roman governor, Pontius Pilate. The use of the name Jesus Christ needs some clarification. It is often used as if Jesus was his first name and Christ was his surname. However, Christ is a title that was given Jesus. It is the English equivalent of the Greek term *kristos,* which means anointed, or in Hebrew, *mashiyach* or messiah.[9] Many non-believers not only don't believe that Jesus was God, but also believe he was mythical and never really existed. Yet there is evidence—though sparse—outside the Bible that supports his existence as a human who walked the Earth.

Archaeological research reveals that, during the time of Jesus' adolescence and early adulthood, Nazareth was a poor village of fewer than 400 people. Jesus worked there as a *tekton.* This Greek word is typically translated as carpenter, but it also refers to craftsman, woodworker, or even day laborer. His work was considered below that of a peasant, since the *tekton* did not own land. The irony in the nineteenth century is that Christian Americans placed private land ownership near the top of the American dream list and coerced Native Americans—who strongly believed in community ownership of land—into farming small plots of land they were forced to own.

The most important day for Christians is Easter. The Easter story is both appalling and amazing—the stunning betrayal of Jesus by one of his disciples, the triple denial by Peter, his best friend, and the horrific crucifixion. That tragedy is followed by a stunning reversal three days later.

Christians' belief that Jesus rose from the dead is a game changer. His teachings became even more important because a person who rose from the grave, who demonstrated his power over death, and who has proven his divine authority demands attention. And what Jesus says demands a response. Many subsequent Christian actions have been greatly beneficial, but unfortunately, some have come in twisted forms, often to the detriment of non-Christians—the Doctrine of Discovery, pro-slavery, Indian reservations, ethnic cleansing, cultural if not actual genocide, and Manifest Destiny.

In the Bible, on the third day after his death, Jesus showed his followers his hands and side, which bore the marks of the crucifixion and the pierce of the lance. These were necessary credentials for the identity of the risen Lord. That had implications for all Christians. It meant that Jesus carried upon himself visible marks of his human life—he remembered human suffering. There is a mystery of the two natures of Jesus: human and divine. The human one was raised from the dead and the divine one suffered for human pain.

Mainstream Christian theology has accepted the mystery that Jesus was both fully human and fully divine at all times. However, this was not accepted by the men of the Enlightenment, including many of our most famous thinkers, especially Thomas Jefferson, who did not believe in miracles or the Trinity—that Jesus was God.

In Europe, the teachings of Jesus were often ignored or subjugated due to greed. When Jesus witnessed injustices—ignoring the sick, the mistreatment of the powerless, and other earthly inequalities—he preached against them with divine inspiration and because his heart was human. When Christian believers listen to Jesus, they are listening not only to God who cares for the poor but also to a human being who knew the poor and who was poor himself.[10]

The Apocalyptic Jesus

A point of contention between Jews and Christians has always been their definition of the Messiah. Before Christianity, no Jews believed that the Messiah would suffer and die. For them the Messiah would be a figure of grandeur and power who would implement God's purposes on Earth in a dominating way. Jews did not understand the passages of Scripture that referred to the suffering of God's righteous one as a reference to the Messiah. And none of these passages (Isaiah 53; Psalm 22) mentions the Messiah.[11]

Jesus was a Jewish rabbi, but his actions and teachings enraged those who taught traditional Jewish religion. For example, Jesus touched lepers, who were considered outcasts, and in a strong patriarchal society he welcomed women as his disciples. Jesus mingled with the poor, the weak, and the sick and called on the wealthy and powerful to repent and reform. Jesus' power was shown through selfless service, healing the sick through miracles, and the ultimate sacrifice on the cross. He taught a radical ethics, one that called on people to turn away from revenge and retributive justice to an ethic of love and forgiveness. The New Testament teaches that one of the main reasons Jesus came to Earth was so that men could repent and accept him as their personal savior. They would then secure a place in heaven. Jesus said, "It is not the healthy who need a doctor, but the sick. I have not come to call the righteous, but sinners to repent" (Luke 5:31).

Since the historic publication over a century ago of Albert Schweitzer's masterpiece, *The Quest of the Historical Jesus,* most scholars in Europe and North America have understood Jesus as a Jewish apocalyptic prophet.[12] Most churchgoers know little about this, but those attending the leading seminaries and divinity schools in this country have studied it for years. Who is the apocalyptic Jesus and what did he teach? Professor Bart D. Ehrman has written extensively on the subject. He explains Jesus this way:

> Like other apocalypticists of his day, Jesus saw the world in dualistic terms, filled with the forces of good and evil. The current age was controlled by the forces of evil—the Devil, demons, disease, disasters, and death; but God was soon to intervene in this wicked age to overthrow the forces of evil and bring in his good kingdom, the kingdom of God, in which there would be no more pain, misery, or suffering. Jesus' followers could expect this kingdom to arrive soon—in fact, in their lifetimes. It would be brought by a cosmic judge of the earth, whom Jesus called the Son of Man (alluding to a passage in the Jewish Scriptures, Daniel 7:13-14). When the Son of Man arrived there would be a judgment of the earth, in which the wicked would be destroyed but the righteous rewarded. Those who were suffering pain and oppression now would be exalted then; those who had sided with evil and as a result were prospering now would be abased then. People needed to repent of their evil ways and prepare for the coming of the Son of Man and the Kingdom of God that would appear in his wake, for it was to happen very soon.[13]

Prolific author and Catholic priest Henri Nouwen very much understood the apocalyptic Jesus. Those who tout the prosperity gospel set Christians up for a fall and disillusionment. Nouwen eloquently wrote:

Many people live with the unconscious or conscious expectation that eventually things will get better; wars, hunger, poverty, oppression, and exploitation will vanish; and all people will live in harmony. Their lives and work are motivated by that expectation. When this does not happen in their lifetimes, they are often disillusioned and experience themselves as failures.

But Jesus doesn't support such an optimistic outlook. He foresees not only the destruction of his beloved city Jerusalem but also a world full of cruelty, violence, and conflict. For Jesus there is no happy ending in this world. The challenge of Jesus is not to solve all the world's problems before the end of time but to remain faithful at any cost.[14]

The principal sources of information about Jesus are the Gospels of the New Testament. The Gospels, although written anonymously, have been traditionally ascribed to four men: two of Jesus' disciples—Matthew, the tax collector, and John, the son, Zebedee—and two companions of other apostles—Mark, the secretary of Peter, and Luke, the traveling companion of Paul. Mark was the first gospel written in 65-70 CE (Jesus died around 30 CE); Matthew and Luke's in 80-85 CE; and John's in 90-95 CE. The Gospel of Mark was the first of the three synoptic gospels—the majority of both Matthew and Luke were based on information from Mark.

There were other gospels, like the Coptic Gospel of Thomas, that were not included in the New Testament because they were considered filled with heresy at the time the New Testament was being compiled. The Gospel of Thomas is one of the greatest archaeological finds of the twentieth century. It presented a Gnostic view of a material world that was evil and created by an inferior deity. Religion's goal was to acquire the knowledge (Greek: *gnosis*) to escape this fallen world. Dualism was an important Gnostic concept in which some humans were merely matter and destined to die and others possessed a spark of the divine. The aim of Gnostics was to find the knowledge to allow those with sparks of the divine to leave this world and return to their spiritual home. Thus, salvation was obtained through self-knowledge. The Gospel does not contain an account of Jesus' life, crucifixion, or resurrection, but only his secret teachings.[15]

In Gnostic followers, we find the first Christian elitists. They believed they possessed a higher spiritual knowledge, similar to Christian racists who would wreak havoc on non-Christians over the centuries. John was one of the first to combat the Gnostic teachings in the late first-century Christian churches. He wrote in 2 John 7, "Many deceivers have gone out into the world, those who do not confess that Jesus Christ has come in the flesh; any such person is the deceiver and the antichrist."

Because the Gospels were written in Greek, not Aramaic, they appear to have been compiled outside of Palestine. Sources like John and Luke indicate that the Gospels were written by scribes on reports that were handed down, either orally or in writing, from earlier Christians and that ultimately these reports went back to eyewitnesses.

The earliest readers of the Gospels found their authors' names to be unimportant. It may come as a surprise to many Christians that the first time the Gospels had names attributed to them came about 120-130 CE in the writings of an obscure author named Papias who claimed that the apostle Peter would speak about Jesus' words and deeds as the occasion demanded, and that Mark, his secretary, later wrote the stories down but not in order. He also claimed that Matthew wrote the sayings of Jesus in Hebrew and that everyone interpreted them as they could. He said nothing about Luke or John.[16]

Even though Matthew is the first book to appear in the New Testament, it was not the first book written. Those books were penned starting in the 50s CE by the apostle Paul, and Thessalonians I was his first book. Paul's letters to Christians provided guidance, explained doctrine, encouraged fellow believers, and explained the significance of Jesus' crucifixion and resurrection. Paul, more than Jesus, can be seen as a founder of the Christian religion. His view was the atonement theory, which is based on the concept that we are born with original sin and inherit our sinful nature from our fallen ancestors, Adam and Eve. We can be saved only by God's grace through Jesus. To make our salvation possible, Jesus sacrificially took our sins on himself.

The Gospels were written between the years 50 and 95 CE. The New Testament achieved its current form around the fourth century. It should be noted that we don't have the originals of any of the books of the New Testament. The copies, in Greek, were made, in most instances, centuries later.[17]

The message that Jesus taught about sharing was certainly consistent with the Native American's belief in community ownership of possessions. Under the Allotment Act in the late nineteenth century, the U.S. government would force Indians to own private property. In Matthew 19, Jesus tells a wealthy man to sell his riches, give them to the poor, and follow Him. Jesus, who often taught by using parables, ends his lesson in Matthew by pointing out that to live the way God desires, followers need to share in everything, including homes, relationships, and property.

While these passages were overlooked by Europeans and Americans, other messages weren't. They would have a profound and often dismal impact on all Native Americans and other non-Christian races. For centuries, Jesus' words provided Christian missionaries the rationale not only for spreading their religion worldwide but also converting heathens to Christianity. Greed was made more acceptable when dealing with heathens. If the savages didn't want to accept the Christian way to heaven, then they deserved hell on Earth and beyond. In the white man's mind and heart, his Christian God wanted His followers to own the West. Manifest Destiny and social Darwinism were born.

The Way to the Father

One of the most profound passages by Jesus is in John 14:6 where He proclaimed, "I am the way and the truth and the life. No one comes to the Father [God] except through me." In Acts 4:12—most likely written by Luke—this foundational statement is reinforced: "Salvation is found in no one else, for there is no other name under heaven given to me by which we must be saved." Paul confirmed the exclusivity in 1 Timothy 2:5: "For there is one God and one mediator between God and men, the man Jesus Christ."

In *The Problem of Pain*, the great Christian apologist and defender of the faith C. S. Lewis summarized the struggle that many Christians and non-Christians have with the exclusivity of Jesus being the only way to God:

> And it has been admitted throughout that man has free will and that all gifts to him are therefore two-edged. From these premises it follows directly that the Divine labor to redeem the world cannot be certain of succeeding as regards every individual soul. Some will not be redeemed. There is no doctrine which I would more willingly remove from Christianity than this, if it lay in my power. It has the full support of Scripture and, especially, of Our Lord's own words; it has always been held by Christendom; and it has the support of reason. If the game is played, it must be possible to lose it. If the happiness of the creature lies in self-surrender, no one can make that surrender but himself (though many can help him to make it) and he may refuse. I would pay any price to be able to say truthfully "all will be saved."[18]

The Great Commission

In King David's "Song of Praise" he states, "Therefore I will praise you, O Lord, among the nations; I will sing praises to your name" (2 Samuel 22:50). It has been called the greatest evangelical passage in the Old Testament. These words would inspire Jesus.

A profound statement by Jesus would lead to all sorts of distortions by Christian colonial powers. Crusaders, conquistadors, missionaries, and governments would use his command to justify taking lands from heathen races—usually people of color. At first, heathens reasoned that if they converted, white Christian aggression would end, but as time passed, even conversion didn't lead to retention of their lands. By then, Manifest Destiny and racism commanded white Christians to seize any lands they deemed God wanted them to have, and if there was profit to be made—God was good. Matthew 28:16-20 explains the Great Commission:

> Then the eleven disciples went to Galilee, to the mountain where Jesus had told them to go. When they saw him, they worshiped him; but some doubted. Then Jesus came to them and said, "All authority in heaven and on earth has been given me. Therefore go and make disciples of all nations, baptizing them in the name of the Father and of the Son and of the Holy Spirit, and teaching them to obey everything I have commanded you. And surely I am with you always, to the very end of the age."

In his classic *The Screwtape Letters,* C. S. Lewis wrote about human nature in a fallen world through Satan's eyes:

> Once you have made the World an end, and faith a means, you have almost won your man, and it makes very little difference what kind of worldly end he is pursuing. Provided that meetings, pamphlets, policies, movements, causes, and crusades matter more to him than prayers and sacraments and charity, he is ours [Satan's]—and the more "religious" (on those terms) the more securely ours. I could show you a pretty cageful down here.[19]

After Jesus Christ

In the early Christian movement, even though books were important, almost always they were read aloud in social settings, such as in worship. They were read aloud so that the illiterate could hear, understand, and even study them. Despite the fact that early Christianity was by and large made up of illiterate believers, it was a highly literary religion.[20] It should be noted that in Roman Palestine the best guesstimate is that something like three percent of the population could read, and they resided in the larger cities and towns. The majority of people outside urban areas hardly ever saw a written text. Populations in smaller towns and villages may have had a literacy level of about one percent. Those who did learn to read did so in Hebrew or Aramaic and not Greek.[21]

Both early Christian and Native American oral cultures very likely changed as they circulated by word of mouth. The concern for verbal accuracy is found exclusively in written cultures where, in most cases, accounts can be checked to see if they are consistent. Before the printing press, however, the Bible was reproduced by hand by scribes who could easily alter the text depending on what their patron desired. We have no original Bible.[22] Many Christians would counter this statement by saying each word in the Bible is divinely inspired.

Among all the pagan sources that come down to us from the centuries following Jesus' death, he is mentioned only twice by Pliny the Younger and once by Tacitus. The first-century Palestinian historian Flavius Josephus gives us a bit more information but, again, only enough to support the claims of the New Testament. That is, that Jesus was known as a teacher and doer of great deeds who acquired a faithful following but was crucified at the instigation of Jewish leaders under Pontius Pilate, when Tiberius was emperor. Nor is there much additional information to be gleaned from the twenty-three other books of the New Testament outside of the Gospels, including the writings of Paul.[23]

From the first century CE, we have hundreds of documents written by pagan authors for all kinds of reasons, as well as numerous public inscriptions and considerable archives of private letters. In none of these extensive library records is Jesus ever mentioned at all. As enormous an impact as Jesus has made on Western culture over the past 2,000 years, in his own day, his impact appears to have been practically nonexistent. He was an unknown legend in his time.[24]

Our earliest recorded references to Jesus in pagan sources comes from the early second century, and only two references are documented between 30-130 CE. The first is from the Roman governor, Pliny the Younger, of the province of Bithynia-Pontus, modern-day Turkey. He mentions a group of Christians who are followers of "Christ, whom they worship as a God."[25]

The second, and more substantial, reference comes in the writings of a friend of Pliny, the famous Roman historian Tacitus. In his history of Rome, *The Annals* (115 CE), Tacitus discusses an incident that had happened fifty years earlier, when Emperor Nero torched the city of Rome to enable him to develop his own architectural plans for the city. When Nero became suspected of perpetrating the arson, he had the Christians, who were generally despised by the populace, rounded up, charged with the arson, and executed in various heinous ways. Tacitus mentions that they were followers of "Christ," who, he notes, was crucified by Pontius Pilate, when Tiberius was the emperor. No other certain references to Jesus exist by any pagan author within a century of his death.[26]

The surviving Jewish sources are also of little use in reconstructing the life of Jesus. The main source for the history of Palestine at the time was Flavius Josephus, a Jewish aristocrat who was a general in the northern part of Israel, Galilee, during the Jewish uprising against Rome in 66-70 CE. Josephus wrote a twenty-volume work on the history of the Jews from Adam and Eve to his own time, called the *Jewish Antiquities*. In brief references, Josephus notes that Jesus was called by some the Messiah and that he had a brother named James. In another reference, Jesus was known to be a wise man who did spectacular deeds and had a following among both Jews and Gentiles. He was brought up on charges by the Jewish leaders, appeared before Pontius Pilate, and was crucified. His followers formed a community that continued to thrive, first in Judea, then elsewhere, even in Rome.[27]

Christianity Becomes Complicated: The Early Christian Theologians

Christianity's first theologians, called the apostolic fathers, consisted of persons who interpreted and applied the apostolic message in the first apostleless generation, which was besieged by false gospels and attacks from pagan skeptics. They wrote primarily to exhort, encourage, and instruct Christian churches in the transitional time after the deaths of the apostles. The apostolic fathers included Clement, Ignatius, and Polycarp. They were writers of the second century who attempted to defend Christianity against pagan opponents such as Celsus.[28]

In the mid-second century, a rich Greek shipbuilder arrived in Rome and made a large donation to the Roman church. His name was Marcion, and he was the first Christian known to produce an actual "canon" of Scripture—

a collection of books that constituted the sacred texts of the faith. He idolized Paul and considered him the only true apostle. Marcion would be eventually declared a heretic for a number of divergent beliefs. One of them was that he believed there were two different Gods: the harsh God of the Jews who created the world and called Israel to be his people, and the God of Jesus who sent Christ into the world to save people from the wrathful vengeance of the Jewish creator God.[29]

In his canon, Marcion included ten letters of Paul that were available to him and the Gospel of Luke. There was no Old Testament. However, by the end of the second century there were Christians who were insisting that Matthew, Mark, Luke, and John were the Gospels—no more or less. The four Gospels were inspired by Irenaeus in his classic *Against Heresies,* who wrote, "It is not possible that the Gospels can be either more or fewer in number than they are. For, since there are four zones of the world in which we live, and four principle winds, while the Church is scattered throughout the world, and the pillar and ground of the Church is the Gospel . . . it is fitting that she should have four pillars. . . ."[30]

During the first two centuries of the church, there were no church buildings, and followers met in members' homes. It's very likely that the members who hosted these meetings were some of the wealthier individuals in the community, since most people living in urban areas lived in small, cramped apartments.

The second and third century's leading apologists—defenders of the faith—were Origin, Athenagoras of Athens, Tertullian, and Justin Martyr, who stressed the authority of reason. They believed reason could yield an increasingly accurate understanding of God's will. They were trying to influence relatively humane Roman emperors such as Marcus Aurelius to take Christianity seriously, if not as true.[31]

Athenagoras of Athens is credited with presenting one of the first theological explanations of the doctrine of the Trinity, writing, "We acknowledge God, and a son his Logos, and the Holy Spirit united in essence—the Father, the Son, and the Spirit of effluence, as light from fire."[32] Tertullian, who was born in 150 CE in Carthage, wrote expositions on both the doctrines of the Trinity and the humanity and deity of Christ, and laid down the foundation for later official church orthodoxy in both the East and the West.[33] His *Against Praxas* provided a fairly clear statement of this organic monotheism: "All [three—Father, Son, and Holy Ghost] are of One."[34] What the Trinity means is still argued today. In the Age of Enlightenment, the Unitarian Church, Thomas Jefferson, and others argued against the divinity of Jesus. Jefferson produced his own gospels void of any of the stories of the miracles performed by Jesus.

The final steps in the formal canonization process and creation of the New Testament took place in the late fourth century. The first list containing all twenty-seven books, Matthew through Revelation, and no others, was produced by Athanasius, bishop of Alexandria and leading defender of orthodoxy, in his Easter letter to Christian congregations in Egypt in 367 CE.[35]

Christian Rome

The Roman Empire reached far from Italy. Roman ships docked at 250 ports. A quarter of a million miles of roads—each twenty-three feet wide—were built throughout Europe, Africa, and the Middle East. Commerce and the word of Jesus traveled along them. There is perhaps no event in the history of Christian theology that is more surprising and influential than the conversion of the Roman Empire to Christianity. At the end of the third century and the beginning of the fourth, the persecution of Christians increased throughout the Empire. At that time, the portion of citizens and subjects of the Empire who were Christians was probably no more than five percent.[36] Spectacles of death in Roman arenas were so popular all across the Empire that they built 251 amphitheaters. The Coliseum, the largest ever built in Rome, was finished in 80 CE and had a seating capacity of 50,000 to 80,000 spectators. By one estimate, at least 200,000 people died in the arena. More died in other amphitheaters.[37]

After becoming emperor in 306 CE, Constantine seven years later issued the Edict of Malan, which officially declared imperial toleration of Christianity. He gradually began to favor Christians and Christianity over other religions. He never did make Christianity the official religion of the Empire, and he remained the high priest of the official pagan religion of the Empire until his baptism just before his death in 337 CE. Hoards of unconverted pagans flooded into Christian churches merely to gain status in the eyes of the imperial court and the large bureaucracy under Constantine.[38]

Constantine left Rome in 330 CE and built a new Rome in the East as the new imperial capital of the Empire. He chose the city of Byzantium—today's Istanbul in Turkey—and renamed it after himself, Constantinople. Throughout his life, one of his main projects was to build the most beautiful city the world had ever seen and place at the center his own great palace and cathedral. After the sack of Rome in 410 CE, Constantinople became the new center of Christianity. The Eastern and Western parts of the Empire would diverge and ultimately yielded in 1054 to two forms of Christianity, Roman Catholic and Eastern Orthodox.

Christians Battle Over Predestination and Free Will

Arius of Alexandria and his followers declared that salvation was a process of being joined with God by grace and free will, and Jesus was not truly God.[39] To combat him, a council of bishops convened in 325 CE in Nicaea in modern-day Turkey. The nature of Jesus was a central issue, and they produced the Nicene Creed, which proclaimed belief in the Trinity: God the father, Jesus the son, and the Holy Spirit. Arius rejected the Nicene Creed, taking the position that although Christ was the son of God, he was not divine. Arius died a heretic, and his followers who rioted were put to the sword. Over 3,000 Christians died at the hands of fellow Christians—more than all the victims in three centuries of Roman persecution.[40]

Free will was one of the most important ideas that led to the rise of the West. Ancient societies believed in fate. Belief in free will led directly to valuing the right of the individual to freely choose, with the result that medieval Europe rejected slavery, the first to do so without external compulsion. However, during the colonial period, they had no problem subjecting people of color outside of Europe to slavery.

Augustine of Hippo, born in 354 CE in northern Africa, is considered the true father of the Western approach to theology. His theology centered around "its emphasis on the absolute supremacy of God and the accompanying absolute helplessness and dependency of the human soul on the grace of God."[41] Many Christians today associate predestination with the sixteenth-century Protestant reformer John Calvin. However, the broader perspective is Augustine's monergistic ideas of Providence and salvation in which God is the sole active agent and energy, and humans—both collectively and individually—are instruments of God's grace or wrath. Augustine's God is an all-determining reality whose power is its main characteristic. Man didn't choose God; God chose him. On the predestination of the saints, Augustine affirmed what later generations of theologians would come to call unconditional election and irresistible grace. As Roger E. Olson wrote in *The Story of Christian Theology*, ". . . God chooses some of the human mass of perdition to receive the gift of faith by grace and leads others to their deserved damnation."[42]

According to Augustine, children are born guilty of the sin of Adam and Eve and are corrupt from birth. Baptism is necessary to wash away that guilt, heal that corruption, and reduce a person into the life of salvation within the church. Later Augustine suggested that unbaptized infants who died may go to a place called limbo, which was neither heaven nor hell.

Augustine believed that the notion of free will was entirely compatible with the doctrine that God knows ahead of time what choices we will make. God knows what we will freely decide to do but does not interfere; it remains up to us to choose virtue or sin. Augustine's views were still held in high regard in the thirteenth century by Thomas Aquinas, who taught that "a man can direct and govern his own actions" and that "the rational creature participates in the divine Providence not only in being governed but also in governing."[43] The great controversies over original sin, free will, predestination, and grace that consumed the Western church for over 100 years continued down through subsequent centuries.

Pelagius was born in Britain in 350 CE and arrived in Rome around 405 CE. He was labeled a heretic by the church and by Augustine because he denied original sin, denied that God's grace is essential for salvation, and preached sinless perfection through free will apart from grace. In his book, *On Free Will,* he wrote, "Evil is not born with us, and we are procreated without fault."[44] He did believe that we are all born into a world corrupted by sin, and we all tend to sin due to the bad examples shown us by our parents and peers. If everyone does sin, it is simply because they freely and willfully choose to repeat what Adam did.

Thus we come to the fundamental parting of the ways in theology. Most Christian theologians today believe in free will, but some follow Augustine and see his view as compatible with predestination. They reason that free will is there whenever we do what we want to do even if our wants and wishes are predetermined by something other than ourselves. It's complicated. Christ's missionary commandment was fulfilled with the conversion of Germans, Celts, and Slavs after Christianity had been firmly established as the state religion of the Roman Empire.

The Fall of the Roman Empire

Sacked by the Gothic army of King Alaric in 410 CE, the city of Rome fell. The population of the city plummeted from 500,000 in the year 400 CE to about 50,000 in 600 CE.[45] Rodney Stark stated in *How the West Won* that "the fall of Rome was, in fact, the most beneficial event in the rise of Western civilization, precisely because it unleashed so many substantial and progressive changes."[46]

There were many reasons for the fall of the Roman Empire in the fifth century; among them were apathy, bureaucratic absolutism, and defense of a 10,000-mile frontier. The Dark Ages were characterized by famines and plagues, including the Black Death in its recurring pandemics that repeatedly decimated the population.

Even though they were bloodthirsty, the Huns, Goths, Franks, and Saxons were all devout Christians. Their missionaries found teaching pagans the lessons of Jesus to be an almost hopeless task. For medieval Christians, death was the penalty for hundreds of offenses, particularly those against property. Soldiers for Christ swung their swords freely.

The Holy Roman Empire was born on Christmas Day 800 CE when Pope Leo III in a ceremony in St. Peter's in Rome crowned Frankish King Charlemagne as Holy Roman Emperor. The intent was to resurrect the Roman Empire in the West. In fact, it conferred religious and moral authority to the illiterate Charlemagne and protection to the bishops in Rome. Over the next thousand years, forty-five Holy Roman Emperors attempted to oversee a patchwork of kingdoms, duchies, and imperial cities. There was never a nation-state with centralized political control but a collection of many kings and centers of patronage.

The Holy Roman Empire at one time was composed of most of German-speaking Europe and for centuries was led by the Vienna-based Habsburgs. At the end of World War I, the Habsburg Empire was the second-largest state in Europe after Russia. At one time or another, it had covered the continent from the North Sea to the Balkans and from Silesia to Sicily, encompassing at least part of twelve present-day countries. In 1278, Rudolf, the first Habsburg, took control of Austrian lands, and the last emperor, Charles I, was exiled to Switzerland in 1919.[47]

The last Holy Roman Emperor, Francis II, elected to dissolve his empire rather than allow it to be taken over by Napoleon. On August 6, 1806, an imperial herald galloped through the streets of Vienna to a magnificent medieval church in the center of the city. He ascended to a balcony and blew his silver trumpet, declaring the end of the Holy Roman Empire. Many would not miss it. In 1787, James Madison quipped that it was "a nerveless body; incapable of regulating its own members; insecure against external dangers; and agitated with unceasing fermentation in its own bowels."[48]

For over 900 years, during the Middle Ages and Dark Ages, from approximately 475 CE to 1450, the Catholic Church in the West produced little in the way of great theology. Theology in the West after Augustine tended to look to objective, written authorities such as Scriptures, creeds, and canonical laws to settle disputes and guide its development. Western Christians came more and more to see theology as a kind of philosophy. However, Eastern Orthodox theology never divorced itself from divine liturgy. The worship of the Church was considered by Eastern orthodox Christians to be the major aspect of tradition, which was the ultimate source of all theology. The liturgy maintained the Church's identity and continuity in the midst of a changing world.[49]

The Western Church believed in predestination, while the Eastern Church believed in free will. Eastern bishops and theologians interpreted Jesus' statement that he would build his church on the rock, Simon Peter, meaning Peter's faith. The Western Church interpreted Jesus to mean that the church should be located in Rome because that is where Peter was a bishop, and Jesus had given the keys of the kingdom of heaven to Peter (Matthew 16:18-19). They believed that all bishops of Rome had primacy over the entire Church of Jesus Christ until he returned.[50]

In some ways much of medieval Christianity had more in common with paganism. Of the seven cardinal virtues named by Pope Gregory I in the sixth century, only three were Christian—faith, hope, and charity—while the other four—wisdom, justice, courage, and temperance—were adopted from the pagans Plato and Pythagoras. A transition in attitudes was unfolding.

The crowning of kings in Christian medieval Europe led to them claiming that they ruled by divine right. Likewise, the Vatican and the Catholic Church took a similar stance. No religion is immune to individual interpretation. One pope proclaimed, "The Church is independent of any earthly power, not merely in regard to her lawful end and purpose, but also in regard to whatever means she may deem suitable and necessary to attain them." A cardinal stated, "The Church is not susceptible of being reformed in her doctrines. The Church is the work of an incarnate God. Like all God's work, it is perfect. It is, therefore, incapable of reform."[51]

The common people in medieval times were not only isolated physically, but they were also poorly informed of events outside their villages. They lived mainly in darkness lit occasionally by fire. In Europe, their anonymity approached the absolute. So did their mute acceptance of it. Their descendants either adopted the surname of the local lord—a custom later followed by American slaves—or took the name of an honest occupation: Miller, Taylor, or Smith.

In the Middle Ages, common people had little to no awareness of time—a fact that seems foreign to us in modern times where life revolves around schedules and appointments. They were frequently unaware of which century they were living in. Much like Native Americans, their lives revolved around the passing of the seasons and such cyclical events as religious holidays, harvest times, and local celebrations. There were no clocks or calendars. During some periods, very little of positive effect happened.[52]

However, even then there was an agricultural revolution with the development of a new plow and a new, more efficient harness for horses. Water and wind power were harnessed more efficiently, which led to improved water mills, and water power was used for sawing lumber and stones, grinding knives and swords, pounding cloth, hammering metal, and drawing wire. Thirteenth-century artists in northern Europe were the first to use oil paint and put their work on stretched canvas rather than on wood or plaster. These advancements led to the average medieval European being healthier and more energetic, and probably more informed and educated than the average Roman.[53]

On the downside, medieval Europe was a war zone. Pope Urban II addressed an assembly of knights gathered outdoors at Claremont in 1095 to propose the first Crusade, and he told them, "Christian warriors, who continually and vainly seek pretexts for war, rejoice, for you have today found a true pretext. . . . Soldiers of Hell, become soldiers of the living God."[54] He called on the knights to free Jerusalem from Muslim rule and make it safe again for Christian pilgrims to visit their holy city. The Muslims had controlled Jerusalem since 638 CE, but—ironically given the Pope's rhetoric—they had allowed Christians to make the pilgrimage to Jerusalem through the centuries and welcomed the revenue that was derived from waves of Christians.[55]

Slavery ended in medieval Europe only because the Church extended its sacraments to all slaves and then banned the enslavement of Christians and of Jews. However, slavery reappeared with a vengeance in the New World. The Church responded vigorously, with sixteenth-century popes issuing a series of angry demands against New World slavery. But the popes had no serious temporal power there, and their vigorous opposition was fruitless. The theological conclusion that slavery was sinful was unique to Christianity.[56]

Catholic priests led humanitarian efforts throughout the world. The thirteenth-century merchant's son St. Francis of Assisi lived a life of poverty, begging, preaching, and caring for lepers. He served as an inspiration for Franciscans. In the sixteenth century, Ignatius of Loyola founded the Society of Jesus, or Jesuits, a religious order requiring vows of poverty, chastity, and obedience. Their focus on education resulted in the founding of a number schools, including many highly regarded colleges and universities.

As they later did with heathen Native Americans in the New World, Catholic monks converted German barbarians and subsequently the Vikings. But an important lesson was to be learned about conversion that would help explain one of the reasons Native Americans were resistant. Sociologists have shown that doctrines are of secondary importance in the initial decision to convert. Paul's conversion on the road to Damascus may be the exception. Social pressure plays a role in conversion, primarily when people feel compelled to align their religious behavior with that of their friends and relatives. It is not about encountering attractive doctrines. Put more formally, "People tend to convert to a religious group when their social ties to members outweigh their ties to outsiders who might oppose the conversion, and this often occurs before a convert knows much about what the group believes."[57]

Sociologists make the point that conversion is primarily an act of conformity, and is a matter of relative strength of social ties pulling the individual toward or away from a group. To convert someone, you must be or become his or her close and trusted friend. After people convert to a new religion, they're excited about converting their friends and relatives. This is achieved through social networking. According to many sociologists, sudden mass conversions in response to sermons, like those claimed in Africa and South America by white evangelists, just don't happen. Evangelists would fervently disagree. Social scientists totally refute any notion of mass psychology and collective consciousness. They contend that successful conversion of a large population, especially one as diverse as New World natives, takes generations. Nonetheless, conversion met with some success south of the U.S. border where large populations of Catholics now live.[58]

The two most important Catholic theologians were Augustine of Hippo (354-430 CE) and Thomas Aquinas, who was born in 1225 in his family's castle in Italy. He was the bright light in Christian theology during the Dark Ages. Aquinas used logic and reasoning to help people understand Christian thought. His teachings were the beginning of the Age of Enlightenment. Theology professor Roger E. Olson wrote, "One name stands out above all others as the scholastic thinker par excellence: Thomas Aquinas. It is impossible to overestimate his importance for the story of Christian theology and especially for the story of Roman Catholic theology. There he remains the standard, the norm, well into the twentieth century."[59]

Aquinas stressed the important principle that the grace of salvation was a pure gift given by God and can't be earned through works. He followed Augustine's doctrines closely, especially predestination. God causes everything except evil, that is, a lack of goodness. God even controls free will. Aquinas wrote, "God, therefore, is the first cause, who moves causes both natural and voluntary. And just as by moving natural causes He does not prevent their actions from being natural, so by moving voluntary causes He does not deprive their actions of being voluntary; but rather is He the cause of this very thing in them, for He operates in each thing according to its own nature."[60]

Like Augustine, Aquinas believed free will was compatible with predestination. Free will was doing what one wants and was consistent with not being able to do otherwise. Predestination became the theological basis for Manifest Destiny that supported taking Native American lands. God's design was for America to expand from sea to shining sea. No theologian was more influential in inspiring expansionists in the American West.

Two of the most significant events in the fourteenth century were the Black Death (1346-1351) and the Hundred Years War (1337-1453). The Black Death, or bubonic plague, caused by the bacteria *Yersinia pestis*, began in China around 1346 and hit the Middle East and North Africa in 1347. Merchant ships brought the dread disease to Europe, and for four years, starting in 1348, it spread from southern Europe to the northern countries. In 1351, Pope Clement VI figured that almost 24 million people, or about thirty percent of the total population, had been killed by the disease.[61]

Many Christians believed it was the end times, and many may have been influenced by Revelation 9:18, which predicted that a third of mankind would be killed by a plague. The Italian philosopher and literary intellectual Francesco Petrarch (1304-1374) reported to a friend of "empty houses, derelict cities, ruined estates, fields strewn with cadavers, a horrible and vast solitude encompassing the whole world."[62]

During medieval times, church attendance was very low, even in Italy. Many believed that God had spread the plague to punish humanity. Priests appeared helpless to heal the sick. King Magnus II of Sweden said, "God for the sins of man has struck the world with this great punishment of sudden death. By it, most of our countrymen are dead."[63] That reasoning would also be used to explain away Native American deaths from disease. From the third to the ninth century, the Roman Catholic Church gradually shifted from allowing laypeople to anoint the sick at any time to permitting only priests to anoint just those close to death. With so much death from communicable disease, the ritual became a last rite to forgive the dying, rather than a rite for healing the sick.[64]

Today, the Roman Catholic Church has more members than any other church at 1.1 billion followers. The majority live in Europe and America. There are 68 million Roman Catholics in the United States, which makes it the nation's largest denomination. Virtually all Christian churches teach that there are important rituals that serve as powerful channels for God's grace, known as sacraments. The Roman Catholic and Eastern Orthodox churches observe seven sacraments: baptism, confirmation, eucharist, penance, last rites, all holy orders (joining the priesthood), and matrimony.

The Eastern Orthodox Church has about 300 million followers. Many live in Greece, Russia, Ukraine, Romania, Bulgaria, and Serbia. There is a greater emphasis on mystical practices by Orthodox Christians. In their theology, humans aim to achieve the Osos, which is understood as a union of the individual with God. Practices such as meditation cultivate consciousness of God and enable people to become more Christ-like. A distinctive feature of Orthodox worship services is their reliance on chanting. As opposed to Catholic services, which feature spoken prayer readings as well as singing and organ music, Orthodox services are almost exclusively chanted.

By the end of the Middle Ages, there were only the Roman Catholic Church and the Eastern Orthodox Church. Martin Luther and Protestants were in the future. It would be Protestants with their numerous denominations who would establish the first colonies in America and bewilder Native Americans in the West with the realization that the Europeans' behavior didn't always match their religious beliefs.

CHAPTER THIRTEEN

The Faith of Our Fathers: Religion in America

The only natural argument of any weight, for the immortality of the soul, takes its rise from this observation, that justice is not extended to the good, nor executed upon the bad, man in this life; and that, as the Governor of the world is just, man must live hereafter to be judged..
—JONATHAN EDWARDS, *MISCELLANEOUS OBSERVATIONS ON IMPORTANT THEOLOGICAL SUBJECTS*

In 2011, an ABC–Washington Post poll found that, by a sixty-six percent to twenty-nine percent margin, Americans think, "Political leaders should not rely on their religious beliefs in making policy decisions." I sympathize with the five percent who didn't answer. To speak of a politician "relying" on religious beliefs assumes that those beliefs are external to the one who holds them, a body of doctrines to which he mindlessly defers. Refusing to "rely" on his religious beliefs, conversely, would require the believer to cease being himself; it can't be done.
—BARTON SWAIM, *THE SPEECHWRITER: A BRIEF EDUCATION IN POLITICS*

Like the wind, faith is something you feel but cannot see. Throughout the fourteenth and fifteenth centuries, European culture was in a state of religious and political turmoil. Nationalism was on the rise, the bubonic plague was decimating the population, and the Church was falling into ruin. The great dream of a unified Europe led by the Italian pope and the emperor working together was fading quickly as the Church came under the control of French kings. The papacy moved to France for most of the fourteenth century. All part of the Holy Roman Empire, kings of nations went to war against one another. The low point was reached in the Great Schism of the West when three men simultaneously laid claim to the office of the pope (1378-1417).[1]

Life of the common man was low on hope and high on toil from sunup to sundown. In 1500, there were seventy-three million people in Europe, and twenty million of them lived in what was known as the Holy Roman Empire, which by that time was mainly Germany and her bordering territories. It was also known as the First Reich.[2]

The church fathers of the Middle Ages believed that to be a really committed Christian, one had to reject ordinary work and family life and withdraw to a monastery to live a life of prayer and contemplation. The way to reach the higher levels of spiritual life was by renunciation and deprivation of physical wants. These ideas were not derived from the Bible but from Greek philosophy. Many of the church fathers were deeply influenced by Platonism, including the writings of Clement of Alexandria, Origin, Jerome, and Augustine.

The Renaissance that began in the fourteenth century gathered strength in the sixteenth century and came to prominence in the next century. It was led by the cultural leaders in Europe as a revolt against corrupt and self-serving rulers and clergyman, and there was a mood of individualism among the arts. Human creativity led Europe out of the Dark Ages into an era of prosperity, beauty, and enlightenment.

The Renaissance—which preceded the European Enlightenment—was a return to the cultural and intellectual forms of the ancient Greeks. European art, literature, and architecture were all influenced by the classical era of the Greeks and sometimes of the Roman Empire. Colonized nations sprouted an array of common values, including materialism, extreme individualism, moralizing, and the philosophical sense of superiority expressed in nationalistic exceptionalism. These ethics would be in direct contrast to the values of the New World peoples they would soon invade.[3]

But there was a pessimistic side to the Renaissance, where elitists looked at what they perceived as lesser cultures as degenerate. This notion continued for centuries. Pastor Cotton Mather in Boston wrote that the natives were "doleful creatures who were the veriest ruines of mankind, which were found on the earth."[4] Even Indian sympathizer Roger Williams viewed tribes as "the wandering Generations of Adam's lost posteritie, having lost the true and living God their maker, have created out of the nothing of their owne inventions many false and fained Gods and Creators."⁵ Degeneration theory crept its way into the belief system of modern ethnography and scientific racism.⁶

The rise of Western civilization can be attributed to the pursuit of knowledge, which was led by the Christian commitment to theology. This may surprise many today since theology is in disrepute among Western intellectuals. The basis of theology was the pursuit of knowledge in an effort to more fully understand God. Theology has sometimes been called the science of faith because it consists of formal reasoning about God. Theology produces an image of God as a conscious, rational, supernatural being of unlimited power and scope. Science is about things, and theology is about words.⁷

Harvard scholar Charles Homer Haskins stated that "universities, like cathedrals and parliaments, are a product of the Middle Ages."⁸ In other words, they were products of the medieval church. The first university was founded in Bologna around 1088 just before the first Crusade. The University of Paris was founded about 1150, followed by Oxford around 1167 and Cambridge in 1209. Through the course of the fourteenth and fifteenth centuries, fifty-two universities were founded in Europe.⁹

During the Middle Ages, the most important center of learning was the University of Paris, which boasted the most outstanding medieval intellectuals. Thomas Aquinas (1225-1274) was the most admired medieval scholar and served as regent master of theology at the university. John Calvin was also a graduate. As social science professor Rodney Stark noted, "The great scientific achievements of the sixteenth and seventeenth centuries were produced by a group of scholars notable for their piety, who were based in Christian universities, and whose brilliant achievements built on an invaluable legacy of centuries of scholastic scholarship."¹⁰

If the Renaissance could be summed up in one word it would be humanism, but it was not secular. It placed prime importance on cultural creativity of the human person and rejected the Augustinian pessimism about humanity that had dominated for 1,000 years. Thus the arts and sciences became known as the humanities.

The great theologian of the Renaissance was Erasmus of Rotterdam, who produced a critical Greek New Testament in 1514. It was the basis for Martin Luther's German translation and provided all scholars throughout Christendom with the means to interpret as well as translate the New Testament. Before Erasmus, biblical scholars usually used the Latin Vulgate, which was the authoritative text of the Roman Catholic Church but a relatively poor translation.¹¹

According to historian William Manchester, who was critical of the Catholic Church, "At any given moment the most dangerous enemy in Europe was the reigning Pope. . . . Ruthless in their pursuit of political power and personal gain, they were medieval despots who used their holy office for blackmail and extortion. . . . Popes and cardinals hired assassins, sanctioned torture, and frequently enjoyed the sight of blood."[12]

The sixteenth-century Roman Catholic Church was wealthy and powerful. While early Christians had atoned for their sins by confession, absolution, and penance, it became possible to erase transgressions by buying indulgences. In Rome, the contributions were welcomed and, in the beginning, used to finance hospitals, cathedrals, and crusades. But eventually the Holy Fathers permitted those who had violated God's commandments to buy release from purgatory, thus encroaching on the sacrament of penance. In 1450, Thomas Gascoigne, chancellor of Oxford, scornfully noted, "Sinners say nowadays: 'I care not how many evils I do in God's sight, for I can easily get plenary remission of all guilt and penalty by an absolution and indulgence granted me by the Pope, whose written grant I have bought for four or six pence.'"[13]

Martin Luther and the Rise of Protestantism

But winds of change slammed Europe like a tsunami on October 31, 1517. At the University of Wittenberg, an Augustinian monk named Martin Luther (1483-1546) nailed his ninety-five theses, or points for debate, to the cathedral church door in the city where he taught. He was disgusted by the sale of indulgences. Also, he would denounce the Roman Church for bleeding Germany, observing, "Every year more than 300,000 gulden [gold coins] find their way from Germany to Rome, quite uselessly and fruitlessly; we get nothing but scorn and contempt."[14]

Luther proposed radical changes in both practice and doctrine. He demanded an end to indulgences. In addition, he proclaimed that the sipping of the communion wine should be taken by the whole congregation and not just the priest. He championed a personal relationship with God.

He believed that justification came through faith alone, which is itself a gift of grace from God. This was the beginning of the third great schism in Christendom. The first was the split between East and West in 1054, and the second was a medieval struggle between two and then three popes from 1378 to 1417. Now, the third was unfolding, and it would cause a division between Roman Catholic and Protestant churches in Europe beginning around 1520 with Luther's excommunication from the Church of Rome.[15]

Cut off by the Church, Luther turned to German princes for support. He believed that the clergy should lead and support the church community without having a higher spiritual status and that people should have a direct connection with God. He wanted to have people read the Bible for themselves. In 1534, he published his own German translation. It was the first social movement in which printed materials played an important role—the printing press was only just coming of age. Eventually, the bound book would sit near the top of the pile of humanity's greatest inventions.[16]

Technology has always played an important part in the spread of religion. In Roman times, it was the thousands of miles of roads built throughout Europe that spread Christianity as far north as Scotland. The Protestant Reformation of the sixteenth century was dependent on fifteenth-century technology in the form of Johannes Gutenberg's printing press. Protestantism relied on this technology to spread the word. The Reformation, relying heavily on published material, spread not only Christianity but in time the ability for the common person to read and write. Thus, the publication of scientific and philosophical material led to the Enlightenment. Skeptics like Copernicus and Galileo redefined humanity's place in the universe.

Between 1517 and 1520, Luther turned out thirty pamphlets and short essays and boldly announced the new age with the phrase, "The time for silence has passed." However, only five percent of Germans in this era could read. The Reformation was a middle- and upper-class phenomenon that left the masses virtually untouched. A study of prominent Reformation leaders found that nearly all of them were, or had been, university professors.[17] These urban groups formed the base of Luther's recruitment. He complained in 1529, "Dear God, help us! . . . The common man, especially in the villages, knows absolutely nothing about Christian doctrine; and indeed many pastors are in effect unfit and incompetent to teach. Yet they all are called Christians, or baptize, and enjoy the holy sacraments—even though they cannot recite either the Lord's prayer, the Creed or the Commandments. They lived just like animals."[18]

The three major Protestant principles that separated it from the Church of Rome and its theology were salvation by grace through faith alone, Scriptures above all other authorities for Christian faith and practice, and the priesthood of all believers.[19]

Even though many of the late medieval scholastic theologians and humanists accepted free will as part of their view of salvation, Luther championed predestination, which he considered to be "very strong wine, and solid food for the strong."[20] Like the Catholic tradition, he also defended infant baptism, which the Anabaptists opposed. They did not consider infant baptism true baptism at all.

In 1546, at the Council of Trent, Roman Catholic authorities fought back with excommunication for anyone who printed any material on sacred matters without Church approval. However, their threats were not effective and only led to the weakening of their authority. This was due in large part to Luther's ability to not only print sacred material but also distribute it. Publishers all over Europe, saw a lucrative business opportunity and capitalized on it. In Wittenberg alone, publishers were producing ninety books a year between 1517 and 1546. By 1520, Luther had become a famed author throughout Europe, which protected him from being punished—like Jan Hus and John Wycliffe had been—by the Catholic Church.[21]

Clearly, Reformation was not about religious freedom of choice. It was just a matter of pulling back from one belief system and embracing another. King Henry VIII and his Anglican Church were notorious for burning, beheading, and hanging a number of dissenters, including Lutherans.

In the early centuries of Christianity, poverty was considered a virtue for it meant a lack of concern for the values of the world and a concentration on the afterlife. In the centuries after the Protestant Reformation, poverty was considered indicative of sloth and other sins. It was seen as proof of the individual's degeneration. The expression "poor but honest" no longer was a valid description. Instead, if a person was poor, it was because he was dishonest and God had refused to bless his labors.[22] Clearly, Native Americans were not a blessed race.

European Wars

Throughout the Middle Ages, the perpetual tug of war was waged between the church and state, between pope and emperor, with one dominating for a period, then the other getting the upper hand. An important turning point came after the Reformation. The split in the medieval church had fractured the religious unity of Christendom. In the past it was assumed that everyone living within a certain nation or geographical region should belong to the same religion. As a result, for more than 100 years, beginning in the late sixteenth century and continuing throughout most of the seventeenth century, Europe found itself embroiled in religious wars. Many people had to flee persecution in their homeland, becoming religious refugees. When people saw that Christians were willing to shed blood over religious differences, they began searching for an alternative basis for their social order. They sought a purely secular arena of discourse, away from religion, that would function as neutral territory to bring peace to warring religious factions.[23]

In 1524, the German Peasants' War initiated by Lutheran radicals lasted only a year but resulted in 100,000 deaths. Next came the Schmalkaldic War during the reign of the Holy Roman Emperor Charles V, who tried to once again force Catholicism on Germany. He was opposed by a number of Lutheran princes. The Peace of Augsburg in 1555 recognized Lutheran principalities, but peace didn't last long.[24]

Two of the most harrowing religious wars were the French Civil Wars of the late sixteenth century and the Thirty Years' War of the early seventeenth century, both bloodbaths that were characterized by ghastly massacres and assassinations. Beginning in 1618, the Thirty Years' War devastated Germany by wiping out a third of the towns and a third of the population, but many Protestant regions survived. Catholics hated Protestants and Protestants hated Catholics. Both hated Jews.[25]

The human calamity of the religious wars ended Europe's shared sense of Christian culture. During these dark decades, European armies and the states heavily taxed their citizens. In 1635, France collected 2,000 tons of silver to pay for war. Political theory slowly broke free from Christian moral philosophy and oriented itself toward "reason of state."

In reality, the so-called religious wars of the period were more motivated by dynastic ambition. Emperor Ferdinand II urged his generals to rally their troops with the "pretext of religion."[26] Cynicism ruled the day. The universal Christian church and empire were gone forever. In 1648, the Treaty of Westphalia ended the Thirty Years' War. However, there arrived a new age of ruthless sovereignty that brought profit and power but also moral and cultural loss.

With Christian nations in disarray, the Islamic Ottoman Empire was the force of the age, spanning from distant Persia, across the defunct Byzantine Empire, into Hungary, and across North Africa. The Habsburgs of central Europe warred against them for generations.

Calvinism

Luther never published a systematic theology, so his thoughts in some ways remain incoherent. Systematic theology was presented by the Swiss reformers in what is called reformed theology. Its true father was Ulrich Zwingli

(1484-1531), who became overshadowed by his younger counterpart John Calvin (1509-1564). It was Calvin who organized, systematized, and articulated reformed theology. Zwingli affirmed that those individuals who ended up damned forever in hell were determined by God for that fate.[27] He did not believe that infants were born guilty of Adam's sin. While baptized children may all be assumed to be saved, they would need to confirm their election for themselves by the age of conscience by public confession of faith. For his efforts, Zwingli was killed at the hands of the Catholics and his body quartered and burned. Martin Luther, who had regarded Zwingli as a rival, called his death at the stake, "A triumph for us."[28]

John Calvin was a French theologian who moved to Geneva, Switzerland, and developed the doctrine of original sin by arguing a position of predestination, whereby some people are saved by God's grace for reasons known to God alone while others are predestined for damnation. Calvinism ultimately achieved the status of state religion in Scotland and was influential in England and the United States.[29] Calvin's theology is the foundation of the reformed churches. Historian William Manchester colorfully described Calvin:

> Calvin was the inverted image of the freewheeling, permissive, high-living popes whose excesses had led to Lutheran apostasy. Frail, thin, short, and lightly bearded, with ruthless, penetrating eyes, he was humorless and short tempered. The slightest criticism enraged him. Those who questioned his theology he called "pigs," "asses," "riffraff," "dogs," "idiots," and "stinking beasts."[30]

Manchester also described penalties for disobedience. Calvinists forbade dancing, singing, makeup, jewelry, swearing, gambling, hunting, and drunkenness. Two-time offenders were fined, and continued disobedience could end in excommunication and banishment from the community. Other penalties were just wildly bizarre: a father who named his newborn son Claude spent four days in jail; so did a woman who wore her hair at an immoral height; a child who struck his parents was beheaded; and any single woman discovered to be pregnant was drowned. When Calvin's stepson was found in bed with another woman and at another time his daughter-in-law was caught with another man behind a haystack, all four were executed.[31]

Most Protestant sects abolished priestly celibacy, often the priesthood itself, the cult of the Virgin Mary, relics, confession, and Christmas. In the

English-speaking world, Christmas was abolished in Scotland in 1563 and in England after the Puritans took power in the 1640s. It returned with the Restoration in 1660, but the celebrations never regained their medieval and Elizabethan abandon.

Calvinism Challenged

In the late sixteenth century, the Dutchman Jacob Arminius (1560-1609) was struggling with his Roman Catholic heritage and the domination of his homeland by Catholic Spain. He supported a small group of rebels who had united several provinces of the Netherlands against Spanish rule. Throughout the 1590s, Arminius and rigid Calvinists in Holland came into increasing conflict. The young preacher openly began to contradict Calvin's view of predestination. The stance against predestination taken by Arminius in his *Declaration of Sentiments* was described by theology professor Roger E. Olson: "He argued that it is contrary to the nature of the gospel itself since it treats people as being saved or not saved completely apart from their being sinners or believers. They are saved or damned first (in God's first decree) and only then made believers or sinners. . . . It is repugnant to God's nature as love and to human nature as free."[32]

Even a larger spat occurred across the English Channel. Martin Luther and Henry VIII have often been linked as leaders of the Reformation, but in many ways that is incorrect. Luther revolted on theological grounds, while Henry remained a faithful Catholic with one exception. He rejected the pope not on religious grounds, but on political ones.

His problems with Rome began in 1527 when Henry decided to dissolve his eighteen-year marriage to Queen Catherine, the daughter of Ferdinand and Isabella of Spain. He needed a male heir, which hadn't happened with his present wife. If there were no male heir, England would probably be at civil war again. The War of the Roses between the Yorkists and Lancastrians had ended just six years before his birth.

Since in 1519 Henry had fathered a boy by his mistress, Elizabeth Blount, he knew the problem was with Catherine and not him. He sought an annulment from Rome. The thought of a royal divorce did not sit well with Pope Clement. Nonetheless, Henry had fallen in love with Anne Boleyn, and the messiest divorce in history ensued.

Anne, a woman in waiting, became pregnant before she was married to Henry VIII. The king moved to make Thomas Cranmer, a Cambridge theologian, his Archbishop of Canterbury with a new level of power. The archbishop thereafter ruled that the pope was incompetent to grant dispensation. He declared Catherine a divorcée and secretly married Henry to his mistress, Anne. In 1533, with the support of parliament, Henry confiscated all Catholic Church lands in England. In November 1534, he abandoned Rome completely and founded the Church of England, also known as the Anglican Church—in America it became the Episcopal Church. He appointed himself and his successors as its supreme head.[33]

Some consider the Anglican Church Protestant since it shares with the Lutheran and Calvinist churches features such as commitment to scripture as primary authority, acceptance of the sacraments of baptism and communion, and prayer in the vernacular. The Anglican Church also shares features with the Catholic Church, such as acceptance of the Nicene Creed, the apostolic succession of bishops, and some of the same ritual and imagery. The Church of England contributed the King James Bible, published in the early seventeenth century after its sponsor James I. It has been called the most celebrated book in the English-speaking world.

Radical Reformation/Quakers

The Radical Reformation included Protestants of sixteenth-century Europe who believed in the principles of separation of church and state, renounced coercion in the matters of religious belief, rejected infant baptism in favor of believer's baptism, and emphasized the experience of regeneration—that is, being born again. Many embraced Christian pacifism and simple lifestyles. One group became known as Mennonites and another as Hutterites. The largest group was the Baptists. They refused to baptize infants. In general, they were opposed to unconditional predestination as championed by Augustine, Luther, Zwingli, and Calvin.

Another group that departed radically from the traditional Christianity of Catholics and Protestants was the Quakers, who traced their origins back to England in the mid-seventeenth century. Like the Anabaptists, Quakers were committed to pacifism. Quakers believed that God could speak directly to human beings in a quiet voice.

William Penn (1644-1718), born in London and a student at Oxford, in 1667 became a member of the Society of Friends, the Quakers. He argued for a far more liberal policy of toleration in England and in 1682 founded his colony in the New World.

A mistake that William Penn wished to avoid pertained to the Indians. Both Virginia and Massachusetts had offended and alienated different tribal groups. Both had suffered from costly Indian wars. Even before coming to America, Penn sent agents ahead to let the Delaware Indians know of his intention to occupy the land, only, he assured them, "with your love and consent." "I am well aware," Penn added, "of the unkindness and injustice that Indians have suffered from previous English settlers and traders. But I am not such a man, as is well known in my country."[34]

In laying out the city of Philadelphia, the City of Brotherly Love, Penn charged his commissioners to "be tender of offending the Indians. . . . But soften them to me and the people; let them know that you are come to sit down lovingly among them."[35]

The colony flourished economically and by 1750 proved to be the major center for Lutheranism, German reform, and Presbyterianism in the colonies. Quakers believed that the command of Christ to "love your enemies and bless them that persecute you" meant at the very least that followers of Christ could not in good conscience take up arms for the purpose of killing those enemies and persecutors.[36]

Pennsylvania made two critical contributions. First, it offered religious liberty on a wider scale than had been available anywhere before. It also demonstrated that religious liberty and economic progress could go hand in hand. By the time of the American Revolution, Philadelphia had become the cultural capital of America, a center of light and learning as well as of prosperity. Throughout the nineteenth century, Quakers would be leaders in defending Native Americans. President Grant would appoint them as Indian agents to replace their corrupt predecessors, albeit with mixed results.

Puritans and the New Israel

The seventeenth and eighteenth centuries witnessed the rise in England of Puritanism and Methodism. These were two movements that would have a profound effect on the Native Americans in the New World—Puritans with the Eastern tribes and Methodists in the American West. Puritanism began as the opposition party to Anglicanism within the Church of England under Queen Elizabeth I. At its foundation was the theology of Calvin. Its greatest preacher and thinker was Jonathan Edwards (1703-1758) of New England, who would bridge the two main Puritan groups in New England—Presbyterianism and Congregationalism—before Puritanism lost favor in the mid-eighteenth century.[37]

As Puritanism faded in England, others who did not immigrate to America settled into nonconforming denominations: Congregationalists,

Presbyterians, and Baptists. Baptists were those Puritan separatists who chose to give up on infant baptism and embrace the Anabaptists' practice of believer's baptism.

In the colonies, Puritans believed that, like Israelites, they too were blessed by God and that their Puritan church was the new Israel. When they made their exodus from England in the 1630s, the Puritans sought a new world where the Christian Commonwealth, modeled after Calvin's Geneva, could be built unhindered by the godless crown and impure state church. North America was the promised land, and they sought to occupy it for God and His kingdom. Calvinists insisted that all honest work—not just religious or ecclesiastical work—glorified God, and that therefore the layman could fulfill his calling in the secular realm just as any priest could fulfill his in the church. Higher education was valued as a way for laymen to fulfill their gifts.

Founded in 1636, Harvard testified to the Puritans' deep dedication to education. The school was permeated with the religious commitment that characterized the colony as a whole. Its 1646 rules stipulated that every student "shall consider the main end of his life and studies to know God and Jesus Christ which is eternal life." Students were required to read their Bibles twice every day, study the Scriptures carefully, and be prepared "to give an account of their proficiency therein, both in theoretical observations of language and logic, and in practical and spiritual truths."[38]

In 1701, Connecticut followed with the establishment of a "Collegiate School" that became Yale College and later Yale University. Congregationalists launched their school first at Saybrook and then in 1716 moved the institution to New Haven. The institution got its name from Elihu Yale, who responded to a plea from Cotton Mather to contribute to the institution. Yale, like Harvard, dedicated itself from the beginning to "the liberal and religious education of suitable youth . . . under the blessing of God."[39] In 1746, Presbyterians established the College of New Jersey, which later took the name Princeton. Its clergyman president, John Witherspoon, was the only minister to sign the Declaration of Independence. Anglicans would respond in 1784 by launching Columbia University in New York City.[40]

Issues other than education had to be addressed in the colonies. Evil had to be eliminated. Salem's witches of the 1690s were equally deluded and harmless, but Puritans hung about twenty innocent victims. The Salem trials were a minor, provincial example of a far more fascinating worldwide phenomenon of hatred that extended to racism. They have since achieved mythic status in the United States. The key witnesses were pubescent hysterics or vengeful opportunists. Accusations were personal vendettas cloaked as righteousness.[41]

In New England, Puritanism thrived for about a century, but by the 1730s it had weakened considerably. Congregational and Presbyterian churches stood at the centers of every city and town, but their influence had faded. Most citizens were not faithful followers of the original Puritan ideals.

The First Awakening

By 1700, the majority of citizens of New England were not members of the established churches even though they were required to attend church regularly. Jonathan Edwards (1703-1758) tried to stem the growing tide of Arminianism—basically free will—that was becoming popular with this group by preaching that free will was absurd.

Most every American knows the dark side of the Puritans' efforts in the New World. What is less appreciated is that the Puritans also carried an ideal of America having a higher calling. At the time when Puritans were losing their way and were seeking power and fortune, Edwards reined them back in to their true purpose. He encouraged New Englanders to multiply and gain control of this new, wild paradise. In addition, Edwards urged them to treat the natives with justice and love. He strongly condemned the mistreatment of Native Americans and called for payments to the tribes for lands taken from them. This was an affront to his congregation, and he was asked to leave his Northampton pulpit. His banishment resulted in him living for some time in the wilderness among the Indians.

Edwards was a model for modern-day evangelicals and a formulator of a Christian worldview for the New World. He championed integrating a deep Christian faith with a rigorous and disciplined intellectual life. He preached that knowledge comes to us by what may be called a "sense of the heart." "Spiritual wisdom and grace is the highest and most excellent gift that ever God bestows on any creature," Edwards declared. Furthermore, "it is not a thing that belongs to reason. . . . It is not a speculative thing, but depends on the sense of the heart."[42] Edwards joined Puritan theology to evangelical piety and practice, which made for a powerful combination that long shaped the religious and intellectual life of New England.[43]

After he lived among the Indians, he settled in the frontier community of Stockbridge, Massachusetts, as minister and missionary to Native Americans. In 1757, he was chosen to be president of Princeton College in New Jersey. Unfortunately, one month after his inauguration he died of smallpox contracted from variolization with live smallpox virus. He was an ardent opponent of Arminian theology and other views opposed to the Puritan heritage, but never engaged in witch hunts. As Roger E. Olson stated, "No theologian in the history of Christianity held a higher or stronger view of God's majesty, sovereignty, glory, and power than Jonathan Edwards."[44]

By 1740, Congregationalists had well over 400 churches, concentrated largely in Massachusetts, Connecticut, and southeastern New Hampshire. Anglicanism had little more than half that number, and its churches were spread throughout the South as well as widely scattered in colonies north of the Chesapeake region.[45]

John Wesley (1703-1791), who would become the most influential Arminian in history, was born in Epworth, England. He attended Oxford University where he studied for the ministry in the Church of England. With George Whitefield (1714-1770) and his brother Charles Wesley, John founded what they called the Holy Club. The critics labeled them Methodists because they were perceived as trying to discover and practice a method of spirituality.[46]

By the time John Wesley died in 1791, Methodism was a full-blown dissenting denomination in England. In North America—where it was a tiny new sect at the time—the cradle of Methodism was Maryland. After the American Revolution, it grew to be the dominant Christian denomination by the time of the Civil War.

In pre-Revolutionary America, the religious landscape was dominated by churches that rested on legal establishment: the Congregationalists in New England and the Episcopalians in New York, Virginia, Maryland, North and South Carolina, and Georgia. Typically, the state collected tithes that all citizens were legally required to pay, whether they attended the established church or not. The state also laid out new parish boundaries, subsidized new church construction, maintained parish properties, paid clergymen salaries, hired and fired them, and even took measures to suppress dissenters.

Baptist preachers, for example, were sometimes jailed and beaten. In many colonies, government positions were limited to church members. Ultimately this weakened the churches. Monopolies tend to be lazy, whether they are churches, businesses, or schools. The established clergy often lived like members of the gentry, enjoying ample time for leisure activities.

By contrast, evangelical ministers were enthusiastic activists, throwing themselves into ceaseless efforts to spread the gospel—the Great Commission. A writer comparing American free churches with England's established churches observed that legal establishment made the clergy "indolent and lazy," since a person with guaranteed income would never "work as hard as one who has to exert himself for a living." As a result, the writer concluded, the Americans had a threefold advantage: "They have more preachers, they have more active preachers, and they have cheaper preachers than can be found in any part of Europe."[47]

Nancy Pearcey, in *Total Truth,* further explains:

> Finally, the established churches tended to be the first to drift into theological liberalism. The wealthier the church, the more likely its clergy were to enjoy social status and formal academic training—and thus also the more likely to welcome liberalism emerging from European universities at the time. Well before the American Revolution, leading scholars at Harvard and Yale had become Unitarian. Instead of exhorting their congregations to repent and be saved, they delivered eloquently styled lectures on "reasonable religion," with the supernatural elements increasingly stripped away. When the First and Second Great Awakenings broke out, the liberal clergy firmly opposed them, declaring themselves on the side of "Reason" against the revivalists' "religion of the heart."[48]

The best description of religion in America before the Revolution and the First Awakening would be that church members were a distinct minority, and in Puritan theology the focus was on God, the Father. Jesus, the man, had almost no role to play. Eighty-five percent of the people who declared their independence in 1776 were Puritans, and to them, Jesus was a marginal figure at best. Puritans were God-fearing rather than Jesus-loving people. It would only be after the Second Awakening in the first third of the nineteenth century that Jesus was liberated from Calvin, much like the colonists had been liberated from George III. Jesus rose up and overthrew his Father as a dominant person in the Trinity.

Wesley placed God's love at the center of his preaching, as opposed to Edwards who made everything revolve around God's glory. Wesley's four essential sources and tools of theology were Scripture, Reason, Tradition, and Experience.[49] He placed a strong emphasis on reason and tradition. He defended infant baptism against the Baptists. His theology was thoroughly Arminian at a time when many evangelicals, including his friend and fellow evangelist George Whitefield, considered Arminianism almost a heresy. This eventually led to the split between the Wesley brothers and Whitefield. The Methodists charted a course for renewal that included an emphasis on

Christian experience of conversion and the ideal of Christian perfection. Emphasis was placed on a personal relationship with Jesus, which was to be lived out through services to others.

The First Great Awakening began when George Whitefield, a staunch Calvinist, made a sensational appearance in the American colonies. He preached at camp meetings in the open air, in the fields, in the streets, anywhere he could gather an audience. Thousands attended meetings that weren't just saving people but were saving the nation. Whitefield pioneered a new preaching style, an actor preacher, as opposed to a scholar preacher. He raised his arms, stamped his feet, acted out Bible stories, and wept aloud. Whitefield became the most famous person in the English-speaking world, with the exception of the king himself.[50]

The entire experience was novel and contrary to the somber, reserved preaching fashion of the day. To promote his tours, Whitefield pioneered the use of mass marketing, borrowing heavily from marketing techniques in the commercial world of his day. When he planned to visit a city, he would send out assistants up to two years in advance to distribute flyers and line up facilities. The evangelist would also issue a constant stream of advance publicity. Historian Harry Stout sums up Whitefield's novelty by calling him America's first modern celebrity.[51]

The young preacher's sermons had an electric effect on the audience. The church was filled to capacity everywhere he spoke. A pleasantly surprised Whitefield wrote, "People hung up on the rails of the organ loft" and "climbed upon the roof of the church" in order to hear him.[52]

Even the reserved Benjamin Franklin was mesmerized. He described Whitefield's preaching as an "excellent Piece of Music" and recalled attending a sermon to raise funds for Whitefield's Georgia orphanage, writing, "I perceived he intended to finish with a collection, and I silently resolved he should get nothing from me." But as he listened to the sermon his emotions took over. Franklin, the author of "A fool and his money are soon parted," wrote, "[Whitefield] finished so admirably that I emptied my pockets wholly into the collector's dish, gold and all."[53]

Organizers of the Awakenings insisted that a mere intellectual understanding of theological principles was not enough. What was needed was a change of heart, or a new birth. This idea came from Europe, which had rejected the Enlightenment focus on reason to embrace the emerging romantic focus on feelings. "Our people do not so much need to have their heads stored, as to have their hearts touched,"[54] wrote Jonathan Edwards in 1743, the preeminent theorist of the First Great Awakening. The emphasis on emotion was perhaps inevitable, given that most people in the colonial era were at least nominally Christian, which meant that the primary goal of the Awakenings was to counter spiritual coldness and indifference.

The reach of the First Awakening was uneven. It was most effective in Massachusetts, Connecticut, Rhode Island, Pennsylvania, New Jersey, and Virginia, but was less influential in New York, Delaware, the Carolinas, New Hampshire, Maryland, and Georgia. Right before the Revolution, only seventeen percent of adults were church members, and spiritual lethargy was common.[55]

Even though Whitefield died before the American Revolution, his biographer Thomas S. Kidd contended that he was profoundly influential on the American nation's founding fathers. Kidd wrote that Whitefield "saw and met more people in Britain, Ireland, and America than any other person of the era."[56] A great orator keeps his audience's attention fixed on himself. What set Whitefield apart was his ability to keep it fixed on God.

The Second Awakening

The First Awakening came before the American Revolution, while the Second Awakening came after, at a time when the Revolution was becoming the template for the way people thought about virtually every area of life. It became common for leaders in the Second Awakening to transfer the rhetoric of independence uncritically from the political sphere to the religious sphere. In the First Awakening, revivalists had not attacked the church structure or learning per se, but only the abuses attributed to the clergy who were part of the privileged class.

By contrast, in the Second Awakening, church authority itself was denounced as tyranny. Creeds and liturgies were rejected. Many began to argue that the American Revolution was not yet complete: we have cast off civil tyranny, they said, but now we need to cast off ecclesiastical tyranny. The priesthood of all believers was taken to mean religion of the people, by the people, and for the people. Abolitionists gained inspiration.

Most opponents of the revival movement, whether orthodox Calvinists or Unitarians, tended to be Federalists and held a political philosophy closer to the older view of classical republicanism. By contrast, supporters of the revival movement, especially Methodists and Baptists, tended to be Jeffersonian, sharing its deep aversion to elitism and placing its trust in the common folk. They knew that Jefferson himself was a Deist, who took a razor to the New Testament and snipped out all of the supernatural elements, leaving only Jesus' moral teaching intact. Yet they supported Jefferson's presidential bid in 1800. Their attitude was summed up by Samuel Miller, an evangelical Presbyterian, who announced that he would "much have Mr. Jefferson President of the United States than an aristocratic Christian."[57]

But it was hard to get a good grasp on America's religious character. In a 1797 treaty with Muslim Tripoli, now Libya, initiated by George Washington and completed by John Adams, the founders declared that "the Government of the United States is not in any sense founded on the Christian Religion." They wanted to make it clear that they had no problem with Islam. Almost a century later, in 1892 the U.S. Supreme Court called the United States a "Christian nation."[58] It's clear in the United States that the importance of Jesus from the beginning of the nation onward has been associated with political calculations, economic changes, and cultural trends.

Increasingly, as the Second Awakening gained momentum, the populist preacher became a performer, stringing together stories and anecdotes, often from his own life. This method engaged the audience's emotions, while subtly enhancing the speaker's own image by highlighting his own ministry and spiritual experiences. The outcome of all this was the rise of personality cults, the celebrity system that has become so entrenched in evangelism. In 1817, a critic of the revivalists wrote, "They measure the progress of religion by the numbers, who flock to their standard; not only by the prevalence of faith, and piety, justice and charity."[59]

The evangelical movement was divided into two wings. The first wing was populist. It had a strong revivalist style that downplayed doctrine and appealed to ordinary folk. Strongest in the Southern states, this wing included mostly Baptists, Methodists, and the restoration movement—Church of Christ and the Disciples of Christ.

The second wing was the rationalist and scholarly. It was centered in the North and included evangelicals within the Congregational, Presbyterian, and Episcopalian churches. They ignited evangelical fervor within these denominations' traditional emphasis on theology and scholarship. The populist stream has become dominant today in terms of sheer numbers and influence within the churches.

The evangelical movement grew out of the First and Second Great Awakenings, embracing a revivalist style of preaching and an emphasis on personal conversion—born again. Classic Protestantism stemming from the Reformation defined the Christian life largely in terms of participation in the church's corporate worship and liturgy. Some religious groups lost members due to the revivalist movement—Catholics, Lutherans, German

Reformed, Dutch Reformed, and old-style Presbyterians. These are sometimes called the confessional churches.

The evangelical church has been remarkably effective in Christianizing American society. Religious adherence in America has actually increased significantly since the colonial period. The common stereotype that in colonial times virtually everyone belonged to a church turns out to be false. The corresponding stereotype that in the modern world, religion is withering away is likewise false. At the time of the American Revolution, the three most popular denominations were Congregationalists (55 percent), Episcopalian (20.4 percent), and Presbyterian (19 percent). Yet by 1850, Congregationalism had virtually collapsed. The Episcopalians had suffered greatly, partly because they supported England during the war, and many returned to the homeland. The religious adherence in 1776 was 17 percent; by 1870 it was 35 percent, by 1890 it was 45 percent, and in 1988 it was 62 percent.[60]

The most striking growth took place among the Baptists and Methodists. During the Revolutionary War, most Methodist preachers returned to England at John Wesley's command, so they were starting over again. Even so, they enjoyed phenomenal success. By 1850 they had become the largest Protestant denomination, accounting for thirty-four percent of all church members in the country. Some historians have called the nineteenth century the "Methodists Age." In 1906, they were overtaken by the Baptists. In 1831, the Frenchman Alexis de Tocqueville wrote, "There is no country in the world where the Christian religion retains a greater influence over the souls of men than in America."[61] The nineteenth century has also been widely referred to as "the evangelical century."[62]

Religion in the West and Nineteenth-Century America

In 1850, only half of America had been settled. States such as Michigan, Missouri, and Texas were the frontier. The dynamics of frontier life continued to shape much of American culture right up to the dawn of the twentieth century. The West was rough and dangerous. People were moving West faster than social institutions could keep up with them. Often there were no schools, no churches, no local governments, and no families, but large numbers of single men.

Texas, for example, in the nineteenth century was subject to a series of governments—Mexican, Texan, Confederate, and American—that could be generously described as fitful. In that context, church groups helped foster a coherent statewide culture and supplemented the skeletal public sector by building schools, orphanages, and hospitals.

Methodists and Baptists found a stronger footing than Presbyterians or Episcopalians during the state's period of rapid expansion after Reconstruction. In *Rough Country,* Robert Wuthnow explained that the former two denominations were less strict on theological matters and offered the average wayward Texan a better bargain: "the immeasurable reward of otherworldly salvation attainable at the relatively low cost of appearing occasionally at the mourner's bench."[63]

In 1840, Alexis de Tocqueville noted that those going west were "adventurers impatient of any sort of yoke, greedy for wealth, and often outcasts from the states in which they were born. They arrive in the depths of the wilderness without knowing one another. There is nothing of tradition, family feeling, or example to restrain them."[64] He added, "When you think of the frontier you should picture towns filled with male drifters, gamblers, confidence tricksters, whores, and saloon keepers, and without churches, schools, or respectable women."[65]

Evangelical preachers, especially Methodist circuit riders—like James Finley (1725-1795) in Pennsylvania and later William Wesley "Brother Van" Orsdel in Montana (1848-1919)—broke with the older pattern of using sermons to instruct, and began to use their sermons to produce a conversion experience. Instead of talking about a gradual growth and faith through participation in a church, evangelicals began to preach a sudden, one-time conversion as the only sufficient basis for claiming to be a Christian.

In the state-supported churches and in wealthier churches, generally the training for pastors was a long, expensive process that led to a chronic shortage of clergy, thus giving them considerable bargaining power over salary and location. Many simply refused to relocate to unsettled frontier areas filled with heathen savages.

By contrast, the Methodist circuit preachers became a legend on the frontier. They traveled constantly, virtually living in the saddle. Similarly, most Baptist preachers were simple farmers, ministering to their own neighbors. Many had only minimal theological education, speaking the same language as the people they were trying to reach. The circuit riders brought moral stability to communities where the faithful started Sunday schools, distributed books, built orphanages, and tended to the imprisoned.

The revivalist concern for the poor and outcast reached even to slaves. At the time of the Revolutionary War, few blacks, whether slave or free, were

Christians. The preaching styles of the Methodists and Baptists were simple, direct, and dramatic. Thousands of African Americans turned to the Gospel because of them. Instead of imposing a solemn, restrained style of worship, they encourage spontaneous singing, chanting, and shouting, affirming the rich heritage of folk expression among African Americans. Meanwhile, what happened to the established churches? They went into a slow but steady process of decline that has continued to our day.

The focus on an intense conversion experience was highly effective in bringing people to faith. But it also tended to redefine religion in terms of emotion, while contributing to a neglect of theology and doctrine in the whole cognitive element of belief. Second, the use of plain language and simple folksongs was highly effective in reaching ordinary people. The revivalists suggested that being theologically educated equated with being spiritually dead. One of their favorite themes was poking fun at the educated clergy back East. Many evangelicals uncritically absorbed the individualism that was coming into vogue in American political life, and simply transferred it to the church. This did not reflect biblical teaching so much as a political philosophy of the day. Revivalism led to a new model of leadership. The pastor was no longer a teacher who instructed the congregation, but a celebrity who was able to inspire mass audiences.

In many evangelical churches, women began to outnumber men, often by two to one. When the British novelist Frances Trollope visited America in 1832, she commented that she had never seen a country "where religion had so strong a hold upon the women or a slighter hold upon the men."[66]

In the early 1800s, said one historian, "New England ministers fervently reiterated their consensus that mothers were more important than fathers in forming 'the tastes, sentiments, and habits of children,' and more effective in instructing them." As a result, "mothers increasingly took over the formerly paternal task of conducting family prayers."[67] The churches were releasing the men from the responsibility of being religious leaders. They were turning religion and morality into the domain of women, something soft and comfortable, not bracing and demanding. Charles Elliot Norton of Harvard spoke for many at the time when he complained of the intellectual flabbiness—what he called the "unmanliness"—of religion.[68]

The new definition of masculine virtue reflected in part the influence of Darwin's theory of evolution—survival of the fittest. For if humans evolved from the animal world, the implication was that the animal nature is the core of our being. This was a startling new concept: from antiquity, virtue had been defined as the exercise of restraint of the lower passions by the higher faculties of the rational spirit in the moral will. But now, in a stunning reversal, the animal passions were held up as the true self.

The rise of social Darwinism in the mid-1800s exalted the survival of the fittest in nature. This equated out West into the white man winning over the red man. "It is a new sensation to come to see man as an animal—the master animal of the world," wrote John Burroughs (son of the author of *Tarzan*).[69] Social Darwinism emphasized "the triumph of man over man in primitive struggle."[70]

Even churches sensed a problem and began recasting religion in a more masculine tone. For too long religion had been the domain of women, tinged with sentimental piety. In 1858, an *Atlantic Monthly* article scolded parents, saying that if a son was "pallid, puny, sedentary, lifeless, joyless," then he was directed to the ministry, while on the other hand the "ruddy, the brave, and the strong" were directed to secular careers.[71]

According to historian James Turner, the scholarly wing of evangelicalism became the most powerful influence in nineteenth-century American culture.[72] The Presbyterians alone established forty-nine universities prior to the Civil War—more than any other denomination—thereby dominating American education. Presbyterians led the late nineteenth-century conservation movement and the creation of the national park system. John Muir, the naturalist responsible for founding the Sierra Club in 1892, was a lapsed Presbyterian who sermonized about the preservation of natural beauty. So, too, the administrations of four Presbyterian-raised presidents—Benjamin Harrison, Grover Cleveland, Theodore Roosevelt, and Woodrow Wilson—used the Interior Department to enact a series of policies to preserve the nation's natural resources. According to author Mark R. Stoll in *Inherit the Holy Mountain*, "Presbyterian determination to conquer avarice and save society, rather than Congregational reverence for the New England town, gave the nation its national conservation and preservation laws."[73]

When America was a young nation, the clergy were often the most highly educated members of the community. The congregation looked up to them and respected their intellectual expertise. According to historian Martin Marty, in the nineteenth century, religion in America "accepted a division of labour." On one hand, "religion acquiesced in the assignment to address itself to the personal, familial, and leisured sectors of life" (the private dimension). On the other hand, "the public dimensions—political, social, economic, cultural—were to become autonomous," and were eventually taken over by non-Christian ideologies.[74]

Nancy Pearcey summarized the boxed-in believers, writing, "No longer were religious leaders the public spokesman of society, as they had once been. Instead, they were permitted to appear in public only to perform the limited role of inspiring and legitimatizing the larger culture. They could perform invocations and benedictions—like opening prayers in Congress—but they were not welcome to comment on the substance of legislation; that would be 'meddling' in politics. Visitors from other countries were amazed at the way the clergy in America were boxed in."[75] The ever-observant Tocqueville commented, "In America, religion is a distinct sphere, in which the priest is sovereign but out of which he takes care never to go."[76]

The overall pattern of evangelicalism's history is summarized by historian Richard Hofstadter in a single sentence. To a large extent, he writes, "the churches *withdrew* from intellectual encounters with the secular world, *gave* up the idea that religion is a part of the whole life of intellectual experience, and often *abandoned* the field of rational studies on the assumption that they were the natural province of science alone."[77]

He mentions three factors. One, churches and seminaries themselves largely withdrew from intellectual confrontation with the secular world, limiting their attention to the realm of practical Christian living. Two, they gave up the idea that Christianity gives a competency framework to interpret all of life and scholarship. Three, in the process, they abandoned an entire range of intellectual inquiry. They gave in to the demand that the academic disciplines must be religiously and philosophically autonomous, without realizing that it was just a cover to introduce new philosophies like positivism and naturalism.

For Christians, Jesus saved, but culture ruled. Words and deeds often didn't match up. In nineteenth-century America, the period where Christian Manifest Destiny ideology justified the destruction of the Native American's way of life, Christian institutions in their weakened state were increasingly not a factor in Indian policy. Missionaries or church representatives might be called to Indian reservations to convert Indians, become agents, or help educate them, but not to Washington, D.C., to help implement government policies regarding the vanishing race.

Religion has come to refer to the public realm of institutions, denominations, official doctrines, and formal rituals, while spirituality is associated with the private realm of personal experience. The pervasive sense emphasized by evangelicals that faith is by definition individual and subjective, ironically may be the prime reason for the loss of credibility on the part of religious institutions in our day.

Pulitzer Prize–winner Jon Meacham reflected on the dualism of religion: "Our finest hours—the Revolutionary War, abolition, the expansion of the rights of women, fights against terror and tyranny, the battle against Jim Crow—can partly be traced to religious ideas about liberty, justice, and charity. Yet theology and Scripture have also been used to justify our worst hours—from enslaving black people to persecuting Native Americans to treating women as second-class citizens."[78]

Religion remains the great "Mystery." Whether you're a Catholic, Baptist, or atheist, when near death, faith is questioned. Raymond Barfield, MD, professor in the schools of both medicine and divinity at Duke University, works with dying children on cancer wards. Very learned in religion and science, Barfield brilliantly summarized the mystery, writing, "The short version is that I am more like Thomas Aquinas, who considered God to be the most incomprehensible of all the things we seek. An infinite God will never be known by me, because I am finite. . . . For Aquinas everything that is good, beautiful, and true finds its ground in the unfathomable God, and every exploration of goodness, beauty, or truth is an exploration into God that helps you comprehend more. But you never stop growing in comprehension, which is why God is incomprehensible."[79]

Part III

Thomas Jefferson: Winning the West

CHAPTER FOURTEEN

A Revolution: The Enlightenment, Scientific Revolution, and the Romantic Movement

Enlightenment is man's emergence from his self-imposed immaturity. . . . Nothing is required for this enlightenment . . . except freedom; and the freedom in question is the least harmful of all, namely, the freedom to use reason publicly in all matters.
—IMMANUEL KANT, *WHAT IS ENLIGHTENMENT?*

Arts and sciences gild the chains of civilization.
—JEAN-JACQUES ROUSSEAU

Great minds talk about ideas, average minds talk about things, and small minds talk about people.
—PETER SELGIN, *BY CUNNING & CRAFT*

It was an impressive group. In 1791, at the request of President George Washington, who was at Mount Vernon, Thomas Jefferson had brought together in Philadelphia senior officers of the American government to discuss some urgent matters. After dinner, while sipping wine, the group turned their attention to general concerns. Present were John Adams, Alexander Hamilton, Attorney General Edmund Randolph, and Secretary of War Henry Knox.

Soon there was a difference of opinion in regard to the British system of government. Much to Jefferson's surprise, in the warmth of the evening candlelight, Adams championed it, stating, "If some of its defects and abuses were corrected, it will be the most perfect constitution of government ever devised by man." Hamilton agreed with Adams, opining that "it was the most perfect model of government that could be formed: and that the correction of its vices would render it an impractical government."[1]

Other differences of opinion had surfaced at dinner. Jefferson had decorated the walls of his residence in Philadelphia with a collection of portraits that included Sir Francis Bacon, John Locke, and Sir Isaac Newton, all prominent men of the Enlightenment Age. Hamilton had no idea who the men were, and Jefferson recalled, "I told him they were my trinity of the three greatest men the world had ever produced, naming them."[2]

Enlightenment Philosophy

In the eighteenth century, countries in Europe developed a set of institutions, including strong property rights, free trade, freedom of religion, press freedom, and limits on government. The spontaneous results of this combination of rules were a rush in technological innovation, rising income, and recognition of civil liberties—at least for whites. Layers of ideas, images, and feelings inundated brains and took on new meaning over time. The mind was a page to be filled with enlightened ideas, and the written word in that period revealed the evolution of it.

The lives of such Founding Fathers as George Washington, John Adams, Thomas Jefferson, James Madison, and Benjamin Franklin demonstrate the close relationship of the American Revolution and the American Enlightenment. Their desires were decisive to the Revolution's direction and outcome. Likewise, the Enlightenment cast a long shadow throughout the nineteenth century on America's attitudes and actions toward Native Americans. The Enlightenment is often cast as the age of reason, but in many ways it favored sociology and psychology over rational philosophy and religion.

As the medieval era emerged into the Renaissance, beginning roughly in the 1300s, there was a movement for the complete emancipation of reason from revelation. That burst into full force in the Enlightenment in the 1700s. The quintessential polymath and Renaissance man was Italian Leonardo da Vinci (1452-1519). Best known as an artist, da Vinci was also an inventor and scientist with interests in medicine, music, geology, astronomy, and much more. His science was approached by observing natural events and not by theoretical explanations.[3]

The aim of the Enlightenment was a rejection of all external authority and discovery of truth by reason alone. Impressed by the stunning successes of the Scientific Revolution, men and women of the Enlightenment elevated science to the sole source of genuine knowledge. Claiming to liberate the verifiable from the noncognitive, it insisted that nature was the sole reality and scientific reason the sole path to truth. Whatever was not susceptible to scientific study was pronounced an illusion and a fraud. Great minds like Francis Bacon, René Descartes, John Locke, Voltaire, and Isaac Newton influenced the world by publishing compelling treatises. They directly challenged the authority of the Roman Catholic Church.

Most of the early modern scientists were Christians and believed that matter was not preexisting but had come from the hand of God. There has always been a tension between religion and science. It is even more pronounced today, when even Christian schools teach that the heart is what we use for religion, while the brain is what we use for science.

Secularists reinforced the schism by claiming that their theory did not reflect any particular philosophy—that it was just the way all reasonable people think. The notion that it was possible to strip the mind of all prior assumptions and religious commitments in order to get down to the bare, unvarnished truths of reason came from the Enlightenment. It was expressed most forcefully in the seventeenth century by René Descartes.[4]

The boldness of the Enlightenment lay in the thinking that reason was a transcendent power for providing infallible knowledge. Reason became nothing less than an idol, taking the place of God as the source of absolute truth. Descartes helped to establish a form of rationalization that treated reason not merely as a human ability to think rationally but as an infallible and autonomous source of truth.

Both Descartes (1596-1650) and scientist-mathematician Isaac Newton (1642-1717), major intellectual catalysts of the Enlightenment, laid the foundation for a new way of thinking and a new view of the natural world that emphasized skepticism over faith and uniformity over divine interventions. Nonetheless, they both considered themselves Christians. Professor of theology Roger E. Olson acknowledges those beliefs in his description of the Enlightenment: "It looked very much like Thomas Aquinas's lower sphere of theology—a collection of concepts about God, the soul and morality knowable by reason apart from grace, faith and special revelation."[5]

René Descartes was born in France and trained as a lawyer, but early on became a military officer in the Dutch States Army. He studied military engineering and mathematics. Descartes believed all truths were linked to one another. Finding one fundamental truth and using logic would open the way to all of science. He is remembered for the famous line, "I think, therefore I am."[6]

During his twenty years in the Netherlands, he revolutionized mathematics and philosophy. Philosophy for him embodied all knowledge. "Thus, all Philosophy is like a tree, of which Metaphysics is the root, Physics the trunk, and all the other sciences the branches that grow out of this trunk, which are reduced to three principles, namely, Medicine, Mechanics, and Ethics. By the science of Morals, I understand the highest and most perfect which, presupposing an entire knowledge of the other sciences, is the last degree of wisdom."[7]

For him, dualism suggested that the mind controls the body, but the body can also influence the mind when people act out of passion. He considered ethics as the highest form of science and believed in God and free will. Even though Descartes was a devout Catholic, his theological beliefs were based on reason. Pascal accused him of Deism and stated, "I cannot forgive Descartes; in all his philosophy, Descartes did his best to dispense with God. But Descartes could not avoid prodding God to set the world in motion with a snap of his lordly fingers; after that, he had no more use for God."[8]

In 1663, the Catholic Church banned Descartes' books due to his shifting allegiance from God to humanity. His skeptical approach dramatically changed the course of Western philosophy and set a course for modernity. He believed a person can make his own laws and take his own stands. This provided the basis for the Enlightenment's emancipation from God and the Church.[9]

By far, the most influential intellectual of the Western world during his lifetime and for decades afterward was John Locke (1632-1704). Locke was born twelve miles from Bristol, England, to Puritan parents. He attended Christ Church, Oxford, and read the works of René Descartes with much interest. He eventually received a bachelor of medicine in 1674.

Locke believed in separation of church and state, which, along with his arguments concerning liberty and the social contract, influenced a number of outstanding individuals including Jonathan Edwards, Voltaire, Thomas Jefferson, Alexander Hamilton, and James Madison. Thomas Jefferson reproduced one passage from Locke's *Second Treatise* verbatim in the Declaration of Independence.

John Locke's *Common Sense* swept the colonies in 1776. Soon there were 100,000 copies in circulation. It was a direct attack on King George III, who came to power through heredity, which Locke believed was absurd and evil. Using an analogy from the Bible, he said the British monarchy was "one of the sins of the Jews."[10]

All the influential people in England consulted Locke on matters of philosophy, religion, and politics. One of his most important works was his *Essay Concerning Human Understanding*, which was revolutionary in Enlightenment philosophy. Along with Isaac Newton, he founded the empirical school of philosophy that helped shape modern science.

What is little written about today is that one of Locke's main interests was religion. His most important religious writing was *The Reasonableness of Christianity*, published in 1695. His main goal was to demonstrate the essence of divine revelation and to show that Christian belief is fully consistent with reason. In other words, Locke treated Christianity as a matter of intellectual belief. He believed in absolute religious freedom, and as an assistant to Oliver Cromwell, aided in drafting a constitution, titled the Agreement of the People, in 1647.[11]

Even though Locke opposed slavery in his major writings, he was an investor in the English slave trade through the Royal African Company. Some accused him of being a hypocrite. He also helped draft a constitution for the Carolinas that established for farm owners the absolute power over their slaves. At the same time, he wrote that all people were equal and independent, and everyone had a natural right to defend his "Life, Health, Liberty, or Possessions."[12] Most scholars believe that phrase inspired Jefferson when he wrote of "life, liberty, and the pursuit of happiness" in the Declaration of Independence.[13] Locke believed that revolution is not only a right but an obligation in some circumstances. Those words would inspire many who led the colonists in the Revolutionary War.

Unlike Jefferson, Locke was very conservative in regard to the Bible. He believed the entire Bible was within human reason, and miracles were proof of the divine nature of the biblical message. Locke believed that without God, social order would be undermined, leading to chaos. George Washington would totally agree. Locke believed in creation and stated that we have been "sent into the world by God's order, and about his business, we are his property, whose workmanship we are, made to last during his, not one another's pleasure."[14]

Matthew Tindal (1657-1733) followed in Locke's footsteps, and in 1730 wrote *Christianity as Old as the Creation: Or, The Gospel a Republication of the Religion of Nature,* which came to be known as the Deists' bible. He concluded that real Christianity is nothing more than a rational ethical system set against a vaguely theistic background. He concluded that religion has no real need of any special revelation, grace, or savior. His publication profoundly influenced leading American thinkers such as Benjamin Franklin and Thomas Jefferson.[15]

Tindal also influenced Thomas Paine (1737-1804), a leading proponent of democratic revolutions and separation of church and state. Paine's *The Age of Reason,* published in 1794, moved beyond the others to an anti-Christian natural religion. A century later, Theodore Roosevelt labeled Paine "that filthy little atheist," as he viewed all Deists as closet atheists.[16]

Deists were religious thinkers of Europe and North America in the post-Reformation period who championed human reason and natural religion over faith and revelation. It was a view of religious knowledge that placed common principles of human reason and common religious ideas of humanity at the center. Deism was most consistent with the basic impulses both of Protestantism and the new philosophy and science of the Enlightenment. Its basic principle can be summed up this way: "Nothing should be accepted as true by an intelligent being, such as man, unless it is grounded in the nature of things and is in harmony with right reason."[17] This principle generally expressed the universal theme of the Enlightenment.

Deists believed in God, but their conception of God is the God of nature, the creator and architect of the universe. In general, they did not believe in a God who intervenes in daily affairs, or one with whom people have a personal relationship—unlike evangelicals today. Most Deists rejected beliefs like the virgin birth, incarnation, the Trinity, resurrection, and the atonement theory of Christ's crucifixion.

Protestant movements viewed reason as corrupted by sin and in need of healing by grace in order to grasp divine truths. Protestant theologians and church leaders saw the Deists as guilty of an unwise yielding of Christianity to accommodate Enlightenment modes of thought. The Enlightenment movement may be summed up as:

1. An emphasis on the power of reason to discover the truth about humanity in the world.
2. Skepticism toward the venerable institutions and traditions of the past.
3. Emergence of a scientific way of thinking that offered intellectuals a viable alternative approach to knowledge from that which had dominated medieval thought.[18]

Deists defended these three main ideas. First, they viewed Christianity as completely consistent with reasonable, universally assessable natural religion and morality. They viewed the doctrine of the Trinity as clearly incompatible with natural religion, and therefore they essentially ignored it. Another common belief was that true religion was primarily about social and individual morality. The third idea was that a good Deist who is intelligent and enlightened should be skeptical toward all claims of supernatural revelations and miracles. If Native Americans were puzzled by Christianity, Deism, the religion of the Enlightenment, would bewilder them.

Inspired by these beliefs, in 1774 the first Unitarian congregation was formed in London at Essex Chapel. In North America, the first Unitarian church was King's Chapel, founded in 1785 in Boston. In the 1790s, a number of Congregational churches in both England and the United States became Unitarian. By 1825, the official denomination was formed as the American Unitarian Association, and Harvard Divinity School became its official seminary. While its members remained small in number, many U.S. presidents and congressmen have claimed it as their spiritual home.[19]

The Enlightenment was an age of science and development of modern technology. Scholars began to assert the logic and importance of cause-effect relationships. They developed scientific notions of natural law. These intellectuals modified the grounds of human knowledge away from, for example, the traditional teachings and dogmas of the church to such objective processes as rational observation, empirical verification, and logical inference.

In terms of religious belief, scholars of the Enlightenment recognized that in earlier times, people naïvely appealed to divine agency to explain natural phenomena that seemed mysterious. A number of biblical scholars were heavily influenced by the Enlightenment and moved to a rationalistic view of the Gospels. According to these scholars, the miracles of the Bible obviously didn't happen. That stance was wholeheartedly embraced by Thomas Jefferson.

One of the assumptions of the Enlightenment had to do with dualistic perceptions of reality. European and American forms of dualism had their roots in ancient Greece. Dualism is a way of perceiving reality within a framework of two opposing rudiments, such as spirit and flesh, mind and body, mind and matter, good and evil, virtue and vice, or Christian and heathen.

The opposite is holism. The worldview of Native Americans was holistic and embraced harmony. All creation was considered both good and spiritual. In the dualistic worldview, however, only the spirit was considered to be good. Creation was considered to be either evil or less spiritual. Western

Enlightenment compartmentalized the world by separating humanity from nature and then dividing those partial realities into extrinsic categories. This unnatural divide lent itself to the old dualistic system of the material world versus the spiritual world. This meant trouble for the indigenous peoples, and often that trouble arrived in the name of Christianity, greed, and politics.

The Scientific Revolution

Ever since the first migrations out of Africa, adapting to new frontiers has been part of human nature. However, the idea that the human experience includes the freedom to explore, whether on Earth, in space, or in works of literature, is of relatively recent origin. The least of the soul's faculties, as Plato wrote in *The Republic*, was imagination. This was consistent with Aristotle's *Rhetoric* in which he rejected the idea of speculative writing. He wrote, "Nobody can 'narrate' what has not yet happened."[20]

The average educated European in the early seventeenth century believed in witches and werewolves, bloodletting, signs from God and comets that portended evil, and the notion that blood could soften diamonds. The typical individual trusted traditional authorities over experience and had no concept of studying nature. But only a century later, that had changed. Belief in werewolves and witches had vanished, and scientists were peering through telescopes and microscopes. Many owned a pendulum clock and a barometer and respected experience as an authority. The physical world was now all about facts, experiments, evidence, theories, and laws of nature. Nature was now an intelligible and controllable network of causes and effects, a storehouse of knowledge that humans could set out to discover and use. Slowly science became an autonomous republic of its own, with its own values and virtues.[21]

For some 300 years after the Scientific Revolution, Christianity and science were thought to be completely compatible and mutually supporting. The publication *De Revolutionibus Orbium Coelestium*, written in 1543 by Nicolaus Copernicus (1473-1543), is usually considered the beginning of the Scientific Revolution. Most scientists were Christian believing that matter was not preexisting but had come from the hand of God. Thus, a pastor collecting biological specimens was a common sight in the countryside. The stunning complexities of nature revealed by science were not feared as a challenge to belief in God but hailed as a confirmation of his wisdom and design. Scholars as diverse as Copernicus, Kepler, Newton, Boyle, Galileo, Harvey, Ray, and Browne felt called to use their scientific gifts in praise to

God and service to humanity. The application of science, medicine, and technology was justified as a means of reversing the effects of the fall by alleviating suffering and toil.[22] The harmony between science and religion collapsed abruptly in the nineteenth century when Charles Darwin published his theory of evolution. It was yet another blow to white and Native American relations.[23]

However, matters were different before the Scientific Revolution. During the Middle Ages, Copernicus shocked the world. The Polish physician and astronomer, after years of observing the night skies, came to the heretical conclusion that the Earth was not the center of the universe but was rotating on its own axis and orbiting around a stationary sun once a year, which was contrary to the Church's stance that the sun revolved around the Earth.

Pope Leo X was a humanist and early on actually sent Copernicus a letter of support. However, the scientist's thoughts were not well known until after he died. Then his conclusions were either laughed at or openly denounced. Martin Luther wrote, "People give ear to an upstart astrologer who strove to show that the earth revolves, not the heavens or the firmament, the sun and the moon. . . . This fool wishes to reverse the entire scheme of astrology; but sacred Scriptures tell us that Joshua commanded the sun to stand still, not the earth."[24] Chiming in, John Calvin quoted the ninety-third Psalm, "The world also is stabilized, that it cannot be moved," and he asked, "Who will venture to place the authority of Copernicus above that of the Holy Spirit?"[25]

Italian philosopher and astronomer Giordano Bruno (1548-1600) added in 1584 in his *De I'Infinito Universo e Mondi* (On the Infinitive Universe and Worlds) that the universe was boundless and could contain any number of inhabited worlds. This again challenged the Aristotelian view that the Earth was the center of the universe. The Church had Bruno burned at the stake for these heresies. Within a few decades, his ideas were being widely accepted throughout Europe.

But the controversy would not go away. Galileo Galilei (1564-1642), a founding father of the Scientific Revolution, agreed with Copernicus and Bruno and also identified four moons circling around Jupiter. Meanwhile, Johannes Kepler (1571-1630), a German mathematician, published his three laws of planetary motion.

Galileo was born in Pisa, Italy, and early on considered becoming a priest, but at his father's insistence he enrolled at the University of Pisa for a medical degree. Later, he was appointed the chair of mathematics there.

Even though he was a pious Roman Catholic, Galileo had three children out of wedlock.[26]

Galileo confirmed heliocentrism, which prompted his findings to eventually be submitted to the Roman Inquisition in 1615. He was found in violation of the Council of Trent. The Inquisition found that Galileo's conclusion that the Earth orbits the Sun "receives the same judgment in philosophy and . . . in regard to theological truth it is at least erroneous in faith."[27] When he persisted in publishing his work, in 1616 the Inquisition ordered for him ". . . to abandon completely . . . the opinion that the sun stands still at the center of the world and the earth moves, and henceforth not to hold, teach, or defend it in any way whatever, either orally or in writing."[28]

For over a decade, Galileo avoided the subject, but his *Dialogue Concerning the Two Chief World Systems* once again stirred the ire of the Inquisition. In 1633, he was put on trial, and under the threat of torture, Galileo admitted that he had not told the truth about a revolving earth. As he was leaving the court, he muttered, "E pur simuove" ("and yet it does move").[29]

For the rest of his life, he was placed under house arrest and his *Dialogue* was banned. All his present and future publications were also banned. Suffering from insomnia and blindness, Galileo died in disgrace. Two hundred years later, Thomas Henry Huxley, in a eulogy to Galileo, characterized the Church as "the one great spiritual organization which is able to resist, and must, as a matter of life and death, resist, the progress of science and modern civilization."[30]

Another key figure in the Scientific Revolution that swept Europe was Johannes Kepler. In 1609, as court astronomer to Emperor Rudolf II of Prague, Kepler used the amazing naked-eye observations of his predecessor Tycho Brahe to discover that the planets orbit the Sun in elliptical paths, disproving the belief in circular orbits that had been held since Aristotle's time and strengthening the arguments for a heliocentric universe. Kepler was a deeply religious Lutheran whose scientific work was filled with spiritual beliefs. He consulted horoscopes and believed that the cosmos was a living organism possessed of a soul. Like most people of his time, he also believed in witches—his mother Katharina was accused of being a witch and was tried in Württemberg, starting in 1615.[31]

As the seventeenth century progressed, the frontiers of science and literature became closely interconnected. John Milton wove Galileo's discoveries into *Paradise Lost*. The poet wrote that Satan's shield "Hung on his shoulders like the moon, whose Orb / Through Optic Glass the Tuscan Artist views."

A contemporary of Galileo, Francis Bacon (1561-1626) was born in London and attended Trinity College, Cambridge, under the tutelage of Dr. John Whitgift, future Archbishop of Canterbury. Besides Bacon becoming attorney general and lord chancellor of England, he was also a philosopher, scientist, and author. He promoted scientific methodology, and in 1733, Voltaire, a guiding force of the Royal Society (which was founded under King Charles II in 1660), spoke of Bacon as the father of the scientific method.[32]

Credited with establishing the inductive method of science, Bacon stated that the reason earlier ages got their science all wrong was that they deducted their ideas about nature from metaphysical speculations. Genuine science must start not with the philosophy but with facts, followed by reasoning strictly through induction. Soon, his method was applied to virtually every field of thought: science, political philosophy, moral theory, and even biblical interpretation. Its central concept was even enshrined in the Declaration of Independence in the phrase, "We hold these truths to be self-evident." Where did the idea of self-evident truths come from? It came from Bacon's Common Sense Realism.[33]

For Bacon, standing at the dawn of the Scientific Revolution, the main enemy had been Aristotelian philosophy. The Londoner taught that science must start by clearing past ideas—by delivering the mind from all the metaphysical speculation, all perceived notions of truth, all the accumulated superstition of the ages. "With minds washed clean from opinions," in his words, we sit down with the facts "as little children and let the facts speak for themselves—then compile them inductively into a system."[34] Author Nancy Pearcey stated in *Total Truth*, "The very notion that facts 'can speak for themselves' would send contemporary philosophers into babbling fits about paradigm shifts and conceptual frameworks."[35]

Applied to biblical interpretation, the Baconian method stipulated that the first step is to free our minds from all historical theological formulations: Calvinist, Lutheran, Anglican, or whatever. We confront the biblical text as a collection of facts that speak for themselves and then compile individual verses inductively into a theological system. Statements in Scripture were treated as analogous to facts in nature, noble in exactly the same way.

Among the most influential to embrace the Baconian method were the old-school Presbyterians at Princeton. It is important to realize that the term *science* had not yet acquired the narrow, specialized meaning it has today. Instead it meant any form of systematized knowledge, so the term was applied even to subjects like politics, morality, and theology. Theology was known as the queen of sciences. This explains why so many clergymen at the time assumed that a scientific method like Bacon's could be applied to theology.

After the Revolutionary War, the only public authority to which one could credibly appeal was science because, ideally, at least science was democratic. By following the scientific method, one was not supposed to submit to any established authority; each individual could thus examine the evidence and decide for himself. Applied to theology, the Baconian method claimed that the Bible was accessible to everyone who cared to look at its facts—an idea that appealed to a newly born democratic culture, especially in the person of Thomas Jefferson.

However, some lamented the Church's loss of the wisdom provided by some of their greatest stars throughout Church history: Augustine, Aquinas, Luther, and Calvin. By adopting the Baconian method, many American evangelicals lost the intellectual riches of two millennia of theological reflection. But they didn't care—for them religion was all about emotion.

Because of their Baconian view of knowledge, nineteenth-century evangelicals tried to build a moral science based on empirical and rational grounds alone. One philosophy textbook put it as an approach based on an entirely naturalistic view of human nature. In doing so, however, they opened the door to full-fledged philosophical naturalism—nature is all that exists. Philosophers abolished courses on moral philosophy, replacing them with empirically oriented courses on experimental psychology and sociology that spelled out the full implication of a naturalistic view of human nature. The American university had been secularized.

Besides his major influence on philosophy and religion in North America, Bacon played a prominent role in establishing the British colonies of Virginia, the Carolinas, and Newfoundland. He was mainly responsible for drafting the two charters of government for the Virginia Colony.[36]

Later, high praise came from Thomas Jefferson, who wrote, "Bacon, Locke, and Newton. I consider them as the three greatest men that have ever lived, without any exception, and as having laid the foundation of those superstructures which have been raised in the physical and moral sciences."[37]

The Scientific Revolution swept Europe at the end of the Renaissance, and continued until the end of the eighteenth century, influencing those involved with the Enlightenment. There was significant progress in the fields of mathematics, physics, biology, chemistry, and astronomy, which had profound effects on society and the European understanding of nature.[38]

One of the most important publications during the Scientific Revolution was Isaac Newton's 1687 *Principia,* which described the laws of motion and universal gravitation. His laws replaced the Greek view that had dominated science for 2,000 years. Science became its own discipline and was viewed as having practical implications.[39]

Christianity—especially after the Reformation—played a pivotal role in the rise of the Scientific Revolution, as history professor Peter Harrison noted:

> Historians of science have long known that religious factors played a significantly positive role in the emergence and persistence of modern science in the West. Not only were many of the key figures in the rise of science individuals with sincere religious commitments, but the new approaches to nature that they pioneered were underpinned in various ways by religious assumptions. . . . Yet, many of the leading figures in the Scientific Revolution imagined themselves to be champions of the science that was more compatible with Christianity than the medieval ideas about the natural world that they replaced.[40]

Taking the lead from Bacon, scientists in the Age of Enlightenment presented theories and then set out with research to prove them. The research had to be observable, so it focused on material things. It generally avoided philosophical matters such as the existence of God. The Enlightenment was the age of secular humanism, and to some, God was an unprovable hypothesis.[41]

Nonetheless, the star of the Scientific Revolution, Isaac Newton (1642-1727), wrote far more on theology than he did on physics. He spent a considerable amount of time calculating the Second Coming—which he determined to be 1948. Earlier, Johannes Kepler was also deeply interested in biblical questions and worked out the date of the Creation, which he calculated to be 3992 BCE.[42]

Isaac Newton is widely considered one of the most influential scientists of all time. He was born in the county of Lincolnshire, England, on Christmas Day, December 25, 1642. He attended Trinity College, Cambridge, and while at the time the college teachings were based on the works of Aristotle, in his spare time he also read works by Descartes and Galileo.

After he received his master of arts and became a fellow of the College of the Holy and Undivided Trinity, in 1667 Newton stated that "I will either set Theology as the object of my studies and will take holy orders when the time prescribed by the statutes [seven years] arrives, or I will resign from the college."[43] During that time, a fellow at either Cambridge or Oxford was required to take holy orders and become an ordained Anglican priest. But since a Lucasian Professor of mathematics could not be active in the church, he was exempted from ordination requirements.[44]

Newton is credited with developing calculus, binomial theorem, the law of universal gravitation, and laws of motion, among others. Later in life, in the 1690s, he wrote a number of works on the Bible. He corresponded with John Locke on many of these matters. Although some scholars have stated Newton did not believe in the Trinity, his biographer Sir David Brewster stated that Newton certainly did. Like many other leaders of the Enlightenment, he saw no conflict in being a Christian who benefitted from slavery. He invested heavily in the South Sea Company, which traded in slaves, but lost a large fortune when the enterprise failed.[45]

Newton was the second scientist to be knighted; the first was Francis Bacon.[46] In a 2000 survey of members of Britain's Royal Society, Newton was picked as the greatest scientist of all time, with Einstein coming in second.[47] He is commemorated on a monument in Westminster Abbey that was completed in 1731. The Latin inscription on the base translates:

> Here is buried Isaac Newton, Knight, who by a strength of mind almost divine, and mathematical principles peculiarly his own, explored the course and figures of the planets, the paths of comets, the tides of the sea, the dissimilarities in rays of light, and, what no other scholar has previously imagined, the properties of the colours thus produced.
>
> Diligent, sagacious and faithful, in his expositions of nature, antiquity and the holy Scriptures, he vindicated by his philosophy the majesty of God mighty and good, and expressed the simplicity of the Gospel in his manners. Mortals rejoice that there has existed such and so great an ornament of the human race! He was born on 25 December 1642, and died on 20 March 1727.[48]

At the center of scientific progress was England. It was at the heart of the Industrial Revolution, which began in Britain in 1750 and in no small part happened there because of greater political and economic liberty. The standard of living of the average person in Britain doubled from 1750 to 1850. More goods were being produced by far less labor. Machines could be thanked for that. In England, the upper middle class, the bourgeoisie, believed that status and power should be achieved through merit rather than inheritance. They were highly supportive of education and liberty.

Centuries earlier, the Magna Carta had guaranteed the property rights of British citizens, and they saw the basis of liberty through individual property rights. This was a foreign concept to Native Americans, and would be a serious point of contention when the U.S. government insisted on individual property and not collective ownership for them.

Industrialization took place in America at breakneck speed between 1780 and 1830. The term *scientist* was first coined in 1833. In the early stages, whole families went to work in the factory, but soon it became evident that industrial work was shockingly different from the older family-centered work culture. To many, the world of industry seemed to be a social Darwinist war of each against all. Some have even suggested that Darwin's concept of the survival of the fittest was merely an extrapolation into biology of the competitive efforts of early industrialism.[49]

The emerging world of industrial capitalism fostered a new definition of virtue. Previously the good man was the one who exercised self-restraint and self-sacrifice for the sake of the common good. The capitalist world seemed to require each man to function as an individual in competition with other individuals. In this new context, it was appropriate, even necessary, to act under the impulse of self-interest and personal ambition. Greed was a virtue.

Adam Smith's *The Wealth of Nations* treated self-interest as a universal natural force, analogous to the force of gravity and physics. There emerged a new vision of the individual as free from settled social bonds, free from generational ties to the past, free to find his own place in society through open competition. Eventually, the values of the colonial period were actually turned upside down. The Puritans had viewed passions as a threat to social order, requiring control and self-restraint for the public good. But by the end of the nineteenth century, male passions and self-interest came to be viewed in a positive light—as the source of equality and economic prosperity.

In fact, the word *competitive* now entered the English language for the first time. Until then, English did not even have a word for a person who relished the challenge of a contest. By the end of the nineteenth century, competition—inspired by Darwin's survival of the fittest—had become an obsession among American men. It was firmly believed that free competition was the engine of prosperity and political life.[50]

As the nineteenth century progressed, the Baconian view filtered down from the realm of abstract ideas and began to be expressed in the institutional structure of the university itself. Universities that had been founded by Christian churches, like Harvard, Princeton, Columbia, and Yale, began pushing theology off into a separate department instead of allowing it to permeate the curriculum as a whole. Religion became an extracurricular activity that students pursued in their private time on the side—like going to chapel or participating in Christian student groups. Religion was being removed from the curriculum where public knowledge was taught and relegated to the private sphere of subjective experience. In the curriculum, religion was replaced by the humanities, which were supposed to fill the vacuum by dealing with higher questions of meaning, morality, and spiritual life.

The Romantic Movement Challenges Science

Yet scientific materialism with its vision of a mechanistic universe, the Age of Enlightenment, and the Industrial Revolution were unattractive to many people, and this galvanized a reaction known as the Romantic Movement. The Romantics responded by trying to preserve some cognitive territory for things that were not reducible to scientific materialism, including religion, morality, the arts, and humanities. Romanticism rejected the philosophy of materialism in favor of the philosophy of idealism, which says that ultimate reality is not material but mental or spiritual.[51]

In an affront to religion, Romanticists rejected its intellectual component. They also rejected rationalism. The movement became widely popular in American politics, philosophy, and art. It appealed to a wide audience and saw an increase in female authors and readers. But Romanticism made a fatal concession—it largely conceded the study of nature to mechanistic science and sought only to carve out a parallel arena for the arts and humanities.[52]

The first person to reject Enlightenment notions of progress and civilization was Jean-Jacques Rousseau (1712-1778), the flamboyant Swiss rebel who gave birth to Romanticism. Rousseau was born in Geneva, the heart of Calvinism. If there ever was an intellectual, European champion of Native Americans, it was Rousseau. He rejected the idea of private property ownership that during the nineteenth century the American government would embrace and become part of the American Dream. Rousseau wrote:

> The first man who, having fenced in a piece of land, said 'This is mine,' and found people naïve enough to believe him, that man was the true founder of civil society. From how many crimes, wars, and murders, from how many horrors and misfortunes might not anyone have saved mankind, by pulling up the stakes, or filling up the ditch,

and crying to his fellows: Beware of listening to this imposter; you are undone if you once forget that the fruits of the earth belong to us all, and the earth itself to nobody.[53]

Rousseau believed that only in nature were found uncorrupted morals, and he claimed that the highest stage of human development was what was found in savages. Savages were an ideal balance between brute animals and decadent civilization:

This period of the development of human faculties, maintaining a middle position between the indolence of our primitive state and the petulant activity of art egocentrism, must have been the happiest and most durable epoch. The more one reflects on it, the more one finds that this state was the least subject to upheavals and the best for man, and that he must have left it only by virtue of some fatal chance happening that, for the common good, but never to have happened. The example of savages, almost all of whom have been found in this state, seems to confirm that the human race had been made to remain in it always; that this state is the veritable youth of the world; and that all the subsequent progress that has been in appearance so many steps towards the perfection of the individual, and in fact for the decay of the species.[54]

Although Rousseau never used the term *noble savage,* many associate him with it because of his beliefs. The oxymoron first appeared in the English language in Dryden's play, *The Conquest of Granada* (1672). Benjamin Franklin championed the idea that all races, including Native Americans, had virtue. Bruce E. Johansen, author of *Forgotten Founders: Benjamin Franklin, the Iroquois, and the Rationale for the American Revolution,* wrote:

Franklin's writings on American Indians were remarkably free of ethnocentrism, although he often used words such as "savages," which carry more prejudicial connotations in the twentieth century than in his time. Franklin's cultural relativism was perhaps one of the purest expressions of Enlightenment assumptions that stressed racial equality and the universality of moral senses among peoples. Systematic racism was not called into service until a rapidly expanding frontier demanded that enemies be dehumanized during the rapid, historically inevitable westward movement of the nineteenth century. Franklin's respect for cultural diversity did not reappear widely as an assumption in Euro-American thought until Franz Boas and others revived it around the end of the nineteenth century. Franklin's writings on Indians expressed the fascination of the Enlightenment with nature, the natural origins of man and society, and natural (or human) rights. They are likewise imbued with a search (which amounted at times almost to a ransacking of the past) for alternatives to monarchy as a form of government, and to orthodox state-recognized churches as a form of worship.[55]

But times were changing. In 1853, Charles Dickens, in his weekly magazine *Household Words,* wrote a scathing and sarcastic review in response to George Catlin's art exhibit in London that featured Indians. Romanticism was fading in favor of Realism and so was the idea of a noble savage. Dickens, who would become one of the most famous authors of his time, expressed the belief held by many in the United States as the country grabbed up more land out West:

> To come to the point at once, I beg to say that I have not the least belief in the Noble Savage. I consider him a prodigious nuisance and an enormous superstition. . . . I don't care what he calls me. I call him a savage, and I call a savage a something highly desirable to be civilized off the face of the earth. . . . The noble savage sets a king to reign over him, to whom he submits his life and limbs without a murmur or question and whose whole life has passed chin deep in a lake of blood; but who, after killing incessantly, is in his turn killed by his relations and friends the moment a gray hair appears on his head. All the noble savage's wars with his fellow-savages (and he takes no pleasure in anything else) are wars of extermination—which is the best thing I know of him, and the most comfortable to my mind when I look at him. He has no moral feelings of any kind, sort, or description; and his "mission" may be summed up as simply diabolical.
> . . . .
> To conclude as I began. My position is, that if we have anything to learn from the Noble Savage, it is what to avoid. His virtues are a fable; his happiness is a delusion; his nobility, nonsense. We have no greater justification for being cruel to the miserable object, than for being cruel to a William Shakespeare or an Isaac Newton; but he

passes away before an immeasurably better and higher power [i.e., that of Christianity] than ever ran wild in any earthly woods, and the world will be all the better when this place knows him no more.[56]

Perhaps General Phil Sheridan was inspired by Dickens, who lived an ocean apart, when he said, "The only good Indian is a dead one." Opinions had certainly changed from the height of the Romantic Age.

Rousseau's *The Social Contract*, published in 1762, was one of the most important works on political philosophy. The opening line is: "Man is born free, and everywhere he is in chains. Those who think themselves the masters of others are indeed greater slaves than they." In his mind, man competing with his fellow man was part of a degenerate phase of society. When the individual is his own author of the law, he can remain free. Therefore, true followers of Jesus would not make good citizens in a country full of laws. Even more ire developed in Calvinist Geneva when Rousseau rejected the doctrine of original sin—so central to Calvinism. Rousseau found his spirituality in nature and viewed God as impersonal creator, as did many Deists of the time.[57]

In his book *Rousseau and Revolution,* author Will Durant countered others who asserted that Rousseau had little influence on America and its Founding Fathers, writing, "The first sign of his political influence was in the wave of public sympathy that supported active French aid to the American Revolution. Jefferson derived the Declaration of Independence from Rousseau as well as from Locke and Montesquieu. . . . The success of the American Revolution raised the prestige of Rousseau's philosophy."[58]

As the nineteenth century unfolded, the American West of the Louisiana Purchase found its father in President Thomas Jefferson as his representatives, Lewis and Clark and their Corps of Discovery, headed up the Mississippi in their search for a passage to the Pacific Ocean. For the Indians, a perfect storm was brewing.

Even more devastating than smallpox, the beliefs in men's minds that led to the Renaissance, Enlightenment, Scientific Revolution, Industrial Revolution, and the Reformation would be played out on one of the grandest of stages. For a fleeting moment, Romanticism provided Native Americans with some hope that they would be treated as equals. The words of Thomas Jefferson that all men are created equal would be encouraging, but not for long.

The elitists saw Indians as mentally inferior, on par with apes. Men of the Enlightenment saw God in nature but had no time for Indian myths and legends. If they left behind the miracles of Jesus, the most famous man ever, they certainly discounted the gods and myths of the savages. The Scientific and Industrial Revolutions affirmed the white man as superior and also provided the firepower to prove it.

It would be the century of Manifest Destiny and of Christians of many beliefs reuniting in the Eden that was the American West. Social Darwinism championed survival of the fittest, which no doubt was a white man, and the white man was greedy. Greed almost always trumps, as Abraham Lincoln stated in his first inaugural address, "the better angels of our nature."

If Indians could have been pushed into the ocean, they probably would have been. Instead, the heathens, or what was left of them after disease, starvation, and death—at the hands of soldiers, frontiersmen, and settlers—were placed in barren gulags called reservations. After a century of broken promises and broken treaties, the final indignation would be the white man chipping away at the Indians' landholdings on the reservations.

CHAPTER FIFTEEN

All Men are Created Equal: Thomas Jefferson and His Legacy

Bacon, Locke, and Newton . . . I consider them as the three greatest men that have ever lived, without any exception, and as having laid the foundation of those superstructures which have been raised in the physical and moral sciences.
—PRESIDENT THOMAS JEFFERSON

Jefferson's legacy in American religion is at least as long as it is in American politics. More than anyone else, Jefferson was responsible for setting the ground rules for religious practice in the United States.
—STEPHEN PROTHERO,
CHAIR OF THE DEPARTMENT OF RELIGION AT BOSTON UNIVERSITY

The lives of such Founding Fathers as Benjamin Franklin, John Adams, Alexander Hamilton, Thomas Jefferson, James Madison, and George Washington demonstrate the overlapping nature of the American Revolution, religion, the Scientific Revolution, and the American Enlightenment. And because they were such central players, their desires were in fact decisive to the Revolution's direction and outcome. They were also influential in the direction Americans took in dealing with Native Americans. During the Revolution, the British fought for their king, but the American rebels fought for their lives and God.

Jefferson was a visionary zealot with a mind that roamed at the speed of thought. He never for a moment believed that conflict was to be just about ends. It was always to be about building a better world, one in which, not coincidentally, every person would be free to worship his or her own God. The often tragic nature of history teaches us that while we should never give up our principles, we must also realize that we cannot maintain our principles unless we survive. Most strategic choices are between lesser and greater evils. Jefferson was an idealist who chafed at the cynicism of realists, and he consistently argued that U.S. policies had to honor the country's basic moral values as well as its crucial geopolitical interests.

In 1790, three Quaker-inspired petitions favoring emancipation—and endorsed by an aged Benjamin Franklin—were introduced in Congress. Some members, like Madison, kept a low profile and quietly hoped the issue would go away. Others, like James Jackson of Georgia, exploded. If the Quakers loved blacks so much, he shouted in a rant to fellow members in Congress, let them go to Africa. He also cynically pronounced that in Africa they could marry and be given in marriage and have a motley race of their own. Fergus M. Bordewich, author of *The First Congress,* believed that the failure to act on emancipation was the most consequential failure of the First Congress. Many members of Congress loathed slavery but feared that the new government could not risk an open debate on the subject without splintering the country. They believed that attaining emancipation was like opening a rusty door: it would take several swings before finally opening. That was Jefferson's conclusion, and he has been roundly criticized for it ever since. He believed that, in time, an enlightened America would abolish slavery. He has also been castigated by many evangelicals today for taking religion out of government—a move that was intended to spare Christian denominations from persecution in Virginia by a state government controlled by Anglicans. They also have accused him of not being a Christian.[1]

The Jefferson Bible

By March 10, 1804, Jefferson's forty-six-page volume had been completed. Years later, he recalled, "It was the work of two or three nights only at Washington, after getting thro' the evening task of reading the letters and papers of the day." Jefferson titled the work *The Philosophy of Jesus of Nazareth extracted from the account of his life and doctrines as given by Matthew, Mark, Luke and John. Being an abridgment of the New Testament for use of the Indians unembarrassed with matters of fact or faith beyond the level of their comprehensions.* Although this booklet was lost after his death, Jefferson often read from it in the evenings as he searched for moral insights.[2]

One biographer has called Jefferson "the most self-consciously theological of all America's presidents."[3] His religious writings demonstrate Jefferson's deep devotion to Jesus and his moral teachings, which for Jefferson was the basis for true religion.

Jefferson was born an Anglican, but even as a boy he started questioning the doctrine of the Trinity. Jefferson had been inspired from the works of his friend Joseph Priestley (1733-1804), the preeminent Anglo-American scientist and a leading theologian who in 1782 published *An History of the Corruptions of Christianity*. Like all good men of the Enlightenment, Priestley championed science to demystify the world and ultimately undermine the political and religious leaders who promoted superstition to maintain their authority. He believed that the Trinity, the Virgin birth, Original Sin, and predestination, among others, were corruptions and prevented people from understanding and embracing Christian faith. Priestley became an object of hate by other Christian leaders for his belief in Unitarian ideas, criticisms of the established church, and admiration of the revolution taking place in France.[4]

After Priestley's home was burned in England, in 1794 he moved to the United States with the support of Jefferson and Dr. Benjamin Rush. Rush, a famous Philadelphia physician, scientist, and humanitarian, was a deeply religious man raised in the evangelical Presbyterian tradition that swept the mid-Atlantic provinces beginning in the 1730s. At the heart of his faith was a personal and emotional communion with God, fellowship with fellow believers, and reliance on the Bible versus the teaching of learned clergyman.

Inspired by Priestley's 1803 publication *Socrates and Jesus Compared*, Jefferson wrote *Syllabus of an Estimate of the Merit of the Doctrines of Jesus, Compared with Those of Others* and sent it off to Rush. He divided the development of moral thoughts into three sections: ancient Greek and Roman philosophers, moral principles of the biblical Jews, and the teachings of Jesus of Nazareth. In Jefferson's view, Jesus had made the moral duties of affection, benevolence, and philanthropy incumbent on all mankind.

Jefferson's list of corruptions included Original Sin, the Virgin birth, the atonement, predestination, salvation by faith, bodily resurrection, and the Trinity.[5] He believed the Trinity was a concoction of priests, ministers, kings, and popes in an effort "to filch wealth and power to themselves," who had perverted the pure morals of Jesus into "an engine for enslaving mankind."[6]

Jefferson, who at the time was being accused of being an atheist by many religious leaders in the United States, explained his beliefs to Rush, writing, "They are the result of a life of inquiry and reflection, and very different from the anti-Christian system, imputed to me by those who know nothing of my opinions. To the corruptions of Christianity, I am indeed opposed; but not to the genuine precepts of Jesus himself. I am a Christian, in the only sense in which he wished any one to be; sincerely attached to his doctrines, in preference to all others; ascribing to himself every human excellence, and believing he never claimed any other."[7] While crediting Jesus with bringing the highest moral wisdom, Jefferson denied his divinity. To him, morality arose not from revelation, but rather from the dictates of nature and reason. His God was the God of nature, which was the God of reason. In his thinking, miracles were not consistent with the demands of reason and the laws of nature, and Jesus had not performed them. Besides, miracles showed power over nature that was totally unacceptable to the men of the Enlightenment. However, Jesus was Jefferson's spiritual hero, and he called Jesus "the first of human Sages."[8]

On January 20, 1804, Jefferson ordered two copies of the King James version of the New Testament from a Philadelphia bookseller. Two weeks later, he received a pair of nearly identical volumes published in Ireland in the 1790s. Even though world events such as the Louisiana Purchase and England at war with France preoccupied him, the president had time to work on his Bible.

With razor in hand, he excised New Testament corruptions by Paul and others. Those corruptions included all miracles and all legends surrounding Jesus' virgin birth, crucifixion, resurrection, and ascension. Only about one in ten gospel verses survived Jefferson's razor to produce *The Philosophy of Jesus of Nazareth*.[9]

In 1805, Jefferson ordered two additional copies of the New Testament in English and two in French. However, they remained on his bookshelf until after he retired at Monticello. In 1819, from the different language versions of the New Testaments, he cut out the pages that he believed were uncorrupted by misunderstandings, fabrications, and time and carefully glued them onto loose pages. He again excised passages "of vulgar ignorance, of things impossible, of superstitions, fanaticisms, and fabrications."[10] The Jefferson Bible was structured chronologically, while his earlier 1804 effort was arranged topically. By 1820, Jefferson had finished his work, *The Life and Morals of Jesus of Nazareth Extracted Textually from the Gospels in Greek, Latin, French & English*—known as the Jefferson Bible—and sent the pages to Frederick A. Mayo, a Richmond bookbinder who stitched them together in a red leather binding adorned with gold tooling. The modest book measured eight and a quarter inches tall and just under five inches wide.

Jefferson excluded those elements that could not be supported through reason, that he believed were later embellished, or that seemed superfluous or repetitious across the four evangelists' accounts, the Gospels. In Jefferson's Bible and the earlier revision of Virginia laws, he displayed an extraordinary lack of reverence toward the authorities of the past. Journalist William Duane remarked that Jefferson was "the greatest rubber off of dust" that he had ever encountered.[11] Jefferson believed that man is an engineer of his own fate. He explained his motivation: "The religion-builders have so distorted and deformed the doctrines of Jesus, so muffled them in mysticisms, fancies and falsehoods, have caricatured them into forms so monstrous and inconceivable, as to drive them rashly to pronounce its founder an imposter."[12]

The Life and Morals of Jesus was made for Jefferson's own personal use and was not intended for general publication. "I never go to bed without an hour, or half an hour's previous reading of something moral," Jefferson told his physician when inquiring about his daily routine. He was so private about his religious beliefs that his grandchildren said he never revealed much to them. "I not only write nothing about religion," he told a correspondent, "but rarely permit myself to speak of it." He firmly believed that God meant to reserve the matter of belief to the discernment of the individual, stating, "No man can conform his faith to the dictates of another. The life and essence of religion consists in the internal persuasion or belief of the mind."[13]

While Jefferson was closer to Deism than atheism, he was closer still to Unitarianism. In 1820, he stated his Jeffersonian Creed:

1. That there is one God, and he is all-perfect.
2. That there is a future state of rewards and punishments.
3. That to love God with all thy heart, and thy neighbor as thyself, is the sum of religion.

He felt so assured that everyone would be won over to his creed that he stated, "There is not a young man now living in the U.S. who will not die a Unitarian."[14]

Before his death in 1826, Jefferson left on the bottom of his portable writing desk, the same desk on which he drafted the Declaration of Independence, an attached note from 1825 that read, "Politics, like religion, has its superstitions. These, gaining strength with time, may, one day give imaginary value to this relic, for its association with the birth of the Great Charter of our Independence."[15] The ideas that were self-evident to Jefferson and his colleagues were the concepts of individual rights and equality. It was based not on superstition but on human reason.

Stephen Prothero, chair of the Department of Religion at Boston University, summarized the impact Jefferson had on American religion:

> Jefferson's legacy in American religion is at least as long as it is in American politics. More than anyone else, Jefferson was responsible for setting the ground rules for religious practice in the United States. His commitment to volunteerism, enshrined today in the First Amendment, transformed his nation into the world's most Christianized country. But also opened that country to the religious diversity we see today. . . .
>
> Today, U.S. suburbs are filled with "Golden Rule Christians" who, like Jefferson, believe that the essence of true religion lies in right living rather than right-thinking, and that service to others is the highest form of prayer. . . .[16]

Jefferson hated what Christianity had become, not despite of his love of Jesus, but because of it. And he was able to admire, respect, and perhaps even love, "The first of all Sages" only because he was able to separate the religion of Jesus from the religion of Christianity. Jefferson was not of a sect by himself. Millions of Americans today, Christian and otherwise, harbor similar sentiments. In this sense, Jefferson was a founding father not only of the United States of America but also of today's Jesus nation.[17]

The Statesman

Above all, Thomas Jefferson was a Renaissance and polymath man who embraced the philosophy of the Enlightenment. He spoke Latin, Greek, Italian, French, and Spanish and played the role of farmer, lawyer, legislator, governor, diplomat, first secretary of state, second vice president, and third president. Much the optimist and idealist, he, like all great leaders, championed hope and truly believed the country's finest hours were yet ahead.

At six feet, two and one-half inches tall, Jefferson, a freckled redhead, was gregarious and counted many friends. They were dazzled by the man who was a philosopher, naturalist, scientist, and historian. Those who dined with him described him as a man of curiosity, charm, wit, and laughter.

But he was no bookish pedant. He loved the outdoors, where he raced horses and kept his body fit by walking miles. Three glasses of wine a day helped him unwind as he often spent his evenings reading and catching up with correspondence.[18] For him, America's leaders should be well-educated and the masses enlightened. He had faith in the people—at least white people.

High praise came from Jefferson biographer and Pulitzer Prize–winner Jon Meacham: "Judged by the raw standard of the winning and the keeping of power, however, Thomas Jefferson was the most successful political figure of the first half century of the American Republic. For thirty-six of the forty years between 1800 and 1840, either Jefferson or a self-described adherent of his served as president of the United States: James Madison, James Monroe, Andrew Jackson, and Martin Van Buren. (John Quincy Adams, a one-term president, was the single exception). This unofficial and little-noted Jeffersonian dynasty is unmatched in American history."[19]

Stephen Prothero added, "Thomas Jefferson is revered in the United States today as the author of the Declaration of Independence, the architect of the First Amendment, and one of the saints of American civil religion. Though questions persist regarding his views on race and his relationship with his slave Sally Hemings, he is widely respected nonetheless as one of the nation's great champions of individual freedom."[20]

All these presidents and his followers called themselves Jeffersonians. Originating with Jefferson, they believed that white American men had a right to property and religious freedom, but these rights did not extend to men of color. Jeffersonians placed American farmers at the pinnacle of society. If slaves were needed for them to be successful, then so be it because God approved.

Inspired by the likes of Locke, Vattel, and Grotius, Jeffersonians agreed with the principle that it was acceptable to acquire the Native American lands due to their transient lifestyle. To appease them, they would be given some land—far west of civilization—to cultivate in the hope that someday they could be civilized.

Future leaders were both inspired and disgusted by Jefferson. At a 1962 dinner party honoring all living recipients of the Nobel Prize, President John F. Kennedy paid tribute to the genius of Jefferson, remarking, "I think this is the most extraordinary collection of talent, of human knowledge, that has ever been gathered together at the White House, with the possible exception of when Thomas Jefferson dined alone."[21]

Yet Jefferson had numerous enemies. Many saw him as a fanatic atheist, and others were suspicious of his infatuation with France. During his successful 1800 effort to unseat President John Adams, Jefferson was the recipient of personal attacks seldom seen in U.S. politics. He was called an idiot and a coward. Reverend William Linn, a Dutch reformed minister from New York who hated Jefferson, warned "of a manifest enemy to the religion of Christ, in a Christian nation, would be an awful symptom of the degeneracy of that nation, and . . . the rebellion against God."[22] Undaunted, Jefferson wrote in an 1814 letter, "Our particular principles of religion are subject of accountability to our God alone. I inquire after no man's, and trouble none with mine."[23]

Theodore Roosevelt called him our worst president. In the eyes of the general public today, he is not faring well. Some professors have dropped teaching the writings of Jefferson because he was a racist, slaveholder (nine presidents owned slaves including Washington), and had a slave, Sally Hemings, as his mistress who bore him four children who lived to adulthood.[24] Like the problem with slavery, Jefferson kicked the can down the road in regard to Native Americans. Jefferson understood that it's easy to have courage about things you can't do anything about; so he did things he could do something about.

Stephen E. Ambrose, author of *Undaunted Courage,* in his *To America: Personal Reflections of an Historian,* summarized his critique of Jefferson, writing, "He died with hope, that the future would bring to fruition the promise of equality. For Jefferson, that was the logic of his words, the essence of the American spirit. He may not have been a great man in his actions, or in his leadership, where he did little or nothing to bring about his hope. But in his political thought, he justified that hope."[25]

Every generation finds its failings in past generations, much like the individual finds failings in friends and family. Often, walking in another man's shoes is an uncomfortable fit, and it is easier to criticize than empathize. How many today if transported back to the time of slavery or Indian conflicts would have had the courage to make a stand?

Jefferson biographer Dumas Malone concluded—as did Jon Meacham—that Jefferson understood that societal changes were slow to evolve, and while he had the ideas for a more perfect union, others in the future would be responsible for making it come to fruition. Malone wrote, "Jefferson's vision extended farther and comprehended more than that of anybody else in public life, and, thinking of himself as working for posterity, he was more concerned that things should be well started than that they be quickly finished."[26]

Perhaps Jefferson surmised that one does not surrender a way of life in an instant. That which is lifelong can only be surrendered over an undetermined amount of time. Who determines that time? Well, God does. As a dedicated Deist, Jefferson believed God started the clock then backed away.

Who adjusted the clock when the time was off? Wait for God? Perhaps. Moral maturity is the accomplishment of years, and one can only surrender to the will of God as His will becomes apparent. The fullness of the Spirit—like the fullness of time—is not instantaneous but progressive. Jefferson very much believed that. And he proved to be right. In Garry Wills' Pulitzer Prize–winning *Lincoln at Gettysburg,* he wrote how Abraham Lincoln was inspired by Jefferson's Declaration of Independence to champion freedom for the slaves.[27]

The Life and Times of Jefferson

Thomas Jefferson (1743-1826) was born the third of ten children, at the family home near Charlottesville in the Virginia wilderness. He grew up as a child of privilege on his wealthy family's farm. His father's library included Shakespeare, Jonathan Swift, and Joseph Addison. He also grew up in an elitist, plantation culture where all his family and friends owned slaves. He knew nothing different. One cannot underestimate the long-term influence of one's childhood.

By nine years old, he was studying the classics in French with Reverend William Douglas, with whom he lived for five years. After that, he boarded with Reverend James Maury, who taught him the classics. His education culminated with entering William and Mary College where George Washington, John Marshall, James Monroe, and other famous Americans matriculated.

Most young adults in the 1760s and early 1770s fixed their conversations on the definition of liberty in the nature of representative government. Politics were everything to the young Jefferson. As David McCullough stated in *John Adams,* "Jefferson was devoted to the ideal of improving mankind but had comparatively little interest in people in particular."[28] In the eighteenth century, the newly made Americans came to cherish individualism, innovation, equal legal rights, and the unequal economic results of geographic and social mobility. In many ways, those who believed in American exceptionalism tried to distance themselves from England.

But by the early nineteenth century, America drew closer to England economically and nurtured a middle-class ethos united in Protestant pride and embracing everything English. In Jefferson's world, the leading colonial towns increasingly looked like the newer neighborhoods of London. Reading English books rather than local ones, the elites of America drank tea, wore imported clothing, lived in knockoffs of English mansions, and worshipped in copies of the latest English churches. England was a source of the latest fashions in nineteenth-century America.

The New World was a place to be discovered, but also a place where people discovered themselves. The pursuit of prosperity and liberty for some required others to be poor, subordinated, disposed, and shackled. Indians were killed and relocated, and African Americans worked so that some Englishmen and Americans could get rich in a new land. It was the American Dream.

The Revolutionary War in 1775 and the Declaration of Independence in 1776 were instigated by Jefferson and other revolutionaries who saw themselves as Englishmen who were being denied their rights and benefits. After the French and Indian War, a position by England that particularly infuriated Virginians was London's insistence on giving the king the power to decide the fate of western lands. Previously, the Virginians had been free to speculate in those frontiers.

In 1768, twenty-five-year-old Thomas Jefferson was elected to represent his county in the House of Burgesses. That same year, he started a project to build his new home, Monticello, Italian for "little mountain," a palatial home on a hill designed in the manner of the sixteenth-century Italian architect Andrea Palladio. He contracted for 100,000 bricks for the walls and ordered specially made windows from London. Slaves helped in the construction, along with doing their normal chores of working his fields, cutting his firewood, cooking, washing, saddling his horses, turning down his bed, and waiting on him from morning to night. His inheritance brought him not only thousands of acres of land but also debt, the normal status for a plantation owner.[29]

In 1772, he married Martha Wayles Skelton. For the next forty-one years, he was almost always serving in a public office besides running his extensive farm holdings. Those holdings included owning more than 600 slaves from 1769 to his death. He inherited 150 from his father and father-in-law and bought roughly 20 more. The rest were born into slavery on his lands. From 1774 to 1826, he owned approximately 200 at any one time.[30]

Early in public life, an idealistic Jefferson bravely spoke out against slavery. In 1769 in the House of Burgesses, Jefferson noted, "I made one effort in that body for the permission of the emancipation of slaves, which was rejected."[31] To his credit, Jefferson supported the Act Prohibiting Importation of Slaves of 1807, which stated that no new slaves were permitted to be imported into the United States. In his annual message to Congress on December 2, 1806, President Jefferson stated, "I congratulate you, fellow-citizens, on the approach of the period at which you may interpose your authority constitutionally, to withdraw the citizens of the United States from all further participation in those violations of human rights which have been so long continued on the unoffending inhabitants of Africa, in which the morality, the reputation, in the best interests of our country, have long been eager to proscribe."[32]

Some were surprised when such a young man as Jefferson was placed at the head of the committee for preparing a Declaration of Independence at the First Continental Congress in June 1775. John Adams (1735-1826) explained to a correspondent:

> Mr. Jefferson came into Congress in June, 1775, and brought with him a reputation for literature, science, and a happy talent of composition. Writings of his were handed about, remarkable for the peculiar felicity of expression. Though a silent member in Congress, he was so prompt, frank, explicit, and decisive upon committees and in conversation—not even Samuel Adams was more so—that he soon seized upon my heart; and upon this occasion I gave him my vote, and it all in my power to procure the votes of others. I think he had one more vote than any other, and that placed him at the head of the committee. I had the next highest number, and that placed me the second. The committee met, discussed the subject, and then appointed Mr. Jefferson and me to make the draft, I suppose because we were the two first on the list.[33]

As it turned out, Adams insisted on Jefferson writing the draft. Enlightenment vision along with the importance of the individual is clearly evident in the final product that was edited by Benjamin Franklin (who added "self-evident"):

> When in the course of human events it becomes necessary for one people to dissolve the political bands which have connected them with another, and to assume among the powers of the earth the separate and equal station to which the laws of nature and of nature's God entitle them, a decent respect to the opinion of mankind requires that they should declare the causes which impel them to the separation.
>
> We hold these truths to be self-evident: that all men are created equal; that they are endowed by their creator with certain unalienable

rights; that among these are life, liberty and the pursuit of happiness; that to secure these rights, governments are instituted among men, deriving their just powers from the consent of the governed; that whenever any form of government becomes destructive of these ends, it is the right of the people to alter or to abolish it, and to institute new government, laying its foundation on such principles, and organizing its powers in such form, as to them shall seem most likely to affect their safety and happiness.[34]

Jefferson's God of public religion was not the God of Abraham or God the Father of the Holy Trinity. The Founding Fathers could have used Christian imagery in the Declaration but didn't. The haunting reminder of religious wars prevented it. Jefferson believed it was important that every American find God as they understood it. The public God was the God of everyone, not just Christians. This is a fact not well appreciated today by many Christians.

He reflected on writing the Declaration of Independence, "Neither aiming at originality of principle or sentiment, nor yet copied from any particular and previous writing, it was intended to be an expression of the American mind, and to give to that expression the proper tone and spirit called for by the occasion."[35]

Years later, Jefferson was even sensitive to the atheist or unbeliever in any God. He believed that individual moral conduct was not totally derived from religion. He once asked, "If we did a good act merely from the love of God, and a belief that it is a blessing to him, whence arises the morality of the atheist? It is idle to say, as some do, that no such being exists."[36]

For years, John Adams and Jefferson had a tenuous relationship. One irritating subject for Adams was the notoriety that Jefferson received for the Declaration. In an attempt to devalue the document, Adams called it a "theatrical show" of little substance. Just before the two renewed their friendship, Adams stated, "Jefferson ran away with all the stage effect of that, i.e., all the glory of it."[37]

It was obvious that all men were created equal unless they were men of color like slaves and Indians. London philosopher and realist Jeremy Bentham, in a retort, said that idea was "absurd and visionary. . . . 'All men,' they tell us, 'are created equal.' This surely is a new discovery; now, for the first time, we learn, that a child, at the moment of his birth, has the same quantity of natural power as the parent, the same quantity of political power as the magistrate."[38]

Harkening back to the theme that Americans are God's chosen people and Ecclesiastes 9:11-12, friend John Page encouraged Jefferson, "I am highly pleased with your Declaration. God preserve the United States. We know the race is not to the swift nor the battle to the strong. Do you not think an angel rides in the whirlwind and directs this storm?"[39]

In the late eighteenth and nineteenth centuries, it became increasingly clear to Americans that their civilization was not compatible with the Indians' way of life. Disease and warfare had decimated the indigenous populations as the whites advanced westward, and by the time of the American Revolution, the idea of the "Vanishing American" was born. As historian Robert F. Berkhofer, Jr. wrote, "If Whites regarded the Indian as a threat to life and morals when alive, they regarded him with nostalgia upon his demise—or when that threat was safely past." That truth would certainly play out over the nineteenth century.[40]

In 1776, the colonies were not only facing conflict from the British but also from the Indians. For Virginians, the Cherokee posed a particular problem. The idealistic Jefferson was fascinated with the Indian's language and culture. As he would do for years, he collected Indian artifacts. Devoid of the chains of Christianity, and living in nature, the natives were seen in his idealistic view as noble as long as they hadn't been tainted by whites. But, like most whites, his realistic side saw the need to acquire Indian lands by any means possible and then convert the natives to civil and obedient fellow countrymen.

Any lasting admiration for the Cherokee was severed, however, by what was happening in the real world around Jefferson. A number of tribes were allies of the British and thus were seen, like any other enemy, as a threat to independence from Britain. In August 1776, Jefferson wrote, "Nothing will reduce those wretches so soon as pushing the war into the heart of their country. But I would not stop there. I would never cease pursuing them while one of them remained on this side of the Mississippi."[41] Unpacking his words would suggest that if the Indians stood their ground east of the Mississippi they would be annihilated. Their only alternative was relocating to the West. At that time, the West held few whites, so its capacity to accept eastern Indians into their new home pragmatically seemed the least painful solution, but it was not the final solution.

Understanding American attitudes in 1776 creates a good foundation to understand how they would address the Indian problem in the future. The basis for the Revolution was the Enlightenment, inspired in part by John Locke's call for revolution and liberalism; the Renaissance, which embraced republicanism; the First Great Awakening, which emphasized defiant individualism; and capitalism.

In the fall of 1776, Jefferson, along with the assistance of his trusted friends James Mason and James Madison (who would become Jefferson's successor as president)—heirs to the Enlightenment's notion of "unalienable rights"—would take the idealism of the Declaration of Independence and put it into practical use. Unlike slavery, Jefferson was ready to tackle the thorny issue of separation of church and state. His actions would turn him into a target of hatred that has continued today.

Since Virginia was controlled by the Anglican Church, it was a crime not to baptize infants. Baptists were denied governmental positions whether civil or military. Baptist children could be removed from their homes if their parents did not submit to the Anglican Church's rules. In Jefferson's view—inspired by the Enlightenment and the distrust of organized religion—public funds should not be used to support churches. Jefferson wrote, "Our Savior chose not to propagate his religion by temporal punishments or civil incapacitation." On the contrary, "he chose to . . . extend it by its influence on reason, thereby showing to others how [they] should proceed."[42]

The powerful Anglican Church had enjoyed privileges including economic support by means of public taxes and the commitment of government authority to restrict gatherings of dissenters from the established faith. Jefferson led the successful revolution against legal privilege for religion. In Virginia, he had witnessed the authority of government being used to suppress gatherings for worship by Presbyterians, Baptists, and others and to threaten dissenting preachers with the force of law. Even though in writings like the Declaration of Independence Jefferson spoke of God as the Creator, he was attacked by the Anglican Church for believing in the separation of church and state.

In 1779, Jefferson introduced "a bill for establishing religious freedom" in the Virginia legislature. He wrote, "No man shall be compelled to frequent or support any religious worship . . . whatsoever . . . nor shall otherwise suffer, on account of his religious opinions or belief; but that all men shall be free to profess, and by argument to maintain, their opinions in matters of religion. . . ."[43]

In 1786, under the direction of Jefferson, a law, the Virginia Statute for Religious Freedom, was passed in the Virginia House of Delegates that guaranteed Presbyterians, Baptists, and members of other religions in Virginia the freedom to worship, stating, "No man shall be compelled to frequent or support any religious worship place, or ministry whatsoever, nor shall be enforced, restrained, molested or burdened in his body or goods, nor shall otherwise suffer on account of his religious opinions or belief."[44]

Later, many clergymen warned their congregations that they should hide their Bibles if Jefferson became president and that his election might bring down God's wrath on the new republic. Reverend William Linn, who had served as president of Queens College, now Rutgers University, distributed a widely read pamphlet that proclaimed, "The election of any man avowing the principles of Mr. Jefferson . . . [will] destroy religion, introduce immorality and loosen all the bonds of society."[45]

Matters worsened when renowned patriot and revolutionary Thomas Paine returned to the United States in 1802 and was invited by Jefferson to stay at the presidential mansion in Washington. Paine had been condemned by many Christians as the ungodly author of the *Age of Reason,* which stated Paine's Deist beliefs in God as maker, but rejected the divinity of Jesus and denounced clerical power.

James Mason's formulation that "all men are equally entitled to the free exercise of religion, according to the dictates of conscience" influenced both the Declaration of Independence and the Bill of Rights. Madison wrote nineteen amendments for the Bill of Rights, and in June 1789 Congress passed just twelve. The position of the First Amendment was a historical accident. Amendments on Congressional apportionment and compensation would have been first but were rejected by the states. The Bill of Rights centerpiece is the First Amendment's guarantee that "Congress shall make no law respecting an establishment of religion, or prohibiting the free exercise thereof." Only after passage of the Fourteenth Amendment and related Supreme Court rulings was this warranty explicitly understood in state governments. Religious freedom and his commitment to universal education are two of Jefferson's greatest contributions to our country.[46]

Every one of the Founding Fathers had a slightly different take on church-state separation. Almost all of George Washington's (1732-1799) significant public addresses included religious language. He believed in taxes to support religion, the appointment of military chaplains, and sacred language at public ceremonies.[47] He was consistent in championing religion to build the character of American people. This was not the position of Madison, who would be called a libertarian today. He believed the state should not support religion in any manner and that government should be non-cognizant of religion. He opposed the government singling out religious groups and individuals for special privileges, as was so prominent in Europe.

In his farewell address, Washington again emphasized his belief that the government should support religion so it could build Americans' character, writing, "Of all the dispositions and habits which lead to political prosperity, Religion and morality are indispensable supports. In vain would that man claim the tribute of Patriotism, who should labor to subvert these great pillars of human happiness, these firmest props of the duties of Man and citizens. The mere Politician, equally with the pious man ought to respect and to cherish them. A volume could not trace all their connections with private and public felicity."[48]

Washington, a massive man, large boned and well over six feet tall, had traveled widely in the wilds of western Virginia, and he played a significant role in the first bloody encounter of the French and Indian War. His marriage to Martha—barely five feet tall, stocky rather than dainty, a young widow with two children, but holder of one of the largest fortunes in Virginia—was an ideal match for a man with ambition but only a modest fortune to his name. Washington's evolution from a typical colonial farmer into a Revolutionary patriot, his leadership of the Continental Army, his role at the Constitutional Convention, and his presidency is one of the great American stories. Slavery was no abstraction to the Washingtons, who were among the largest slave owners in Virginia.

In his life, Washington grew increasingly uneasy about slavery in a remarkable evolution for a man of his class, a shift that has been explored in illuminating detail by Henry Wiencek in *An Imperfect God: George Washington, His Slaves, and the Creation of America*.[49] Although black soldiers helped to win the Battle of Yorktown, those who hoped that the patriot's victory might extend the rights of man to the enslaved were doomed to disappointment. In his will, Washington provided for the emancipation, upon Martha's death, of the 123 slaves that he personally owned. Martha held another 153 slaves in her own name but freed none of them, not even those who were married to spouses freed by George. Of her slaves she wrote, "The blacks are so bad in their nature that they have not the least gratitude for the kindness that may be showed to them." If George's attitude about slavery foreshadowed the enlightened values that came to fruition in the nineteenth century, Martha's views were pointed toward the pro-slavery politics of the antebellum South. In this contrast one can see the divided impulses that were present at America's creation and that were eventually destined to collide in the Civil War.[50]

Slavery was an issue filled with emotion. Jefferson remembered his failures in the House of Burgesses and lack of support from delegates to the

Continental Congress who removed his attacks on the slave trade from the Declaration of Independence. Undeterred, at the General Assembly in Williamsburg, Jefferson prepared an amendment that would provide freedom for all slaves born after a certain day, but once they were freed they would have to be deported since he couldn't imagine free whites and free blacks living together. During his retirement, Jefferson reflected on his failed stand and his hope for the future, writing, "Yet the day is not distant when it must bear and adopt it, or worse will follow. Nothing is more certainly written in the book of fate, than that these people are to be free; nor is it less certain that the two races, equally free, cannot live in the same government. Nature, habit, opinion have drawn indelible lines of distinction between them."[51] This stark conclusion also summarized white attitudes toward the Indians.

Jefferson's segregationist notions were put into action by the American Colonization Society, which was also supported by James Madison and James Monroe. The society was founded in 1816, and from 1821 to the Civil War it collected and shipped free blacks in the United States to the all-black colony of Liberia in Africa. Racial segregation for slaves and Indians was the rallying point from the publication of Jefferson's *Notes on the State of Virginia* in 1785 to the first years of the Civil War. White politicians, men of the Enlightenment, scientists, and church leaders all believed non-whites could only reach their full but limited potential by segregating them from Americans. There was also a raw fear and anxiety of racial mixing and racial warfare. Separation was essential because slavery corrupted blacks, and Indians were corrupted by frontier lawlessness. One of the most infamous examples of segregating Indians was the forced removal in 1838-1839 of 10,000 Cherokees to present-day Oklahoma. Jefferson and Madison found support for this stance from prominent medical professionals like Benjamin Rush and David Ramsay.[52]

Philosophy gave way to survival in the late spring of 1781. Governor Jefferson and the Virginia General Assembly moved from Richmond to Charlottesville because they were under threat from the British Army commanded by Lord Cornwallis. Cornwallis had ordered his men to pursue the government to Charlottesville. Home at Monticello, Jefferson rode out to a hillside and through his spyglass saw the British approaching. Having already removed his family from their home, Jefferson mounted his horse and headed to join them. Five minutes later, the British arrived at Monticello and asked where Jefferson was. Fortunately for the governor, the British did not loot his home, although they did drink some of his fine wine. Cornwallis did burn barns and crops and scattered his slaves at some of his other plantations.

By October 1781, with the American victory at Yorktown, the war was essentially over. Even though Jefferson was pleased that the war ended, all was not well at home. His thirty-three-year-old wife Martha was dying. Most likely she was succumbing to tuberculosis or complications following the birth of their daughter, Lucy Elizabeth. The next summer she was confined to her bed. Jefferson was a faithful husband and remained next to her. His children were young at the time: Patsy, nearly ten; Polly, four; and Lucy, an infant. Their mother died on September 6, 1782, and Jefferson took an oath to his dying wife that he would never marry again. A widower with three young children, Jefferson sadly believed his political career was over, but fortunately he was wrong.

The focus of the Constitution was on power and not God. The issues centered around the power of large and small states, between branches of government, and the rights of man. God was not mentioned in the Constitution, nor was any divine power authority. After the ratification of the Constitution in 1789, the framers sat down to work out the Bill of Rights. Modeled after Jefferson's law in Virginia, the First Amendment read, "Congress shall make no law respecting an establishment of religion, nor prohibiting the free exercise thereof."[53] In his *Notes on the State of Virginia* (1785), his only published book, Jefferson once again defended religious freedom, arguing, "It does me no injury for my neighbor to say there are twenty gods or no god. It neither picks my pocket nor breaks my leg."[54]

In May 1784, Jefferson joined John Adams and Benjamin Franklin in Paris to negotiate commercial treaties with European nations. The following year, he replaced Franklin as minister to France (1785-1789). Constantly in debt, Jefferson worried that his salary would not be sufficient for his lifestyle. Most of those debts were to English creditors, as he continued to spend lavishly on shoes, boots, rifles, and scientific instruments. He never denied himself any material possessions or comforts. In Paris he spent more than 200 francs for fifty-nine bottles of Bordeaux—the equivalent of three months wages for an average French worker. He would spend weeks buying a book every day at the finest bookstores in Paris. The merchants had never seen an American so ravenous for books. He also bought a number of paintings, many religious in theme. Before he left France, Jefferson had purchased sixty-three paintings, along with seven terra-cotta busts that he planned to adorn Monticello with. Back in Virginia his beloved Lucy died of whooping cough at two years of age. Of the six children, only two remained alive.[55]

The Northwest Ordinance of 1787 was perhaps the single most important piece of legislation passed by the Confederation Congress. It was based on Thomas Jefferson's proposed Ordinance of 1784. Earlier, in 1778 during the Revolutionary War, the U.S. government had negotiated its first Indian treaty with the Delaware in hope of their support against the British. The United States promised the Delaware statehood, which never happened. Over the next century, the tribe signed a series of eighteen treaties, the result of which left them powerless and dispersed from Canada to Oklahoma.

The Northwest Ordinance of 1787 provided a similar level of security for the Indians. Congress delineated its idea of how landholdings west of the Appalachian Mountains should be governed. The United States promised that "utmost good faith shall always be observed towards the Indians; their landed property shall never be taken from them without their consent." William Henry Harrison, superintendent of the Northwest Indians and governor of Indiana territory, between 1800 and 1812 signed fifteen treaties with tribes who turned over present-day Indiana, Illinois, and a large portion of Ohio and portions of Michigan and Wisconsin at a penny an acre. These treaties were often signed hastily by tribesmen who affixed an X or a pictograph to the treaty without understanding its ramifications. Often the representatives did not represent the majority of the tribe.[56]

The struggle over the issue of slavery was also addressed in the Northwest Ordinance of 1787. The law prohibited slavery north of the Ohio River and east of the Mississippi River. In addition, Jefferson made certain that when the populations of Ohio, Indiana, Illinois, Wisconsin, and Michigan were large enough, the territories would be allowed to become states. The same principles would apply to the Louisiana Purchase territories. After 1787, however, Jefferson did not broach the topic of abolition with deportation; he had concluded it was politically toxic.[57]

Jefferson believed that abolition's time had just not arrived for his generation. But he was optimistic that in future generations enlightened people would do the right thing. Once freed, blacks—who Jefferson viewed as a captive nation—could then be sent back to Africa. Pulitzer Prize–winner Annette Gordon-Reed and Peter Onuf in *"Most Blessed of the Patriarchs"* wrote that Jefferson believed whites would always be prejudiced against men of color, and blacks would not forgive the whites for being enslaved. Blacks would always be second-class citizens, and Jefferson's America was envisioned as a community of white Christian families—each one headed by a patriarch. Blacks and Indians could never really be first-class citizens and part of that family.[58]

In 1787, Jefferson began a sexual relationship with his wife's enslaved half-sister, Sally Hemings, who was light-skinned and described as beautiful. Hemings and Jefferson's wife had the same father. Soon she gave birth to his child, who only lived a short time. Jefferson made a pledge to Sally that their children should be freed at the age of twenty-one. She eventually gave birth to four others who were freed: Beverly, Herriot, Madison, and Eston.[59]

Blacks and whites had participated in interracial sex since the arrival of slaves in America in the 1620s. Another noted politician who didn't hide his relationship with a slave was Kentuckian Richard Mentor Johnson (1780-1850). Johnson, a U.S. Congressman and the famed killer of Shawnee leader Tecumseh, had a long-term relationship with a mulatto slave, Julia Chinn, who he had inherited from his father. They had two daughters together who ended up marrying white men, which caused a public outrage since intermarriage was illegal in Kentucky.[60]

In 1790, Jefferson became the first secretary of state, holding that position until 1791, and in 1797 he became the second vice president of the United States. Two years later, the great George Washington was dead at Mount Vernon. Jefferson planned a grand remodel of Monticello. It would be the most costly project of his life. He tore off the entire second floor and more than doubled the size of the house, which was inspired by a residence he had seen in Paris. Eight rooms increased to twenty-one rooms, many octagonal, that were filled with French accents. The slaves were kept busy.

In his run for presidency in 1800, Jefferson was again attacked for his religious views. A Christian Federalist believed a Jefferson win was a sure way to destroy a Christian America, arguing, "Can serious and reflecting men look about them and doubt, that if Jefferson is elected, and Jacobins get into authority, that those morals which protect our lives from the knife of the assassin—which guard the chastity of our wives and daughters from seduction and violence—defend our property from plunder and devastation, and shield our religion from contempt and profanation, will not be trampled upon and exploded."[61]

President Jefferson and the Indian Problem

At noon on Wednesday, March 4, 1801, Thomas Jefferson was inaugurated as the third president. In the next eight years, Jefferson cut the national debt by one third, cut taxes and spending, cut the military, abolished all internal taxes, founded the U.S. Military Academy in 1802 at West Point, and eased naturalization rules. He soon installed his secretary, Meriwether Lewis, in the East Room of the president's house.

In October 1801, the Danbury Baptist Association honored Jefferson for his views on religious liberty. Jefferson stated, "Believing with you that religion is a matter which lies solely between man and his God, that he owes account to none other for his faith or his worship, that the legitimate powers of government reach actions only, and not opinions. I contemplate with sovereign reverence that act of the whole American people which declared that their legislature should 'make no law respecting an establishment of religion, or prohibiting the free exercise thereof,' thus building a wall of separation between Church and State."[62]

Problems arose on the southern border of the United States in 1802. Secretary of State James Madison estimated that 52 million acres of land—between the thirty-first and thirty-fifth parallels, between the northern border of Spanish Florida and the southernmost border of the new state of Tennessee—were still owned by the Indians. There were claims to some of the land by the French, Spanish, and English. American settlers were migrating onto Tennessee, eastern Georgia, and southern Mississippi lands owned by the Indians. The region was seen as ideal for growing cotton, which had been made more profitable with the invention of the cotton gin in the 1790s. In 1802, Georgia demanded all Indians be removed from the state. Their wishes were approved by the Jefferson administration so that white claims for land west of Georgia would be dropped.

Jefferson suggested establishing trade houses that had earlier been authorized by the Intercourse Act of 1795 to offer goods at cost to Indians. Proponents of the trade houses hoped they would keep Indians loyal to the United States while also compelling Indians to sell their lands when they became indebted from purchasing goods at the trade houses.[63]

However, the pressure continued to remove the Indians farther west. Jefferson's secretary of war, Henry Dearborn, spent a great deal of his time on Indian affairs. Tensions grew on Indian lands all across the trans-Appalachian region. Claiming settler's sovereignty, frontiersmen were gobbling up land all over the area. In negotiations with the Cherokee, who claimed large tracts of land, Dearborn said, "We [the U.S. government] never wish to buy, except when you're perfectly willing to sell."[64] Like many other promises, that would be broken.

The Choctaw posed another obstacle in the southeastern United States in Mississippi, Florida, Alabama, and Louisiana. Dearborn believed that they had an obligation to sell their hunting grounds so Americans could farm it. The Jefferson administration pressured the Indians to sell at a meager price never exceeding two cents an acre. Choctaw leaders ultimately sold

800,000 acres of land and received "15 pieces of strouds [woolen cloth], three rifles, 150 blankets, 250 pounds of powder, 250 pounds of lead, one bridle, one man's saddle, and one black silk handkerchief."[65]

A common tactic used by the Jefferson administration was to foster tribal divisiveness and then negotiate with the most pliable leader, who often didn't represent the entire group of Indians but sold the land anyway. One Indian chief would realize that if he didn't sign the treaty the whites would find another Indian chief to sign, who would then have the power over the entire tribe. Once again, Jefferson's idealistic talk about teaching the Indians farming and educating them was abandoned as he sanctioned threats, intimidation, and bribes to acquire land.

One of Jefferson's greatest challenges was keeping the young country intact. With the resistance he had experienced early in his political career in regard to the issue of slavery, he set that effort aside. Some Deists believed God set things in motion but didn't micromanage matters. Jefferson approached the problem of slavery in a similar manner. Future generations would have to deal with it. Besides, there were still real threats from Spain, Britain, France, and the Indians. He needed to translate his anxiety into action in these matters. The threat of invasion from a foreign country was on the national conscience. Even though the Father of the American West never traveled west beyond Hot Springs, Virginia, he certainly understood the strategic importance of the region.

In 1802, the president read Alexander Mackenzie's *Voyages from Montréal,* a book on the explorer's 1793 travels through Canada to the Pacific. MacKenzie wrote, "It requires only the countenance and support of the British government [to] secure the trade of that country to its subjects. Many political reasons must present themselves to the mind of every [man] acquainted with the enlarged system and capacities of British commerce."[66]

Back in 1783, Jefferson had expressed his fears about the British taking over the West to George Rogers Clark, saying, "I am afraid" that they "have some thoughts of colonizing into that quarter."[67] Jefferson picked his personal secretary, Meriwether Lewis, to find the best route to the Pacific. George Rogers Clark's brother, William, agreed to Lewis' request to help him organize the Corps of Volunteers for North West Discovery. Congress agreed to a disbursement of $2,500 to fund the expedition. In the end, it would cost fifteen times that amount.

CHAPTER SIXTEEN

Father of the American West: Thomas Jefferson and the Corps of Discovery

At his most philosophical and reflective moments Thomas Jefferson envisioned the Corps of Discovery in terms of values—values to be preserved and extended. By finding both the garden and the passage, Jefferson's captains would ensure the continued vitality of the Republic. Jefferson's thoughts about values ran to the virtues of rural life: simplicity, frugality, and independence.
—JAMES P. RONDA, *VOYAGE OF DISCOVERY*

The potential of the United States was, if not limitless, certainly vast— and vastly greater if the nation could add the trans-Mississippi portion of the continent to its territory.
—STEPHEN E. AMBROSE, *UNDAUNTED COURAGE*

In March 1802, France and Britain signed the Treaty of Amiens, which called for the withdrawal of British troops from some of their most recently acquired territories. Napoleon Bonaparte (1769-1821) had expanded French holdings in Europe and won a truce. His success led to his appointment as First Consul for life in France.[1]

Napoleon was born on the island of Corsica to a moderately affluent family. In January 1779, he moved to Autun in the Burgundy region of France to study religion. Five months later he entered a military academy. He eventually rose to power during the French Revolution and dominated

European affairs for years. Along with being one of the greatest commanders in history, Napoleon became one of the most famous politicians in Western civilization.

Not believing in separation of church and state, Napoleon restored the Roman Catholic Church as the majority church in France. He selected the bishops and also controlled church finances. Nonetheless, religious freedoms were expanded to Protestants and Jews. For supporting the Jews, Napoleon was denounced by the Russian Orthodox Church, which formally condemned him as "Antichrist and the Enemy of God."[2]

Like Jefferson and some of the Founding Fathers, Napoleon was a Deist. His brand of Deism believed that God played no part in the day-to-day life of humans. Being a savvy politician, Napoleon understood the power of religion and how to use it to his advantage. He expressed this by saying, "It is by making myself Catholic that I brought peace to Brittany and Vendee. It is by making myself Italian that I won minds in Italy. It is by making myself a Moslem that I establish myself in Egypt. If I governed a nation of Jews, I should reestablish the Temple of Solomon."[3]

Fortunately for the United States, by 1803 Napoleon could not justify holding on to the Louisiana Territory because renewed war with Britain was imminent. He planned to sell the discovery rights of this massive amount of land to the United States. Many in France opposed the deal, including Napoleon's brothers. As Napoleon was soaking in cologne-scented water in his bathtub, his brothers arrived to share their concerns. "You will have no need to lead the opposition," advised Napoleon, "for I repeat there will be no debate, for the reason that the project . . . conceived by me, negotiated by me, shall be ratified and executed by me, alone. Do you comprehend me?" On Monday, April 11, 1803, Napoleon told his finance minister, Barbe-Marbois, "I renounce Louisiana. It is not only New Orleans that I will cede, it is the whole colony without any reservation. I know the price of what I abandon . . . I renounce it with the greatest regret. But to attempt obstinately to retain it would be folly."[4]

Just three years earlier, fading Spain had signed a treaty in London giving France the Spanish territory of Louisiana—more than half of Spain's North American colonies. "I am willing to hope, as long as anybody will hope with me," said Jefferson, that the news was not true, but it was.[5] Through the port of New Orleans traveled much of the commerce from the Mississippi River region that the United States depended on. Jefferson worried, "There is on the globe one single spot, the possessor of which is our natural and habitual enemy. It is New Orleans, through which the produce of three-eighths of our territory must pass to market, and from its fertility it will ere long yield more than half of our whole produce and contain more than half of our inhabitants."[6]

On April 30, 1803, the U.S. Minister to France, Robert R. Livingston, and Virginian James Monroe, who had traveled to France as Jefferson's envoy, signed the treaty that gave control of not only New Orleans but the entire Louisiana Territory to the United States for about $15 million, or three cents an acre. Jefferson, who was mostly interested in purchasing New Orleans, now was stunned with the news that the United States could possess all of the Louisiana Territory. "It is something larger than the whole U.S., probably containing 500 millions of acres, the U.S. containing 434 millions," Jefferson wrote.[7] With the deal out of the way, in May Napoleon declared war on Britain.

The president was concerned about his authority to purchase the land. The so-called Jefferson Rule referred to Jefferson's own assertion that his arguably unconstitutional actions as president, such as the Louisiana Purchase, accurately reflected the intentions of the founders, a principle that became part of the political DNA of later administrations.[8]

According to historian Robert Bothwell in *Your Country, My Country*, the Louisiana Purchase was the decisive event in continental history. It guaranteed that the United States would become a much greater power, with a large reserve of agricultural land in the West that settlers could access through the Mississippi River system.[9]

Jefferson had already planned to send Meriwether Lewis out West before the purchase. As Jefferson absorbed the fact that the United States was now double in size and that Lewis would be exploring American-controlled land, on July 5, 1803, he wrote Lewis, who was about to embark on his expedition, outlining its purpose, "In the journey which you are about to undertake for the discovery of the course and source of the Mississippi, and of the most convenient water communication from thence to the Pacific. . . ."[10]

But Jefferson had more in mind than just discovery of a new passage to the Pacific. He envisioned the Louisiana Territory filled with white settlers who would farm the land and keep it secure for the United States. The final solution for the Indian problem was in the future, but for now if the Indians resisted they would be pushed farther west and into the ocean if needed. In a forceful letter in 1803 to William Henry Harrison, the governor of the Indiana Territory, the president wrote that the Indians "will in time either incorporate with us as citizens of the United States or be removed beyond the Mississippi." If they resisted removal, the United States would retaliate by "seizing... the whole country of that tribe, and driving them across the Mississippi, his only condition of peace."[11]

Jefferson and Meriwether Lewis (1774-1809) shared much in common. Lewis was born in the Blue Ridge Mountains to wealthy parents who owned slaves and large plantations. In time, at age thirteen, he inherited Locust Hill, a Virginia plantation of nearly 2,000 acres, 520 pounds in cash, 24 slaves, and 147 gallons of whiskey. Since there were no public schools, Lewis, like Jefferson, obtained a private education by boarding with several preachers who taught him Latin, mathematics, natural science, and English grammar.[12]

At age eighteen, he considered seminary at William and Mary, but the responsibilities of the plantation required him to tend to his land. He added to Locust Hill by acquiring an 1,800-acre tract on the Red River in Montgomery County along with several other parcels. Low-lying lands were planted in corn to provide food for slaves and animals. More fertile land was planted with tobacco. It was very common to try to acquire more land. George Washington owned tens of thousands of acres in the Tidewater and Piedmont areas and over 63,000 acres of trans-Appalachian land. Jefferson owned 5,000 acres in the Piedmont that was given to him by his father, and his land holdings increased by 11,000 acres when he married his wife.[13]

But Meriwether Lewis was restless and desired adventure. In May 1792, American sea captain Robert Gray had sailed his ship *Columbia* along the Pacific Northwest coast into a river that would take the boat's name. This inspired Jefferson to raise funds to send explorers on an expedition to the Pacific. Lewis contacted Jefferson, who was a family friend, to volunteer. Jefferson recalled that Lewis "warmly solicited me to obtain for him the execution of that object. I told him it was proposed that the person engaged should be attended by a single companion only, to avoid exciting alarm among the Indians. This did not deter him."[14] However, Lewis was just a teenager at the time, and Jefferson chose another man, Frenchman Andre Michaux, whose expedition foundered before reaching the Mississippi River.

At the time of Jefferson's first inauguration on March 4, 1801, there were a little over 5.3 million people in the United States. Twenty percent were slaves. The boundaries of the country stretched from the Atlantic to the Mississippi River and from the Great Lakes to the Gulf of Mexico. The land was sparsely inhabited, with only four roads that spanned the country. The majority of people lived within fifty miles of tidewater. Only ten percent of Americans, about a half million people, lived west of the Appalachian Mountains.[15]

Virginians like Jefferson, Lewis, and Clark viewed the Indian as being a virtuous heathen who was pure and ready to be civilized. In contrast, slaves were seen as sub-humans on the level of an animal. As historian Stephen Ambrose explained:

> Jefferson's attitude toward Indians was the exact opposite of his attitude towards Negroes. He thought of Indians as noble savages who could be civilized and brought into the body politic as full citizens. In 1785, he wrote, "I believe the Indians then to be in body and mind equal to the whiteman." He thought the only difference between Indians and white men was religion and the savage behavior of the Indians, which was caused by the environment in which the Indian lived. Neither did he say that the perceived shortcomings of the Negro—such as laziness or thievery—were caused by their condition as slaves. Keenly interested in Indian ethnology, an avid collector of Indian vocabularies, he had not the slightest interest in African ethnology or African vocabularies.[16]

Jefferson didn't pick the young Lewis initially as an explorer but offered him a position as his secretary. Eleven days before his inauguration, on February 23, 1801, he wrote Captain Lewis about the position, "not only to aid in the private concerns of the household, but also to contribute to the mass of information which it is interesting for the administration to acquire. Your knowledge of the Western country, of the Army and of all its interests & relations has rendered it desirable . . . that you should be engaged in that office."[17] Lewis jumped at the chance to work with Jefferson, and together they spent many evenings often with other guests on matters concerning the army, among other topics.

In 1803, Jefferson's dream of an expedition to the West was taking shape. What to take on the journey required considerable thought, especially in regard to trade goods—not generally gifts—with the Indians. Beads of various colors were an important item: five pounds of white glass beads, twenty pounds of red beads, a large quantity of blue beads, 144 small cheap scissors, 288 brass thimbles, sewing thread, silk, paint, 288 knives, combs, armbands, and ear trinkets.[18]

Their medical advisor was Dr. Benjamin Rush, the most prominent American physician of the day and a signer of the Declaration of Independence. His recommendations showed how primitive Western medicine was at the time. He advised, "When you feel the least indisposition, do not attempt to overcome it by labour or marching. Rest in a horizontal posture. Also fasting and diluting drinks for a day or two will generally prevent an attack of fever. To these preventatives of disease may be added that gentle sweat obtained by warm drinks, or gently opening the bowels by means of one, two, or more of the purging pills."[19] The pills Rush referred to were his patented "Rush's pills" that were used for almost anything that ailed the patient. Containing chamomile, a mixture of mercury, chlorine, and jalap, the pill produced explosive diarrhea. Another important medication was mercury, which was used to treat syphilis. Rush also prepared a medical list with a total cost of $90.69 for drugs, lancets, forceps, syringes, opium, Peruvian bark, potassium nitrate, tartar emetic, laudanum, and calomel.

Lewis wrote to Jefferson, "Dr. Rush has favored me with some abstract queries under the several heads of physical history, medicine, morals and religion of the Indians, which I've no doubt will be serviceable in directing my inquiries among that people." The questions Rush suggested that Lewis ask reveal how little Americans knew about the Plains Indians. The questionnaire asked about diseases and remedies, age of marriage, the state of the pulse at different times of the day, when they woke up, bathing, murder, suicide, intoxicants, and animal sacrifices in their religious ceremonies, among others. Perhaps the most intriguing was evaluating the Indian ceremonies in comparison with those of the Jews.[20]

In the eighth century BCE, the Assyrians dispersed the kingdom of Israel, which gave rise to the life and legend of the Lost Tribes of Israel. One of the most provocative theories regarding the origins of Native American tribes is the belief that they could be somehow linked to the Ten Lost Tribes of Israel. Christopher Columbus proclaimed that the newly discovered Indians were in fact of Jewish origins. Columbus even suggested that Spain could "recruit their bodies and their wealth to assist Europeans in a final crusade to crush Islam and reclaim Jerusalem."[21] Jefferson and Lewis had a lengthy discussion about the Indians of the Plains possibly being the Lost Tribes of Israel after a number of publications made the connection.[22]

The Hope of Israel (1650), one of the first books to suggest that Native Americans were a remnant of the Lost Tribes, was written by a Dutch rabbi and diplomat, Manasseh Ben Israel. The next year, Thomas Thorowgood published his best seller, *Jewes in America, Or, Probabilities that those Indians are Judaical, made more probable by some Additionals to the former Conjectures.* The Lost Tribes idea was favorably accepted by minister Cotton Mather and Quaker leader William Penn. Penn wrote to a friend in England, "I found them [the Indians of the Eastern shore of North America] with like countenances with the Hebrew race; and their children of so lively a resemblance to them that a man would think himself in Duke's place, or Barry Street, in London, when he sees them." Many Protestant evangelicals praised Indians as virtuous and noble in part because of their connection with the Lost Tribes.[23]

More support was garnered after James Adair (1709-1783), a forty-year veteran as an Indian trader in the South, and meticulous chronicler of the Jewish-like features of Native American religion and social custom, in 1775 wrote *The History of the American Indians . . . Containing an Account of their Origin, Language, Manners, Religion and Civil Customs.* The book was arguably one of the most important eighteenth-century works on the southeastern Indians. He presented twenty-three arguments that proved the North American aborigines were descended from the Ten Lost Tribes. He was convinced that their appearance, beliefs, languages, and ceremonies were similar.

Even after the Lewis and Clark Expedition had returned in 1806, there were more publications supporting the connection in the following decades. In 1825, pastor Ethan Smith (1762-1849), a self-proclaimed expert on Jewish history, published *View of the Hebrews,* which discussed the similarity between Native American religious customs and that of ancient Judaism. This was followed by *The Ten Tribes of Israel Historically Identified with the Aborigines of the Western Hemisphere* (1836) by Barbara Simon, *A View of the American Indians* (1828) by Israel Worsely, and *American Antiquities and Discoveries in the West* (1835) by Josiah Priest, among others. Many pointed out the physical similarities between Indians and Jews.

The most popular and controversial of all interpretations on the origins of Native Americans came from Mormon founder and prophet Joseph Smith (1805-1844). His *The Book of Mormon* was allegedly a scriptural account of God's dealings with the remnant of Jewish descendants who had migrated to America during ancient times.

The possibility of a connection between Native Americans and ancient Jewish tribes romanticized the Plains Indians in the minds of many Americans, including Jefferson. It further supported the idea of the noble savage. Conversely, for those who were racist and anti-Semitic, it fueled the concept that Indians were best exterminated.

After spending time with Dr. Rush, Lewis felt comfortable enough to take on the doctor duties on the journey. This was due in part because he had learned from his mother the therapeutic uses of herbs. From his time on the frontier, where no doctors were present, he became proficient in setting broken bones and removing an embedded bullet or arrow. He obviously impressed Rush, who wrote Jefferson, "His mission is truly interesting. I shall wait with great solicitude for its issue. Mr. Lewis appears admirably qualified for it. May its advantages prove no less honorable to your administration and to the interests of science."[24]

Commerce with the Indians was important for winning them to America's side and providing the country with products such as furs. Jefferson made it clear to Lewis that he wanted him to learn the names of the nations, their size, their relations with other tribes, and languages. Being a politician, Jefferson knew the best way to size up a competitor is with charm. "In all your intercourse with the natives," Jefferson advised Lewis, "Treat them in the most friendly & conciliatory manner which their own conduct will admit." At the same time, Jefferson wanted Lewis to let the Indians know who they were dealing with, advising, "Satisfy them of your journeys innocence," but "let them know the power and strength of America." Being a man of the Enlightenment, Jefferson also wanted to discover the flora and fauna of the Louisiana Territory, especially specimens that were not found in the East.[25]

On June 19, 1803, Lewis wrote to William Clark with a request that he join him on the expedition as an officer. Lewis described the expedition to Clark: "My plan is to descend the Ohio in a keeled boat thence up the Mississippi to the mouth of the Missourie, and up that river as far as its navigation is practical with a keeled boat, there to prepare canoes of bark or raw-hides, and proceed to its [Missouri River] source, and if practicable pass over to the waters of the Columbia or Origan River and by descending it reach the Western Ocean."[26]

Also a Virginian, William Clark (1770-1838) grew up in the area that would become Kentucky. Like Jefferson and Lewis, he was a planter and slaveholder. Without formal education, Clark in 1789 joined other Kentuckians to fight in the Northwest Indian War against Indians who were trying to preserve their territory north of the Ohio River. Later, in 1794 at the Battle of Fallen Timbers, Captain Clark commanded a company who drove back the enemy composed of Native Americans and Canadians. That victory essentially ended the Northwest Indian War.[27]

Two years later, Clark resigned his commission due to poor health and returned to his family's plantation near Louisville. Lewis had served under Clark for about six months, but they were not well acquainted. They would become great friends. Clark, a seasoned woodsman, accomplished surveyor, and an excellent waterman, complemented Lewis. It was Clark who brought his slave York on the expedition. In 1807, after his three-year expedition with Lewis and the Corps of Discovery, Clark was appointed by President Jefferson as brigadier general of the militia and the Louisiana Territory, and as the U.S. agent for Indian Affairs. At the time, the government was actively setting up trading posts throughout the territory.[28]

Jefferson dreamed of an ideal America with the Indians living on a vast reserve west of the Mississippi. He often had discussed with Lewis the idea of persuading American pioneers in the upper Louisiana to accept land in Illinois in exchange for their holdings in the West. Thus, everything east of the Mississippi would be free of Indian problems. His naïve idea did not take into account that all the frontiersmen out West would never accept such a ridiculous offer. They were searching for gold, hides, and land opportunities that were available only in the Louisiana Territory.

Voyage of Discovery

By May 1804, Lewis and Clark and the Corps of Discovery were heading up the Missouri River. The great American road show of mercantile and hardware was presented to every tribe they encountered. They also wanted to demonstrate to the Indians that American technology was better than that of their British competitors. Rifles, balls, and powder were much desired by the Indians, who had inferior British shotguns. Along the way, the Corps distributed certificates and medals (like the Jefferson Peace Medal) to Indian chiefs in addition to their trade goods.[29]

It was important to communicate to the Indian tribes that their great leader was now Thomas Jefferson, president of the United States, and not the Spanish or French. Lewis informed them about Jefferson, saying, "Children, your only father; he is the only friend whom you can now look for protection, or from whom you can ask favours, or receive good councils, and he will take care to serve you, & not deceive you."[30]

The first American description of the ceremonial dress of the Plains Indians was documented by an impressed Captain Clark. "The Souix," he wrote, "is a Stout bold looking people (the young men hand Som) & well-made. The Warriors are Verry much deckerated with Plain Porcupin quils & feathers, large leagins & mockersons, all with Buffalow roabs of Different Colours. The Squars wore Peticoats & and a white Buffalow roabes with the black hair turned back over their necks & Sholders."[31]

By October 24, 1804, the expedition was approaching the Mandan villages that were the center of trade for the Northern Plains. In late summer, Indians—Crow, Assiniboine, Cheyenne, Kiowa, Arapaho—who lived far from the villages came to trade along with whites from the North West Company. The Corps would spend the winter of 1804-1805 in a fort constructed in the Mandan area. With Jefferson's interest in Indian languages, the expedition spent some time in the winter gathering vocabularies in an attempt to render words from various Indian languages into an English spelling. Lewis had little interest in Indian myths, legends, or spiritual life. He was more interested in the day-to-day work habits in the villages.

Clark wrote of his Mandan friends, "These are the most friendly, well disposed Indians inhabiting the Missouri. They are brave, humane and hospitable." In contrast, he wrote of the Teton Sioux, "These are the vilest miscreants of the savage race, and must ever remain the Pirates of the Missouri, until such measures are pursued, by our government, as will make them feel a dependence on its will for their supply of merchandise."[32]

Later, in the summer of 1805, Sacajawea, the Indian wife of French Canadian trader Toussaint Charbonneau, helped the expedition locate the Shoshone in what is now western Montana. Without the Shoshone's help, which included a supply of horses and information regarding a passage over the mountains, the expedition probably would've turned around and gone home. By October 1805, they were over the Bitterroot Mountains and headed down the Columbia River where they spent the winter of 1805-1806 after building Fort Clatsop on the rainy and dreary Oregon coast.[33]

On the journey home, Lewis returned on the Missouri River while Clark took a more southerly route down the Yellowstone River. By August 1806, the two had reunited east of where the two rivers join near today's Montana-North Dakota border. By the end of September, they had arrived back in St. Louis. Besides all the rich ethnographic and cartographic information that they were ready to share, they also had described 178 new plants and 122 species and subspecies of animals.[34]

In an 1813 letter, Jefferson wrote one long sentence in praise of Meriwether Lewis:

> Of courage undaunted, possessing a firmness & perseverance of purpose which nothing but impossibilities could divert from its direction, careful as a father of those committed to his charge, yet steady in the maintenance of order & discipline, intimate with the Indian character, customs & principles, habituated to the hunting life, guarded by exact observation of vegetables & animals of his own country, disinterested, liberal, of sound understanding and the fidelity to truth so scrupulous that whatever he should report would be

as certain as if seen by ourselves, with all these qualifications as if selected and implanted by nature in one body, for this express purpose, I could have no hesitation in confiding the enterprise to him.[35]

Four years earlier, on October 11, 1809, Meriwether Lewis, while staying at Grinder's Stand—seventy-two miles from Nashville, Tennessee—shot himself in the head with his pistol. The shot grazed his head. With his other pistol he shot himself in the chest, and the ball passed down through his body and exited near his lower spine. He staggered to the door and called out, "O madam! Give me some water, and heal my wounds." A short time later he died.[36]

Perhaps because of his apparent suicide, history was not kind to him in the nineteenth century. He was basically ignored. From 1889 to 1891, when Henry Adams wrote a multivolume history of the Jefferson administration, Lewis was hardly mentioned. He was finally given some recognition in Thwaites' edition of the journals at the end of the century. His fame has been rising ever since.

It was commonplace for politicians to repeatedly lie and break treaties with the Indians. Ideals are often hard to maintain and implement. Why? In some instances it is because the political opportunist almost always lacks the courage of his or her convictions. Like Jefferson and so many other politicians who followed, it is not necessarily because they had no convictions. It is because convictions are always subordinated to the needs of ambition and ingratiation.

As a man of the Enlightenment, Jefferson's God was the God of nature. His ideal view of the West was nature's people, the Indians, abandoning their way of life as hunter-gatherers and picking up the plow, reading the Bible, and sharing the bountiful land with their Eastern brothers. This willing transformation by the Indians would accommodate the ever-increasing masses of immigrants arriving from Europe. Jefferson opined, "While they are learning to do better on less land our increasing numbers will be calling for more land, and thus a coincidence of interests will be produced between those who have lands to spare, and want other necessaries, and those who have such necessaries to spare, and want lands."[37]

In Jefferson's mind, the harmony of nature was a powerful force that was stronger than human will. The West was America's Eden, and its Father blessed its red and white children. But soon his imagined West would collapse like a house of cards. The War of 1812, in which many of the Indians sided with England, transformed the American view of the noble savage into a bloodthirsty devil. It came as fast as a thief in the night.

In President Madison's 1809 annual message to Congress, he described "our Indian neighbors" as living under a "just and benevolent system" and who were moving rapidly toward civilization. However, by 1811 with the winds of war blowing, his charitable words were nowhere to be found. He informed Congress of "several murders and depredations committed by Indians" in the northwestern wilderness, and of "the menacing preparations and aspects of a combination of them on the Wabash, under the influence and direction of a fanatic of the Shawnee tribe." Two years later during his second inaugural address, the incredulous president was firmly in the camp of Americans who viewed Indians as the bloodthirsty devils who were doing the British's dirty work. He angrily denounced the savages who were "eager to glut their savage thirst with the blood of the vanquished and to finish the work of torture and death on maimed and defenseless captives."[38]

He was referring to Shawnee warrior Tecumseh, whose homeland in northern Indiana Territory had been invaded by white settlers. Tecumseh believed that only a pan-Indian confederacy could defeat the United States.[39] Earlier, President Jefferson had assigned a Quaker to the tribe to aid in civilizing them. He hoped the Indians would soon wear European-style clothing, attend school, and abandon their hunting in favor of farming. The Indians wanted no part of it. Defiantly, from August 1811 to January 1812 Tecumseh traveled from village to village in the Southeast and Midwest. He met with Creek, Chickasaw, Choctaw, Osage, Western Shawnee, and Delaware, among others. His efforts met with little success, and he was defeated along with the British in the War of 1812 by the United States. In 1813, he was killed by American forces. Even the most charismatic of Indian leaders could not keep a multi-tribal military force together for any period of time. Stealthy ambushes or full-scale assaults proved ineffective.[40]

After the war ended, Madison changed course again and stated that "our Indian neighbors" were friends of America once more.[41] While Madison's last words were comforting to the public who were anxious to move west but not anxious to encounter hostile Indians, Jefferson's dream of a Western Eden had forever evaporated. Brian Dippie explained:

> Still, the war and Tecumseh's "conspiracy" to unite all the Western tribes in a grand alliance to oppose American expansion had shattered the comfortable illusion that the Indians would gladly exchange land for civilization. . . .
>
> During the peace talks, a British minister accused the United States government of a total disregard for Indian land title, "thereby

menacing the final extinction of those nations." Stung, the American ministers defended their government's "humane and liberal" Indian policy. But the exchange indicated a growing awareness that the War of 1812 had permanently altered Indian-white relations in North America.[42]

With Americans moving south and west, the idea of the Indians as an independent nation became unacceptable. Independent nations had to be negotiated with and treaties had to be honored. A land grab was much less messy, especially since America could wield its military might against a bunch of scattered, unorganized tribes. They were renegades, and Americans were God's chosen people. Anti-Indian sentiments should not just be thought of as only a form of racism or prejudice. It was a deeply held belief, religious in power, through which America's events were interpreted.

What were the Indians to do? Some did move to Canada, Florida, and farther west on their own. Others saw the pioneers arriving in Illinois and Wisconsin and avoided them. This worked for about a decade. In 1819, the Indian Civilization Fund was established by Congress with an annual funding of $10,000. The focus was acculturation, with the establishment of schools to learn to read, churches to convert the Indians to Protestant Christianity, and model farms. It was all about destroying tribal communal landholdings and bringing peace on the rapidly developing frontier.

Speaker of the House Henry Clay summarized the beliefs of most Americans, saying, "We are powerful and they are weak—to use a figure drawn from their own sublime eloquence, the poor children of the forest have been driven by the great wave which has flowed in from the Atlantic ocean to almost the base of the Rocky mountains, and, overwhelming them in its terrible progress, has left no other remains of hundreds of tribes, now extinct, than those which indicate the remote existence of their former companion, the mammoth of the New World!"[43]

After his second term, on Wednesday, March 15, 1809, President Thomas Jefferson returned home to Monticello. The news arrived of the death of Lewis. Absorbed in his books and running his plantations, Jefferson's well-known affair with his slave Sally Hemings continued. A Vermont visitor, Elijah Fletcher, wrote in 1811, "Mr. Jefferson's tall, spare, straight in body. His face not handsome but savage—I learnt he was but little esteemed by his neighbors. . . . The story of Black Sal is no farce—That he cohabits with her and has a number of children by her is a sacred truth—and the worst of it is, he keeps the same children slaves—an unnatural crime which is very common in these parts—This conduct may receive a little palliation when we consider that such proceedings are so common that they cease here to be disgraceful." In a letter, Josiah Quincy, Jr., of Massachusetts, gave perspective to Jefferson's living situation, writing, "The enjoyment of a negro or mulatto woman is spoken of as quite a common thing: no reluctance, delicacy or shame is made about the matter. It is far from being uncommon to see a gentleman at dinner, and his reputed offspring a slave to the master of the table."[44]

One of Jefferson's many contributions was selling his book collection to our country. The British had burned approximately 3,000 books belonging to Congress in Washington, D.C., during the War of 1812. Jefferson's impressive and rare collection totaled 6,487 volumes, and these formed the basis of the new Library of Congress. The *National Intelligencer* wrote, "For its selection, rarity and intrinsic value, is beyond all price."[45]

Jefferson very much understood the importance of higher education to benefit the long-term goals of the United States. In 1818, he worked with others to establish a university to be built in Charlottesville, Virginia. It would be his last great act of leadership. He stated, "This institution will be based on the illimitable freedom of the human mind."[46] From a terrace at Monticello he could watch the construction through a telescope. Jefferson assisted in the curriculum and pushed for minimal clerical influence.

Standard faculty at the time included a professor of divinity, but Jefferson proposed an ethics professor instead. His first round of selections for faculty appointments caused a public outcry when he selected a number of professors who held religious opinions akin to his own. Joseph Cabell, a legislator who supported Jefferson establishing the university, warned his friend about his unusual selections and that the clergy suspected "that the Socians [Unitarians] are to be installed at the University for the purpose of overthrowing the prevailing religious opinions of the country."[47]

Up until the end, Jefferson remained skeptical of church authorities and the supernatural events of the Bible. He wrote, "It is too late in the day for men of sincerity to pretend they believe in the Platonic mysticisms that three are one, and one is three. . . . But this constitutes the craft, the power, and the profit of the priests. Sweep away their gossamer fabrics of factitious religion, and they would catch no more flies. We should all then, like the Quakers, live without an order of priests, moralize for ourselves, follow the oracle of conscience, and say nothing about what no man can understand, nor therefore believe; for I suppose belief to be the ascent of the mind to an intelligible proposition."[48]

One of Jefferson's greatest worries during the last decade of his life involved his beloved Louisiana Territory. Missouri wanted to become a state, but would it be a slave state or not was the question. Politicians from the Northeast were concerned that if too many slave states entered the Union they would gain control of the government. The Missouri Compromise passed in 1820 under President James Monroe. It regulated slavery in the country's Western territories by prohibiting the practice in the former Louisiana Territory above the thirty-sixth parallel, with the exception of Missouri—it would be allowed to become a slave state.

Today, equality for minorities continues to be a challenging problem. Jefferson, being the visionary he was, understood that the issue of slavery would not be resolved in his lifetime. Showing his frustration, he wrote, "The cession of that kind of property, for so it is misnamed, is a bagatelle which would not cost me a second thought, if, in that way, the general emancipation and expatriation could be effected; and, gradually, and with due sacrifices, I think it might be. But, as it is, we have the wolf by the ear, and we can neither hold him, nor safely let him go. Justice is in one scale, and self-preservation in the other."[49]

In 1826, with failing health, Jefferson continued to read the Bible, his Bible, and the great philosophers of the early ages. He wrote down in words what he considered a fulfilled life: "Adore God. Reverence and cherish your parents. Love your neighbor as yourself, and your country more than yourself [the Golden Rule]. Be just. Be true. Murmur not at the ways of Providence. So shall the life into which you have entered the portal to the one of the eternal and ineffable bliss."[50]

In March 1826, Jefferson drew his last will. He suffered from chronic diarrhea and an enlarged prostate and relied on large doses of laudanum for relief. He was troubled by the disappointing enrollment and unruly students at the University of Virginia along with personal financial debt. The Virginia legislature planned a special lottery to save him from disgrace.

On June 24, Jefferson wrote a letter to the mayor of Washington, D.C., declining an invitation to the Fourth of July celebration. The famous letter would be reprinted all over the country:

> May it be to the world, what I believe it will be (to some parts sooner, to others later, but finally to all) the signal of arousing men to burst the chains under which monkish ignorance and superstition had persuaded them to bind themselves, and to assume the blessings and security of self-government. . . . All eyes are opened, or opening, to the

rights of man. The general spread of the light of science has already laid open to every view the palpable truth, that the mass of mankind has not been born with saddles on their backs, nor a favored few, booted and spurred, ready to ride them legitimately by the grace of God. These are the grounds of hope for others. For ourselves, let the annual return to this day forever refresh our recollections of these rights, and an undiminished devotion to them.[51]

On July 3, Jefferson, who had been unconscious for a day, awoke at seven o'clock in the evening to see his oldest daughter Martha Randolph—the most important person in his life—and his physician, Robley Dunglison, who were keeping watch. He fell back into a slumber but was awoken two hours later by his doctor to be given a dose of laudanum, but he refused it saying, "No, Dr., nothing more." At four in the morning on July 4 he spoke his last words, and at approximately one o'clock in the afternoon on July 4 he died.[52]

That same day, about two and a half hours later, his friend John Adams also died. That two great presidents, Thomas Jefferson and John Adams, would die on the Fourth of July was seen by John Quincy Adams, future president and son of John Adams, as "visible and palpable" manifestation of "Divine favor."[53]

John Adams was not a victim to acquiring material wealth and living a high lifestyle. His estate was worth approximately $100,000 when he died. Conversely, Jefferson died with a debt exceeding $100,000, which was more than the value of Monticello, his plantations, and all his possessions, including slaves. The lottery proved unsuccessful.[54]

His will directed only five slaves freed, and they were members of the Hemings family but not Sally Hemings. Her freedom was arranged by Jefferson's daughter, Martha Randolph, after his death. In order to free Hemings, Jefferson would have had to state it in his will and petition the state legislature for her freedom, and since she was over forty-five years old, he would have had to provide financial support for her. This would have been an admission of his thirty-eight year relationship with her that would humiliate his oldest daughter. In addition, he believed his legacy would be damaged.[55] In January 1827, 130 of Jefferson's slaves were sold at auction on the front lawn of Monticello, along with furniture and farm equipment. In 1831, Jefferson's beloved Monticello was also sold for pennies on the dollar.[56]

It seems that great statesmanship is sometimes not related to financial acumen. The twentieth century's greatest leader of the free world, Winston

Churchill, also was dogged by money troubles. Only a month after becoming prime minister in 1940, Churchill ran out of money to pay his household bills, his taxes, and the interest on his large overdraft. He relied on friends to cover his expenses during the war. This allowed him to pay a number of overdue bills from shirt makers, watch repairers, and wine merchants before he turned his attention to the war. The Last Lion admitted that he was a spendthrift and ran through his inheritances after World War I. Like Monticello for Jefferson, Chartwell, the country house Churchill bought in 1922, ran way over budget with the addition of a new wing, swimming pool, and tennis court.[57] Ever struggling to cover expenses, in 1935 he spent the modern equivalent of $62,000 on champagne. Earlier, in 1914, he was smoking about a dozen cigars a day, costing more than $1,600 a month in today's money. After Churchill became a private citizen in 1946, a group of benefactors purchased Chartwell while affording the Churchills a lifetime tenancy. Churchill's story may give some solace to those disturbed by the private financial problems of the Father of the American West and many other great leaders.[58]

The stone obelisk that marks Jefferson's grave did not mention his great political achievements, including serving as governor of Virginia, minister to France, secretary of state, vice president of the United States, or president of the United States. Nor did it mention him being known as the Father of the American West after the Louisiana Purchase. As a man of the Enlightenment he wanted to be known for his creative contributions in the fields of religion, education, and human freedom:

> Here Was Buried
> THOMAS JEFFERSON
> Author of the Declaration of Independence,
> Of the Statute of Virginia for Religious Freedom,
> And Father of the University of Virginia[59]

Jefferson's religious influence would reach far beyond the Jeffersonian presidents. Abraham Lincoln has been called the spiritual center of American history.[60] Like Jefferson, Lincoln was skeptical of organized Christianity. A young Lincoln read with keen interest Thomas Paine's *Age of Reason* along with other Deists' works. His belief hovered somewhere between evangelical Protestantism and the Enlightenment skepticism that Jefferson embraced.[61] He very much carried forward the Jeffersonian side of American religious life and stated, "When any church will inscribe over its altar as its sole qualification for membership, the Savior's condensed statement of the substance of both the law and Gospel, Thou shalt love the Lord thy God with all thy heart, and with all thy soul, and with all thy mind, and thy neighbor as thyself [the Golden Rule]—that Church I will join with all my heart and soul."[62]

Author Andrew Burstein summed up Jefferson's beliefs: "Morals, well taught, make the world a better place. Dogmas, aggressively promoted, inhibit the honest pursuit of knowledge. . . . If there is a God, no human can affect to know his mind, so what good is there in trying to enforce belief?"[63]

CHAPTER SEVENTEEN

Father of the Removal Policy: Thomas Jefferson and the Doctrine of Discovery

Of all tyrannies, a tyranny sincerely exercised for the good of its victims may be the most oppressive. It would be better to live under robber barons than under omnipotent moral busybodies. The robber baron's cruelty may sometimes sleep, his cupidity may at some point be satisfied; but those who torment us for our own good will torment us without end for they do so with the approval of their own conscience.
—C. S. LEWIS

Under the law of nature, all men are born free and everyone comes into the world with the right to his own person which includes the liberty of moving and using it at his own will.
—THOMAS JEFFERSON IN THE HOWELL SLAVERY CASE, 1770

Thomas Jefferson not only was one of America's main Founding Fathers, but he was also the architect of the Indian removal policy and exercised America's Discovery authority over the Indian nations. It was his idea to move all the Eastern Indian tribes west of their homelands, while at the same time he developed many strategies to apply Discovery policies to the Eastern and Western tribes. His dream was of a continental American empire, and one of the ways of achieving that lofty goal was using the Doctrine of Discovery, among other legal and political tools, to attain it.

The early years of the nineteenth century saw the young nation boasting sixteen states east of the Mississippi River and south of the Ohio River. The Northwest Territory stretched from the Ohio River to the Great Lakes. The map was empty west of the Mississippi. That blank space was a highly contested area where the United States of America competed for control with Britain, Spain, and France. The Mississippi, the trading port of New Orleans, and the uncharted Louisiana Territory were at the center of the strife.

Before he began his state and national political careers, Jefferson was not only a planter but an attorney. From 1767 to 1774, he practiced law full-time. Almost half of the 941 cases he handled during his legal career were land claim disputes that included Indian title, tribal ownership, and the sale of Indian lands. The Doctrine of Discovery was involved in almost all of these cases because Britain and the Virginia Colony protected Indian titles by following its principles. The significant point in regard to Indians was that an individual American could not purchase land from them. In Jefferson's view, only the colony and eventually the state of Virginia held the "sole and exclusive power of taking conveyances of the Indian right of soil."[1] This doctrine came into play when white land seekers headed west and claimed land title under "squatters sovereignty" even though the Indians owned the land. There was no legal basis for whites to make this claim.

Jefferson had an active interest in gaining Indian land titles for purchase by Virginia settlers. He himself had inherited shares in a land speculation company that purchased Indian land in the West. Chronically debt ridden, Jefferson, like all plantation owners, understood that the only way to increase his profits was to purchase more land.

The Doctrine of Discovery in U.S. history was unfortunately underemphasized by historians until the publications by Robert J. Miller, currently professor of law at the Sandra Day O'Connor College of Law at Arizona State University.[2] From the fifteenth century on, as Europeans and Americans explored and plundered new lands, in their minds they were justified under this philosophical policy. They based their principles on religious and ethnocentric beliefs that their culture, religion, and race were superior to all others. When European imperialists headed to the New World, the doctrine provided automatic, immediate full control of property rights along with governmental, political, and commercial rights over native peoples without their knowledge or consent.[3]

In 1630, as the Puritans' ship neared land in America, John Winthrop, the governor of the Massachusetts Bay Company, gave a sermon to the people on board. He made it clear that their mission was both divinely ordained in a manner that was a forerunner of American Manifest Destiny. His famous address, "A Modell of Christian Charity," would eventually be a source to rationalize taking Indian lands:

> The Lord will be our God, and delight to dwell among us, as his oune people, and will command the blessing upon us in all our wayes. Soe that wee shall see much more of his wisdome, power, goodness and truthe, then formally wee haue been acquainted with. Wee shall finde that the God of Israel is among us, when ten of us shall be able to resist a thousand of our enemies; when Hee shall make us a prayse and glory that men shall say of his succeeding plantations, "The Lord make it likely that of New England." For wee must consider that wee shall be as a city upon a hill. The eies of all people are upon us. Soe that if wee shall deale falsely with our God in this worke wee haue undertaken, and soe cause him to withdrawe his present help from us, wee shall be made a story and a by-word through the world. Wee shall open the mouthes of enemies to speake evill of the wayes of God, and all professors for God's sake. Wee shall shame the faces of many of God's worthy servants, and cause theire prayers to be turned into curses upon us till wee be consumed out of the good land whither wee are a goeing.[4]

European and American explorers like Lewis and Clark were doing more than thanking God for safe travels when they planted their national flags and religious symbols in newly discovered lands. The main purpose of these acts of Discovery was to demonstrate their country's legal claim over the lands and natives. Naturally, these claims were vigorously opposed by the natives. From its original thirteen colonies, the United States from 1774 until 1855—when the Pacific Northwest was acquired by the United States—implemented the Doctrine of Discovery as a basis of its land grabs.[5]

Explorers sent out by Jefferson were tasked with defining the borders of the Louisiana Territory and its waterways—specifically the Red River, which today separates Oklahoma and Arkansas from Texas, the Mississippi River, and the Missouri River. The space was inhabited for centuries by kinships that had developed interconnected trade routes. Powerful chiefs who lived in great villages the size of St. Louis had controlled access to these lands. Jefferson's maneuvers are detailed in Julie M. Fenster's *Jefferson's America: The President, the Purchase, and the Explorers Who Transformed a Nation*. As the book's review editor at *True West* magazine, Stuart Rosebrook astutely wrote, "Her conclusions on Jefferson's presidential aspirations for Western expansion will permanently cement any doubts that the Virginian is the father of the American West."[6]

Jefferson personally recruited explorers whose scientific skills were essential for marking borders and claiming new lands. Lewis and Clark were not his only hires. Dr. George Hunter, a prominent Philadelphia chemist, was joined by William Dunbar, a self-taught scientist who was a slave owner on a cotton plantation in the Mississippi Territory, to explore the Ouachita River in the Southwest, which flows in part through today's Arkansas and Oklahoma. Meanwhile, young Zebulon Pike was commissioned by the president to find the source of the Mississippi. On his expedition, as winter closed in over the upper Mississippi, Pike pushed toward Leech Lake in present-day Minnesota through knee-deep snow and despite a severe case of trench foot.

In 1806, as Lewis and Clark made their way back from the Pacific, Thomas Freeman, a surveyor, and Peter Custis, a naturalist and medical student in Philadelphia, were sent by Jefferson to explore the Red River to verify reports that the river might provide a water route to Santa Fe. They didn't know that the river, which flows into the Atchafalaya River east of today's Alexandria, Louisiana, originates in the Texas Panhandle. Jefferson considered the Red River Expedition second in importance only to the Lewis and Clark Expedition. Perhaps his most courageous explorer, Freeman, when more than 600 miles upriver, was confronted by the Spanish army, which had been sent to apprehend him. The Spanish attempted to cross to the American side of the Red River, but Freeman stood his ground and the army retreated without bloodshed. All of Jefferson's men, like the president himself, demonstrated single-mindedness and a stubborn arrogance filled with curiosity to define a new world.[7]

It was of utmost importance to Thomas Jefferson that when Lewis and Clark reached the Pacific Ocean they would undertake the necessary actions in accordance with the Doctrine of Discovery to make claim to the Pacific Northwest. For the next four decades, the United States argued with Russia, Spain, and England that America owned the Northwest because American sea captain Robert Gray in 1792 was the first to discover the Columbia River, the first inland exploration and occupation of the territory was by Lewis and Clark in 1805-1806, and finally, in 1811, Astoria was established as the first permanent settlement in the Northwest.[8]

The Doctrine of Discovery was one of the first international laws, relied upon by colonial powers when conflict arose regarding newly discovered lands. It had its beginnings in medieval times during the Crusades from 1096 to 1271 as Christians sought to recapture the Holy Lands. Earlier, the Roman Catholic Church and its popes had established a worldwide jurisdiction; this was one of the main reasons Christians felt the need to wage a Holy War against the infidels.[9]

One of the fathers of the Doctrine of Discovery was Pope Innocent IV, whose writings in 1240 would be an inspiration for sixteenth- and seventeenth-century legal writers on the Discovery doctrine. The pope declared that it was legitimate for Christians to invade infidel lands. He stated that the natural law rights of non-Christians to elect their own leaders and to own property were trumped by the papacy's divine mandate to care for the entire world. The pope stated that he had the control of the spiritual health of all humans.[10]

Colonies in the New World

As the Spanish and Portuguese invaded the New World, they referred back to the writings of Pope Innocent IV, which stated that the Church had the authority to deprive non-Christians of their property and sovereignty if they would not allow Christian missionaries. The Catholic Church wielded its power by granting Christian kings title and ownership rights in the lands of infidels. This would ensure the Pope's guardian duties over all humans. Thus, by the time Christopher Columbus sailed to the New World, the Doctrine of Discovery was well established and accepted by all colonial powers.[11]

Disputes did arise. In the New World, France and England came to odds over differing Discovery claims. The French and Indian War (1754-1763) resulted in France transferring its Discovery claims in Canada and east of the Mississippi River to England and its claims to lands west of the Mississippi to Spain.[12]

From the beginning, the English colonial governments considered tribal governments as sovereign. While they differed on minor points, each individual colony enacted statutes that gave them the authority of preemptive right to control and regulate sales of Indian lands. In addition, every colony worked to control all trade and commercial activities between the colonists and Indians.[13] After the Revolutionary War, in the Articles of Confederation, Congress tried to sort out each state's claims over the western lands that Britain had ceded to the United States in 1783.

The states would transfer their land claims to the federal government only if Congress agreed to pay off all the states' Revolutionary War debts and if they got a cut in the profits from the sale of western lands. In 1781, Virginia was the first to give up its western land claims, but the process took three more years before Congress approved the deal. Thereafter, the U.S. Congress was the government body that controlled the western Indian lands by the Doctrine of Discovery. Congress had the authority to buy land from the Indian nations and then sell the land to settlers. Also, it had the authority to create new territories and states as long as they agreed to pay the state and national Revolutionary War debts.[14]

The federal Discovery powers were guaranteed in the new Constitution. Article One specifically excluded states and individuals from Indian commercial affairs by granting Congress the authority "to regulate commerce with foreign nations, and among the several states, and with the Indian Tribes."[15] By 1795, Congress was the only government entity interacting with the tribes on trade and commerce. One way of achieving this—which was strongly supported by George Washington and Thomas Jefferson—was the establishment by Congress of federal trading posts across the Indian frontier. From 1795 to 1822, twenty-eight federal trading posts were built; private companies successfully lobbied to end this federal monopoly so that the companies could profit instead.[16]

President Washington created the "Savage as the Wolf" federal policy because he believed the Indians were on the road to extinction as American settlements multiplied and the federal government purchased tribal lands. Dealing with Indian tribes was considered the federal government's main foreign policy issue. After he became president, Thomas Jefferson championed Washington's federal trading program because he believed that keeping private traders away from the Indians would help the government befriend the natives through trade and commerce.

The federal government's understanding of the Doctrine of Discovery was made evident by a statement by Secretary of War Henry Knox (1750-1806) in June 1789. He wrote, "The Indians being the prior occupants, possess the right to the soil. It cannot be taken from them unless by their consent, or by the right of conquest in case of a just war. To dispossess them on any other principle, would be a gross violation of the fundamental laws of nature, and of that distributive justice which is the glory of the nation."[17] With this in mind, over 100 treaties with the Indian nations were signed between 1789 and 1823.

Countering this position were frontier Americans who had no problem taking Indian lands from savages. The governor of frontier Tennessee justified this in 1798, declaring, "By the law of nations, it is agreed that no people shall be entitled to more land than they can cultivate. Of course no people will sit and starve for want of land to work, when a neighboring nation has much more than they can make use of."[18]

The system of creating new territories that eventually became states provided further voices in Congress to obtain native lands by force if necessary. Many seemed to forget the third article of the Northwest Ordinance, which was adopted by the First Federal Congress in 1787 and said, "The utmost good faith shall always be observed towards the Indians; their lands and property shall never be taken from them without their consent; and in their property, rights and liberty, they never shall be invaded or disturbed, unless in just and lawful wars authorized by Congress; but laws founded in justice and humanity shall from time to time be made, for preventing wrongs being done to them, and for preserving peace and friendship with them."[19]

As Robert J. Miller pointed out, there are ten elements to the Doctrine of Discovery. The discovering nation had to be the first to make claim to an unknown property. To gain complete title, that land needed to be occupied. That was the motivation for building forts and settlements occupied by soldiers or settlers. Having laid claim to the land, the claimant had the sole right to buy the land from native people. Unknown to them, the native peoples lost their full property rights and ownership of their lands. Their only right was to occupy and use their land. But that right could last forever if the natives never consented to sell their land. When they sold their land, they could sell it only to the nation that had discovered it. This severely limited Indian ownership rights. They could also only trade with the new owners.[20]

The doctrine provided that the nation that discovered the mouth of a river was given claim over all the lands drained by that river. This had dramatic consequences in America where some rivers are over 1,000 miles long.

Another way of obtaining lands from Indians was by instituting terra nullius and vacuum domicilium. These are legal terms that, in practice, meant that if the indigenous people were not properly using their land—even if it was occupied and had been actively utilized by them—according to European and American law, the land was considered vacant and available for Discovery claims.

As it would be with Manifest Destiny, religion played a significant role in the Doctrine of Discovery. Non-Christians were seen as not having the same rights to land, sovereignty, and self-determination as Christians. Land disputes went to the Bible holders. No doubt this encouraged the discoverers to avoid Christianizing the Indians too quickly if they owned desirable land. Thus, "killing the Indian to save the man" was thoroughly implemented only once the Indian's land had been seized.

The clear importance and constitutionality of the Doctrine of Discovery in the United States came to fruition in the 1823 *Johnson v. McIntosh* Supreme Court decision that defined the doctrine and the basic principles of Indian property rights that are still in use today. This particular case came to court because more than one Anglo-American purchaser claimed title to land previously owned by the Piankeshaw Indians in southern Illinois. They had sold it to speculators in 1775 and once again by treaty thirty years later to the United States. William McIntosh then bought it from the U.S. government. The Supreme Court ruled in his favor.[21]

In summary, the court stated that, under Discovery, when European, Christian nations discovered virgin lands, they immediately gained sovereign and property rights in the land of non-Christians, non-European natives, and of course Indians.[22] The transfer of political, trade, and property rights away from Indian people was achieved whether or not they knew it.[23]

Chief Justice John Marshall (1755-1835) stated, "The United States . . . [and] its civilized inhabitants now hold this country. They hold, and assert in themselves, the title by which it was acquired. They maintain, as all others have maintained, that discovery gave an exclusive right to extinguish the Indian title of occupancy, either by purchase or by conquest; and gave also right to such a degree of sovereignty, as the circumstances of the people would allow them to exercise. . . . Discovery gave title to the government by whose subjects, or by whose authority, it was made against all other European governments, which title might be consummated by possession."[24]

The natives' loss of property and sovereignty rights was justified according to the court by "the character and religion of its inhabitants . . . the superior genius of Europe . . . [and] ample compensation to the [Indians] by bestowing on them civilization and Christianity, in exchange for unlimited independence." The court even went as far as to say that American or European countries could sell or grant their title to property to others even though the lands were still in the possession and use of the natives. In effect, the result was that the lands owned by Indian nations held little economic value, which made it easier for European countries and American settlers to obtain them.[25]

The cornerstone of the Doctrine of Discovery was greed aimed to benefit economic and political interests. It also sometimes avoided expensive wars between European nations over discovered lands. While they might dispute land ownership, Americans and Europeans always agreed that native people lost significant property and governmental rights.

President Thomas Jefferson and the Doctrine of Discovery

President George Washington appointed Jefferson the first U.S. secretary of state in 1789, a position he held until the end of 1793. Jefferson interpreted Discovery powers exactly as the Supreme Court would in 1823 when the term Doctrine of Discovery was first used.

In May 1790, as secretary of state, Jefferson was involved in the question of land ownership in Georgia. Following the Discovery rule, he wrote:

> If the country, instead of being altogether vacant, is thinly occupied by another nation, the right of the native forms an exception to that of the new comers; that is to say, these will only have a right against all other nations except the natives.
>
> Consequently, they have the exclusive privilege of acquiring the native right by purchase or other just means. This is called the right of preemption, and has become a principle of the law of nations, fundamental with respect to America. There are but two means of acquiring the native title. First, war; for even war may, sometimes, give a just title. Second, contracts or treaty.[26]

The Discovery rules were honored by European nations when it came to control of the Louisiana Territory. Since French explorers had traveled north and south on the Mississippi River in the 1680s, France laid claim to the area under Discovery rights. In 1763, France transferred those rights to Spain and England. England received claim to the lands east of the Mississippi and Spain received claims west of the river. A weakening Spain transferred its Discovery claim back to France in 1800. In 1804, after the Louisiana Purchase, Jefferson was uncertain who owned the Oregon country.

Robert J. Miller explained what the Louisiana Purchase really involved:

> You have no doubt read that the Louisiana Purchase was the "greatest real estate deal in history" because the United States paid only "three cents an acre." That statement is false. This is a common mistake that many, many historians and authors have made because they do not understand the Doctrine of Discovery. Thomas Jefferson would have

known that these statements are false, and this discussion proves that point with his own words and with the facts.

... First, the Louisiana Purchase was not a real estate deal. The United States did not buy land in the Louisiana territory because France did not own land in the territory. France and Spain may have owned a few parcels of land where their forts, trading posts, and official buildings were located, but there were very few such sites in the territory. Instead of real estate, the United States purchased what France and Spain did own in the region: their discovery claims to a limited form of sovereign, political, and commercial power over the Indian nations and the real-property right of preemption.[27]

The $15 million paid by the United States bought only the Discovery rights to limited sovereignty over the territory and the right that only the United States could deal with the Indian nations politically and commercially. Jefferson wrote in 1803 that he hoped his country would "endeavor to procure the Indian right of soil, as soon as they can be prevailed on to part with it, to the whole left bank of the Mississippi."[28]

In the end, the United States spent much more than the $15 million it paid to France for the complete fee-simple title. In the next hundred years after the 1803 treaty with France, the United States entered wars with the Indians, negotiated treaties with them, and purchased their land, the fee titles, and then Indians' right of occupancy. It has been calculated that the United States paid almost $300 million to Indian tribes who occupied the Louisiana Territory in treaty payments to buy the land the tribes agreed to sell.[29]

As Meriwether Lewis was preparing for his trip up the Missouri, the United States completed the Louisiana Purchase. Jefferson wanted to make sure Lewis relayed to the Indians that the United States was now in control of their lands. "When your instructions were penned," the president wrote, "this new position [the Louisiana Purchase] was not so authentically known as to effect the completion of your instructions. Being now become sovereigns of the country, without however any diminution of the Indian rights of occupancy we are authorised to propose to them in direct terms the institution of commerce with them. It will now be proper you should inform those through whose country you will pass, or whom you may meet, that their late fathers the Spaniards agreed to withdraw ... that they have surrendered to us all their subjects ... that henceforward we become their fathers and friends."[30]

Jefferson understood, as did almost all Americans at that time, that American territorial expansion would come at the expense of Indian nations and their property rights. He believed God had guaranteed America the right to the Indians lands. In his first inaugural address on March 4, 1801, he stated that America "possessed a chosen country, with room enough for our descendants to the thousandth and thousandth generation . . . [and] an overruling Providence [that] . . . delights in the happiness of man." The man would have to be defined as a white man because there was no real place in his dream for the Indians.[31] Historian James Ronda stated that Jefferson's divine vision "made empire not only possible but somehow almost predetermined."[32] The Puritans called this predestination.

In 1809, Jefferson wrote then-President James Madison praising the U.S. Constitution that allowed American expansion, noting, "No Constitution was ever before so well calculated as ours for extensive empire." Even in 1786 he had dreamed of the thirteen states populating the entire New World, though much of it was occupied by indigenous people, writing, "Our confederacy must be viewed as the nest, from which all America, North and South, is to be peopled."[33]

The idealistic side of Jefferson admired the Indian. He wrote, "I believe the Indian, then, to be, in body and mind, equal to the white man."[34] But that was only for those Indians who had not been tainted by contact with the white man. He dreamed of an American society where the Indians would be assimilated into the white man's culture. In a prediction that he probably knew would never come to pass, he wrote that he hoped the outcome for the Indians would be "to let our settlements and theirs meet and blend together, to intermix, and become one people. Incorporating themselves with us as citizens of the United States, this is what the natural progress of things will, of course, bring on, and it will be better to promote than to retard it. Surely it will be better for them to be identified with us, and preserved in the occupation of their lands." Jefferson voiced concerns about the Indians' poor living conditions, observing, "They are our brethren, our neighbors; they may be valuable friends, and troublesome enemies. Both duty & interest then enjoin, that we should extend to them the blessings of civilized life, & prepare their minds for becoming useful members of the American family."[35] That would probably mean them becoming farmers on small patches of land. What Jefferson hoped for and what really happened were two very different things.

Jefferson's vision of the future of the Indians was presented on March 4, 1805, during his second inaugural address. The Louisiana Purchase in 1803 had been opposed by some and was of questionable legality because the Constitution did not specify the right of a president to purchase such a massive piece of land. As a man of the Enlightenment who placed a premium on progress, reason, and American exceptionalism, Jefferson delivered a racist speech full of ominous overtones for the Indians:

> I know that the acquisition of the Louisiana has been disapproved by some, from a candid apprehension that the enlargement of our territory would endanger its union. But who can limit the extent to which the federative principle may operate effectively? The larger our association, the less will be shaken by local passions; and in any view, is it not better that the opposite bank of the Mississippi should be settled by our own brethren and children, than by strangers of another family? With which shall we be most likely to live in harmony and friendly intercourse?
>
> ... The aboriginal inhabitants of these countries I have regarded with the commiseration their history inspires. Endowed with the faculties and the rights of men, breathing an ardent love of liberty and independence, and occupying a country which left them no desire but to be undisturbed, the stream of overflowing population from other regions corrected itself on the shores; without power to divert, or habits to contend against, they have been overwhelmed by the current, or driven before it; now reduced within limits too narrow for the hunter's state, humanity enjoys us to teach them agriculture and the domestic arts; to encourage them to that industry which alone can enable them to maintain their place in existence, and to prepare them in time for that state of society, which to bodily comforts adds the improvement of the mind and morals. We have therefore liberally furnished them with the implements of husbandry and household use; we have placed among them instructors in the arts of first necessity; and they are covered with the aegis of the law against aggressors from among ourselves.
>
> But the endeavors to enlighten them on the fate which awaits their present course of life, to induce them to exercise their reason, follow its dictates, and change their pursuits with the change of circumstances, have powerful obstacles to encounter; they are combated by the habits of their bodies, prejudice of their minds, ignorance, pride, and the influence of interested and crafty individuals among them, who feel themselves something in the present order

of things, and fear to become nothing in any other. These persons inculcate sanctimonious reverence for the customs of their ancestors; that whatsoever they did, must be done through all time; that reason is a false guide, and to advance under its counsel, in their physical, moral, or political condition, is perilous innovation; that their duty is to remain as their Creator made them, ignorance being safety, and knowledge full of danger; in short, my friends, among them is seen the action and counteraction of good sense and bigotry; they too have their anti-philosophers, who find an interest in keeping things in their present state, who dread reformation, and exert all their faculties to maintain the ascendancy of habit over the duty of improving our reason and obeying its mandates.[36]

However, reality was a different matter. Above all, the one thing that both the white man and Indian cherished was land. It was sacred to the Native Americans. For the white man, land was a means of making a living or profiting. Also, in Jefferson's vision the entire landmass from the eastern United States to the Pacific Ocean needed to be secured not only for the masses of immigrants arriving from Europe but also to keep other colonial powers out of the region. James Ronda stated that Jefferson made the acquisition of tribal lands "the central feature of federal Indian policy."[37]

The dilemma was how to go about acquiring Indian lands with as little conflict as possible. The international Doctrine of Discovery demanded that the federal government purchase the land from the Indians. It then could be distributed to settlers. Thus, Jefferson continually communicated to Indian leaders that he was ready to buy their lands.

Often the Indians did not want to sell their land. Selling the lands west of the Appalachian Mountains had been resisted by an increasingly unified confederation of tribes who occupied the region now known as the Old Northwest. In August 1793, a council of Indians at the foot of the Miami Rapids wrote to the commissioners of the United States, in part:

> Brothers: you have talked to us about concessions. It appears strange that you should expect any from us, who have only been defending our just rights against your invasions. We want peace. Restore to us our country, and we shall be enemies no longer.
>
> Brothers: you make one concession to us by offering us your money; and another by having agreed to do us justice, after having long, and injuriously, withheld it—we mean in the acknowledgment

you have now made, that the King of England never did, nor ever had a right to give you our country, by the treaty of peace. And you want to make this act of common justice a great part of your concessions: and seem to expect that, because you have at last acknowledged our interdependence, we should, for such a favor, surrender to you our country. . . .

We desire you to consider, brothers, that our demand is the peaceable possession of a small part of our once great country. Look back, and review the lands from whence we have been driven to this spot. We can retreat no farther, because the country behind hardly affords food for its present inhabitants; and we have therefore resolved to leave our bones in this small space to which we are now confined.[38]

Bribing Indian political leaders was an effective method to obtain Indian lands. At times, federal employees were directed to drive Indians into debt by selling them goods. This was often achieved at the federal trading posts. In February 1803, Jefferson wrote Indiana Territory Governor William Henry Harrison, "We shall push our trading houses, and be glad to see the good and influential individuals among them run in debt, because we observe that when these debts get beyond what the individuals can pay, they become willing to lop them off by a cession of lands." Three years later, in regard to Cherokee country, Jefferson indicated that getting Indians into debt "is the way I intend to git there countrey for to git them to run in debt to the publick store and they will have to give their lands for payment."[39]

Bribes were also used to keep the peace. In 1791, when he was secretary of state, Jefferson wrote that the "most economical as well as humane conduct towards them is to bribe them into peace, and to retain them in peace by eternal bribes."[40]

Over the next century, bribes would also be commonplace with Indian agents who financially gained from their power on Indian reservations. The situation worsened when Indian agents were given permanent legal status in 1834. Originally, Congress expected the agents to achieve lofty goals even though they lacked the power and money to accomplish them. Congressional instructions in 1802 read, "The motives of the Government to sending Agents to reside with the Indian Nations, are the cultivation of peace and harmony between the U. States, and the Indian Nations generally; the detection of any improper conduct in the Indians or the Citizens of the U. States, or others relating to the Indians, or their lands, and the introduction of the

Arts of husbandry, and domestic manufactures, as means of producing, and diffusing the blessings attached to a well-regulated civil society."[41]

Such expansionists welcomed the decimation of Indian populations by infectious diseases like smallpox. As Indians vanished, their lands became unpopulated and ripe for the application of the Discovery rights of preemption and limited sovereignty over unoccupied lands. No other Indian tribe was allowed to own the land. Jefferson stated, "We have a right to their lands in preference to any Indian tribe, in virtue of our permanent sovereignty over it."[42]

The Removal Act of 1830 was passed during Andrew Jackson's presidency, so he is often blamed for confiscating Indian lands in the eastern United States. However, Jefferson was the architect of the removal policy that Jackson emulated. In August 1803, Jefferson wrote, "The best use we can make of [Louisiana territory] for some time, will be to give establishments in it to the Indians on the East side of the Mississippi, in exchange for their present country . . . and thus make this acquisition the means of filling up the eastern side. . . . When we shall be full on the side, we may lay off a range of states on the Western bank . . . advancing compactly as we multiply." It was clear that after lands east of the Mississippi were full and adjacent lands west of the Mississippi were full that the Indians would be moved again farther toward the West Coast.[43]

This move was unrealistic and cruel to the Indians in the East. Eighty percent of them were farmers who supplemented their crops with hunting. Moving them west of the Mississippi onto lands that they had no clue how to farm was cynical fantasy. Besides, much of the land on the Great Plains was not suitable for farming. Portions of the Northern Plains were called a desert for a reason.

When Indian tribes resisted Jefferson's plan, he advocated for their removal, and if that failed, he called for their extermination and extirpation for the final solution. The Cherokee nation's support of the British in 1776 angered Jefferson to the point that he called for their removal to west of the Mississippi, and if they resisted, his advice was to exterminate them. When he was governor of Virginia during the Revolution, Jefferson ordered Virginia troops to exterminate the Shawnee nation or drive them westward out of the state. As president, in 1807 Jefferson learned of tribal resistance sparked by encroachment of U.S. citizens. He said, "If ever we are constrained to lift the hatchet against any tribe, we will never lay it down till that tribe is exterminated, or driven beyond the Mississippi . . . we shall destroy all of them." In 1813, ex-president Jefferson had not softened his view. The Creek Nation became his latest focus of ire when they resisted loss of their lands. When Indians resisted, his view was that their "barbarities justified extermination" and that the United States must "pursue them to extermination." Jefferson wrote polymath Alexander von Humboldt, one of his and Charles Darwin's heroes, that it "oblige us now to pursue them to extermination, or drive them to new seats beyond their reach."[44]

Since the United States did not have the upper hand with Indians who occupied the Louisiana Territory, Jefferson had to use a softer and gentler approach on them, knowing that, in time, the American government would be in a position to either move them to wherever was the most convenient for American settlers or exterminate them. This more sensitive attitude was conveyed to Meriwether Lewis, who then advised Indians, "[Our great chief] commanded us . . . to undertake this long journey . . . to council with yourselves and his other red-children . . . to give you his good advice; to point out to you the road in which you must walk to obtain happiness. He has further commanded us to tell you that when you accept his flag and medal, you accept therewith his hand of friendship, which will never be withdrawn from your nation as long as you continue to follow the councils which he may command. . . ."[45]

Americans perfected the art of devaluing Native Americans. One of the words often used to describe them was "children." One definition of a child is an immature person who has the hope of someday fulfilling his potential. Christians would counter, pointing out that, in the Bible, use of the term children is endearing, ". . . our Father loves us for He calls us his children. . ." (1 John 3:1). Both views represented dualism where the Indian was either a Christian or heathen, enlightened or savage, etc.

Congress tried to control Indians' commerce with whites, and from 1796 to 1822 it went on to regulate and conduct trade with the Indians. In 1832, Congress prohibited liquor in Indian country. Congress oversaw the punishment of crimes in Indian country and also punished Indian crimes outside that area. Around 1820, it began to fund the education and civilization of the child-like natives.[46]

Lewis and Clark distributed flags and Jefferson Peace medals to many of the natives. Besides being an overt symbol of peace and friendship, the items symbolized in a more subtle manner America's new ownership over the Indians. Jefferson instructed Lewis and Clark to tell the Indians to take "all the flags and medals which you may have received from your old fathers the French and Spaniards, or from any other nation whatever, your father will give you new flags and new medals of his own in exchange. . . . It is not proper since you have become the children of the great chief . . . of America, that you should wear or keep those emblems of attachment to any other great father but himself, nor will it be pleasing to him if you continue to do so."[47]

Other methods were used to prove legal evidence of Discovery-based occupation along the path of Lewis and Clark. Both men spent a good deal of time mapping and documenting features of the landscape. This was done not only to aid future explorers and settlers but also as a well-recognized European ritual of making Discovery claims.

Another way of proving legal evidence was by leaving a document at a site. On March 18, 1806, Lewis and Clark were about to leave Fort Clatsop on the Oregon coast to return to St. Louis. Leaving a document that could be found by another nation would be proof that the Pacific Northwest was America's. They listed the names of all the members of the expedition on the document and also drew a rough map of their route from St. Louis to the Pacific Ocean on the back of the memorial. The document hung in Fort Clatsop, and copies of it were distributed to various Indian chiefs who were instructed to pass them on to any passing ship's captain. "The object of this list is," the document stated, "that through the medium of some civilized person who may see the same, it may be made known to the informed world, that the party consisting of the persons whose names are hereunto annexed, and who were sent out by the government of the U' States in May 1804 to explore the interior of the Continent of North America, did penetrate the same way of the Missouri and Columbia Rivers, to the discharge of the latter into the Pacific Ocean, where they arrived on the 14th day of November 1805, and from whence they departed the [left blank] day of March 1806 on their return to the United States."[48]

One of the memorials survived. On June 12, 1806, the American ship *Lydia* arrived in the Columbia River, and the Indians told the captain about Lewis and Clark's stay. As instructed, the Indians gave him one of the memorials. The memorial made its way by ship to Canton, China, and eventually to Boston where it arrived in May 1807.[49]

Could there have been any better tool for prying the land away from Native Americans than the Doctrine of Discovery? It was based on a 1,000-year-old belief held by Catholic Church leaders that they owned the world, and now was translated by Protestant American politicians—who hated Catholics—to mean that they had the right to control the lands of the American West and its people. What could top that? In time, Manifest Destiny would. It was the American-born Christian doctrine that the West was the new Eden waiting for Christians to populate it and move aside nature's people and its wildlife.

CHAPTER EIGHTEEN

Manifest Destiny: If God is for Us, Then Who Could Ever Stop Us?

Friends and brothers, listen: Where you now are, you and my white children are too near to each other to live in harmony and peace. . . . Beyond the great Mississippi, where a part of your nation has gone, your father has provided a country large enough for all of you, and advises you to remove to it. There your white brothers will not trouble you; they will have no claim to the land, and you can live upon it, you and all your children, as long as the grass grows or the water runs, in peace and plenty. It will be yours forever.
—ANDREW JACKSON TO THE CREEK NATION, MARCH 23, 1829

O thus be it ever when freemen shall stand
Between their lov'd home and the war's desolation!
Blest with vict'ry and peace may the heav'n rescued land
Praise the power that hath made and preserv'd us a nation!
Then conquer we must, when our cause it is just,
And this be our motto—"In God is our trust,"
And the star-spangled banner in triumph shall wave
O'er the land of the free and the home of the brave.
—LAST VERSE, *STAR-SPANGLED BANNER*, FRANCIS SCOTT KEY, 1814

Manifest Destiny was American predestination. Minds were overflowing with the wealth that the West represented. Prosperity brings all sorts of empowerments, just as poverty denies them. It is the empowerment rather than the absolute poverty that is most crucial. Basic freedoms—above all the freedom to lead a life one has reason to value—when achieved, can translate into better health and longer lives. When they are not, the cumulative effects lead to an early grave. That was the future of Native Americans.

By 1800, almost a million settlers were living in the area between the Mississippi River and the Appalachians. Others were encouraged to join them as the federal government purchased land from the Indians and then sold 320-acre tracts to Easterners with twenty-five percent down and four years to pay the balance. In 1804, the minimum tract was reduced to 160 acres at a cost of two dollars an acre.

Two years later, with settlers pouring into the area enticed by cheap land, Congress authorized the building of a road from Cumberland, Maryland, across the mountains to Wheeling, Virginia. Construction on the National Road, as it was nicknamed, began in 1811, and by 1818 it was completed. The road was eventually extended west to Vandalia, Illinois.[1]

Next, the United States focused on Spanish-owned Florida. Spain, weakened and unable to control the Seminole Indians, was ripe for the picking. In 1818, Andrew Jackson led a military force into Florida to punish the Seminoles for depredations along the United States border. Secretary of State John Quincy Adams initiated negotiations with the Spanish minister, Luis de Onís, to purchase Florida. Adams stated that, under Spanish rule, Florida had become "a derelict open to the occupancy of every enemy, civilized or savage, of the United States, and serving no other earthly purpose and as a post of an annoyance to them." In 1819, the Transcontinental Treaty with Spain provided for the transfer of Florida to the United States and unimpeded U.S. title to the Pacific Northwest, but the U.S. relinquished its claim to Texas. In return, the American government agreed to assume payment of $5 million worth of claims that American citizens held against the Spanish government. Both Jackson and Adams believed that God intended America to have Florida.[2]

John Quincy Adams (1767-1848), president from 1825 to 1829, was the first American figure to fashion a detailed strategy intended to harness the country's geographic, military, economic, and moral resources. He was best known as a foreign policy expert and was considered the father of "Realism" in foreign affairs. He understood that it was self-interest, not idealism, that dominated statesmanship. He warned against intervention in the affairs of foreign nations. He never doubted that America's republican experiment was the gift of Providence to the world; rather, he feared that an interfering foreign policy would destroy that gift. He believed, as the Founding Fathers had, that America was predestined to spread across the continent. Adams feared that foreign powers would incite discord among Americans for their own dark purposes and thus sought to rid them from the continent.[3]

Adams long considered slavery an abomination, but he kept his thoughts private because he was not prepared to jeopardize national unity to right a great wrong. He learned that from Thomas Jefferson. Nonetheless, he came to fiercely oppose the annexation of Texas when he saw that it would expand slave power.

James Monroe (1758-1831) ran unopposed in the election of 1821, losing only 1 out of 232 electoral votes, which was cast for then Secretary of State John Quincy Adams. Chief Justice John Marshall administered the oath of office. In his second inaugural address on March 5, 1821, delivered in the recently rebuilt Hall of the House of Representatives, Monroe presented his ideas on how the Indian problem should be addressed:

> The care of the Indian tribes within our limits has long been an essential part of our system, but, unfortunately, it has not been executed in a manner to accomplish all the objects intended by it. We have treated them as independent nations, without their having any substantial pretensions to that rank. The distinction has flattered their pride, retarded their improvement, and in many instances paved the way to their destruction. The progress of our settlements westward, supported as they are by a dense population, is constantly driving them back, with almost the total sacrifice of the lands which they have been compelled to abandon. They have claims on the magnanimity and I may add, on the justice of this nation which we must all feel. We should become their real benefactors; we should perform the office of their Great Father, the endearing title which they emphatically give to the Chief Magistrate of our Union. Their sovereignty over the vast territories should cease, in lieu of which the right of soil should be secured to each individual and his posterity in competent portions; and for the territory thus ceded by each tribe some reasonably equivalent should be granted, to be vested in permanent funds for the support of civil government over them and for the education of their children, for their instruction in the arts of husbandry, and to provide sustenance for them until they could provide it for themselves. My earnest hope is that Congress will digest some plan, founded on these

principles, with such improvements as their wisdom may suggest, and carry it into effect as soon as it may be practical.⁴

Monroe's words were prophetic. Within a few decades, the Indians would reside on reservations with small individual plots and the remaining portions of their lands sold to whites. Educating them would become important, but educating them for what purpose was always elusive and unclear. The president's idea of being a real benefactor translated into taking their lands away from them and distributing them as the U.S. government saw fit.

In tribal speeches over the decades, Indian leaders pleaded with the whites to respect their rights, meeting little success. In 1822, a Pawnee leader named Petalesharo explained to President Monroe, "He [the Great Spirit] made my skin red and yours white; he placed us on this earth and intended that we should live differently from each other. He made the whites to cultivate the earth, and feed on domestic animals; but he made us, red skins, to rove through the uncultivated woods and plains, to feed on wild animals, to dress in their skins. . . ."⁵

By 1823, the American population had exploded to 9.5 million people. But there were concerns that the alliance of Russia, Prussia, Austria, and France might assist Spain in the reconquest of some of her colonies in the New World. France had been rumored to be covetous of Cuba, and Russia was seen as spreading its influence from Alaska down along the Pacific coast. There were also concerns over Britain's intentions.

On December 2, 1823, President Monroe delivered his annual message to Congress, addressing the looming dangers from foreigners. In what would become known as the Monroe Doctrine, the president outlined American foreign policy. First, the United States would stay out of any conflicts in Europe. America also had no interest in European colonies in the New World. He assured Latin American governments, "whose independence we have . . . acknowledged we could not view any interposition for the purpose of oppressing them, or controlling in any other manner their destiny, by any European power in any other light than as the manifestation of an unfriendly disposition towards the United States." He also said, "The American continents, by the free and independent condition which they have assumed and maintain, are henceforth not to be considered as subjects for future colonization by any European powers." He warned Europe that "we should consider any attempt on their part to extend their political system to any portion of this hemisphere as dangerous to our peace and safety."⁶

Jefferson once stated that he liked "the dreams of the future better than the history of the past."[7] His dream of whites settling Indian areas west of the Appalachians was coming to fruition. In 1810, only one out of seven Americans lived west of the Appalachians, but by 1840 more than a third lived there. The reasons were many for settlers to find the area attractive. Unlike their European counterparts, who for centuries were rooted in the same village working the same land and in the same social status, American society had a less rigid class structure, and the opportunity to follow dreams was much greater. After touring America in the early 1830s, Frenchman Alexis de Tocqueville was impressed with Americans' restless, rootless, and ambitious way of life, writing, "In the United States, a man builds a house in which to spend his old age, and he sells it before the roof is on . . . he brings a field into tillage and leaves other men to gather the crops . . . he settles in a place, which he soon afterwards leaves to carry his changeable longings elsewhere . . . the tie that unites one generation to another is relaxed or broken. . . . Every man there loses all trace of the ideas of his forefathers or takes no heed of them."[8]

Andrew Jackson (1767-1845) was elected as president in 1828 with strong support from the planters and farmers in the South and West, along with artisans and factory workers in towns and cities. For many, his election symbolized a victory for the nationalistic West and a vindication of the common man. Born in poverty to Scottish-Irish immigrant parents in the Carolina backcountry, Jackson moved to Tennessee and eventually became a lawyer, land speculator, soldier, politician, and farmer. He was the first president who did not come from a wealthy American family and who lived west of the Appalachian Mountains. His story fit perfectly into the Romantic era where a poor person born in a log cabin could end up in the White House.[9]

During his presidency, Jackson came under immense pressure from Westerners wanting cheaper land. Senator Thomas Hart Benton of Missouri proposed a gradual reduction of the minimum price of public lands of inferior quality from $1.25 to fifty cents an acre. Any unsold land that was so undesirable would be given away free. Also, in what would become known as "squatter's sovereignty," Westerners demanded that men who had settled on public domain before the land was surveyed and offered for sale would be able to purchase their land that they had improved for the minimum price per acre. Neither of these proposals was enacted by the Jackson administration. Jackson did propose that every man should have a chance to obtain land at a price that covered only the cost of a survey and clearing Indian title.

As far as dealing with problems that arose with slaves and Indians, Jackson did very little. He was one of the largest slave owners in the Southwest and philosophically didn't have a problem with whites owning slaves. He basically ignored any Indian rights. They couldn't vote, so their rights were overlooked except by humanitarians concentrated in the Northeast who were affiliated with the anti-Jackson party.

Jackson, with the support of Monroe, Adams, and Congress, vigorously enforced a plan to remove all the Indian tribes to lands west of the Mississippi. He rationalized this by stating that the Indians were unhappy living among the whites and were threatened with extinction. A few years later, President Van Buren agreed and told Congress that the federal Indian policy had been "just and friendly throughout . . . its watchfulness in protecting them from individual frauds unremitting." Reality was quite a different matter.[10]

Fulfilling a campaign promise, in his first annual message to Congress in 1829, Jackson called to enact legislation to remove the "Five Civilized Tribes" of the Southeast—the Cherokee, Creek, Choctaw, Chickasaw, and Seminole—to west of the Mississippi River.

Jackson very much relished the role of the great white father and believed that only removal could save the Indians from extinction. Jackson's plan was to transfer the Indians into the wilderness and then work on educating them and saving them for Jesus. A Jackson supporter wrote, "But it will prove in the end an active enlarged philanthropy. These untutored sons of the Forest, cannot exist in a state of Independence, in the vicinity of the white man. If they will persist in remaining where they are, they may begin to dig their graves and prepare to die."[11] Jackson had been inspired by President Monroe when he gave a message in 1825 that removal "would not only shield . . . [the Indians] from impending ruin, but promote their welfare and happiness." The consequences of staying in the East would lead to their "degradation and extermination."[12]

As head of the Office of Indian Affairs from 1824 to 1830, Thomas L. McKenney (1785-1859) was considered one of the most knowledgeable men in America on Indian character. He was regarded as a good friend by the Indians. In his mind, education would play the major role in civilizing the Indian, and he championed missionary activity among the tribes. He envisioned a future where they would "constitute a portion of 'our Great American family of freemen.'"[13]

For political reasons, in 1829 McKenney reversed course. He stayed in office under Presidents Madison, Monroe, and Adams, but with Jackson's insistence on Indian removal to the West, he became a supporter of that position. Dismissing any chance of the Indian becoming civilized in the East, the politician in him stated, "We once . . . thought it practical to preserve and elevate the character of our Indians, even in their present anomalous relations to the States; but it was 'distance that lent this enchantment to the view.' We have since seen for ourselves, and that which before looked like a flying cloud, we found, on a near inspection, to be an impassable mountain. . . . If the Indians do not emigrate, and fly the causes, which are fixed in themselves, and which have proved so destructive in the past, they must perish."[14]

Two that remained against forced removal were Edward Everett and John Quincy Adams. They were very skeptical of the land offered the Indians in the Great American Desert. The chances of them succeeding at farming there were almost nil. Peleg Sprague, a Whig senator from Maine, embraced Puritan predestination, asserting that if "it is the doom of Providence, that they must perish, let it be in the course of nature; not by the hand of violence. If in truth they are now in the decrepitude of age, let us permit them to live out all their days, and die in peace; not bring down their gray hairs and blood, to a foreign grave." In 1802, John Quincy Adams posed a question that would haunt him decades later during the removal debate: "What is the right of a huntsman to the forest of a thousand miles of which he has accidentally ranged in quest of prey? . . . Shall the fields and valleys, which of beneficent God has formed to teem with the life of innumerable multitudes, be condemned to everlasting barrenness?"[15]

But immigrants were pouring in from Europe, and waiting for the Indians to die off in the East over decades was unacceptable to those in power. Politicians can rationalize anything, and that was true of Lewis Cass, secretary of war, who echoed the Jacksonian perspective, "If they remain, they must decline and eventually disappear. . . . If they're removed, they may be comfortably established, and their moral and physical condition meliorated. It is certainly better for them to meet the difficulties of removal, with the probability of an adequate and final reward, than, yielding to their constitutional apathy, to sit still and perish."[16]

The arguing continued in Congress, but on May 28, 1830, President Jackson signed into law the Indian Removal Act: "An act to provide for an exchange of lands with the Indians residing in any of the States or Territories, and for their removal west of the river Mississippi."[17] Four years later, Secretary of War Lewis Cass was responsible for a new Bureau of Indian Affairs with statutory authority.

Another important piece of legislation passed was the revision of the Indian Trade and Intercourse act of 1802, which altered Indian country to that area in which Indian title was yet un-extinguished outside the boundary of any existing state or territory. Jared Sparks, editor of the *North American Review,* took a dim view of the whole process. He believed removal was necessary, but he prophetically predicted, "After all, this project only defers the fate of the Indians. In half a century their condition on the Mississippi will be just what it now is on this side. Their extinction is inevitable."[18] He saw through the promise in the Removal Act to the emigrant tribes that the United States would "forever secure and guarantee to them, and their heirs or successors, the country so exchanged," because it had a legal out, namely, "provided always, that said land shall revert to the United States if the Indians become extinct, or abandon the same."[19] Those ominous words surely made many Indians worried that the whites would be motivated to see them die off.

Many Cherokee in the Southeast had become civilized and Christianized. That fact was a hard pill to swallow for those who believed it couldn't happen for the very reason that God did not want Christianized Indians. God wanted dead Indians. This belief was challenged in 1829 in the *Cherokee Phoenix,* a newspaper printed in New Echota, Georgia, capital of the Cherokee Nation, as the United States was about to undertake forced removal of the tribe to Indian Territory:

> It is frequently said that the Indians are given up to destruction; that it is the will of heaven that they should become extinct, and give way to the whiteman, the causes which have operated to exterminate the Indian tribes, that are produced as instances of the certain doom of the whole aboriginal family . . . did not exist in the Indians themselves nor in the will of Heaven, nor simply in the intercourse of Indians with civilized man; but they were precisely such causes as are now attempted by the state of Georgia; by infringing upon their rights; by disorganizing them, and circumscribing their limits.[20]

By the time of Jackson's second State of the Union address, the Choctaw and Chickasaw had agreed to removal. From 1800 to 1830, on more than forty occasions white leaders tried to convince the Choctaw to sell their Mississippi homeland. They were successful in obtaining more than 13 million acres by 1830. But the white man's appetite for land was insatiable, and they sought to obtain the remaining 10 million acres. With the signing in September 1830 of the Treaty of Dancing Rabbit Creek, the Choctaw agreed to move west. Tushpa, twelve years old when the tribe was forced to move to eastern Oklahoma, years later related to his son James Culberson their journey. There were about 100 men, women, and children in the band. Kanchi, the seller of the land, lamented, "Sometime back beyond our old homes I heard a man preach from a book that he called the Bible and although that book was read by white men, I believe there is something better in it than the way the white man acts...."[21]

The Seminole, Cherokee, and Creek, however, had refused to part with their land. The opposition Whig party supported their refusal to move. Jackson used questionable rationalization to make it seem that removal was beneficial for all. Several of the tribes had become Christianized in the Southeast, but he still considered them heathens. This led to the obvious conclusion that he equated progress with the advancement of American expansionism and not conversion. And Jackson was ready to use military force to fulfill the nation's Manifest Destiny. At his second annual address to Congress on December 6, 1830, Jackson proclaimed:

> It gives me pleasure to announce to Congress that the benevolent policy of the Government, steadily pursued for nearly thirty years, in relation to the removal of the Indians beyond the white settlements is approaching to a happy consummation....
>
> The consequences of his speedy removal will be important to the United States, to individual States, and to the Indians themselves. The pecuniary advantages which it promises to the Government are the least of its recommendations. It puts an end to all possible danger of collision between the authorities of the General and State Governments on account of the Indians. It will place a dense and civilized population on large tracts of country now occupied by a few savage hunters. By opening the whole territory between Tennessee on the north and Louisiana on the south to the settlement of the whites it will incalculably strengthen the southwestern frontier and render the adjacent States strong enough to repel future invasions without remote aid. It will relieve the whole State of Mississippi and the western part of Alabama of Indian occupancy, and enable those States to advance rapidly in population, wealth, and power. It will separate Indians from immediate contact with settlements of whites; free them from the power of the States; and enable them to pursue happiness in their own way and under their own rude institutions; will

retard the progress of decay, which is lessening their numbers, and perhaps cause him gradually, under the protection of the Government and through the influence of good counsels, to cast off their savage habits and become an interesting, civilized, and Christian community. These consequences, some of them so certain and the rest so probable, make the complete execution of the plan sanctioned by Congress at their last session an object of much solicitude.

Toward the aborigines of the country no one can indulge a more friendly feeling than myself, or would go further in attempting to reclaim them from their wandering habits and make them a happy, prosperous people. . . .

Humanity has often wept over the fate of the aborigines of this country, and Philanthropy has been long busily employed in devising means to avert it, but its progress is never for a moment been arrested, and one by one have many powerful tribes disappeared from the earth. To follow to the tomb the last of his race and to tread on the graves of extinct nations excites melancholy reflections. But true philanthropy reconciles the mind to these vicissitudes as it does to the extinction of one generation to make room for another. In the monuments and fortresses of an unknown people, spread over the extensive regions of the West, we behold the memorials of a once powerful race, which was exterminated or has disappeared to make room for the existing savage tribes. Nor is there anything in this which, upon a comprehensive view of the general interests of the human race, is to be regretted. Philanthropy could not wish to see this continent restored to the condition in which it was found by our forefathers. What good man would prefer a country covered with forests and ranged by a few thousand savages to our extensive Republic, studded with cities, towns, and prosperous farms, embellished with all the improvements which art can devise or industry execute, occupied by more than twelve million happy people, and filled with all the blessings of liberty, civilization, and religion?

The present policy of the Government is but a continuation of the same progressive change by a milder process. The tribes which occupy the countries now constituting the Eastern States were annihilated or have melted away to make room for the whites. The waves of population and civilization are rolling to the westward, and we now propose to acquire the countries occupied by the red men of the South and West by a fair exchange, and, at the expense of the

United States, to send them to a land where their existence may be prolonged and perhaps made perpetual. Doubtless it will be painful to leave the graves of their fathers; but what do they more than our ancestors did or than our children are now doing? To better their condition in an unknown land our forefathers left all that was dear in earthly objects. Our children by thousands yearly leave the land of their birth to seek new homes in distant regions. Does Humanity weep at these painful separations from everything, animate and inanimate, with which the young heart has become intertwined? Far from it. It is rather a source of joy that our country affords a scope where a young population may range unconstrained in body or in mind, developing the power in the faculties of man in their highest perfection. These remove hundreds and almost thousands of miles at their own expense, purchase the lands they occupy, and support themselves at their new homes from the moment of their arrival. Can it be cruel in this Government when, by events which it cannot control, the Indian is made discontented in his ancient home to purchase his lands, to give him a new and extensive territory, to pay the expense of his removal, and support him a year in his new abode? How many thousands of our own people would gladly embrace the opportunity of removing to the West in such conditions! If the offers made to the Indians were extended to them, they would be hailed with gratitude and joy.

And is it supposed that the wandering savage has a stronger attachment to his home than the settled, civilized Christian? Is it more afflicting to him to leave the graves of his fathers than it is our brothers and children? Rightly considered, the policy of the General Government toward the red man is not only liberal, but generous. He is unwilling to submit to the laws of the United States and mingle with their population. To save him from this alternative, or perhaps utter annihilation, the General Government kindly offers him a new home, and proposes to pay the whole expense of his removal and settlement. . . .

May we not hope, therefore, that all good citizens, and none more zealously than those who think the Indians oppressed by subjection to the laws of the States, will unite in attempting to open the eyes of those children of the forest to their true condition, and by a speedy removal to relieve them from all the evils, real or imaginary, present or prospective, with which they may be supposed to be threatened.[22]

There was a major flaw in Jackson's reasoning. White settlers were enthusiastic about settling the West because of the new opportunities it presented. On the contrary, the Indians loved their land and hated the thought of being forced into a foreign territory. The U.S. government previously had signed many treaties with the Indians, but often the Indians didn't understand the ramifications of signing legal documents. In 1832, Sac and Fox Indians who had previously signed treaties that had given up their ancestral land in northwestern Illinois attempted to reclaim it. In a brief and bloody engagement between the tribes and the Illinois militia that became known as the Black Hawk War, the tribes were defeated and banished to west of the Mississippi. Sixty-seven-year-old Sac war chief Black Hawk (1767-1838) was captured, but he eventually went on a tour of the eastern United States where he met President Andrew Jackson. The dignified chief dictated his life story to a government interpreter in 1832. *Life of Ma-ka-tai-me-she-kia-kiak or Black Hawk* (1833) was the first published Native American autobiography. His writing demonstrated how differently Indians and whites viewed land ownership:

> Why did the Great Spirit ever send the whites to this island, to drive us from our homes, and introduce among us poisonous liquors, disease and death? They should have remained on the island where the Great Spirit first placed them. But I will proceed with my story. My memory, however, is not very good, since my late visit to the white people. I have still a buzzing in my ears, from the noise—and may give some parts of my story out of place; but I will endeavor to be correct. . . .
>
> [In 1816] For the first time, I touched the goose quill to the treaty—not knowing, however, that, by that act, I consented to give away my village. Had that been explained to me, I should have opposed it, and never would have signed their treaty, as my recent conduct will clearly prove.
>
> What do we know of the manner of the laws and customs of the white people? They might buy our bodies for dissection, and we would touch the goose quill to confirm it, without knowing what we are doing. This was the case with myself and people in touching the goose quill the first time.
>
> We can only judge of what is proper and right by our standard of right and wrong, which differs widely from the whites, if I have been correctly informed. The whites may do bad all their lives, and then,

if they are sorry for it when about to die, all is well! But with us it is different; we must continue throughout our lives to do what we conceive to be good. If we have corn and meat, and know of a family that have none, we divide with them. If we have more blankets than sufficient, and others have not enough, we must give to them that want. . . .

How smooth must be the language of the whites, when they can make right look wrong, and wrong like right.[23]

The Cherokee approached the loss of their lands differently than had Black Hawk. They focused on European concepts of treaties and laws. The Cherokee were considered the most civilized of all the tribes, and they too resisted removal. The tribal leaders hired William Wirt, former U.S. attorney general, to represent them against the state of Georgia.[24] In 1831 and 1832, they appealed to the U.S. Supreme Court and were successful in retaining rights to their land. Chief Justice John Marshall opined, "Acts of Georgia are repugnant to the Constitution. . . . They are in direct hostility with treaties [which] . . . solemnly pledge the faith of the United States to restrain their citizens from trespassing on it [Cherokee territory]. . . ."[25]

In a scenario that would repeat itself with other tribes, in 1835 a splinter group of Cherokee signed the Treaty of New Echota, agreeing to move. Peter Nabokov, in *Native American Testimony*, wrote, "To present an illusion of tribal consent, Jackson's secret agents bribed, deceived, and intimidated individual Indians, falsified records, squelched open debate, and finally persuaded some tribesmen to sign in favor of removal."[26] Most of the tribe decried this treaty, and even though Andrew Jackson understood that it was illegitimate, it gave the U.S. government the grounds to move the Cherokee.

In 1836, the Cherokee submitted a protest to Congress in a last-ditch effort to retain their lands. It was one of many unsuccessful attempts. The document was received by Congress and published in a number of newspapers that were sympathetic to the tribe. One was *The Friend*, a Philadelphia newspaper directed to Quakers, well-known pacifists who opposed slavery and Indian removal. Their attempts failed and the vast majority of Cherokee were forced to move to Indian Territory, now Oklahoma, in 1838 and 1839, along what has been known as the Trail of Tears. The hazardous death walk saw at least 4,000 Cherokee die along the way. An excerpt from the document pleading their case to Congress well describes the Cherokee's plight:

If treaties are to be thus made and enforced, deceptive to the Indians and to the world, purporting to be a contract, when, in truth, wanting the assent of one of the pretended parties, what security would there be for any nation or tribe to retain confidence in the United States? If interest or policy require that the Cherokees be removed, without their consent, from their lands, surely the president and Senate have no constitutional power to accomplish that object. They cannot do it under the power to make treaties, which are contracts, not rules prescribed by a superior, and therefore binding only by the assent of the parties. In the present instance, the assent of the Cherokee nation has not been given, but expressly denied. . . . It is the express wish of the government of the United States to remove the Cherokees to places west of the Mississippi. That wish is said to be founded in humanity to the Indians. To make their situation more comfortable, and to preserve them as a distinct people. Let facts show how this benevolent design has been prosecuted, and how faithfully to the spirit and letter has the promise of the president of the United States to the charities been fulfilled—that "those who remain may be assured of our patronage, our aid, and good neighborhood." The delegation are not deceived by empty professions, and fear their race is to be destroyed by the mercenary policy of the present day, and their lands wrested from them by physical force.[27]

Americans' lust for land was almost incomprehensible. The Europeans were quite astonished by it. Harriet Martineau (1802-1876), a noted British journalist and political reformer, toured the United States in the 1830s. She produced three books about American society that were favorably received in Britain. While in the United States, however, she supported women's rights and the abolitionist movement, and this led to her widespread condemnation. In an excerpt drawn from a chapter on agriculture in her 1837 volume, *Society in America,* she provided an explanation for American expansionism:

The pride and delight of Americans is in their quantity of land. I do not remember meeting with one to whom it had occurred that they had too much. Among the many complaints of the minority, this was never one. I saw a gentleman strike his fist on the table in an agony at the country being so "confoundedly prosperous"; I heard lamentations over the spirit of speculation; the migration of young men at the back country; the fluctuating state of society from the incessant movement westwards; the immigration of labourers from Europe; and the ignorance of the sparse population. All these grievances I heard perpetually complained of; but in the same breath I was told in triumph of the rapid sales of land; the glorious additions to which had been made by the acquisition of Louisiana and Florida, and the probable gain of Texas. Land was spoken of as the unfailing resource against over manufacture; the great wealth of the nation; the grand security of every man in it. . . .

The possession of the land is the aim of all action, generally speaking, and the cure for all social evils, among men in the United States. If a man is disappointed in politics or love, he goes and buys land. If he disgraces himself, he betakes himself to a lot in the west. If the demand for any article of manufacture slackens, the operatives drop into the unsettled lands. If the citizen's neighbours rise above him in the towns, he betakes himself where he can be monarch of all he surveys. An artisan works, that he may die on land of his own. He is frugal, that he may enable his son to be a landowner. Farmers' daughters go into factories that they may clear off the mortgage from their fathers' farms; that they may be independent landowners again. All this is natural enough in a country colonised from an old one, where land is so restricted in quantity as to be apparently the same thing as wealth. It is natural enough in the young republic, where independence is the highest political value.[28]

Manifest Destiny

Although Manifest Destiny was not used to define American expansion to the Pacific Ocean until 1845, it was clearly in place after the Revolutionary War. The phrase was not a new idea but grew out of the principles and legal elements of the Doctrine of Discovery. Expansionism heated up during the 1820s and was fueled by the Second Great Awakening, which reminded and convicted American Protestants that God wanted them to spread the word of his salvation. Every human from sea to shining sea needed to be spiritually converted to Christianity, and this would usher in a millennium of peace on Earth. The heathen Indians were not the only challenge. There was a vivid strain of anti-Catholicism in the movement. Romanticism inspired Americans to look to the great American frontier for its identity.

America's Manifest Destiny was first delineated in 1839 in the *United States Democratic Review,* a journal with close ties to the Democratic party.

American exceptionalism was announced to the world. From the seventeenth century onward, writers had asserted that their city upon a hill was unique in history and destined by God to spread in both land and cultural influence. In the article "The Great Nation of Futurity," the dramatic ambitions by the author expressed those of America, ". . . the far-reaching, the boundless future will be the era of American greatness. In its magnificent domain of space and time, the nation of many nations is destined to manifest to mankind the excellence of divine principles; to establish on earth the noblest temple ever dedicated to the worship of the Most High—the Sacred and True. Its floor shall be a hemisphere—its roof the firmament of the star-studded heavens, and its congregation an Union of many Republics, comprising hundreds of happy millions, calling, owning no man master, but governed by God's natural and moral law of equality, the law of brotherhood—of 'peace and goodwill amongst men.'"[29]

In the famous 1845 essay, "Annexation," promoting the annexation of Texas, the *Democratic Review* proclaimed that foreign powers were thwarting "the fulfillment of our manifest destiny to overspread the continent allotted by Providence for the free development of our yearly multiplying millions."[30] Thus it introduced the term Manifest Destiny to the public. It went on to assert that God had preordained expansion across the continent, and that American exceptionalism had to be protected against foreign powers such as Britain and France to achieve God's will. American expansionism was seen as natural and inevitable, with benefit to all. It was justified by Anglo-Saxon superiority over other races. In *Manifest Destiny and American Territorial Expansion,* Professor Amy S. Greenberg noted, "In reality, there was nothing predestined about manifest destiny. It was a self-serving ideology that achieved a variety of purposes, few of which were noble. Land speculation had helped drive expansion since the colonial era."[31]

The term immediately became extremely popular with the masses. It fed into Americans' ideology that they were racially and culturally superior to non-whites. Since God was on their side, whites expected Indians to yield to their desires, which normally centered on obtaining their land. Prior to 1830, Americans had justified taking lands from the savages because they were not farming and improving it. But there was a clear change in rationale after the ethnic expulsion of the civilized Cherokee who had both improved and farmed their land. Becoming civilized was no longer the determining factor in the equation. It was race.

Historians have agreed that there are three basic themes to Manifest Destiny: the American people and their institutions had a special Christian virtue; their mission was to redeem and remake the world in the image of America; and there was a divine destiny for whites under God's direction to accomplish this wonderful task.[32] Bringing more land under white control meant spreading Christianity and its democratic institutions over the entire North American continent.[33]

With God on their side, settlers marched west and occupied the frontier regions of the Mississippi, Missouri, and Illinois Rivers that flowed into new territories soon to become states: Arkansas, 1836; Michigan, 1837; Florida, 1845; Iowa, 1846; and Wisconsin, 1848. Initially the vast area beyond Missouri and Arkansas that stretched to the Rocky Mountains was of no interest to the settlers. Explorers had reported that the land was too arid for farming, and cartographers labeled it as the Great American Desert. With that in mind, white Americans presented it as a permanent gift to the Indians. The whites felt they had enough land east of Indian Country.[34] But their generosity would not last. One New Jersey politician shouted, "Make way, I say, for the young American buffalo. He has not yet got land enough."[35]

The first area outside the United States where settlers moved in great numbers was Texas. Stephen F. Austin was among its biggest promoters, and he obtained a huge land grant from Mexico and planted the flourishing colony on the banks of the Brazos River. By 1830, eastern Texas was occupied by nearly 20,000 whites and 1,000 slaves from the United States. That same year, the Mexican government prohibited further immigration from the United States and stopped the importation of slaves. In addition, they placed heavy duties on American goods. To make matters worse, General Santa Anna (1794-1876), who seized political power in Mexico, refused to give Texas statehood.

On March 2, 1836, Texas declared its independence from the old Mexican Constitution. Santa Anna marched into Texas with a large army and exterminated a small garrison of Texans at the Alamo mission in San Antonio. On April 21, 1836, at the Battle of San Jacinto, General Sam Houston and his army defeated the Mexicans and took Santa Anna prisoner. The defeated general was forced to sign a treaty recognizing Texan independence. Subsequently, the new Republic of Texas framed a constitution that was ratified in September 1836. There was overwhelming support to join the United States.

The first American contacts with California were made by merchant ships that traded along the coast and by whale boats stopping for supplies. By then, Franciscan friars had built a chain of missions along the coast from

San Diego to San Francisco. By 1838, the Mexican government deprived the missions of their lands and the mission system soon fell apart.

Thomas O. Larkin, a prominent merchant, arrived in Monterey in 1832 and built a flourishing trade. He tirelessly promoted American immigration to California. By the 1840s, a few immigrants began to leave the Oregon Trail near the Snake River to follow the California Trail across the Nevada desert and the Sierra Nevada to the Sacramento River Valley. More followed, and soon America would set its sights on adding California to the Union.

In 1844, Henry Clay of the Whig party ran against Democrat James K. Polk of Tennessee. Manifest Destiny was the main issue in the campaign. The Polk administration championed the annexation of Texas, which, in December 1845, was admitted to statehood.

James Knox Polk (1795-1849) was born in North Carolina. His father was a slaveholder, and his mother was a descendant of a Scottish religious reformer. In 1813, he enrolled at the Zion church near his home and eventually attended the University of North Carolina. He studied law in Nashville and became the speaker of the house in the state legislature and governor of Tennessee. Under his presidential administration, the U.S. Naval Academy and the Smithsonian Institution opened.[36]

Mexico was furious over the annexation of Texas and broke off diplomatic relations with the United States. Disputes over the southern and western boundaries of Texas were also a source of contention. Polk looked with a covetous eye on New Mexico and California and hoped to purchase these areas from Mexico. He explored the possibility of resuming diplomatic relations with them, but the Mexican government was collapsing. A new revolutionary government came to power, snubbing any idea of making a deal. Polk sent his war message to Congress on May 11, 1846, and soon the United States had declared war on Mexico. An old nemesis, Santa Anna, had regained power in Mexico and moved north to attack General Zachary Taylor, who in time pushed back Santa Anna's forces to Mexico City.

A third American campaign commanded by General Winfield Scott landed near Veracruz in March 1847, and after its surrender, the American forces moved on to Mexico City. In September, American troops forced their way into the city and soon thereafter it surrendered. On February 2, 1848, the Treaty of Guadalupe Hidalgo transferred California, New Mexico, and the Rio Grande boundary for $15 million to the United States and provided for the assumption of the claims of United States citizens against Mexico.

Manifest Destiny along with American successes in acquiring new lands had many urging the U.S. government to seize all of Mexico. One supporter of Manifest Destiny asked why the United States should "resign this beautiful country to the custody of the ignorant cowards and profligate ruffians who have ruled it for the last twenty-five years?"[37] But for now, America had reached its predestined destiny. The treaty with Mexico had added more than a half-million square miles of territory. God was good.

Another area of potential expansion was Oregon country. During the 1830s and early 1840s, merchants, fur trappers, and missionaries awakened Americans to the potentialities of the region, which the United States already had a fairly solid claim to. James K. Polk supporters had threatened to go to war with Britain over the right of ownership of Oregon even though war with Mexico was looming. In January 1846, Democrats were pushing for war against Britain. Whig Congressman Robert Winthrop of Massachusetts spoke out against military action and the idea of Manifest Destiny:

> There is one element in our title, however, which I confess that I have not named, and to which I may not have done entire justice. I mean that new revelation of right, which has been designated as the right of our manifest destiny to spread over this whole continent. It has been openly avowed, in a leading administration journal, that this, after all, is our best and strongest title; one so clear, so preeminent, and so indisputable, that if Great Britain had all our other titles in addition to her own, they would weigh nothing against it. The right of our manifest destiny! There is a right for a new chapter in the law of nations; or rather in the special laws of our own country; for I suppose the right of a manifest destiny to spread, will not be admitted to exist in any nation except the universal Yankee nation! This right of our manifest destiny, Mr. Speaker, reminds me of another source of title which is worthy of being placed beside it. Spain and Portugal, we all know, in the early part of the sixteenth century laid claim to the jurisdiction of this whole northern continent of America. Francis I [King of France in the early sixteenth century] is related to have replied to this pretension, that he should like to see the clause in Adam's Will, in which their exclusive title was found. Now, Sir, I look for an early reproduction of this idea. I have no doubt that if due search be made, a copy of this primeval instrument, with a clause giving us the whole of Oregon, can be somewhere hunted up. Perhaps it may be found in that same Illinois cave in which the Mormon Testament has been discovered. I commend the subject to the attention of those in that neighborhood, and will promise to withdraw all

my opposition to giving notice or taking possession, whenever the right of our manifest destiny can be fortified by the provisions of our great First Parent's last will and testament![38]

Polk decided to abandon war and tried to compromise with Britain. In July 1845, he notified the British minister in Washington, Richard Pakenham, that the United States was willing to renew its offer to divide Oregon along the forty-ninth parallel. But Pakenham held firm and wanted the division at the Columbia River. In the end, the British government concluded that it wasn't worth going to war over the extra land, which in their view had been depleted of resources. In fact, the Hudson's Bay Company had already transferred its headquarters from Fort Vancouver on the Columbia hundreds of miles north to the Fort Victoria area on Vancouver Island.

In June 1846, the treaty was signed that divided Oregon country at the forty-ninth parallel as the United States had requested, but it retained for the British all of Vancouver Island and the right to navigate the Columbia River. Many in America were relieved that war had been averted with the British since the United States was still at war with Mexico.

In 1849, Congress established the Department of the Interior, which took over the management of the Indian Bureau. Jefferson Davis, who eventually would be secretary of war, championed the civilian jurisdiction over Indian affairs. Earlier, Davis had resisted the Indian Bureau, leaving it under the control of the War Department, but now he said, "Happily for them, honorably for us, the case has greatly changed, and is, I hope, before distant day, to assume a character consonant with the relations of guardian and ward, which have been claimed by us as those existing between our Government and the Indian tribes."[39]

Almost all who had debated the subject of the Indian removal to the West by 1850 realized that there would be no sanctuary there for the Indians. Millions were immigrating to the United States from Europe, and the government needed and wanted homesteaders. In 1853, the chairman of the House Committee on Indian Affairs warned, "The whites can no longer be kept out of Indian country. The plains and prairies to the Rocky Mountains have nearly ceased to echo the lowing of the buffalo; the crack of the emigrants' whip, the merry jest and joyous laugh of the Caucasian man, now ring through the vast wilderness."[40]

And no one had a good plan to civilize the Indian. In 1848, Reverend David Lowery, a missionary to the Winnebago, concluded that the Indian removal policy was severely flawed. He did not believe it was a foregone conclusion that the future for Indians was extinction. The problem was that isolating the Indian had just not worked.

The government's answer was a reservation system, which won support in the late 1840s. Full implementation took place by 1853. States where whites were flooding in used reservations to protect at least some land from the homesteaders. The government viewed the Indians as their guests on these reservations. By 1863, Indian reservations were regarded as "the fixed policy of the government."[41]

The end of the Civil War allowed renewed government attention to the Indian problem. As Brian Dippie concluded in *The Vanishing American,* "The Civil War did serve, however, as a dividing line between dominant philosophies in Indian affairs. Before 1860, segregation was still the rule; after 1865, assimilation was increasingly the order of the day. The vanishing American had defied the prophecies of the past. Whites had shed their rhetorical tears in vain. The Indians' continued presence was a fact that could not be evaded."[42]

With its acquisitions in the South and West, the United States had now taken a form recognizable today. It was a big country that eagerly greeted European immigrants. Between 1830 and 1860, the population increased from 12,866,000 to 31,443,000. Even with this impressive growth, the country was still sparsely settled and lacking manpower in many areas. Rapid acceleration in immigration began in the mid-1840s. In 1820, there were only 8,385 immigrants from Europe, and in the decade before 1840, fewer than 600,000 crossed the Atlantic. That ballooned to over 75 million toward the end of the nineteenth century.[43]

The "Old Immigrants" from the 1820s to the 1870s came mainly from Great Britain, Scandinavia, and Germany. They typically spoke English, were literate, Protestant, and blended fairly easily into American society. Conversely, the "New Immigrants" from the 1870s to the 1920s, arriving predominantly from southern and eastern Europe, were typically poorer and less educated than the earlier immigrants. Many were Jewish. In the 1850s, Catholics—many from Ireland—accounted for only five percent of all Americans, but by 1910 that percentage had more than tripled.[44]

In Europe, over 2.5 million Jews were forced out of their homelands by government persecution and economic hardships. Austria attempted to ban Jews from marrying. America also took part in persecuting certain foreign "unwanteds." Instead of Jews, overt racism was directed toward the Chinese. The Immigration Act of 1882 directly banned the immigration of all Chinese people to the United States and called for a one-year prison sentence and a $500 fine for any person attempting to smuggle Chinese laborers into the country. This act certainly would have made European Jews nervous. Would they be the next to be excluded? The answer was, eventually, yes. In 1924, a pivotal year in the history of American Judaism, the U.S. Congress cut the torrent of Jewish immigration to a trickle with the passage of the Johnson-Reed Act.[45]

Toward the end of the nineteenth century, the old doctrine of Manifest Destiny that fueled the conquest of California and Oregon in the 1840s was supplemented with a new model. Earlier, simple faith that God had chosen Americans to own the land from the Atlantic to the Pacific was surpassed by scientific racism, exemplified by social Darwinism based on survival of the fittest. American imperialists now cast a covetous eye on natives and backward peoples in tropical climates. Science, more than God, validated American desires. The fittest to rule were those who had the power and craft to do so. America was the superior breed; Aryan and Teutonic were labels often associated with this idea.

However, religion was still important in validating Manifest Destiny. Josiah Strong (1847-1916), an evangelical leader and social reformer, believed America had divine sanction. In 1885, he wrote in his popular book, *Our Country*, that he pictured the American branch of the family moving "down upon Mexico, down upon Central and South America, out upon the islands of the sea, over upon Africa and beyond." Professor John W. Burgess of Columbia University added that the Teutonic nations had "the mission of conducting the political civilization of the modern world." Darwinian lecturer and writer John Fiske shared with many philosophers the idea that English-speaking people, because of Manifest Destiny, should establish sovereignty of the seas and bestow the blessings of benevolent rule and superior institutions on the less fortunate people around the globe.[46]

The words of God and Darwin in the last half of the nineteenth century worked harmoniously together to confirm that the killing of hostile Indians was justified and to condone placing those who survived into a life of no hope on reservations. Indian reservations, in a way, were America's national zoos, but they were attractions no white man wanted to attend. *Merriam-Webster's Dictionary* defines zoo as (a) a garden or park where wild animals are kept for exhibit; or (b) a place, situation, or group marked by crowding, confusion, or unrestrained behavior.

CHAPTER NINETEEN

Cleansing the West: Religion, Steel, and Romance

To Americans who had just won their independence from one empire, it seemed that God had cleared the way for His chosen people to build their own empire in the West, just as He had when the Pilgrims landed in Massachusetts Bay in 1620 in the wake of an epidemic that had depopulated the East Coast. The Revolution meant a new nation had its eyes on the West; smallpox cleared the West for occupation. George Washington crossing the Delaware is a more comfortable image of nation building than smallpox stalking Indian lodges, but they are two sides of the same coin in explaining how the West became "American."
—COLIN G. CALLAWAY, *ONE VAST WINTER COUNT*

Missionaries, after learning some of the religious myths of tribes they encountered, solemnly declared that the inhabitants of the new continent were the Ten Lost Tribes of Israel. Indians thus received a religious-historical identity far greater than they wanted or deserved. But it was an impossible identity. Their failure to measure up to the Old Testament standards doomed them to a fall from grace. They were soon relegated to the status of a picturesque species of wildlife.
—VINE DELORIA, JR., *CUSTER DIED FOR YOUR SINS*

For the Indians it was the perfect storm. Enlightenment philosophy embraced by Jefferson and many succeeding presidents was followed by Christian Manifest Destiny. Other Americans looked to romanticizing the

West for affirmation of American exceptionalism—certainly a gift from God. Americans believed that the West had the potential of Eden regained and that Eden was to be populated by white settlers at the expense of the indigenous people. Some, like Abraham Lincoln and Ulysses S. Grant, would eventually question that premise. But before the Civil War, America guided by Manifest Destiny gobbled up Florida, Texas, the Southwest, California, and Oregon as the major controversy was whether a new state would be a free state or a slave state.

In 1831 and 1840, Alexis de Tocqueville was the first writer to note the "exceptional nature" of the United States. Although the exact term—American exceptionalism—was not used until the 1920s, it was evident in Tocqueville's *Democracy in America:*

> The position of the Americans is therefore quite exceptional, and it may be believed that no democratic people will ever be placed in a similar one. Their strictly Puritanical origin, their exclusively commercial habits, even the country they inhabit, which seems to divert their minds from the pursuit of science, literature, and the arts, the proximity of Europe, which allows them to neglect these pursuits without relapsing into barbarism, a thousand special causes, of which I have only been able to point out the most important, have singularly concurred to fix the mind of the American upon purely practical objects. His passions, his wants, his education, and everything about him seem to unite in drawing the native of the United States earthward; his religion alone bids him turn, from time to time, a transient and distracted glance to heaven. Let us cease, then, to view all democratic nations under the example of the American people. . . .[1]

American exceptionalism traditionally has been held to reside in a series of values and institutions: universities, churches, personal liberty, jury trials, uncensored newspapers, regular elections, habeas corpus, open competition, and yes, religion, philosophy, medicine, and science. The ignorance of our time is to assume that these ideals are somehow the natural condition of an advanced society. History paints a different story.

The Second Great Awakening rose to prominence in the first half of the nineteenth century and inspired religious fervor. It was paralleled by Romanticism filled with emotion that was directed toward God and experienced by the average citizen through art and literature. Both rejected the Enlightenment philosophy characterized by rationalism and Deism.

In *The Vanishing American,* Brian Dippie described white attitudes early in the nineteenth century, writing, "Eighteenth-century intellectuals knew that history moved in cycles, and that societies rose and fell with the regularity of the turning wheel of time. But the red man's history was racial, not social: as a type of mankind he was destined to vanish, leaving no trace behind. . . . The Vanishing American, in short, represented a perfect fusion of the nostalgic with the progressive impulse."[2]

The frontier spirit of the American West was molded by cheap or free land for whites. Until the Civil War, the Indians had been segregated, but as the West filled up, eventually the Indians needed to be Christianized and assimilated into American society even though they had been relegated to reservations, continuing the reality of segregation.[3]

Religion and the West

Under the influence of Thomas Jefferson, the American Revolution had removed government from any significant role in religion and, to a lesser extent, limited religion's role in influencing government. But Protestant religious forces mounted a powerful counteroffensive in the first half of the nineteenth century. Thomas Paine had died a lonely death, which was symbolic of the fading influence of extreme Deists on American religion. Organizations such as the American Bible Society (1816) and the American Sunday School Union (1824) rose to combat faithlessness. Out West, Sunday school was the only institution that taught children reading and writing. It often existed for years before the establishment of a church in the community. The tools of the Protestant Second Great Awakening were missionaries, Bibles, teaching people to read and write, revivals, and a commitment to duty, character, and what's right.

To give philosophical expression to their faith, most evangelicals of the nineteenth century called on the services of a philosophy imported from Scotland called Common Sense Realism, which was immensely popular across the entire intellectual landscape in America at the time. Common Sense Realism has even been called the official philosophy of nineteenth-century America.[4]

Common Sense Realism was brought to America by Presbyterian minister John Witherspoon (1723-1794), who left Scotland in 1768 to become a Founding Father and president of Princeton University, then called the College of New Jersey. From Princeton, this philosophy spread through the academic world of the day. Common Sense Realism was crafted by the Scottish philosopher Thomas Reid (1710-1796) in response to the radical skepticism of a fellow Scott, David Hume (1711-1776). The core claim of Common Sense Realism was that undeniable or self-evident truths of experience provided a firm foundation upon which to build the entire edifice of knowledge. By common sense, Reed did not mean practicality or horse sense, as we use the term today, but rather those truths known by universal human experience common to all humanity. Most nineteenth-century thinkers included among the self-evident truths many of the basic teachings of Christianity, such as God's existence, his goodness, his creation of the world, and God's desire for Christians to reign supreme over heathens. These were taken to be self-evident to reasonable people.[5]

Andrew Jackson (1767-1845) was in the middle of the great religious revival of the nineteenth century, but he wouldn't take sides. Jackson cautiously wrote, "All true Christians love each other, and while here below ought to harmonize; for all must unite in the realms above. . . . Amongst the greatest blessings secured to us under our Constitution is the liberty of worshiping God as our conscience dictates." As a student of Jefferson, he acknowledged the importance of individual freedom in religious matters. At another time, he stated, "All Christians are brethren, and all true Christians know they are such because they love one another. A true Christian loves all, immaterial to what sect or church he may belong."[6]

Most Americans remained in the Congregational, Presbyterian, Baptist, and Methodist churches or joined evangelical sects that proliferated during the century. The most successful were the Methodists, whose itinerant ministers rode a circuit of several congregations in distant settlements throughout the West and preached to the level of the common man. A religious frenzy spread from the East to the West. At camp meetings, many repented and were converted to Christianity. A push for every human in America to be converted and saved was the thrust of the Second Great Awakening. The different denominations with their different theologies were received by the Indians as confusing and hypocritical.

The greatest preacher of the revival era was Reverend Charles G. Finney (1792-1875). Like George Whitefield and Jonathan Edwards before him, Finney, professor of theology and president of Oberlin College, promoted revivals in the growing towns of the West and also in major cities in the East. To him, salvation was important, but it's what you did after salvation that mattered on Earth. One had to work as well as believe, and out West that work meant sending missionaries and converting the heathen Indians to Christianity. There was never much regard or understanding of the Indians' rich religious traditions.

Education became the cornerstone for the welfare of the common man and the Indian. A crusade for free, tax-supported public education emerged in the early nineteenth century. At the time, the children of the poor obtained their elementary education at home or in a church. Children of the rich were educated in private schools or from tutors. The battle for public education peaked in the two decades after the 1830s. Eventually public elementary education was established. Through education, public officials believed that lowly whites and Indians would understand the importance of land ownership. In 1848, Horace Mann, secretary of the Massachusetts Board of Education, stated, "Nothing but Universal Education can counterwork this tendency to the domination of capital and the severity of labor. Once the working man has his position improved, he will naturally want to acquire property." Education, Mann concluded, "is the great equalizer of the conditions of men—the balance wheel of the social machinery. . . . It does better than to disarm the poor of their hostility toward the rich: it prevents being poor."[7] In the spirit of the Enlightenment, a resolution was adopted by the Mechanics Union of Trade Associations of Philadelphia in 1830 declaring "that there can be no real liberty without a wide diffusion of real intelligence. . . . [U]ntil means of equal instruction shall be equally secured to all, liberty is but an unmeaning word, and equally an empty shadow."[8]

An important aim of Christian leaders was the establishment of not only churches but colleges. These were the bases to educate missionaries who then could spread throughout the West. The rising power of churches was no more evident than in the founding of a number of schools of higher education. Congregationalists and Presbyterians together founded Western Reserve (1826) in Ohio, Knox (1837) in Illinois, Grinnell (1847) in Iowa, and Ripon (1851) in Wisconsin. The emerging powerful Methodists constructed early frontier schools like McKendree (1835) and DePaux (1837) in Indiana, and Ohio Wesleyan (1842). Not to be outdone, the Baptists built Denison (1832) in Ohio, Shurtleff (1835) in Illinois, and Baylor (1845) in Texas. Roman Catholics started St. Louis University (1832) in Missouri, St. Xavier (1842) in Illinois, and Notre Dame (1844) in Indiana. Episcopal schools included Ohio's Kenyon (1826) and the University of the South in Tennessee (1858).[9]

But Christianizing the American West was a mixed bag. Yale President Timothy Dwight (1752-1817), who visited western New England, noted that the pioneers "cannot live in regular society. They are too idle, too talkative, too passionate, too prodigal, and too shiftless to acquire either property or character."[10] He would speak for later clergy who explored the Louisiana Territory. Congressman Edward Everett (1794-1865) was appalled at the lack of integrity and good faith in regard to America's policies toward the Indians. He noted a number of treaties that had been violated and concluded, "We shall sign and seal, but we shall not perform. Let them go to Texas; let them join the Comanches, for their sakes, for ours."[11]

However, others—especially Methodists and Baptists—perceived the West as filled with promise. In 1832, Congregationalist Lyman Beecher brought his family to Cincinnati. He believed that by the end of the century there would be as many as 100 million people living in the region between the Appalachian Mountains and the Mississippi River, and that without Christianity the region would fall into barbarism. As he heard tales from travelers returning from New Orleans, St. Louis, and the Pacific Ocean, he confessed that then "did I perceive how God, who seeth the end from the beginning, had prepared the West to be mighty."[12]

Missionaries Out West

The English missions were never as successful as those of the Spanish and the French. Catholic missionaries held comparatively more enthusiastic opinions of the Indians. In turn, the Indians were more welcoming to the flexibility of the Catholic Jesuits than the rigidity of the Puritans and were attracted to the ceremonies of Catholicism, versus the dull services of the Protestants.

Inspired by the biblical Great Commission and injunction (Matthew 7:16, "to know them by their fruit"), Christian missionaries spread throughout the West. Besides their efforts to convert Indians to Christianity, missionaries supported local printing and newspapers, education, and local voluntary organizations in rural Western communities.[13] While their intentions were often good, missionaries brought Indians together in close quarters where God and, unfortunately, germs might reach them. The latter was more successful.

There were few American missionaries serving the Indians before the War of 1812. Afterward, national missionary societies garnered enough finances to support a number of missions among the Indians. Beginning in 1819, Thomas McKenney, head of Indian Affairs and the War Department, used $10,000 appropriated by Congress to subsidize missionary societies. They built schools that instructed Indian children on agriculture and domestic arts. It was a situation where there was little separation between church and state. This relationship continued until after the Civil War. The goal was to reshape Indians into model Americans who farmed the land during the week and attended church on Sunday. If they could read and write, then they could participate in government decisions as American citizens. Citizenship for all Indians would not be attained until 1924.

In 1823, one Christian missionary society delineated its vision of Manifest Destiny:

> Let then, missionary institutions, established to convey to them the benefits of civilization and the blessings of Christianity, be efficiently supported; and with cheering hope, you may look forward to the period when the savage shall be converted into the citizen; when the hunter shall be transformed into the mechanic; when the farm, the workshop, the School-House, and the Church shall adorn every Indian village; when the fruits of Industry, good order, and sound morals, shall bless every Indian dwelling; and when throughout the vast range of country from the Mississippi to the Pacific, the red man and the white man shall everywhere be found, mingling in the same benevolent and friendly feelings, fellow-heirs to a glorious inheritance in the kingdom of Immanuel.[14]

More than almost any others, missionaries viewed the Indian way of life as incompatible with Christianity and civilization. They pushed for larger budgets and more missionaries. The government was a willing participant because it saw Christianizing the Indians as the only practical way of dealing with them. In 1846, a missionary to the Eastern Sioux stated, "As tribes and nations the Indians must perish and live only as men! With this impression of the tenancy of God's purpose as they are being developed year after year, I would labor to prepare them to fall in with Christian civilization that is destined to cover the earth."[15] Thanks to private and government funding, missionary organizations became large bureaucracies but with little to show for their efforts.

Through public propaganda, settlers, profiteers, and policymakers espoused missionaries as bringing Christianity and civilization to the savages. In reality, they knew also that religion was an effective way of subduing the natives for economic advantage and land acquisition, and that missionaries could possibly aid in a peaceful conquest. The words of John Winthrop in New England rang true for those whites heading west: "As for the Natives in New England, they inclose noe Land, neither had any settled habitation, nor any payment Cattle to improve the Land by, and soe have noe other but a Naturall Right to those Countries. Soe if we leave them sufficient for their use, we may lawfully take the rest, there being more than enough for them and us."[16]

In 1804, Reverend Gideon Blackburn (1772-1838) was welcomed by Cherokee leaders as he built a Presbyterian school among them. In the spirit of cooperation, Chickasaw chiefs asked for farmers and blacksmiths to live with them in their villages so they could teach their young men new skills. The openness of the Indians encouraged churches and missionary societies to support educational, vocational, and religious work among these groups. Missionary groups were seen as being able to civilize Indians at a lower cost than the U.S. government. In an optimistic tone, in 1823, one mission board member concluded, "The American savages are capable of being both civilized and Christianized."[17]

At the beginning of the nineteenth century, a group of Protestant missionaries proposed the establishment of "model Zions." They envisioned outposts in the wilderness where Indian children could be housed and instructed in Christian values and education away from the toxic effects of their Indian villages. In his annual message in 1818, President Monroe picked up on the missionaries' idea and wrote that it was "indispensable that their independence as communities should cease, and that the control of the United States over them should be complete and undisputed." A year later, Congress passed a bill providing "the civilization of the Indian tribes adjoining the frontier settlements." A sum of $10,000 annually was appropriated for the employment of people of good character to instruct the Indians in agriculture and teach their children the basics of reading, writing, and arithmetic. This was the start of the first government involvement in tribal internal affairs.[18]

Less than a decade after the Louisiana Purchase, the Missionary Societies of Massachusetts and Connecticut sent members westward to report on the state of religion and morals in the territory. The news wasn't good. "The state of society in this country is very deplorable. The people are entirely ignorant of divine things, and have been taught only to attend mass and count their beads." Their Catholic counterparts found the conditions no better. They reported that the newly appointed Roman Catholic bishop, Louis William Dubourg, "mourns over the depravity and wickedness of this place."[19]

That news prompted the Baptists and Methodists to head west to bring Christianity to the heathens. By 1850, the Methodists had built more churches than any other group in western lands, including Mississippi, Louisiana, Texas, Arkansas, Tennessee, Ohio, Indiana, Illinois, Michigan,

Wisconsin, and Iowa. But they didn't stop there. By mid-century, missions reached all the way to California and Oregon Territory. The Oregon missions were launched by the Congregationalists (Samuel Parker, 1833), the Methodists (Jason Lee, 1834), and the Presbyterians (Henry Harmon Spalding and Marcus Whitman, 1835-1836; Cushing Eells and Elkanah Walker, 1838).[20]

Not to be outdone, by 1850 the Baptists had attracted 1 million members out West. They evangelized to both the new settlers and the Indians they were displacing. Isaac McCoy, a missionary, argued for the creation of an Indian territory in the West to insulate the natives from greedy, encroaching white traders. Well before mid-century, the Cherokee, Creek, Choctaw, and Chickasaw were all living in Indian Territory, which would become Oklahoma. He envisioned an even larger, permanent territory in the West where Indians could be educated and Christianized.

In 1818, Cyrus Byington (1793-1868) organized the Presbyterian mission to the Choctaw Indians. The purpose was to not only preach the gospel but also teach the Native Americans to learn English and assimilate into the white culture. He began his work in a classroom in Mississippi. The Indian students were given American names and issued American clothing. The boys learned agriculture, dairying, horticulture, and animal husbandry. The girls learned kitchen duties, sewing, mending, and washing clothes. Byington wrote a friend, "The children are docile, silent, obedient, and ready to perform any kind of labor. They are active and useful."[21]

Byington was especially effective in converting the Choctaw because he had learned their language and preached to them in their native language. He even wrote several books in Choctaw. In 1833, the U.S. government moved the Choctaw to southeastern Oklahoma. Two years later, Byington arrived and organized a church at Eagle Town. In time, there were five more churches planted. While he was there, he translated the Bible into Choctaw. Soon 2,700 Indians were converted, and by 1860 more than ten percent of the Choctaw tribe had joined a Presbyterian congregation. Another ten percent became members of other churches. His success was an exception and not the rule. By 1925, the Native American Christian community stood at a paltry 35,000.[22]

One of the key elements of Manifest Destiny was that Americans were destined to bring enlightenment to the West. The West was a grand and needy venue where unbelieving whites and Indian heathens could be converted to Christianity. It was also a religious battlefield where Protestant leaders envisioned the conquering of Catholicism. To the north in Canada were French Catholics, and to the south in Mexico were Hispanic Catholics. The Second Great Awakening inspired Protestants to battle the ever-increasing Catholic immigrants, especially those from Ireland, who were making the West their new home.

Presbyterian pastor Lyman Beecher (1775-1863) was a passionate crusader against the Catholics. He believed Catholic immigrants from Europe would undermine American freedom. For him, the final battle for religious superiority and control would take place in the American West. When he became president of Lane Theological Seminary in Cincinnati, in 1832, the city was considered part of the West. He traveled throughout the Northeast, raising funds to build Protestant institutions across the trans-Appalachian West. Caught in the middle of the battle were Native Americans who were puzzled and dismayed with these religious battles. In an 1835 plea for the West, Beecher summarized the conflict with the Catholics:

> If this nation is, in the providence of God, destined to lead the way in the moral and political emancipation of the world, it is time she understood her high calling, and were harnessed for the work. . . .
>
> It is equally plain that the religious and political destiny of our nation is to be decided in the West. There is the territory, and there soon will be the population, the wealth, and the political power. The Atlantic commerce and manufactures may confer always some peculiar advantages on the East. But the West is destined to be the great central power of the nation, and under heaven, must affect powerfully the cause of free institutions and the liberty of the world.
>
> The West is a young empire of mind, and power, and wealth, and free institutions, rushing up to a giant manhood, with the rapidity and a power never before witnessed below the sun. If she carries with her the elements of her preservation, the experiment will be glorious—the joy of the nation—the joy of the whole earth, as she rises in the majesty of her intelligence and benevolence, and enterprise, for the emancipation of the world.
>
> It is equally clear, that the conflict which is to decide the destiny of the West, will be a conflict of institutions for the education of her sons, for purposes of superstition, where evangelical light; of despotism, or liberty. . . .
>
> We must educate! We must educate! Or we must perish by our own prosperity. If we do not, short from the cradle to the grave will be our race. . . . And let no man of the East quiet himself, and dream

of liberty, whatever may become of the West. Our alliance of blood, and political institutions, and common interests, is such, that we cannot stand aloof in the hour of her calamity, should it ever come. Her destiny is our destiny; and the day that her gallant ship goes down, our little boat sinks in the vortex!

. . . .

Since the irruption of the northern barbarians [Catholics], the world has never witnessed such a rush of dark-minded population from one country to another, as is now leaving Europe, and dashing upon our shores. . . . Clouds like the locust of Egypt are rising from the hills and plains of Europe, and on the wings of every wind, are coming over to settle down upon our fair fields. . . .

"The spirit of the age" . . . is moving on to put an end in Europe to Catholic domination, creating the necessity of making reprisals abroad for what liberty conquers at home. Their policy points them to the West, the destined centre of civilization and political power once their own, and embracing now their ancient settlements and institutions and people, and not a little wealth—bounded on the north by Catholic population, and on the south by a continent not yet emancipated from their dominion, and agitated by the at present successful conflicts of the Catholic priesthood to extinguish free institutions and reconstruct those of despotic power.[23]

Beecher's fame would be eclipsed by his daughter, who was the seventh of nine children. She directed her energies toward abolishing slavery and did not embrace her father's positions on religion or race. By the time the family moved to Cincinnati in 1832, she was twenty-one years old. Four years later she would marry Calvin Ellis Stowe, a biblical scholar and Lane Theological Seminary's first professor. In 1850, Harriet Beecher Stowe (1811-1896) left Cincinnati and soon was working on *Uncle Tom's Cabin* from a shabby home in Brunswick, Maine. Her story first appeared as a serial in *National Era,* an anti-slavery paper, starting in 1851. On March 20, 1852, it was published in a two-volume book form. A week after publication, 10,000 copies had been sold. Within a year, just in the United States, more than 300,000 more were printed. In England, over 1.5 million copies were sold in a little over a year, and eventually the book appeared in thirty-seven languages.

Harriet Beecher Stowe saw the Civil War as a conflict to end slavery. She became impatient with President Lincoln when he didn't announce emancipation soon enough for her liking, and she traveled to Washington, D.C., after he finally stated that the slaves would be freed. She was welcomed at the White House, where Lincoln supposedly said, as he shook her hand, "So this is the little woman who made this big war."[24]

The Roman Catholics entered a West where their missions had been built centuries ago. The legendary Father Junípero Serra (1713-1784), a Franciscan friar, supervised a number of missions in California from San Diego to San Francisco. His main purpose was to bring the Catholic faith to native peoples, but the Spanish government also used these missions to secure California as their territory under the Doctrine of Discovery.

Born in Petra, Mallorca, by the 1740s Serra was disenchanted as a teacher and followed the path that over 15,000 priests and members of Catholic religious orders took from 1493 to 1822 in leaving Spain for the New World.[25] After landing in Puerto Rico in 1749, he preached in Mexican missions from 1758 to 1768. In 1769, he arrived in San Diego and took control of the seventeen missions founded between 1697 and 1767 in California. One year later, he relocated to Monterey and eventually to Carmel where he baptized over a thousand natives.[26]

From the beginning, many natives resisted the Catholics' call to conversion. Indians were forced to help build the missions, and their cultures were devalued or ignored. In 1780, Serra wrote, "That spiritual fathers should punish their sons, the Indians, with blows appears to be as old as conquest of the Americas; so general in fact that the Saints do not seem to be any exception to the rule."[27] Many Native Americans today resent how their ancestors were treated at the missions. Serra biographers Rose Marie Beebe and Robert M. Senkewicz explained the rationale of Serra and other Fathers in using physical punishment, writing, ". . . his belief in potentially salvation-bringing effects of punishment led him consistently to approve flogging, a very common eighteenth-century form of punishment for a variety of offenses, and a punishment that was regarded by colonial military officials as particularly suitable for native peoples."[28]

Father Serra spent thirty-four years as a dedicated missionary to the Indians in Mexico and California. He believed his treatment of the Indians was a better alternative than the oppression by colonial soldiers and settlers who exploited them. A realist, Serra has been called a saint and a sinner. He cared deeply for the Indians and honestly believed he was doing what was best for them.

Many missionaries were used by their governments to keep the natives under control until their land could be seized and settled by whites, as explained by Beebe and Senkewicz: "The missionaries, as we have seen, genuinely believed they were protecting the native peoples from exploitation by unscrupulous and potentially cruel settlers. But in the actual working-out of Spanish expansion in eighteenth-century New Spain, the practical function of the missions was to prepare the indigenous population for the arrival of settlers by teaching them skills that would make them useful and assimilated ranch hands."[29]

Like Jefferson and many others, Serra suffers from critics who place twenty-first-century values on incomparable worlds of the past. On September 23, 2015, Pope Francis canonized Father Serra at the Basilica of the National Shrine of the Immaculate Conception in Washington, D.C., during his first visit to the United States. It was the first canonization ceremony to be held in this country.

Nineteenth-century Roman Catholics believed that their church with the pope as its head was the one true moral and spiritual authority on Earth. One of the most famous Catholic priests was Father Pierre-Jean De Smet (1801-1873), who was born in Catholic Flanders, now Belgium. His life serving the Indians would be a testimony not only to his devotion to them but also to the challenges that missionaries of any denomination faced out West. In 1821, he sailed for America and spent most of the 1820s at the Jesuit seminary in Missouri, where he became a priest in 1827. In 1839, he was ministering to the Potawatomi Indians at Council Bluffs on the Missouri River. He was disillusioned by the effects of alcohol on the Indians.

During the 1830s, there was a fabled story of four delegations of Salish-led Indians living in the Bitterroot Valley in what is now western Montana who trekked all the way to St. Louis in order to obtain the Bible or plead with the Jesuit missionaries to serve their homeland with the Word. The first delegation headed east in 1831. The last three delegations were primarily Salish. One delegation found Father De Smet at Council Bluffs in 1839. Noted Missoula artist Edgar Paxson (1852-1919)—most famous for his massive *Custer's Last Stand*—memorialized their journey in his famous 1912 painting *Seeking the White Man's Book* or *After the Whiteman's Book* (see the dust jacket for his oil masterwork of the same subject). The mural, 81 inches by 47 inches, hangs in the House Lobby in the capitol in Helena, Montana. (The five other 1912 Paxson murals that accompany it are *The Border Land, Lewis at Black Eagle Falls, Pierre de la Verendrye, Lewis and Clark at Three Forks,* and *Surrender of Chief Joseph*.[30]) The comforting image justifies Manifest Destiny and the taking of Indian lands. The intention was historical airbrushing to teach new generations of whites that the Indians were indeed willing partners in conversion and desiring to become civilized like whites. Who would doubt that conclusion if the seekers were inspired enough to walk all the way to St. Louis to embrace Christianity?

In 1840, De Smet made the first of many trips to visit Indians in the West, especially the Flathead. He was welcomed by them in the Bitterroot Valley of western Montana, and he was impressed by them, writing that the tribe members "are scrupulously honest in their buying and selling; they have never been accused of committing a theft. . . . Lying is hateful to them beyond anything else. . . . Their plight, always a jovial humor, very hospitable, and helpful to one another in their duties."[31]

St. Mary's Mission to the Flathead, which was fashioned after the seventeenth- and eighteenth-century Paraguayan Reductions (Jesuit settlements for indigenous people), was viewed by Father De Smet as a wilderness kingdom in the untainted frontier of the Rocky Mountains. He tried diligently to find similarities between Catholic theology and Salish beliefs and practices: the sacramental and transformative power of chant, prayer, and devotional hymns; the veneration of sacramental objects and sacred sites; the use of water and incense for purification and for transporting prayers to the spirit world; feast days; and the mediating power of guardian spirits. He was one of the few religious figures in the West who honored Indian beliefs.

The Jesuits were sophisticated educators and taught in native languages, using aids such as pictures, charts, music, and drama. They asked Indian leaders to help them convert others by being models and mentors. De Smet was optimistic that Indian hunters could be transformed into peaceful Christian farmers.

In October 1841, he observed, "The nation of the Flatheads appear to be a chosen people—'the elect of God.' . . . It would be easy to make this tribe the model for other tribes—the seed of 200,000 Christians, who would be as fervent as were the converted Indians of Paraguay. Among them, dissensions, quarrels, injuries, and enmities are unknown."[32] This optimistic report may have been influenced by his need to have the Catholic overseers continue to financially support him.

But the Salish harbored many disagreements with the Catholics, including the concept of sin and hell, and the importance of European social, political, and economic values. They wanted none of the Catholics' wishes for them to become farmers or make peace with their hated enemy, the Blackfeet. They did not understand why a loving God would send his children to hell. Likewise, they had no understanding of the attractiveness of a heaven where there were no relatives or bison.

Relations between the Jesuits and the Salish worsened when the Jesuits established a mission to the Blackfeet. Feeling betrayed, the Salish believed the Christian medicine that gave them power to win wars was now being shared with their enemies. Soon they were back to their Indian beliefs. After 1846, Victor, the principal chief of the Bitterroot Salish and friend of the Jesuits, was unable to get his people to listen to the missionaries anymore. In frustration, in 1850, the Jesuits closed the mission and sold their buildings and farm to a local trader. St. Mary's Mission to the Salish did not reopen until 1866.[33]

The missionaries in many instances were overwhelmed by miners, settlers, military officers, and government treaty negotiators. Disarray led to warfare and dispossession. Father De Smet's missionary career ended in 1848 when he was called back to be an administrator for the Missouri Jesuits.

Father De Smet's most controversial role involved a mission to the camp of Sitting Bull during the Fort Laramie Treaty negotiations in 1868. He failed to convince Sitting Bull of the government's good intentions, but in the end there was enough support for a treaty. In less than a decade, the U.S. government had broken it.

De Smet wrote that it was disgusting to call Native Americans savages because he found high culture in their community but warned that this could change when they "learned the vices of the whites."[34] No one had more hope and optimism for a bright future for the Native Americans than did Father De Smet. He lived among the Indians for many years. He spent the last thirty-five years of his life in St. Louis. Frustrations mounted when, after the Civil War, President Ulysses S. Grant adopted an Indian peace policy that assigned Protestant missionaries across most of the West, even in areas where there were Catholic missionaries. Toward the end of his life, De Smet became disillusioned with the U.S. government. In many ways he felt that both the Indians and Catholics were outsiders in America.

But times were changing. By 1850, due to massive immigration from Ireland caused by a potato famine, the Roman Catholic Church became the largest denomination in the country—a title they have not given up even today. Of the 5 million immigrants who settled in America from 1815 to 1860, 2 million came from Ireland.[35]

The missionaries never wavered in their commitment to saving the Indians. If Jesus was the only way to heaven, and the Great Commission demanded them to spread the good word, then their calling could not waiver. But there was a practical dilemma. Should the Indians be civilized first or should the heathens be converted to Christianity first? There seemed to be no consensus. The Jesuit's efforts were directed toward conversion first, but their French countrymen believed they should be civilized as Frenchmen and then converted. Puritans, in their no-nonsense approach to life, saw a clear path to salvation only after the savage had been civilized.

But for many Americans, missionaries were too idealistic. A religious writer reflected the view of the masses: "There seems to be a deep rooted superstition . . . that the Indians are really destined, as if there were some fatality in the case, never to be Christianized, but gradually to decay till they become totally extinct."[36] Many Protestant realists believed in predestination, which meant God wanted the Indians to vanish. It was certainly more comforting to white Christians if God wanted the Indians turned away at the gates of heaven.

Jefferson, the Father of the American West, would have approved of the way the West was developing religiously. While being more secular than the East, with a low percentage of formal affiliation with religious institutions, the West was certainly pluralistic, with Protestant, Catholic, Jewish, and Russian Orthodox religions worshipping freely without government intervention. Protestants set out to extend the institutions and programs of the Second Great Awakening across the West, but early on they ran into resistance from Mormons, Mexicans, Chinese, Japanese, Russians, and native peoples. The Asians brought with them Shinto, Confucian, Taoist, Buddhist, and folk beliefs. The disappearance of a recognizable Protestant norm became the norm in the West.

From the 1860s to the 1880s, tribes were increasingly confined to reservations. Early in the 1860s, churches began lobbying the Indian Bureau in Washington for franchises over the respective reservations. In a move that the Indians would find frustrating, one reservation would be assigned to the Lutherans, another to the Roman Catholics, another to the Methodists, and another to the Episcopalians. One of the few social activities permitted on reservations was the church service. Many missionaries didn't realize that it was less the reality of their religion and more the threat of extinction that brought converts to them. Indian congregations were established in nearly every reservation west of the Mississippi.[37]

One of the white man's burdens was his calling to educate and civilize the world. Missionaries equated Christianity with Western culture and its apparent superiority over other cultural forms. This belief was supported by progress in science and technology. However, after almost 500 years of active missionary efforts, only three to five percent of native populations today are born-again Christians. On some reservations that figure is less than one percent.[38]

The Industrial Revolution: The Best Ideas Come from Solving Common Problems

Science and technology during the Industrial Revolution produced marvels.[39] Scottish-born James Watt (1736-1819) made perhaps the largest contribution to technology when he designed a superior steam engine in 1765. The steam engine was one of the greatest inventions of all time.[40] In 1804, Oliver Evans (1755-1819) of Philadelphia, a leader in American technology and automation, developed a high-pressure steam engine that was adaptable to a great variety of industrial purposes. Soon it was being used not only in steam navigation but to run sawmills, flour mills, and common printing presses. Mills no longer needed to be located on rivers, and once cumbersome machines no longer needed to be powered by horses.[41] In 1828, steam power replaced water power at many cotton mills. Steam power led to the building of 240,000 miles of railroads to carry powerful railroad engines.[42]

Simeon North (1765-1852), from Middletown, Connecticut, revolutionized the American clock industry, and Connecticut manufacturers were soon mass-producing inexpensive clocks for a national market. His genius was using interchangeable parts for a variety of different timepieces. His techniques were adapted by gun makers. In England, Henry Cort (1741-1800) made advancements in milling iron that increased tensile strength and the speed of production. Soon, steam-powered railroads were crisscrossing Europe and America, while steamboats chugged up their great rivers. In 1811, four years after Robert Fulton's (1765-1815) *Clermont* made its celebrated voyage up the Hudson River, New Yorker Nicholas J. Roosevelt (1767-1854) launched the steam-powered *New Orleans* at Pittsburgh and sent it on a successful voyage down the Ohio and Mississippi Rivers. Steamboats eventually ran from St. Louis up the Missouri to Fort Benton in what would become Montana in the heart of Indian country. The Erie Canal was completed in 1825. In 1838, Samuel Morse (1791-1872) demonstrated his telegraph, and five years later Congress authorized the building of an experimental line from Washington, D.C. to Baltimore.[43]

The Industrial Revolution was in complete swing by the time of the Revolutionary War. Starting around 1760, it transformed Western civilization and was no more evident than in the development of railways. Commercial railways started in Great Britain in the 1820s with the mechanized transport of freight. By the 1830s, passenger service proved profitable. Central European countries imported British technology in the late

1840s. By 1854, more than 1,200 miles of track crisscrossed central Europe. The railways proved critical for national defense, cultural improvement, as a safety net to avoid regional famine, and for national prestige.[44]

By the 1830s, Americans were calling for a railroad to be built from New York City to the Great Lakes and on to Oregon and the Pacific Coast. In 1853, Congress authorized funds to survey a possible transcontinental route. A number of transcontinental railroads were completed in the second half of the nineteenth century: the Union Pacific (1869); Central Pacific (1869); Southern Pacific (1883); Northern Pacific (1883); Atchison, Topeka & Santa Fe (1885); and the last, the Great Northern (1893). Once they were completed, thousands of miles of feeder lines spread throughout the various regions.[45]

American society became enchanted with science and technology. Many Americans concluded that it was science and reason abetted by free markets and democracy—and not religion and nature—that were the drivers of justice and freedom. Scientific rationalization, which favored systematic observation and hypotheses testing, could make people better at abstract thinking and in seeing inconsistencies between abusive practices and the values they purported to hold. In its own way, science played its part in the abolitionist movement.

In its own way, too, the railroad played its part in destroying the West known to Native Americans. From 1820 to 1920, the largest destruction of animal life in world history was unfolding. One of the wonders of the world was being reduced to a blank slate. By the 1880s, pronghorns and wild horses would be the only large animals left. In the nineteenth century, the Great Plains was a slaughterhouse. After the Civil War, 20,000 game hunters shot 10 million bison alone, in addition to most of the other big-game animals. Many hunters arrived by train and steamboat.[46]

No technology had a greater effect on the West than the development of more efficient firearms. Superior firepower often wins battles, and those battles took place between whites and Indians, whites and whites, and Indians and Indians. All were searching for the latest and best guns to win the day. It seemed that God favored the stronger army, and usually a stronger army meant the one with the best guns.

"We showed them many curiosities and the air gun which they were much astonished at," wrote William Clark in 1804.[47] The noiseless gun was nicknamed the "great medicine" for its smokeless firepower, and it certainly impressed the Indians on the Corp of Discovery's journey west. American technology improved rapidly after that first meeting. Over the next century there would be literally hundreds of different models and makes of rifles, shotguns, and handguns.[48] The hunter out West became an American idol who exemplified the strenuous life and survival of the fittest.[49]

Today, there an estimated 300 million firearms in America, and many carry the name of legendary manufacturers like Samuel Colt (1814-1862), Daniel Wesson (1825-1906), Horace Smith (1808-1893), Oliver Winchester (1810-1880), and John Browning (1855-1926). In the early 1800s, the federal government was the main customer of the gun makers. Eli Whitney (1765-1825) secured a contract in 1798 to supply the U.S. government with 10,000 muskets that were the first to be mass-produced with interchangeable parts. Before and after the Civil War, gun manufacturers survived by supplying millions of guns to foreign countries. From 1868 to 1880, settlers out West preferred less expensive, more durable muskets over newer multiple-shot weapons, but that soon changed.[50]

The Colt Paterson, manufactured in the late 1830s, was the first practical revolving pistol, and it revolutionized handguns from then on. Sam Colt's first firearm was soon used against Comanches by the early Texas Rangers. It also saw service in Florida's second Seminole War (1835-1842), the Mexican War (1846-1848), and the California gold rush. Even more successful was the 1851 Colt Navy revolver, a ball six-gun with nearly a quarter of a million sold between 1850 and 1873.[51]

The 1852 and 1853 slant-breech Sharps carbine was popular with the U.S. military and was nicknamed the "Beecher's Bible" after Henry Ward Beecher (1813-1887), an antislavery minister and brother of Harriet Beecher Stowe. He stated that there was more moral power in one Sharps carbine than in 100 Bibles. Out West it became a popular weapon with the professional bison hunters.[52]

A well-received Civil War gun was the 1860 Colt Army revolver, which had sales upward of 200,500 from 1862 to 1873. It found favor with the U.S. cavalry, Wells Fargo agents, and the Texas Rangers. One of the most famous guns of the West after the Civil War was the "Yellow Boy" 1866 Winchester .44 caliber lever-action rifle. Over 170,000 left the factory between 1866 and 1898. Bloody Knife, Custer's Arikara scout, rode into the Battle of the Little Bighorn with a Yellow Boy, facing his Indian enemies who also carried the same tack-adorned rifle.

Another perhaps lesser-known but extensively used rifle was the Springfield Allin Conversion 1866 rifle, considered one of the most powerful single-shot rifles in the West. Hide hunters like William F. "Buffalo Bill" Cody (1846-1917) appreciated its power and accuracy. A professional hunter could kill as many as 150 animals a day, which by mid-century had severely thinned the herds on the Great Plains. Those defending attacks on Wyoming's Bozeman Trail in the Hayfield and Wagon Box Fights in 1867 used this weapon too, with great efficiency.[53]

Colt found another success with the famous 1873 Colt single-action army revolver. From its first introduction, it became a favorite with those living on the frontier. With over 192,000 in production by the end of the nineteenth century, it was the best-selling firearm in the period. The so-called Peacemaker was preferred by lawmen, outlaws, and cowboys, including legends of the West like Wyatt Earp, Bat Masterson, John Wesley Hardin, and the Daltons, who relied on it in gunfights.

Not to be outdone, Winchester came out with its 1873 rifle. It was their first centerfire gun and proved so successful that it was manufactured from 1873 until 1919 with well over half a million manufactured by the turn of the century. The most famous and recognizable rifle of the American frontier, the Winchester 73 was a favorite of Pat Garrett, William F. Cody, famed Montana rancher Granville Stuart, Butch Cassidy, and Billy the Kid.

The rifle considered to have destroyed the Plains Indians' nomadic way of life more than any other firearm was the 1874 Sharps buffalo rifle. From 1871 until 1881, it reliably killed the Indians' main source of food and clothing along with other big game. Famous lawman Bill Tilghman and Martha "Calamity" Jane Canary helped to make the 1874 Sharps famous.[54]

Many important firearms followed as the Indians' way of life in the West slowly came to an end, including the Remington revolver (1875), Winchester rifle (1876, a favorite hunting rifle of Theodore Roosevelt), Colt double-action revolver (1877), Winchester rifle (1886), and the Winchester shotgun (1887), among others.

Most technological breakthroughs came from tinkering. The nineteenth century fostered a lot of tinkerers. No fewer than twenty-three people deserve credit for inventing some version of the incandescent bulb before Thomas Edison (1847-1931). The same is true of other inventions. Elisha Gray (1835-1901) and Alexander Graham Bell (1847-1922) filed for a patent on the telephone on the very same day. There were six different inventors of the thermometer, three of the hypodermic needle, five of the electric telegraph, four of photography, five of the steamboat, and six of the electric railroad. Most inventions are one endless chain of parallel instances. The marriage of reason and revelation produced a civilization of technological mastery and racist ideology.[55]

Painting with a Dirty Brush: The Artistic Expression of the Philosophy of Romanticism

With its jagged mountains, pristine forests, raging rivers, endless plains, and open sky, the massive territory that made up the American West was bound to inspire the imagination of artists. Many artists and photographers used landscapes to make statements that forged or reinforced opinions about nationhood, cultural identity, Native Americans, and the environment. Paintings and photographs may be aesthetically pleasing, but they all contain messages, overt or subliminal. English-born painter Thomas Hill (1829-1908) became rich and famous for his grand paintings of Yosemite and the Sierra Nevada in a time known as the heyday for landscape painters. In 1844, Hill moved as a teenager to Taunton, Massachusetts. After his first trip to California in 1861, he accompanied famed photographer Carleton Watkins (1829-1916) to Yosemite, and their art significantly influenced the decision by Congress in 1864 to protect Yosemite Valley from development. It was the first large-scale example in America of park land (in this case, to be administered by the state) being set aside for preservation and public recreation.[56] Art supported and solidified Manifest Destiny in the minds of Easterners.

Industrialization and disillusionment with life sparked Romanticism and a nostalgia for the past when life was simpler. In the first half of the nineteenth century, scores of experimental communities sprang up throughout the United States, led by reformers who wanted to focus on the biological family as the fundamental unit of society. They championed society without private property, much like the Indians did. While industrialized America focused on building an earthly Eden, reformers built utopian villages: Mother Ann Lee (1736-1784) founded Shaker colonies in the late eighteenth century; Robert Owen (1771-1858) established a commune in Indiana in the 1820s; George Ripley (1802-1880) created Brook Farm outside of Boston in the 1840s; Étienne Cabet (1788-1856) launched the Icarian Experiment in Illinois around 1850; and John Humphrey Noyes (1811-1886) founded the Oneida Perfectionist Society in upstate New York in 1848. Like Romanticism, utopian villages slowly lost favor after 1850 with the stark realism of the Civil War.[57]

Art can set us free, but it can also reinforce a society's preconceptions—as in religious art or Romantic verse—and can even be a means of enforcing them. Art is another form of philosophy, and it makes us think about what it is to be human. In the nineteenth century, a real human was an educated, white Christian.

The Romantic era spurred the development of concert halls, symphony orchestras, natural history museums, and even restaurants. More abstract themes of Romanticism included: childhood as a remarkable stage of life; living closer to nature to make one both more innocent and more authentic; artists as prophets; artists' self-expression; the realization that biological species evolved; and thinking of society itself as a corrupt force, aided by technology and commerce.

Nearly every aspect of public and private life was transformed between 1760 and 1860. Isaiah Berlin (1909-1997), historian of ideas, called Romanticism "the greatest single shift in the consciousness of the West."[58] The movement was understood mainly from its poetry, literature, music, and art. Romanticists were fascinated with exotic and remote cultures, including those of the Indians. They personalized religious beliefs and were critics of society. In art, they portrayed grand landscapes. Their generation witnessed a roaring acceleration of science and technology and a relentless drubbing by industrial urbanization of nature and the individual. Romanticists resisted this.

Supporters of the Enlightenment affirmed that reason could regulate and explain the world, even perfectly govern human society. But reason alone could also lead to totalitarian ideologies as it did in the American West. The Enlightenment vision was of a static world, while the Romantic vision was of a dynamic one, beyond formulaic understanding. Romanticism revealed that reason has limits while still paying tribute to it. Romanticists distrusted rational distinctions, instead embracing feeling over fact and dismantling assertions of truth. Society was a source of evil. Thus, Native Americans were tainted once they were introduced to the white man's world.

Romanticism rejected religion's intellectual component and also rationalism. It therefore complemented the emotions-based Second Great Awakening. Romanticism became widely popular in American politics, philosophy, and art. It appealed to a wide audience and saw an increase in female authors and readers. Art and literature proved to be an effective form of propaganda to sell the West as the new home, the new Israel, but just for white Americans.

Art mirrors philosophy. Neoclassicism coincided with the age of Enlightenment in eighteenth-century art. It was a revival of the styles of classic antiquity and began in 1760 as an opposition to the fashionable Baroque and Rococo styles. Rococo paintings emphasized excessive ornamentation, while Neoclassicism was based on the principles of simplicity and asymmetry as seen in the art of Rome and ancient Greece. As Neoclassicism faded, it was replaced by Romanticism where emotions were elicited by powerful visual images. Beautiful pieces of two- or three-dimensional art were gifts from a Christian God.

Early painters of the American West, such as portrait painter Charles Bird King (1785-1862), Indian gallery painter George Catlin, and Seth Eastman (1808-1887), romanticized the Indian's way of life before civilization ruined it. Catlin wrote, "Nature has nowhere presented more beautiful and lovely scenes, than those of the vast prairies of the West and of man and beast no nobler specimens than those who inhabit them—the Indian and the Buffalo—joint and all original tenants of the soil, and fugitives together from the approach of civilized man; they have fled to the Great Plains of the West, and there, under an equal doom, they have taken up their last abode, where their race will expire and their bones will bleach together."[59]

German-born American painter Albert Bierstadt (1830-1902) exemplified American Romanticism. A strong emphasis was placed on the individual imagination and emotion of the artist. This was summarized by German painter Caspar David Friedrich (1774-1840), who stated that "the artist's feeling is his law," and by poet William Wordsworth (1770-1850), who explained that poetry should be "the spontaneous overflow of powerful feelings."[60] Nature was king for Romanticists, especially the effects of nature upon the artist when he was alone and surrounded by it. Romantics did not trust the human world—a fact stressed by Rousseau. Only through nature could you become morally and mentally healthy. Conversely, Indians untainted in nature could be morally poisoned by contact with American civilization.

If one artist exemplified Romantic art it was British landscape painter Joseph Mallord William Turner (1775-1851), who was known as "the painter of light" and whose art was a preface to Impressionism. He was one of the most influential painters and arguably the greatest British painter of the nineteenth century. Influential art critic John Ruskin described him as the artist that "stirringly and truthfully measures the moods of nature."[61] Since light to Turner was God's spirit, he concentrated on the play of light on water and radiance in skies with ephemeral atmospheric effects. The concept of the sublime in Romantic landscape paintings—that sense of being overwhelmed by the immensity, beauty, and even threat of nature—was expressed in paintings by Turner and by such American artists as Bierstadt, Thomas Hill (1829-1908), and Thomas Moran (1837-1926).

The influence of American Romantic art on the American psyche cannot be overemphasized. The American West was grand and stunningly beautiful—a gift to Christians from God, there for the taking. It fueled Manifest

Destiny. How did the average Easterner learn about the West? Perhaps the most effective way was art. By mid-century, there were literally tens of thousands of prints of landscape paintings published by private publishers and the U.S. government. In addition, books and periodicals like *Harper's* used landscape illustrations lavishly. The finest representations of the prophetic frontier landscapes were those of the Hudson River School, whose most important paintings were completed between 1855 and 1875. One of the best-known paintings was *Mount Ktaadn* (1853) by Frederic Edwin Church (1826-1900), even though the setting was pure fantasy.[62]

Frederic Edwin Church was born in Hartford, Connecticut, and became a leading figure in the second generation of the Hudson River School of painters and one of the chief competitors of Albert Bierstadt. In the 1850s and 1860s, Church was one of America's most famous landscape painters. He was the only pupil of Thomas Cole (1801-1848), who was the founder of the Hudson River School. The Hudson River artists depicted landscapes with realistic, detailed, and often idealized portrayals of nature filled with Romanticism. The artists believed that American landscapes were the manifestation of God's work. They were inspired by J. M. W. Turner and the Düsseldorf School of Painting in Germany.[63]

Another noted artist of the Hudson School was Worthington Whittredge (1820-1910). Whittredge was born on a farm near Springfield, Ohio. In 1849, he studied at the Royal Academy in Düsseldorf, Germany, and spent five years there. His style evolved into the meticulous recording of naturalistic details. After painting Eastern landscapes, he headed west to the Rockies for new inspiration. Three trips to the West resulted in the production of some forty paintings. Along with Bierstadt, he is considered one of the painters of Luminism, an offshoot of the Hudson River School. Popular in the 1850s to 1870s, Luminism was characterized by the effects of light on landscapes, often through the use of an aerial perspective, while concealing brushstrokes. One of Whittredge's most noted paintings is his 1876 *On the Cache La Poudre River, Colorado*.[64]

Bierstadt, Hill, and Moran were part of what would be called the Rocky Mountain School of Landscape. Besides being master landscape artists, the three were also masters of self-promotion. By the mid-nineteenth century, there were few urban areas west of St. Louis, Missouri—the fourth-largest city in the United States. Easterners hungered for images of the discovered lands of the western plains and mountains.

Landscape painters were well positioned to satisfy that desire. Landscape photographers were not. While photography had been invented in 1839 by

Louis Daguerre (1787-1851), it had its limitations for many years. The ambrotype (1854) and tintype (1858) were created using silver salts on metal but produced only one copy. Glass plate negatives followed that could generate endless copies, but still the quality of the prints was limited by camera and film-development technology. Collotypes, mechanical prints, were popular by 1869. Collotype variations included the albertype, heliotype, and artotype. However, early on they were less bright, with decreased definition and tonal quality when compared to prints developed from glass negatives.[65]

In the 1860s and 1870s, landscape photography simply lacked visual impact. There was no "wow" factor. This left the landscape painters of the period with little competition, and they took full advantage. The land rush was on for Bierstadt, Hill, Moran, and others.

Born in Solingen, near Düsseldorf, Germany, Albert Bierstadt was the most famous and financially successful Western landscape painter of the second half of the nineteenth century. But by the time of his death in 1902, he was all but forgotten. His most productive years were from the 1860s until the end of the 1880s.

The Bierstadt family moved to New Bedford, Massachusetts, when Albert was two years old. In 1853, he returned to Düsseldorf to study at the Royal Academy. Eventually fame and fortune came Bierstadt's way after trips out West. *Base of the Rocky Mountains, Laramie Peak* (1860), *The Rocky Mountains, Lander's Peak* (1863), *Mount Hood, Oregon* (1865), *Looking Down Yosemite Valley, California* (1865), *Storm in the Rocky Mountains, Mt. Rosalie* (1866), *The Domes of the Yosemite* (1867), and *Among the Sierra Nevada Mountains, California* (1868), all massive in size, were perfect examples of Romanticism in painting, which the curious public could not get enough of. Bierstadt's large-scale scenery complemented with the effects of light made for great cinematic entertainment and profit for the artist. An expert marketer, Bierstadt promoted *The Rocky Mountains, Lander's Peak* with a single painting exhibition, pamphlet, engraving, and tour, copying the earlier success of Frederic Church. Americans were emboldened and inspired by these masterworks. Bierstadt's paintings sold for as much as $25,000.[66]

The other famed Rocky Mountain School artist was Thomas Moran (1837-1926), who succeeded Bierstadt as the preeminent landscape artist of the last several decades of the nineteenth century. Born in England in 1837, Moran was living in Philadelphia with his family by 1853. In 1871, Moran's big break came when he accompanied Dr. Ferdinand Hayden (1829-1887) on his U.S. Geographical and Geological Survey of the Territories to the Yellowstone region. Federally funded, with additional support from Jay Cooke (1821-1905), director of the Northern Pacific Railroad, and *Scribner's Monthly*, the Hayden Expedition spent over forty days documenting more than thirty sites. Moran's paintings, along with photographs by famed photographer William Henry Jackson (1843-1942), helped convince Congress in 1872 to establish Yellowstone National Park as the world's first national park. One of his masterworks in oil, *Grand Canyon of the Yellowstone* (1872), measured a massive seven by twelve feet and was purchased by the government that year for $10,000. It would not be his last trip to Yellowstone country.[67]

In 1873, Moran accompanied John Wesley Powell (1834-1902) on his trip to the Grand Canyon of the Colorado River. Again, Congress purchased a second, equally grand landscape painting titled *Chasm of the Colorado*. Two years later, Moran completed his third masterpiece, *Mountain of the Holy Cross*, a view of a famous Colorado peak with a cross of snow on its side. By 1876, Moran was rivaling Bierstadt as the major landscape artist in America.

Moran also faced a similar fate as his fellow artists. His *Shoshone Falls* (1900) was exhibited at the Pan-American Exposition in Buffalo, New York, but in 1901, art critic Charles Caffin spoke for many who stated that his preference was no longer for the grand and panoramic in nature. Moran never again attempted another painting on a grand scale after the harsh criticism. The times and the market had changed. When he died in Santa Barbara in August 1926 at age eighty-nine, Moran was fondly described in his obituaries as the "dean of American landscape painters" and "the father of National Parks."[68]

By the 1880s, the Indians had been relegated to reservations, and railroads were crisscrossing the West. The mystique of the West was diminishing. Those artists who invented the past, like Charles M. Russell (1864-1926), would soon garner high prices for their work. The Rocky Mountains, Yosemite, the canyonlands of the Southwest, and Yellowstone were becoming domesticated into tourist attractions that could be reached by rail. The heroic artist-explorer had been diminished to "an armchair traveler's convenience." Bierstadt was discarded to the art-historical trash pile.[69] The idea of the noble savage had faded, and Romanticism in art slowly started losing favor. Rejecting Romanticism, artists of the Realism movement portrayed real contemporary people and situations with truth. Well, at least truth as they saw it. With the West rapidly being developed, its allure and the mystique of the noble savage evaporated.

Romanticism in Literature

The idea of the noble savage was a product of the nineteenth century. Romantics felt nostalgia and pity toward the Vanishing Indian. A staple of American Romantic literature was the theme of life and death of the last living member of a tribe. The first to express this was poet Philip Freneau (1752-1832) in the 1780s.

In Europe, Romantic writers voiced keen disappointment in the dreary prospects available in the world of their day and longed for vanished times of romance and adventure. Leading Romantic authors included Jules Verne (1828-1905), William Morris (1834-1896), and Robert Louis Stevenson (1850-1894).

In the United States, the popularity of Romantic literature was undeniable. Washington Irving's (1783-1859) *The Legend of Sleepy Hollow* (1820) and *Rip van Winkle* (1819) were followed by James Fenimore Cooper's (1789-1851) *Leatherstocking Tales* (1823), which mythicized the noble savage. Both authors were inspired by the writings of Rousseau. A third writer of extraordinary talent, Edgar Allan Poe (1809-1849), with his somewhat pessimistic view of the world, contrasted the first two. Later, Henry Wadsworth Longfellow's (1807-1882) long poem *The Song of Hiawatha* (1855) set his Indian Prometheus in the picturesque forest before the coming of the white man's civilization.[70]

At the forefront of American Romanticism, Cooper established the Indian as a specific literary type around the world. Eleven of Cooper's numerous novels featured Indians. Like many of his contemporary authors, he had little personal contact with Native Americans, and thus confused languages, names, and customs. For romantic purposes, Indians at times were shown to be good and at other times shown to be bad. He admitted, "Few men exhibit greater diversity, or, if we may so express it, greater antithesis of character, than the native warrior of North America. In war, he is daring, boastful, cunning, ruthless, self-denying, and self devoted; in peace, just, generous, hospitable, revengeful, superstitious, modest, and commonly chaste. These are qualities, it is true, which do not distinguish all alike; but they are so far the predominant traits of these remarkable people as to be characteristic."[71]

The Last of the Mohicans (1826) by James Fenimore Cooper was a stellar example of Romantic literature bemoaning the loss of the Vanishing American. His doubts about the value of progress and the superiority of the civilized life harkened back to many European Romanticists who placed

Indians as the ideal. Cooper explored his misgivings in the *Leatherstocking Tales: The Pioneers* (1823), *The Prairie* (1827), *The Pathfinder* (1840), and *The Deerslayer* (1841). He used the American frontier for his setting. It was a romantic, unrealistic frontier where the hero, Natty Bumpo, embodied the courage, nobility, innocence, and naturalness supposedly characteristic of men who lived in the wilderness. His recurrent theme was that if the noble savage could avoid being tainted by the white man's world, he may have a chance to survive. In the nineteenth century, this was known as the "law of vices and virtues," and it colored every discussion on the Indian.[72] The law is well summarized by Brian Dippie: "By mixing with us . . . [the Indians] imbibe all our vices, without emulating our virtues—and our intercourse with them is decisively disadvantageous to them."[73] When Jefferson was queried about the reason the Indians were vanishing, he blamed, in part, alcohol abuse of "spirituous liquors, the small-pox, war, and an abridgment of territory to a people who lived principally on the spontaneous productions of nature."[74]

George Catlin viewed the Indian as very much poisoned by the onslaught of white civilization. Indians who had had contact with the white man were considered corrupted, while those devoid of contact were considered uncorrupted. It was the uncorrupted that he wanted to capture and paint for posterity so that a future America could know the first Americans. The untouched Indians he encountered on the frontier were not the "drunken, naked and beggared" ones who lived in civilization, he critiqued. "But amongst the wild Indians there are no beggars—no drunkards—and every man, from a beautiful natural precept, studies to keep his body and mind in such a healthy shape and condition as will at all times enable him to use his weapons and self defense."[75]

To complement his Indian paintings, which visually stressed their nobility, Catlin published letters and notes on the manners, customs, and conditions of the North American Indians. He added a tabular statement at the end of the publication—in the spirit of dualism—that compared how the Indians' vices—secondary traits—obtained from contact with the white man, and his virtues—original—which were inherent. A few examples of original/secondary traits he noted were social/taciturn, independent/dependent, sober/drunken, rich/poor, landholders/beggars, modest/diffident, handsome/ugly, and free/enslaved, to name a few. A number of characteristics did not change and were seen in both groups. They included hospitable, charitable, religious, worshipful, honorable, grateful, brave, revengeful, jealous, and cruel.[76]

Eventually, transcendentalist writers emerged as Romanticism slowly faded. Ralph Waldo Emerson (1803-1882) believed that the writer should look to the life of the common man, who was the finest product of this new nation. He should turn away from "the great, the remote, the romantic," and "sit at the feet of the familiar, the low. . . ."[77] In the 1850s, American writers took his advice.

With a country that was fracturing over slavery and to a lesser degree the final solution for the Indian problem out West, writers tackled philosophical questions like the nature of man and the source of the evil that they saw as a powerful force in the world. Some of America's greatest writing was produced in the novels of Nathaniel Hawthorne (1804-1864) e.g., *The Scarlet Letter* (1850) and Herman Melville (1819-1891) e.g., *Moby Dick* (1851); and the poetry of Walt Whitman (1819-1892) e.g., *Leaves of Grass* (1855).

Drawing his themes from nature and the common people, in his preface to *Leaves of Grass* Whitman expressed the humane, democratic idealism that was emphasized in his poetry, writing, "Love the earth and sun and the animals, despise riches, give alms to everyone that asks. . . . Hate tyrants, argue not concerning God, have patience and indulgence toward the people, take off your hat to nothing known or to any man or number of men."[78]

As Robert F. Berkhofer, Jr. wrote:

American nature was beautiful for its wildness, its great expanse, and its unspoiled picturesqueness, but it was equally or even more beautiful in the eyes of many Whites for what it promised to become—a land of farms and a treasure house of resources for exploitation. Regardless of whether the Indian was savage or noble, he would inevitably be replaced by White civilization and its benefits. The transition from wild, savage nature to a cultivated, domesticated garden in the American West was believed to be as certain as the westward movement of progress had been in European history.[79]

CHAPTER TWENTY

The Descent of Man: Scientific Racism

Science without religion is lame, religion without science is blind.
—ALBERT EINSTEIN, *SCIENCE AND RELIGION*

Once your mind is inhabited with a certain view of the world, you will tend to only consider instances proving you to be right. Paradoxically, the more information you have, the more justified you will feel in your views.
—NASSIM NICHOLAS TALEB, *THE BLACK SWAN*

Ota Benga, Child of Scientific Racism

Visitors to the monkey house were treated to the extraordinary sight of a four-foot, eleven-inch, brown-skinned young man displayed for their entertainment along with the chimpanzees, orangutans, and baboons. Sometimes as many as 500 spectators crowded around him to gawk. Adults laughed at him and children hooted as Ota Benga—somewhere between fifteen and twenty-three years old—wove mats and hammocks, shot his bow, and attended to his pet parrot. He was quite the sensation.

It's unsettling today to think that another human would be subjugated to such a demeaning situation. Did this injustice transpire some time prior to the Civil War in some backwater burg? Actually, it was at the pinnacle of scientific racism, whose theories had developed over the prior hundred years. The date was September 1906 at New York's Bronx Zoo, which was among the largest metropolitan zoos in the world and comprised 265 acres, boasting some 4,000 animals. Ten years earlier, the Boone and Crockett Club founded the New York Zoological Society—later the Wildlife Conservation Society—which, with the support of its secretary, Madison Grant (1865-1937), and others, developed the zoo. Grant would become one of the major supporters of eugenics.[1]

Ota Benga represented scientific proof of the semi-human nature of black Africans and Native Americans, and some hypothesized that he may have been the missing link between man and ape. Clergymen who thought the exhibit hostile to Christianity and a promotion of Darwinism soon protested to zoo officials. A *New York Times* editorial in an era of an American heart of darkness where scientific racism, colonial arrogance, and Barnum-like showmanship all met at the turn of the twentieth century defended the depiction of Benga as a lesser human:

> We do not quite understand all the emotion which others are expressing in the matter. . . . It is absurd to make moan over the imagined humiliation and degradation Benga is suffering. The pygmies . . . are very low in the human scale, and the suggestion that Benga should be in a school instead of the cage ignores the high probability that school would be a place . . . from which he could draw no advantage whatever. The idea that men are all much alike except as they have had or lacked opportunities for getting an education out of books is now far out of date.[2]

The little man who wound up in a cage for three weeks at the zoo was acquired in the Belgian Congo with the support of the National Geographic Society by a would-be anthropologist and failed missionary named Samuel P. Verner (1873-1943). Verner believed Ota Benga was an ideal candidate for an example of Darwin's *The Descent of Man* as an educational exhibit at the Louisiana Purchase/St. Louis World's Fair of 1904. It's ironic that the majority of buildings were constructed by black workers, and some blacks were involved with architectural design with no credit.[3]

After the Spanish-American war in 1898, the United States acquired new territories, including Guam, the Philippines, and Puerto Rico. The fair was the perfect showplace to prove scientific racism since imperialistic, white America was controlling ever greater lands where non-whites lived. Some of the territorial natives were coerced into coming to the fair and were placed in exhibitions showing their inferiority.

Taking up almost 1,270 acres, the fair, twice the size of the 1893 World's

Columbian Exposition in Chicago, emphasized the superiority of the white race and the success of American empire building. Huge exhibition halls lined a reflecting pool and were adorned with massive outdoor sculptures by America's leading sculptors. Works included *Destiny of the Red Man* by Adolph Weinman, *The Sioux Chief* by Cyrus Dallin, *The Buffalo Dance* by Solon Borglum, and *Cowboy on a Tear (Coming through the Rye)* by Frederic Remington. Over 19 million visitors flocked to the exposition from April 30, 1904, to its closing on December 1, 1904.[4]

In 1895, Verner traveled to the Congo as a missionary but soon became more consumed with acquisitions than conversions to Christianity. He collected everything from tribal masks and musical instruments to chimpanzees and, ultimately, Africans. Later, Verner boasted that he had saved Ota from being eaten by cannibals, but he may have just purchased him at a slave market similar to those where, even today, pygmies are victimized by neighboring peoples in the Congo and adjoining countries.

With possession of seven other young men and boys in addition to Benga, Verner headed to the World's Fair where they were featured—at the University of Man's display—in a kind of ethnographic slideshow that included Ainu from northern Japan, Filipino tribesmen, Zulus, Eskimos, and American Indians, including Apache warrior Geronimo (1829-1909), who had participated in the last and the longest of the Indian wars during the Apache outbreak preceding his surrender in 1886. Each display had a corresponding species classification on an information plaque that presented Darwinian theory in an interesting way that would be appealing and informative to schoolchildren.[5]

Franz Boas (1858-1942), a noted German American scholar, objected to the exhibition because he thought it degraded the subjects and was racist in its assumptions. But, as Pamela Newkirk writes in *Spectacle: The Astonishing Life of Ota Benga,* such "high-minded debates were for the academic elite. For the general public, the site of a barely clad, presumably primitive people assembled across the fairgrounds was evidence enough of Caucasian superiority. . . . The reality—that the delegation comprised captured African children—if considered at all, was understood merely as a means to a scientific end."[6]

The exhibition turned out to be one of the major attractions at the World's Fair. After the fair ended, Verner returned the Africans to the Congo except for Ota Benga, who decided to return to the United States to live. Ms. Newkirk speculated that he feared remaining in the Congo because of the brutality of its Belgian rulers who were killing natives at genocidal proportions.

Verner, a terrible businessman, was penniless and working as a ticket taker in the New York subway to make ends meet. He abandoned Ota at the Museum of Natural History. William T. Hornaday, who embraced scientific racism, jumped at the opportunity to have the African displayed at the Bronx Zoo. Madison Grant was thrilled with the acquisition and being an influential eugenicist, he believed displaying Ota would support his desire to cleanse America of inferior races. His writings on race would later be admired and placed in action by Adolf Hitler.

William Temple Hornaday (1854-1937), a close friend of Theodore Roosevelt, was one of the leading wildlife conservationists in the country. He was born in Indiana and in 1882 was named chief taxidermist at the National Museum in Washington, D.C. Later, he became the first superintendent of the National Zoological Park, now known as the Bronx Zoo.

In 1896, when the Boone and Crockett Club helped establish the New York Zoological Society, Hornaday was chosen as its first director. Limited to 100 members, the Boone and Crockett Club was established in 1887. At the founding dinner held at Theodore Roosevelt's home, distinguished members included Senator Henry Cabot Lodge, Francis Parkman, Owen Wister, Albert Bierstadt, George Bird Grinnell, and Hornaday.[7]

Unlike other zoos, Hornaday stressed natural habitats for animals rather than cages and focused on North American game animals. Shortly after Hornaday became chief taxidermist for the U.S. National Museum in Washington, D.C., he asked his friend Laton Alton Huffman (1854-1931), famed Miles City, Montana, pioneer photographer, to collect sagebrush and buffalograss to send to the museum for a bison display. Hornaday was deeply disturbed by the decimation of bison in the West. For Hornaday, the bison—not the Indian—was the symbol of the American West.[8] In 1905, he founded the American Bison Society, which placed rescued herds in several sites in the American West.[9]

Throughout the years, Hornaday made a number of trips to eastern Montana, where he spent part of his time hunting and exploring with Huffman. One of his trips proved significant when he returned to the National Museum with bits of fossilized bone from the badlands of Montana. In 1902, he encouraged Kansas-born paleontologist Barnum Brown (1873-1963) to travel to the Hell Creek region of eastern Montana, where Brown discovered one of the greatest deposits of fossil bones ever, and eventually excavated the bones of the first *Triceratops* and *Tyrannosaurus Rex* dinosaurs ever discovered. Brown reported one skull was so large that it barely went through the doors of a Northern Pacific boxcar in Miles City.[10]

Sadly, Hornaday had more sympathy for the animals of the American West than he had for non-white humans. After being placed in a cage, Benga was startled by the diversity of animals at the Bronx Zoo. He was right next to an orangutan named Dohong who pedaled around on a tricycle. Benga spent his days weaving straw and rope. To improve his socialization skills, Benga was encouraged to sleep with the chimpanzees. Hornaday wrote an article on him for the October 1906 edition of the Zoological Society *Bulletin* entitled "African Pygmy," which was followed by the article "The Collection of Lizards."[11]

On opening day, September 8, 1906, massive crowds gathered to see Hornaday's prize exhibit. Visitors were amused and frightened by Benga's teeth that were filed into the shape of arrowheads. By now, *The New York Times* had changed its position on such an exhibition. White children were laughing and taunting Benga in his cage, and the *Times* opined that it was not morally right to put an African on display in such a pseudo-scientific way.

Reverend Dr. R. S. MacArthur of Calvary Baptist Church organized a movement to free Benga. He charged that the African was little more than a prisoner in the zoo. Reverend James Gordon, superintendent of the Howard Colored Orphan Asylum in Brooklyn, complained, "Our race, we think, is depressed enough, without exhibiting one of us with apes. We think we are worthy of being considered human beings, with souls."[12] New York Mayor George B. McClellan, Jr. dismissed the objections and refused to meet with the irate clergymen. Hornaday appreciated his support and wrote to him, "When the history of the zoological park is written, this incident will form its most amusing passage." A reporter tracked down Verner, who defensively claimed that "the only restriction that is put on him is to prevent him from getting away from the keepers. That is done for his own safety."[13] Soon the powerful Hearst press mounted a publicity campaign against the exhibit and declared it to be in bad taste.

Hornaday was incredulous. Even though Benga was forced to pose with monkeys and touted as a cannibal—schoolchildren threw raw meat at him—Hornaday said in defense of the exhibit, "We are taking excellent care of the little fellow. He has one of the best rooms in the primate house." Another time he exclaimed, "I do not wish to offend my colored brothers' feelings or the feelings of anyone for that matter. I am giving of the exhibition purely as an ethnological exhibit. It is my duty to interest visitors to the park, and what I have done in exhibiting Benga is in pursuance of this. I am a believer in the Darwinian theory."[14]

On September 16, 1906, more than 40,000 visitors came to the monkey house to see Ota Benga. As a special treat for zoo goers, Benga, with a keeper by his side, was allowed to wander around the park. *The New York Times* reported, "They chased him about the grounds all day, howling, jeering and yelling. Some of them poked him in the ribs, others tripped him up, all laughed at him." Benga was heard saying, "Me no like America, me like St. Louis."[15]

The next day, with criticism mounting, Hornaday relented. "Enough!" he said. "Enough! I have had enough of Ota Benga, the African pygmy. Ring up the Brooklyn Howard Colored Orphan Asylum. Tell them that they can get busy tinkering with his intellect. I'm through with him here."[16]

Benga was sent to the rural campus on Long Island where he was taught math and a few hundred English words and was introduced to the New Testament. The asylum's sponsors intended for him to be trained in the ministry so that he could go back to Africa as a Christian missionary. This did not come to fruition. Like a dog, he was fed scraps in the kitchen away from the children's view. His chain-smoking was perceived as a bad influence on the other young people, and so in 1910, he was transferred to Lynchburg, Virginia, where he lived as the guest of a black seminary.

Similar to native children who attended off-reservation Indian schools, Benga had his name changed to Otto Bingo in hopes he would assimilate better into American society. At the seminary he worked in a tobacco factory and entertained the local boys with stories of elephant hunts and other memories of life in Africa. In March 1916, he committed suicide by shooting himself with a pistol through the heart. Most likely he was consumed with humiliation and homesickness. Upon hearing of Benga's death, an unsympathetic Hornaday wrote, "Evidently, he felt that he would rather die than work for a living."[17]

Verner submitted so-called scholarly articles for publication in order to raise money, and he lectured to American audiences in defense of Belgian rule in the Congo. He had little success in seeking commercial concessions for himself in Africa and was last heard of working in a U.S. government mailroom in the Panama Canal Zone.

Hornaday's good friend Theodore Roosevelt had called for Americans to live the strenuous life. Those who were weak or perceived as inferior were not well tolerated. As the early twentieth century unfolded, government-run eugenic offices opened all over the nation. In 1910, there was a eugenics record office founded by wealthy industrialists. The weak needed to be weeded out so that the nation could be filled with a superior race. This was the basis of a theory called social Darwinism and was the forerunner of Nazism. In the first thirty-five years of the twentieth century, thirty-two states adopted laws that allowed sterilization of defective humans. More than 60,000 Americans were sterilized in the early twentieth century because of epilepsy, stuttering, or being supposedly mentally inferior. Through Ota Benga's story, we cannot escape the painful insights into such human tragedies, including those of Native Americans, created by racism, colonialism, Manifest Destiny, and American exceptionalism.

Scientific Racism

Ethnocentric judgment, an evaluation of one people's qualities by another people, is as old as ancient times. As a social doctrine, racism was an invention of Europeans in modern times as they became colonial powers. It justified their actions. For racists, physical characteristics are an indicator of moral and mental qualities that allows grouping into either inferior or superior races. Over the years, racism has resembled a metastatic cancer. It doesn't return, it just becomes detectable again.

Scientific racism, manifested most dismally in exaggerated claims about the capacity of so-called science and medicine to explain—or explain away—human intelligence and nature, was perhaps the most serious intellectual disease of the nineteenth century. Its destructive force toward Native Americans was almost as devastating as smallpox. It involved some of the post-Renaissance's most profound thinkers, as well as an extraordinary cast of charismatic figures, not a few of them charlatans and rogues. They were all driven by ambition to confirm white supremacy, but attempts to do so rested heavily on false analogies and wishful thinking. Science without direction from a moral compass leads to tragic results.

Scientists are not limited by their imagination but by how good their measuring devices are. With their eyesight, measuring tape, large egos, and the need to be right, physicians, philosophers, clergy, naturalists, anthropologists, and anatomists presented their case for the white man being the superior animal on Earth. Men of many stripes constructed theories of intelligence that provided a rationale for their nostrums. The Negro was at the bottom of human development. Native Americans were just a step above.

It may seem quite odd today, but 200 years ago both religion and science took it for granted that life originated all the time. It is just one example of errors in reasoning. The spontaneous generation of life from nonliving matter was a commonplace view in keeping with natural philosophy going back through Aquinas to Augustine and Aristotle, who observed the emergence of maggots from spoiled meat and other forms of decaying organic matter. Augustine found the issue intriguing enough to wonder whether Noah could have saved himself a lot of bother gathering pairs of every species to survive the flood, since animals can be born, without the union of sex, from inanimate things.[18]

Scientific racism became popular in the mid-nineteenth century and remained so for the next hundred years. It was based on the simplistic idea that different physical attributes determined the superiority or inferiority of a race. Some of the physical attributes that aided in the evaluation of humans included skin color, interior cranial size, skull shape, and facial features, among others. Thus, different races had different IQs. This pseudoscience was debunked after the Holocaust in World War II.

Scientific racism had its roots in ancient times. In the fifth century BCE, Hippocrates wrote *Airs, Waters, Places* in which he declared that dark people were cowards and white people were courageous fighters.[19] During the Age of Enlightenment, many debated monogenism, which contended that all races have a single origin, versus polygenism. Polygenism claimed each race had separate origins; this notion gained popularity among secular, racist groups. Monogenism was accepted by Jews, Christians, and most Muslims.

Scientific polygenism became increasingly accepted during colonial expansion by European countries in the late 1600s and early 1700s as explorers in the New World encountered different races. In the Age of Enlightenment, elite thinkers devalued the Bible and found biblical monogenism ridiculous. One of the era's great thinkers, Voltaire, believed that each race had separate origins, as he laid out in his *Essay on the Manner and Spirit of Nations and on the Principal Occurrences in History* in 1756:

> It is a serious question among them whether the Africans are descended from monkeys or whether the monkeys come from them. Our wise men have said that man was created in the image of God. Now here is a lovely image of the Divine Maker: a flat and black nose with little or hardly any intelligence. A time will doubtless come when these animals will know how to cultivate the land well, beautify their houses and gardens, and know the paths of the stars: one needs time for everything. . . .[20]

> The Negro race as a species of men differ from ours as the breed of spaniels is from that of greyhounds. The mucous membrane, or

network, which nature has spread between the muscles in the skin, is white in us and black or copper colored in them.[21]

John Mitchell (1711-1768) was an American physician and botanist who was well known for his eighteenth-century map of eastern North America. Born in Virginia, Mitchell in 1744 published through the Royal Society in London an influential paper, *An Essay upon the Causes of the Different Colours of People in Different Climates.* In it, he made the startling claim that the first race on earth had been a brown or reddish color. He opined "that an intermediate tawny color found amongst Asiatics and Native Amerindians" was the "original complexion of mankind," and thus other races obtained their skin color by living in different climates."[22] John Hunter (1728-1793), a Scottish surgeon, believed the sun turned humans black. He had observed that a burn would turn black skin white and concluded that Negroes were originally white.[23] His conclusions were incorrect. The white skin that occurs after a burn is due to an inflammatory reaction named post-inflammatory hypopigmentation.

Thus, variations among races could be explained by natural causes. Indians were molded by their social and physical environment. This theory pleased the monogenetic supporters, Jeffersonians and Christians. After all, all men were created equal. Jefferson's friend, Philadelphia doctor Benjamin Rush, summarized the environmentalism theory: "Human nature is the same in all Ages and Countries; and all differences we perceive in its character and respect to Virtue and Vice, Knowledge and Ignorance, may be accounted for from Climate, Country, Degrees of Civilization, from Government, or other accidental causes."[24]

Rush also believed black skin was a hereditary skin disease, which he called negroidism, and it could be cured. Blacks and Indians, to his thinking, were really white but were burdened with a form of non-contagious leprosy that darkened the skin. In a sympathetic tone, Rush stated, "Whites should not tyrannize over blacks, for their disease should entitle them to a double portion of humanity." But then he added, "However, by the same token, whites should not intermarry with them, for this would tend to infect posterity with the 'disorder'. . . . Attempts must be made to cure the disease."[25] He was also incorrect.

Time and time again polygenists emphasized the beauty of the white race and the ugliness of the black race. In Germany, Christoph Meiners (1747-1810), a philosopher and historian, segregated humans into two divisions: the beautiful white race and the ugly black race. Ugly races were seen as immoral and animal-like. With little knowledge of Native Americans, he concluded that they were of inferior stock because of their skin color. Thus, they couldn't adapt to different climates or accept different lifestyles, and when they had a life change, it brought on melancholy. He concluded that, like animals, Indians could live off any type of food and couldn't control their consumption of alcohol. He bought into the myth that was perpetuated by the Spaniards that the Indian's skin was so thick that a sword blade would shatter on contact, and the red man's skull was thicker than an ox.[26]

The fixation on skin color continued with claims made by Samuel Stanhope Smith (1751-1819), a Presbyterian minister and the seventh president (from 1795 to 1812) of the College of New Jersey, now Princeton University. During his presidency, his second edition of *Essay on the Causes of Complexion and Figure in the Human Species* (1810) opposed racism. He suggested that the difference in races were mainly environmental and that outdoor field slaves were darker pigmented than indoor domestic slaves in the South because they weren't exposed to the higher culture of their white owners. This ridiculous conclusion implied that if the slaves were around white culture long enough, their skin would turn white. More likely, white owners were impregnating their slaves, which led to lighter-skinned offspring, or sun exposure just darkened the skin. The confident Smith concluded that black skin was nothing more than a huge freckle that covered the entire body by an oversupply of bile induced by living in tropical climates.[27] The baseless claims were endless. His career at Princeton was controversial, and when he resigned, he stated, "If reason and charity cannot promote the cause of truth and piety, I cannot see how it should ever flourish under the withering fires of wrath and strife."[28] Truth, like beauty, is in the eyes of the beholder.

Polygenism gained further credence during the nineteenth century under the influence of Georges Cuvier (1769-1832), a French naturalist and proponent of scientific racism. Christians rationalized seizing lands from natives because it was God's will, while science articulated the need for civilized races to subdue barbarians so that they someday could be civilized. Cuvier divided the races into Caucasian, Mongolian, and Ethiopian. Adam and Eve were white Caucasians who were the original race, while Mongolians and Ethiopians appeared approximately 5,000 years ago after a major catastrophe.[29] Of course the whites were assigned to be the most physically beautiful and intellectually advanced race.

During the British "Imperial Century" from 1815 to 1914, more than 400 million people and 10 million square miles of land were added to the

British Empire. Formal control over its colonies, many inhabited by people of color, was more easily justified with the support of scientific racism.[30]

In the first half of the nineteenth century, Scottish anatomist Robert Knox (1791-1862) relied on his skull studies to argue, in *The Races of Men* (1850), that the different races were actually different species. His colleague James Hunt (1833-1869) in Britain championed white supremacy in *On the Negro's Place in Nature* (1863).[31] Scottish physician John Crawfurd's (1783-1868) notion that different races had been created separately by God for different climate zones became widely accepted.[32]

In the United States, Charles Caldwell (1772-1853)—best known for founding the University of Louisville School of Medicine—argued that there were four different human species created separately by God: Caucasian, Mongolian, American Indian, and African.[33] Natural scientist Samuel George Morton, Egyptologist George Gliddon, surgeon Josiah Clark Nott, and paleontologist/geologist Louis Agassiz all were credited for bringing polygenism into mainstream scientific acceptance.

Samuel George Morton (1799-1851) was a physician born in Philadelphia, brought up as a Quaker, and later a practicing Episcopalian. He published a number of books from 1823 to 1851, but he is best known as the father of the American school of ethnography that claimed that each race of humans was a separate species. Even though he was an Episcopalian, he argued against the creation story of the Bible. Instead, he claimed that the Bible supported polygenism.[34] After studying mummies in Egypt, Morton claimed that intellect of each race was determined by skull size—larger brain, larger intellect. With one of the largest collections of skulls in the world, he published his findings in three volumes between 1839 and 1849. *Crania Americana; or, a Comparative View of the Skulls of Various Aboriginal Nations of North and South America* (1839) presented evidence that Caucasians were the superior species while Negroes were the most inferior. Indians' brains were in the middle between Caucasians and Negroes. A wise God had placed each separate species in his own homeland. Indians were described as "averse to cultivation, and slow in acquiring knowledge; restless, revengeful, and fond of war, and wholly destitute of maritime adventure."[35] Oliver Wendell Holmes praised Morton for "the severe and cautious character" of his studies that "from their very nature are permanent data for all future students of ethnology."[36]

In 1867, the U.S. surgeon general urged medical officers to collect crania from dead Indians out West when they were collecting specimens of Indian weapons, clothing, and medicines. Other collectors gathered bones from graveyards, battlefields, and hospitals that filled "bone rooms" in major natural history museums around the country. The Smithsonian alone by 1898 had more than 450,000 bone specimens. Two-thirds of the bones collected were those of Native Americans. Ales Hrdlicka (1869-1943), the first Smithsonian curator of physical anthropology, oversaw the collection and eagerly collected brains and skeletons of deceased Native Americans who had taken part in the living ethnographic displays at the St. Louis World's Fair in 1904. His subsequent guidebook demonstrated how he categorized specimens: whites and other civilized people, primitive peoples like Indians, and extinct peoples and early man.[37]

Franz Boas (1858-1942) pioneered modern anthropology and would be called the "Father of American Anthropology." As a professor at Columbia, he was a staunch opponent of scientific racism and demonstrated in publications that cranial size and shape were significantly dependent on health and nutrition. He further debunked scientific racism by showing that human behavior is reliant on cultural differences and not genetics. Thus, there was no process of stages to a higher culture.[38]

Nott and Gliddon—inspired by Morton, who had died three years earlier—published the major ethnological landmark work of the period titled *Types of Mankind; or, Ethnological Researchers* (1854). Josiah Clark Nott (1804-1873) was a medical doctor born in South Carolina who owned nine slaves and stated that "the negro achieves his greatest perfection, physical and moral, and also greatest longevity, in a state of slavery."[39] George Gliddon (1809-1857) was an English-born American whose chief work was *Ancient Egypt* (1850) and was deeply influenced by Morton's craniometry. Morton had sent Gliddon over 100 Egyptian crania specimens.

Nott confidently wrote that each human race was an independent creation—polygenism—and was anchored to a certain locale. This explained why the Indians were so resistant to moving. With this explanation by well-respected scientific authorities, the forced removal of the Indians to different lands, even though they resisted, was deemed acceptable because Indians were not smart enough or civilized enough to know where they should belong.

In the section of his book titled "Comparative Anatomy of Races," Nott wrote:

> Intelligence, activity, ambition, progression, high anatomical development characterized some races; stupidity, indolence, immobility, savagism, low anatomical development characterize others. Lofty

civilization, in all cases, has been achieved solely by the "Caucasian" group. Mongolian races, save in the Chinese family, in no instance have reached beyond the degree of semi-civilization; while the Black races of Africa and Oceanica no less than the *Barbarous* tribes of America have remained in outer darkness for thousands of years. . . .

Furthermore, certain savage types can neither be civilized or domesticated. The *Barbarous* races of America (excluding the Toltecs) although nearly as low an intellect as the Negro races, are essentially untamable. Not merely have all attempts to civilize them faded, but also every endeavor to enslave them. Our Indian tribes submit to extermination, rather than wear the yoke under which our Negro slaves fatten and multiply.

It has been falsely asserted, that the Choctaw and Cherokee Indians have made great progress in civilization. I assert positively, after the most ample investigation of the facts, that the pure-blooded Indians are everywhere unchanged in their habits. Many white persons, settling among the above tribes, have intermarried with them; and all such trumpeted progress exists among these whites in their mix breeds alone. The pure-blooded savage still skulks untamed through the forest, or gallops athwart the Prairie. Can any one call the name of a single pure Indian of the *Barbarous* tribes who—except in death like a wildcat—has done anything worthy of remembrance?[40]

In a dim view of the future of Indians, Nott wrote, "It is as clear as the sun at noon-day, the last of these Red men will be numbered with the dead. To one who has lived among American Indians, it is in vain to talk of civilizing them. You might as well attempt to change the nature of the buffalo."[41] So influential was his publication that polygenism inspired a school of thought called "pluralists," which by the time of the Civil War was generally accepted throughout America.[42] Advancing social evolution was closely associated with mental capacity, and mental capacity was determined by cranial size.

The Harvard elite supported and agreed with Nott's conclusions. Shortly after Custer was killed at the Little Bighorn in 1876, Theodore Roosevelt entered Harvard, where he would mingle among brilliant but racist Americans. Oliver Wendell Holmes, Sr. taught at Harvard until 1882. Holmes was born in Cambridge, Massachusetts, in 1809. His father was a minister of the first Congregational Church in Boston. Trained as a physician, Holmes very much endorsed Manifest Destiny and racism. He wrote that God had created the Indian, "this sketch in red crayons of a rudimental manhood to keep the continent from being a blank until the true Lord of creation should come to claim it."[43] Logically then, the true Lord wanted his white children to have his land. Roosevelt as president would appoint Holmes' son, Oliver Wendell Holmes, Jr. (1841-1935) to the U.S. Supreme Court in 1902.

The famed historian Francis Parkman (1823-1893) was sometimes seen in the Harvard library working on Montcalm and Wolfe. Roosevelt would dedicate his *The Winning of the West* to Parkman. Parkman was born in Boston to Reverend Francis Parkman, Sr., who was a minister of the Unitarian New North Church in Boston. Junior enrolled at Harvard at age sixteen and before graduation traveled to Europe for eight months on a grand tour. Parkman is best known as the author of *The Oregon Trail: Sketches of Prairie and Rocky-Mountain Life* (1849). Only twenty-three, in 1846 he traveled the Oregon Trail, collecting experiences for his book. The most important part of the book was the three weeks he spent hunting bison with a band of Oglala Sioux. He had a dim view of the Indians after his time with them, as noted by Brian Dippie. "He spent six months on the Oregon Trail," Dippie writes, "one with the camp of Oglala Sioux, and concluded that the Indian was a 'thorough' savage ruled by uncontrollable passions, especially vengeance; a braggart and liar; a stoic; a man of limited mental range; childlike and capricious; yet, withal, beautiful in physique and possessed of a martial ardor that saved him from 'lethargy and utter abasement.'"[44]

Parkman definitely did not espouse the noble savage image that earlier James Fenimore Cooper had made famous. After his adventures out West, he wrote, "For the most part, civilized white man can discover very few points of sympathy between his own nature and that of an Indian. With every disposition to do justice to their good qualities, he must be conscious that an impassable gulf lies between him and his red brethren. Nay, so alien to himself do they appear, that having breathed for a few months the magic air of this region, he begins to look upon them as a troublesome and dangerous species of wild beast, and if expedient, he could shoot them with as little compunction as they themselves would experience after performing the same office upon him."[45]

Through his writing, polygenic racist Parkman fused scientific racism with literature in the post–Civil War era. The same year that Parkman traveled the Oregon Trail, *DeBow's Review,* a regional monthly periodical with wide circulation in the South, was first published. Early on, its first editor, James D. B. DeBow (1820-1867), wrote the majority of the articles.

When it was first published in New Orleans as the *Commercial Review of the South and West* prior to the Civil War, it had many attributes of a *Farmer's Almanac*. It defended slavery and, in the 1850s, urged the South to resume the African slave trade because slavery gave the Negro hope, but for the Indian with advancing civilization there was none. "It is otherwise with the Negro than with the Indian," the magazine stated in 1854. "The former, in the state of slavery for which he is created, under the favoring care of the superior race, cannot be civilized or made a white man by any length of culture, but his condition can be ameliorated, and he indirectly enjoy the benefits of civilization. But the stern, proud Indian cannot be enslaved. The type of the savage beasts among whom he lives, like them he will disappear before the new tide of human life now rolling from the East, and with the buffalo, will have vanished the red man of America."[46]

Alexis de Tocqueville had a similar view and wrote, "The servility of one dooms him to slavery, the pride of the other to death."[47] Black abolitionists Frederick Douglass and Henry Highland Garnet moved to distance themselves from the idea of an adaptable Indian. Douglass (1818-1895), a prominent social reformer, orator, and statesman, was born a slave in Maryland but escaped to the North and eventually became a preacher in 1839. Six years later, he published his famous autobiography *Narrative of the Life of Frederick Douglass, an American Slave*. Many whites questioned his authorship since they believed a black man could not write such a brilliant book. He was an accomplished orator and in 1854 spoke to Western Reserve College about how the Negro easily adapted to any country and climate that he lived in. "Their tenacity of life, their powers of endurance, their malleable toughness, would almost imply a special interposition on their behalf. The 10,000 horrors of slavery, striking hard upon the sensitive soul, have bruised, and battered, and stung, but have not killed. The poor bondman lifts a smiling face above the surface of a sea of agonies, *hoping on, hoping ever*. His tawny brother, the Indian, dies under the flashing glance of the Anglo Saxon. *Not* so the Negro: civilization cannot kill him. He accepts it—becomes a part of it."[48]

Henry Highland Garnet (1815-1882) was also an abolitionist, minister, and orator, although not quite as famous as Douglass. He was also born a slave in Maryland, and in 1842 became the pastor of the Liberty Street Presbyterian Church in New York. In 1868, he was appointed president of Avery College in Pittsburgh, Pennsylvania. In an 1848 speech echoed later by Douglass, he stated, "The Red men of North America are retreating from the approach of the white man. They have fallen like trees on the ground in which they first took root, and on the soil which their foliage once shaded. But the Colored race, although they have been transplanted in a foreign land, have clung to and grown with their oppressors, as the wild ivy entwines around the trees of the forest, nor can they be torn thence."[49]

However, not all clergy viewed that the future of the Indian was extinction, and one proclaimed in an optimistic tone, saying, "Savages of America are capable of civilization, as the savages of Africa." One pastor saw all races in America someday becoming one big happy family, optimistically intoning, "It has pleased Almighty God to bring the shores of America and to bestow upon us as a free gift, the passion of the French, the logic of the Teuton, the Scotsman's perseverance, the fiery eloquence and sturdy sinews of the Irishman, Englishman's great head in purse, the Negro cheerfully toiling under the torrid sun, the patient industry of the Chinese, the Spaniard's gravity, and the indomitable spirit of the Indian warrior—the excellencies of all the families of the earth combined in our American nationality."[50]

This sentiment in the 1870s was a harbinger of a change in American policy toward the Indians. The forced relocation of Indians in the West away from major urban populations in the East that had dominated American policy since the 1820s would eventually change. In 1887, with most of the conflicts in the West over, American policy moved to assimilation. Increasingly, there was the notion that the Indians could be educated and assimilated in American society. The mind was not fully formed at birth but a tabula rasa written on by experience and reflections upon experience. There was hope for the heathen savage. That did not mean, however, that racism was waning.

Just at the time the Bible was under assault from European intellectuals, Charles Darwin published the *Origin of Species* in 1859. In America, even though most citizens were engaged with the Civil War, the publication roiled the faithful. Many believers reconciled their faith with Darwin's ideas about evolution by holding that, at some point in the making of the human species, God invested his creatures with a soul.

Darwin, a pioneering geologist as well as the greatest of all biologists, in his *Origin of Species* and other writings, would inspire in the 1870s the idea of social Darwinism—a modern name—that argued that the strong should see their wealth and power increase, while the weak should see their wealth and power decrease. Of course, this gave further support to white Americans that the American West belonged to them. No scientist in the history of Western civilization had a greater impact on how different races viewed each other. While Newton and Einstein are often mentioned as the greatest scientists of all time, their contributions were difficult for the general population to understand and grasp their relevance. That's not the case for Darwin. Fundamentalist Christians were irate with him for destroying the creation story of Adam and Eve, while he became the symbol of the power of scientific racism that is still felt today.

CHAPTER TWENTY-ONE

Survival of the Fittest: Charles Darwin Explains Evolution

The Chase is among the best of all national pastimes. It cultivates that vigorous manliness for the lack of which in a nation, as in an individual, the possession of no other qualities can possibly atone.
—THEODORE ROOSEVELT, THE WILDERNESS HUNTER (1893)

The race is not to the swift or the battle to the strong, nor does food come to the wise or wealth to the brilliant or favor to the learned; but time and chance happen to them all. Moreover, no man knows when his hour will come: As fish are caught in a cruel net, or birds are taken in a snare, so men are trapped by evil times that fall unexpectedly upon them.
—ECCLESIASTES 9:11-12

In 1831, because space was tight on the ship *Beagle*, Charles Darwin (1809-1882), as he was packing his bags, asked the captain if he could take the Bible, Milton, and Alexander von Humboldt's (1769-1859) *Personal Narrative* (1815), the seven-volume account of Humboldt's travels in Latin America thirty years earlier. The publication made him known everywhere. Humboldt's epic publication was like the Bible to Darwin, and he was pleased when the captain gave a positive nod. The book inspired Darwin to volunteer for the voyage, and Humboldt's words governed everything he saw. "I am at present fit only to read Humboldt," Darwin wrote from Brazil. "He like another Sun illumines everything I behold."[1]

Darwin wasn't the only one mesmerized by Humboldt's achievements.

He was a godlike inspiration to Thomas Jefferson, Henry David Thoreau, John Muir, Frederic Edwin Church, John Charles Fremont, John James Audubon, Sir Charles Lyell, and Louis Agassiz. In 1803, after plunging through colonial archives and examining ancient civilizations, native tribes, and rich forests that the Spanish had demolished in their greed for gold and timber, Humboldt had a greater appreciation for the tragedy of imperialism. He would be called the second Columbus.

Humboldt was born in Berlin to a wealthy Prussian family. Right before his thirtieth birthday, he started on a five-year exploration of Latin America that not only changed his life but made him a legend. During his trip, he formulated the revolutionary idea that the natural world was a web of life. He urged other scientists and artists to follow his path and leave their desks to explore nature.

Humboldt next traveled to Washington, D.C., where he was excited to meet President Thomas Jefferson, who was one of his heroes. The delight was mutual, as Jefferson not only shared his scientific and botanical interests, but also pumped Humboldt for information on Latin America. A brief trip to Monticello followed, where a lifelong friendship began.[2]

After returning to Europe in 1804, Humboldt enthusiastically experimented, lectured, and wrote dozens of books. Many were translated into other languages and became international best sellers. He became the most famous scientist of his age.

Humboldt's final work was *Cosmos,* in which he discussed all he knew about art, nature, history, and all branches of science. Starting in 1845, the first of five volumes was published when Humboldt was seventy-six years old. His readers were taken on a fantastic journey from far-off nebulae to the center of the Earth. Along the way, the polymath covered geography and poetry, the migration of the human races, and the magic of the aurora borealis. The second volume immersed its readers in a discussion of the mind, human history, Hindu philosophy, medieval understanding of nature, Hebrew text, voyages of discovery, and landscape paintings.

The young Romantic landscape artist, American Frederic Edwin Church, was greatly influenced and inspired by the second volume, which stressed the importance of landscape painting in bringing together nature, science, and imagination. Church first went to South America in 1853 for a seven-month stay and returned four years later. In April 1859, long lines formed outside his Manhattan studio waiting to see his famous *The Heart of the Andes,* a massive 5½-by-10-foot oil canvas. Church hoped that Humboldt could see his painting and wrote to him about it. The celebrated scientist never saw the painting. He died at age eighty-nine before the letter arrived. Church told a friend that hearing the news "touched me as if I had lost a friend."[3]

As an even greater sensation than his personal narrative, *Cosmos* had sold 80,000 copies by 1851 and excited an entire new generation about natural science. Emerson called him "one of those wonders of the world, like Aristotle . . . who appear from time to time, as if to show us the possibilities of the human mind."[4]

In 1859, the year Humboldt died, Charles Darwin published his great scientific treatise *On the Origin of Species by Means of Natural Selection, or the Preservation of Favoured Races in the Struggle for Life.* He put forth the epic idea that evolution was by natural selection. At the time of a revised 1869 edition, economist Herbert Spencer coined the term *survival of the fittest,* which eleven-year-old Theodore Roosevelt embraced the rest of his life. Darwin was his hero, and he inspired young Roosevelt to become an amateur ornithologist. It was appealing to the future president that man had evolved from apes.

Three years before the publication of *On the Origin of Species,* a Neanderthal skull was discovered in Germany. British biologist Thomas Huxley went on a lecture circuit to present proof that man was a primate and a direct descendent of apes. Little did the famed scientist know that up to five percent of modern human DNA is from the Neanderthal. Soon he was the leading interpreter of Darwinism. Not long before he died, Roosevelt wrote about his childhood and stated, "Thank heaven I sat at the feet of Darwin and Huxley."[5]

Theodore Roosevelt was the West's president. He was a Rough Rider, a rancher in Dakota Territory, and a wilderness warrior for the conservation of hundreds of millions of acres of pristine land throughout the West.[6] As a disciple of Darwin, he very much promoted the idea of dominant world races over aboriginals. While he could call Indians in his *The Winning of the West* "cunning and stealthy" and "the tigers of the human race," he believed that by assimilating into the white culture they could improve their lot in life. However, he was a strong believer in social Darwinism, and it was up to the individual Indian tribes to survive. He had a low opinion of the Sioux, and in true Darwinian form he wrote, "We must turn them loose, hardening our hearts to the fact that many will sink, exactly as many will swim."[7]

Late in his last term in the White House, Roosevelt planned a grand hunting trip to Africa. It would generate the classic *African Game Trails,* illustrated by America's sporting and wildlife artist, Philip R. Goodwin.[8] Like Darwin who traveled with Humboldt's book on the *Beagle,* Roosevelt packed books for his adventure. Before he left for Africa in 1909, he wrapped Darwin's *On the Origin of Spec*ies and *Voyage of the Beagle* along with Huxley's essays in a waterproof cover to avoid damage on the forthcoming safaris. T. R. spent considerable time studying Darwin's teachings.[9]

On February 25, 1909, only two days before he created his federal bird reservations, Roosevelt wrote to James Joseph Walsh, a professor of physiological psychology who had dedicated his book *Catholic Churchmen in Science* to Roosevelt, "I think the trouble about Darwinism is that people confound it with evolution. I suspect that all scientific students now accept evolution, just as they accept the theory of gravitation, or the general astronomical scheme of the solar system and the stellar system as a whole; but natural selection, in the Darwinism sense, as a theory, evidently does not stand on the same basis. It must be tested, as the atomic system is tested, for instance."[10]

Charles Darwin's theories had a profound effect on how America viewed what they perceived as the lesser races. The white, colonial domination of so many lands where colored people lived was proof that they were the superior race. Darwinism linked whites and Indians closer in origin since they evolved from a similar source. However, this didn't bring any greater respect for them. Darwinism gave further support to scientific racism in a white world that demanded it. White America didn't have to rely on God and Manifest Destiny anymore to justify racism. They had science and medicine to affirm their superiority over Native Americans.

The Life of Darwin

February 12, 1809, is one of the most important dates in American history. That day, Abraham Lincoln was born in Hodgenville, Kentucky, and the Great Emancipator would go on to be considered by many as the greatest of all American presidents. Across the Atlantic in Shrewsbury, England, Charles Darwin, the fifth of six children, was born on the same date to a prominent wealthy financier and doctor, Robert Darwin, and his wife Susannah Darwin. His father's father, Erasmus Darwin, was a Deist and noted abolitionist.

A loner and sullen as a child, especially after the death of his mother when he was eight years old, Darwin could be seen taking walks alone and reading in his room. As a child, he was influenced by an unusual combination of the teachings of the Church of England and the Unitarian Church that was particularly popular in the industrial heartland, where men were proud to be self-made and independent thinkers. As previously noted, Unitarians rejected the miracles of Jesus and believed that the discovery of the truth about God and Jesus must come through independent study and reflection rather than church indoctrination. With his older brother Erasmus, Charles attended the nearby Anglican Shrewsbury Boarding School.[11]

In October 1825, Charles and Erasmus entered the University of Edinburgh medical school, which was considered one of the finest in the world. Many of America's most outstanding physicians had trained there. While in medical school, he and his brother visited a number of Edinburgh churches, and he enthusiastically wrote to his sister, "What part of the Bible do you like best? I like the Gospels. Do you know which of them is generally reckoned to be the best?"[12]

At Edinburgh, enrolled in a natural history course, Darwin was taught a conservative kind of geology by Robert Jamieson that the Earth had been formed first in water and then was shaped through a number of major catastrophes. In his second year of medical school, he joined a natural history group that debated orthodox religious concepts of science.[13]

But conflict with his anatomy teacher Robert Edmund Grant, along with other problems at medical school, prompted Darwin to drop out, and in 1829 he enrolled at Christ's College, Cambridge, to be educated as an Anglican parson. It was a move inspired more by Darwin's father than the young man's interest in religion. However, neither medicine nor religion was intellectually stimulating enough for him. He became passionate over insect collecting, which gained the admiration of the country's two greatest entomologists—the Reverend Frederick William Hope and James Francis Stephens. Identifying and studying insects in time also became boring, and he moved on to other interests.

By the time he finished Cambridge, he had become a Bible scholar, and in his 1879 *Autobiography* wrote, "Whilst on board the *Beagle* I was quite orthodox, and I remember being heartily laughed at by several of the officers (though themselves orthodox) for quoting the bible as an answerable authority on some point of morality. I suppose it was a novelty of the argument that amused them. But I had gradually come, by this time, to see the Old Testament from its manifestly false history of the world, with Tower of Babel, the rainbow as a sign, etc. etc., and from its attributing to God the feelings of a revengeful tyrant, was no more to be trusted than the sacred books of the Hindoos, or the beliefs of any barbarian."[14]

Darwin left Cambridge in June 1831, and several months later he was on the HMS *Beagle* with Captain Robert Fitzroy. The purpose of the expedition was to chart the coastline of South America.[15] His father objected to the multiyear voyage, stating that it was a waste of time. Darwin felt free to explore the world because he knew he was going to be a wealthy man from his mother's Wedgwood legacy, which he would receive when he was twenty-five, and he knew eventually he would also inherit his father's fortune, which in today's money was equal to a few million dollars.[16]

With Charles Lyell's (1797-1875) just published and revolutionary *Principles of Geology,* Darwin anxiously anticipated exploring rocks in the New World. Geology seemed to satisfy his enjoyment of collecting, identifying, and classifying material. Native Americans believed God was found in all plants, animals, and inanimate objects, even rocks. Darwin appreciated this connectivity and mystery. He understood that plants and animals were "bound together by complex relations." The great naturalist John Muir (1838-1914) concurred and said, "When we pick up one thing in the universe we find it hitched to everything else."[17]

Lyell's system championed the long-term evolution of the Earth's surface, which supported his direct observations of rock formations. He was the first to estimate that the Earth was over 300 million years old, and he coined the terms Pleistocene, Paleozoic, Mesozoic, and Cenozoic. The Pleistocene lasted from around 2.6 million years ago to about 11,700 years ago, when the last glaciation period waned. In the New World, the late Pleistocene saw large land mammals similar to those seen in Africa. After his presidency, Theodore Roosevelt headed a hunting expedition to Africa, imagining what the American West must have been like in ancient times. On his train ride from Nairobi in 1910, he viewed large exotic beasts and commented that it was a "railroad through the Pleistocene."[18]

Suffering from severe seasickness, an inspired Darwin still wrote voluminous notes on marine invertebrates and insects. Having read about the geology of the Earth was nothing like actually recording it in person. He traveled from the coastal plains of South America to the high Andes and the coral reefs of the Indian Ocean. New volcanic land on the Galapagos Islands awed the young scientist as he trekked over lava fields that poured into the ocean. It became clear in his mind that the Earth was much older than the biblical 6,000 years.

His around-the-world adventure ended when the *Beagle* reached Falmouth, Cornwall, on October 2, 1836. In less than two years, he was made secretary of the Geological Society of London, and he soon published his first scientific papers on geological topics. It was then that he started formulating, in secret, the possibility of the transmutation of species and soon the theory of natural selection. Before Darwin published *On the Origin of Species* in 1859, evolutionary ideas were known as transmutation. Basically, higher animals like mammals developed from a common ancestor. Fish, reptiles, and birds branched off along the way. In 1809 in France, Jean Baptiste Lamarck (1744-1829) presented his theory of *Transformisme* in *Philosophie Zoologique*. He did not believe in a common ancestor for animals but that different forms of life were created by spontaneous generation. He was wrong.

On January 29, 1839, Darwin married his cousin Emma Wedgwood, a devout Christian who insisted they attend church together. He became anxious, anticipating how Emma would accept his evolutionary theories. Over his lifetime, Darwin suffered from a number of nervous conditions that caused nausea, crying, ringing of the ears, exhaustion, and "dying sensations."[19] Some were brought on at the time from his rejection of creation in Genesis and of conventional Christianity. He related these doubts to his future wife over the objections of his father. He recalled, "Before I was engaged to be married, my father advised me to conceal carefully my doubts, for he said that he had known extreme misery thus caused with married persons. Things went on pretty well until the wife or husband became out of health, and then some women suffered miserably by doubting about the salvation of their husbands, thus making them likewise to suffer. My father added that he had known during his whole long life only three women who are skeptics."[20]

From the time of his marriage to the death of his father in 1848, Darwin's doubts transitioned to a complete rejection of all Christianity—he still believed in a god—and he stated, "I can indeed hardly see how anyone ought to wish Christianity to be true; for if so the plain language of the text seems to show that men who do not believe, and this would include my Father, Brother and almost all my friends, will be everlastingly punished. And this is a damnable doctrine."[21] His convictions were confirmed in 1851 when his ten-year-old daughter Annie died. "Thus disbelief crept over me at a very slow rate, but was at last complete. The rate was so slow that I felt no distress, and have never since doubted even for a single second that my conclusion was correct."[22]

For Darwin, creation theories were essentially "old think." His final theory was quite simple but logical. It was obvious that plants and animals differed. Breeders of plants and animals for generations had shown that many of the variations were heritable. Most animals and plants produced more offspring than they generally needed to replace themselves. That resulted in a huge waste. For example, a female fish might produce more than 1 million eggs in a season. Likewise, the subsequent oversupply of humans produced a struggle for existence in an unforgiving world. The end result was a selection of more favorable races. This evolutionary diversity resulted in natural selection over a long period of time.

Variations in a species were due to spontaneous mutations that were inheritable. Those who inherited the best variations survived and thrived, while those less fortunate eventually died off. It was "survival of the fittest." And of course, white Europeans were ruling the world because they were the fittest. Darwin summarized his ideas behind natural selection in his fourth chapter of *On the Origins of Species:*

> If during the long course of ages and under varying conditions of life, organic beings vary at all in the several parts of their organisation, and I think this cannot be disputed; if there be, owing to the high geometrical powers of increase of each species, at some age, season, or year, a severe struggle for life, and this certainly cannot be disputed; then, considering the infinite complexity of the relations of all organic beings to each other and to their conditions of existence, causing an infinite diversity in structure, constitution, and habits, to be advantageous to them, I think it would be a most extraordinary fact if no variation ever had occurred useful to each being's own welfare, in the same way as so many variations have occurred useful to man. But if variations useful to any organic being do occur, assuredly individuals thus characterised will have the best chance of being preserved in the struggle for life; and from the strong principle of inheritance they will tend to produce offspring similarly characterised. This principle of preservation, I have called, for the sake of brevity, Natural Selection.[23]

Fortunately for Darwin, by 1859, geologists had established a much older Earth in opposition to creation. This supported the process of natural selection over long periods of time. He described how he came to this position on the first page of *On the Origin of Species:*

> When on board H.M.S. *Beagle,* as naturalist, I was much struck with certain facts in the distribution of the inhabitants of South America, and in the geological relations of the present to the past inhabitants of that continent. These facts seem to me to throw some light

on the origins of species—that mystery of mysteries, as it has been called by one of our greatest philosophers. On my return home, it occurred to me, in 1837, that something might perhaps be made out on this question by patiently accumulating and reflecting on all sorts of facts which could possibly have any bearing on it. After five years' work I allowed myself to speculate on the subject, and drew up some short notes; these I enlarged in 1844 into a sketch of the conclusions, which then seemed to me probable: from that period to the present day I have steadily pursued the same object.[24]

In *Origin of Species* Darwin summarized the core ideas of several authors of books that he had read in the 1830s and 1840s.[25] Along with his publications, these powerful books altered the understandings of their age. At the time, new technologies—steamships, railways, and telegraphs—were altering the conception of the natural world in transforming the pace of life. These publications stressed that science was not inconsistent with religious faith, but rather an engine to further faith. Publications included *Consolations and Travel* (1830) by Humphry Davy, president of the Royal Society of London; *Preliminary Discourse on the Study of Natural Philosophy* (1831) by John Herschel, astronomer and co-inventor of photography; *On the Connection of the Physical Sciences* (1834) by Mary Somerville, who believed that the study of mathematics was the highest form of theology; *Reflections on the Decline of Science* (1830) by inventor and mathematician Charles Babbage; the three-volume *Principles of Geology* (1830-1833) by lawyer turned geologist Charles Lyell, who was sickened by the notion of transmutation or evolution of species; and *Constitution of Man* (1828), reissued in 1836, by George Combe, a self-educated legal clerk who popularized the theory of phrenology, which stated that the brain was the organ of thought and the shape of the skull a guide to a man's mental character. All of these authors were members of English society and attended the same parties, discussed science together, and reviewed one another's books.[26]

Along with Darwin—at least at the time the books were written—all of these authors believed that there was a connection between the sciences, that the Earth was older than previously believed from the Bible, that God created the world by uniform natural law, and that He built lawful changes into his original creation. These views aided Darwin into framing his theory of evolution by natural selection in a way his readers could accept. The presentation was so successful that within two decades after the publication of *Origin of Species,* most British scientists and most of the public accepted that species evolved. However, like all scientific theories it was not an absolute, final truth because theories are always subject to change. All theories are works in progress.

In *The Descent of Man,* published in 1871, Darwin made it clear that he wanted to debunk polygenism, writing, "If I have erred in giving to natural selection great power, which I am very far from admitting, or in having exaggerated its power, which is in itself probable, I have at least, as I hope, done good service in aiding to overthrow the dogma of separate creations."[27] The first reference to the Creator in *On the Origin of Species* made clear his beliefs:

> He who believes in separate and innumerable acts of creation will say, that in these cases it has pleased the Creator to cause a being of one type to take the place of one of another type; but this seems to me only restating the fact in dignified language. He who believes in the struggle for existence and the principle of natural selection, will acknowledge that every organic being is constantly endeavoring to increase in numbers; and that if any one being vary ever so little, either in habits or structure, and thus gain an advantage over some other inhabitant of the country, it will seize on the place of that inhabitant, however different it may be from its own place.[28]

In *The Descent of Man,* Darwin argued against the scientific racists who stated that whites, blacks, and Indians were different races and created separately, observing, "It may be doubted whether any character can be named, which is distinctive of the race and his constant. . . . [T]hey graduate into each other, and . . . it is hardly possible to discover clear, distinctive characters between them. . . . As it is improbable that the numerous, and unimportant, points of resemblance, between the several races of man, in bodily structure and mental faculties (I do not here refer to similar customs) should all have been independently acquired, they must have been inherited from progenitors who had the same characters."[29]

Because of survival of the fittest and natural selection, Darwin did see a time when civilized races would dominate. "At some future period," he wrote, "not very distant as measured by centuries, civilised races of man will almost certainly exterminate, and replace, the savage races throughout the world. At the same time the anthropomorphous apes, as Professor Schaaffhausen has remarked, will no doubt be exterminated. The break between man and his nearest allies will then be wider, for it will intervene between man in a more civilised state, as we may hope, even than the Caucasian, and some ape as low as a baboon, instead of as now between the negro or Australian and the guerrilla."[30]

The Church was concerned with many points of Darwin's new evolution theory in that it denied a role for the Creator in the diversification of life, and it required an Earth much older than 6,000 years. Darwin held his ground, however, and believed that even the whole idea of God and religion might have an evolutionary origin and character:

> There is no evidence that man was aboriginally endowed with the ennobling belief in the existence of an Omnipotent God. On the contrary there is ample evidence, derived not from hasty travelers, but from men who have long resided with savages, that numerous races have existed and still exist, who have no idea of one or more gods, and who have no words in their languages to express such an idea. The question is of course wholly distinct from that higher one, whether there exists a Creator and Ruler of the universe; and this has been answered in the affirmative by the highest intellects that have ever lived.
>
> If, however, we include under the term "religion" the belief in unseen or spiritual agencies, the case is wholly different; for this belief seems to be almost universal with the less civilized races. Nor is it difficult to comprehend how it arose. As soon as the important faculties of the imagination, wonder, and curiosity, together with some power of reasoning, had become partially developed, man would naturally have craved to understand what was passing around him, and have vaguely speculated on his own existence.
>
> The moral nature of man has reached the highest standard as yet attained, partly through the advancement of the reasoning powers and consequently of a just public opinion, but especially through the sympathies being rendered more tender and widely diffused through the effects of habit, example, instruction, and reflection. It is not improbable that virtuous tendencies may through long practice be inherited. With the more civilised races, the conviction of the existence of an all-seeing Deity has had a potent influence on the advancement of morality. Ultimately man no longer accepts the praise or blame of his fellows as his chief guide, though few escape this influence, but his habitual convictions controlled by reason afford him the safest rule. His conscience then becomes his supreme judge and monitor.

Nevertheless the first foundation or origin of the moral sense lies in the social instincts, including sympathy; and these instincts no doubt were primarily gained, as in the case of the lower animals, through natural selection.[31]

As we have seen and will see, Darwin's theory of natural selection was used by others in many situations for purposes quite different from those intended by Darwin for science itself. Shortly after its publication, *Origin of Species* was hotly debated at Oxford in 1860 and in the United States at meetings of the American Academy of the Arts and Sciences, the Boston Society of Natural History, and the Cambridge Scientific Club. Leading scientists in the debate were Asa Gray (1810-1888), professor of botany at Harvard University; William Barton Rogers (1804-1882), geologist and one of the founding professors of the Massachusetts Institute of Technology; and Jean Louis Rodolphe Agassiz (1807-1873), professor of zoology at Harvard. Agassiz was the heir to Humboldt's legacy as the world's greatest naturalist—a title that Darwin would soon own. Gray and Rogers hated Agassiz because he was hogging the limelight and was a blatant self-promoter of his beliefs.

Agassiz grew up in Switzerland and studied with Cuvier and Humboldt in Paris. In 1847, he immigrated to the United States and became a professor of zoology and geology at Harvard, a school of less than 400 students. He would head up the Lawrence Scientific School and found its Museum of Comparative Zoology. Over the years, he made important findings in zoology, geology, and glaciology. He was the first to scientifically present the concept that the Earth had experienced an ice age.[32]

Agassiz was a strong believer in creationist ideology. When Darwin's *Origin of Species* was published, he denounced the book and message as atheism even though he was not a churchgoer. In his "Essay on Classification" (1857), Agassiz wrote, "The combination in time and space of all these thoughtful conceptions exhibits not only thought, it shows also premeditation, power, wisdom, greatness, prescience, omniscience, Providence. In one word, all these facts in their natural connection proclaim aloud the One God, whom man may know, adore, and love; and Natural History must in good time become the analysis of the thoughts of the Creator of the Universe."[33] The essay was included in the first two quarto volumes published of his epic *Contributions of the Natural History of the United States*. Ten volumes were planned, but Agassiz completed only four. His goal was to "endeavor to make myself understood by all."[34] A Unitarian, Agassiz believed in an extremely conservative version. The European polygenic view of creation was that each plant and animal arose from discrete centers and then spread out geographically over time. His view was that each species stayed in the area where they were created and didn't spread far from that.

Early in his career, he believed that all humans were one species. His student Edward Sylvester Morse, who later was a committed Darwinian, wrote about Agassiz in his diary on April 26, 1860: "Splendid lecture by Prof this morning on the absurdity of believing that Adam and Eve were the first created and the only ones. It was a masterly lecture and was listened to with great attention."[35]

But that all changed when he moved to America where he saw Caucasian, Arctic, American Indian, and Negro people. Agassiz would write extensively on polygenism. He contended that there were a number of separate species of humans who were created on land in specific areas: Europeans in Europe, Africans in Africa, Australian aboriginals only in Australia, and Native Americans only in America. He believed the book of Genesis recounted the origin of the white race only, and the writers of the Bible knew of humans only in their particular area. They were unaware of other creations in distant lands. This was heralded by Southern slave owners and Indian haters as further proof of white superiority. Agassiz concluded that no species currently living had existed before the Pleistocene Age. Like his mentor Cuvier, he believed that all fossil species were from older creations and were not the ancestors of any present living plants or animals.

Cuvier and Agassiz believed in waves of spontaneous generation.[36] This "catastrophism" paradigm was seen as reflecting the creation and extinction of new species by an array of dramatic and unnatural dei ex machina. In contrast, uniformitarianism presumed that the world—organic and inorganic—proceeded via processes currently operating over a long period of time. This theory eventually won out because it provided enough time for evolution by natural selection from mutations to create the present plant and animal world.

Recently (at the time of this writing), catastrophism has been enjoying a comeback. Its supporters make the point that life didn't so much unfold smoothly over hundreds of millions of years as lurch chaotically in response to diverse crises and opportunities, such as too much oxygen, too little carbon dioxide, too little oxygen, too much carbon dioxide, too hot, too cold. Darwinists would contend that these catastrophic environments merely helped describe the conditions within which evolution by natural selection had proceeded, and evolution remains driven by the differential reproduction of certain genetic constituents over others.[37]

When Agassiz died in 1873, *Harper's Weekly* wrote that no death save that of Lincoln had elicited such heartfelt expressions of sorrow.[38] Yet the ideas of polygenism and catastrophism soon lost credibility, and Darwin became the greatest naturalist in the world. He had theorized, and paleontologists soon provided evidence, that man had descended from apes. Many in the Christian community found this unacceptable. After the Oxford debate in 1860, Frederick Temple, one of the authors of *Essays and Reviews*, delivered a sermon at the University Church of St. Mary encouraging compromise and conciliation. He preached that a man of science didn't need to be a nonbeliever, saying, "The student of science now feels himself bound by the interests of truth, and can admit no other obligation. And if he be a religious man, he believes that both books, the book of nature and the book of Revelation, alike come from God, and that he has no more right to refuse to accept what he finds in one than what he finds in the other."[39]

How times had changed. Before the Scientific Revolution, all scientists were clerics, and science was closely allied with magic and astronomers. As science developed, it espoused that certain knowledge is based on certain facts. This was in contrast to the facts of theology, which were based on spiritual faith. There is a certain irony that Charles Darwin was buried in Westminster Abbey not far from Isaac Newton. But this Gothic structure was more than a famous religious building. It has been the place of coronation and the burial site for famous Englishmen for centuries.

Darwin's Legacy

To understand white attitudes toward Native Americans in the second half of the nineteenth century is to understand Darwinism and scientific racism. Theodore Roosevelt's views toward the West were a combination of his lifelong support for Darwinism and Manifest Destiny. Roosevelt, more than any other, is the president we associate with the West in this period. He lived for a time in North Dakota where he ranched and hunted. Later, as president he would set aside several hundred million acres in the West to be enjoyed by the public. To know Roosevelt's mind is to understand America's attitudes toward Native Americans.[40]

Six years after Roosevelt died, Charles Scribner's Sons in 1926 published *The National Edition of Roosevelt's Works* in a twenty-volume set. Volumes eight and nine reproduced *The Winning of the West*, an account of the exploration and settlement of our country from the Alleghenies to the Pacific. Drawing from his experiences in Dakota Territory from 1883 to 1886, Roosevelt dedicated the book to Francis Parkman, "To whom Americans who feel a pride in the Pioneer history of their country are so greatly indebted." The publication was well received by the American public when it was first published in a two-volume set in 1889. In 1894, a third volume was completed and followed by a fourth volume in 1896. They were issued and reissued under the general title of *The Winning of the West*, as either a six-volume set or a three-volume set, all with the same text.

Albert Bushnell Hart (1854-1943), the historian, writer, and teacher known by some as the "Father of American history," wrote an introduction in the 1926 edition titled "Roosevelt as Pioneer." Hart was a classmate and friend of Theodore Roosevelt's at Harvard and in 1883 was hired by Harvard to teach its only course on American history. He retired the year that the edition was published. He spent a period of his life collecting written material by Roosevelt and would eventually be called the "Theodore Roosevelt Cyclopedia."[41] Hart's introduction revealed the perception of historians of the day on what transpired in the nineteenth century:

> Indian wars in the main arose from Indian lands, or rather from wild lands which were claimed both by Indians and by white settlers. Then and now, much baseless sympathy is gone out to the Indians as driven from their ancestral lands by the insatiable white man. Roosevelt says on that point: "There were a dozen tribes, all of whom hunted in Kentucky and fought each other there, all of whom had equally good titles to the soil, and not one of whom acknowledged the right of any other; as a matter of fact they had therein no right, save the right of the strongest.... The white settler ... does not feel that he is committing a wrong, for he knows that the land is really owned by no one." On the other hand, these lands from which the Indians drew much of their food and clothing; and large areas, such as the permanent villages of the Creeks and Cherokees, they had a kind of homestead title.
>
> If there is a text to *The Winning of the West*, it is that the coming in of the whites was not to be stayed by any force in America. They could not remain on the wild land except in opposition to the Indians; war and war to a finish was therefore inevitable. As Roosevelt puts it: "The conquest and settlement by the Whites on Indian lands was necessary to the greatness of the race and to the well-being of civilized mankind. It was as ultimately beneficial as it was inevitable ... all that can be asked is that they shall be judged as other wil-

derness conquerors, as other slayers and quellers of savage peoples are judged." To his careful account of the massacre of Moravian Indians at Gnadenhutten, he sternly adds that no Indian tribe could expect to exist, however harmless, if it forswore self-defense. It cannot be denied that the settlers in general had no interest in attempts to civilize and Christianize Indians. What they wanted was an Indianless Eden.[42]

For Hart, who idolized Roosevelt and was one of the most respected American historians, there was no shame or regret of advanced and civilized whites taking the lowly savages' land. America's actions were supported historically by the colonial aggression of France, England, and Spain, as he stated later in his introduction: "All this is not foreign to American history. The vast movement by which this continent was conquered and peopled cannot be rightly understood if considered solely by itself. It was the crowning and greatest achievement of a series of mighty movements, and it must be taken in connection with them. Its true significance will be lost unless we grasp, however roughly, the past race-history of the nations who took part therein."[43]

In chapter one of *The Winning of the West,* titled "The Spread of the English Speaking Peoples," Roosevelt addressed the controversy that still rages today—how numerous were the Indians before the white man arrived:

The Indians have shrunk back before advances only after fierce and dogged resistance. They were never numerous in the land, and exactly what their numbers were when the whites first appeared is impossible to tell. Probably an estimate of half a million for those within the limits of the present United States is not far wrong; but in any such calculation there is of necessity a large element of mere rough guesswork. Formerly writers greatly overestimated their original numbers, counting them by the millions. Now it is the fashion to go to the other extreme, and even to maintain they have not decreased at all. This last is a theory that can only be upheld on the supposition that the whole does not consist of the sum of the parts; for whereas we can check off on our fingers the tribes that have slightly increased, we can enumerate scores that have died out almost before our eyes. Speaking broadly, they have mixed but little with the English (as distinguished from the French and Spanish) invaders. They are driven back, or die out, or retire to their own reservations;

but they are not often assimilated. Still, on every frontier, there is always a certain amount of assimilation going on, much more than is commonly admitted. . . .

To this I can testify of my own knowledge as regards Montana, Dakota, and Minnesota. The mixture usually takes place in the ranks of the population where individuals lose all trace of their ancestry after two or three generations; so it is often honestly ignored, and sometimes mention of it is suppressed, the man regarding it as a taint. But I also know many very wealthy old frontiersmen whose half-breed children are now being educated, generally at convent schools, while in the Northwestern cities I could point out some very charming men and women, in the best society, with a strain of Indian blood in their veins.[44]

In terms of Manifest Destiny, Roosevelt later in *The Winning of the West* described in religious symbolism the spirit of the white settlers who led the strenuous life that he so much admired:

Of course, in each case there was also very considerable movement directly westward. They were a sturdy race, enterprising and intelligent, fond of the strong excitement inherent in the adventurous frontier life. Their untamed and turbulent passions and the lawless freedom of their lives made them a population very productive of wild, headstrong characters; yet, as a whole, they were a God-fearing race, as was but natural in those who sprang from the loins of the Irish Calvinists. Their preachers, all Presbyterians, followed close behind the first settlers, and shared their toil and dangers; they tilled their fields, rifle in hand, and fought the Indians valorously. They felt that they were dispossessing the Canaanites, and were thus working the Lord's will in preparing the land for a race which they believed was more truly His chosen people than was that nation which Joshua led across the Jordan. They exhorted no less earnestly in the bare meeting-houses on Sunday, because their hands were roughened with guiding the plow and wielding the axe on the week-days; for they did not believe that being called to preach the word of God absolved them from earning their living by the sweat of their brows. The women, the wives of the settlers, were of the same iron temper. They fearlessly fronted every danger that men did, and they worked quite as hard.[45]

Famed poet and novelist Hamlin Garland (1860-1940) also wrote an introduction to *The Winning the West,* titled "Roosevelt As Historian," that appeared in volume eight. Garland was born in Wisconsin and in 1922 won the Pulitzer Prize for the biography *A Daughter of the Middle Border.* Earlier, he had serialized a biography of Ulysses S. Grant in *McClure's* magazine before publishing it in book form in 1898.[46] As might be expected, Garland also was an avid admirer of Roosevelt, as demonstrated in the opening paragraphs of the introduction:

> In rereading Roosevelt's *The Winning of the West,* I am more deeply impressed than ever before with their literary quality as well as with the new material which they contain. He not only read widely and carefully in certain unpublished valuable records of the period which he set out to cover, but throughout this reading and consequently throughout his writing he remains remarkably fair-minded and convincing. . . .
>
> The special qualities which Roosevelt brings to the writing of these volumes are clarity of insight, sympathy, and a sense of fair dealing which he expresses nobly in his judgments of both red man and white. By reason of this Western experience of which he speaks, he was able to understand both the Iroquois and the pioneer, and to be just to all the participants in the long war which won and held the West.
>
> He is indeed almost repellently faithful in transmitting to the reader an understanding of the vengeful struggle which went on for more than one hundred years between the advance-guard of white settlement and the rear-guard of red barbarism, a struggle which was inevitable as it was far-reaching. He perceives it as a novelist might see it.[47]

Some may take exception today to Garland's statement about Roosevelt being fair-minded. In Roosevelt's chapter three of volume nine, Part Two, titled "The Indian Wars," his prose smacked of racism and social Darwinism:

> In these treaties we have been more than just to the Indians; we have been abundantly generous, for we have paid them many times what they were entitled to; many times what we would have paid any civilized people whose claims was as vague and shadowy as theirs. . . . No other conquering and colonizing nation has ever treated the original savage owners of the soil with such generosity as the United States.

Nor is the charge that the treaties with the Indians have been broken, of weight itself; it depends always on the individual case. Many of the treaties were by the whites and broken by the Indians; others were broken by the whites themselves; and sometimes those who broke them did very wrong indeed, and sometimes they did right. No treaties, whether between civilized nations or not, can ever be regarded as binding in perpetuity; with changing conditions, circumstances may arise which render it not only expedient, but imperative and honorable, to abrogate them.

Whether the whites own the land by treaty, by armed conquest, or, as was actually the case, by mixture of both, mattered comparatively little so long as the land was won. It was all-important that it should be won, for the benefit of civilization and in the interests of mankind. It is, indeed, a warped, perverse, and silly morality which would forbid a course of conquest that has turned whole continents into the seats of mighty and flourishing civilized nations. All men of sane and wholesome thought must dismiss with impatient contempt the plea that these continents should be reserved for the use of scattered savage tribes, whose life was but a few degrees less meaningless, squalid, and ferocious than that of the wild beasts with whom they held joint ownership. It is as idle to apply to savages the rules of international morality which obtain between stable and cultured communities, as it would be to judge the fifth century English conquest of Britain by the standards of today. Most fortunately, the hard, energetic, practical men who did the rough pioneer work of civilization in barbarous lands, are not prone to false sentimentality. The people who are, are the people that stay at home. Often these stay-at-homes are too selfish and indolent, too lacking in imagination, to understand the race-importance of the work which is done by their pioneer brethren in wild and distant lands; and they judge them by standards which would only be applicable to corrals and their own townships in parishes. . . .

The most ultimately righteous of all wars is a war with savages, though it is apt to be also the most terrible and inhuman. The rude, fierce settler who drives the savage from the land lays all civilized mankind under a debt to him. American and Indian, Boer and Zulu, Cossack and Tartar, New Zealander and Maori—in each case the victor, horrible though many of his deeds are, has laid deep the foundations for the future greatness of a mighty people.[48]

With these powerful and succinct statements by the American West's favorite president and spokesman, it's not difficult to understand white attitudes toward the Indians from the time of the Civil War to the turn of the century: congregating them on reservations, killing the Indian to save the man, caging Ota Benga in a zoo, rising support for eugenics, and delaying citizenship for all Native Americans until 1924.

Both Parkman's *Oregon Trail* and Roosevelt's *The Winning of the West* were published by the Putnam family. George Palmer Putnam (1814-1872) was born in Maine and founded G. P. Putnam in 1848. His highly successful company would go on to publish works by such famed authors as Washington Irving, James Fenimore Cooper, and Edgar Allan Poe. His sons, George and John, inherited the business when he died in 1872 and changed the name to G. P. Putnam's Sons.[49]

George Haven Putnam also wrote an introduction to *The Winning of the West* in volume nine, titled "Roosevelt, Historian and Statesman." Apparently, Roosevelt wrote most of his book at the Putnam offices on 23rd Street in New York City. Roosevelt was not only an author and client, but a partner of the publisher. Putnam described Roosevelt's motivation for writing the book, observing, "In 1888, when he began the writing of *The Winning of the West,* Roosevelt was expecting to devote some years to his historical work. He was ambitious, as he told me, to do for the record of the southwest territories of our continent what Parkman had done for the explorations and settlements of the northwest."[50]

Eventually, Roosevelt dissolved the partnership. Putnam noted he left the publisher after a few years with no regrets. He needed his stake in the business to keep his cattle ranch in Dakota Territory solvent. Bad weather had financially hurt the ranchmen. Putnam wrote, "He scolded me later for not having refused to pay him off. 'The publishing undertaking,' he said, 'was a good investment, but the money that you return to me went into the prairie and has never come back.'"[51]

Darwin's influence continued into the twentieth century. The Progressive Era in America was underway, and it inspired a history textbook called *Civic Biology*. With its teaching of Darwin's evolution, it was banned by the Tennessee state legislature. This didn't prevent a twenty-four-year-old science educator from teaching from the book. State prosecutors indicted John Thomas Scopes for his rebellious behavior. He was convicted, but that judgment was later overturned with the help of the American Civil Liberties Union.

Civic Biology was far from precise science. Inspired by scientific racism of the nineteenth century, it taught that the Negro and Indian were beneath the Caucasian, who was the highest example of human development. It also advocated eugenics on the basis of race. The book's author, George Hunter, wrote, "If such people were lower animals, we would probably kill them off to prevent them from spreading."[52]

In his book *Imbeciles,* Adam Cohen profiled the 1927 *Buck v. Bell* case in which the U.S. Supreme Court upheld Virginia's right to sterilize the mentally ill. Carrie Buck was a supposedly feeble-minded woman who had been raped as a teenager. She and her mother had spent time as inmates in the Virginia State Colony for Epileptics and Feebleminded. Her baby from the rape was placed in foster care. Buck was ordered sterilized to prevent any more offspring. Justice Holmes, writing for the majority, opined that "three generations of imbeciles are enough."[53]

Some challenged the Progressives, but the U.S. courts—with such famed jurists as Louis Brandeis, William Howard Taft, and Oliver Wendell Holmes—upheld the states' sterilization policies. Sterilization became so popular that, in time, many healthy offspring of criminals were also sterilized; only later did authorities reconsider whether a criminal mind could be inherited. Darwin's doctrine of survival of the fittest played out in a new, twisted form.

In *Illiberal Reformers,* Thomas C. Leonard showed how progressive Darwinism led to state hospitals and asylums filled with a combination of mentally and physically inferior humans—the sick, the old, and repeat criminals—who were subjected to forced sterilization. Over time, this was the fate of tens of thousands of inmates.[54]

Many doctors and jurists were all in for eugenics, which inspired economists to consider eugenics for those who were not deemed productive. Making matters worse, legislation was passed that made it illegal to pay wages below a mandated level, but only white skilled laborers qualified for the best jobs, leaving blacks and Native Americans unemployed.

A nonprofit, the Eugenics Records Office, impressed Europe's Nazis. The Third Reich's Law for the Prevention of Hereditarily Diseased Offspring, which was formulated from a blueprint issued by a lab in Cold Springs Harbor, New York, led to the sterilization of hundreds of thousands of Europeans. That, along with Hitler's Panzers, blasted away at the dikes of civilization. Only after Americans saw eugenics taken to an extreme, resulting in genocide, did eugenics in the United States begin to abate.

In almost all cases of eugenics, the human categories classified as inferior paralleled the race rankings that scientists had established. In many respects, laws were made to protect the weak from the strong, but in this case the law failed. So much of scientific racism had nothing to do with science and medicine but more on biased assumptions. One of the brightest thinkers of the nineteenth century wrote, "The very essence of an instinct is, that it is followed independently of reason." His name was Charles Darwin.[55]

Part IV

The Golden Rule, or the Golden-Ruled?
Custer: the Son of the American West

CHAPTER TWENTY-TWO

The Better Angels of Our Nature: Custer and the Fight to Make the Union Whole

We are not enemies, but friends. We must not be enemies. Though passion may have strained, it must not break our bonds of affection. The mystic chords of memory, stretching from every battlefield and patriot grave to every living heart and hearthstone all over this broad land, will yet swell the chorus of the Union, when again touched, as surely they will be, by the better angels of our nature.
—ABRAHAM LINCOLN'S FIRST INAUGURAL ADDRESS
MONDAY, MARCH 4, 1861

In years long-numbered with the past, when I was verging upon manhood, my every thought was ambitious—not to be wealthy, not to be learned, but to be great. I desired to link my name with acts & men, and in such a manner as to be a mark of honor—not only to the present, but to the future generations.
—GEORGE ARMSTRONG CUSTER

George Armstrong Custer was a war lover. The Civil War was the great event in his life. He won national prominence and thoroughly enjoyed himself during those four bloody years.
—STEPHEN AMBROSE, CUSTER AND CRAZY HORSE: THE PARALLEL LIVES OF TWO AMERICAN WARRIORS

It's the moral choices that excite and disturb. There lies free will. Those special human behaviors unleashed when some people are placed in charge of others in realms like the Civil War or the American West without real law. The Civil War was a contest of the survival of the fittest and served to bolster Northerners' attitudes of Manifest Destiny, scientific racism, and social Darwinism. It was the proving grounds for Union military leaders whose next task was winning the West. The Civil War and Indian wars were a two-part play with the same actors starring in both tragedies that had underlying tones of conflicts over religion and property rights. At the center of both were men of color who had little say about the outcome.

The Indian wars were about America's consolidation of power and later about the relocation of the Indians who survived to reservations. The most effective way to destroy people is to deny and obliterate hope and their own understanding of their history. It's not surprising that Custer was a racist—it would be surprising if he wasn't. What is more satisfying to a Darwinist than to kill the fittest? What motivates war? Ideology and theology do, and in cultures of honor, answering an affront. In most wars, of course, material rewards—land and plundered goods—also have been major motivations.

The people who participate in historic events behave the way they do within societal values of their cultural milieu. Journalists and historians record their facts through one lens of knowledge about the world, and then through another of perceived readers' expectations. This basic truth about the nature of truth itself creates frustrations and challenges for writers, but when a good story emerges, triumph is experienced. That good story—repeated hundreds of times in publications—is the story of George Armstrong Custer.

Even though Custer was one of the most celebrated military officers of the Civil War, mainstream historians tend to ignore or minimize that fact and often emphasize his erratic personality when they write their stories. Thus, in John M. Blum's *The National Experience: A History of the United States,* a standard college history textbook, in the thirty pages dedicated to the Civil War, Custer is not mentioned. His single entry in the textbook is not flattering: "At the Battle of the Little Bighorn on June 25, 1876, the rash young General George A. Custer and 265 men were wiped out in the general's first, and last, stand in the new Sioux war."[1] In other words, Custer was unstable and inexperienced, which led to his defeat.

Perhaps Ken Burns' 1990 Civil War television documentary educated Americans on that bloody tragedy—three quarters of a million Americans were slaughtered—like no other source. In September 1994, *The First Vintage Civil War Library Edition,* "the complete text of the best-selling narrative history of the Civil War—based on the celebrated PBS television series," by Geoffrey Ward with Ric Burns and Ken Burns, was published. Custer has four entries. The first is an entry on July 3, 1863, on the third day of Gettysburg. The Union cavalry stopped Confederate Jeb Stuart under the command of Robert E. Lee, "thanks in part to a series of headlong charges by a 23-year-old general, George Armstrong Custer."[2] For the entry on October 18, 1864, at the Battle in the Shenandoah Valley, a victory for Union soldiers, the authors noted, "At the victory, General George Armstrong Custer lifted his little commander [Sheridan] off the ground and danced with joy."[3] On April 9, 1865, Palm Sunday, Lee surrendered at Appomattox. The articles of surrender were signed at the McLean house in the front parlor by Grant and Lee. The authors wrote, "Behind him, Union officers began to bargain over Wilmer McLean's parlor furniture. Sheridan paid $20 for Grant's table; Custer rode off with another table over his head."[4] Actually, Sheridan purchased the signing table and gifted it to Custer's wife, Libbie, in appreciation for her husband's outstanding service during the war. Custer did not steal a table. And the last entry, regarding the Grand Review of the Armies parade on May 23, 1865, in Washington, D.C., again painted Custer in an unfavorable light, noting, "Only General George Armstrong Custer disturbed the formal majesty of the occasion, managing to pass the reviewing stand twice, once when he seemed uncharacteristically unable to control his horse and galloped past the dignitaries far ahead of his men, his long yellow hair whipping in the wind, and again after he had wheeled and returned to the head of this column."[5] Yet again, 2005 Pulitzer Prize–winner Doris Kearns Goodwin's almost 950-page book, *Team of Rivals: The Political Genius of Abraham Lincoln,* makes no mention of Custer.[6] In *The Man Who Saved the Union: Ulysses Grant in War and Peace* by H. W. Brands, Custer gets brief mention—for the famous bear hug of Sheridan and his encounter with Lee at Appomattox. Sheridan's gift of the signing table is not mentioned. Custer finally received his national recognition when T. J. Stiles won the Pulitzer Prize for his 2015 masterpiece, *Custer's Trials.*

Custer spent his life distancing himself from his modest roots. His father, Emmanuel Custer—like most Americans—believed if you were white, worked hard, and believed in God then anything was possible. He was a devout Methodist blacksmith and loved Andrew Jackson, who as president refused an offer to become a member of an upper-class Presbyterian church. Jackson wrote, "A true Christian loves all, immaterial to what sector church he may belong."[7] Methodism was the most popular denomination at that time, attracting a large portion of the working class. Custer was pressured by his family, wife Libbie, and her family to undergo conversion. Toward the end of the Civil War, he went through the motions, but probably only so he could appease them all.

Libbie's father, the wealthy and well-respected Judge Daniel Bacon—until the Civil War made Custer a national star—didn't approve of Libbie marrying him. They married on February 9, 1864. He then congratulated Custer and told his son-in-law that he placed salvation as the most important thing in life. The judge wrote that Libbie "is made so happy by marriage, I am made like happy. . . . You are all I can desire or wish and I am not without pride at your well earned and fully appreciated reputation."[8]

On February 5, 1865, Custer accepted Jesus Christ as his personal savior in the Presbyterian Church in Monroe, Michigan, that Libbie and her family attended. The Christian idealist would expect conversion to be a life-changing experience, bringing a change of heart and activation of will, but that didn't happen.

Custer's father showed no disappointment that his son had chosen the Presbyterian Church over his Methodist Church for his spiritual conversion. He was pleased that his son had finally come to the Lord. "I will say that you have no superiors and I am proud that I am the father of such a noble boy," Emmanuel wrote. "You have clumb up the ladder of fame and honor your self what a great satisfaction it is to me." Like the judge, his father also placed Custer's conversion as his most proud moment for his son, even though by that time he was a famous Civil War general. He prayed that Custer would "stick to and defend the . . . banner of King Jesus."[9]

A Star is Born

Custer was born on December 5, 1839, in a log house on the corner of Main and Liberty Streets in the small burg of New Rumley in east-central Ohio. Today, an impressive bronze is the centerpiece of the Custer Memorial located along State Route 646. His mother, Maria Ward Kirkpatrick, was Emmanuel's second wife—his first wife died in their sixth year of marriage. Several sons died before George Armstrong was born, and as a toddler he was nicknamed "Autie" after struggling to say Armstrong.

Emmanuel's strong opinions greatly affected his son. He was a Democrat who believed in individualism and equality for white men only. As a common laborer, he was suspicious and not trusting of the wealthy or of colored people. A daughter-in-law wrote, "You are well aware how father Custer feels over the 'niger' question," and "You know well father Custer's antipathy to the negro."[10] Like his father, Custer despised the Republican party and very much supported the right of Southern slave owners to transport their slaves into the Western territories.

Custer's father's dream for his son's future would never have included West Point. He believed that honest work was done with the hands, and he was satisfied to be a blacksmith. At age nine, Armstrong was apprenticed with Joseph Hunter, a furniture maker, but after three years he left the mentorship. After further schooling, in 1855 at age fifteen, he taught school at a private academy and eventually in a public school outside of Cadiz, the seat of Harrison County in Ohio. Custer had a passion and aptitude for writing.

Unlike his father, Custer dreamed big and wrote a letter to Republican Congressman John A. Bingham, requesting an appointment to West Point. In a December 12, 1856, letter to his half-sister Lydia Ann Reed, who lived in Monroe, Michigan, he wrote, "Mothers much opposed to me going there but Father and David [older half-brother] are in favor of it very much. I think it is the best place that I could go. I will get $28 per month for five years and be getting a good education at the same time and when I come out I will get five years pay ahead. I think I am lucky in getting the appointment which I think I am certain of now."[11]

Custer wrote her that the sons of some of the greatest men of America went to West Point. In reality, less than five percent of the cadets in that era had wealthy parents. He understood that the flamboyant and the extremely visible is the way society judged heroes. Heroes delivered visible results and didn't care about the process. Sons of farmers, merchants, and the professions made up the bulk of attendees.[12]

It was a demographically diverse group with cadets matriculating from all over the country. Like other colleges, the coursework included science, ethics, and a foreign language like French with an emphasis on memorization and recitals in front of the class. In addition, classes in engineering and military coursework were part of the curriculum. On January 27, 1858, Custer wrote his half-sister, Ann, and her husband, David, that "my class which numbered over 100 when we entered in June is now reduced to 69. This shows that if a person wants to get along here he has to study hard."[13]

Custer knew that he could never be at the top of his class, and the only way to satisfy his ego was to present an attitude of indifference. One of his fellow cadets recalled, "Custer said that there were but two positions of distinction in a class—head and foot; and as he soon found that he could not be head he determined that he would support his class as a solid base."[14] Testing poorly, Custer excelled in demerits—considered academic marks—which also affected his class ranking. Even though he was noted for his legendary pranks that carried a tone of cruelty and provided him with further demerits, his charismatic personality won over many friends. After their time at West Point, his roommate, Tully McCrea, wrote, "A whole-souled generous friend, and a mighty good fellow, and I like him. The great difficulty is that he is too clever for his own good. He is always connected with all the mischief that is going on and never studies any more than he can possibly help. He has narrowly escaped several times."[15] Still, Custer could be defensive and hold a grudge if he felt he was being underappreciated by friends or family.

On one occasion, the alternative to studying was cheating. After being at West Point three and a half years with poor academic marks, Custer attempted to steal one of his instructor's examination notebooks. Upon hearing his teacher's footsteps, Custer ripped the sheet of questions out of the notebook and hid them. Obviously, the instructor understood what happened and changed the tests. Custer and thirty others failed the examination. He also flunked re-examination. A dozen were dismissed from school, but inexplicably he was not. He believed this was another example of his luck and specialness.[16]

Custer enjoyed pursuing women and basked in their flirting with him. McCrea wrote, "He is a handsome fellow, and very successful ladies' man. Nor does he care an iota how many of the fair ones break their hearts for him."[17] On August 29, 1859, after returning to West Point after two months of summer break, he was treated by a surgeon for gonorrhea.[18] This was not an uncommon malady for young men of the time when it was common for young men to pay for sex with prostitutes. Randall Fuller, a professor of English at Tulsa University, critically described Custer's time at West Point, writing, "There he drank and gambled and whored. . . ."[19]

On June 24, 1861, Custer graduated last in a class of thirty-four. With 192 demerits, he was within 8 of the yearly limit. He ended up with a total of 726, which was the highest among any classmate. His class graduated a year ahead of schedule in order to supply officers for the Civil War, which had begun on April 12. Lincoln had taken office on March 4 and immediately had to deal with secessionists who on March 4 organized the Confederate States of America. They selected Jefferson Davis as their president.[20]

Much is made of Custer finishing last in his class at West Point, as if high marks in class equate to great leadership in the field. Other leaders also struggled with the rigors—and rigidity—of academic life. Winston Churchill, considered by many the greatest leader of the twentieth century, was another who was not at the head of the class. At Harrow College, J. E. C. Welldon, who became headmaster in 1886, was impressed by

Churchill's ability to recite lines, but he struggled scholastically in other areas like Greek and Latin. In fact, it took Churchill three attempts to get accepted in September 1893 at the Royal Military Academy at Sandhurst. After the second failed attempt, he retained a well-known crammer named Captain James. He was finally accepted for a cavalry cadetship that required lower marks than one for the infantry. While he did well in history and chemistry he struggled in other areas and lamented, "I had to find another useful card." After fifteen months, he finished 8th out of 150.[21]

Eisenhower was Allied Supreme Commander in World War II and became the thirty-fourth president. He is perhaps the greatest American general of the twentieth century. In 1910, Eisenhower entered West Point, where his studies were narrow and technical with emphasis on civil and military engineering. The method of teaching had not changed since the war of 1812. Every day the cadets recited approved answers to standard questions. Each response was carefully graded. It was all rote learning. He excelled in calculus, but as Eisenhower biographer Stephen Ambrose wrote in *Eisenhower: Soldier and President,* "In other subjects, Eisenhower was content to stay in the middle. He preferred enjoying his classmates to competing with them."[22]

Like Custer, Eisenhower also enjoyed pranks. Ambrose wrote, "His own favorite story about a cadet prank centered on the sometimes absurd literalness of the regulations and orders. Eisenhower and another plebe, named Atkins, were guilty of an infraction. The cadet corporal who caught them, named Alder, ordered them to report to his room after tattoo in 'full-dress coats,' meaning a complete dress uniform. The two plebes decided to do exactly as ordered, and that night reported to Adler wearing their coats and not another stitch of clothing."[23]

Close to graduation from West Point, Custer wrote, "It is my great expectation to fight for my country and to die for it if need be. The thought has often occurred to me that I might be killed in this war; and if so, so be it."[24]

Slavery and a House Divided

Before 1700, Christians paid little attention to the souls of slaves or Native Americans. They were not considered fully human and were incapable of learning. This led to a lack of interest in proselytizing slaves. By 1750, about twenty percent of the American population was African or of African descent.[25]

At the end of the seventeenth century, the influential Puritan preacher Cotton Mather vigorously supported slave conversion and rejected racial inferiority based on color. He stated, "How canst thou Love thy Negro, and be willing to see him ly [lie] under the Rage of Sin, and the Wrath of God?" He was so sure of his position that he published pamphlets on the need to Christianize and held the "Society of Negros" on Sunday night at his home with the intention of converting the attending Africans.[26]

Soon afterward, Mather's contemporary, Samuel Sewall, who had served as a judge during the Salem witch trials, challenged the widely held belief that Africans had been condemned to everlasting slavery by the Bible. Organized anti-slavery activity began with Quakers, who held that every human being possessed a godly inner light that made enslavement a sin against God himself. By the mid-eighteenth century, Quaker meetings from the Carolinas to New England were calling on their own members to free their slaves, and they soon began urging abolition upon non-Quaker slave owners as well.

During the First Great Awakening, George Whitefield championed the conversion of slaves to Christianity. In 1740, he circulated a pamphlet that asked, "Are your children anyway better by Nature than the poor Negroes? . . . Blacks are just as much, and no more, conceived and born in Sin, as White Men are. Both, if born and bred up here, I am persuaded, are naturally capable of the same religious improvement."[27]

Although North American colonials generally avoided forced conversions, the treatment of African slaves was an enormous exception. Slave owners were at first ambivalent about converting their slaves, but once church leaders argued that loyalty to one's master was part of the Christian ethic, the conversion of African Americans ensued. Yet, for all the sordid circumstances of slaves' initial encounter with Christianity, the black church thrived. Today, descendants of slaves are the most religiously devout group in the United States.[28]

Increasingly, the Quakers were joined by numerous Northern evangelicals, whose revivalist approach to abolition infused new passion into the movement, demanding that society as a whole—not just individuals—cleanse itself of the sin of slavery. Perhaps even more important than religious reasons, the ideas about liberty and the rights of individuals that inspired the American Revolution also animated abolitionists. Religion has never been independent of cultural influences.

By the 1820s, every Northern state had ended slavery, and by the 1830s, abolitionist bastions in New York and New England were electing their members to local and state offices, creating a base of power to begin influencing national politics. Even if some of the more outspoken abolitionists were evangelical, most evangelicals were not outspoken abolitionists. In general, Northern evangelicals did not differ from Southern evangelicals in racial views, except that they tended to oppose slavery.

Although Congress rode out a number of crises over slavery's westward expansion from 1820 to 1850, the intensified hostility between the free North and slavery's defenders in the South would soon fracture the prevailing party system, leaving a vacuum that would be filled in the South by secessionists and in the North by political men who gradually came to embrace anti-slavery's goals.[29]

Early in our nation's history, one of the most challenging questions was this: Were America's millions of slaves property or were they human beings with intrinsic rights? John Marshall, chief justice of the U.S. Supreme Court from 1801 to 1835, made his views known on slavery in an obscure case involving a captured Spanish slave ship, the *Antelope*. The Spanish-licensed ship and its slaves were seized by the *Arraganta,* a privateer flying the Uruguayan flag, after leaving Africa. After stealing more slaves from Portuguese ships, the *Arraganta,* carrying more than 300 chained Africans, and the hijacked *Antelope* crossed the Atlantic back to Brazil. The *Antelope* with 281 captives was seized near St. Augustine on June 29, 1820, by the *Dallas,* a U.S. Navy cutter. At issue was the legal standing of the captives. The United States maintained that the Africans were free under the 1819 Slave Trade Act. Both Presidents James Monroe and John Quincy Adams, who successively held office during the proceedings, distanced themselves from the case due to the volatility of the slavery issue.

One of the lawyers arguing in front of the Supreme Court that the slaves were human beings with natural rights was lawyer Francis Scott Key of "Star-Spangled Banner" fame. Marshall's court held that slavery was detestable but not contrary to law. He concluded that slavery was condoned by custom and by the Constitution. Thus, Marshall declared, "This court must not yield to feelings which might seduce it from the path of duty, and must obey the mandate of the law." Marshall's court ruled that the United States could not interfere with the slave laws of other nations. That ruling opened the way for almost continuous international slave trafficking between 1825 and 1866. More than 1.5 million enslaved Africans were transported to the Americas during this period.[30]

Having become more openly anti-slavery, in 1841 John Quincy Adams concluded that the Marshall court had been hypocritical, and he declared that the Declaration of Independence was the final arbiter of law. But his sentiments were not shared by the Supreme Court. The year Custer started

West Point, *Dred Scott v. Sandford* was heard by the U.S. Supreme Court. Dred Scott (1799-1858) was a black slave who sued for his freedom along with that for his wife and two daughters, claiming that they should be free because they had lived in Illinois and the Wisconsin Territory for four years—both slave free. The Supreme Court, however, in a seven-to-two decision, wrote that no one of African ancestry could claim citizenship in the United States, and therefore he could not bring suit in federal court. At that time, the court had a number of Southern judges. In 1863 at Gettysburg, Abraham Lincoln—in the spirit of Jefferson—affirmed that the nation was conceived in liberty and dedicated to the proposition that all men are created equal.[31]

Those who defended slavery characterized the North as greedy Yankee capitalists and idealized the South as an agrarian hierarchy of a white master and his African slaves whom God had predestined and approved by natural law. The rationale that whites were extremely charitable to lift their inferiors out of barbarism was applied to all people of color, including Indians.

As Edward E. Baptist wrote in *The Half Has Never Been Told*, slavery was woven into the fabric of early nineteenth-century capitalism. Bankers supported it with loans that were used to expand slavery, which then earned lucrative profits for them in the rich cotton-growing areas of the Deep South.[32]

Usually when profits are to be made, morality is not part of the equation. In the year 1800, there were 1 million slaves, but prior to the Civil War that number had swollen to about 4 million. The commercial development of the Mississippi River Valley was totally dependent on slavery and land. Without slavery, the land was worthless. Slaves were the slave owners' gold. By the 1820s, the 2 million slaves then in the United States were worth more than $1 billion or about twenty percent of all the wealth owned by all U.S. citizens. They were a commodity like wheat, cotton, and pork bellies, with markets for them throughout the South.

Defenders of slavery claimed that emancipation would lead to widespread miscegenation even though race mixing in the South was already common. Rape of enslaved women by their white owners was not unusual. By 1860, there were hundreds of thousands of biracial people (known at the time as mulattoes) that made up about thirteen percent of the nation's black population. There was no crime against rape by the slave owner, who had full rights to do whatever he wanted to do with his property.

Part of antebellum Manifest Destiny was a vision by many Americans of a transcontinental nation, which included the spread of slavery all the way to the Pacific Ocean. Many of the Founding Fathers were slave owners, although President Andrew Jackson was the only one who personally drove a convoy of chained slaves. Emancipation would leave the South economically flattened after the Civil War.[33]

Onward Christian Soldiers

Forcing Indian tribes to move west of the Mississippi opened up lands that could be worked by slaves. From 1824 to 1832, the Philadelphia-based Bank of the United States increased loans to slave owners sixteen times over. When the economy survived the Panic of 1837, slavery by the 1850s mushroomed with the new wave of "Negro fever" that doubled the price of slaves in relation to that of other goods. On the eve of the Civil War, slavery was robust.

The pro-Southern President James Buchanan (1791-1868), in his January 1861 State of the Union address, was less worried about the secession crisis in South Carolina and spent more time expressing his hope of acquiring Cuba for the United States—a longtime goal of slave owners who sought an opportunity to expand slavery.[34]

On March 4, 1861, in Abraham Lincoln's (1809-1865) inaugural address, he asked America for "intelligence, patriotism, Christianity, and a firm reliance on Him, who has never yet forsaken this favored land." A few weeks earlier in Montgomery, Alabama, Confederate President Jefferson Davis called on the same God to tear apart the country, saying, "Reverently let us invoke the God of our fathers to guide and protect us in our efforts." The question of who God was really for haunted Lincoln, who wrote, "The will of God prevails. In great contests each party claims to act in accordance with the will of God. Both may be, and one must be wrong. God can not be for, and against the same thing at the same time. . . . By his mere quiet power on the minds of the now contestants, He could have either saved or destroyed the Union without a human contest. Yet the contest began. And having begun He could give the final victory to either side any day. Yet the contest proceeds."[35]

Since Columbus first landed in the New World, Christians had rationalized their immoral behavior toward men of color by interpreting the Bible in a way to support it. Shakespeare once wrote, "The devil can cite Scripture for his purpose." The abolitionists quoted Exodus 21:16 and Deuteronomy 24:7 to support their case against slavery: "Whoever steals a man, whether he sells him or is found in possession of him, shall be put to death."

It wasn't until the second quarter of the nineteenth century, in response to a new breed of abolitionists, that Southern whites invoked the Bible and

Christian ideals in a systematic defense of slavery.[36] From 1846 until the Civil War, every man who achieved the rank of bishop within the Methodist Episcopal Church, South, was a slave holder.[37] Pro-slavery advocates found support in a story in Genesis 9:20-27 about Noah, who, after the flood, became drunk on wine and passed out naked in his tent. One of his three sons, Ham, found him and told the others, much to Noah's disgust. Noah cried out, "Cursed be Canaan [a son of Ham's]; a slave of slaves shall he be to his brothers." Over time, legend developed that the sons of Ham were dark skinned, and thus the Bible supported slavery.

A number of pastors embraced scientific racism and believed slaves were born to a certain permanent low level in life by God's design. They argued that Abraham, the father of faith, held slaves without God's disapproval (Genesis 21:9-10) and that slavery was widespread throughout the Roman world, yet Jesus never spoke against it. The apostle Paul specifically commanded slaves to obey their masters (Ephesians 6:5-8), and Paul returned a runaway slave, Philemon, to his master (Philemon 12).

The charitable and evangelical reasons proffered in support of slavery were that slavery removed people from a culture that worshipped the devil and practiced witchcraft and other evils; brought people to a Christian land where they could hear the gospel; enabled Christian masters to provide religious instruction to their slaves; placed people where they were treated with kindness; functioned such that it was in the slave owners' own interest to treat their slaves well. Social reasons were also used: slaves were like women who were supposed to play a subordinate role (Ephesians 5:22, 1 Timothy 2:11-15); slavery is God's mean of protecting and providing for an inferior race; and abolition would lead to slave uprisings and bloodshed and anarchy.[38] Many passages regarding slavery in the Bible contradict each other, so subsequent interpretations were tainted by tradition, reason, racism, science, medicine, and personal experience.

Historian Forrest G. Wood explained the role of economics, writing, "Cynical though it may sound, it is not an exaggeration to submit that the critical factor in determining who opposed slavery and who supported it was, with every church that claimed a national constituency, a consequence entirely of political and economic factors. All of the Christian conviction in the world could not dent the purse of one slaveholder."[39]

During mid-century, the only thing that seemed to derail Manifest Destiny, nationalism, and a sense of invincibility was slavery. The United States had ended the slave trade in 1808, but the question of the future of the existing slaves continued unanswered. At the Presbyterian General

Assembly in 1818, there was a unanimous declaration against slavery. Participants declared, "We consider the voluntary enslaving of one part of the human race by another as a gross violation of the most precious and sacred rights of human nature; as utterly inconsistent with the law of God . . . totally irreconcilable with the spirit and principles of the gospel of Christ."[40] William Lloyd Garrison's radical newspaper, the *Liberator*, founded in 1831, provided a national voice for abolitionists.

The myth that church leaders in the North were all abolitionists is one of the major falsehoods in American history. For example, in 1855, Dutch reformed minister Samuel B. How (1790-1868) championed slavery for the North and declared that the Bible stated that there was no sin in slavery. He argued that the Bible taught "that there are rights of property; that there are masters and there are slaves, and bids us to respect the right of the master, and not to covet his man-servant or maid-servant" (Exodus 20:17). He confidently added that "the desire and the attempt to deprive others of property which the law of God and the law of the land have made it lawful for them to hold, is to strike a blow at the very existence of civilization and Christianity." Roman Catholic Bishop John England (1786-1842), in Charleston, South Carolina, agreed with How that God supported slavery and explained that natural law supports "a state in which one man has dominion over the labour and the ingenuity of another to the end of his life."[41] These racist views did not bode well for Native Americans.

Christianity could be the best friend of either the slave supporter or the abolitionist. Christians ushered slaves via the Underground Railroad to freedom, while other Christians gathered to recapture slaves who had run away from their rightful owners. Lincoln lamented that both "read the same Bible, and pray to the same God."[42]

From the time of Custer's birth until the Civil War, the Methodist, Baptist, and Presbyterian churches were torn apart because of the slavery issue. In 1843, the Methodist anti-slavery convention in Boston offended sister churches in the South. One year later, the sixty-year-old Methodist Church, the largest denomination in the country, ended being a single church. It split into two branches along north and south lines. It wouldn't be until 1939 that the two branches came together again. In 1845, the Baptist Church also separated into a northern and southern body. The Southern Baptists outnumbered their Northern counterparts. Twelve years later, the Presbyterians also divided. Libbie Custer's father saw his Michigan Presbyterians lead the way against slavery. Harriet Beecher Stowe pleaded with the North and South in her 1852 *Uncle Tom's Cabin* to repent of the respective injustices and cruelties before it was too late. She wrote, "A day of grace is yet held out to us. . . . The Christian church has a heavy account to answer."[43]

No political figure did more than Abraham Lincoln (1809-1865) to preserve our Constitution or infuse it with the principles of Jefferson's Declaration of Independence. Lincoln has been called by one historian, "the spiritual center of American history." His journey through Christianity symbolizes America's same journey. Very much in the tradition of Jefferson, Lincoln was suspicious of institutional Christianity and was not a churchgoer. "When any church will inscribe over its altar as its sole qualification for membership," Lincoln stated, "the Savior's condensed statement of the substance of both the law and gospel 'Thou shalt love the Lord thy God with all thy heart, and with all thy soul, and with all thy mind, and thy neighbor as thyself' [the Golden Rule]—that Church will I join with all my heart and soul."[44]

Like Jefferson, Lincoln embraced Thomas Paine's *Age of Reason* and other deistic works, and as Jon Meacham wrote, "Throughout his life Lincoln often seemed to inhabit a 'twilight' of belief and doubt somewhere between evangelical Protestantism and Enlightenment skepticism. As a freethinking questioner of standard creeds and institutional traditions, Lincoln carried forward the Jeffersonian side of American religious life."[45]

Lincoln, along with his wife Mary Todd (1818-1882), also sought solace in spiritualism as they dealt with the carnage of the Civil War and were haunted by the death of their three-year-old son Eddie in 1850 and their eleven-year-old son Willie in 1862. Mediums visited the White House at least eight times during Lincoln's presidency to hold séances.[46] Communication with the dead was the basis for modern spiritualism and originated in upstate New York in 1848 when the three Fox sisters supposedly transmitted messages from the great beyond. Spiritualism became popular during the Civil War for those who were in despair over their loved ones slaughtered in the conflict.[47]

Lincoln was alienated from his father and, like Custer, hated manual work. The Founding Fathers acted as surrogate fathers to Lincoln. Their ideas about liberty, equality, and slavery gave him the strength eventually to oppose slavery. Besides Thomas Paine, Lincoln saw George Washington as a champion of liberty and a leader in moral reformation. Jefferson was another influential Founding Father, but Lincoln found Jefferson's refusal later in life to campaign publicly against slavery extremely disappointing. When Lincoln debated Senator Stephen Douglas in 1854, both men interpreted the intentions of the Founding Fathers differently. Douglas insisted that they had left each state free to allow slavery or not and that the Declaration's concept of equality applied only to white men. In contrast, Lincoln argued that they had meant it when they said *all* men are created equal.[48]

Lincoln believed from reading the Bible that the Civil War was the national atonement for the offense of slavery. Early on, a young Lincoln struggled mightily over the issue of slavery. During the 1830s as a state legislator, he made his first public statement on slavery when the legislature passed a resolution that censored abolitionism and confirmed the right to own slaves. Since many of the voters were from the South, the vote was 77-6, with Lincoln being one of six dissenters. The resolution stated, "We highly disapprove of the formation of abolition societies" and hold "sacred" the "right of property in slaves."[49] Lincoln also believed, however, that Congress did not have the power to interfere with slavery in states where it was historically established. There would have to be a constitutional amendment. He wrote, "If slavery is not wrong, nothing is wrong."[50] Decades earlier, Jefferson had faced the same personal dilemma.

In 1858 Lincoln—compassionate, intelligent, and a literary genius—prepared for another try for the U.S. Senate. His opponent from the Democratic Party again was Stephen Douglas. One of the questions at the time was what to do with free blacks in America. Again harkening back to Jefferson, Lincoln supported sending them back to Africa after compensating slave owners, as proposed earlier by Edward Bates and Henry Clay. "My first impulse," Lincoln stated, "would be to free all the slaves, and send them to Liberia, to their own native land."[51]

Initially, as president, he still believed in allowing blacks to return to their homeland. However, he did not want to offer direct emancipation because it would alienate the border states whose backing was critical for winning the war. The Republicans needed the tenuous support of Northern Democrats. His position was embraced by most of the voters in the North.[52] Lincoln commented that voluntary colonization could occur, "at someplace, or places, in a climate congenial to them. It might be well to consider, too, whether the free colored people already in the United States could not, so far as individuals may desire, be included in such colonization."[53]

Lincoln asked Ben Butler, a former Union general and Massachusetts politician, to determine the logistics of deporting the slaves. Butler reported, "Mr. President, I have gone carefully over my calculations as to the power of the country to export the Negroes of the South and I assure you that, using all your naval vessels and all the merchant Marine fit to cross the seas with safety, it will be impossible for you to transport to the nearest place . . . half as fast as Negro children will be born here."⁵⁴

Lincoln's idea of colonization outraged many abolitionists in the North, including Frederick Douglass and Salmon P. Chase, who wrote, "Let the sword make a nation of 4 millions of black men free, and let them be free, as free as the white man."⁵⁵ Early in his presidency, Lincoln had almost no concept that the black man was equal to the white man and that America was his home too.

Lincoln finally came around to the idea of freeing slaves with his Emancipation Proclamation that set January 1, 1863, as a date for all slaves in the rebellious states to be free, roughly 3.5 million blacks. In his address, he reached back to Thomas Jefferson and his Declaration of Independence for his proclamation of equality. It did not cover the roughly 425,000 slaves in the loyal border states. Many in his cabinet were shocked by the boldness of the proclamation. Edward Bates, one of the more conservative cabinet members, supported it on the condition that the free slaves unconditionally be deported to Central America or Africa. Bates believed amalgamation would eventually bring "degradation and demoralization to the white race." He pushed for treaties with foreign governments to accept the slaves and hoped the treaties would "provide for the just and humane treatment of emigrants—e.g., ensuring an honest livelihood by their own industry . . . and guaranteeing to them 'their liberty, property and the religion which they profess.'"⁵⁶ Blacks deserved Jefferson's promised "life, liberty, and the pursuit of happiness," but only in a foreign country.

The Emancipation Proclamation was a game changer. In Europe, especially England, popular support swelled for the Union. Even those workers in textile mills in England who had suffered financially because of the lack of cotton from the South sent messages of support to Lincoln. Karl Marx said it was "the most important document in American history since the establishment of the Union."⁵⁷

The Civil War

Lincoln's presidency was troubled from the beginning. When he was elected, there were thirty-three states in the Union, but by the time of his inauguration on March 4, 1861, six had already left. South Carolina led the way on December 20, 1860. At 4:30 A.M. on April 12, 1861, the Confederates opened fire on Fort Sumter, starting the Civil War. In 1861 and 1862, momentum lay with the Confederacy. European public opinion was strongly against slavery and saw the American war as part of a universal struggle between the forces of human rights and oppressive privilege. French liberal intellectual Edouard Laboulaye (1811-1883) warned, "Should liberty become eclipsed in the new world, it would become night in Europe, and we shall see the work of Washington, of the Franklins, of the Hamiltons, spit upon and trampled underfoot by the whole school which believes only in violence."[58]

When Lincoln arrived in Washington, D.C., it had been in the past a major regional slave market with a large number of shackled slaves often sent from the Capitol trudging toward local slave pens. Now, in the antebellum era, there was a total reversal, and Washington became a magnet for free men and women who soon made up a majority of its black population. Even slaves were commonly allowed to hire themselves out, paying their masters a fixed sum and keeping the rest for themselves. Over time, free blacks founded schools, small businesses, and self-help organizations, gradually forming the core of the city's black middle class.[59]

Ulysses S. Grant (1822-1885), an 1843 graduate of West Point, was back home in Galena, Illinois, after serving in the peacetime army and working as a clerk in his father's tannery. His future adversary, Robert E. Lee, four days after Sumter fell, was offered by Lincoln field command of the entire Union army, but the next day Virginia voted to secede. On April 23, 1861, Lee accepted command of the Confederate Army of Virginia. Eventually the western counties of Virginia rejoined the Union as the new state of West Virginia.[60]

Robert E. Lee (1807-1870) was related to some of the most famous Virginia families—Lees, Carters, Randolphs, and Harrisons. His father, Light Horse Harry Lee, was a good friend of George Washington and one of his favorite lieutenants. Lee graduated second in his class of 1829 at West Point. In Mexico, he was once said to have reprimanded young Captain Grant for slovenly dress. He was an honorable man who was faithful to his wife and never drank, swore, or smoked. He was a devout Christian and prayed often. He never owned a slave himself, and in the middle of the war he freed those slaves who had belonged to his father-in-law.

Lee's march to the top was plodding compared to Grant's meteoric rise. He spent over three decades in the U.S. Army, creeping up from lieutenant captain to lieutenant colonel. He was not initially accepted by the Rebel gray. He was characterized as a bureaucrat, too cautious, and too old. That all changed on the last day of May 1862 when fate handed him the command of the Army of Northern Virginia. Within thirteen months, he won a series of spectacular victories—the Seven Days, Second Manassas, Fredericksburg, Chancellorsville—before he faltered at Gettysburg in July 1863.[61]

The head of the Union Army of the Potomac—100,000 untrained volunteers—was General George McClellan (1826-1885). Those who served under him, including Custer, loved him. He had a flamboyant and egotistical personality much like Custer and loved to be called the "Young Napoleon." McClellan told his wife, "You have no idea how the men brighten up when I go among them. I can see every one glisten. Yesterday they nearly pulled me to pieces in one regiment. You never heard such yelling."[62] Later, McClellan was made general-in-chief as well as the commander of the Army of the Potomac. True to form, McClellan assured Lincoln, "I can do it all."[63]

Like many who misjudge war, Lincoln believed that the secession crisis would resolve quickly after the Southerners understood the foolishness of it all. However, the Battle of Bull Run turned out to be a disaster for the Union. "Little did I conceive," William Howard Russell wrote of Bull Run and the impact that it had by the end of 1861, "of the greatness of the defeat, the magnitude of the disaster which it had entailed upon the United States. . . . So short-lived has been the American Union, that men who saw it rise may live to see it fall."[64]

The Union effort was not going well, and on March 11, 1862, McClellan was dismissed as general-in-chief of the federal armies so he could concentrate on upcoming battles in Virginia. Grant was having more success. He had seized Paducah, Kentucky, and thus the Union controlled access to the Tennessee and Cumberland Rivers. In the winter of 1862, he won victories at Fort Henry on the Tennessee and Fort Donelson on the Cumberland. On April 6, 1862, Grant was encamped with 42,000 Union troops near Pittsburg Landing, Tennessee. Brigadier General William Tecumseh Sherman (1820-1891) had recovered from depression—some thought even psychosis—earlier that winter and now was encamped with his Ohioans not far from a little Methodist church built of logs named Shiloh. The Confederate Army of Mississippi attacked, and during the ensuing battle Sherman was wounded twice and had three horses shot from under him. "Well, Grant," Sherman said. "We've had the devil's own day, haven't we?" His good friend Grant replied, "Yes. Yes. Lick 'em tomorrow."[65]

Counting both Union and Rebel forces, a total of 100,000 men fought at Shiloh, with tragic results. The casualty rate was twenty-five percent. The press criticized Grant as a butcher. He now, like many others, understood that this would be a prolonged war, writing, "Up to the battle of Shiloh I, as well as thousands of other citizens, believed that the rebellion against the government would collapse suddenly and soon if a decisive victory could be gained over any of its armies . . . but [afterward] I gave up all idea of saving the Union except by complete conquest."[66]

Even though it was considered a Union victory, Grant lost his command. General Henry W. Halleck, now named general-in-chief of the federal armies, assumed field command and spread the rumor that Grant had been drinking heavily. Today, some scholars do not believe that Grant had a reliance on heavy drink, but instead had an inability to hold even a dram of liquor. A discouraged Grant contemplated resigning and heading to St. Louis, but his friend Sherman convinced him not to, saying, "You could not be quiet at home for a week when armies are moving."[67] Sherman added, "I then begged him to stay, illustrating his own case by my own. Before the battle of Shiloh, I had been cast down by a mere newspaper assertion of crazy, but that single battle had given me new life. . . . I argued with [Grant] that . . . if he remained, some happy accident might restore him to favor and his true place."[68]

The war was draining the federal government, and by the end of 1862 it was spending $2.5 million a day on the conflict. To raise money, Congress enacted the first income tax, established the first national banking system, and started printing the first national currency—called greenbacks. It also passed an internal revenue act. The Morrill Act transferred federal lands to states so that colleges could be built.

In order to stimulate the economy, Congress awarded public lands to homesteaders and railroaders so a transcontinental line could be completed. The Homestead Act of 1862 provided more than 1 billion acres of land for the landless, but much of the land ended up in the hands of greedy capitalists who had no intention of tilling the soil. As Civil War historian and biographer C. Vann Woodward wrote, "Many of them, like Tom Scott and Andrew Carnegie, got their start in war supply operations. They proceded with their conquest of an untamed West in much the same ruthless fashion with which Sherman had proceded across Georgia. In the manners and morals and in the ethics of gluttony the Gilded Age entrepreneurs were more than a match for the Gilded Age politicians, with whom they worked hand in glove."[69]

In August 1862, in response to pressure by the abolitionists, Lincoln stood firm and said, "My paramount object in this struggle is to save the Union, and is not either to save or to destroy slavery. If I could save the Union without freeing any slave, I would do it; if I could save it by freeing all the slaves, I would do it; if I could save it by freeing some and leaving others alone, I would also do that."[70]

On September 15, 1862, Lee, in command of 18,000 Confederate troops, took up a position east of the town of Sharpsburg, Maryland, next to the Potomac River and next to a little stream called Antietam Creek. McClellan and his army of 95,000 Union soldiers grouped across the creek. As the battle pursued, Lee stopped his invasion since he was heavily outnumbered. Eager for a decisive victory, Lincoln wired McClellan, "God bless you and all with you. Destroy the rebel army if possible." But as was typical, McClellan hesitated, and Lee and his men escaped.[71]

Still, Lincoln believed that, since Lee's army had been driven off Union soil, it was a message from God, saying, "God had decided the question in favor of the slaves." Five days after the battle, on September 22, 1862, Lincoln issued his Emancipation Proclamation. He said, "If my name ever goes into history, it was for this act." Jefferson Davis called it the "most execrable measure recorded in the history of guilty men."[72]

By the end of 1862, the Union had the largest army in the world. The Confederates had the second largest. This prevented any foreign interference. Besides, England and France opposed slavery. John Stuart Mill wrote, "The triumph of the Confederacy would be a victory of the powers of evil which would give courage to the enemies of progress and damp the spirits of friends all over the civilized world. [The American Civil War] is destined to be a turning point, for good or evil, of the course of human affairs."[73]

The realities of war were haunting. The camps were cauldrons of disease. The sanitary commission inspector reported that camps were "littered with refuse, food and other rubbish, sometimes in an offensive state of decomposition; slops deposited in pits within the limits or thrown out broadcast; heaps of manure and offal to the camp." Scurvy, dysentery, diphtheria, typhoid, and pneumonia killed more than fighting did. Medical care was primitive. A Confederate physician remembered, "All complainants were asked the same question. 'How are your bowels?' If they were open, I administered a plug of opium, if they were shut, I gave a plug of blue mass."[74]

According to military historian Stephen Ambrose, on the Confederate side, 94,000 died in battle and 164,000 died from disease. On the Union side, 110,000 died in battle and 225,000 died from disease.[75]

The Civil War was a bloodbath in part because the weapons were ahead of tactics. The .58-caliber rifle, with its soft lead bullet at low velocity, tore humans apart. When a bullet hit, it shattered the arm or leg. Amputation was the only alternative. In the South especially, there was a shortage of chloroform, so many of the soldiers had their limbs sawed off totally awake. If a soldier got hit, he immediately opened his shirt to see if it was directly into the abdomen, which he knew was a death sentence. Blood poisoning was common. Although Custer touted his saber charges, there was little morbidity or mortality from them. There were almost no bayonet wounds in the Civil War.[76]

There were many desertions. Soldiers were conflicted between duty and self-interest and torn between movements that were larger than themselves and their primal fear. At the time of Bull Run, cowards were often branded with a "C," initially on the hip but later on the face or forehead. President Lincoln, showing empathy for deserters who ran away, advised a judge advocate general, "Deal gently with these leg cases . . . for no doubt many a pair of cowardly legs has run away with the valiant heart."[77] He may have imagined what it felt like to hear the slap of bullets into the meat of a person next to you and see bloody human body parts scattered underfoot, and nevertheless have to march ahead toward a fierce enemy not far in front of you. Many leaders were not as lenient, and execution remained an established punishment for desertion even into the twentieth century. Custer would embrace this harsh form of punishment out West.

In May 1863, under General Joseph Hooker's command, the Union army lost 17,000 men at Chancellorsville. It was Lee's masterpiece. A shaken Lincoln cried out, "My God! My God! What will the country say?" For Lee it was a brilliant victory, but 13,000 of his men were either dead or disabled. The most noted death was that of Stonewall Jackson who, after having his arm amputated, died of infection.[78]

By 1863, Lincoln believed the key to winning the war was taking Vicksburg, Mississippi. The Confederates controlled 100 miles of the Mississippi River from Vicksburg south to Port Hudson, Louisiana. That control allowed east-west movement of crops and livestock from Texas to the Confederate armies as far east as Virginia. But he had not found his general yet. All had proven unsatisfactory—Winfield Scott, Irvin McDowell, George McClellan, John Pope, George McClellan again, Ambrose Burnside, and Joseph Hooker.

At the end of January 1863, Grant and 45,000 men were assigned by Lincoln to capture Vicksburg. With progress slow and stories of Grant drinking heavily, Edwin Stanton sent Charles Dana, an administration investigator, to report what was going on. At first, Dana was critical of the operation, but he soon changed. William Sherman was described as Grant's best lieutenant, "a very brilliant man and an excellent commander of corps. Sherman's information was great, and he was a clever talker. . . . What a splendid soldier he is!"[79]

General Halleck directed Grant to head south of Vicksburg to meet up with Nathaniel Banks and his troops before attacking, but Banks got delayed for a week. Grant took the greatest gamble of his career by attacking without waiting for Banks. Unlike Custer, who in June 1876 would also not follow orders, Grant was successful. Grant was known for taking the fight to the enemy with relentless fervor.

A jubilant Lincoln wrote Grant, "I do not remember that you and I ever met personally. I write this now as a grateful acknowledgment for the almost inestimable service you have done the country." The president had initially doubted Grant's strategy, saying, "I thought it was a mistake. I now wish to make the personal acknowledgment that you were right and I was wrong."[80]

As the battle for Vicksburg raged on (from May 18 into the first week of July), Lee decided his Army of Northern Virginia would again try to invade the North by attacking Pennsylvania, which would force Grant to remove his forces. This set the stage on July 1 for the greatest battle ever fought in North America—Gettysburg. By the second day of the battle, 65,000 Confederates confronted 85,000 Union troops. On the third day, Custer made a name for himself by leading his troops on multiple charges against Jeb Stuart, thwarting the Confederates' plans. By the time the carnage was over, almost a third of the soldiers—51,000—were lying dead and rotting. The count showed 23,000 casualties for the North and 28,000 for the South. Lee lamented, "All this has been my fault. It is I who have lost the fight."[81]

A Union soldier recalled the horrific day, writing, "The dead bodies of men and horses had lain there, putrefying under the summer sun for three days. . . . Corpses swollen to twice their original size, some of them actually burst asunder with the pressure of foul gases and vapors. . . . Several humans or inhuman corpses sat upright against a fence, with arms extended in the air and faces hideous with something very like a fixed leer, as if taking a fiendish pleasure in showing us what we essentially were and might at any moment become."[82]

These graphic details were countered with the jubilation of a victory for the North. Elisha Rhodes (a Union soldier whose wartime writings became famous through their inclusion in Ken Burns' PBS Civil War documentary) joyously wrote in his diary, "July 4, 1863. Was ever the Nation's Birthday celebrated in such a way before? I wonder what the South thinks of us Yankees now! I think Gettysburg will cure the Rebels of any desire to invade the North again." The next day, after hearing more good news, he added, "Glorious news! We have news that Vicksburg has fallen! We have thousands of prisoners and they seem to be stupefied with the news."[83]

The reality, however, was that, for the North to ensure victory, more men would be needed. A draft was instituted that would add 300,000 new Union troops. All men between ages twenty and forty-five were required to sign up, and those inducted would be committed to three years' service. Many criticized the law as a rich man's bill. Any man that came up with $300 and found someone to substitute for his service was exempt. In a variation of "survival of the fittest," the exemption could be called the "survival of the richest." Every president from the time of the Civil War until a young Theodore Roosevelt took office had some appointment in the military during the Civil War except for Grover Cleveland, who found someone to serve in his place. Other prominent men, including Andrew Carnegie, J. P. Morgan, and the fathers of Theodore and Franklin Roosevelt, found others to serve in their place. The fact that Theodore Roosevelt's father never served in the Civil War haunted him for his whole life. It was one of the reasons that he led the strenuous life and served so gallantly in the military. Though he loved his father deeply, Roosevelt was ashamed that he was essentially a draft dodger.

In 1863, the Union found a supply of new soldiers in the free black population. Many were hesitant to accept them in the military. Sherman cautiously said, "I have had the question put to me often, 'Is not a negro as good as a white man to stop a bullet?' Yes: and a sand-bag is better; but can a negro do our skirmishing and picket duty? Can they improvise bridges, sorties, flank movements, etc., like the white man? I say no." His view was countered by Lincoln and Grant who said yes, "I have given the subject of arming the Negro my hearty support. This, with the emancipation of the Negro, is the heaviest blow yet given the Confederacy. . . . By arming the Negro we have added a powerful ally. They will make good soldiers and taking them from the enemy weakens him in the same proportion they strengthen us."[84]

By the fall of 1863, Lincoln was so impressed with the forty-one-year-old Grant that he named him commander of all the Union armies between Appalachia and the Mississippi. Grant thanked Sherman and McPherson for his success. Sherman returned the compliment, saying, "The chief characteristic in your nature is the simple faith in success you have always manifested, which I can liken to nothing else than the faith a Christian has in his Saviour. This faith gave you victory at Shiloh and Vicksburg."[85]

Lincoln's choice proved to be a wise one. Grant won another victory at Chattanooga. An officer recalled, "When Grant arrived we began to see things move. We felt that everything came from a plan."[86] Both Sherman and General Phil Sheridan (1831-1888) took part in the battle. Sherman was a superb strategist but not much of a field fighter. Sherman had attended West Point three years before Grant where he was known as a quick study in class but unreliable outside it. His average demerits per annum were about 150. Sherman and Sheridan gained a reputation as two of the fiercest warriors in the war. They would bring that same energy eventually to the Indian battles out West.[87]

Grant's rise to the country's warrior hero had been a long and circuitous one. He was born Hiram Ulysses Grant on April 27, 1822, in a cabin at Point Pleasant, Ohio. His father, Jesse, ran a tannery and supported Henry Clay, a Whig, who opposed Democrat Andrew Jackson. He was a sensitive and shy young boy who felt more comfortable in the company of horses. Schoolbooks had little interest to him, and he loved reading the works of Washington Irving and James Fenimore Cooper like so many other youth—such as Custer—in that era.

He entered West Point in 1839 with the hope of a stable vocation. Weighing only 120 pounds, Grant was an average student and failed to get the cavalry assignment that he wanted. Tuberculosis ran in the family, and the last six months of school he suffered from a severe cough that led to weight loss.

In 1848, he married Julia Dent, the sister of his West Point roommate, and they eventually had three sons and a daughter. He jumped from job to job, running a grocery store and then trying to make money by selling potatoes. Julia's father gave her sixty acres. In time, he managed the Dent farm, which entailed managing slaves. A friend remembered, "He was not a hand to manage Negroes. He couldn't force them to do anything. He was just so good and good tempered, and besides, he was not a slavery man."[88] Grant consistently lost money as a farmer. In St. Louis, he met Sherman, and the two lamented how poorly they had done in private life. Sherman said, "West Point and the regular Army aren't good schools for farmers, bankers, merchants, and mechanics."[89]

The future president began to drink. Other vocations also proved to be failures, including jobs as a bill collector, realtor, and firewood salesman on the streets of St. Louis. His realtor partner, Harry Boggs, recalled the winter of 1858-1859, writing, "I can see him now as he used to sit humbly by my fireside. He had no exalted opinion of himself at any time, but in those days he seemed almost in despair."[90]

The war saved Grant from obscurity, and a series of victories not only propelled him up the military ranks but also stamped him as a national hero.

In May 1861, he was a civilian on $2 per diem, but nine months later he was a major general scoring victories from Belmont to Fort Donelson and earning the nickname "Unconditional Surrender Grant." War makes gods.

Grant's gift was military service. He was a clear thinker and dogged in his methodical approach to battle. He had the ability to visualize the battlefield and pinpoint his enemy's weaknesses. His physical appearance was the opposite of Custer's. Elisha Rhodes commented, "General U. S. Grant is a short, thick-set man and rode his horse like a bag of mail. I was a little disappointed in the appearance, but I like the look of his eye."[91] Both Custer and Grant were most successful making war. As Grant biographer H. W. Brands wrote, "He knew he had never been good at anything but war, and now that another war [the Civil War] had begun, he wouldn't miss it for the world. And this war, unlike the Mexican war, was one he could believe in. The Union was a cause to stir the heart of any patriot."[92]

Charles Dana, after observing Grant at Vicksburg, wrote:

> Grant was an uncommon fellow—the most modest, the most disinterested, and the most honest man I ever knew, with a temper that nothing could disturb, and a judgment that was judicial in its comprehensiveness and wisdom. Not a great man, except morally, not an original or brilliant man, but sincere, thoughtful, deep, and gifted with courage that never faltered; when the time came to risk all, he went in like a simple-hearted, unaffected, unpretending hero, whom no ill omens could deject and no triumph unduly exalt. A social, friendly man, too, fond of a pleasant joke and also ready with one; but liking above all a long chat of an evening, and ready to sit up with you all night, talking in the cool breeze in front of this tent. Not a man of sentimentality, not demonstrative in friendship, but always holding to his friends, and just even to the enemies he hated.[93]

In 1864, Lincoln's old nemesis, George B. McClellan, accepted the Democratic nomination for the presidency. He routinely called Lincoln "the original gorilla" and deeply resented the president for removing him from command of the Grand Army of the Potomac. Without further military successes, Lincoln believed he would be beaten in the election. Sherman seemed to be the only one of Grant's commanders who was still making any progress. "Grant stood by me when I was crazy," Sherman said, "and I stood by him when he was drunk; and we stand by each other always."[94]

With victories at Gettysburg, Vicksburg, and Chattanooga, in 1864 Lincoln made Grant general-in-chief of all Union armies. On May 6, 1864, Sherman's Grand Army of the West headed south from Chattanooga into Georgia with 98,000 men under his command. His march through Georgia and the Carolinas in the autumn of 1864 and early 1865 remains a byword for savagery.[95] There was devastation and destruction, fire and brimstone. Sherman came to be seen as the personification of evil.[96]

It was the march to the sea and burning of Atlanta that distinguished Sherman (1831-1888) as a Civil War general. He was second in significance only to Grant. He broke the South's will to resist and Southerners' belief that it could survive as a confederacy. He was an innovator in his understanding of logistics and topography. Both Custer and Sherman put on a show as flamboyant as those staged by Buffalo Bill Cody. Again and again, he outflanked the enemy with his superb grasp of terrain honed while stationed in the antebellum South. Like Dwight Eisenhower, Sherman knew how to drill his men and keep them focused on their mission. Secretary of War Edwin Stanton and others pressured Sherman to use African Americans as combat soldiers, but he resisted. Black troops were handed shovels instead. As a racist, Sherman saw them as too inferior to be successful in battle. He would carry his racism into destroying the Native American culture and clearing the way for the transcontinental railroad. He advocated extermination, not assimilation.[97]

At the end of August, the Confederates had abandoned Atlanta. With 45,000 men, Sheridan attacked the Confederates in the Shenandoah Valley. Sheridan became known as the most relentless officer Grant commanded. It paid off with a victory. Lincoln was elated with Sherman's capture of Atlanta and Sheridan's victory in the Shenandoah Valley.

The November presidential election proved successful for Lincoln and was bolstered by solid support from his Union Army. With Atlanta secure, on November 16, 1864, Sherman moved toward the coastal city of Savannah. Along the way, his army destroyed almost everything in its path, and on December 21 Savannah fell to the Union forces.

Over 25,000 slaves marched alongside Sherman's troops, hoping the troops would protect them from Confederate snipers. Sherman wrote, "The whole army of the United States could not restore the institution of slavery in the South. They can't get back their slaves, any more than they can get back their dead grandfathers. It is dead."[98] Their desperation was evident in a letter by an Indiana officer, who wrote, "It was very touching to see the vast numbers of colored women following after us with babies in their arms, and little ones like our Anna clinging to their tattered skirts. One poor creature, while nobody was looking, hid two boys, five years old, in a wagon, intending, I suppose, that they should see the land of freedom if she couldn't."[99]

At the end of 1864, Lincoln was delighted with Union progress, crowing, "Grant has the bear by the hind leg while Sherman takes off its hide." Sherman wasn't done. In early 1865, he moved northward toward the Carolinas. Then, vindictively, he said, "When I go through South Carolina it will be one of the most horrible things in the history of the world. The devil himself couldn't restrain my men in that state." The fact was not lost on Union soldiers that South Carolina had led the way in leaving the Union.[100] On January 31, Congress voted 119 to 56 to pass the Thirteenth Amendment to abolish slavery and sent it to the states for ratification.

Ironically, Lee in desperation urged the Confederate Congress to authorize black troops, which they did on March 13, 1865. Within days, there was a new Confederate battalion made up of two companies of black hospital orderlies and three companies of white convalescents.

Grant now commanded nearly 1 million troops, as opposed to Lee who led fewer than 100,000. Lee had seen enough bloodshed and finally surrendered to Grant at the McLean house near the Appomattox Courthouse in Virginia. A Seneca Indian on Grant's staff, Lieutenant Colonel Ely Parker, wrote the articles of surrender for the two commanders to sign.

Both Grant and Lee shared a number of characteristics that helped them succeed: close relationships with their officers, tactical creativity, outstanding decision-making, seizing initiative, and exemplary leadership. They also shared a few shortcomings: infrequent overconfidence, unclear orders, and costly frontal assaults. After the war, Grant said of Lee, "I never ranked Lee as high as some others in the Army. I could never see in his achievements what justified his reputation."[101] Both stubbornly refused to admit the obvious—they were each other's greatest opponent.

Lincoln's end came on April 15, 1865, after being shot in the head on the prior evening, Good Friday, at Ford's Theatre. Four days earlier, he had addressed a crowd outside the White House about the difficult issue of reconstruction, and he publicly endorsed black suffrage for the first time. After hearing Lincoln's words, John Wilkes Booth turned to a friend and said, "That means nigger citizenship. Now by God I'll put him through! That is the last speech he will ever make."[102]

African Americans missed Lincoln perhaps more than the whites. They referred to him as their Moses, their father, and their benefactor. Lincoln's funeral train allowed mourners a substitute for the loss of each Union soldier who died so far away from home. Lincoln's coffin stood for every soldier who didn't get a proper burial. Christians had a dilemma because they ascribed their wartime victory to God's will, but what about Lincoln's assassination? Some saw him as a Jesus figure, a sacrificial lamb for the sin of slavery. He was atonement for the nation's sins and the last casualty of the Civil War. Jesus Christ died for the world. Lincoln died for his country.

But others saw it as God's message to stiffen Northern resolve to make sure blacks obtained real citizenship rights and to block any chance that the Confederates could come into power. They rationalized that perhaps God removed Lincoln because he was too empathetic and merciful to impose the measures that the radical Republicans favored.[103]

The Fourteenth Amendment granting citizenship to blacks was opposed by the new president, Andrew Johnson (1808-1875), who had ironically supported abolition, saying, "This is a country for white men, and, by God, as long as I am President, it shall be a government for white men."[104] The law bypassed Indians, who were not subject to federal jurisdiction. They would have to wait until 1924 before they were recognized as citizens in their own country.

Before Custer was the "Son of the American West," he was a Civil War hero with an impressive record. That war developed him into the man who fought to win the West.

CHAPTER TWENTY-THREE

A Civil War Legend Unleashed: Custer Revealed

Never, never, never believe any war will be smooth and death easy, or that anyone who embarks on that strange voyage can measure the tides and hurricanes he will encounter.
—WINSTON CHURCHILL

During war, generals become as close to gods on earth as we are ever likely to see.
—WINSTON GROOM, THE GENERALS

His personal moral character has stood in for the moral character of the United States.
—T. J. STILES, CUSTER'S TRIALS

No one is the same size as history, no one's that big. But Custer came close. Custer, like most Northerners, fought for reunification and not abolition. The regular experience of death was the hallmark of his life. Custer's first commission was as second lieutenant of the 2nd U.S. Cavalry Regiment on July 18, 1861. Even though he arrived late to the first major battle of the Civil War, Bull Run, and was mainly a noncombatant, Custer wrote to his roommate, Tully McCrea, who was still at West Point, that he was the last to leave the battlefield and was almost taken prisoner. Custer was never satisfied with his impressive achievements on the battlefield. He always had to make them more grandiose to his family, friends, and public.

Who did Custer model himself after? That man was George McClellan

(1826-1885), commander of the Army of the Potomac. He was the most senior general in the U.S. Army even though he was only thirty-five years old in 1862, at the time when Custer joined the general on his personal staff as an aide-de-camp. He gave Custer his first big break and became Custer's idol. In March 1862, Custer wrote, "I have more confidence in General McClellan than in any man living. I would forsake everything and follow him to the ends of the earth. I would lay down my life for him."[1]

Short in stature, McClellan—his nickname was "Little Mac"—was born in Philadelphia to a prominent surgeon who was one of the founders of Jefferson Medical College. He entered West Point at fifteen—the institution waived its normal minimum age of sixteen—and finished second in his class of fifty-nine cadets in 1846. His best friends were from Southern aristocratic families. Like Grant, he served in the army that captured Mexico City in 1847. Considered by historians as a poor general and insubordinate to Lincoln, McClellan, after running unsuccessfully against the president as a Democratic presidential nominee in 1864, later served as governor of New Jersey.[2]

Both McClellan and Custer could be charismatic when they wanted to be, and both surrounded themselves with admirers. Historian Richard Slotkin wrote, "McClellan's headquarters was a closed circle, an echo chamber filled with followers and acolytes who praised his every decision as masterful."[3] Custer's superior was also obsessed with his physical appearance and public adoration. He basked in the flattery of some who called him a genius with extraordinary judgment. And of course, like Jesus, he considered himself a divine medium to the world. McClellan commented to General Burnside, "I can almost think of myself as a chosen instrument to carry out his schemes." He shared with his wife, Ellen, "I feel that God has placed great work in my hands. My previous life seems to have been unwittingly directed to this great end."[4]

Custer's mentor seemed to have no boundaries to his grandiosity and didn't care if he shared his disdain for his superiors. Thus, McClellan characterized Secretary of War Stanton as "without exception the vilest man I ever knew or heard of." Lincoln was dismissed as "an idiot," "gorilla," and "a well-meaning baboon." The day after Custer joined the staff, McClellan wrote his wife in regard to Lincoln and his supporters, "It is perfectly sickening to deal with such people & you may rest assured that I will lose as little time as possible in breaking off all connection with them."[5] He wrote his father-in-law, "I confess to prejudice in favor of my own race, & can't learn to like the odor of either Billy Goats or Niggers."[6] In McClellan's mind, he was the only one fit to be president of the United States.

For many Northerners, fighting the war had little to do with ending slavery. As McClellan wrote early in the conflict, "Help me to dodge the nigger—we want nothing to do with him. I am fighting to preserve the integrity of the Union & the power of the Govt—on no other issue. To gain that end we cannot afford to raise up the negro question."[7] Manifest Destiny and racism were embraced by many of the soldiers of the Northern army, including Custer.

As McClellan led battles, he suffered terrible losses, as during the Seven Days Battles against Robert E. Lee's troops. Historian James M. McPherson wrote, "The 30,000 men killed and wounded in the Seven Days' equaled the number of casualties in all the battles in the Western theater—including Shiloh—during the first half of 1862."[8] Very much charmed by McClellan, Custer defended his idol in a letter to his sister. "I lost several friends in the various engagements and lament their loss," Custer wrote. "It is better to die an honored death than to live in dishonor."[9] McClellan appreciated the hero worship, and years later wrote of Custer, "In those days Custer was simply a reckless, gallant boy, undeterred by fatigue, unconscious of fear, but his head was always clear in danger, and he always brought me clear and intelligible reports of what he saw when under the heaviest fire."[10]

Even though his performance in battle was considered disappointing, McClellan seemed to have no limits to his hubris. This was no more evident than in July 1862 when Lincoln visited him and his staff, including Custer, at Harrison's Landing. McClellan had prepared an opinion letter about the rebellion that he handed to Lincoln to read in front of him:

> I earnestly desire . . . to lay before your excellency, for your private consideration, my general views concerning the existing state of the rebellion.
>
> It should not be a war looking to the subjugation of the people of any State in any event. It should not be at all a war upon population, but against armed forces and political organizations. Neither confiscation of property, political executions of persons, territorial organization of States, or forcible abolition of slavery should be contemplated for a moment. . . . Military power should not be allowed to interfere with the relations of servitude, either by supporting or impairing the authority of the master. . . .
>
> A declaration of radical views, especially upon slavery, will rapidly disintegrate our present armies.[11]

As the war progressed, Custer's courage and success in battles heightened his fame. On September 17, 1862, McClellan faced Lee in a battle at Antietam (the Confederates called it Sharpsburg) that would be noted as a place where, in one day, more Americans died than in any other battle in American history to date. Custer's luck held that day. He was on McClellan's staff instead of leading the charge as he often did. Six thousand men died and another 17,000 were wounded on both sides—more than the losses of the War of 1812 and the Mexican war combined. The battle was poorly executed by McClellan, and he missed opportunities to crush Lee's armies. He was often timid in making needed advances. On September 19, the Confederates fled to the South. Despite the heavy losses and inconclusive result, Antietam was considered a Union victory, which gave Lincoln the opportunity to issue the Emancipation Proclamation.[12]

The battle was also noteworthy for being the first to demonstrate the power of photography. Today, it is difficult to appreciate the profound impact photography had on Americans for generations following the Civil War. Photography could either dazzle you or give you nightmares. Forever romanticized, war (for those not involved) was a noble endeavor even if it resulted in death or disability. Carnage of a sort so old—an uncivil affair in which fists, strangulations, and stompings supplemented bullets and bayonets—just did not register in the American psyche. That all changed in 1862. The shocks of the Civil War to the American nervous system were brutal and unprecedented, not least because it was the first conflict in history memorialized in photography. People could follow in realistic detail the four years of killing and destruction, and grieve for the missing by holding images of them taken at a precise moment in the past.[13]

Mathew Brady (1822-1896) was one of the greatest photographers of the nineteenth century. In October 1862, the exhibition at his New York gallery of photographs taken several weeks earlier at Antietam was a turning point in America's appreciation of the camera's power to record horror. Masses lined up around the block and waited for hours to examine in a somewhat macabre way what could now be seen up close. A reviewer wrote in *The New York Times,* "Mr. Brady has done something to bring home the terrible and earnestness of war. If he has not brought bodies and laid them in our dooryards and along our streets, he has done something very like it. . . . By the aid of the magnifying glass, the very features of the slain may be distinguished."[14]

Mathew Brady photographed over a dozen presidents and almost every noted person in America during his professional career. The Ohio generals who visited his New York studio included Ulysses S. Grant, William T. Sherman, Philip H. Sheridan, and Custer. Much to Custer's delight, a never-ending supply of images of Custer appeared in newspapers around the country during the war.

Custer especially loved having his picture taken. It was even better than looking in the mirror. Over the years, numerous portraits of Custer and photographs of Custer with others, especially Libbie, were taken by some of America's greatest photographers. Even though his parents were strapped for cash, Custer would rather spend thirty dollars or more on a picture of himself than help them out. On November 6, 1863, Custer wrote, "I'm extravagant in many ways. I lost ten dollars today that I bet on a horse race with Gen. Kirkpatrick. . . . Between you and me I could keep a family with the money I spend needlessly."[15]

Biographer T. J. Stiles described Custer's soaring ego, writing, "The phenomenon of stardom itself appealed to him. He wanted those things that were forbidden and pleasurable. He wanted admirers. He wanted embellishment. He wanted to control how others saw him. Like a star actor."[16]

Custer Through the Looking Glass

T. J. Stiles commented on the young West Point graduate's character at the beginning of the Civil War in the regular army, noting, ". . . Custer was individualistic, romantic, and impulsive. This contrast would color the rest of his life. He was perhaps the truer representative of the young republic, but the Army foreshadowed its future."[17]

Historian Paul Andrew Hutton wrote, "My feelings on Geronimo are that he was a self-centered narcissist just like General George Custer. That's why I admire him."[18] Custer was indeed a textbook narcissist, and that is the key to understanding him. This is not a criticism, but a psychiatric diagnosis that's not difficult to make. There is no more impactful expression of narcissism than racism, either in an individual or a nation.

The Greek myth of Narcissus is the origin of the term *narcissist*. Narcissus rejected the romantic advancements from the lovely mountain nymph Echo, who, for a number of reasons, was also punished by the gods. She was left with a voice but condemned to a life of wandering. The gods, at a revengeful Echo's pleading, punished Narcissus by making him fall in love with his own image reflected in a pool. Narcissus yearned to possess himself, which he couldn't do. He couldn't pull himself away from looking at his own image and eventually starved to death and fell in the water, never to be seen again. His flaw was he could never love another human except himself.[19]

Because of his grandiose conception of himself, the narcissist needs a continual supply of those he charms to maintain specialness, exaggerated importance, and a sense of superiority. That's because he often has secret feelings of insecurity, shame, vulnerability, and humiliation. Custer was embarrassed about his humble beginnings. It's healthy to have some narcissism because without it, no one could develop self-esteem or better themselves in life. The most outstanding leaders typically harbor a healthy ego. Narcissism becomes pathologic when the person can think of no one other than himself and his satisfaction. Certain professions attract those with narcissistic personality disorder. They include politicians, actors, public ministry, and the military, among others.[20]

Narcissists seek a captive audience—like soldiers and church members—forced to give them repetitive approval. The narcissist has an exaggerated sense of self-importance and entitlement and expects to be recognized as superior even without achievements that warrant it. He exaggerates his achievements and talents. He feels he is free to be exhibitionistic, and pranks and jokes are common. He believes in his own superior wisdom and doesn't tend to discuss ideas but imposes them. He is preoccupied with fantasies about success, power, brilliance, beauty, or the perfect mate. He is charming to those who are charmed by him, but is ruthless toward those who don't buy into his hubris. Thus he can be competitive, vindictive, devaluing, and vengeful. When confronted, he acts defensively and looks ahead to the future with no remorse, blaming any mistakes on others. He wants to be surrounded only by yes people, and so his closest associates often secure their positions through connections and boot licking.

When dealing with the public and journalists, the narcissist tends to exaggerate and lie. He has little ability to control his desires and can be impulsive and brash. What is so attractive to the charmed is that he appears to be in command of every situation and speaks with certainty in a tone of authority. By being clever, charming, seductive, persuasive, and self-assured, the narcissist presents an impressive aura.

Those who are charmed by the narcissist are looking for someone to make them feel special. Psychiatrist James Masterson calls them "closet narcissists" who don't invest in their own feeling of grandiosity but in an omnipotent other. It makes them feel special. Libbie would eventually come out of the closet, and for almost sixty years after her husband's death continued to bask in her and her husband's past glory.[21]

People around a narcissist feel he or she has star quality. A narcissist wants to be admired more than loved. As T. J. Stiles wrote of Custer,

"He yearned to be accepted, to be admired, to belong."[22] To attract attention, the person is often a flashy or an eccentric dresser. The men frequently have trophy wives who like to feel special by flirting.

Soldiers can be a warehouse of narcissistic supply because they often need someone outside themselves to motivate them. Those who are entranced by the narcissist become loyal followers of the charmer and in an indirect way gain some of the sense of specialness in themselves by their strong attachment to the charismatic person. They look for a savior figure. The game for the narcissist is always domination, not cooperation.[23]

The fifth edition of the *Diagnostic and Statistical Manual of Mental Disorders* (DSM) lists nine criteria for narcissistic personality disorder (NPD). They have remained unchanged over the last twenty years. An individual needs only five of them for the diagnosis: 1) has a grandiose sense of self-importance; 2) is preoccupied with fantasies of unlimited success, power, brilliance, beauty, or ideal love; 3) believes that he or she is special and unique and can only be understood by, or should associate with, other special or high status people or institutions [like the military]; 4) requires excessive admiration and is highly susceptible to flattery; 5) has a sense of entitlement; 6) is interpersonally exploitative; 7) lacks empathy; 8) is often envious of others or believes that others are envious of him or her; and 9) shows arrogant, haughty behaviors or attitudes.

Some have suggested, in regard to racism, that the United States represented a narcissistic country. In *American Narcissism: The Myth of National Superiority,* author Wilber W. Caldwell wrote, "Historically, these notions of superiority spring from myths of the unique abundance and regenerative power of the new land; from visions of chosen-ness, mission, and high destiny; from indelible lessons of frontier self-sufficiency; from a developing sense of American isolation and uniqueness, and finally from the perceived universality of American ideology."[24]

Custer and Libbie

For Custer, his first love was himself, and that love was only completely consummated when he was in battle. Everything about war was narcissistic supply. So it's not surprising that even after all the horror he had experienced during the Civil War, Custer didn't want it to end. He wrote to his cousin Augusta Ward on October 2, 1862, only two weeks after Antietam:

> You asked me if I will not be glad when the last battle is fought. So far as the country is concerned I, of course, must wish for peace, and

will be glad when the war is ended, but if I answer for myself alone, I must say that I shall regret to see the war end. I would be willing, yes glad, to see a battle every day of my life. Now do not misunderstand me. I only speak of my own interests and desires, perfectly regardless of all the world besides, but as I said before, when I think of the pain & misery produced to individuals as well as the miserable sorrow caused throughout the land I cannot but earnestly hope for peace, and at an early date. Do you understand me?[25]

Both Custer biographers T. J. Stiles and Stephen Ambrose characterized Custer as a romantic. Stiles' main thesis was that Custer was a man out of time who did not adjust well to the cultural changes that the war had set in motion. In this context, synonyms for romantic include idyllic, sentimentalist, and marked by the imaginative or emotional appeal of what is heroic, adventurous, and idealized. Custer was a primitive and obsolete figure in an age dominated by Darwin. Ambrose wrote, "Custer wallowed in romanticism. As with so many nineteenth century romantics, he was unmoved by the deaths of thousands but tremendously affected by the suffering of one."[26] However, from a psychiatric standpoint, war provided his narcissistic supply like nothing else in life. His romantic persona was a veneer to his underlying personality disorder. Better examples of romantics are James Fenimore Cooper, Albert Bierstadt, and Charles M. Russell.

On November 7, 1862, in a snowstorm at the headquarters' camp at Rectortown, Virginia, a messenger brought orders that Major General Ambrose Burnside would be replacing McClellan. McClellan's inflammatory behavior toward his superiors, including Lincoln, finally got him fired. As the year ended, Captain Custer took a break from the war and headed back to his sister's home in Monroe, Michigan. Without any specific work, Custer worried about his future.

His attentions were directed toward women like Fannie Fifield and Libbie Bacon, though not always pleasantly. Once, while Custer dallied in the Fifield family parlor, Libbie arrived and was abruptly confronted by Custer because she had been drinking a little beer. She defended herself. Custer didn't hesitate to direct his anger toward others when he didn't control the situation. It was not uncommon for him to send inflammatory notes to friends and relatives who didn't give him the attention he thought he deserved.[27]

As it became clear to him that his military advancement would rely more on the Republican president and his generals, Custer distanced himself from his idol, McClellan. By April 1863, Brigadier General Alfred Pleasonton was now his superior. He informed his sister Ann of his new staff position and mentioned his shock that the general had a black, female cook named Hannah. In the letter to her, he assumed that his sister would share his disgust in eating food prepared by a black woman. In the same letter, so as not to act too enamored and vulnerable concerning Libbie, he wrote, "There are not more than a dozen girls in Monroe who I like better than Libbie and that is the truth."[28]

As might be expected, when his increase in rank didn't happen, Custer rationalized, "A rule which I have always laid down—never to regret anything after it is done." Stiles noted, "But his refusal to regret indicates an indifference to the effects of his actions on others. He refused to admit he was wrong, lashing out sarcastically at his accusers. When cornered by his transparent guilt, he tried to trivialize or dismiss his misdeeds."[29]

As the war dragged on, Lincoln continued to look for a general that would end it. Joseph Hooker was replaced by Major General George Meade. Pleasanton received a promotion, and he in turn pushed for Custer to become a brigadier general—quite an achievement for such a young soldier. In late June 1863, Custer received the good news that his promotion had finally been approved. He wrote, "To say I was elated would faintly express my feelings. I well knew that I had reason to congratulate myself."[30]

One of the ways Custer expressed his specialness and grandiose sense of self-importance came in the form of showy dress. He donned a broad-brimmed felt hat tilted to one side that covered the origin of his long, blonde curly locks. His jacket—double breasted to designate he was a general—was made of black velveteen adorned with gold piping. His sailor's shirt with a broad rectangular blue collar with white trim was complemented by a gaudy red tie wrapped around his neck. The package was completed with high cavalry boots highlighted with gilt spurs. The charmed loved it, while others were less certain about his garb. One officer with a critical eye commented, "This officer is one of the funniest-looking beings you ever saw. His aspect, though highly amusing, is also pleasing, as he has a very merry blue eye, and a devil-may-care style."[31]

The papers fed his ego. The *Monroe Commercial* wrote, "We have not a more gallant man in the field. Whenever there is a daring expedition to be undertaken or hard fighting to be done, he is ever among the foremost."[32] After Gettysburg, the Monroe paper quoted the *Philadelphia Inquirer*, which described Custer as "conspicuous among the bravest of the brave. Young, dashing, impulsive, his golden, curly locks, and gay velvet undress jacket, made him a shining-mark for the Rebel sharp-shooters; but he came out of the fire unscathed and unharmed. This young officer has a bright future before him."[33]

Libbie had found the man to make her feel special. With her thick, dark hair and attractive face and figure, she delighted in men admiring her. If war was where Custer was fulfilled, it was the attention of men that fulfilled her ego. As her biographer Shirley Leckie noted, "Nothing delighted her more than attracting men."[34] Custer won her over with his charm. "C [Custer] has quite spoiled me," she wrote. "Everything I said or did was remembered or treasured by him."[35] Another time she wrote, "Every other man seems so ordinary beside my own particular *star*."[36]

The "boy general with the golden locks" was named after a preacher. His father was content to be a blacksmith and a farmer. After all, Christ was a carpenter, and David was a shepherd. Custer was not a churchgoer like his father, and if he wanted to seek God in solid form he could look in the mirror or at the latest photograph taken of him by Brady. In the summer of 1863, his sister Ann fretted over this and wrote him a long letter, saying, "My Dear Brother O how much I wish you were a Christian. You have often said you was happy. I don't think there is any true happyness in the world with out religion."[37] Custer used religion as a tool and an effective mode of charming targeted individuals. As Stiles described, "Armstrong remained a creature of the senses, not the spirit. He filled his heart with temporal things, with fighting, promotion, friendship, music, dancing, gambling, and love—and lust."[38]

Libbie was pleased that Custer didn't drink, but she had no problem letting him know that she didn't appreciate his swearing and gambling. Custer's father, his father-in-law, sisters, and Libbie pressured him to accept Jesus Christ as his personal savior. Even though he did convert, most likely it was more show than anything. The real goal was appeasing them. After conversion, there was no noticeable change in his behavior. In fact, as the years went by, his grandiosity ballooned. The conversion of the soul is the miracle of the moment, but the manufacture of a saint is the task of a lifetime. Perhaps Custer didn't live long enough.

Custer's charm worked on Libbie. In January 1864, before she was married, Libbie wrote of her future husband, "I no longer walk in the shadow, but in bright sunshine. . . . I do not say Armstrong is without faults. But he never tastes liquor, nor frequents the gaming-table, and though not a professing Christian that respects religion."[39]

Initially not approving of Libby's marriage to Custer, on February 9, 1864, Judge Bacon walked his daughter down the aisle of the Presbyterian church in Monroe, Michigan. They received a Bible and a gold watch as wedding gifts from the judge. Custer's war fame and charisma had won him over too. Emmanuel Custer was equally awed and wrote his son a few months before the marriage, "The hand of the Lord has been over you and around you. Nothing else could have saved you. We should look and trust him and be very thankful for his goodness and mercy shoan toward us."[40] Methodism and its church was everything to a devout Christian like Emmanuel. It was his identity. Yet any reservations about Custer being married and converted in the Presbyterian Church melted away as his son became a national sensation. It seems Custer's brilliance shone so brightly on all around him that they fell in line.

The Letters

As was common until recent times, people communicated then by writing long letters to each other. In the Custers' case, those letters could reach forty-five pages or more to Libbie. At times, their writings to each other were intense and sexual. Letters are a treasure trove for historians, and the Custers' are among the best sources of understanding their personalities.[41] While Custer was away at war, Libbie became one of the leading Washington socialites. She took every advantage of cashing in on her husband's fame. She traveled in the circle of some of the most prominent people in Washington and participated in all of the right balls. She wore the most attractive dresses she could afford so she could charm every male she met. She was the charmer and other men were the charmed. They were her narcissistic supply.

To let folks back home know he was taking Christianity seriously—even though he wasn't—Custer wrote to Libbie on April 22, 1864, from Virginia, "At four this afternoon I had Divine service at Headquarters. There were three chaplains present in a large congregation from the regiments. The Chaplain of the 5th made a beautiful prayer, invoking the divine blessing on your boy, spoke of the responsibility resting on me and prayed that I might be guided by grace from above and become, not only a powerful instrument in suppressing the rebellion, but a shining leader in the Christian army."[42] In reality, the center of his devotion was always himself.

In a May 1, 1864, letter to Libbie, Custer tried to explain to her that, inwardly, God had touched him, but there was no external evidence because he didn't want to be a hypocrite like so many Christians:

> I suppose my little one has been to church to-day. Among the traits of her character I first learned to love was her religious earnestness.

I have always felt an utter contempt for those who, under the cloak of piety, conceal base designs. The infidel has a stronger claim on my respect than he who professes insincerely. It may seem strange to you, dear girl, that I, a non-professing (tho not an unbeliever) Christian, should so ardently desire you to remain so. I have never prayed as others do. Yet, on the Eve of every battle in which I have been engaged, I have never omitted to pray inwardly, devoutly. Never have I failed to commend myself to God's keeping, asking Him to forgive my past sins, and to watch over me while in danger . . . and to receive me if I fell, while caring for those near and dear to me. After having done so all anxiety for myself, here or hereafter, is dispelled. I feel that my destiny is in the hands of the Almighty. This belief, more than any other fact or reason, makes me brave and fearless as I am. You might ask why, then, I have not become a member of some religious organization. It would take too long to tell. You are the first to whom I have ever made this explanation . . . I want you to know me as I am.[43]

As he embellished his fighting, Custer inflated his devotion. In his letters to Libbie, he danced effortlessly between impressing her with his piety and more endeavors. On May 16, 1864, from Rexall's Landing, James River, Virginia, he wrote:

Suffice it to say that our brigade has far surpassed all its previous exploits, and that your Boy was never before the object of such attention, and has succeeded beyond his highest expectations . . . and is only sorry that he cannot be with you to tell you all. Wilson proved himself an imbecile and nearly ruined the corps by his blunders. Genl. Sheridan sent for me to rescue him (Wilson) from these, though I was in a different part of the field. And after severe and bloody fight which I had command of nine regiments I cut my way through the enemy's lines and opened a way for the Corps to safety. The 1st Vermont, now under Wilson, sent over to our brigade and asked if they could not obtain "a pair of Custer's old boots" to command them. One of Genl. Sheridan's highest staff officer said "Custer saved the Cavalry Corps," and Genl. Sheridan told Col. Alger "Custer is the ablest man in the Cavalry Corps." (This is for you only, my little one. I would not write this to anyone but you. You may repeat it to our own people in Monroe, but not anyone in Washington).

I thought of you in every battle, and was sorry you would be caused anxiety on your Boy's account.[44]

In another May letter to Libbie from Virginia, Custer bragged, "I continue to receive the most flattering compliments in regard to our late battles, but you need have no fears regarding my vanity."[45] The problem with flattering a narcissist is that it isn't endearing, but empowers the recipient to even higher levels of grandiosity.

But his ego had started to grate on Libbie because it was focused too much on him and not her. She was beautiful, smart, and highly educated. She had attended Young Ladies Seminary and Collegiate Institute where she was valedictorian.[46] Her sun was just as bright as Custer's. The best way to relate that to him was to let him know that other men agreed with her assessment. As psychiatrist James Masterson noted, "The narcissist often has a low self-esteem that is a defense against insecurity and abandonment. The narcissist is not as certain as he or she looks. The illusion of stability is sustained by appearance."[47] Libbie's mother died when she was a teenager and that sense of abandonment was a thread of self-doubt woven throughout her life.

In a letter to Custer earlier in 1863, Libbie related how a "handsome young man" had stared at her at church, making her blush, and she admitted, "I am susceptible to admiration." Later, at a New Year's Eve party at her seminary, she wrote to her future husband that she had "made a conquest—a young man from New York who insisted on kissing her cheek."[48]

Now, Custer's egotistical letters from Virginia were countered in a June 1864 letter from Washington about her continued fixation after marriage on other men in which she wrote, "If I were a young unmarried lady here I should flirt, I am afraid, but I have no desire to do so. Tho still enjoying gentleman society nobody could misconstrue my laughing and talking as flirting. I know, my dear, that tho I have a pretty face it is my husband's reputation brings me so much attention."[49] Custer immediately replied, "You know what ample cause I have had to be suspicious or doubtful in regard to the conduct of women. One would naturally suppose my youthful experience would make me ever watchful. But I would as soon harbor a doubt of my Creator as of my darling little wife." Trust and piety was his message.[50]

Thrilled with the comments, Libbie backed off the jealousy theme and projected the faithful housewife in a letter to Custer on June 10, 1864, from Washington, writing, "Col. Gray can't say enough in praise of you. He told Judge Christiancy you are the most perfect gentleman he ever met. He never heard you say a word against anyone. Oh my darling, what have I not endured in torture for the past fortnight. I will learn to be brave, but you know, dear, I can't learn all at once. . . . Autie, I do get along so nicely with my sewing. I am surprised at the ease with which I can make my clothes. I think of the days of peace when little children's voices will call to us. I can hardly wait for my little boy and girl. I send you a little picture I have drawn . . . Dear Father, do you think you will look that way?"[51]

Receiving the much-needed praise, Custer made an about-face and shrewdly changed the focus from him to his faithful caring housewife, penning, "With thoughts of my darling and with the holy inspiration of a just and noble cause I gladly set out to discharge my duty to my country with a willing heart. Need I repeat to my darling that while living she is my all, and if Destiny wills me to die, wills that my country needs my death, my last prayer will be for her, my last breath will speak her name and that Heaven will not be Heaven till we are joined together. Write to Monroe and tell them of my absence. Yours through time and eternity, Autie."[52] Yes, he certainly would've wanted to let friends and family back home know of his love for her and his country. It's telling that in three sentences he used "my" nine times.

She was charmed, and in another June letter wrote words that were music to his ear, saying, "Oh, Autie, if you could have seen how their faces lighted up when they learned who I was . . . they shook my hand. . . . I can feel it yet."[53] Libbie was married to a star. A month later, Custer, who was finally given a break from fifty consecutive days of marching and fighting with Sheridan's troops, informed Libbie on July 1, 1864, from Petersburg, Virginia, where his allegiances truly were:

> While I am still as strongly wedded to the "noble profession of arms" as I ever have been and hope ever to be, I frequently discover myself acting as an umpire between my patriotism and my desire to be and remain with my darling. I wonder at the strength of my love of country and my desire to serve her, in view of the sacrifices I make to carry out my idea of duty to my government. I do not enter the Army, as some do, leaving wealth, position, comfortable home—but I do infinitely more, I separate myself from my heart's darling. But it will not always be so. A better time is in store for us.[54]

But the flattery, as is often the case, wasn't enough. Libbie wrote that same month to Custer from Washington:

Mr Ph. mails my letters every morning and brings me mine. When he saw my spirits rise at getting one he called loudly for postage. I gave him the answer I always give to gentlemen hinting at such a salute—I'm married. Had I not been. . . . Mr K. was here to-night. Very cordial. Too much so, for I avoided his attempt to kiss me by moving aside and offering him a chair. Any lady can get that man to do anything. But all I want is that he shall take me on that trip, to you. . . .[55]

On August 21, 1864, with his ego obviously threatened, Custer, writing from Berryville, Virginia, attempted to impress Libbie:

But imagine my surprise as I watch the retreating enemy to see every man, every officer, take off cap and give "Three Cheers for General Custer!" It is the first time I ever knew of such demonstration except in the case of General McClellan. I certainly felt highly flattered. The commander is a graduate of West Point long before my time, and yet as enthusiastic over your boy as if he were a youth of eighteen.

After the battle I heard "By G—d Custer is a brick!" "Custer is the man for us!" And other expressions somewhat rough but hearty.

Genl. Merritt was present during part of my engagement, but never gave me an order or suggestion, even. The battle was called by many "the handsomest fight of the war," because fought on open ground, and successful.[56]

The dueling narcissists continued, and in the fall Libbie wrote, "Robert N called on me and told me how well I was looking. I was so pleased, for I am not indifferent to compliment and have feared of late I was growing right homely.[57] In another letter, she wrote, "I guess you'd like to know who's been taking your girl around? Well, he's very nice, but he's Mrs G's beau. I like Major P. very much; he is intelligent and refined, but he cannot really love his wife or he wouldn't be taking other ladies to the theater."[58]

When threatened, Custer invoked the Lord and soon wrote to Libbie, "A few days ago Dr. Ruliston, the Corps surgeon, was congratulating me on my successful fight near Front Royal. . . . He's a religious man and withal a perfect gentleman. . . . After speaking of my narrow escape he asked if I felt grateful & had returned thanks for my preservation. How glad I was to reply in the affirmative and to add that I invariably offer my thanks to Him Whose shield protects me and Whose wisdom guides me and directs my judgment."[59]

Libbie soon wrote, "Mr Bagg says I am 'very well preserved.' They all think I looked just as I did. I know you will be glad your vain little wife has passed muster with such critics. Oh, Autie, they are all surprised I am such a sempstress. To think I made and fitted the calico myself. They think it is so commendable, now that I have plenty of money to get it done."[60]

In the last days of the war, Custer was still emphasizing the spiritual. However, once the war was over, that would end:

> We had an engagement with the enemy at Ashland, and there my preservation from death, or being maimed, crippled, for life, was miraculous, and strengthens my grateful dependence on the Merciful Being Who has so often shielded me. . . . May I live to glorify Him and keep His commandments! . . .
>
> Chaplain Holmes—he is one of my aides now—exclaimed "thank God." To which my grateful heart responded Amen.
>
> The evening after Waynesboro I invited Chaplain Holmes to my tent, for prayers and to read a Chapter. He and I alone with God gave thanks for the victory He has vouchsafed our arms.
>
> I read a chapter every night—except last night when it was raining and I had no light.[61]

In March 1865, posting from White House Landing, Virginia, Custer continued his spiritualism:

> Col. Capehart sent his band to serenade me this evening. They played "Auld Lang Syne" and "Home Sweet Home." And Oh, how lonely I felt for my little one. I do not complain, for that I should deem a sin. God has been more than kind to me, and I humbly trust I may ever have a grateful spirit for His goodness. . . . Oh, I forgot to tell you: I have not uttered a single oath, nor blasphemed, even in thought, since I saw you, so strictly I've kept my resolution.[62]

Custer had won over Chaplain Holmes, and on March 21, 1865, from White House, Virginia, Holmes wrote Custer a glowing letter about his military genius and how his glorious name would be in the history of war. He attributed Custer's luck to God shielding him. Custer couldn't wait to send this letter on to Libbie so she could share it with friends and family. Upon receiving the letter, Custer's father wrote Libbie in March 1865:

Well, Libbie, I received your welcome letter. I need not tell you of our anxiety. . . . You know from experience. Also you know to Whom to look for help. I feel every day more and more under obligation to my Savior for such good boys. I have all the confidence in the world in my son Auty, surrounded, as he is by temptation. Counsel Thomas. I want my son above all to be a good soldier of our Savior. We send our love and you send it to the boys. Your affectionate father.[63]

Victory

By Custer's side at the final battle between Grant and Lee at Appomattox was Tom Custer (1845-1876), his younger brother. Tom had enlisted as a private in 1864 and advanced quickly with help from his brother. By November 1864, Tom was on Custer's staff. Nepotism was commonplace, and General Phil Sheridan's brother served on his staff. Lincoln's son was on Grant's staff. But Tom's brother was demanding and he commented, "If anyone thinks it is a soft thing to be a commanding officer's brother he misses his guess."[64]

Of course, Custer loved being idolized by yet another person, especially when it was his brother. Custer's whole staff was composed of those who worshipped him. There was no room for dissenters. Modeling himself after his brother, Tom Custer was also a risk taker and mounted a heroic charge in the Appomattox campaign. He was so aggressive that Custer had to put Tom under arrest in order to get him to go to the rear to be treated by a surgeon after being shot in the face and neck. Custer made sure that the higher-ups knew about Tom's bravery. That led to Tom's first Congressional Medal of Honor.[65]

At the end of the war, the ultimate compliment was handed to not only Libbie but her husband. After the signing by Lee and Grant of the surrender documents at the McLean house at Appomattox, General Sheridan paid for the little pine signing stand with two $10 gold pieces. He handed it to Custer to present to his wife. Custer was so delighted that Sheridan recounted to the Illinois Commandery of the Loyal Legion in Chicago that "the delighted Custer rode off, like a boy, balancing the table on his head." On April 10, 1865, Sheridan wrote to Libbie from Appomattox Courthouse, Virginia, "My dear Madam—I respectfully present to you the small writing-table on which the conditions for the surrender of the Confederate Army of Northern Virginia were written by Lt. General Grant—and permit me to say, Madam, that there is scarcely an individual in our service who has contributed more to bring this about then your very gallant husband. Yours very respectfully, Phil. H. Sheridan, Major General."[66]

By March 1866, Custer's term had concluded. His pay as a major general in the volunteers, $8,000 a year, was discontinued. He automatically reverted to rank and rating in the regular army at $2,000 a year, with a small allowance for living quarters. He was twenty-seven years old. As T. J. Stiles wrote, "Custer undeniably served his country, yet he pursued his own agenda all the while."[67]

There was victory for the North and defeat for the South. Shelby Foote (1916-2005), born in Greenville, Mississippi, took twenty years to write his classic three-volume, 3,000-page narrative, *The Civil War*. No one has ever explained better why the Civil War is still so meaningful, writing, "But the Civil War defined us as what we are and it opened us to being what we became, good and bad things. And it is very necessary, if you're going to understand the American character in the twentieth century, to learn about this enormous catastrophe of the nineteenth century. It was the crossroads of our being, and it was a hell of a crossroads."[68] He pointed out that Southerners have a perpetual sense of defeat not shared by any other region in America.

In many ways, the Civil War defined the East, Midwest, and South during the late nineteenth century. Likewise, the Indian wars defined the American West. Like the Southerners, the Indians also have a sense of defeat that the white man really never understood or appreciated. Again, Shelby Foote astutely noted, "We think we are a wholly superior people. If we'd been anything like as superior as we think we are, we would not have fought that war. But since we did fight it, we have to make it the greatest war of all times. And our generals were the greatest generals of all time. It's very American to do that."[69]

For Custer, his church was the army, his pulpit his horse, his Bible his saber, and his congregation his troops. All the carnage was trumped by the glory not of God but of war. He was a general, he was God on Earth. Those living east of Eden now set their gaze to the West. The Golden Ones would soon rule. Custer was America: proud, exceptional, a leader, enlightened, and narcissistic. He was the Golden Boy in the Golden country. But both didn't play by the Golden Rule.

Nationalism strengthened after the Civil War, as noted by Foote: "Before the war, it was said, 'the United States are. . . .'" Grammatically, it was spoken that way and thought of as a collection of independent states. After the war, it was always 'the United States is. . .'—as we say today without being self-conscious at all. And that sums up what the war accomplished. It made us an is."[70]

CHAPTER TWENTY-FOUR

American Idols: Grant and Custer after the Civil War

Ulysses Grant emerges as a genius in battle and a steadfast president who met the daunting challenges of his time with principled leadership and great physical and moral courage. As a beloved commander in the field, he made the often unpopular sacrifices necessary to win a brutal war. As a victorious general, he worked valiantly to protect the rights of freedmen in the South. And as a visionary politician, he gave Native Americans unprecedented power to shape their own fate even as the realities of Manifest Destiny brought an end to their way of life.
—H. W. BRANDS, THE MAN WHO SAVED THE UNION: ULYSSES GRANT IN WAR AND PEACE, BACK COVER

The largest themes in American history emerge in the most intimate details of his [Custer's] life.
—T. J. STILES, CUSTER'S TRIALS

The line between luck and skill—and between gambling and investing—is rarely as clear as we think.
—ADAM KUCHARSKI, THE PERFECT BET: HOW SCIENCE AND MATH ARE TAKING THE LUCK OUT OF GAMBLING

Parallel Lives of Grant and Custer

After the Civil War, devastation was spread widely throughout the South. Its people were depressed and worn out, and its economy was in shambles.

Conversely, the North was empowered as industrialization surged, enhancing its wealth as millions from Europe flocked to the United States to participate in the American dream. But all was not well. John Wilkes Booth had assassinated Lincoln and had organized a conspiracy that targeted Andrew Johnson and William Seward. Johnson was spared when his assassin lost his nerve. Seward was assaulted in his bed and stabbed nearly to death. Grant took special precautions on his train ride back to Washington that spared his life. The day after Lincoln's assassination, he received an unsigned note that read, "General Grant, thank God, as I do, that you are still live. It was your life that fell to my lot, and I followed you on the cars. Your car door was locked, and thus you escaped me, thank God!"[1]

With Lincoln's death, Andrew Johnson (1808-1875) became the new president. In 1864, the Tennessee Democrat had been added to Lincoln's ticket only to help him attract votes from certain regions in the South so he could be reelected. As a politician, Johnson had little going for him. Oliver Temple said, "Johnson's life was full of stormy passions. It had no rest, and but little sunshine in it. He was strong and self-willed; had excessive confidence in his own power; was obstinate and dogmatic, and had little respect for the opinion of others."[2]

Grant, for his part, championed amnesty for Confederate officers and men. The Thirteenth Amendment passed Congress in January 1865 and made slavery illegal. Under Johnson's reconstruction plan, the Southern states needed to accept the amendment to return to the Union. However, Johnson opposed black citizenship. He said, "This is a country for white men, and, by God, as long as I am President, it shall be a government for white men." Against his opposition, the Republicans drafted the Fourteenth Amendment, which stated, "All persons born or naturalized in the United States, and subject to the jurisdiction thereof, are citizens of the United States and of the State wherein they reside." Thus, blacks were granted citizenship but not Native Americans because they were not subject to federal jurisdiction.[3]

Custer could be cold and cruel, charming by design, and arrogant by instinct. He and distress walked together after the Civil War. Often a man is defined not by where he was born and raised but where he dies. Midwesterner Lincoln died in the East on Good Friday for America's sins. Midwesterner Custer died in the West during the Sun Dance, also for America's sins. Winston Churchill and Custer shared at least one common trait. When asked after World War II how her husband managed to do so much, Churchill's wife, Clementine, said, "He never did anything he didn't want to do, and left someone else to clear up the mess."[4] The same could be said of Custer. After his stellar performance in the Civil War, Custer could ask, "Everything I've ever wanted has come true, now what?" For much of the rest of his life, he could ask, "Everything I've ever wanted has fallen apart, now what?"

Legends of Custer's fall started sixteen days after Lee's surrender at Appomattox and ten days after Lincoln's death. At age twenty-five, he stole a prized horse, Don Juan. The horse's owner, Richard Gaines of Charlotte County, Virginia, estimated the horse to be worth $10,000. It was a showy horse that Custer knew would be just perfect for the May 23 and May 24, 1865, Grand Review celebrating the Union armies' triumph with a march through Washington, D.C. Tens of thousands of spectators lined Pennsylvania Avenue to take in the great parade. On the first day, veterans of the Army of the Potomac were led by General George G. Meade down the famous street as individual bands preceded every brigade. Children cheered as horsemen rode almost a dozen wide, curb to curb.[5]

Custer was in his element. The gallant hero received flowers from women and cheers from everyone. Mayhem broke out when a young lady threw a wreath of flowers at him. Don Juan, not yet comfortable with his new rider, reared and plunged and bolted away. Being an expert horseman, Custer quickly gained control as onlookers applauded. The *Harrisburg Weekly Patriot & Union* described his wild ride as "like the charge of the Sioux chieftain," and the crowds cheering after he gained command of the horse as "the involuntary homage of the every-day heart to the man of romance. General Custar [sic] should have lived in a less sorted age." The incident is often cited by Custer detractors who wrongly use it as an example of his unhinged personality.[6]

Phil Sheridan was unable to participate in the parade because the state of Texas was still battling Union forces under the direction of Edmund Kirby Smith. Grant's victory at Vicksburg had cut off Texas from the other Confederate states and this led to the Lone Star State's defiant stance. Custer was preparing a cavalry division to march on Texas, but General-in-Chief Ulysses S. Grant instructed Sheridan to demand that Custer relinquish possession of Don Juan. As he would often do, Sheridan defended Custer, who was his most reliable officer, and told Grant that he had instructed his officers to take Confederate horses wherever found. Covering for Custer only empowered him.

The Texas campaign was a disaster, as Custer led five regiments of troops who were inexperienced in combat and wanted to go home and restart their lives after the war. To complicate matters, supply lines were inadequate and food became scarce. This led to some of his men scrounging for food, infuriating Texas civilians. Custer's discipline included flogging, head shaving, and mock executions. He court-martialed those who deserted. Custer commented, "Desertions became numerous and of daily occurrence. . . . As many as twelve have deserted from the same regiment in one night. Unless some action had been adopted which would check the system of desertion . . . the entire command would have in short time disappeared."[7]

Many of his troops hated Custer. Gone were those who fought for honor, manhood, comrades, adventure, and duty in the Civil War. War was hell, especially when your leader was Custer. George Stover, of the 7th Indiana, recalled, "It was a common occurrence to see soldiers at any time in the day draw up and shoot at Custer and his staff. General Custer asked, 'Who in the hell was doing that shooting?' I told him there would be more. . . . He was in the camp of the 7th Indiana, whose men he had whipped for killing a beef."[8] Gone was the charmer and his charmed. One of Custer's greatest fears had come to fruition—the loss of his grandiosity in the eyes of the public. In 1868, the *Des Moines State Register* wrote, "The men of the 1st Iowa Cavalry remember this Custer. His memory will be a stench in their nostrils, and that of their 'children's children to the remotest generations.'"[9] Custer was in the habit of collecting critical newspaper editorials and flew into fits of rage over them.

Rumors of assassination attempts on Custer's life circulated back East, and Grant ordered Sheridan to dismiss Custer. Again, Custer's mentor convinced Grant not to end Custer's command. As resistance to Union forces ended in Texas, on January 27, 1866, Custer and Libbie boarded a crowded steamship bound for New Orleans. His time as major general in the U.S. volunteers—organized during the Civil War—ended, and he reverted to his permanent regular army rank of captain. Fifty thousand Union troops had served in Texas, but only 10,000 remained there to keep order.[10]

Since the Civil War, Custer had a black maid, Eliza Brown—who would be with Libbie and him out West—but he never warmed to blacks. Eliza at times was Libbie's only female company. However, both Libbie and all the Custer men were deeply racist. Libbie wrote home, "You are well aware of how father Custer feels over the 'nigger' question." Armstrong and Tom loved to play racist jokes on their father. One Christmas Libbie wrote, "Everybody gathered round to see him [Emmanuel] open a box containing a nigger doll baby."[11]

Racist Custer wrote to Libbie's parents from Texas:

Planters are everywhere losing extensive and valuable crops owing to the fact that the negros refuse to labor and there is no means by which they can be compelled to do so. . . . A contract has no binding affect whatever upon the negro. . . . Negro troops are also being mustered out rapidly, and I hope will continue until the last of the race has laid down the musket and taken up his more appropriate implement the shovel & hoe. There are white men, veterans, anxious and willing to fill up the Army to any limit desired. To them the preference should be given. I am in favor of elevating the negro to the extent of his capability and intelligence . . . but in making this advancement I am opposed to doing it by correspondingly reducing or debasing any portion of the white race. And as to entrusting the negroes of the Southern states with that most sacred and responsible privilege, the right of suffrage, I should as soon think of elevating an Indian chief to the popedom of Rome. All advocates of Negro suffrage should visit the Southern States and see the class of people upon whom they desire to confer the privilege.[12]

Now as a regular army captain, his hubris was replaced with self-doubt and uncertainty about the future. Too much fame too early in life left Custer rudderless. The year after leaving Texas, he wrote Libbie a reflective letter, "My every thought was ambitious, not to be wealthy, not to be learned, but to be great. I desired to link my name with hacks and men, and in such a manner as to be a mark of honor, not only to the present, but to future generations."[13]

Finding much-needed purpose and adulation hopefully would come for him in the form of Washington politics. President Andrew Johnson's opposition to secession by the South was interpreted by Republicans as support for the first Civil Rights Bill. Nothing could be further from the truth. Historian Eric Foner wrote about Johnson and his racist supporters' views, observing, "The key to post-war politics, they believed, lay in changing the focus of debate from slavery to race."[14] Like Custer, McClellan, and many Northerners, Johnson tolerated the end to slavery, but denounced suffrage for the newly freed slaves.

Before the subcommittee on the Joint Committee on Reconstruction, Custer explained that leniency to past slaveholders had diminished their understanding of the enormity of the sin they had committed by leaving the Union. Custer warned, "There is a very strong feeling of hostility towards the freedmen as a general thing," and, "A system of laws regulating labor would be passed which would virtually place the freedmen under the entire control of their former owners."¹⁵ His warnings were critical in raising extreme doubt that the Southerners could be trusted to treat the freedmen fairly without federal oversight.

By vetoing the Civil Rights Bill on March 27, 1866, Johnson offended the Republican party that was responsible for him being elected vice president. Custer supported Johnson and believed the bill to be unconstitutional. Custer wrote to Libbie, "I think if I stay here much longer and Andy Johnson remains firm, the Constitution will be able to stand alone," and added, "My confidence in the strength of the Constitution is increasing daily while Andy is as firm and upright as a tombstone. . . . He has grown . . . . He is a very strong Union man."¹⁶

Custer's stance was well received by adoring and influential businessmen on Wall Street who doted on him. They entertained him at the posh Manhattan Club on Fifth Avenue and invited him to a session at the stock exchange. He accompanied friends to masked balls where he charmed the women and gave Libbie a dose of her own medicine. As she had assured Custer during the war that her flirting never led to anything inappropriate, Custer—known for his never forgetting a slight—now returned the favor. He wrote Libbie that he and his West Point friends visited "pretty-girl-waitress saloons. We also had considerable support with females we met on the street—'Nymphs du Pave' they are called . . . sport alone was our object. At no time did I forget you." As she was caring for her sick father back in Monroe, he wrote about another party where he engaged a voluptuous woman in a low-cut dress, "I have not seen such sites since I was weaned."¹⁷

Enjoying New York, a city he loved, was expensive and, if he was to make it his home, he needed a good source of income. He talked to Grant about becoming a mercenary for Benito Juarez who was fighting a revolution in Mexico against France's puppet ruler there, Maximilian I. Custer secured a letter of recommendation from Grant that stated Custer "rendered such distinguished service as a cavalry officer during the war. There was no officer in that branch of service who had the confidence of General Sheridan to a greater degree than General C. and there is no officer in whose judgment I have greater faith than in Sheridan's."¹⁸ However, Secretary of State William Seward blocked his plan to head to Mexico. Matters worsened with Libbie's father's death on May 18, 1866.

In July, Congress passed an act that capped troops at 54,302. With only 2,835 officer positions and a flood of applicants for them, Custer's dream of securing a permanent rank as general evaporated. At the end of the month,

Don Juan died of a stroke after a month earlier winning first prize over six thoroughbreds in a race. His hope of selling the horse for $10,000 was gone—another bad omen.[19]

With a thin supply of troops out West, Grant organized new black regiments and needed officers to lead them. Custer was elevated to lieutenant colonel in the 9th U.S. Cavalry, Colored. That did not set well with Custer, who contacted Grant about a transfer. Custer also contacted Secretary of War Edwin Stanton and President Johnson for assistance. He requested that "I may be appointed Colonel of one of the new infantry regiments, provided I cannot be appointed Colonel of Cavalry, but in whatever branch of the service I may be assigned I most respectfully request to be attached to an organization composed of white troops as I have served and wish to serve with no other class." A racist, Johnson believed he had found a political supporter in Custer and granted the transfer. Both would oppose the Fourteenth Amendment. It's ironic that Custer's disdain for blacks redirected his career on a trajectory that would lead him someday to his fate at the Little Bighorn.[20]

Returning the favor, Custer and Libbie joined President Johnson, who had boarded a train on August 28, 1866, on a speaking tour of the North known as a "swing around the circle." Some of the cabinet members and Grant were also traveling with the president. Grant's mood was somber because he did not support many of Johnson's positions. That was not the case for Custer. He was quickly alienating himself from loyal Unionist supporters back in Libbie's hometown of Monroe. The September 20 edition of the *Monroe Commercial* stated, "It is a matter of painful regret to all who still hold to the views upon reconstruction which he expressed in his testimony, to see him now so fully espouse the cause of the very rebels whom he fought."[21] Custer also lost support from Grant, who was offended by his comments. Custer misjudged the political winds, as the Republican party won a large majority in both houses of Congress in the midterm elections, and President Johnson would eventually be impeached.

While in office, Johnson attempted to obstruct the enforcement of the Reconstruction Acts, which led the Republicans to launch an impeachment effort. As Johnson and the Republicans battled in Washington, conflicts were escalating out West. In 1860, gold and silver had been discovered in parts of Nevada, Colorado, Idaho, and Montana. Easterners flocked to those regions and set up permanent camps. The Oglala Chief Red Cloud, at Fort Laramie, said, "The Great Spirit raised both the white man and the Indian. I think you raise the Indian first. He raised me in this land and it belongs to me. The white man was raised over the great waters, and his land is over there. Since they cross the sea, I have given them room. There are now white people all about me. I have but a small spot of land left. The Great Spirit told me to keep it."[22] Red Cloud and Crazy Horse led attacks on routes traveled by white men heading to Montana.

As general-in-chief, Grant was in charge of dealing with the Indian problem. In the summer of 1865, he sent his good friend Sherman to St. Louis to head up the army forces in the West. Sherman's solution to the problem was to divide the West into separate districts, with the Sioux restricted north of the Platte River, west of the Missouri River, and east of the road to Montana. The Cheyenne and other tribes would have their own districts. Sherman wrote Grant, "This would leave for our people exclusively the use of the wide belt, east and west, between the Platte and the Arkansas, in which lie the two great railroads and over which passes the bulk of travel to the mountain territories. As long as these Indians can hunt the buffalo and antelope within the described limits we will have the depredations of last summer and, worse yet, the exaggerations of danger raised by our own people, often for a very base purpose."[23]

Comparing the dishonest agents of the Indian Bureau of the Department of the Interior to the rogue traders of the Civil War, Grant pushed to bring the traders under his military control. He told Sherman, "The Indian Bureau should be transferred to the War Department, and Indian agencies, from among civilians, abolished. . . . No license should be given to traders among them. Keeping arms and munitions from them, trade and all other articles would weaken them more rapidly than campaigns."[24]

Grant convinced Secretary of War Edwin Stanton and President Johnson to let military officers determine who the peaceable Indians were. Some of the officers dealt harshly with the Indians, and in 1867 this led to Indian raids on forts and settlements. Sherman became resigned to the fact that there would be no peace and wrote Grant, "This conflict of authority will exist as long as the Indians exist, for their ways are different from our ways. Either they or we must be masters of the Plains. . . . I have no doubt that our people have committed grievous wrong to the Indians, and I wish I could punish them. But it is impractical. . . . Both races cannot use this country in common. . . . One or the other must withdraw."[25]

A dilemma arose when the Johnson administration allowed traders to continue their corrupt ways and Congress refused to provide financial support to the military. With no financial backing, Grant instructed his officers to retreat from the forts in the valley of the Powder River. He wrote Sherman, "It will be well to prepare at once for the abandonment of the posts Phil Kearney,

Reno, and Fetterman, and to make all the capital with the Indians that can be made out of the change.... I fear that, by delay, the Indians may commence hostilities and make it impossible for us to give them up."[26]

In military retreat, Grant urged Sherman to head up a peace commission. The previous autumn, Sherman had been frustrated at Fort Laramie when Red Cloud had boycotted the talks. Red Cloud would not negotiate until the whites had left the Powder River. In the summer of 1868, the army abandoned the Powder River forts. Red Cloud and his warriors then burned the forts down. He kept his word and traveled to Fort Laramie and signed a treaty that Sherman had prepared. The treaty in part stated, "The Government of the United States desires peace, and its honor is hereby pledged to keep it. The Indians desire peace, and they now pledged their honor to maintain it."[27]

Narrowly escaping impeachment, Johnson vowed to finally enforce Reconstruction laws in the South, but his political career was in shambles. Grant's name was forwarded as the Republican nominee for the 1868 presidential election. His opponent was Horatio Seymour, the Democratic governor of New York. Grant was victorious, winning the popular vote by 300,000 of nearly 6 million votes cast.[28]

Grant's victory continued a tradition of generals being rewarded for military victories with the presidency: George Washington in the Revolutionary War, Andrew Jackson in the War of 1812 and in conflict with the Spanish in Florida, William Henry Harrison in the War of 1812, and Zachary Taylor over the Mexicans. Democracy and the American way of life were achieved not by inspirational and idealistic values but by military force. That was the case when dealing with the British, the Spanish, the Mexicans, and finally the Indians.[29]

Even though he was a military man, Grant was seen by different delegations of Indians as more sympathetic to their plight than previous presidents. In his mind, the Indian wars were caused by the corruption and mismanagement within the Indian Bureau that remained under the Interior Department. Under his administration, a new Indian commission was created and composed of prominent philanthropists and others who wanted to see the Indians treated with respect. The new commission stated:

> The history of the government connections with the Indians is a shameful record of broken treaties and unfulfilled promises. The history of the border white man's connection with the Indians is a sickening record of murder, outrage, robbery, and wrongs committed by

the former as a rule, and occasional savage outbreaks and unspeakably barbarous deeds of retaliation by the latter as the exception. . . . In our Indian wars, almost without exception, the first aggressions have been made by the white man.

In addition to the class of robbers and outlaws who find impunity in their nefarious pursuits upon the frontiers, there is a large class of professedly reputable men who use every means in their power to bring on Indian wars, for the sake of the profit to be realized from the presence of troops and expenditure of government funds in their midst. They proclaim death to the Indians at all times, in words and publications, making no distinction between the innocent and the guilty. They incite the lowest class of men to the perpetration of the darkest deeds against their victims, and, as judges and jurymen, shield them from the justice due to their crimes. Every crime committed by a white man against an Indian is concealed or pilliated; every offense committed by one Indian against a white man is borne on the wings of the post or the telegraph to the remotest corner of the land, clothed with all the horrors which the reality or the imagination can throw around it.[30]

Grant's commission placed the Quakers in charge of around half of the Western Indian agencies. The Quakers had led the battle for abolition because of their religious beliefs. Under the so-called Quaker or peace policy, the Indians were still expected to be confined to reservations, and those resisting the reservation were considered hostile and presumed to be at war with the government. The peace policy sought, first, to place the Indians upon reservations as rapidly as possible, where they could be provided for in such a manner as the dictates of humanity and Christian civilization required. Grant said, "Indians should be made as comfortable on, and uncomfortable off, the reservations as it was in the power of government."[31]

Corrupt agents were replaced by men dedicated to God who were presumed to be honest. The intent was to make sure the Indians got the distribution of annuities and rations that they deserved. A board of Indian commissioners, independent of the Interior Department, was created in 1869 to supervise Indian affairs. Lacking the power to make the changes they wanted, the board slowly lost favor and by the early 1880s was replaced by the old patronage system. Many Westerners rejected the Grant peace policy as overly sentimental and lacking realistic goals.

The Quaker policy would eventually influence the education of children on and off Indian reservations. In 1873, the secretary of interior summarized the long-term goals of the plan:

> Being thus placed on reservations, they will be removed from such contiguity to our frontier settlements as otherwise will lead, necessarily to frequent outrages, wrongs, and disturbances of the public peace. On these reservations they can be taught, as fast as possible, the arts of agriculture, in such pursuits as are incident to civilization, through the aid of the Christian organizations of the country now engaged in this work, cooperating with the Federal Government. Their intellectual, moral, and religious culture can be prosecuted, and thus it is hoped that humanity and kindness may take the place of barbarity and cruelty. . . . [It] is the further aim of the policy to establish schools, and then through the instrumentality of the Christian organizations, acting in harmony with the Government, as fast as possible, to build churches and organize Sabbath schools, whereby these savages may be taught a better way of life than they have heretofore pursued, and be made to understand and appreciate the comforts and benefits of a Christian civilization, and thus be prepared ultimately to assume the duties and the privileges of citizenship.[32]

For most of the other agencies, Grant appointed army officers to replace Interior Department agents. Grant took Sherman's advice to separate the Indians from the whites on the frontier to reduce confrontations. The Indians were given reservations, for their exclusive use only, in perpetuity. The idea of reservations originated in the 1850s. The Indians would have their own self-government aided by the advice of Quakers and education professionals. Initially, there was success with the Sioux and other Plains tribes who accepted the land on the reservations. One of the legacies of the 1870s was the total control by the agents and complete dependence of the Indians on the government.

With the tribes now considered wards of the state and not independent governments, the agents in many cases disregarded tribal authority and established their own native police force with native courts that answered to the agents. In 1871, the federal government became responsible for the education of Indian children and made specific appropriations for this purpose. By 1872, the government had placed men from thirteen separate religious groups to oversee seventy-three Indian agencies around the country.[33]

One of the many men who told Grant that the inevitable fate of the

Indian was not extinction was Benson J. Lossing, a popular historian during the period. In an 1870 article titled "Our Barbarian Brethren," he urged Americans to treat the Indian as a man and their brother. He opined that if Americans had treated the Indians by the Golden Rule "they might have acquired as clear a charter for permanent existence as other children of the All-Father."[34] Many Darwinists and theologians agreed that the Indian's fate was not necessarily extermination. Christian missionaries had faith that the Indians could be educated and converted to Christianity.

In 1862, a leading journal of theology and literature, the *Boston Review*, published an article expressing this sentiment by stating that "the extinction of the Indian race is not, from the nature of things, an inevitable necessity." Using Christian free will as a guide, the author separated Indians into two classes—dualism—that had moral choices. "Those that would be saved to adopt civilization and those that would be doomed to vanish if they didn't abandon their way of life. . . . Their only choices civilization or extinction, and this must be made at once."[35]

In contrast, Brigadier General James H. P. Carleton believed that the Indians were decreasing rapidly, but believed in Calvinistic predestination for the Indian. In 1865, he wrote that their rapid decline was Providential for those "which the Almighty originates, when in their appointed time He wills that one race of men—as in lower animals—shall disappear off the face of the earth and give place to another race. . . . The races of the mammoths and the mastodons, and the great sloths, came and passed away!"[36]

The Doctrine of Discovery was circumvented on March 3, 1871, when President Grant signed a law that abandoned the Indian treaty system because the United States no longer acknowledged that they were dealing with sovereign nations. The act stated, "No Indian nation or tribe within the territory of the United States shall be acknowledged or recognized as an independent nation, tribe, or power with whom the United States may contract a treaty."[37] The law resulted in saving the United States a considerable amount of money that was being spent on treaties with the Indians when the country was reeling from the cost of the Civil War and Reconstruction. It also recognized that Indians were essentially wards of the state, and their improvement would be achieved only through assimilation, education, and Christianization. These goals were in line with Grant's policies directed toward a people whose future was not extermination. This placed his army in a precarious situation, as summarized by General William T. Sherman in 1870: "There are two classes of people, one demanding the utter extinction of the Indians, and the other full of love for their conversion to civilization and Christianity. Unfortunately the army stands between and gets the cuffs from both sides."[38]

Grant was more optimistic than Carleton had been. Red Cloud (c1822-1909) was impressed with Grant's new agents and visited him in Washington in 1872—the same year Grant signed the law establishing Yellowstone National Park. The Sioux chief suggested a place on the White River as a location for the new agency headquarters. Grant and many others understood that if the Indians did not settle down on the reservations they would probably be killed by white settlers. It was their only chance for survival.

The president welcomed Red Cloud and his delegation, but was concerned that the place Red Cloud chose was within the limits of Nebraska. He thought they might be happier in Indian Territory. He warned the Indian delegation:

> They will find that the whites are in number as the blades of grass upon the hill side, and their number increases every day. They come from other countries in greater numbers, every year, than the whole number of Indians in America. . . .
>
> We want to do for you and your people all we can to advance and help them, and to enable them to become self-supporting. The time must come when, with the great growth of population here, the game will be gone, and your people will then have to resort to other means of support. While there is time we would like to teach you new modes of living that will secure you in the future and be a safe means of livelihood. I want to see the Indians get upon land where they can look forward to permanent homes for themselves and their children.[39]

Concerned about white encroachment, Grant raised the possibility of future relocation, saying, "If any time you feel like moving to what is known as Cherokee country [Oklahoma] which is a large territory with an admirable climate, where you would never suffer from the cold and where you could have lands set apart to remain exclusively your own, we would set apart a large tract of land that would belong to you and your children. We would at first build houses for your chiefs and principal men, and send men among your people to instruct them so they could have houses for shelter. We would send you large herds of cattle and sheep to live upon, and to enable you to raise stock."[40]

If the Indians were agreeable to assimilation, Grant said, "We would send, if you so desire, Indians who have been accustomed to live with white men, who would instruct you in growing and raising stock until you know how to do it yourselves. We would establish schools, so that your children would learn to read and to write, and to speak the English language, the same as white people, and in this way you and your people would be prepared, before the game is gone, to live comfortably and securely.... I say this only for you to think about and talk about to your people. Whenever you are ready to avail yourself of this offer, then you can talk to us and we will do what I say. All the treaty obligations we have entered into we shall keep with you unless it is with your own consent that the change is made, or so long as you keep those obligations yourself."[41]

Grant made similar promises to other Sioux chiefs. Chief Spotted Tail was impressed with Grant's kindness and before he left said, "I hear that in a few months there will be an election for a new president. I hope you may be successful. This would please me very much, for you have been very kind to my people." Grant reassured the chief, "However the election may result, I hope there will be no change in the Indian policy."[42]

George Stuart, a member of the Indian commission, was instructed by the president that "if the present policy toward the Indian can be improved in any way, I will always be ready to receive suggestions on the subject. But if any change is made, it must be on the side of the civilization and Christianization of the Indian. I do not believe our Creator ever placed different races of men on this earth with the view of having the stronger exert all its energies in exterminating the weaker. If any change takes place in the Indian policy of the government while I hold my present office, it will be on the humanitarian side of the question." His lofty ideals would in time give way to real-world conflicts.[43]

A month after Spotted Tail's visit, Grant discussed his new Indian policy in his annual message. He noted that it had reduced the expense of management and attacks on white settlements. Manifest Destiny and assimilation was the theme of his second inaugural address delivered in early March 1873, in which he said, "Under Providence I have been called a second time to act as executive over this great nation.... I do not share in the apprehension held by many as to the danger of governments becoming weakened and destroyed by reason of their extension of territory. Commerce, education, and rapid transit of thought and matter by telegraph and steam have changed all this. Rather do I believe that our Great Maker is preparing the world, in His own good time, to become one nation, speaking one language, and when armies and navies will be no longer required."[44]

Because genocide was not known as a word until the 1940s, the "war of extermination" was its forerunner. Grant continued his message, which was directed specifically to his Indian policy:

> To bring the aborigines of the country under the benign influences of education and civilization. It is either this or war of extermination. Wars of extermination, engaged in by people pursuing commerce and all industrial pursuits, are expensive even against the weakest people, and are demoralizing and wicked. Our superiority of strength and advantages of civilization should make us lenient toward the Indian. The wrong inflicted upon him should be taken into account and the balance placed to his credit. The moral view of the question should be considered in the question asked, can not the Indian be made a useful and productive member of society by proper teaching and treatment? If the effort is made in good faith, we will stand better before the civilized nations of the earth and in our own consciences for having made it. . . . These things are not to be accomplished by one individual, but they will receive my support and such recommendations to Congress as will in my judgment best serve to carry them into effect. I beg your support and encouragement."[45]

Grant's noble words were somewhat silenced by real-world scandals. Millions in public money were fraudulently siphoned to a New York City Democratic ring of William Tweed and his Tammany Hall cronies. Another scandal involved the Union Pacific, in which federal funds were illegally subverted to subcontractors who paid off some members of Congress in their company stock.

In addition, an embarrassing situation revolved around William Belknap, who controlled the concessions at army trading posts in the West. His second wife lived beyond her husband's $8,000 per year salary and arranged to share in the profits at the posts. While he may not have known about the kickbacks to begin with, Belknap continued to receive them even after his wife's death. In 1875, the Democrats gained control of the house and launched an investigation into Belknap's affairs. The disgraced war secretary soon resigned.

With the election approaching in 1876, Grant's minister to England, Robert Schenck, was forced to resign when he promoted investments in which he had a personal stake. Next was Secretary of the Navy George Robeson, who had hundreds of thousands of dollars in his bank account that he couldn't explain. Secretary of the Interior Columbus Delano also resigned when it was revealed that his son was profiting illegitimately from his father's position. Closer to home, Grant's younger brother Orvil was paid by the government for surveying lands in Wyoming territory, a task that he failed to do. A Congressional investigator asked the chief clerk of the Cheyenne office about the federal survey and confirmed that Orvil had never set foot in Wyoming. These scandals and others soured the American public on government and its ability to carry out programs with integrity. Adding to the problems were settlers out West who continually attempted to confiscate land intended for the Indian.[46]

Grant's administration was further shaken when the Panic of 1873 destroyed the financial markets. The panic centered around Jay Cooke, who had underwritten securities for the Northern Pacific Railroad, among others. He pitched $100 million of railroad construction bonds to prospective buyers. The Northern Pacific route would run from Lake Superior to Puget Sound through what he called the Eden of the continent. He was unable to sell tens of millions of bonds, which led to him closing his company headquarters in Philadelphia on September 18. This led to a collapse of financial houses around the country. No one knew at the time that the nation would be in a depression for the next ten years. Much like the Great Depression of the 1930s, homeless Americans would wander the country seeking jobs. Those who had jobs would strike for living wages. The crisis of the Civil War and Reconstruction was now replaced with the first crisis of the Industrial Age.

America looked west to the vast riches it held as a way out of the economic catastrophe. Many Easterners, especially in the large urban areas like Philadelphia, looked sympathetically toward the Indian as their lands were systematically taken from them. Westerners who were in bitter confrontation with the savages thought the Easterners naïve and unrealistic. Settlers, cowboys, miners, and trappers found support from their local news outlets and famous writers like Mark Twain, who viewed the Indian with disgust. In 1870, Twain wrote about the Indian, "His heart is a cesspool of falsehood, of treachery, and of low and devilish instincts. With him, gratitude is an unknown emotion; and when one does him a kindness, it is safest to keep the face toward him, lest the reward be an arrow in the back. To accept of a favor from him is to assume a debt which you can never repay to his satisfaction, though you bankrupt yourself trying. The scum of the earth."[47]

In an essay titled "The Literary Offenses of Fenimore Cooper," Twain criticized him for over-romanticizing the Indian, writing, "No, other

Indians would have noticed these things, but Cooper's Indians never notice anything. Cooper thinks they are marvelous creatures for noticing, but he was almost always in error about his Indians. There was seldom a sane one among them."[48]

A Dakota newspaper in 1874 expressed most Westerners' views about their land:

> This is God's country. He peopled it with red men, and planted it with wild grasses, and permitted the white man to gain a foothold; and as the wild grasses disappear when the white clover regains footing, so the Indian disappears before the advance of the white man.
>
> Humanitarians may weep for poor Lo, and tell of the wrongs he has suffered, but he is passing away. Their prayers, their entreaties, can not change the law of nature; can not arrest the causes which are carrying them on to their ultimate destiny—extinction.
>
> The American people need the country the Indians now occupy; many of our people are out of employment; the masses need some new excitement. . . . An Indian war would do no harm, for it must come, sooner or later.[49]

With the country in recession, the prospect of gold in the Dakota Black Hills was a potential way for the country to recover. A group from Nebraska touted the Black Hills as the place to be settled by the whites, which would improve the general welfare of the country. Newspapermen and western Congressmen agreed, along with Phil Sheridan, who was in charge of the security of the West. Skeptical of Grant's peace policy, Sheridan believed in the extermination of the Indians. He was famously known for stating that the only good Indian was a dead Indian. In May 1874, Sheridan was eager to send Custer to the Black Hills and wrote Sherman from his Chicago headquarters, "I would like to start Colonel Custer with the column of cavalry out, about 15 June, to examine the Black Hills country. . . . This country is entirely unknown, and the knowledge of it might be of great value in the case of Indian troubles."[50]

An expedition to the Black Hills was opposed by Bishop William Hare, who was one of the pastors on Grant's peace commission. He warned Grant, "Such an expedition would, almost beyond a doubt, provoke an Indian war." He went on to explain that the Black Hills were sacred to the Sioux and off-limits to whites. Hare added, "An invasion of the Black Hills means,

I fear, or at least will surely result in, war, and war to the knife."⁵¹ Interior Secretary Delano agreed and said a war with the Sioux would be deplorable and undo efforts for peaceable relations.

With his administration in trouble from scandal and the economy a shambles, the pragmatic side of Grant authorized Sheridan to dispatch Custer to the Black Hills. Custer confirmed that there were gold deposits in the Black Hills. In the spring of 1875, Grant summoned Red Cloud and Spotted Tail to Washington to convince them to give up the gold region. He informed them that gold seekers were coming and there was nothing he could do to stop it, saying, "I do not propose to ask you to leave the homes where you were born and raised, without your consent. Every year this same difficulty will be increased unless the right of the white people to go to that country is granted by you; and it may in the end lead to hostilities between Indians and the white people without any special fault on either side." A skeptical Red Cloud told Grant that he had enough troops to keep speculators out of his sacred lands, but the chief knew that would not happen. He entered negotiations with the U.S. government.⁵²

Sitting Bull and Crazy Horse did not enter into negotiations, and when a flood of miners arrived in the Black Hills, they resisted the intruders. Grant's generals pushed for a fight with the Indians. Sheridan wrote Sherman, "We might just as well settle the Sioux matter now. It will be better for all concerned."⁵³ Knowing what's right is easy, but doing right is the challenge. Civil rights were only for those in civilized country.

Grant relinquished, and in the spring of 1876 he directed Sherman and Sheridan to send the 7th Cavalry into the Yellowstone Valley to subdue hostiles. But Grant did not want Custer to lead the campaign. The president perceived Custer as a reckless showboat with little regard for authority from his commanders. Since Custer had political aspirations, many condemned Grant's orders as personally motivated against Custer. In the end, he allowed Custer to join the 7th Cavalry but insisted General Alfred Howe Terry have formal command of the expedition.

After the disaster at the Little Bighorn, Sherman wrote Grant on July 8, 1876, lamenting the decision. "For some reason as yet unexplained," he penned, "General Custer, who commanded the seventh cavalry and had been detached by his commander General Terry at the mouth of the Rosebud to make a wide detour up the Rosebud, a tributary of the Yellowstone, across to the little Big Horn, and down it to the mouth of the Big Horn, the place agreed on for meeting, attacked en route a large Indian village with only a part of his force, having himself detached the rest with a view to intercept the expected retreat of the savages, and experienced an utter annihilation of his immediate command."⁵⁴

Grant always regretted his decision to allow Custer to rejoin the 7th Cavalry and concluded that Custer's hubris had led to his and his men's death. He told a reporter, "I regard Custer's massacre as a sacrifice of troops, brought on by Custer himself, that was wholly unnecessary. He was not to have made the attack before affecting the junction with Terry and Gibbon. He was notified to meet them on the 26th, but instead of marching slowly, as his orders required in order to effect the junction on the 26th, he entered upon a forced march of eighty-three miles in twenty-four hours, and thus had to meet the Indians alone on the 25th."⁵⁵ With the death of so many men, Grant's administration took another blow.

Civil War veterans from both the North and South rallied behind Grant and volunteered to avenge Custer's death. Congress approved the request for more men to reinforce Terry. Soon Sitting Bull, Crazy Horse, and their followers would be back on the reservation.⁵⁶ We'll see more of Custer out West in the next chapter.

John Eaton, commissioner of the Bureau of Education, was a representative of the Department of the Interior at the Centennial Exposition in Philadelphia in 1876. It was his task to prepare a statement on the trends in Indian population over the preceding decades. But his numbers conflicted with others. Even so, he placed great importance on population numbers in determining the plight of the Indian and saw hope for their future:

> The solution of the problem of the Indian civilization depends greatly on the conclusions reached respecting Indian population. If, as is generally believed, the Indians are a vanishing race, doomed to disappear at a not remote period, because of their contact with civilization . . . then the efforts in behalf of their civilization will assume, in most minds, a sentimental aspect. . . . But, on the contrary, it is shown to be true that the Indians, instead of being doomed by circumstances to extinction within a limited period, are, as a rule, not decreasing in numbers, and are, in all probability, destined to form a permanent factor, an enduring element of our populations, the necessity of their civilization will be at once recognized, and all efforts in that direction will be treated as their importance demands.⁵⁷

As Brian Dippie points out in *The Vanishing American,* "Population estimates were obviously highly unreliable, and virtually worthless as indicators of the Indians' racial destiny."[58]

Most likely Grant was relieved when he relinquished his office to Rutherford Hayes in 1877, but, unfortunately for the Indians, his absence led to a dimmer view of their future. In 1880, a somewhat bitter Colonel John Gibbon, who had survived the Battle of the Little Bighorn, described the Indian as a "wild animal" and wrote, "Philanthropists and visionary speculators may theorize as they please about protecting the Indian . . . and preserving him as a race. *It cannot be done.* Whenever the two come in contact . . . the weaker *must* give way, and disappear. To deny this is to deny the evidence of our own senses, and to shut our eyes to the facts of history."[59]

In 1882 in Massachusetts, George Ellis published *The Red Man and the White Man in North America* and wrote that while the Indian was not declining yet, he lamented their inevitable extinction. "If I am competent to infer from the mass of what I have read," Ellis wrote, "the consenting opinion and judgment of the very large majority of men of actual knowledge and practical experience of the mature Indians is that they cannot be civilized—that the race must perish either by violence or decay. The final catastrophe, it is said, has been forecast, prepared for, and is steadily advancing to its dismal close."[60]

Sherman published *Memoirs of General William T. Sherman, Written by Himself in 1875,* which some believed was critical of his old friend Grant. But after Grant read the book he approved of Sherman's every word, saying, "You cannot imagine how pleased I was. . . . Sherman is not only a great soldier but a great man. He is one of the very great men in our country's history. . . . As a writer he is among the first. As a general I know of no man I would put above him. . . . There is not a fault line in Sherman's character."[61] This was high praise for Sherman from an American who was the most popular military hero since Andrew Jackson.

Because of his popularity, in January 1881, Samuel Clemens, aka Mark Twain (1835-1910), approached Grant about publishing his memoirs. In the summer of 1884, Grant's long history of smoking and drinking caught up with him with the onset of oral cancer. He initially experienced some scratchiness in the back of his throat, which changed in time to pain. When he noticed swelling in his throat, he sought the advice of a throat specialist who prescribed gargles and ointments with little benefit.

Sensing his mortality, Grant, who had mulled over the idea of a memoir, now decided to sign a contract because the royalties would provide funds for his family after he was gone. He contacted William Sherman, who said he had been paid $25,000 for his. Grant was close to signing a contract with *Century* when Mark Twain intervened. The author of *Tom Sawyer* and *Huckleberry Finn* said, "Sell me the memoirs, General. I am a publisher. I will pay double the price. I have a checkbook in my pocket; take my check for $50,000 now and let's draw the contract."[62] Soon, Clemens' publishing firm, Charles L. Webster & Co., received a signed contract from Grant to publish his autobiography.

Clemens was raised in Hannibal, Missouri, which was made famous in his writings. He grew up as a Presbyterian but was critical of organized religion. He wrote, "Faith is believing what you know ain't so," and "If Christ were here now there is one thing he would not be—a Christian."[63] He worked as a riverboat pilot and, two weeks before the Civil War broke out, joined the Confederate Missouri State Guard. Once war was declared, he and a friend headed west. At the time, Colonel Ulysses S. Grant was the head of the Union regiment in Missouri.[64]

In the summer of 1885, Grant's health from throat cancer deteriorated. His weight plummeted to 125 pounds and his voice was reduced to a whisper. Clemens visited him on a number of occasions at his home on 66th Street in New York. By mid-June, Grant had almost finished his two-volume book, titled *Personal Memoirs of Ulysses S. Grant*. His family had moved him to a summer cottage a few miles north of Saratoga Springs. He delivered his second volume to Charles L. Webster, Twain's nephew by marriage, on July 18. Five days later he died of starvation due to the inability to eat food.

In *Mark Twain: A Life,* Ron Powers wrote that the publication of Grant's memoirs was "the most successful business enterprise of Mark Twain's life, as well as the greatest bequest to American culture outside his own works."[65] Later, financial disaster hit Twain when he invested $300,000 into a new invention, the Paige typesetting machine, which was prone to breakdowns. With the invention of the linotype, the Paige became obsolete. Twain lost almost all his royalties from his writings and his wife's inheritance. In 1894, he would declare bankruptcy.

Shortly after the publication of Grant's memoirs in 1885, Charles L. Webster & Co. presented his wife with her first royalty check of $200,000, which was the largest single royalty payment in the history of publishing to that time. She would eventually receive $450,000 (equivalent to almost $12 million in today's money) in royalty fees from the sale of hundreds of thousands of copies of Grant's book. Mark Twain netted $200,000. The work is considered one of the great masterpieces of military literature.[66]

Feeling confident, Twain signed Pope Leo XIII to a $100,000 contract for the rights to his biography. Upon publication in 1887, *The Life of Pope Leo the XIII* appeared in six different languages and was widely publicized. Webster & Co. had projected sales of over 100,000, but only several hundred were sold. This also contributed eventually to Twain's bankruptcy.[67]

Grant historian H. W. Brands wrote, "American Indians recalled Grant as the president whose peace policy offered a distinct alternative to the aggressive exploitation favored by his predecessors and most of his contemporaries. The Indians, like African Americans, could not claim lasting success for Grant's endeavors on their behalf; his struggle for minority rights against majority hostility or indifference was a battle he couldn't win. But he waged a good and honorable fight."[68]

CHAPTER TWENTY-FIVE

Son of the American West: Custer, O Fallen Star

How you have fallen from heaven, O shining star, son of the morning! You [Satan] have been thrown down to the earth, you who destroyed the nations of the world.
—ISAIAH 14:12

I could whip all the Indians on the Continent with the Seventh Cavalry.
—GEORGE ARMSTRONG CUSTER, JUNE 25, 1876

Ho-ka hey! It is a good day to fight! It is a good day to die! Strong hearts, brave hearts, to the front! Weak hearts and cowards to the rear.
—CRAZY HORSE, JUNE 25, 1876

The simplest answer, usually overlooked, is that the army lost largely because the Indians won. To ascribe defeat entirely to military failings is to devalue Indian strength and leadership.
—ROBERT UTLEY

Certain people and events achieve iconic status. More than just famous, they speak to Americans about who they are as a people and a nation. Truths about them, and arguments about them, are truths and arguments about ourselves. Over the decades, Custer has served as a symbol of American notions of heroism and individualism, and fears of hubris. And, of course, he himself has become a battleground in the debate over the conquest and dispossession of American Indians. He has been treated as a convenient stand-in for large historical developments and high level policy decisions—as has the Little Bighorn.
—T. J. STILES, *CUSTER'S TRIALS*

Victories are celebrated and defeats are studied. Most often we learn more from losing than from winning. The core issue facing the United States in regard to Native Americans was how to use incredible power with self-restraint. America failed the Indians and itself. When diplomacy fails, the world is governed by military force, and a primary purpose of the military is to kill people. The American West was a place where manhood could be celebrated while carefully walled off from society and accountability from those back East. It was the days of wooden prairie schooners and iron men. To destroy the enemy you have to destroy hope—hope of winning, hope of a better life, and hope for their God. Hope is an anchor to the soul, and only hope can overcome evil. Once you remove hope, evil wins; when you have nothing to lose, violence results. Peter Nabokov wrote in *Native American Testimony*, "But this Vanishing Indian idea ignored the fact that, despite centuries of forced migration, debilitating warfare, rampaging epidemics, and psychological resignation, over three hundred thousand enumerated Indians were still alive in 1865. They survived in official reservations and in tiny, little known enclaves with no federal recognition."[1]

Custer had fought the good fight in the Civil War. The nation was one again, but far from whole. For many, Lincoln's assassination on Good Friday felt like a sacrifice for the national sin of slavery. The next fight would not be the good fight for Custer. From the end of the Civil War to the end of his life in 1876, his personality would fragment and slowly self-destruct. People do what they know how to do. Politicians and military leaders don't have a vast repertoire. When they get in a jam, they just do what they've always done, even if it's not working anymore. And for Custer it didn't work anymore at the Little Bighorn. On a sunny June day, the 7th Cavalry rode into a "ravine as dark as death" (Psalm 23:4). God was not at their side—another was. A good story needs a villain, and in Custer, history found one. Good villains drive ratings and book sales. Perhaps that is why other U.S. military officers and atrocities out West are little remembered today.

Unremembered Atrocities

Even though George R. Crook (1830-1890) committed one of the most heinous acts—"The Severed Heads Campaign"—in American military history, he is overshadowed by the myth and legend of Custer.[2] Historian Paul Andrew Hutton has shed light on Crook's actions.

Like so many other outstanding Civil War military officers—Custer,

Grant, Sherman, and Sheridan, who called Ohio their home—Crook participated in the Indian wars. Upon graduation in 1852 from West Point, he ranked near the bottom of his class. His early assignments took him to Oregon and California where he had his first fights with Indians. In 1857, on the Pitt River Expedition, he was almost killed by one of their arrows. There was no love lost between him and the "savages." By the time of the Civil War, he was promoted to colonel of the 36th Ohio Volunteer Infantry. After a number of Civil War battles, in February 1865 he was captured and held as a prisoner of war in Richmond by the Confederates until there was a prisoner exchange a month later.[3] After the war, Crook fought Indians in the Northwest, and President Ulysses S. Grant eventually promoted him to be in command of the Arizona Territory.[4]

He was the darling of the press and politicians for subduing the Apache after he declared an end to the first Apache campaign on April 9, 1873. An impressed Grant promoted him two grades to the rank of brigadier general, and the Arizona press praised Crook, calling him the "Napoleon of successful Indian fighters." Likewise, Crook congratulated his troops who had "outwitted and beaten the wiliest of foes . . . and finally closed an Indian war that has been waged since the days of Cortez."[5]

However, all was not well, as Hutton noted. With the Apache subdued, a new reservation was created at San Carlos as an extension of the White Mountain Reservation, with headquarters at Camp Apache. As happened on so many reservations, the Indians were cheated out of their rations by a crooked agent. In this case it was interim agent Dr. R. A. Wilbur. After a permanent agent, Charles Larrabee, arrived in March 1873, he discovered that Wilbur had spread vicious rumors about him to the point that three Apache, Chunz, Chan-deisi, and Cochinay, planned to kill Larrabee. Larrabee tried to appease them by giving them more rations from his storehouse, but in May, one of the Apache shot Lieutenant Almy in the head. More shots rang out and chaos ensued. Larrabee was so distraught that he resigned and turned over San Carlos to the army.

Because the Apache had left their assigned agencies, a tarnished Crook was under pressure to make them return. Not wanting to be displaced from the pedestal many had placed him on, Crook ordered bounties on the Indians much like wolf hunters who were paid bounties for pelts. In this case, he wanted the Indians' heads, and he wanted them right away, stating, "The more prompt these heads are brought in the less liable other Indians, in the future, will be to jeopardize their heads."[6] Apache scouts aided the military in hunting them down.

Crook was pleased when the heads started coming in, and on June 23, 1873, he wrote, "Recent telegram from Babcock says that John Daisy's [Chan-deisi's] head was brought into Apache the other day, which leaves now only Chunz's head on his shoulders.... Start your killers as soon as possible after the head of DelChe [sic] & Co."[7] Success was achieved when Chunz and six of his friends had their heads placed on display at the San Carlos post parade grounds.

Soon Delshay's head was also on display but at two different places. One would assume this deception by at least one party would infuriate Crook, but instead he was amused, saying, "When I visited the Verde reservation, they would convince me that they had brought in his head, and when I went to San Carlos, they would convince me that they had brought in his head. Being satisfied that both parties were earnest in their beliefs, and the bringing in of an extra head was not amiss, I paid for both parties."[8]

Decapitating defiant Apache, along with starvation, demoralized those living off the agency, and eventually they slowly returned. As Hutton stated, "Crook's brutal tactics had proven eminently successful—despite their rather Medieval methods—and brought about a brief peace in Arizona territory."[9]

During the Great Sioux War of 1876-1877, General Crook was in command of the Big Horn and Yellowstone Expedition at Fort Fetterman in northeastern Wyoming territory. As Custer headed west from Fort Abraham Lincoln in western North Dakota Territory, Crook and his troops were supposed to meet up with him, but they were driven back to Fort Fetterman. One can only imagine what might have happened at the Battle of the Little Bighorn if Crook had arrived as planned.

Eventually, Crook returned to Arizona where he was made head of the Department of Arizona. The Apache named him "Great Wolf." He was unable, however, to bring Geronimo into captivity, and in 1886, this cost him his command to General Nelson A. Miles, who captured the Apache leader and for all purposes ended the Apache wars. That conflict has the distinction of being the last of all the Indian wars.[10]

Still, Crook continued up the promotion ladder to the rank of major general, and President Grover Cleveland promoted him to command the military division of the Missouri two years later. In his final years, a somewhat remorseful Crook and Nelson Miles championed the fair treatment of Indians. Sioux war chief Red Cloud said of him, "He, at least, never lied to us. His words gave us hope."[11] Other army officers joined in to bolster the public's opinion of the Indian, including "race educators" like

O. O. Howard and Richard Pratt, and ethnologists like John Wesley Powell and Garrick Mallery.[12]

The grisly act of cutting the heads off of Indians who disobeyed military orders was one of many barbaric and heinous acts toward Native Americans. During the Civil War, the Dakota War of 1862 occurred because of U.S. treaty violations and corruption by Indian agents. On August 17, in retaliation, an Indian hunting party in Minnesota killed five settlers who were on a hunting expedition. That escalated to the Dakota attacking settlements along the Minnesota River. In Abraham Lincoln's second inaugural address, he reported that no less than 800 men, women, and children had died. Even though the U.S. Army was occupied with the Civil War, they responded, and by December 1862, soldiers had taken 1,000 Dakota prisoners. A trial in early December ended with the conviction of 303 Sioux prisoners of murder and rape, and they were all sentenced to death. President Lincoln, consumed with the Civil War, still took time to personally review the trial records. Henry Whipple, the Episcopal bishop of Minnesota, traveled to Washington, D.C., to plead with Lincoln for leniency. Two hundred sixty-four prisoners' terms were commuted, but thirty-eight Dakota were publicly hanged on December 26, 1862, in Mankato, Minnesota—the largest mass execution in U.S. history. Their chief's skull and scalp were triumphantly displayed in St. Paul.[13]

In his book *American Carnage: Wounded Knee, 1890*, historian Jerome A. Greene described the events leading to the killing of over 200 Indians—men, women, and children. But he noted that there were many other massacres, writing, "The December 28, 1890, encounter between U.S. Army and Lakota Sioux [at Wounded Knee, not premeditated] came in the wake of several other massacres of native peoples during that period—all of them undeniably premeditated—as punitive forces operating under the auspices of the United States forcibly subjected the Indians to the national will."[14] Those encounters included, in January 1863, troops killing 250 Shoshone in their village at Bear River in Washington Territory (in Idaho); in November 1864, 150 southern Cheyenne and Arapaho slaughtered by the cavalry at Sand Creek, Colorado; and in January 1870, 250 Piegan men, women, and children killed on the Marias River in northwestern Montana territory.[15]

Colonel John Milton Chivington, who led the attack at Sand Creek said, "Damn any man who sympathizes with Indians! . . . I have come to kill Indians, and believe it is right and honorable to use any means under God's heaven to kill Indians. . . . Kill and scalp all, big and little; nits make lice."[16] In 1865, at a Congressional testimony, John S. Smith stated, "I saw the bodies of those lying there cut all to pieces, worse mutilated than any I ever saw before; the women cut all to pieces . . . with knives; scalped; their brains knocked out; children two or three months old; all ages lying there, from sucking infants up to warriors. . . . By whom were they mutilated? By the United States troops. . . ."[17] Kit Carson added, "Jis to think of that dog Chivington and his dirty hounds, up thar at Sand Creek. His men shot down squaws, and blew the brains out of little innocent children. You call sich soldiers Christians, do ye? And Indians savages? What der yer 'spose our Heavenly Father, who made both them and us, thinks of these things? I tell you what, I don't like a hostile red skin anymore than you do. And when they are hostile, I fought 'em, as hard as any man. But I never yet drew a bead on a squaw or papoose, and I despise the man who would."[18] No charges were brought against Chivington after a Congressional investigation, but it did end his political aspirations.

In *Blood on the Marias: The Baker Massacre,* historian Paul R. Wylie described the attack by Major Eugene Baker and his troops from the 2nd Cavalry on a Piegan Indian village on the Marias River in Montana Territory. The village was mainly inhabited by women, children, and old men dying from smallpox. Guides informed the drunk commander that he was attacking the wrong village, but he struck anyway. *The New York Times* called the massacre, "A more shocking affair than the sacking of Black Kettle's camp on the Washita" by Custer two years earlier.[19]

None of these tragic events is well remembered today and neither are the military officers who participated in them. Only the Battle of the Little Bighorn has the distinction of being one of the most famous and most extensively documented battles in American history. The question is why? Since his death on June 25, 1876, in southeastern Montana, Custer has been treated differently by each generation. In many ways this is a reflection more on the attitudes of historians who present facts but sometimes not the truth.

Why is the Custer story still relevant? In 1876, at least for a day, America's faith in all of its religious, philosophical, medical, and scientific ideologies was shaken to the core. Native Americans rejoiced with trembling. How to deal with it? Custer was portrayed as a martyr, crazy, betrayed, cavalier, stupid, evil, good, valiant, reckless, and on and on. It seems like everyone has their own opinion. Perhaps he was a symbol of something greater. In *Custer Died for Your Sins: An Indian Manifesto* (1969), Vine Deloria, Jr. wrote that Custer had to die to atone for the white man's treatment of Native Americans:

The most popular and enduring subject of Indian humor is, of course, Gen. Custer. There are probably more jokes about Custer and the Indians than there were participants in the battle. All tribes, even those thousands of miles from Montana, feel a sense of accomplishment when thinking of Custer [probably not the Crow]. Custer binds together implacable foes because he represented the Ugly American of the last century, and he got what was coming to him.

Some years ago we put out a bumper sticker which read "Custer Died for Your Sins." It was originally meant as a dig at the National Council of Churches. But as it spread around the nation it took on additional meaning until everyone claimed to understand it and each interpretation was different.

Originally, the Custer bumper sticker referred to the Sioux Treaty of 1868 signed at Fort Laramie in which the United States pledged to give free and undisturbed use of the lands claimed by Red Cloud in return for peace. Under the covenants of the Old Testament, breaking a covenant called for a blood sacrifice for atonement. Custer was the blood sacrifice for the United States breaking the Sioux treaty. That, at least originally, was a meaning of the slogan.[20]

Vine Victor Deloria, Jr. (1933-2005), born in South Dakota near the Oglala Lakota Pine Ridge Indian Reservation, was a historian, theologian, activist, and author of a number of other books, including *American Indian Policy in the Twentieth Century* (1985) and *God is Red: A Native View of Religion* (1994). His father was an Episcopal archdeacon and missionary, and Deloria was a product of reservation schools. He graduated from Iowa State University and served in the Marines during the 1950s before earning a degree in 1963 from the Lutheran School of Theology in Illinois. Later, he earned a law degree from the University of Colorado, Boulder, in 1970. Perhaps no one in his generation knew more about both Christian and Indian religions.

However, there is more to atonement than just a blood sacrifice, as theologian Larry Shelton noted in *Cross & Covenant,* writing:

> Forgiveness involves, in the Old Testament at least, not only the sacrificial ritual, but the attitude of repentance as well, which includes the making of restitution and continued faithful obedience to the expectations of the covenant with God. Thus the blood of the sacrifice is only part of the covenant of forgiveness process, and we should

not interpret "blood" literally as the essence of atonement. Instead, we understand it is a synecdoche in which "blood" means the entire atonement process. The prevailing popular understanding of atonement is that God's wrath is propitiated, or appeased, so that he can then be implored to forgive sinful humanity. But both textual and grammatical evidence refutes this assumption. In the Bible, God is never the object of the terms of atonement, propitiation, or reconciliation. Humanity is the object of these terms, all of which have to do with changing attitudes.[21]

Custer got killed, and his blood was shed, but you can't kill Manifest Destiny, scientific racism, nationalism, and social Darwinism with a bullet. Without restitution, unforgiven sin continues today, and perhaps that is one of the reasons that so much has been written about Custer and the Battle of the Little Bighorn. In a way, the hundreds of publications on Custer represent our national repentance and restitution.

Into the West—The Gambler

Custer felt a visceral fascination with the natural world. Wilderness, especially big wilderness, is where wildness most often happens. Wilderness is where evolution occurs because it is where we can find an alternative to, and solace from, our cluttered civilized lives. For Custer, wilderness was heaven to his romantic notions. In its simplest form, wilderness allows other creatures their rights on this planet and the opportunity to experience the survival of the fittest. It was the proving grounds for determining who was the fittest. Custer knew that it is in the little things and in the lonely places that we prove ourselves capable of the big things. At times, he lacked subordination but not sense. The ultimate temptations occur in the wilderness and can be deadly. But it's worth the gamble because when you do what you fear most, you can do anything.

World War II General Erwin Rommel, the "Desert Fox," made a distinction between a gamble and a risk. There is only a chance of success with both, but the difference is that with risk, if you fail, you can recover. Your reputation can be recovered with no long-term damage. In a battle your resources will not be depleted, and you can fall back to your original position with acceptable losses. However, with a gamble, defeat often leads to problems that spiral out of control. When taking a gamble, if difficulties occur, it becomes harder to retreat. The stakes are too high and you can't afford to lose. When you try harder to rescue the situation, you often make matters worse and sink deeper into a hole that you can't get out of. Custer became good at gambling and failing, whether it was stealing Don Juan, investing in a silver mine, stock speculating, betting on horse races, or fighting Indians. It is essential as a leader to take risks, but as Custer found out, gambling is a fool's game. It can get you killed.[22]

The Heart of the Great Plains

Like other wars, the wars against Native Americans were motivated by ideology and theology. In most wars, of course, material rewards—land and plundered goods—also have been a major motivation. All this was true as the Indians lived their final years in freedom on the Plains.

On a new assignment, Custer and Libbie arrived at Fort Riley, Kansas, in the middle of October 1866. The Union Pacific Railroad had extended its tracks westward within ten miles east of the fort. The railroad had been incorporated with President Lincoln's approval on July 1, 1862, by an act of Congress called the Pacific Railroad Act of 1862. It was constructed from Council Bluffs, Iowa, to meet the Central Pacific railroad line being extended eastward from San Francisco. Built mainly by Irish laborers during the Civil War, the two lines would join on May 10, 1869, at Promontory Summit, Utah.

The U.S. government built a number of forts on the central and southern Plains to defend white settlers against Indian attacks. Many of the forts in Kansas were on the railroad route. Fort Leavenworth in the upper northeast portion of Kansas was built in 1827 and was the oldest active U.S. Army post west of Washington, D.C. It was also the base of the African American buffalo soldiers who were part of the 10th Cavalry Regiment formed on September 21, 1866. For those heading west—soldiers, surveyors, missionaries, and settlers—it was a forward destination.[23]

Fort Riley, established in 1853 and 137 miles west of Fort Leavenworth, was named after Major General Bennett C. Riley, who led the first military escort along the Santa Fe Trail. Its purpose was to protect settlers and traders who traveled along the Oregon, California, and Santa Fe Trails. The "Great Migration" had started in 1843 with settlers heading west on the Oregon Trail and accelerated with the discovery of gold in California in 1849 and in Colorado in 1859.

Westward expansion in the mid- to late nineteenth century is a cherished institution of American history. The successive phases of the frontier, first the frontiersmen and the pioneers, then the farmers and the towns, were unfolding in this period. The unromantic facts were that life was hard on the Great Plains. Many settlers couldn't afford the land parcels granted in Kansas, and life was made more challenging with droughts and grasshoppers destroying crops. Many Americans were displaced by the American Civil War and subsequently encroached on Indian Territory in southeastern Kansas. They were squatters. It was a fact for whites that when they came into that country, the Indians had to move, and the government had to move them farther west. The most aggressive settlers knew they had to get to these lands first because the most desirable were taken early.

The Easterners brought with them cholera, whooping cough, and the ultimate killer, smallpox, which quickly devastated Indian populations. In 1887, Fort Riley became the site of the United States Cavalry School and the starting point to reach other forts. Fort Hays, 149 miles west of Fort Riley, was completed on October 11, 1866, to protect Union Pacific Railway workers. It was named after General Alexander Hays, who was killed at the Battle of the Wilderness during the American Civil War. Like many of the forts, Fort Hays was more like a town with limestone buildings. It did not have a wall surrounding it. During the Indian wars, it was the base of operations for military forces and also a supply point. A number of other forts encircled it.[24]

From Fort Hays, one could travel north 201 miles to Fort McPherson in Nebraska, west 125 miles to Fort Wallace, or south 347 miles to Fort Sill. Fort Wallace was built in 1865 to help defend settlers against Cheyenne and Sioux raids. Fort McPherson—also known as Fort Cottonwood—was completed in October 1863 and was named after Major General James B. McPherson. It provided protection for settlers along the Oregon and California Trails between Fort Kearney and Colorado. Fort Sill—thirty miles south of the 1868 Washita massacre—was built in 1869.[25]

After being at Fort Riley for only a few weeks, on November 9, 1866, Custer left for Washington to appear before an examining board that evaluated him for possible promotion to lieutenant colonel. Libbie did not travel with him, and a rift was becoming apparent between them. None of his daily letters to her were reproduced in her memoirs or preserved in her archival collection. The implication is that she didn't want the public to know about their problems. He had been seen in the company of famed Italian actress Adelaide Ristori, and reports of multiple affairs reached Libbie.[26]

In his time in Kansas, Custer had a number of encounters with Pawnee, Comanche, Sioux, Cheyenne, Arapaho, and Kiowa. The first was during the Hancock Expedition that marched out of Fort Riley on March 27, 1867, west toward Fort Hays. At the end of the Civil War, General Winfield Scott Hancock (1824-1886) had been assigned to supervise the execution of the Lincoln assassination conspirators. In 1866, he was promoted and given a command based out of Fort Leavenworth.

Even though the force was less than half the size of a full-strength brigade, the expedition visually was impressive, accompanied by famous civilian scouts like Wild Bill Hickok, and with Custer commanding the cavalry. Sherman had made it clear to Hancock that the purpose of the expedition was to make the Indians behave, ordering him "to go among the Cheyennes, Arapahos and Kiowas . . . and notify them that if they want war they can have it now; but if they decline the offer, then impress on them that they must stop their insolence and threats."[27] The Sand Creek Massacre had increased Indian hostilities in the area.

Custer reported to Hancock that a group of Indians had headed north after killing three men at Lookout Station. The expedition made contact with some hostiles and burned a vacated Indian village, but nothing else was accomplished. Hancock's time in Kansas was brief, not because of his unsuccessful expedition, but because President Johnson was displeased with Republican generals' governance of Reconstruction in the South. He perceived them as too sympathetic to the freed slaves. Johnson was most unhappy with Phil Sheridan and had him switch assignments with Hancock, who was a Democrat. Sheridan reported to Fort Leavenworth and Hancock to New Orleans.[28]

Custer seemed preoccupied—Libbie was more on his mind than fighting Indians. With a sense of guilt from his sexual sins, Custer appealed to her, using the religious angle that had worked so well for him during the Civil War, but that he had seldom used since. On April 25, 1867, he wrote her about praying to God, "That I may be worthy, and be led to pursue such a moral life" as a role model for others. Looking for forgiveness, he included a poem, *"Blest, indeed, is he who never fell... / Strong's temptation, willing are the feet / That follow pleasure; manifold her snares / ...Pardon, not wrath, is God's best attribute."*[29]

She did not write back. Other letters to her suggested multiple affairs. He comforted her by writing that his love for her drove "all thoughts even of them from my mind. . . . I never thought of a single girl to whom I ever paid the slightest attention with any feeling but that of supreme indifference, and without wishing to see them, have cared nothing if I never met either of them again."[30] The charmer had been caught charming the wrong women.

Once again, Sherman came to the rescue and escorted Libbie from Fort Riley part of the way to Fort Hays. With patrons like Sheridan and Sherman, Custer time and time again wasn't held accountable for bad behavior. On May 17, Libbie arrived, but the Custers' world had been going sideways. Their new problem became his troops. Before she arrived, he manically demanded a dress parade every evening and was excessive about the troops keeping the camp clean. Swearing was banned, and Custer demanded his officers to arrest soldiers for petty crimes. Impulsively and for unclear reasons, he marched some of his troops to Lookout Station, but no Indians were found.

With Custer becoming unhinged, on May 15, Captain Albert Barnitz wrote of an impending mutiny, saying, "General Custer is very injudicious in his administrations, and spares no effort to render himself generally obnoxious. I have utterly lost all the little confidence I ever had in his ability as an officer—and all admiration for his character, as a man, and to speak the plain truth I am thoroughly disgusted with him! He is the most complete example of a petty tyrant I have ever seen. You would be filled with utter amazement, if I were to give you a few instances of his cruelty to the men, and discourtesy to the officers."[31]

Two days later, with many troops affected by scurvy—lack of vitamin C—six men left their post for less than an hour to purchase some canned fruit, a source of the vitamin. Harkening back to his punishment in Texas, Custer had their heads shaved on one side and then paraded them through camp for the rest of the enlisted men to see.

To make matters worse, a severe thunderstorm flooded Big Creek and Fort Hays, drowning several men. (The fort was eventually relocated a dozen miles upstream to a safer location.) Libbie returned to Fort Riley, but Custer remained behind. On May 3 and again on May 21 he received marching orders from the 7th Cavalry's senior officer, Colonel Andrew Jackson Smith, to head north to Fort McPherson on the Platte River and then west and eventually south to Fort Wallace. Smith's orders read, "The object of the expedition is to hunt out and chastise the Cheyenne and that portion of the Sioux who are their allies between the Smoky Hill and the Platte." But Custer's need to see Libbie superseded his need to follow the commands of his superiors. He finally suppressed his desires and headed out on June 1, 1867, for a seven-week march.[32]

As Custer and his troops meandered toward the Platte, Pawnee Killer and other Sioux hostiles escaped. Sherman believed Pawnee Killer was responsible for a number of attacks in the area. Custer believed that a small group of irresponsible Indians were causing most of the problems in the area, but Sherman wrote to Grant on June 11 that all of them needed to pay the ultimate price:

> It is an inevitable conflict of races, one that must occur where a stronger is gradually displacing a weaker. The Indians are poor and proud. They are tempted beyond the power of resistance to steal of the herds and flocks they see grazing so peacefully in the valley. To steal they sometimes must kill. We in our time cannot discriminate—all look alike, talk alike, and under the same passions act alike, and to get the rascals, we are forced to include all. . . . Hostilities between the races will continue till the Indians are all killed or taken to a country where they can be watched.[33]

Bad omens were in the air. The Indians vanished like ghosts, and before they got to Fort McPherson, a drunk officer, Wyckliffe Cooper killed himself with a gun. Not concerned about his men or Indians, Custer wrote to Libbie to meet him at the westernmost outpost of Fort Wallace. Custer's march to Fort Wallace presented him with his first chance to engage an Indian party of Cheyenne and Oglala, but instead of a fight, Custer wanted to talk with their leader, Pawnee Killer. Outwitting Custer, Pawnee Killer convinced him and his 7th Cavalry to follow the Indians to their camp. As the troops followed, the Lakota leader left them in the dust.

With a white regiment desertion rate of around thirty-three percent after the Civil War, it came as no surprise that between July 6 and July 8, thirty-four men deserted Custer. On July 7, twelve men deserted with their arms and equipment, prompting Custer to order Major Joel Elliott to shoot them. Three of the deserters were shot and loaded into a wagon along with unarmed prisoners for the trip back to camp. Custer would not allow the doctor to treat the deserters, and one of the privates died from his gunshot wound.

As they progressed south toward Fort Wallace, they found Sherman's messenger Lieutenant Lymen Kidder and his eleven-man escort lying dead, scalped, skulls broken, and mutilated. Pawnee Killer was the most likely culprit, which made his earlier deception even more humiliating to Custer. The final blow came when Custer arrived at Fort Wallace on the evening of July 13, and Libbie wasn't there. Against orders, Custer with seventy-five handpicked men headed east toward Fort Hays in search of Libbie. You can't jump out of the basement window—but Custer did. He was arrested for desertion; the man who so harshly punished deserters had deserted himself.

Custer's court-martial started on the morning of September 17, 1867, in Fort Leavenworth, Kansas. Witnesses told the judge that Custer and his escort of men headed for Fort Hays on July 16. During the march, there had been an Indian attack on Custer's rear guard before reaching Downer's Station where Custer and his men were to spend the night. Later, a detachment of seven men were sent back to the site of the attack to find Custer's personal horse. Five of the men returned and reported that they had been attacked by Indians. Two soldiers were missing. Custer's group headed for Fort Hays anyway, before the two men were recovered by the station commander Arthur B. Carpenter—one was dead and the other wounded. In an August 16 letter to his mother, Carpenter wrote:

> You have probably heard of that conceited upstart called Gen. Custar [sic]. He came through here about the middle of the last month. . . . While at dinner his rearguard was attacked about 3 miles west of here, and those who came and reported two killed. Custar remained unconcerned—finished his dinner, and moved on without saying a word to me about the bodies, or thinking of hunting the Indians.[34]

Carpenter wrote that he was angry that Custer had abandoned the two men, assuming they were both dead. He wrote his mother that the wounded man "says that he would have died before morning if I had not sent out and brought him in. That is General Custer out and out. . . . I hope for the good of the service he will be dismissed."[35]

Custer cared little for his men or the consequences of his desertion. All that he was concerned about was seeing Libbie at Fort Riley. Absence had made their hearts grow fonder. It had not been a comfortable time for Libbie there. Black soldiers from the 38th Infantry were arriving in increasing numbers, and a fire on the Plains had almost burned down her home. Libbie wrote, "The early days of their soldiering were a reign of terror to us women, in our lonely, unprotected homes. I was very much afraid of a Negro soldier." She called them "darkies" and compared them to apes and monkey acrobats and characterized them as lazy and careless.[36]

She had forgiven him, and he had similar sentiments. Libbie wrote Rebecca Richmond, saying, "He took a leave himself, knowing none would be granted him. When he ran the risk of a court-martial and leaving Wallace he did it expecting the consequences . . . and we are determined to not live apart again, even if he leaves the Army otherwise so delightful to us."[37]

Seemingly not in touch with reality, Custer, during the recess of the trial, on September 26 wrote a friend that everything was working out charmingly. Sheridan wrote him a letter of support reporting that everyone in Washington "regarded my trial as an attempt by Hancock to cover up his failures."[38]

On November 8, 1867, the verdict at Custer's court-martial was announced. Custer was found guilty of absence without leave, neglecting to look for the two men shot at Downer's Station and pursue their Indian attackers, and ordering to shoot dead any deserters, three of which were severely wounded and denied medical treatment on Custer's order. He was also found guilty of causing the death of one of the deserters, Private Charles Johnson. Murder charges were determined to be a matter for a civil trial and not a military trial. He was sentenced "to be suspended from rank and command for one year, and forfeit his pay proper for the same time."[39] It would be up to Grant to refer Custer for a murder trial in a civilian court.

Grant disliked Custer, but he did not refer him for a murder trial, which spared his life. He did make his displeasure known, as reported in the *Leavenworth Bulletin:* "General Grant, in reviewing the case, declared that the decision of the Court Martial was altogether too lenient."[40] The then-conservative *New York Times,* a champion of Custer, came to his defense:

> There is considerable astonishment expressed at the result of the trial. General Custer's anxious to have it stand, as it gives him a respite he has desired for a long time, not perhaps in this precise way. . . . It may be, too, that some of this wished-for leisure time will be devoted to the preparation of a work that will be decidedly interesting to those who have followed the fortunes of the General through his campaigns. . . .
>
> General Custer is, to those who know him intimately, the very beau ideal of an American cavalry officer. He is a magnificent rider, fearlessly brave, a capital revolver shot, and without a single objectionable habit. He neither drinks, swears, nor uses tobacco in any form. His weakness, if he has one, is a fast horse, to get all the speed out of which there is no better man than the long-haired hero of Shenandoah.[41]

Custer and Libbie stayed in Leavenworth until the spring of 1868. Both believed the verdict was without substance and the punishment was too severe. They blamed it on General Hancock, a weak man who had to blame his failings on Custer. In an October 1867 article in *Turf, Field and Farm*, Custer berated Hancock, who he characterized as not having the gifts to battle Indian hostiles. In subsequent articles, he counted himself as being educated in the ways of the frontier by Indian and civilian scouts, and touted his understanding of the Indians' way of life. In another newspaper he rebuked the court-martial findings and said Hancock had handpicked many of the jurors. Jealousy, he explained, was the reason for the guilty verdict. Hancock went on to be the Democratic nominee for president of the United States in 1880.

These inflammatory statements against the integrity of the military were grounds for another court-martial. Again, the decision rested on Grant's shoulders, but he was distracted with his own personal problems. President Johnson was unpopular, and the Republicans were looking for someone to run for president. Many wanted Grant, the war hero. Johnson had disregarded the Tenure of Office Act when he fired Secretary of War Edwin Stanton on February 21, 1868. That, along with the president resisting Reconstruction, angered the Republicans. Three days later, the House of Representatives impeached Johnson—a first in American history.

Calls for Custer's court-martial went ignored by Grant who worried that it would give the appearance of punishing a Johnson supporter by his political rival. Rewarded narcissism in an individual or a nation is a dangerous thing. Once again, Sheridan came to the aid of Custer. Unaccountability reaps grandiosity and hubris. Earlier he had let the Custers live in his large house at Fort Leavenworth after they were commanded to leave military quarters. Sheridan directly pleaded for mercy on Custer to Grant:

> He feels very sensibly [i.e., deeply] his punishment and I think would, if he were re-instated, make a better officer than if the sentence were carried out to its full extent. He held high command during the Rebellion and had difficulty in adapting himself to his altered position. There was no one with me who I more highly appreciated than General Custer. He never failed me, and if his late misdeeds could be forgotten, were overlooked on account of his gallantry and faithfulness in the past, it would be gratifying to him and to myself, and benefit to the service.[42]

In May 1868, Custer, who was still living at Fort Leavenworth, wrote a friend about a new petition for his court-martial. He and Libbie were together and that's all that mattered. They hosted a number of parties throughout the previous winter and spring. They then moved back to Monroe where Custer worked on his memoirs. On September 24, Sheridan wired him from Fort Hays informing him that he wanted him back to join eleven companies of his regiment that were to leave on an expedition in October toward the Wichita Mountains to confront hostiles who were raiding settlements.

Yielding to pressure from his generals, Grant decided not to court-martial Custer. On October 4, Custer returned to Fort Hays. After confrontations to the west of the fort, Sheridan looked south along the Washita River in Indian Territory to crush Indian hostiles. Custer and his 7th Cavalry headed directly south in a move, Sheridan intended, "to strike the Indians a hard blow and force them on the reservations set apart for them, and if this cannot be accomplished to show to the Indian that the winter season would not give him rest." He would teach them a lesson so that "these Indians, the enemies of our race and of our civilization, shall not again be able to begin and carry on their barbarous warfare." Custer understood that if the Indians did not surrender, then they would be annihilated.[43]

The Indians were fighting a guerrilla war of attack and disappear. Traditional battles between forces such as took place in the Civil War were unknown on the frontier. Thus, the gallantry of the Civil War was replaced by attacking Indian villages inhabited by not only warriors but also old men, women, and children at night in the winter. It was a form of terrorism and was quite effective.

The Washita village would be attacked by 800 soldiers divided into four separate columns—a tactic right out of the textbook at West Point. Major Joel Elliott would swing east to the left side of the village, Captain William Thompson would lead men west around the village to the south side, and Captain Edward Myers would also swing west and remain there. Thus the village would be totally surrounded at the time of the attack. Eight years later at the Little Bighorn, these same tactics would fail Custer, with catastrophic results.

Before dawn on November 27, 1868, the sounds of soldiers' cheers and the melody of "Garryowen" rang out through the valley as the 7th Cavalry charged. Unbeknownst to them, one of the chief proponents of peace with the whites, Black Kettle, was in the village. The leading Southern Cheyenne for peace had survived the Sand Creek Massacre to now be shot dead, along with his wife, Medicine Woman. It took only a few minutes to destroy the village. All the Cheyenne men were executed. Some soldiers gunned down women and children as they ran for their lives. When

Custer found out, he ordered them to stop shooting at them. After around 100 villagers were killed, the lodges were burned. Downstream and not far from the village was a massive encampment of about 6,000 Arapaho and Southern Cheyenne. Concerned that they would be surrounded by an overwhelming force, Custer ordered retreat even though Elliott and his men were missing.[44]

It was a hollow victory for Custer. Women and children had been massacred, along with the peace-loving Black Kettle. To make matters worse, Elliott and his men were dead, killed by the Indians. Two weeks later, Sheridan and Custer returned to find Elliott and seventeen of his men's frozen bodies riddled with bullet holes and arrows. This dampened Sheridan's earlier elation over the victory and embittered soldiers, including Frederick Benteen, toward Custer.

Fearing further attacks from Sheridan, the Indians began surrendering, which prompted him to establish Fort Sill in 1869 at the base of the Wichita Mountains. A confident Custer next hunted Indians near the mountains. There were still 1,400 Cheyenne that had not surrendered. Slowly, they too would surrender, broken, malnourished, and sad. One scout reported, "I never saw such heart-broken, hopeless expressions on the face of another human being."[45]

Many of the hostiles were taken to Camp Supply. The young Indian girls spent the evenings in the tents of the army officers and were raped by them. Custer picked one of the most beautiful for his enjoyment, seventeen-year-old Monahseetah, who entertained him throughout the winter until Libbie arrived in the spring.[46]

Controversy arose in late December 1868 over the Washita incident, with some newspapers calling it a massacre. Even *The New York Times,* while stating that it wasn't a massacre, did admit that it was "a pretty murderous affair. . . . Nothing is said of a single [male Cheyenne] being captured—from which we may guess that all were dispatched." T. J. Stiles lays some of the blame on Custer's superior, writing, "In any event, Custer only struck Black Kettle's band because Sheridan refused to allow any Cheyennes a refuge at Fort Cobb. This order led directly to Black Kettle's death, and Sheridan issued it long before Custer first set out from Camp Supply."[47]

Sheridan hated hostile Indians and had ordered Custer "to destroy their villages and ponies; to kill and hang all warriors, and bring back all women and children." As Stiles further points out, "Ever since the Nuremberg trials, orders have not been considered justification for crimes against humanity. . . .

The very existence of the United States was predicated on the disposition of the indigenous. If Custer was wrong, ultimately it was because the nation was wrong. Many believe it was. But he was no outlier."[48]

Republican Grant was now in the White House, and George, Libbie, and Tom Custer were enjoying pleasant times at Fort Hays. Hunting parties arriving by rail were entertained by company commander Colonel Nelson Miles (1839-1925) and the Custers. Some were sent by Sheridan, who knew his friends would be impressed with a celebrity like Custer.

But all was not well in the military. Before Andrew Johnson relinquished his office on March 3, 1869, he decimated the army by cutting the regiments almost in half. This meant that, in the West, Indian fighting almost came to a halt. This lull prompted a visit by Custer to some of his friends in Chicago. Like his promise to Libbie to halt inappropriate relationships with other women, his promise to curtail his gambling went unfulfilled. His gambling addiction had become a serious matter between the two of them as evidenced in a letter to Libbie in which Custer wrote, "You may laugh at me, perhaps taunt me with the remark that I am unable to carry out the resolution. I have often heard you express the idea that I was incapable of doing it."[49] The fighting continued.

His next fiasco was investing in a mining operation, the Stevens Lode Silver Mine, in the Rocky Mountains west of Denver. It was an ill-conceived get-rich scheme in which Custer needed investment money from others since he had little of his own. As he was hustling investors, Custer wrote Libbie of a number of women who were flirting with him. Libbie returned the favor by corresponding with other men. Nonetheless, Custer stayed in New York scrounging up money for his silver mine. By the fall of 1871, his dream of investors putting up hundreds of thousands of dollars was burst when he could raise only $12,000. After a year, his scheme failed when financiers stopped investing.[50]

Custer, the Renaissance Man

With funds cut from the military, in September 1871 Custer was relegated to chasing bootleggers and breaking up Ku Klux Klan gatherings in his new post at Elizabethtown, Kentucky. Even though the Fifteenth Amendment had been ratified in 1870, giving blacks the right to vote, the South was still filled with acts of discrimination. Custer was on the side of the discriminators and cared little to chase the Ku Klux Klan around the countryside. This did not endear him to Grant.

Seeking celebrity and financial reward as an intellectual author of the West in the era of Darwinism, Custer now became the amateur Darwinist, anthropologist, geologist, and delineator of battles with the Indians. It was a time when many authors—including Custer—used semicolons and commas instead of periods, resulting in single sentences that could fill a page. Even so, Custer was marketable.

There was a postwar boom in the popularity of magazines. In 1865, there were only 700 magazines published in the United States, but that number had nearly doubled to 1,200 by 1870. By 1885, there would be 3,300. Readers in the East and South were developing more interest in happenings of the West as it experienced rapid growth in industry, transportation, political power, and white culture. Magazines endlessly carried stories of the romance of the West. The most popular literary journals were *Harper's* and *Scribner's*.[51]

The payments to contributors averaged five to ten dollars a page. Mark Twain garnered two cents a word from *Galaxy*. It was next to impossible to make a living writing for periodicals. Income of $2,000 a year was considered comfortable for the average American, but to achieve that the writer would have had to sell an article every week. With the explosion of periodicals, editors were hungry to fill their pages and accepted articles that were poorly written by untrained writers. But that gradually changed so that by 1877, magazines like *Putnam's*, *Galaxy*, and *Atlantic* were featuring articles written by trained, professional journalists.

Custer worked with editor Francis Church at his *Galaxy* offices in New York. Eventually, the serialized articles would be compiled into the book *My Life on the Plains,* published in 1874 by Sheldon and Company, New York. As T. J. Stiles wrote, "He developed a fascination with natural history, and collected fossils in the West. He paid attention to new thinking about the geological origins of the Earth and the theory of evolution, as presented by Charles Darwin in the *Origin of Species* in 1859. But his essays were also the work of an amateur, a gentleman hobbyist of the old school."[52]

Custer described in flowery words the beauty of the Wichita Mountains that he had viewed while chasing Indians:

> Here are to be seen all the varied colors which Bierstadt and Church endeavored to represent in their mountain scenery. . . . The air is pure and fragrant, and as exhilarating as the purest of wine; the climate enchantingly mild; the sky clear and blue as the most beautiful sapphire, with here and there clouds of rarest loveliness, presenting to the eye the richest coral mingling of bright and varied colors;

delightful odors are constantly being wafted by; while the forests, filled with the mockingbird, the colibri, the hummingbird and the thrush, constantly put forth a joyful chorus, and all combined to fill the soul with visions of delight and enhance the perfection and glory of the creation. Strong indeed must be that unbelief which can here contemplate nature in all her purity and glory, and, un-awed by the sublimity of this closely connected testimony, question either the divine origin or purpose of the beautiful firmament.[53]

As an anthropologist, Custer rebuked James Fenimore Cooper's unrealistic depiction of the Indian:

Cooper, to whose writings more than to those of any other author are the people speaking the English language indebted for a false and ill-judged estimate of the Indian character, might well have laid the scenes of his fictitious stories in this beautiful and romantic country.

It is to be regretted that the character of the Indian as described in Cooper's interesting novels is not the true one. But, as in emerging from childhood into the years of a mature age, we are often compelled to cast aside many of our earlier illusions and replace them by beliefs less inviting but more real, so we as a people, with opportunities enlarged and the facilities for obtaining knowledge increased, have been forced by a multiplicity of causes to study and endeavor to comprehend thoroughly the character of the red man. So intimately has he become associated with the Government as ward of the nation, and so prominent a place among the questions of national policy does the much mooted Indian question occupy, that it behooves us no longer to study this problem from works of fiction, but to deal with it as it exists in reality.

Stripped of the beautiful romances with which we have been so long willing to envelop him, transferred from the inviting pages of the novelist to the localities where we are compelled to meet with him, in his native village, on the war path, and when raiding upon our frontier settlements and lines of travel, the Indian forfeits his claim to the appellation of the *noble* red Indian. We see him as he is, and so far as all knowledge goes, as he ever has been, a *savage* in every sense of the word; not worse, perhaps, than his white brother would be, similarly born and bred, but one whose cruel and ferocious nature far exceeds that of any wild beast of the desert.

. . . . In him, we find the representative of the race whose origin is as promises to be a subject forever wrapped in mystery; a race incapable of being judged by the rules or laws applicable to any other known race of men; one between which it and civilization there seems to have existed from time immemorial a determined and unceasing warfare—a hostility so deep-seated and inbred with the Indian character that in the exceptional instances where the modes and habits of civilization have been reluctantly adopted, it has been at the sacrifice of power and influence as a tribe, and the more serious loss of health, vigor and courage as individuals.[54]

In a nod to Darwinism and the belief that Indians were the Lost Tribes of Israel described in the Old Testament, Custer wrote in his "The American Indian" chapter:

By closely studying the customs, costumes, faith and religious traditions of the various tribes, a striking homogeneity is seen to exist. At the same time and from the same sources we are enabled to discover satisfactory resemblances between certain superstitions and religious rites practiced among the Indian tribes and those which prevailed at one time among the ancient Persians, the Hebrews and the Chaldeans. They who adhere to the belief of disparity of origin may readily adduce arguments in refutation of an opposite theory. The apparent similarity found to exist in the customs, dress and religious rights of different tribes may be partially accounted for by their long intercourse under like circumstances, the effect of which would necessarily be an assimilation in beliefs and usages to a greater or less degree.[55]

. . . . Each tribe had its peculiar customs, whether of war, the chase or religion. They exhibited some close resemblances as well as widely different traits of character. That they sprang from different nations rather than from a single source seems highly probable.[56]

. . . . Many of the Indian customs and religious rites closely resemble those of the Israelites. In many tribes, the Indians offer the first fruits of the earth and of the chase to the Great Spirit. They have also certain ceremonies at stated periods. Their division of the year corresponds with the Jewish festivals. In some tribes, the brother of the deceased husband receives the widow into his lodge as his legitimate wife. Some travelers claim to have seen circumcision practiced among certain tribes. Another analogy between the Jews and the Indians is seen in their purifications, baths, anointings, fasts, manner of praying; and abstaining from certain quadrupeds, birds and reptiles considered impure.[57]

.... Then again, the medicine man of the tribe, who is not, as his name implies, the physician, but stands in the character of high priest, assumes a dress and manner corresponding to those of the Jewish high priest.[58]

.... In studying the Indian character, while shocked and disgusted by many of his traits and customs, I find much to be admired and still more of deep and unvarying interest. . . . Study him, fight him, civilize him if you can, he remains still the object of your curiosity, a type of man peculiar and undefined, subjecting himself to no known law of civilization, contending determinedly against all efforts to win him from his chosen mode of life. He stands in the group of nations solitary and reserved, seeking alliance with none, mistrusting and opposing the advances of all.

.... Civilization may and should do much for him, but it can never civilize him. A few instances to the contrary may be quoted, but these are all susceptible of explanation. No tribe enjoying its accustomed freedom has ever been induced to adopt a civilized mode of life, or as they express it, to follow the white man's road.[59]

.... Nature intended him for a savage state; every instinct, every impulse of his soul inclines him to it. The white race might fall into a barbarous state, and afterwards, subjected to the influence of civilization, be reclaimed and prosper. Not so the Indian. He cannot be himself and be civilized; he fades away and dies. Cultivation such as the white man would give him deprives him of his identity. Education, strange as it may appear, seems to weaken rather than strengthen his intellect.[60]

Toward the end of the chapter, Custer expressed his view on the role of disease in decimating the Indian population, writing, "But little idea can be formed of the terrible inroads which diseases before unknown to them have made upon their numbers. War has contributed its share, it is true, but disease alone has done much to depopulate many of the Indian tribes. It is stated that the smallpox was first introduced among them by the white man in 1837, and that in the short space of one month, six tribes lost by this disease alone twelve thousand persons."[61]

In the next chapter, titled "General Hancock's Campaign," Custer had his chance to humiliate his old nemesis. He belittled the spring 1867 Hancock Expedition, alleging, "None, perhaps, of late years has excited more general and unfriendly comment, considering the slight loss of life inflicted upon the Indians. . . ."[62] At the same time, he championed the military's charity toward the Indian. "On the contrary," he wrote, "the army is the Indian's best friend, so long as the latter desires to maintain friendship. It is pleasant at all times and always interesting to have a village of peaceable Indians locate their lodges near our frontier post or camps."[63]

In a favorable tone toward the Indian, Custer also wrote, "If I were an Indian, I often think that I would greatly prefer to cast my lot among those of my people who adhered to the free open plains, rather than submit to the confined limits of a reservation."[64]

Some newspapers wrote positive reviews. The *Independent* wrote, "General G. A. Custer . . . administers a well-deserved rebuke to Fenimore Cooper." The *San Francisco Chronicle,* which wanted to please its land-grabbing readers, opined, "The subject is narrowed down to the simple proposition, either the progress of civilization must be stayed or the red man must be driven away or exterminated."[65] *Turf, Field and Farm* described his writing as "stirring." The *Massachusetts Ploughman* agreed that Custer "tells a story of adventure with great spirit, and in a way to command readers." Others were not so kind. *The Literary World* characterized his stories as "not very interesting," and the *New York Tribune* found it boring, remarking, "General Custer's 'My Life on the Plains' has apparently no end."[66]

Financial success had always eluded Custer, and his writing proved to be no different. By the end of 1872, his monthly serialized articles in *Galaxy* had garnered him a modest $1,200. His ego would need to be satisfied once more in battle. This time it would be on the Northern Plains.[67]

Destroying Graceland

By 1873, survey parties from the Northern Pacific Railroad, headquartered in Minnesota, were in the Yellowstone River Valley in eastern Montana. The Sioux and Cheyenne believed this was another example of breaking the Fort Laramie Treaty. On April 10, 1873, the Custers and the 7th Cavalry set up camp outside the capital, Yankton, in southeastern Dakota Territory. By the summer of 1873, they had relocated to the newly built Fort Abraham Lincoln on the Missouri River near present-day Bismarck, North Dakota.

Dakota country brought a new nickname for the "Son of the American

West." Evan S. Connell, author of *Son of the Morning Star: Custer and the Little Bighorn,* wrote about how he received the name:

> In Dakota Territory five years later the Arikaras christened him Son of the Morning Star, or Child of the Stars. At least that is how he might have received the name. Maybe the Crow scout White Man Runs Him, who also was known as Son of the Morning Star, conferred this—his own name—upon Custer. Whether a Ree or a Crow first called him that, Son of the Morning Star must be regarded as a child of Dakota Territory; but symbolically it seems right to say he was born at dawn in Oklahoma beneath the bright soft light of Venus. No matter how he got the name, he liked to be called Son of the Morning Star. Without doubt he liked it better than several names the troopers called him: Hard Ass, Iron Butt, Ringlets.[68]

This was the land of Lakota warrior Crazy Horse (c1842-1877), who had made a name for himself on December 21, 1866, when he and his men ambushed and killed army soldiers in what has been called the Fetterman Massacre. Crazy Horse and his warriors became almost a mythical force on the Northern Plains and were much feared by the military. At that time, while the U.S. military was still a threat, the Lakota more frequently battled their enemies—Blackfeet, Pawnee, and their most hated rival, the Crow. But by 1873, it was clear to Crazy Horse that the coming railroad posed the most serious threat to their freedom.

Custer had a few skirmishes with the Lakota during the summer but inflicted casualties on only a few dozen warriors. Libbie had returned to Monroe for a visit when Custer wrote her an inflated letter about himself, especially about him protecting the Northern Pacific engineers. "My little girl never saw people more enthusiastic," he wrote. "The expedition would've turned back long ago and abandoned the enterprise . . . had not your Boy stepped generally to the front."[69] With their relationship mended, a bored Libbie in a letter to Custer gave him the adulation he so desperately craved, penning, "So monotonous so commonplace and besides I see every day that great ambition I have for you and how I bask daily in the sunshine of your glory."[70] In another letter she wrote, "Autie, your career is something wonderful. Can you realize what wonders come constantly to you while other men lead such tame lives?"[71]

The most efficient way to destroy an enemy, especially when not fighting against a traditional, organized army, is to destroy their food source.

Most recently, a prime example would be the use of Agent Orange during the Vietnam War from 1961 to 1971 in what was called Operation Ranch Hand. The aerial herbicide was authorized by President John F. Kennedy in November 1961, and over the years almost 20 million gallons of the defoliant destroyed the jungles and rural areas of Vietnam, eastern Laos, and Cambodia, with the objective of depriving guerrillas of food and cover. Results were disappointing. Agent Orange has proved to have had disastrous effects on the natives and U.S. military who were exposed to it.[72]

By destroying the bison herds, whites not only destroyed the Indians' food source, but also their source for shelter and clothing. It was the most effective way to destroy their hope. The railroads were the most efficient way to bring hunters out West to kill the bison. Twenty thousand hunters killed 10 million bison after the Civil War. Robes and other parts of the animal could then be transported east to markets. Historian Paul Hutton wrote, "Sheridan wanted quickly to reduce the buffalo population so as to terminate the hunting right."[73] Indians themselves were enticed to kill the bison for their robes, with hefty bounties paid by whites.

The ultimate insult to the Indians came when, in the summer of 1874, Custer led an expedition to their sacred Black Hills, looking for gold and a place to locate a fort. Many believed this also broke the Fort Laramie Treaty. Rumors that he had found gold in the Black Hills were reported widely in newspapers throughout the United States. His fame again was on the rise. Additional notoriety came with the publication that fall of *My Life on the Plains.*

With the country in a depression, the discovery of gold was great news. Beyond that, many saw the fertile place as a fine area for white settlement. Sherman told a reporter, "Well, I don't know about the minerals, but there is evidently an immense and viable region to be open to civilization, and the Army alone can do it."[74] At that time, the Sioux were still considered the owners of the Black Hills, and the army made anemic attempts to keep white prospectors and settlers out of the area.

By the summer of 1875, thousands of gold seekers were spreading over the Black Hills like ants. Libbie was visiting Monroe, and Custer went on to New York. It was there he heard about government negotiations with the Sioux to obtain the Black Hills.

But his mind was on his finances, and he approached a lecture agency. Custer was in deep financial trouble. On $398,983 in transactions, he had lost $8,578 on bad stock trades with no way to repay. Libbie did not know about his debts, but when she joined him in New York in the fall of 1875, money was tight. She wrote Tom Custer in late December, "The holidays have been rainy, gloomy. I did not have half the fun I had anticipated, looking in at the shop windows. On Christmas morning I went to church, but came back weary, disgruntled."[75]

With the influx of whites in the Black Hills and under political pressure, Grant relinquished and stopped enforcing his order to keep trespassers out of the Black Hills. His decision was made easier when his inspector, E. C. Watkins of the Office of Indian Affairs, reported that Sitting Bull and his bands were as wild and savage as when Lewis and Clark had passed through the Northern Plains. He wrote that they were defiant and contemptible and encouraged Grant to take action against them since there were only a few hundred warriors that could be easily crushed by a thousand troops.[76] Interior Secretary Chandler advised Sioux agents to inform Sitting Bull that he must report to the reservation by January 31, 1876. Because it was the winter, few of the Indians received word, and this gave the War Department an excuse to deal forcibly with the hostiles.

However, Secretary of War William Belknap had more pressing problems over illegal kickbacks he and his wife were receiving. On March 1, 1876, Belknap was willing to confess but was not allowed to. The next day, articles of impeachment were drawn up. Grant accepted Belknap's resignation. Congress continued to investigate the Belknap situation and also graft by Orvil Grant, the president's brother. Custer testified against Orvil, much to the delight of the Democrats. In addition, Major Lewis Merrill, who had actively pursued the Ku Klux Klan in South Carolina, much to the ire of Custer, was accused by Custer of a bribe from the state legislature.

T. J. Stiles summarized Grant's feelings toward Custer: "President Grant could not have been surprised by Custer's participation in the Congressional offensive. It was typical of his self-dramatizing, self-righteousness, partisanship, and recklessness in insulting the chain of command. For the first time, though, Custer attacked Grant himself—or so it seemed from Grant's perspective. The president had long disdained Custer; now he saw him as an enemy."[77]

Custer's reckless behavior took many forms. He planted bogus political stories in newspapers; he accused Grant's own family of corruption; on hearsay, he denigrated an officer in his own regiment; and for political gain, he supported the Democratic Party against his commander-in-chief. To make matters worse, there was a question of corruption by Sheridan regarding a corn transaction at Fort Abraham Lincoln.[78]

Custer was ready to leave Washington at just the time he was to testify in the Belknap investigation. Grant demanded Custer be replaced as commander at Fort Abraham Lincoln. Sheridan suggested General Terry. Custer tried to plead his case to Grant, but the president would not see him. Custer then boarded a train to Chicago and on to St. Paul. Sherman was furious that Custer had left without seeing Grant and had Custer pulled off the train before he left St. Paul for Fort Abraham Lincoln.

Still a media darling with some, Custer was defended by the *New York World* as a victim of political vindictiveness. "President Grant has to-day performed an act which appears to be the most high-handed abuse of his official power which he has perpetrated yet," the paper wrote.[79] It claimed that Custer was the only man qualified who could lead the expedition against the Indians. On May 4, 1876, with all the scandals involving his administration in Washington, Grant allowed Custer to return to Fort Abraham Lincoln, but he was to remain there and not join the expedition.[80]

General Alfred Terry (1827-1890) came to Custer's defense, but Sheridan remained unconvinced. Custer's biggest supporter had finally had enough of his shenanigans. Sheridan wrote Grant, "I am sorry Lieutenant Colonel Custer did not manifest as much interest by staying at his post to organize & get ready his regiment & the expedition as he does now to accompany it . . . & I sincerely hope if granted this time it will have sufficient effect to prevent him from again attempting to throw discredit on his profession and his brother officers."[81]

Under pressure, Grant caved and allowed Custer to join Terry. Sherman telegrammed Terry, "Advise Custer to be prudent, not to take along any newspaper men, who always work mischief, and to abstain from any personalities in the future. Tell him I want him to confine his whole mind to his legitimate office, and trust to time. That newspaper paragraph in the *New York World* of May 2 compromised his best friend here, and almost deprived us of the ability to serve him."[82]

The Great Sioux War

The primary officers in charge of the Great Sioux War were Commanding General William T. Sherman in Washington, D.C., and his subordinate, Lieutenant General Philip H. Sheridan, Commander of the Military Division of the Missouri, with offices in Chicago, Illinois.

With Custer back East, "the Great Sioux War" officially began on March 17, 1876, when Brigadier General George Crook's Big Horn Expedition attacked a village of Northern Cheyenne under Chief Old Bear along the

Powder River in southeastern Montana. The 400 soldiers of the 2nd and 3rd Cavalry believed they were attacking Crazy Horse. Infuriated, the Northern Cheyenne joined forces with the Sioux. This was the first of nine separate expeditions that generated ten major army-Indian encounters.⁸³

Next was Crook's failed Battle of the Rosebud on June 17. One stream west of the Rosebud River was the Little Bighorn. The Little Bighorn was the site of one of the largest gatherings of Indians in the history of the West. Almost 8,000 people congregated to hunt and to partake in their religious ceremonies. Many had responded to Sitting Bull's invitation to join free Indians in Montana and leave the Great Sioux Reservation in western South Dakota in the spring of 1876. They had been on the reservation for as long as eight years since the Laramie Treaty of 1868. Besides looking forward to hunting and the June Sun Dance, many of the young men yearned for a fight against the Crow.

In June, the hot, dry weather scorched the eastern Montana prairie grass and turned it from forest green to straw yellow. Hunkpapa, Blackfeet, Sioux, Oglala, Minneconjou, and San Arc congregated to celebrate the Sun Dance. As Native American author James Welch wrote in *Killing Custer*, "This ceremony, common to all plains tribes, took place during the Moon of Making Fat (June) or the Moon of Blackening Cherries (July) always during the full moon, for it lit up the ignorance of the black sky. The Lakotas called the ceremony *wiwanyag wachipi*, or dance looking at the sun. Today it is called the Sun Dance."⁸⁴

Chief Sitting Bull (c1831-1890) took part in this Sun Dance, which may have been the largest in history. Toward the end of the ceremony, Black Moon caught the chief as he fainted. When Sitting Bull regained consciousness, he whispered to Black Moon. Black Moon told the participants, "Sitting Bull wishes to announce that he has just heard a voice from above saying, 'I give you these because they have no ears.' He looked up and saw soldiers and some Indians on horseback coming down like grasshoppers, with their heads down and their hats falling off. They were falling right into our camp."⁸⁵

Welch explained, "The people were happy with this vision, for they knew what the words meant. The soldiers had no ears to listen to the truth that the Sioux and Cheyenne wanted to be left in peace to hunt and to be together on the ground of many gifts. The soldiers who wanted war were coming to their camp and would be killed there. The announcement was clear enough. The people rejoiced. Wakan Tanka would protect them."⁸⁶

On May 17, 1876, all twelve companies—750 officers and enlisted men—of the 7th Cavalry paraded through Fort Abraham Lincoln as the military band played "Garryowen." The Custer brothers, George, Tom, and Boston; the soon-to-be infamous Reno and Benteen; Bloody Knife; twenty-one Arikara scouts; three Gatling guns; and 150 wagons headed west. The day before, Sheridan had wired Terry, "I believe it to be fully equal to all the Sioux which can be brought against it, and only hope they will hold fast to meet it. . . . You know the impossibility of any large number of Indians keeping together as a hostile body for even one week."[87] Libbie camped with them the first night and the next morning, May 18, said her final goodbye. Custer and his troops were killed on June 25, 1876.[88] The next day the myths, legends, and lies would begin.

Crazy Horse and Gall's forces totaled 2,500 warriors. Custer's companies attacked with 225 soldiers. In *Crazy Horse and Custer,* military historian Stephen Ambrose delineated Custer's mistakes: He refused Terry's offer of four companies of the 2nd Cavalry; he badly underestimated his enemy more in terms of fighting capability than number; he attacked one day too soon and should've waited for Gibbon; he did not know his enemy's position, strength, or location; and he couldn't outflank Crazy Horse's flanking force.[89] Ambrose wrote, "The conclusion is inescapable. At the Little Bighorn, Custer was not only outnumbered; he was also outgeneraled."[90]

The dean of Western historians, Robert M. Utley, who has studied the battle as thoroughly as anyone, wrote:

> Sitting Bull's significance at the Little Bighorn lay not in flaunting bravery, or directing the movements of warriors, or even inspiring them to fight. It lay rather in a leadership so wise and powerful that it drew together and held together a muscular coalition of tribes, one so infused with his defiant cast of mind that it could rout Three Stars and annihilate Long Hair. Never had the Sioux and Cheyennes triumphed so spectacularly, and never would they again. For that, more than any other chief, they could thank Sitting Bull.[91]
>
> . . . . Then on June 25, 1876, history merged with legend to award George Armstrong Custer immortality. The Battle of the Little Bighorn cut short a career that would have gained occasional mention in the histories of the Civil War and the western frontier. Instead, it made the slain Custer's name a household word then and forever after—an icon in the public imagination, at times bright, at times tarnished, but never in danger of decay.[92]

Vine Deloria wrote that all tribes felt a sense of accomplishment when

Custer died, but that was not entirely true. Many of the Crow lamented Custer's death. Plenty-Shield explained to Frank Bird Linderman:

> My man, Goes-Ahead, told me that he felt afraid when he saw so many lodges. He, with the two others, Hairy-Moccasin, and White-Man-Runs-Him, turned here, going up the creek that white men call Reno. They met Son-of-the-Morning-Star coming down this Creek, and told him what they had seen. They said that there were more Lacota, more enemies, than there were bullets in the soldier's belts, that there were too many to fight.
>
> "But Son-of-the-Morning-Star was going to his death, and did not know it. He was like a feather blown by the wind, and *had* to go."
>
> She pressed her fist against her forehead, and bent her head. "Tst, tst, tst! He would not listen," she murmured. "And he was brave; yes, he was a brave man."
>
> "Two-Bodies, a half-breed interpreter, listened," she went on [probably Mitch Boyer]. He spoke to Son-of-the-Morning-Star, saying, 'You can yet get safely away.'
>
> "But the soldier chief wanted to fight. He *had* to fight, because he had to *die*. And this made others die with him," she added, speaking slowly and with deep feeling.
>
> "My man, Goes-Ahead, told me that Son-of-the-Morning-Star drank too often from the straw-covered bottle, and that as soon as Two-Bodies told him that he might yet get away he made a big mistake by dividing his blue horse-soldiers into three parties, sending two of them away from him."[93]

Many implied that if Crook had not been defeated on the Rosebud and had joined Terry, Gibbon, and Custer, the catastrophe would not have occurred. Subsequently, the Indians broke up into small bands, with some heading south toward the Bighorn Mountains and others heading back to the reservations. Crook eventually received reinforcements and on August 31 started chasing some of the Indians into Dakota Territory. Soon the hostiles were out of supplies and near starvation. His troops eventually confronted American Horse, who died that night from gunshot wounds.

General Terry and Colonel Gibbon, under orders from General Sheridan, built a cantonment at the mouth of the Tongue River on the Yellowstone under the command of Colonel Nelson A. Miles. Miles had many encounters with Sitting Bull in the fall of 1876 until Sitting Bull and his followers entered Canada. In November, under the direction of Crook, Colonel Ranald S. Mackenzie at dawn attacked a major village of Northern Cheyenne under Chiefs Dull Knife (Morning Star) and Little Wolf in the Bighorn Mountains.

On January 7, 1877, Miles' men battled the Sioux and Cheyenne in the upper Tongue River Valley. After the Battle of Wolf Mountains, it was clear that the hostiles' days were numbered.

In the dead of winter, there was little game, and the warriors' families were starving. By springtime, tribesmen from Crazy Horse's and Dull Knife's villages headed toward the Red Cloud and Spotted Tail agencies in Nebraska and also to agencies in Dakota Territory along the Missouri River.

The last holdout was Lame Deer, but after Miles led a dawn attack on May 7, 1877, on his village, the proud warrior surrendered. That marked the end of major engagements and the Great Sioux War. In 1881, Sitting Bull surrendered at Fort Buford, Dakota, at the confluence of the Yellowstone and Missouri Rivers.[94]

Historian Jerome A. Greene wrote that official records showed that there were a total of 408 military casualties in the Great Sioux War. Two hundred eighty-three soldiers and scouts were killed and another 125 wounded. The majority of losses occurred under Custer's command. The number of Indians killed were 150 and 90 wounded, with many more noncombatant losses. According to Greene, "Despite the eighteen months of sporadic fighting, it was the Little Bighorn, the largest and most controversial engagement, that captured and maintained the fascination of the American public as it continues today. . . ."[95]

Alongside Custer that fateful day on June 25, 1876, were Manifest Destiny, social Darwinism, scientific racism, and American exceptionalism. Doubts about them were short lived, and they quickly rebounded in the minds of white Americans. The Western frontier was officially over in 1890, and the Indians were relegated to reservations.

The power of the Sun Dance and the Spirit of the West met the power of the U.S. military, and at least for one day, the spirits ruled. Even though her husband left her in debt, Libbie spent the rest of her life creating his legend in her books on her star. In 1885, *"Boots and Saddles," or Life in Dakota with General Custer* was published. Next was *Tenting on the Plains* in 1887 and finally, *Following the Guidon* in 1890. She died on April 4, 1933, on Park Avenue in New York, almost fifty-seven years after her husband. Many held back their criticism toward Custer until she passed.

Without lament, L. Frank Baum (1856-1919), famed author of *The Wonderful Wizard of Oz*, became a spokesman for white racists and survival of the fittest. Baum was born in New York to a devout Methodist family. His father, Benjamin, was a wealthy businessman who made some of his fortune providing barrels during the Pennsylvania oil rush. Frank grew up on a palatial estate where his father bought him a printing press, which led to several small publications. Later, he was an actor on stage, and his indulgent father built him a theater in 1880. In July 1888, he headed to Aberdeen, Dakota Territory, and became editor of the local newspaper, the *Aberdeen Saturday Pioneer*.

On December 20, 1890, five days after the killing of Sitting Bull, he wrote an infamous tribute:

> Sitting Bull, the most renowned Sioux of modern history, is dead. He was not a Chief, but without Kingly lineage he arose from a lowly position to the greatest Medicine Man of his time, by virtue of his shrewdness and daring.
>
> He was an Indian with the white man's spirit of hatred and revenge for those who had wronged him and his. In his day he saw his son and his tribe gradually driven from their possessions: forced to give up their old hunting grounds and espouse the hard-working and uncongenial applications of the whites. In these, his conquerors, were marked in their dealings with his people by selfishness, falsehood and treachery. What wonder that his wild nature, untamed by years of subjection, should still revolt? What wonder that a fiery rage still burned within his breast that he should seek every opportunity of obtaining vengeance upon his natural enemies.
>
> The proud spirit of the original owners of these vast prairies inherited through centuries of fierce and bloody wars for their possession, lingered last in the bosom of Sitting Bull. With his fall the nobility of the Redskin is extinguished, and what few are left are a pack of whining curs who lick the hand that smites them. The Whites, by law of conquest, by Justice of civilization, are masters of the American continent, and the best safety of the frontier settlements will be secured by the total annihilation of the few remaining Indians. Why not annihilation? Their glory is fled, their spirit broken, their manhood effaced; better that they die than live the miserable wretches that they are. History would forget these latter despicable beings, and speak, in latter ages of the glory of these grand Kings of Forrest and plain that Cooper loved to heroize.

> We cannot honestly regret their extermination, but we at least do justice to the manly characteristics possessed, according to their lights and education, by the early Redskins of America.[96]

After the Wounded Knee Massacre, on January 3, 1891, he was inspired to write:

> The peculiar policy of the government in employing so weak and vacillating a person as General Miles to look after the uneasy Indians, has resulted in a terrible loss of blood to our soldiers, and a battle which, at best, is a disgrace to the War Department. There has been plenty of time for prompt and decisive measures, the employment of which would have prevented this disaster.
>
> The Pioneer has before declared that our only safety depends upon the total extermination of the Indians. Having wronged them for centuries we had better, in order to protect our civilization, follow up by one more wrong and wipe these untamed and untamable creatures from the face of the earth. In this lies safety for our settlers and the soldiers who are under incompetent commands. Otherwise, we may expect future years to be as full of trouble with the Redskins as those have been in the past.
>
> An Eastern contemporary, with a grain of wisdom in its wit, says that "when thou whites win a fight, it is a victory, and when the Indians win it, it is a massacre."[97]

His newspaper failed that same year, and he moved to Chicago. In 1900, he published the classic book *The Wonderful Wizard of Oz,* which became a best-selling children's book.

Native Americans fought not only for their survival with the U.S. military but also against much more powerful forces. One of the reasons Ohioan George Armstrong Custer and the Battle of the Little Bighorn is still in the conscience of the average American citizen is that it is a powerful symbol of the shortcomings of humanity. Foolishness leads to the short perspective and wisdom to the long perspective. Custer searched for pleasure, profit, and popularity. He failed.

The quintessential question regarding the Battle of the Little Bighorn is not why Custer lost. He attacked an enemy composed of an overwhelming number of superior warriors. The Indians were well rested and were defending their wives and children. They were highly motivated, unlike the

U.S. troops who were exhausted from Custer's relentless journey from Fort Abraham Lincoln.

The real question is why Custer attacked in the first place with the belief that he would be victorious. He'd gambled in the Civil War and won. Since that time, his gambling had left him in debt. In his mind, he never lost on himself. He needed a personal win like he had in Washita to satisfy his narcissistic ego. Hubris (from the Greek word of same spelling) is defined as excessive pride or self-confidence. Synonyms include arrogance, conceit, haughtiness, self-importance, egotism, and superiority. In Greek tragedy, hubris is excessive pride toward or defiance of the gods, leading to nemesis.

In his *Hubris: The Tragedy of War in the Twentieth Century*, historian Alastair Horne laid out a central theme of how earlier victories lead later to overestimates of military capabilities and military misadventures. These types of disasters have been occurring since the beginning of man. He stated that it is partly motivated by racial contempt for the enemy. Six examples of hubris leading to military failure that he presented were Sushima, Nomohan, Moscow (German attack), Midway (Japanese overconfidence after Pearl Harbor), McArthur in Korea, and the French at Dien Bien Phu.

In his epilogue, Horne concluded that hubris is a social epidemic and not just an illness infecting warlords and tyrants. He reminded us that the ancient Greeks understood the "terrible penalties that befall those who release from Pandora's Box the dormant Bacillus of hubris."[98] Hubris is the narcissist's guiding force, and on June 25, 1876, Pandora's Box was opened, and Custer was killed.

Professor Randall Fuller wrote, "While alive, Custer was an often controversial celebrity, alternately praised for his heroism and condemned for his political meddling and poor treatment of military subordinates. Upon his death, he ceased to be a human personality entirely and became instead a blank screen upon which to project collective fantasies about individual heroism in an era increasingly defined by mass culture."[99]

CHAPTER TWENTY-SIX

The Children of Manifest Destiny and Shifting Shadows: Education to Kill the Indian

After all this, the white man had concluded that the only way to save Indians was to destroy them, that the last great Indian war should be waged against children. They were coming for the children.
—DAVID WALLACE ADAMS, *EDUCATION FOR EXTINCTION: AMERICAN INDIANS AND THE BOARDING SCHOOL EXPERIENCE 1875-1928*

Soap and education are not as sudden as massacre, but they are more deadly in the long run.
—MARK TWAIN

Education without values, as useful as it is, seems rather to make man a more clever devil.
—C. S. LEWIS

Jim Thorpe, American Hero

He was a superstar. In 1950, the Associated Press voted him the "greatest athlete" and the "greatest football player" of the first half of the twentieth century. His Indian name was Wa-Tho-Huk, meaning "bright path." James Francis "Jim" Thorpe (1887-1953) was the most famous Indian to ever attend the Carlisle Indian Industrial School in Carlisle, Pennsylvania. There he would be coached by Glenn Scobey "Pop" Warner (1871-1954), one of the most noted football coaches in American history.[1]

Thorpe was born near the town of Prague, Oklahoma, and baptized in the Catholic church. He kept the faith all his life. His father, Hiram Thorpe, had an Irish father and a Sac and Fox Indian mother. His mother, Charlotte Vieux, was also of mixed race with a French father and a Potawatomi mother. Jim attended the Sac and Fox Indian Agency School in Stroud, Oklahoma, with his twin brother Charlie, who died of pneumonia when he was nine years old. Because Jim ran away from school a number of times, he was sent to an Indian boarding school in Lawrence, Kansas. Two years later, his mother died of complications from childbirth, which left him despondent. He found work at a horse ranch.[2]

His big break came when he entered the Carlisle Indian School in 1904 where a number of coaches were impressed with his athletic prowess. Later in the school year, his father died of blood poisoning from a hunting accident. Distraught, Jim left school, but he eventually returned to Carlisle.

In 1907, he participated in almost every sport at Carlisle, including track, football, baseball, and lacrosse. In addition, he won the 1912 intercollegiate ballroom dancing championship. But it was football that brought him the earliest athletic recognition. In 1911, he played running back, defensive back, place kicker, and punter and led his team to an upset victory over a top-ranked Harvard team. The inscription on the Carlisle game ball read, "1911, Indians 18, Harvard 15." A year later, he led Carlisle to another upset victory over Army. One of the Army players, Dwight D. Eisenhower, recalled the game in a 1961 speech, saying, "Here and there, there are some people who are supremely endowed. My memory goes back to Jim Thorpe. He never practiced in his life, and he could do anything better than any other football player I ever saw." Nonetheless, newspapers used racist comments in chronicling his athletic accomplishments like "Jim Thorpe on rampage" or "Indians scalp Army," and later, *The New York Times* ran a headline, "Indian Thorpe in Olympiad; Redskin from Carlisle Will Strive for Place on American Team."[3]

All-American honors followed in 1911 and 1912. In 1912, he attended the summer Olympics in Stockholm, Sweden, and won gold in the pentathlon and the decathlon. Thorpe was crowned the greatest athlete in the world. But all was not well. In January 1913, the *Worcester Telegram* published a story about Thorpe playing professional baseball before the Olympics. At the time, it was against the rules for professional athletes to compete in the Olympics, and he was stripped of his medals. Many believed he lost his medals because he was a mixed blood. White athletes also played professionally but were craftier at avoiding getting caught.

Thorpe moved forward in his life, with outstanding professional careers in baseball, football, and basketball. During the Depression and after his athletic career was over, he found some work as an extra in the movies. Other jobs included construction worker, bouncer, ditch digger, and security guard. His personal life was uneven, and he married three times. Alcoholism was a constant companion.

On March 29, 1953, *The New York Times* ran Thorpe's obituary titled "Jim Thorpe is Dead on West Coast at 64." (Thorpe was actually sixty-five at the time of his death.) The sympathetic story read in part:

> Los Angeles, March 28—Jim Thorpe, the Indian whose exploits in football, baseball and track and field won him acclaim as one of the greatest athletes of all time, died today in his trailer home in suburban Lomita. His age was 64.
>
> Thorpe was eating dinner with his wife when he suffered a heart attack. . . .
>
> Hero of the 1912 Olympic Games at Stockholm and a towering football figure, Jim Thorpe was probably the greatest natural athlete the world has seen in modern times. . . .
>
> Thorpe came back from Stockholm with $50,000 worth of trophies. They included a Viking ship presented to him by the Czar of Russia, and gifts from King Gustaf.
>
> A month later the new American sports idol was toppled from his high pedestal when the Amateur Athletic Union filed charges of professionalism against him, accusing him of receiving pay for playing summer baseball with the Rocky Mount Club in the Eastern Carolina League. The amount of money was negligible, helping to tide him over at school, but the American Olympic committee offered its apologies and sent back the gifts and medals lavished upon the young man to whom President Theodore Roosevelt had cabled long messages of congratulation. . . .
>
> In the summer of 1949, Warner Bros. started work on a motion picture entitled "Jim Thorpe—All-American," with Burt Lancaster in the athlete's role. The picture reached Broadway in the summer of 1951.

In October 1982, the International Olympic Commission reinstated Thorpe's 1912 Olympic medals. Sadly, the original medals had been stolen from a museum and never recovered. Commemorative medals were presented to two of his children.

Education for Extinction

Jim Thorpe may have been the most famous Indian to ever have been educated at Carlisle, but his notoriety had nothing to do with his classroom education. His success was bittersweet for educators and reformers at the time. His fame brought prestige to the off-reservation schools at a time when their importance was in decline, but it was athletic in nature and not scholastic. For generations, educators toyed with different methods of teaching Indian children skills that would aid in assimilating them into the white man's world. They adopted combinations of simple rules aimed at solving their immediate Indian problem without a long-term perspective. Most proved ineffective. Rules without relationships leads to rebellion.

One of the earliest tribes to offer traditional education to its children was the Cherokee in Indian Territory—now Oklahoma. By 1868, sixty-four schools provided secondary education, with a number of them offering both male and female students an education at Christian seminaries. Tribal culture and the Cherokee language were minimized, as was any vocational training.[4]

Following the Civil War, there was a rush of Episcopalians, Presbyterians, Quakers, Baptists, and Roman Catholics who went west to educate Indian children not only in reading and writing but also Christianity. The Indians were bewildered as different denominations fought over doctrine and jurisdiction over them. A pastor might preach about the evils of liquor on Sunday, and the rest of the week his parishioners would bring liquor into the villages. Mixed messages led to failure.

Besides educating and Christianizing Indian children, one of the government's goals was to instill a sense of patriotism, as expressed by Indian Commissioner Thomas J. Morgan:

> It is of prime importance that a fervent patriotism be awakened in [the children's] minds. . . . They should be taught to look upon America as their home and the United States government as their friend and benefactor. They should be made familiar with the lives of great and good men and women in American history, and be taught to feel pride in all their great achievements. They should hear little or nothing of the "wrongs [done] the Indians," and of the injustice of the white race. If their unhappy history is alluded to it should be to contrast it with the better future that is within their grasp.[5]

In 1882, Indian reformers Herbert Welsh and Henry Pancoast traveled from Philadelphia to Sioux country in Dakota Territory and visited mission schools in Yankton and Santee where the children were learning their ABCs on slate tablets. Pancoast, inspired by seeing the children being educated by white men, wrote:

> In front of the school-house, a ring of Indian children playing Jacob and Rachel. I can see now the free, unconscious grace of their motions, and hear the childish giggles and screams of laughter, and the funny little accent which they shouted "Jacup" and "Rashel."
>
> I looked at these children and thought of the hideous record of the righteous greed and bloody retaliation that makes up the sad story of their race, and of the lives that lay before them that they thought of so little. Yet to look at them is to hope. Mournful and oppressed as the condition of the race is, it may be that out of the darkness and the bondage "a little child shall lead them."[6]

Believing that Indian children could be assimilated into white civilization, the two reformers formed the Indian Rights Association in 1883. The goal was "to secure the civilization of the two hundred and ninety thousand Indians of the United States [inclusive of the thirty thousand natives of Alaska], and to prepare the way for their absorption into the common life of our own people."[7]

The group met in 1883 at the Lake Mohonk Conference, which was inspired by prominent Quaker philanthropist Albert K. Smiley. William Torrey Harris, U.S. Commissioner of Education, was asked at the conference whether an Indian was civilized:

> No, he is at the tribal stage. He is at the patriarchal stage. Civilization below the patriarchal stage would not be above the brutes. Above that comes the village community, and many who believe in socialism would like to have us go back to that. Above the village community comes feudalism, wherein the individual is ground into subordination, so that division of labor can be established. No yellow race has passed through it. The black race is not passed through it except as it has come into the house of bondage. The nations of Europe and America have passed through it. It is a great thing to go through these stages.[8]

His views were supported by an agent to the Utes at the White River Agency in Colorado who was skeptical about the ability to civilize Indians.

He wrote, "Civilization has been reached by successive stages: first was the savage, clearly that of these Utes; next the pastoral, to which a few have now extended; next the barbaric; and finally the enlightened, scientific, and religious." Little value was place by whites on Indian traditions and beliefs.[9]

The great debate in the 1880s was how to educate Indian children. They represented the future hope of those who wanted to civilize Indians because they believed the older Indians were not educable. In 1886, the commissioner to the Utes, Thomas J. Morgan wrote:

> It is food for thought to note the number of handsome, bright-eyed children here, typical little savages, arrayed in blankets, leggings, and gee-strings, their faces hideously painted, growing up in all the barbarism of their parents. A few years more, and they will be men and women, perhaps beyond redemption, for, under the most favorable circumstances, but little can be hoped from them after grown and matured, weeded and steeped in the vices of their fathers. It is rather the little children that must be taken in hand and cared for and nurtured, for from them must be realized the dream, if ever realized, of the philanthropist and of all good people, of that day to come when the Indian, a refined, cultured, educated being will assume the title of an American citizen, with all the rights, privileges, and aspirations of that favored individual.[10]

Education would lead to self-sufficiency, saving the government money. It was also cheaper than fighting them. Secretary of Interior Henry Teller calculated that, in a ten-year period, battling the Indians cost $22 million, which was four times more than it would have been to educate 30,000 children for a year.[11]

Commissioner Morgan harkened back to the idealistic words of Thomas Jefferson, who declared that uncivilized Indians retarded both white settlement and national prosperity. Morgan wrote:

> A wild Indian requires a thousand acres to roam over, while an intelligent man will find a comfortable support for his family on a very small tract. When the rising generation of Indians have become civilized and have learned how to utilize the land they live on, a vast domain now useless can be thrown open to settlement and become the seat of great farms, happy homes, thriving towns and cities, and vast mining and commercial industries. Barbarism is costly, wasteful and extravagant. Intelligence promotes thrift and increases prosperity.[12]

Easterners believed that the Protestant work ethic was nowhere to be found in the Indians' way of life. Conversely, Indians were baffled that the white man measured success by how much wealth he accumulated. Besides the children being taught how to read, write, and speak the English language, there were instructional books on how to learn practical skills and trades. But white educators were frequently frustrated by their inability to motivate Indian children to become competitive and hard-working. One noted, "A string of text-books piled up in the storehouses high enough to surround the reservation if laid side-by-side will never educate a being with centuries of laziness instilled in the race."[13]

Surely, the Protestant work ethic could be instilled in the Indian if they were Christianized. One Indian educator wrote, "A really civilized people cannot be found in the world except where the Bible has been sent and the gospel taught; hence, we believe that the Indians must have, as an essential part of their education, Christian training."[14]

Increasingly, it was understood that the Indians were not bound for extinction, and education was essential. Education came in the form of new schools that were supported by funds from Congress. A year after Custer died, Congress began appropriating money for the purpose of Indian education. It started in 1877 with $20,000, and by 1900 Congress had appropriated $2,936,080 for the year. School enrollment ballooned from 3,598 Indian children in 1877 to 21,568 in 1900. In 1884, only twenty-five percent of Indian children were being educated, but by 1926 that number had increased to eighty-three percent.[15]

No longer was the U.S. Army fighting the Indian tribes. Now it was an army of Christian schoolteachers. Meryl Gates, president of the Lake Mohonk Conference in 1891, declared:

> That is the army that is going to win the victory. We are going to conquer barbarism, but we are going to do it by getting at the barbarism one by one. We are going to do it by the conquest of the individual man, woman, and child which leads to the truest civilization. We are going to conquer the Indians by a standing army of school-teachers, armed with ideas, winning victories by industrial training, and by the gospel of love and the gospel of work.[16]

Models

Earlier, in the 1860s, a total of forty-eight reservation day schools were located on the outskirts of Indian villages. Their main goal was teaching the

English language. Whites concluded that they were unsatisfactory because they did not champion assimilation. Too much time was spent under the influence of their family at home. Many Indian parents were opposed to the educational process, which led to chronic absenteeism and runaways. In 1878, one agent argued, "It must be manifest to all practical minds that to place these wild children under a teacher's care but four or five hours a day, and permit them to spend the other nineteen in the filth and degradation of the village, makes the attempt to educate and civilize them a mere farce."[17]

To address the problem, by the late 1870s, reservation boarding schools became popular and were located at agency headquarters, usually away from most students' parents. The curriculum was divided into four primary grades and four advanced grades, and half the day was dedicated to basic subjects and the other half to vocational training. The boys worked on the school farm where they learned to raise horses and livestock and also blacksmithing, carpentry, and harness making. The girls were trained in housekeeping.

The influence of the family was minimized because the students spent eight to nine months at the boarding school and were allowed to see their parents only in the summer and for some holidays like Christmas. Problems arose when the children were not at school and they relapsed into the old tribal ways. In 1879, one agent to the Wichita lamented, "How soon they seem to forget all they have been taught, after they returned to camp."[18] Another frustration was that they would leave school healthy at Christmas break but return with contagious diseases like body lice and bedbugs. In addition, family visits made the children homesick once they returned to school.

To alleviate these problems, some suggested that the boarding school should be kept in session year-round so the children could avoid the savage influence of their parents. But another more radical idea gained favor—the education of children away from the reservation. P. P. Wilcox, the agent to the San Carlos Apache, stated, "On the reservation no school can be so conducted as to remove the children from the influence of the idle and vicious who are everywhere present. Only by removing them beyond the reach of this influence can they be benefited by the teaching of the schoolmaster."[19]

Ethnic Cleansing Through Off-Reservation Boarding Schools

The mastermind of the off-reservation boarding school was not a college professor or a Christian reformer. His name was Lieutenant Richard Henry Pratt (1840-1924), and his first students would be a bunch of Indian prisoners jailed at Fort Sill in Indian Territory. The prisoners were made up of thirty-four Cheyenne, two Arapaho, twenty-seven Kiowa, nine Comanche, and one Caddo who had been arrested for their hostilities during the so-called Red River War of 1874.[20]

After serving in the Civil War on the Union side, Pratt returned to his hometown of Logansport, Indiana, where he went into the hardware business. Like Custer, Grant, Sheridan, and so many other ex-military officers, he found civilian life was not fulfilling. In March 1867, he was commissioned as a second lieutenant in the 10th U.S. Cavalry, which was composed of all blacks except for the officers. He spent eight years in the West fighting Indians and came to believe that assimilation was the only way they were going to survive.

In the spring of 1875, his Indian prisoners were transported from Fort Sill to Fort Leavenworth, Kansas, where Pratt was assigned to supervise their removal to prison at St. Augustine, Florida. Upon arriving there at Fort Marion, Pratt came up with the idea that he would create a school to teach civilization to the Indians. Soon they were wearing discarded army uniforms and sporting short haircuts. Pratt personally met with them every day and lectured them on embracing the white man's civilization. He believed giving them increased freedom would create responsibility and encourage a work ethic. To inspire them to strive for individual achievement, he gave each one of them their own savings account.

Next, he hired Sarah Mather, a retired teacher and former director of a girl's boarding school. She was extraordinarily talented and inspired other teachers to join her. In the summer of 1876, Pratt proudly wrote to General Sheridan, "I have a two-hour school daily with an average of fifty pupils, divided into four classes, with a good teacher for each. The teachers work from the purest and the best motives of Christian charity and, as a consequence, successfully."[21]

With the ability to read at a basic level, the pupils next were indoctrinated with the Bible and God. Weekly prayer meetings were filled with the music of Christian hymns, and they were encouraged to attend local church services. Episcopal bishop Henry Benjamin Whipple visited the prison and was inspired by what he saw. He wrote, "I was never more touched than when I entered this school. Here were men who had committed murder upon helpless women and children sitting like docile children at the feet of women learning to read. Their faces have changed. They have all lost that look of savage hate, and the light of a new life is dawning on their hearts. . . . They seem to hang upon my words as if I were a messenger of life from heaven."[22]

Most likely, there were some true converts, and visitors believed a miracle had occurred. Indeed, this surely was the model to bring Indians into the white man's civilization after decades of searching for the right method. Famed author Harriet Beecher Stowe visited the prison in April 1877 and was stunned by the transformation from bloodthirsty warriors to model students. The savage now looked prim and proper, well disciplined, and ambitious. She wrote in one of her articles for the *Christian Crisis*, "Now there was plainly to be seen among them the eager joy which comes from the use of a new set of faculties. . . . Might not the money now constantly spent on armies, forts, and frontiers be better invested in educating young men who shall return and teach their people to live like civilized beings?"[23]

With the support of the secretary of the interior, the commissioner of Indian Affairs, affluent congressmen, and the secretary of war, Pratt was authorized to matriculate 125 students for a new Indian school. The school would be located at an unused military barracks at Carlisle, Pennsylvania. By September 1879, he and Miss Mather were searching for students in the Dakotas—especially the Sioux at the Pine Ridge and Rosebud agencies. On November 1, 1879, Jim Thorpe's alma mater, the U.S. Training and Industrial Indian School at Carlisle, opened. Pratt proudly declared, "I believe in immersing the Indian in our civilization, and when we get them under, holding them there until they are thoroughly soaked."[24]

In a strange way, Richard Henry Pratt's face, scarred and dimpled from smallpox as a child, was a comforting sight for the bewildered and sad Indian children shuffling onto the grounds of the school. Generations of Indians carried the same disfigurements he did from a virus that had traveled to America with the first Spanish ships that explored the New World. Memories of their beloved families—many who had been inflicted with the dreaded disease—and home country out West flashed through their consciousness as the superintendent welcomed them. The endless train ride was behind them, and they had no understanding of what lay ahead.

Upon arriving, many of the new students were photographed in their savage state with long, greasy hair, dirty clothing, and moccasins. Later photographs showed the symbolic and literal transformation they underwent when their hair was cut and they donned white children's clothing. Members of the House Committee on Indian Affairs and the Board of Indian Commissioners were shocked by the transformation Pratt achieved at Carlisle. The prior hardware store owner would remain as the most important force in educating Indians for the next twenty-five years.[25]

Like so many others, he believed that he understood the Indians better than most and had little time to listen to suggestions on improving his programs. Detractors, and there were many, characterized him as a sour, arrogant narcissist. He was the prototypical ethnic cleanser who held little value in traditional Indian rituals or ceremonies, but importantly, he did not believe that Indians were racially inferior. He is credited with the famous line, "Kill the Indian in him and save the man." New government regulations aided Pratt by denying Indian social customs and religious rituals like the Sun Dance. The Oglala held their last Sun Dance in 1881, and the Kiowa held their last one six years later.

Pratt believed the Indians' inferiority was due to them growing up in a different culture and could be erased with education. He wrote, "It is a great mistake to think that the Indian is born an inevitable savage. He is born a blank, like the rest of us. Left in the surroundings of savagery, he grows to possess savage language, superstition, and life. We, left in the surroundings of civilization, grow to possess a civilized language, life, and purpose. Transfer the infant white to the savage surroundings, he will grow to possess a savage language, superstition, and habit. Transfer the savage-born infant to the surroundings of civilization, and he will grow to possess a civilized language and habit."[26]

Some criticized Pratt's school because it didn't allow Indian students to attend school with white children. How would they ever assimilate? One positive outcome was that the Indian children from different tribes intermixed at Carlisle, which often resulted in lasting friendships and a better respect for other Indians' traditions. When they were old enough, the Indians often married others from different tribes, and this formed a sense of shared identity labeled "Pan-Indianism."

Pratt defended school segregation by stating that his students were eventually integrated by his outing system that allowed students to leave school and work around the state of Pennsylvania on farms.[27] At first, they were allowed off campus only in the summer, but soon one-year sabbaticals were introduced. He resisted having Indians educated in the West because he believed it would just lead to more segregation. His dream scenario would be to distribute the entire population of Indian children around the country into white family homes. The Carlisle slogan was "To civilize the Indian, get him into civilization. To keep him civilized, let him stay."[28]

Secretary of the Interior Carl Schurz disagreed with Pratt and believed off-reservation schools should be in the West. The first was located in Oregon. In 1884, off-reservation schools also opened in Chilocco, Oklahoma; Genoa, Nebraska; Albuquerque, New Mexico; and Lawrence,

Kansas. By 1902, there were twenty-five schools, all of which were in the West, except for Carlisle. Schurz's reasons for western locations were the expense of shipping children back East, the importance of appreciating their home country, and a familiarity with the area they would someday return to. In 1885, the school superintendent at Albuquerque wrote, "The parents may often visit their children, and thus grow accustomed to their improvement, and so that the children may spend each year a long vacation at their homes."[29]

The Student's Perspective

The separation of children from their parents was heart-rending. A young Lakota Sioux, Plenty Kill, later named Luther Standing Bear (1868-1939), left his family in the fall of 1879 and was the first Indian boy to step inside the Carlisle Indian School grounds. In time, he would become a great writer of such classics as the 1928 *My People, the Sioux*—the first of three volumes intended to introduce readers to his tribe.

Upon boarding a steamer for the East, he recalled, "It was a sad scene. I did not see my father or stepmother cry, so I did not shed any tears. I just stood over in a corner of the room we were in and watched the others all crying as if their hearts would break."[30]

His fear and loss of hope was palpable in his recollection of his trip:

> When I had reached young manhood the warpath with the Lakota was a thing of the past. The hunter disappeared with the buffalo, the war scout had lost his calling, and the warrior had taken his shield to the mountain-top and given it back to the elements. The victory songs were sung only in the memory of the braves. So I could not prove that I was a brave and would fight to protect my home and land. I could only meet the challenge as life's events came to me. When I went East to Carlisle School, I thought I was going there to die . . . I could think of white people wanting little Lakota children for no other reason than to kill them, but I thought here is my chance to prove that I can die bravely. So I went East to show my father and my people that I was brave and willing to die for them.[31]

Many of the parents of the Indian children were totally opposed to them being sent off to school. The reservation agent's solution was withholding food rations or jailing the parents. On the Fort Peck Reservation in

Montana, one of the agency police drove to a noncompliant parent's home and threw them in the guardhouse jail. In actions that are reminiscent of World War II Germany, the children were rounded up by agency police and shipped to their destination by train. In 1886, an agent to the Mescalero Apache wrote:

> Everything in the way of persuasion and argument having failed, it became necessary to visit the camps unexpectedly with a detachment of police to remove the children, willing or unwilling. Some hurried their children off to the mountains or hid them away in camp, and the police had to chase and capture them like so many wild rabbits. This unusual proceeding created quite an outcry. The men were sullen and muttering, the women loud in their lamentations, and the children almost out of their wits with fright.[32]

Forced removal led to village unrest and increased tribal fractionalism. In 1902, Hamlin Garland noted:

> Each tribe, whether Sioux, or Navajo, or Hopi, will be found to be divided . . . into two parties, the radicals and the conservatives—those who are willing to change, to walk the white man's way; and those who are deeply, solemnly skeptical of all civilizing measures, clinging tenaciously to the traditions and lore of their race. These men are often the strongest and bravest of their tribe, the most dignified and the most intellectual. They represent the spirit that will break but will not bow. And, broadly speaking, they are in the majority. Though in rags, their spirits are unbroken; from the point of view of their sympathizers, they are patriots.[33]

Once the children of Manifest Destiny reached Carlisle, all evidence of their past ethnicity was eliminated. Part of their manhood was destroyed when their long hair was cut short. From a practical point, short hair made it easier to keep head lice under control, but on an ideological level, the whites believed that long hair was symbolic of savagism. One of the most poignant examples of the terror instilled in the children was recorded at the Pine Ridge boarding school:

> "They are cutting the hair!" Through doors and windows the children flew, down the steps, through the gates and over fences in a

mad flight for the Indian villages, followed by the mob of bucks and squaws as though all were pursued by a bad spirit. They had been suspicious of the school from the beginning; now they knew it was intended to bring disgrace upon them.³⁴

The next step in saving the man was the elimination of Indian clothing. Two plain suits, with an extra pair of pants, were provided according to Indian service regulations. Each girl was given three dresses. Underwear, night clothes, and boots were also provided as needed. However, the children were often not given the clothing that they were supposed to be issued. Tattered clothing went unmended and feet quickly outgrew shoes. The children lost their individual identity since they all wore similar, uniform clothing.

When the children arrived, they were given new names that were easier for the whites to pronounce. Surnames were given because someday it would make identifying who owned private property easier. Some of the most popular new names given by the agents were those of presidents, vice presidents, and famous people of the day. Common last names were Lincoln, Grant, Sheridan, and Sherman. In his 1905 book *The Middle Five: Indian Schoolboys of the Omaha Tribe*, Francis La Flesche described how a teacher allowed his school class to pick an Indian boy's name:

> The teacher looked serious, then we became scared. After a moment his face relaxed, and he said in a pleasant tone, "We must have the name of the new boy on the Register, but we cannot have any name that is unpronounceable. We shall have to give him an English name. Will you suggest one?"
>
> A number of hands went up and as many historic names were offered and rejected. Finally it was determined to call him William T. Sherman and that name was entered upon the Register.³⁵

Luther Standing Bear wrote that, not soon after he arrived at Carlisle, an interpreter said, "Do you see all these marks on the blackboard? Well, each word is a white man's name. They are going to give each one of you one of these names by which you will hereafter be known." One by one, each boy stepped forward and with a long pointer touched a name that was then written on tape and placed onto his shirt.

> When my turn came, I took the pointer and acted as if I were about to touch an enemy. So we all had the names of white men sewed on

our backs. When we went to school, we knew enough to take our proper places in the class, but that was all. When the teacher called the roll, no one answered his name. Then she would walk around and look at the back of the boys' shirts. When she had the right name located, she'd make the boy stand up and say "Present." She kept this up for about a week before we knew what the sound of our name was.[36]

Punishment and Illness

Many of the children ran away from the schools. In 1901, Pratt reported that forty-five children were dropped for running away. For those misbehaving, a number of punishments awaited them. When caught, some children had their hands switched and some were placed in isolation for a day in the school chapel. More severe punishment included whipping or working the girl's laundry. Some were thrown in the school jail. Other misbehaving boys might be dressed in girl's clothing and forced to march back and forth in the schoolyard for long periods of time. These forms of punishment were supplemented with palm slapping, standing in the corner, scrubbing the floors, cleaning the school grounds, and wearing a dunce hat. If they spoke their native language, they were forced to brush their teeth with harsh lye soap, which could leave the inside of their mouth raw.[37]

The type and severity of punishment varied from school to school. Throughout Canada and the United States, reports of discipline now considered shocking included children eating their own vomit, being whipped naked until becoming unconscious, having sewing needles pushed through their tongues, scalding with boiling water, shocking with electricity, and rubbing faces with human excrement.[38]

Some didn't run away and showed their defiance by setting their school on fire. To combat the problem, buckets of water were often placed throughout the school's rooms. Fire drills were commonplace. Eventually, arsonists were prosecuted. In 1886, the agent at Fort Stephenson said, "Fires during the winter months were of frequent occurrence."[39]

Lone Wolf, a Blackfeet, recollected the misery of being at school:

School wasn't for me when I was a kid. I tried three of them, and they were all bad. First time was when I was about 8 years old. The soldiers came and rounded up as many of the Blackfeet children as they could. The government had decided we were to get White Man's education by force.

It was very cold that day when we were loaded into the wagons. None of us wanted to go and our parents didn't want to let us go. Oh, we cried for this was the first time we were to be separated from our parents. I remember looking back at Na-tah-ki and she was crying too. Nobody waved as the wagons, escorted by the soldiers, took us toward the school at Fort Shaw. Once there our belongings were taken from us, even the little medicine bags our mothers had given us to protect us from harm. Everything was placed in a heap and set afire.

Next was the long hair, the pride of all the Indians. The boys, one by one, would break down and cry when they saw their hair thrown on the floor. All of the buckskin clothes had to go and we had to put on the clothes of the White Man.

If we thought that the days were bad, the nights were much worse. This was the time when real loneliness set in, for it was then we knew that we were all alone. Many boys ran away from the school because the treatment was so bad but most of them were caught and brought back by the police. We were told never to talk Indian and if we were caught, we got a strapping with a leather belt.

I remember one evening when we were all lined up in a room and one of the boys said something in Indian to another boy. The man in charge of us pounced on the boy, caught him by the shirt, and threw him across the room. Later we found out that his collar-bone was broken. The boy's father, an old warrior, came to the school. He told the instructor that among his people, children were never punished by striking them. That was no way to teach children; kind words and good examples were much better. Then he added, "Had I been there when that fellow hit my son, I would have killed him." Before the instructor could stop the old warrior he took his boy and left. The family then beat it to Canada and never came back.[40]

Frequently, the best pieces of meat were taken by the school employees, and the children got only the necks and ribs. While food shortages varied from school to school, many children suffered from malnutrition. One report concluded that "28% of the girls and 69% of the boys were underweight."[41]

This led to increased susceptibility to communicable diseases. Some children resorted to stealing food or running away. Under these harsh conditions, epidemics of tuberculosis, trachoma, measles, pneumonia, mumps, and influenza spread quickly throughout the schools. Many children were buried on the school grounds, while others were released to die at home. In 1897, the superintendent at Crow Creek, South Dakota, reported to Washington, D.C.:

> When a pupil begins to have hemorrhages from the lungs he or she knows, and all the rest knows, just what they mean, in spite of everything cheerful that can be said or done. And such incidents keep occurring, at intervals, throughout every year. Not many pupils die in school. They prefer not to do so; and the last wishes of themselves and their parents are not disregarded. But they go home and die, and the effect in the school is much the same. Four have done so this year. As many more have gone out who undoubtedly will never be able to return; and others, and still larger numbers, have had hemorrhages from the lungs, or the terrible scrofulous [tuberculosis] swellings which we know, and they know, practically certify to their fate. Keeping them in school at all sometimes becomes a rather painful task.[42]

It wasn't until 1908 that the government got serious about trying to combat tuberculosis in the schools. A Smithsonian Institution study showed that almost twenty percent of the students on five reservations carried the disease, which prompted Commissioner Francis Leupp to state that "the tuberculosis scourge is the greatest single menace to the future of the red race."[43]

Curriculum for Civilization

The first task in civilizing Indian children was teaching them the daunting task of writing, reading, and speaking English. This progressed not unlike the education received by white children in the early grades. Often, however, the best methods of teaching were not administered, and intimidation was a common and easy incentive to force children to learn. Luther Standing Bear remembered the agonizing task of having to stand in front of his class and read paragraphs of English: "Even for the sixth and seventh times I read. I began to tremble and I could not see my words plainly. I was terribly hurt and mystified. But for the eighth and ninth times I read. It was growing more terrible. Still the teacher gave no sign of approval, so I read for the tenth time! I started on the paragraph for the eleventh time, but before I was through, everything before me went black and I sat down thoroughly cowed and humiliated for the first time in my life and in front of the whole class!"[44]

Certain subjects were totally new to the students, such as arithmetic, where they spent their time learning numbers and simple measurements. The importance of linear measurements seemed odd to them since their world was made up of circles—tipis, stars, the moon, and the sun. Also, Luther Standing Bear had learned that the Earth was flat with four corners and seemed unable to grasp the concept that it was a sphere spinning on an axis. His belief was similar to those in the early Catholic Church who taught that the sun revolved around a flat Earth. Centuries earlier, heretics were killed by the Catholic Church for declaring that the Earth revolved around the sun. Now it was the children's turn to be punished. The tension that the white man felt between religion and science was also felt by the students. The Hampton (Virginia) Institute's newspaper reported:

> A teacher in endeavoring to overthrow the Indian belief that the earth is flat, stands still, and that the sun passes over and under it every twenty-four hours, said, in conclusion, "So you see, it is the earth that goes around while the sun stands still." A tall boy asked, "Then what for you tell us one story about man in the Bible—I forget his name—strong warrior—fight all day, but get dark so can't fight, and he say 'Sun stand still.' What for he say that if Sun all time stand still."[45]

By 1890, many of the schools used Horace E. Scudder's book, *A History of the United States of America*. White-Indian relations were presented in the dualistic manner of the oxymoron noble savage versus civilized man. One passage in the book read, "While the tribes differed from one another, all the Indians were in some points alike. They were brave, but they were treacherous. They never forgave an injury. They could bear hunger and torture in silence, but they were cruel in the treatment of their captives. They were a silent race, but often in their councils some of their number would be very eloquent."[46]

The students read in their history books that at the time of Columbus their ancestors were ignorant barbarians whose worth was only that of a servant. Custer's defeat was described as a massacre by the Indians. The teachers made it clear to their students that Manifest Destiny could be obtained only by the subjugation of their race.

The teachers' task was difficult because the children had learned from their parents and grandparents not to trust the white man. One reflective teacher explained that she found it difficult to teach the students history because of the guilt of "the sins of her father to answer for before each class."

Still, she wrote that she "wants to encourage her pupils to be civilized like the white man, to embrace his religion, and follow his example, and yet has to put into his hands a history of broken promises and of a civilization as far from Christianity as the Indian himself is."[47]

The Indian office provided guidance for the frustrated teachers:

> Always seek to create a spirit of love and brotherhood in the minds of the children toward the white people, and in telling them the history of the Indians dwell on those things which have showed nobility of character on the part of either race in their dealings with the other. . . . Whenever acts of injustice must be related, show to the pupils that the guilt of the persons committing them does not attach to the whole race, for in every people, no matter how virtuous, there are always a large number of the unconscientious and the cruel.[48]

There is evidence that at least some students embraced the idea that the progression of civilization was from savages like his people, through barbarism, and finally to the white man's civilization. A certain type of brainwashing was achieved, as evidenced by two essays written by Indian students at Hampton Institute:

> The Caucasian is the strongest in the world. The semi-civilized have their own civilization, but not like the white race.
> The savage race kept their own ways, and they may have had these occupations; they were hunted, fished, and foughted to the other people. They beat too.
> The white race have three occupations agriculture, manufacturing and commerce.

The other essay:

> The white people they are civilized; they have everything and go to school, too. They learn how to read and write so they can read newspaper.
> The yellow people they half civilized, some of them know to read and write, and some know how to take care of himself.
> The red people they big savages; they don't know nothing.[49]

The emphasis on ethnic cleansing continued throughout their education, and the students were even reminded on their graduation day by

Philip Garrett, a member of Board of Indian Commissioners, about the importance of the white man's God and their need to assimilate into the white man's world:

> The path that lies before you is somewhat different from that of most of those around you. They belong to races which have been gradually developing their own civilization by a power from within, stimulated, as it were, by mere sunshine and rain; you are a race thrown by the Providence of God in the pathway of a mighty and resistless tide of civilization, flowing Westward around you. So mighty is the flood, that resistance is fruitless, and the only choices between submission and destruction on the one hand, were joining the flood and floating with it, on the other. . . . But great is the force of example and imitation. You are in the midst of an advanced civilization, which serves you as an object lesson. You have a unique opportunity to show the marvelous change that can be brought in a single generation by the aid of good schools, and the lessons of centuries.[50]

After graduation from Carlisle, Pratt relied on his outing program to place students. Wary Easterners were hesitant to board the children. It seems their idealism for racial equality and assimilation was strongest when they didn't have to deal with the problem themselves. Relying on Christian charity, Pratt gave an impassioned plea at a Congregational church in New England to take the children in as farm workers. In the 1890s, he started placing the children in industrial and urban settings, which gave them an opportunity to learn skills other than farming.

Many of the homes that accepted the children were owned by Quakers in the East. Would the placement be as easy out West? Off-reservation schools like Haskell, Carson, Albuquerque, Phoenix, and the Sherman Institute soon developed their own outing programs. Without good Christian homes to be placed in, many of the children were exploited. Fifty to 100 students at a time were sent out in work gangs on ranches and farms. These programs were very similar to the convict leasing system. Blistering heat scorched them from sunrise to sundown, and they slept at night in barns. Their future was understood to be that of common laborers and household servants with little chance for future advancement.

According to 1897 government guidelines, students starting out in a new job as farm hands were to be paid one cent per hour—the average was fifteen times higher for the white man. After two years experience, their pay was raised to 1.5 cents per hour. Those in industrial shops could receive as much as three cents per hour after three years.[51]

The children returning home from school after graduation received a mixed reception. Wearing the latest styles of the whites, the children were a stark contrast to their traditional parents on the reservation. Agent Albert Kneale wrote, "I have seen these girls, when they first cast eyes upon their parents, stare in abject horror, then as the truth dawned upon them, burst into tears. I've seen parents glance fleetingly on these visions of civilized loneliness, then turn away in disgust, returning to their homes, leaving the children to shift for themselves."[52]

Besides being ostracized, the new graduates could be the object of community ridicule and were pressured to return to the traditional ways on the reservation. Those that had converted to Christianity at boarding school tried to share their faith, with little success. Charles Clifford, a former Hampton student, preached to a group of Ghost Dancers at Pine Ridge that they were following a false religion, but had little success:

> Because when I told them the story of our Savior, they would compare it with the story of their Christ, and say that he is the same Christ come again the second time to save the Indians from the land of bondage, like Moses saved the children of Israel from the land of the Egyptians. They were told by their prophets that this Christ came to whites the first time to prepare them for the life to come, but they despised Him and hung him up on a cross and put Him to death, so he gave up this work among the whites, who are slowly starving the Indians to death to get them out of their way.[53]

Frank Black Hawk felt unprepared to answer questions from Indians at Standing Rock Reservation and wrote a letter to his school:

> But they asked me many questions I was not able to answer. Here's some of the questions they asked me. If God made men and women his own image why is it they are so many different colors of nations in the world and why did the white people killed Jesus Christ? You say he was the son of God and could do everything. Why he did not save himself when they was going to kill him? And what is the reason his Father did not save him when he prayed so many times, and so hard? All of these I was not able to answer and many others.[54]

Not only was their newfound Christianity of little benefit on the reservation, but all of their practical industrial training was found to be worthless and impractical. They had been trained to tailor suits and repair fancy dress shoes. One of Pratt's Florida prisoners, Quoyonah, after settling back at Fort Sill, Oklahoma, wrote Pratt about his predicament:

> You first taught me the white man's road. I am now very poor and disconsolate. All you gave me is gone, and if you can send me any clothes or something to work in I will be thankful. I have no tools to work with, or plows to work the ground to make corn. Can you send me some? I am again a Comanche. I was compelled to go back to the old ground, though I did not want to, but I had no pants and had to take leggings. I never have any money, for I cannot earn it here, and my heart told me to come to you for help, and perhaps you could send these things to me. I have no piece of ground for my home, and now when I want to work the white man's road and learn it, I have nothing to do it with. I am working first on this man's ground, then on somebody else's, and I am never settled in any place. I have made great many rails so you see I have not forgotten what you told me. I haven't a horse of my own. I am very poor. When you come to see us I shall have nothing to show you—no corn—no house—nothing at all. A poor country and a bad ground. I don't sleep well. I am afraid.[55]

Government officials combated the poor reception the children were receiving at home by devaluing life on the reservation. One wrote, "Children leaving even the best of training schools for their homes are like swine returning to their wallowing in filth, and barbarism."[56]

One of the biggest obstacles to assimilation was the Indians' resistance to owning private property. Reformers pushed for the allotment of Indian land in severalty—individual ownership—as a way to end tribal connections and provide a source of income as farmers. After Rutherford B. Hayes became president, the government shifted back to a less lenient approach to the Indian situation. That continued with the Garfield and Arthur administration under which political patronage was controlled by the Bureau of Indian Affairs. Quaker agents that the Grant administration had appointed were replaced by those owed political favors.

In 1887, Congress passed the General Allotment Act, also known as the Dawes Act, named after Senator Henry Dawes of Massachusetts. "There can be but little doubt that this is one of the most vital and important steps ever taken by Congress in its dealings with the Indians," stated the Indian Rights Association to its members.

Passage of the Dawes Act on February 8, 1887, created Indian Citizenship Day, also known as Franchise Day, to impress upon the Indian children their opportunity to own land. With private ownership came citizenship. To encourage the students, the special day was filled with speeches by politicians, pageants, and dramatizations. One of the staff at Carlisle wrote a conciliatory poem to address the mistaken belief of many Indians that to attain American citizenship they had to give up their land. In part, the poem read, "But welcomed the ruling, if now by our losses, we gain thousand fold in a better estate. A man may be chief in the empire of reason. Education, not land, makes a citizen great."[57]

Each Indian family received 160 acres—a single person was given 80 acres if they were over eighteen, and if under eighteen they were allotted 40 acres. The Red Lake Chippewa and the Arizona Navajo argued successfully that they could not make a living on such a small parcel of land and were provided with more acreage. Many other tribes could have made the same argument in areas that were considered desert on the Great Plains.[58]

To protect the Indians from greedy whites, the government held the actual deed for twenty-five years, during which the land could not be sold. Along with land ownership came citizenship status, but Indians then became subject to the criminal and civil laws of the state or territory where they resided. Indian courts were set up to handle minor crimes such as polygamy and theft. An unfortunate part of the law was that any land surplus could be sold to white settlers. The proceeds from the sale were to be used for educating and civilizing Indians. This resulted in almost no land for future generations of Indians.[59] By the time the allotments finally ended in 1934, American Indians had lost 98.4 percent of their land since they had come to the aid of the Pilgrims 300 years earlier.[60]

Resistance to the white man's way of life, including his schools on the reservations, motivated the whites to recruit men to serve as Indian police. By 1890, fifty-nine reservations had their own police. The police served as role models for the children entering school because they had their hair cut short, wore white man's clothing, and did not participate in traditional Indian ceremonies. The Indian police became infamous in December 1890 on the Standing Rock Reservation when they shot dead Sitting Bull after he resisted arrest. Agent James McLaughlin had feared that Sitting Bull was going to leave the reservation and take part in the Ghost Dance.[61]

It took almost a decade for the Allotment Act to reach all the reservations. Opposing the law, representatives of about twenty tribes in present-day Oklahoma met to form an all-Indian state. Congress countered with the Curtis Act of 1898 that abolished their tribal governments and left Indians no legal say in the allotment process.

The first to be directly affected by a reduction in their reservation were the Iowa Indians. After they received their allotments, ninety percent of their land was still available for sale to white homesteaders. By 1900, the American Indian population hit an all-time low at 237,000. In 1901, when Theodore Roosevelt became president, he praised the Allotment Act as "a mighty pulverizing engine to break up the tribal mass."[62]

The Allotment Act didn't result in the level of assimilation expected, much to the dismay of reformers. Its failure inspired Frances Campbell Sparhawk in 1906 to write, "What concerns us to-day is to find out what is the matter with the Indian, what keeps him from assimilating with his surroundings, why we cannot absorb two hundred and fifty thousand Indians into all our millions and never know where they are."[63]

Many pointed to the reservation as the reason for the lack of assimilation. The Indian living situation there was likened to being in prison. One observer wrote, "Imagine everything that is opposed to all that is American or modern in detail, especially in principle, and you have an Indian reservation."[64] In 1903, another critic wrote, "Is it any wonder twenty-five years of education have not solved the Indian problem when the educated young men and women must choose to be either farmers, herders, or agency employees, and have to live under the blighting and deadening restraints and influences of the Reservation, the corrupting examples of immoral employees, and the despotism of the agent, where the corner-stone of free civilized society—government by law—has been omitted?"[65]

Famed author and ethnologist George Bird Grinnell, who understood the Indian better than most, predicted that allotment would be a failure, and he was proven correct. He wrote, "In many cases allotment has proved the greatest misfortune that could come to the Indians, and . . . it is often an absolute bar to their progress."[66] Westerners knew that much of the land that was allotted to the Indians was not suitable for farming. A large proportion was considered desert, receiving less than ten inches of precipitation a year. Thus, the government set the Indian up for failure and resignation. Grinnell wrote that the Allotment Act convinced the Indian that "work was useless because work in the white man's way brought him no return."[67]

Grinnell's friend Theodore Roosevelt believed it was a matter of survival of the fittest. In 1892, he commented on the Allotment Act, "It must not be done too quickly, for he will then be helpless and perish, nor must it be delayed too long, for he will then become accustomed to being petted and cared for and will be too weak to stand when finally left alone. When it is done, we must be prepared to see a great many of the Indian sink under the strain. . . . We must protect and guard them up to a certain point; but all the while we must be fitting them as we best can for rough contact with the world."[68]

To his credit, Roosevelt opposed those who championed the idea that Indian children should be stripped of all evidence of their culture. As president, he called the short-hair rule a "misfortune" and said that the Indian dances were "perfectly proper to keep up and even encourage." In addition, Indian songs and poetry could have a benefit, "not merely for the good it will do them, but for the chances that great good will be done thereby in the end to the whites." The Carlisle philosophy of "kill the Indian to save the man" had little support from President Theodore Roosevelt.[69]

At the end of Roosevelt's term in 1909, his commissioner of Indian Affairs, Francis Leupp, had cut the twenty-six off-reservation boarding schools down to twenty. Pratt was retired by then, but that did not keep him from voicing his disapproval. The reservation schools were certainly less expensive to run, and by 1913, 78.3 percent of all Indian children were in school—26,028 in public schools, 27,584 in government schools, and 5,109 in mission schools.[70]

With the institution of the Dawes Act, Indians saw not only their non-allotted land sold off, but white swindlers and land thieves gained control of their allotted land. Over the next four decades, the 138 million acres of land in tribal hands at the time of allotment plummeted to a mere third of that total. In addition, provisions were not made for future generations of Indians, so the offspring did not inherit enough land to provide for a sustainable life.[71]

Children of a Greater God

Among American educators, many were skeptical that Indian children could ever lead integrated lives with whites. There was a sense of urgency among Christian leaders to convert the children before they were led astray by pagan gods. In their view, misguided rituals like the Ghost Dance had led to the Wounded Knee Massacre in December 1890. The quicker to Jesus the better, and if life on Earth was not promising for the

Indian children, at least they had the next life in a Christian heaven to look forward to. In the 1890s, the Office of Indian Affairs' rules stated, "Pupils of Government schools shall be encouraged to attend the churches and Sunday-schools of their respective denominations." That encouragement led to children attending three Sunday services, a Wednesday evening prayer meeting, and daily morning and evening prayers. In 1894, Superintendent of Indian Schools William Hailmann exalted, "Prayer, song, and Bible reading should be wholly free from mystifying illusions and sentiments, but rich and forceful in the simple earnestness with which they lead the heart to God, to virtue, to benevolence, to reverence, to self-abnegation, and to devotion."[72]

As David Wallace Adams wrote in *Education for Extinction,* "An inordinate amount of time was spent on moral training. In the eyes of educators, Indian children were products of cultures that placed little emphasis on 'virtue' at least as it was understood in the context of Christian ethics. . . . In particular, Indian children needed to be taught the moral ideals of charity, chastity, monogamy, respect for the Sabbath, temperance, honesty, self-sacrifice, the importance of pure thoughts and speech—indeed, an almost endless array of personal characteristics important to the formation of 'character.'"[73]

While the educators and pastors seemingly were pleased with the conversion of the schoolchildren, their students were often skeptical of the entire process. Helen Sekaquaptewa was typical of the majority:

> I remember one preacher especially, although they were all about the same. I couldn't understand a thing he was talking about but had to sit and listen to a long sermon. I hated them and felt like crying. If I nodded my head going to sleep, a teacher would poke me and tell me to be good. It seemed as if this preacher would talk all night. He put a great deal of emotion into his sermons. He would work himself up to a climax talking loud and strong, and then come down to a whisper, and I would think, "Now he is going to stop." But no, he would start all over again and go on and on.[74]

If Christianity bewildered the children, so did American society in general. In 1893, the World's Columbian Exposition was held in Chicago to honor Columbus' arrival in the New World in 1492. For the Indian children, it was a celebration of the destruction of their culture. A world once lit only by fire was now electrified.

The exposition was highlighted by technology. Inventions and manufacturing advances could be seen throughout the grounds. The horizon was dominated by a large Ferris wheel, and electric lights were everywhere. Indoor exhibits featured the first fully electrical kitchen, fluorescent lamps, and the forerunner to the zipper. New edibles included Crackerjacks, Cream of Wheat, Juicy Fruit gum, Quaker Oats, Shredded Wheat, Pabst Blue Ribbon beer, and Aunt Jemima pancake mix.

America was proud of itself. Earlier, the 1876 Centennial International Exhibition was the first official world's fair in the United States and was held in Philadelphia from May 10 to November 10 to celebrate the hundredth anniversary of the signing of the Declaration of Independence in Philadelphia. It too had a number of products first displayed to the public, including Alexander Graham Bell's telephone, the Remington typographic machine, Heinz ketchup, and a precursor to the electric light.

At the 1893 exposition, Frederick Jackson Turner (1861-1932), one of the most noted historians of his generation, read before the American Historical Association his paper "The Significance of the Frontier in American History." He presented his belief that the spirit and success of the United States from the colonial era to 1890 was directly tied to the country's westward expansion. The land had been free for the taking.

Much influenced by Charles Darwin, he preached an evolutionary model where distinct American characteristics had emerged from the West and not from the East. The uniquely American rugged identity occurred on the border between civilization and the savagery of the wilderness. Turner's "Frontier Thesis," which characterized the West in terms of individualism, frontier violence, and rough justice, influenced for generations the writers and producers of popular histories, novels, and eventually movies. He cared little about the Indians and had no sympathy for them as victims. When he died in 1932, sixty percent of university history departments in the United States were teaching courses in frontier history inspired by Turner.[75]

Turner eventually also put forth essays on sectionalism, which were collected after his death into the *Significance of Sections in American History*, which won the Pulitzer Prize in history in 1933. He argued that different ethno-cultural groups had distinct settlement patterns, and this reflected itself in politics, economics, religion, and society.[76]

Although Turner saw no need for churches in the West, his writings played well to a Christian nation that knew from the Bible that the first home God placed humans in was the garden. A place of solitude like the West made it sacred—Jesus retreated to the wilderness to experience God alone. The Bible is full of the importance of place. Place was also important to Indians, who created sacred locations—far away from Carlisle—to meet their gods. Pratt understood this. It reinforced his belief that the education of the Indians needed to be achieved far from their homes.

Indian Pride, Carlisle Football

By the time Jim Thorpe played football for Carlisle, the sport had been played there for a number of years. At first, Pratt resisted allowing the boys to play football and relinquished only after demanding two conditions: the Indian boys must be models of sportsmanship and bring honor to their race and, on a more practical level, they needed to promise that they would beat the best football teams in the land. Pratt warmed to football because it brought a kind of notoriety to Carlisle that his educational gains just didn't match.

In 1894, the Indians played their first full season. In 1895, they played the University of Pennsylvania, Navy, Bucknell, and Yale. In 1899, Pratt sought the advice of Walter Camp (1859-1925) and signed Glenn Scobey Warner (1871-1954), who had been the captain of his football team at Cornell and had coached at the University of Georgia, Iowa State University, and Cornell University. His salary at Carlisle was $1,200, which was an extraordinarily high salary for that time. Except for a three-year interlude, "Pop" Warner was the coach at Carlisle until 1914. In 1907, Carlisle beat the University of Pennsylvania, University of Minnesota, University of Chicago, and Harvard, resulting in a 10-1 win-loss season. There would be four more seasons where the team won ten games or more.[77]

After leaving Carlisle, Warner coached four teams to national collegiate championships: 1915, 1916, and 1918 with Pittsburgh, and 1926 with Stanford. Warner is credited in part with bringing to college football the screen pass, spiral punt, single- and double-wing formations, and the use of shoulder and thigh pads. He was inducted into the College Football Hall of Fame as a coach in 1951.

Pratt believed football gave the Indians a chance to show that they could compete not only on the field but in the white man's society. Notoriety for many universities today comes from their athletic teams, especially football, basketball, and track. Pratt commented, "Nothing we have ever done has so much awakened the attention of the country to the possibilities of the Indian."[78]

As many believe today, Pratt saw sports as a way for young men to learn teamwork, hard work, self-control, self-reliance, discipline, and winning.

And sports championed what Darwin, Custer, and Theodore Roosevelt held dear, "the survival of the fittest." On a more symbolic level, for Pratt football was an endeavor of gaining yardage or land. James Oliver Robertson provided one reason why football is the most popular of American sports. It "ritualizes," he said, "the moving frontier, and the teamwork, cooperation, and individual heroism necessary to resist the moving frontier. Football players are pioneers and Indians at the same time."[79]

But racism was never far away. One reporter commented on the Harvard-Carlisle contest in 1896:

> Never was there a spectacle so calculated to impress an imaginative mind. All the manifold interests of the present and the past, the near and the far, were collected on the instant on Soldiers' Field. Over 500 years of education were represented by the young palefaces in crimson, while centuries of fire and sun worship, medicine men incantations, ghost dances and mound building were flooded before the inner vision by the appearance of the young men from Carlisle. Every glance at their swarthy faces and crow-black hair wafted the mind back to days of Pontiac, King Philip, Samoset, to the time of Hannah Dustin's escape, to Lovewell's war and Marquette's trips of discovery in a fabric of birch bark.[80]

Newspapers relished reporting events from the gridiron in demeaning verbiage. The *Chicago Chronicle* wrote that the University of Illinois' "palefaces had its line shot and shattered by arrowlike plunges and its advances balked as a tomahawk would stop the rush of an unarmed opponent." The *Philadelphia Press* characterized the Princeton-Carlisle game as the "fiercest struggle ever witnessed . . . the tug, the strain, the resounding thwack of shoulders on head and knee on hip, the crunching of shoes on fallen limbs, told of a struggle in which race was matched against race. And the race with a civilization and history won the day."[81]

Custer's heroic stand against the sly Sitting Bull and wild Crazy Horse symbolically was relived in the *Boston Globe*'s report on the Harvard-Carlisle football game. "Custer's last stand on the Little Big Horn was never more fiercely assailed," gushed the story, "than was the stand of the Harvard eight. . . . There was piling and crunching and tumbling and twisting like that of a drive of logs in ugly water, but the men of Harvard stood as firm as a hill. At them went the Indians like buffalo charging through a prairie fire, but the human wall could not be breached." The Indians were defeated 4-0.[82]

Next it was the *New York Herald*'s turn to use racial slurs when it reported the 1896 Yale-Carlisle game that Yale barely won. The Kiowa, Comanche, and Apache:

> whooped and grunted and tore holes through Yale's rush line, through which they poured like fire water from a bunghole, or buffalo through a mountain canyon. . . . All along the side lines danced the medicine men, with their buckets and sponges and incantations, praying and conjuring in their native tongue, and doctoring everybody that needed it. . . .
>
> Three thousand spectators saw the delirious battle. They saw Yale hurled back foot by foot, and yard by yard. They saw the half-wild men, whose ancestors made things pleasant for us in the olden times with tomahawk and scalping knife, knocking the breath out of the pale faced lad whose fathers took their muskets afield to protect themselves from possible scrimmages.[83]

Both sides were haunted by the ghosts of the past. Pop Warner was disappointed that his Indian players never possessed school spirit to the extent that his white teams had at other schools. He recalled, "When playing against college teams, it was not to them so much the Carlisle school against Pennsylvania or Harvard, as the case might be, but it was Indian against the White Man." At another time he said, "It was not that they felt any definite bitterness against the conquering white, or against the government for years of unfair treatment, but rather they believed the armed contest between red men and white had never been waged on equal terms. . . . If there was one team that the Indians like to beat more than another, that team was the Army."[84]

In the early twentieth century, only a small percentage of the American public went to college, around eight percent in 1920. A pressing question nationally was how to get more people to support the idea of college. One of the major forces that arose was football. Newly built stadiums started drawing tens of thousands of fans. The football game was supplemented with halftime shows with music played by marching bands. Indians became closely associated with football because they represented objects of racial repulsion, but conversely they were also symbols of masculinity. They were semi-humans that could barely restrain violence—a quality attractive to football fans. But it wasn't just the violent savage that was attractive. Once again, the more-than-century-old idea of the noble savage came into play.

In 1920, the University of Illinois launched a capital campaign to build a new football stadium. The promotional pamphlet was filled with Indian symbolism that included a Sioux in full headdress wearing a loincloth and boots with a peace pipe raised in one hand. The pamphlet stated, "No temples have these ancient Indians left us, and no books. But we have a heritage from them, direct through the pioneers who fought them and learned to know them. It is the Great Heart, the fighting spirit, the spirit of individualism, of teaching our children to be free but brave and to have a God—for these are the laws of our tribe."[85] Not to be left out, the Boy Scouts of America and the YMCA adopted Indian dances and survival skills set in the wilderness.

Pop Warner and Jim Thorpe not only elicited for the Indian a feeling of respect but also of potential superiority. At the time, blacks were the brunt of racism, and their strength and masculinity was not admired. Instead, they were perceived as brutes and ridiculed. The fighting Sioux of North Dakota adopted the Indian moniker in 1930 after it was determined that Sioux footballers were more likely to beat the bison of North Dakota State. Today's Stanford Cardinals were once the Stanford Indians. Florida State has been able to keep the Seminoles as its mascot because the university received approval from the Seminole nation.[86]

Resentment runs deep, and, in many ways, athletics did little to erase America's racist past. For both sides, football was more than a sport; it churned with great symbolism. As David Wallace Adams wrote, "So Indian-white football was more than just a game. Football is about boundaries, crossing boundaries, and defending boundaries. It was about another time and space. It was about the frontier and about Crazy Horse and Custer. It was about history and about myth. Indian-white football was deep play."[87]

Reality

Pratt had an increasingly difficult time convincing policymakers that his students were assimilating into white society. By the spring of 1886, reformers received bad news. Indiana Congressman William Holman, chair of a special committee to investigate the results of the Indian schools, reported that returned students mostly reverted to barbarism. Illinois Congressman Jay S. Cannon, a member of the committee, reported that his investigation concluded that "we could not find that there was one student of all the hundreds educated at Carlisle or Hampton or any of the schools off the reservation but had gone back to their savage life in a very short time."[88] Their report was bolstered in 1892 by a publication by sociologist Frank Blackmar that found only three of sixty-seven Cheyenne and Arapaho who were former students at Haskell "were pursuing anything beyond the life of an ordinary Indian." Many were practicing the Ghost Dance and partaking of peyote.[89]

In 1901, Commissioner of Indian Affairs William Jones confirmed the failure of the nation's Indian policy. Over the past thirty-three years, he reported, the government had spent more than $240 million in an attempt to civilize Indians. Assimilation had failed, Jones said, and most Indians were living on reservations and had reverted back to their tribal traditions. It was time to reassess. Confusion on what to do next prevailed.[90]

Between 1900 and 1920, a strong case was made to close the off-reservation schools. It became clear to officials that Indians were not going to be able to rapidly assimilate or assimilate at all, and separating children from their parents was cruel and uncivilized. Pratt's model had encouraged Indian dependency on the government, and more emphasis should be attempted to make the Indian children proud of their past.

In a total reversal, scientific racism and eugenics gained increased popularity. It was now believed by some that it wasn't environment but inherited racial characteristics that would keep the Indians primitive. One racist speaker at the 1909 National Education Association meeting proclaimed, "The races of men feel, think, and act differently not only because of environment, but also because of hereditary impulses."[91]

In 1902, Hamlin Garland attacked the off-reservation schools, saying, "The theory that to civilize the red man it is necessary to disrupt families and to smother natural emotions by teaching the child to abhor his parents is so monstrous and so unchristian that its failure was foretold to every teacher who understood the law of heredity."[92]

Reformers moved away from traditional education for Indian students and more into vocational training for actual jobs. An important advance was a move to embrace and celebrate Indian culture into the school programs. Indian arts and crafts were added to the vocational training. Navajo students were encouraged at rug weaving and silversmithing, Pueblo at pottery, and Cheyenne at beadwork. Their works provided a much-needed source of income. In 1905, Navajo rug sales accounted for twenty-five percent of tribal income. Reliance, pride, and hope were generated through these endeavors.

An attempt at assimilation began in the early 1890s when the Indian office offered local public schools ten dollars per capita per quarter to accept Indian students. Progress was slow, and by 1896 only 303 Indian students were enrolled in public schools.[93]

In the early twentieth century, there was an explosion of children attending public school and a dramatic drop in those attending government schools. Particularly hard hit were the boarding schools. As might be expected, Pratt resisted this transformation, and he spent most of the 1890s attacking reformers. Until the end, he was convinced that off-reservation schools were the only way to achieve assimilation. He lashed out at the Indian Bureau and told audiences that it would be better if there never had been one. On June 15, 1904, Pratt was informed that his services were no longer needed. He was essentially fired. Conditions at Carlisle deteriorated, and in the fall of 1918 it was closed.

A comparison of the distribution of Indian students by institutional type provided by the *Annual Report of the Commissioner of Indian Affairs* of the years 1900 and 1925, respectively, reveals some interesting trends. The number of Indian students enrolled in government schools with off-reservation boarding was 7,430 and 8,542; reservation boarding, 9,604 and 10,615; day schools, 5,090 and 4,604; public schools, 246 and 34,452; and other (mission, private, and state institutions), 4,081 and 7,280.[94]

In *Education for Extinction,* David Wallace Adams concluded:

> In the final analysis, the boarding school story constitutes yet another deplorable episode in the long and tragic history of Indian-white relations. For tribal elders who had witnessed the catastrophic developments of the nineteenth century—the bloody warfare, the near-extinction of the bison, the scourge of disease and starvation, the shrinking of the tribal land base, the indignities of reservation life, the invasion of missionaries and white settlers—there seemed to be no end to the cruelties perpetrated by whites. And after all this the schools. After all this, the white man had concluded that the only way to save Indians was to destroy them, that the last great Indian war should be waged against children. They were coming for the children.[95]

Citizenship for the Indian came finally in 1924, but it was a mixed blessing, as described by Brian Dippie in *The Vanishing American:*

> Finally, on June 2, 1924, President Calvin Coolidge signed into law an act making "all noncitizen Indians born within the territorial limits of the United States" citizens thereof. Even this act was a compromise of sorts. The Supreme Court in the case of *United States v. Nice*

(1916) had ruled that "citizenship is not incompatible with tribal existence or continued guardianship, and so may be conferred without completely emancipating the Indians or placing them beyond the reach of congressional regulation adopted for their protection." Thus, the Indian citizenship act did not resolve the legal complexities of the red man's special status, nor did it substantially alter the Bureau of Indian Affairs' jurisdictional authority over reservations. But a measure that had been so contentious and at times apparently so unattainable had won approval only a week after Congress passed the quota act restricting immigration in the United States. That alone was enough to make the Indian citizenship act a cause for celebration. It was the symbolic high point of the assimilationist era.[96]

Shining the light on all the dark corners of American history is painful, even more so when children are in the shadow lands. As C. S. Lewis warned, "Since it is so likely that children will meet cruel enemies, let them at least have heard of brave knights and heroic courage. Otherwise you are making their destiny not brighter but darker." What a shame that the Indian children's heroes had been silenced.

CHAPTER TWENTY-SEVEN

Lamentations of the Fall: Genocide, Ethnic Cleansing, and Post-Traumatic Stress Disorder

Each one is tempted when by his own evil desire, he is dragged away and enticed. Then, after desire has conceived, it gives birth to sin, and sin, when it is full grown, gives birth to death.
—JAMES (BROTHER OF JESUS) 1:14-15, *NEW TESTAMENT*

It's impossible to consider living without ideals. However, when ideals lead to ideology, that's a very dangerous thing. Ideology then leads to creating the image of an enemy, and it leads to the murder and massacre that we've seen since the beginning of time.
—MICHAEL HANEKE

Genocide has two phases: one, destruction of the national pattern of the oppressed group; the other, the imposition of the national pattern of the oppressor.
—RAPHAEL LEMKIN, THE MAN WHO COINED THE TERM GENOCIDE IN 1944

No one who ever studied western history can cling to the belief that the Nazis invented genocide.
—WALLACE STEGNER

No sustained policy of genocide was ever promoted by colonial, state, or federal governments in the United States.
—GARY CLAYTON ANDERSON, *ETHNIC CLEANSING AND THE INDIAN*

America's dealing with Native Americans in almost every area of life has been an abject failure. First pushed west and then relegated to reservations, the Indians who weren't killed by communicable diseases or starved to death by the elimination of their food source—the bison— were killed by the military if they remained hostiles. The violent deaths of Sitting Bull and Crazy Horse on reservation land robbed children of their legendary heroes. For many, "kill the Indian" didn't mean kill just their ethnicity but literally kill them. For those reformers who imagined a day when Christian Indians would blend seamlessly into American society, their dreams never materialized. To "save the man" for them meant converting the heathen savage to Christianity. Failure was achieved in that respect also. Only about five percent of Native Americans are born-again believers.[1] Many Native Americans still think of Christianity as a white man's religion. Indian religions, myths, and legends have survived. It seems that for many, "to save the man" meant saving the white man so he could end up with the red man's land. Native American and Alaska Native populations today struggle in a society whose main connection with them is the Indian casino. They are forgotten and forlorn. Statistics support this statement.

Numbers

When estimating North American native population totals, many historians use a conservative figure of 10 to 20 million Indians before Columbus. By 1900, the Indian population was only 237,080 people. In the early 1800s, California was home to an estimated 260,000 Indians, but by 1900 there were only 20,000.[2] The 1990 census revealed twenty-three percent of the native population live on reservations, while seventy-seven percent live in urban areas. There are 557 federally recognized tribes or nations, and 220 of those are in Alaska. That number changes with time. Approximately 200 native tribes have become extinct, and there are 250 different native languages and dialects still spoken on a daily basis—Apache and Lakota are as different from Navajo and Mohawk as Norwegian is from Japanese.[3]

Here is the lasting legacy of the eighteenth century. The 2012 U.S. Census Bureau's American Community Survey estimates that there are 5,226,034 American Indians and Alaska Natives (AI/AN) comprising 1.7 percent of the total U.S. population. The average life expectancy of a Native American male is seventy-one years—seven years less than his white counterpart. In 2012, the ten states that had the greatest number of AI/AN, in descending order, were California, Oklahoma, Arizona, Texas, New Mexico, Washington, New York, North Carolina, Florida, and Alaska. In 2010, there were 324 federally recognized American Indian reservations. The median income of AI/AN households in 2012 was thirty percent lower than the entire nation. The AI/AN group has the highest poverty rate of any racial group at 29.1 percent, compared to 15.9 percent for the entire nation.[4]

The Bureau of Indian Education (BIE) directly operates 58 elementary and secondary schools for AI/AN students, and another 125 are operated by tribes under BIE contracts or grants. The Bureau of Indian Affairs (BIA) also funds 26 tribal colleges and universities, and BIE directly operates 2 post-secondary schools. As of 2006, there were only 2,380 Bureau of Indian Affairs and tribal uniformed officers to cover the over 56 million acres of tribal lands.[5]

During the 2010-2011 school year, there were 49,152 students in BIE schools and 644,000 Indian students in the U.S. public school system—comprising one percent of the total public school population. The suspension rate was almost double compared to white males. Only 13.3 percent of Native Americans had undergraduate degrees. In 2011, twenty-one percent of AI/AN students reported alcohol consumption on school property compared to four percent of white students. The dropout rate was double that of white students. In 2012, thirty-nine percent of AI/AN students who started in 2005 as first-time, full-time students at four-year institutions [college] actually graduated, compared to sixty percent of similar white students.[6]

AI/AN youth are arrested at a rate three times the national average, and seventy-nine percent of the youth in Federal Bureau of Prisons custody are AI/AN. Approximately seventy-five percent of deaths of AI/AN youth from ages twelve to twenty are violent, including intentional injuries, homicide, and suicide. Fifty-six percent of AI/AN fourth-graders knew some information about their tribe's or group's history, traditions, arts, or crafts. Thirty-three percent of AI/AN eighth-graders had reading teachers that integrated AI/AN culture and history into reading/language arts instruction at least once a month.[7]

Federal services for Native Americans include the Indian Health Service (IHS), which provides federal health care services to Native Americans. A tribe or tribal organization operates more than half of the Indian health programs and are contracted from IHS. Annual Congressional appropriations have met only fifty-two percent of American Indian and Alaska Natives' health care needs. Mortality rates from alcoholism are 514 percent higher than the general population. Suicide rates are more than double, and teen suicide rates are the highest of any population group in the United States. Diabetes is 177 percent higher than the entire population, and tuberculosis incidence is 500 percent higher.[8] Since being relegated to reservations, Native Americans have suffered more from suicide, heart disease, lung disease, obesity, alcoholism, and diabetes because of social disadvantages—mainly having little control over their lives. Empowerment is crucial to improving health.[9]

So What's the Controversy?

Indians never have fit nicely into the American dream. Racism emboldened public and private leaders to destroy their way of life. It was self-evident that God predestined the land for white, Christian, civilized citizens. The allure of the West was expressed in Romantic art and literature—very effective propaganda tools. It played into the notion of God beckoning whites from the East to Eden. But if you want to get an idea of a country's temperament, ethics, and national elegance, you need to look at it when the nation is under tests of severe circumstances, not under the regular rosy glow of daily life.

The controversy over what happened to the Indians, whether it was ethnic cleansing or genocide, has been feverishly debated for decades. In the dominant camp of genocide writers are David E. Stannard (*American Holocaust: The Conquest of the New World*, 1993); Ward Churchill (*A Little Matter of Genocide*, 1998; *Struggle for the Land*, 2002; and *Kill the Indian, Save the Man*, 2004); and Andrew Woolford, ed. (*Colonial Genocide in Indigenous North America*, 2014), among many others.[10]

Author Wallace Stegner believed, "No one who ever studied western history can cling to the belief that the Nazis invented genocide."[11] Others would disagree with that statement. Rodney Stark, the co-director of the Institute for Studies of Religion at Baylor University, in *How the West Won: The Neglected Story of the Triumph of Modernity* (2014), championed modernity propelled by Christianity as entirely the product and savior of Western civilization, and rejected genocide. He wrote:

> I use the term modernity to identify that fundamental store of scientific knowledge and procedures, powerful technologies, artistic achievements, political freedoms, economic arrangements, moral sensibilities, and improved standards of living that characterize Western nations and are now revolutionizing life and the rest of the world. For there is another truth: to the extent that other cultures

have failed to adopt at least major aspects of Western ways, they remain backward and impoverished.[12]

... What happened in the New World was an unpreventable catastrophe; grumblings about the intentional spread of disease are unwarranted. As historian Stafford Poole put it, "the term [genocide] applies to a calculated, deliberate extermination of an identifiable people for racial or other reasons...." There are other terms to describe what happened in the Western Hemisphere, genocide is not one of them.[13]

Historian Gary Clayton Anderson would say that term was ethnic cleansing. The idea behind ethnic cleansing of the Indian was if you could erase his way of life, then he would be like a blank slate or piece of clay that could be transformed into the white man. In *Ethnic Cleansing and the Indian: The Crime That Should Haunt America* (2014)—one of the most recent and well-thought-out publications to address the genocide versus ethnic cleansing controversy—he made the case against genocide and for ethnic cleansing. He wrote, "Genocide will never become a widely accepted characterization for what happened in North America, because large numbers of Indians survived and because policies of mass murder on a scale similar to events in central Europe, Cambodia, or Rwanda were never implemented."[14] He concluded, "Genocide did not occur in America primarily because moral restraints prevented it."[15]

Anderson described the six most famous attacks on Indians that killed about 1,800 natives as "war crimes" but not genocidal massacres. Those attacks were the 1637 attack by the English on the Pequot, the 1859 massacre of over 300 northern California Indians, the 1863 massacre of a Shoshone village at Bear River, the 1864 massacre of Cheyenne at Sand Creek, the 1870 Baker massacre of a Piegan village in Montana, and the 1890 massacre of Lakota Indians at Wounded Knee.[16] Custer's attack at Washita could be added.

In his 2015 *Custer's Trials,* T. J. Stiles agreed with Anderson and wrote:

> The words "extermination" and "extinction" often appeared in discussions of American Indians. The white public in the West, Sherman wrote to Grant in 1867, "are clamorous for extermination, which is easier said than done, and they have an idea that we are moved by mere human sentiments."
>
> Sentiments played no part in his or Sheridan's thinking, but neither did genocide. Sherman often spoke outrageously (as when he

seemed to reject extermination for mere practical reasons, "easier said than done"), but his ruthlessness did not extend to indiscriminate massacres—just discriminating ones. "I would not hesitate to approve the extermination of a camp" that sent out "thieving, murdering parties," he specified, "but I would not sanction the extermination" of the band that remained quiet.[17]

While controversial, Anderson's writing continued the conversation of how the destruction of the cultures of many Indian tribes could take place in a Christian nation. We can see the results of man's words and actions, but not his thoughts. Perhaps, that is the way of nations too. Anderson concluded that ethnic cleansing was a policy by the U.S. government to save, not destroy, Indians. Without ethnic cleansing, Indian survival would have been much less.[18]

Disagreeing with that conclusion is Matt Ridley, evolutionary biologist and member of the British House of Lords, who wrote in *The Evolution of Everything* (2015) that generally the best thing we can do to make the world a better place is absolutely nothing. Whenever we think someone should do something about something, our minds automatically turn to a religious deity, political leader, a government agent, a corporate CEO, an organization's director, or an institution's governing board. Blank-slate theories of personality, intelligence, gender, and sexuality, which have dominated the social sciences until very recently, insisted that parents, schools, and culture were the dominant shapers of these most central characteristics of who we are. Therefore, if we want to improve the nation or Native Americans, we must design better conditions in which to raise our children, that is, Pratt's school model. But according to Ridley, the overwhelming scientific evidence now shows that these traits come mostly from within, not without, and the social engineering schemes to make people smarter, happier, or anything else are destined to fail. Gifting entitlements to targeted groups only makes them and future generations dependent. Perhaps that's why Pratt's off-reservation schools indeed failed. Ridley's conclusions would not have been well received by those like Pratt who believed they were smarter than the masses. They thought that most Indians were not capable of self-governance and fancied themselves as intelligent social designers.[19]

In his review of Anderson's book in the *Western Historical Quarterly*, Brendan Lindsay took issue with Anderson's conclusions. Lindsay expressed concern over Anderson's tight legal definition of genocide but the lack of one with ethnic cleansing. He also wrote that Anderson ignored the role of the settlers as a genocidal force and concluded, "His claim that Indians survived in part because of, not in spite of, U.S. policy stretches credulity.... Anderson succeeds in his stated goal of promoting awareness of crimes committed against Native Americans. But in proving his claims regarding ethnic cleansing in the absence of genocide, he falls short."[20]

Benjamin Madley's essay in the February 2015 *American Historical Review* also rejected key points in Anderson's interpretation, especially in the definition of genocide and also the involvement of government officials in the colonial and national eras who promoted it.

Clyde Ellis, in a somewhat compromising review in *Montana: The Magazine of Western History*, wrote, "He [Anderson] recognizes the horrific and intentional nature of ethnic cleansing, and he catalogs a damning litany of massive and violent land cessions, forced removals, and coercive assimilation policies that wreaked havoc in Indian country. And if that litany of events fails in Anderson's estimation to amount to genocide, he nonetheless finds it a deeply troubling and profoundly immoral legacy that demands scrutiny."[21]

So what is one to make of this controversy? Perhaps a closer look at the history of the term *genocide* and what type of people committed it will be helpful.

What is Genocide All About?

It may come as a surprise to many that genocide is a relatively new term that came into existence in the fall of 1944. That year, the 674-page *Axis Rule in Occupied Europe* was published by the Carnegie Endowment for International Peace. Genocide made its debut on page 79: "Genocide—a new term and new conception for destruction of nations." The author was a Polish-born lawyer who had fled war-torn Europe for the United States in 1941. Raphael Lemkin (1900-1959), after his arrival, had heard a radio address by Winston Churchill on "the barbaric fury of the Nazis.... We are in the presence of a crime without a name."[22] In 1948, Lemkin successfully lobbied the United Nations to establish the Convention on the Prevention and Punishment of the Crime of Genocide, which became a landmark in international human rights law and defined the crime for the first time.[23]

Lemkin trained in law at Lviv, Ukraine, at the city's university. His contemporary, Jewish lawyer Hersch Lauterpacht (1897-1960), was born in Lviv, and both eventually were present at the Nuremberg trials after the war, where their pioneering legal concepts were used against the Nazis. Lemkin became a Zionist advocate as a student and young lawyer. In 1948, Lauterpacht proposed a draft of the Israeli Declaration of Independence and became the chair of international law at the University of Cambridge. They differed on how to respond to murderous anti-Semitism hatred. Lauterpacht was more interested in protecting individuals with his notion of "crimes against humanity," while Lemkin cared more about protecting groups.[24]

Having lost much of his family to the Holocaust, Lemkin was inspired to invent a name that would match the crime and spent most of the rest of his life crusading for its acknowledgment. In his search for a uniquely memorable neologism, he took inspiration from George Eastman's creation of the wildly popular brand name, Kodak. In September 1888, Eastman formally registered his invented word "Kodak" as a trademark. When asked what Kodak meant, Eastman explained:

> "Kodak." This is not a foreign name or word; it was constructed by me to serve a definite purpose. It has the following merits as a trademark word:
> First. It is short.
> Second. It is not capable of mispronunciation.
> Third. It does not resemble anything in art and cannot be associated with anything in the art except the Kodak.[25]

Lemkin's word is a hybrid that combined the Greek *genos,* meaning people or nation, with the Latin-derived suffix *-cide,* or killing. He had earlier rejected other possibilities, including established terms like barbarity and ethnocide. While he was dreaming of a word to use, he circled, "The Word" on his scribbled writing pad and connected it with a line to another circled phrase, "Moral Judgment." His hope was that the word *genocide* could unite people to keep it from ever happening again—it didn't.[26]

Here is his first definition:

> Genocide has two phases: one, destruction of the national pattern of the oppressed group; the other the imposition of the national pattern of the oppressor. This imposition, in turn, may be made on the oppressed population which is allowed to remain, or upon the territory alone, after the removal of the population and colonization of the area by the oppressor's own nationals.[27]

In 1947, the secretary general of the newly formed United Nations retained Lemkin to spearhead a committee of experts whose responsibility was drafting a law to define, prevent, and punish the crime of genocide. Lemkin's expanded classification included:

1. Physical genocide—direct and immediate extermination; and "subjection to conditions of life which, owing to lack of proper housing, clothing, food, hygiene and medical care or excessive work or physical exertion are likely to result in the debilitation and death of individuals; mutilations and biological experiments imposed for other than curative purposes; deprivation of the means of livelihood by confiscation, looting, curtailment of work, and the denial of housing and of supplies otherwise available to the other inhabitants of the territory concerned."[28]
2. Biological genocide—"sterilization, compulsory abortion, segregation of the sexes or obstacles to marriage," and any other policies to prevent births.[29]
3. Cultural genocide—this is the central characteristic of his original 1944 meaning of genocide and includes "forced transfer of children . . . forced and systematic exile of individuals representing the culture of the group . . . prohibition of the use of the national language . . . systematic destruction of books printed in the national language, or religious works, or the prohibition of new publications . . . systematic destruction of historical or religious monuments, or their diversion to alien uses and destruction or dispersion of objects of historical, artistic, or religious value and of objects used in religious worship."[30]

Lemkin would have used, at the least, cultural genocide for what happened to the Indians. However, he believed there could be no separation of cultural, physical, and biological genocide, and he warned against minimizing the effect of cultural genocide:

> A culture's destruction is not a trifling matter. A healthy culture is all-encompassing of human lives, even to the point of determining their time and space orientation. If a people suddenly lose their "prime symbol," the basis of culture, their lives losing meaning. They become disoriented, with no hope. As social disorganization often follows such loss, they are often unable to ensure their own survival. . . .

The loss and human suffering for those whose culture has been healthy and is suddenly attacked and disintegrated are incalculable.[31]

Lemkin submitted his draft of the law in November 1947, but it was modified by the Soviet Union, who had political groups removed from the list of protected classes, and by the United States, who curiously deleted cultural genocide. A revised draft was eventually adopted on December 9, 1948, by the United Nations General Assembly. The second article of the 1948 Convention on the Prevention and Punishment of the Crime of Genocide defined genocide as being "any of the following acts committed with intent to destroy in whole or in part, a national, ethnical, racial or religious group, as such:"

(a) Killing members of the group;
(b) Causing serious bodily or mental harm to members of the group;
(c) Deliberately inflicting on the group conditions of life calculated to bring about its physical destruction in whole or in part;
(d) Imposing measures intended to prevent births within the group;
(e) Forcibly transferring children of the group to another group.

Ward Churchill wrote, "Here the country was in violation of every one of the criteria posited in the convention's second article."[32]

George Eastman seems to have had more luck with his invented word "Kodak" retaining its fidelity than did Lemkin with "genocide." No one calls a Canon, Nikon, Polaroid, or cell phone camera a Kodak. Not so for genocide. It seems that since the word was invented, its definition has taken on a life of its own. Genocide "experts" adjust its meaning with metronomic regularity. In 1959, Pieter N. Drost, a Dutch law professor, started this game. By the time of the 2002 Rome Statute of the International Criminal Court, which meets in the Hague in the Netherlands, over a dozen new definitions had been put forth by noted individuals.

To address the problem, the International Criminal Court adopted in Article 6 the five acts of genocide defined in the 1948 UN definition. Gary Clayton Anderson wrote, ". . . European and later Americans who committed general acts of dispossession against—or even 'eliminatory' acts—would likely face the charge of 'ethnic cleansing' as defined in Article 7, which has the broad title 'Crimes against Humanity.' On some occasions Article 8, 'War Crimes,' might also apply."[33] Article 7, section 2, paragraph d defines ethnic cleansing as "deportation or forcible transfer of population," which means forced displacement of the persons concerned by expulsion or other coercive acts from the area in which they are lawfully present, without grounds permitted under international law.[34]

Lemkin was not the first to attempt to prevent national atrocities. Swiss businessman Henri Dunant (1828-1910), the founder of the Red Cross, is credited for being the man behind the adoption of a universal moral code of warfare. In 1864, having witnessed the bloodshed and suffering at the 1859 Battle of Solferino in northern Italy, Dunant gathered together representatives of more than a dozen governments. They became the first signatories of the original Geneva Convention. By the end of the year, twelve states had signed it, including Italy, France, Sweden, Denmark, and Spain. They were soon followed by Britain in 1865 and Russia in 1867.

Interestingly, the United States did not sign the Geneva Convention until 1882, which—by chance or not—coincided fairly closely with the end of Indian hostilities out West. That America should own Indian lands was a deeply held belief, religious in its power, through which the West's events were interpreted. For many whites, Indians were the embodiment of original sin, the destroyer of Eden, and all of history was a battle of disparate races struggling for space, land, and power. Signing the Geneva Convention could wait.[35]

Why Genocide?

Many believe that only the Nazis and psychopaths committed genocide.[36] Ethnic cleansing is seemingly more humane. Many believe it's the worst a Christian America could be guilty of. It should be a sobering fact that the greatest toll in human lives over the past century came not from terrorism, not from conventional war, but from genocide. In Abram de Swaan's enlightening book, *The Killing Compartments* (2015), he took a close look at genocide since the nineteenth century. Globally, since the late 1800s, over 100 million lives have been taken on genocidal killing sprees. That is four times the toll of combatants in all regular wars in the same period.

De Swaan pointed out that annihilation is always aimed at a despised ethnic or social group; it is often carried out with extreme and intimate brutality; and it is carried out with the intent of exterminating an entire population. For civilized societies, these nefarious endeavors almost always unfold far from urban areas—Indian wars out West and Nazi concentration camps in Eastern Europe.

Genocide is not rare and examples abound: mass murders of 1 million

Congolese villagers by Belgian troops—who Ota Benga feared—and mercenaries at the turn of the twentieth century, the annihilation of millions in Stalin's Great Terror of the 1930s, the rape of Nanjing, the Holocaust, the massacre of 1 million Hindu Bangladeshis by the Pakistani Army in 1971, the demise of 1 to 3 million Cambodians (twenty-five percent of the population) during Pol Pot's four-year reign, and recent episodes of ethnic mass murder in Guatemala, Rwanda, and the former Yugoslavia. The reign of terror in North Korea continues, with over 1 million lives taken in the last twenty years. And then we have ISIS.

All of us grasp for explanations of why genocide occurs. Several quick and easy answers have become standard explanations. The first is that mass murderers are psychopaths and aberrations of society. According to Abram de Swaan, however, scholarly research is almost unanimous in agreement that the portion of psychopaths among mass murderers is in fact no greater than the rest of the population—five percent.[37]

Before engaging in the slaughter of unarmed civilians—like Indian villages filled with women and children—most perpetrators had never before harmed a living soul. Soldiers retire and never physically hurt another person again. Most return to be functional members of their society and are devoted fathers and loving husbands with successful jobs. In psychological terms, they are mentally and socially well integrated.

Another misconception is that of the "situational view," that if any of us were put under the same circumstances, we might have done the same thing. Thus, it's the situation that causes ordinary people to commit extreme evil. But this doesn't take individual psychological disposition into account. This view was made famous by social psychologist Stanley Milgram (1933-1984) in his obedience studies at Yale University in the early 1960s[38] and by political theorist Hannah Arendt's (1906-1975) reporting of the 1961 trial of Adolf Eichmann.[39] It seems to absolve the perpetrators of personal responsibility. What is rarely mentioned in the accounts of Milgram's study is that many subjects did not obey their superiors—one-third refused to follow orders. In the military, not following orders would get you court-martialed. For some, the only alternative was desertion.

In his 2015 book *The German War,* Nicholas Stargardt related three fundamental findings. The overwhelming majority of Germans saw their war from beginning to end as a war of national defense. Second, and contrary to common interpretations of the regime, the German people were never united either for or against Nazism. Third, and most disturbing, almost from the beginning, the German people were aware of the genocidal savagery of their own armed forces and government. Evidence of guilty knowledge pervades the reports, and private correspondence and diaries offer abundant confirmation. The evidence is massive and compelling. Only the top-secret compulsory euthanasia killings of the unfit inside Germany initially escaped widespread notice until the Bishop of Münster, Count Clemens August Graf von Galen (1878-1946), famously denounced them in a sermon on August 3, 1941.[40]

Snapshots by villagers and tourists of the mass murder of Russian Jews by SS units backed by the German army were leaked to the homeland from June-July 1941 onward. The deportation of Germany's own remaining Jews to killing sites and death camps in the fall and winter of 1941 was impossible to hide. Foreign radio had long since broken the regime's media monopoly, and from mid-1942, the BBC offered its many German listeners detailed accounts of Germany's death factories in the East. Catholic and Protestant denominations made no effort to intercede for German Jews. One of the exceptions was Lutheran pastor and famous theologian, Dietrich Bonhoeffer.[41] For his efforts, he was hung with a wire in prison by the Nazis at the end of the war. Stargardt noted that the majority of German POWs interrogated in 1944 by Allied forces professed unshakable loyalty to their leaders even as Germany went down in ruin.

What causes genocidal social attitudes to arise and become acceptable in the first place? Swaan tackles this troubling question. Ordinary people become capable of committing genocide because of a very specific set of social and psychological steps. Mass murderers almost always work in large teams (e.g., massacres by U.S. Cavalry), within a supportive social context (e.g., Manifest Destiny, scientific racism, group think, and social Darwinism), and are comfortable knowing that they won't be punished for their actions (no accountability in the American West, e.g., Custer). Most striking is the observation that they almost never felt remorse for their actions afterward. It made it easier then, for the cavalry to go to the next Indian village and destroy it or spend their downtime forcing themselves on Indian women.

Survivors of mass annihilation campaigns suffer psychological consequences for the rest of their lives. In the case of the Indians, they've suffered for generations. In earlier wars, some combat veterans developed shell shock, as it used to be called; now we use the term post-traumatic stress disorder (PTSD). But the people committing genocide don't suffer from this. They do just fine. In the 1980s, several Israeli psychologists sent out questionnaires to hundreds of psychiatrists, therapists, clergymen, and physicians in Germany and other European countries asking if any Holocaust perpetrators had ever expressed feelings of guilt or sought help for lingering aftereffects of their crimes.[42] Only one instance was recorded: a German soldier was haunted by the eyes of the six-year-old Jewish girl he stabbed to death on his commander's orders as she ran toward him in the Warsaw ghetto with her arms outstretched.[43]

The lack of remorse is unsettling because one would conclude that a normal person would feel guilt or at least emotional trauma. Swaan explains this by seeing genocidal murder as fundamentally an act of extreme social and psychological compartmentalization. In almost all cases that he reviewed, there was a prior period of social indoctrination where the state presented itself as the aggrieved victim of historical injustice.

His findings would apply to the Indian wars. The Eastern media outraged Americans with reports of Indian atrocities toward white settlers—especially pioneer women and children. What followed was a growing demarcation of the target population socially, legally, and physically. Before massacres in the West by the U.S. military, propaganda campaigns continually painted the Indians—the victims—as the real aggressors, threats to the very existence of the state and its people, and the alien other—savage, heathen, barbarian, and so on.

One of the most fascinating points of Swaan's book was that the actual killing almost always took place in a physically separated location that allowed the perpetrators to view their acts somehow distinct from their normal lives in the social and psychological norms of civilized society. The U.S. government's policy of removing Indians west of the Mississippi and away from civilized America certainly made it easier to later destroy Indian villages far from public scrutiny. Thus, the atrocities were confined to well-defined locations and episodes. Meanwhile, the rest of the civilization—those living far away from the American West—could continue in their daily lives where the workweek was complemented with church on Sunday. Basically, it was out of sight, out of mind. Military leaders like Custer, Baker, and Crook could kill out West and then return to the East to enjoy star treatment, plays, concerts, and horse racing. Their Indian victims underwent "disidentification" as being sickly, subhuman, savages, heathens, and cowardly animals. They were often made to suffer before being killed.[44]

As it is used in society today, the term genocide is almost universally first associated with Nazi Germany and the killing of millions of Jews. For many, ethnic cleansing avoids this association and is more acceptable than even cultural genocide. No matter what the label, any individual in a target group would be expected to suffer mental problems.

Perhaps the worst casualty is being forgotten. Both have occurred today in Native Americans.

Post-Traumatic Stress Disorder Among the Military and Native Americans

Indian cultures certainly experienced both physical and psychological trauma. Their forced removal, at first from the East to west of the Mississippi and then onto reservations after repeated massacres, would make any human race or society feel persecuted and psychologically damaged. Much like our returning veterans of the Vietnam War, Native Americans faced a surprisingly deadly environment in captivity. Both felt a lack of intimacy and low level of trust in a sprawling and anonymous society where people can get away with dishonesty and misbehavior. In *Tribe: On Homecoming and Belonging* (2012), Sebastian Junger sees PTSD in veterans due to them missing the moral universe of their old warrior tribe. There is no civilian tribe that feels right for them to join. The same could be said of Native Americans on reservations who no longer had the traditional homecoming dance ceremonies known as pow wows.[45]

Adverse effects due to trauma were documented in combat soldiers as early as the sixth century BCE. One of the first documentations of PTSD-like effects in civilians occurred in the seventeenth century when Samuel Pepys wrote about the Great Fire of London in 1666 and described how that tragedy affected the city's residents.[46]

What we call today post-traumatic stress disorder (PTSD) was known in Civil War veterans as "soldiers' heart" or "irritable heart," and in the South African Anglo-Boer War (1899-1902) as "disordered action of the heart." In the twentieth century, labels for combat and civilian traumatic stress included battle fatigue, combat fatigue, war neurosis, shell shock, combat stress reaction, traumatic neurosis, post-Vietnam syndrome, rape trauma syndrome, child-abuse syndrome, and battered wife syndrome.[47]

At the end of the 1800s, Freud, Janet, Charcot, and Breuer suggested that PTSD resulted from an emotional response to environmental events. Skeptics doubted this condition and believed patients were malingerers seeking compensation. Others attributed post-traumatic symptoms to pre-existing psychological dysfunction.

Increasing knowledge of chronic psychological problems was gathered after World War II from Holocaust survivors, Hiroshima and Nagasaki atomic bomb survivors, and survivors of railway disasters. It wasn't until

Vietnam veterans showed PTSD—when the term was first applied in war—that clinicians understood that significant long-term psychological problems could develop in people with sound personalities when exposed to horrific stressors. In 1980, PTSD became a distinct diagnosis by the American Psychiatric Association in the third edition of the *Diagnostic and Statistical Manual of Mental Disorders* (DSM-III), which classed it as an anxiety disorder based on frequent symptoms of persistent anxiety, hypervigilance, exaggerated startle response, and phobic-like avoidance behaviors.[48]

In 2013, new revisions (DSM-5) were made to the diagnosis including that it is no longer an anxiety disorder but placed in a new trauma-specific category. Traumatic events were expanded to include actual or threat of death, serious injury, or sexual assault. Fear, helplessness, or horror as initial trauma response was removed because this was found unrelated to PTSD development. Symptom clusters expanded from three to four: re-experiencing, avoidance, negative cognitions and mood, and arousal. To be considered PTSD, symptom duration was reduced from three months to one month (if symptoms abate in a month or less, it's considered acute stress disorder).[49]

The horrific experiences of many of the Indian tribes during the nineteenth century certainly placed many of them in the PTSD diagnosis. It was common for them to lose faith in their medicine men and shamans when they did not protect them from smallpox, other diseases, or white invaders. Spiritual alienation is frequently reported in patients with this condition. Combat veterans have great difficulty in reconciling their religious beliefs with the events they witnessed in the war zone. Many stated that they abandoned their religious faith altogether.

The prevalence of this condition among Indian villages may be better understood by statistics that have been gathered recently. It's significant that there is no ethnic difference in regard to the likelihood of developing PTSD—it isn't just a white man's condition. A survey in the United States from 2001 to 2003 of 5,692 participants eighteen years of age or older found lifetime PTSD prevalence rates of 6.8 percent overall—3.6 percent in men and 9.7 percent in women.[50] Research has also shown that about 40 percent of North Americans are exposed to at least one traumatic event in their lifetime. So it's clear that only a minority of persons exposed to traumatic experiences develop PTSD. An underappreciated risk factor for the condition is the sudden, unexpected death of a loved one, which alone can lead to PTSD. Such causes are often overlooked because of a focus on combat, rape, and assaultive violence. For years, Indian villages experienced terror from military attacks by the U.S. Cavalry.[51]

One of the most important questions regarding Indian culture since the time of the reservations has been why Native Americans have not better assimilated into American culture. Other minorities have more readily blended in. An enigma for years is why Indians have high unemployment and alcoholism, low college attendance, and only a small percentage who have converted to Christianity.

One important and underappreciated factor in the lack of Indian assimilation into white culture is transgenerational trauma, which was first identified and reported in 1966 after clinical observations of offspring of Holocaust survivors.[52] This was followed by many other reports supporting what has been called "survivor syndrome," which is a condition transmitted from one generation to the next. Cognitive and affective symptoms common to survivors and their children include distrust of the world, impaired parental function, chronic despair, inability to communicate feelings, pervasive fear of danger, separation anxiety, and overprotectiveness within a narcissistic family structure. Survivor syndrome has been well documented in survivors and their offspring of genocides in Rwanda, Nigeria, Cambodia, Armenia, and the former Yugoslavia. This has also been observed in the offspring of disaster victims, in impoverished high-crime urban environments, and in other environments where trauma exposure is prevalent.[53]

A number of mental health conditions co-occur with PTSD, including depression (in sixteen percent of cases), generalized anxiety disorder (eleven percent), substance abuse (ten percent), social phobia (seven percent), panic disorder (six percent), and obsessive-compulsive disorder (four percent).[54] A 2000 study found that eighty-six percent of men and seventy-seven percent of women with PTSD had a high likelihood of anxiety disorder, affective disorder, and substance abuse disorder. The greatest symptom decrease occurs during the first twelve months following exposure. A substantial minority continue experiencing PTSD for decades. About half will have a remission between two and ten years post event.[55]

In combat, the most common traumatizing event is witnessing someone badly injured or killed or unexpectedly seeing a dead body. For Indians, war was often close at hand because the U.S. military brought war right to where they lived—villages at Washita, Sand Creek, the Marias River, Wounded Knee, and the Little Bighorn are prime examples. The U.S. military subjected Indian villages to a form of terrorism because the natives never knew when they were going to be attacked. The Indian wars weren't conflicts of large battles undertaken by massive opposing military forces as seen in the Civil War. The Indian women and children especially were exposed to gruesome sights including the death, mutilation, and suffering of friends and family members. With terrorism, the place, timing, and potential victims are usually unpredictable, and the pervasive response of feeling powerless and helpless greatly elevates the risk of perpetual hypervigilance. The objective of the U.S. military was to generate terror and loss of hope in the villages and beyond.[56]

One of the most common characteristics described in Indian populations even today is anger of variable intensity, ranging from mild annoyance or aggravation to fury and rage. The incidence of anger is much higher in individuals experiencing PTSD.[57] Also, for Indian warriors, survival required constant vigilance for potential threats in their environment. Heightened awareness of small changes trained them to respond to threats with aggression and heightened sense of threat perception. Problems arose when Indian warriors returned to civilian life on reservations when their threat perception vigilance remained fully intact and led to the misreading of situations as over-threatening even when a significant threat was absent. Social situations were viewed through an overly negative, hostile, or threatening lens, and this misread could trigger aggressive responses. This in part led to violent interactions on the reservations—the killing of Sitting Bull and Crazy Horse, for example—even with Indian police.[58]

Alcohol abuse is the most frequent co-morbidity in PTSD because alcohol is often used to self-medicate the hyperarousal symptoms associated with PTSD. Alcohol abuse leads to an increased risk factor for aggressive behavior. Alcohol also disinhibits violence in persons with hyperarousal or anger problems.[59]

Combat veterans with PTSD have described feeling unable to relate to civilians, even their own families, and having lost the ability for true connectedness, which leads to a sense of loneliness and isolation.[60] The strongest predictor of increased prevalence of PTSD are combat frequency and intensity; these are a greater risk factor than the actual number of military deployments in predicting adverse mental health outcomes.[61]

All those living in Indian villages with the constant threat of attack from the U.S. military were at risk for developing symptoms that included nightmares, disrupted sleep, changes in appetite, anxiety and fear, heightened startle reactions, depression, irritability, anger, resentment, emotional withdrawal and disconnect from others, and feeling extremely protective of, or fearful for, the safety of their loved ones.[62]

The high suicide rates in Indian populations following smallpox epidemics and military confrontations with the U.S. government were generated from the presence of these overwhelming negative thoughts and hopelessness over the future. When the military destroyed the Indians' way of life and Christian missionaries minimized the Indians' cherished spiritual beliefs, hopelessness ensued. That led to cynicism that killed the idea of merit. On the reservation, merit didn't make you rise; you rose through lies and connections. The young became bitter as they were deprived of idealism that would have helped them rise clearly.[63] Before the white man, there was intertribal warfare, but it didn't generate hopelessness. Instead, young braves looked forward to battling their enemies to bring honor to themselves and pride to their families and tribes. It was their version of the white man's survival of the fittest.

Now What?

To fully understand what is happening to the American Indian today, we should not minimize the trauma that Native Americans have experienced since the first contact with the white man. Arguing over numbers such as the percentage of Indians killed by smallpox versus at the hands of the white man or over the semantics of whether it was ethnic cleansing or genocide, while not unimportant, is a diversion from understanding and addressing the Indians' humanity and dire predicament today.

Only when whites accept that Indians have the full emotional, spiritual, intellectual, and psychological spectrum as whites will we begin to appreciate the pain and hopelessness that is the Indians' experience. Transgenerational post-traumatic stress disorder is real for Native Americans.

In *The Third Reich in History and Memory* (2015), Richard J. Evans concluded that the job of the historian is not to join in with moral debate but to make it possible. There are moral lessons in history, but they are for the readers of historical writing to take, not for the historian to give.[64] For those readers who desire to understand the moral lessons to take from genocide and ethnic cleansing, there is no greater book to digest than *The Sunflower: On the Possibilities and Limits of Forgiveness* (1997) by Simon Wiesenthal with responses by such noted minds as Robert Coles, the Dalai Lama, Matthew Fox, Mary Gordon, Harold S. Kushmer, Dennis Prager, Dith Pran, Desmond Tutu, Harry Wu, and forty-four others. Wiesenthal (1908-2005) is perhaps best known for his work in hunting down Nazi war criminals after World War II. He was imprisoned in a Nazi concentration camp, and one day was taken from his work detail to the bed of a dying SS agent who was haunted by the crimes he had participated in. He wanted to confess to a Jew the atrocities he had committed and wanted forgiveness before he died. Wiesenthal listened but said nothing. There was no forgiveness. What would you do?

What would you have done if you were Wiesenthal? That question was asked to fifty-three distinguished men and women, including theologians, political leaders, writers, jurists, psychiatrists, human rights activists, Holocaust survivors, and victims of attempted genocide in Bosnia, Cambodia, China, and Tibet. Their responses were as varied as their life experiences. *The Sunflower* will compel you to reflect on your own beliefs about religion, philosophy, medicine, science, hate, justice, racism, accountability, and the Golden Rule.

We view the past through the present. From the moment the last Indian was killed by a soldier, accounts of Native American history have reflected the priorities of new generations of historians and the changing politics of the worlds in which they were at work. That's what gives the moral debate its force. We all need to struggle to get things right, and history hopefully does the work on which moral debate will rest. It's easier to do right when we strengthen our mediating institutions that stand between the individual and government, and especially the national government—families, churches, civic organizations, and professional organizations. Every American needs his or her positive influences to help reject hatred and racism and to ensure the American dream is available to everyone.

Notes

INTRODUCTION
(PAGES XVII-XXVIII)

1. I would like to thank the great historian William Manchester (1922-2004), "world lit only by fire;" the noted short story writer Anton Chekhov (1860-1904), "state the problem correctly;" and President Abraham Lincoln (1809-1865), "better angels of our nature" for providing me guidance.
2. Patterson, *The Missouri River Journals of John James Audubon*.
3. Flores, *American Serengeti*, 128-129. In addition, this paragraph was inspired by an informative lecture by Dan Flores titled "The American Serengeti and an Imagery of Loss and Remorse" at a symposium on March 19, 2016, titled "Animals, Arts, and the Environment," held during The Russell auction week in Great Falls, Montana, to support the Charles M. Russell Museum.
4. Plain, "John James Audubon Out West," 15-19; Audubon, *Ornithological Biography*; Irmscher, *Audubon*.
5. Scioli, *Hope in the Age of Anxiety* and *The Power of Hope*.
6. Benson, *Wallace Stegner*.
7. Hunt, *Writing History in the Global Era*.
8. Isaacson, Walter, "Henry Kissinger Reminds Us Why Realism Matters," *Time*, September 6, 2014.
9. Kissinger, *World Order*. This is his 17th book in 60 years.
10. Harari, *Sapiens*.
11. Mann, *1491*, 180.
12. Greene, *American Carnage*.
13. Behbehani, "The Smallpox Story."
14. Ibid., 260.
15. Prothero, *American Jesus*.
16. Miller, *Native America, Discovered and Conquered*.
17. O'Keefe, *Custer, the Seventh Cavalry, and the Little Big Horn*.
18. Stiles, *Custer's Trials*.
19. Adams, *Education for Extinction*, 52.
20. McCullough, *Brave Companions*, xiv.

CHAPTER 1 – OUT OF AFRICA: ORIGIN OF THE RACES (PAGES 3-15)

1. See Anthropology.net, "Peopling Of The Americas: Eva de Naharon, A 13,600 Year Old Skeleton Found Near Tulum, Mexico;" PBS produced a four-part series titled *First Peoples* that originally aired in 2015. It is available from PBS in DVD form.
2. Harbarger, "Decrepit Fish Camps Built on Broken Promises," March 11, 2016. http://www.oregonlive.com/pacific-northwest-news/index.ssf/page/tribal_housing_a_run_of_broken.html#incart_big-photo.
3. Willerslev, "The Ancestry and Affiliations of Kennewick Man," *Nature* 523, 455-458.
4. Callaway, "Ancient Genome Stirs Ethics Debate," 162-163; Douglas W. Owsley, David Hunt, "Clovis and Early Archaic Crania from the Anzick Site."
5. Willerslev, "The Ancestry and Affiliations of Kennewick Man," *Nature* 523, 455-458.
6. A nice review of the DNA findings can be found in *The New York Times* article "New DNA Results Show Kennewick Man Was Native American" by Carl Zimmer, June 18, 2015.
7. Collins, *The Language of God*, 89.
8. Bowman, *Radiocarbon Dating*, 42.
9. Collins, *The Language of God*, 148-149.
10. Gould, *Wonderful Life*.
11. Wignall, *The Worst of Times*.
12. Mann, *1491*, 360.
13. Collins, *The Language of God*, 95.
14. Diamond, *Guns, Germs, and Steel*, 37.
15. Day, "Fossil Reanalysis Pushes Back Origin of *Homo sapiens*;" Fleagle, "Paleoanthropology of the Kibish Formation, Southern Ethiopia: Introduction."
16. Harari, *Sapiens*.
17. Jenner, *A Million Years in a Day*.
18. Ibid.
19. Hershkovitz, "Levantine Cranium from Manot Cave (Israel) Foreshadows the First European Modern Humans," *Nature* 520, 216-219.
20. Shipman, *The Invaders*.
21. Ibid.
22. Harari, *Sapiens*.
23. Pääbo, *Neanderthal Man;* Houldcroft, "Neanderthal Genomics Suggests a Pleistocene Time Frame for the First Epidemiologic Transition," 379-388.
24. Ibid.
25. Houldcroft, "Neanderthal Genomics Suggests a Pleistocene Time Frame for the First Epidemiologic Transition," 379-388; see also Morgan Manella, "Migrating Humans May Have Killed Off Neanderthals by Accident," 4/15/2016, online at Neanderthal Extinction May Be Due to Diseases from Africa-CNN.com.
26. Ibid.
27. Leakey, "Homo Erectus Unearthed," 624-629; Haviland, *Evolution and Prehistory*.
28. Pollard, *Worlds Together, Worlds Apart*, 13.
29. Rose, "New Light on Human Prehistory in the Arabo-Persian Gulf Oasis," 849-883.

30 Brahic, "Humanity's Forgotten Pioneers."
31 Krause, "The Complete Mitochondrial DNA Genome of an Unknown Hominin from Southern Siberia," 894-897.
32 Sawyer, "Nuclear and Mitochondrial DNA Sequences from Two Denisovan Individuals," 15696-15700.
33 Callaway, "First Aboriginal Genome Sequenced." Published online *Nature*, September 22, 2011.
34 Willerslev, "Upper Palaeolithic Siberian Genome Reveals Dual Ancestry of Native American," 87-91.
35 Huerta-Sanchez, "Altitude Adaption in Tibetans Caused by Introgression of Denisovan-like DNA," 194-197. For oxygen loading in red blood cells, see Peterson, "Red Cell Diphosphoglycerate Mutase, Immunochemical Studies in Vertebrate Red Cells, Including a Human Variant Lacking 2, 3-DPG," 953-958.
36 Apanius, "The Nature of Selection on the Major Histocompatibility Complex," 179-224.
37 Davis, *The Compatibility Gene*.

CHAPTER 2 – WHEN THE WEST BELONGED TO GOD: DISCOVERING THE NEW WORLD BEFORE COLUMBUS (PAGES 17-30)

1 Hoffecker, *Human Ecology of Beringia*; Pielou, *After the Ice Age*.
2 Flores, *American Serengeti*, 3.
3 Goebel, "The Late Pleistocene Dispersal of Modern Humans in America," 1497-1502.
4 Ash, *The Emergence of Humans*.
5 Pitblado, "A Tale of Two Migrations: Reconciling Recent Biological and Archaeological Evidence for the Pleistocene Peopling of the Americas," 327-375.
6 Wells, *The Journey of Man*.
7 Mann, *1491*, 180.
8 Diamond, *Guns, Germs, and Steel*, 68-69.
9 Hally, "Chiefdom of Coosa," 227-253.
10 Diamond, *Guns, Germs, and Steel*, 30.
11 Davies, *The Codes of Hammurabi and Moses with Copious Comments, Index, and Bible References*.
12 Mann, *1491*, 31.
13 Nichols, *American Indians in U.S. History*, 33.
14 Stanford, *Across Atlantic Ice*.
15 Mann, *1491*, 19.
16 Raff, "Palaeogenomics: Genetic Roots of the First Americans."
17 Meltzer, *First Peoples in a New World*, 129.
18 Blainey, *A Short History of the World*.
19 Diamond, *Guns, Germs, and Steel*.
20 Calloway, *One Vast Winter Count*, 20.
21 Mann, *1491*, 43.

22 Reich, "The Genetic History of Ice Age Europe."
23 Ibid. See also "Ancient DNA Tells a New Human Story" by Matt Ridley in the May 1, 2015 *The Wall Street Journal*.
24 Mann, 1491, 39; Calloway, *One Vast Winter Count*, 59.
25 Ibid., 35.
26 Blitz, "Adoption of the Bow in Prehistoric North America," 123-145; Whitley, *The Art of the Shaman*, 39, 110.
27 Martin, *The Way of the Human Being*, 21-47.
28 Cunfer, *Bison and People on the North American Great Plains*.
29 Roe, *The North American Buffalo*, 204.
30 Reed, "Writing About Buffalo," 11-16.
31 Flores, *American Serengeti*, 124.
32 Ibid., 126.
33 Ibid., 129.
34 Ibid., 26.
35 Mann, *1491*, 21, 66.
36 Calloway, *One Vast Winter Count*, 70.
37 Ibid., 71.
38 Ibid., 13, 14.
39 Diamond, *Guns, Germs, and Steel*, 100.
40 Ibid., 167.
41 Calloway, *One Vast Winter Count*, 16.
42 Ibid., 17.
43 Ibid., 18.
44 Ibid., 19.
45 Ibid., 21.
46 Mann, *1491*, 294.
47 Goldberger, "Beans for Prevention of Pellagra," 1314; Fenn, *Encounters at the Heart of the World*, 241.
48 Nichols, *American Indians in U.S. History*, 21.
49 Ibid., 22.
50 Mann, *1491*, 304.
51 Calloway, *One Vast Winter Count*, 55.
52 Ibid., 11.
53 Nichols, *American Indians in U.S. History*, 23.
54 Ibid., 24.
55 Ibid.
56 Ibid.
57 Ibid., 25.
58 Calloway, *One Vast Winter Count*, 39.
59 Ibid., 41, 42.
60 Mann, *1491*, 18.
61 In 1975, the Peruvian government adopted a Quechua standardized alphabet. Past spelling of Inca has been updated to Inka.

62 Ibid., 74.
63 Ibid., 367.
64 Stark, *How the West Won*, 239.

CHAPTER 3 – LOST SOULS IN REVELRY: COLLISION OF RACES (PAGES 31-46)

1 See Gaskill, *Between Two Worlds*, for the details of the first American Thanksgiving.
2 Gaustad, *The Religious History of America*, 5.
3 Stark, *How the West Won*, 151.
4 Mann, *1491*, 368, 369.
5 Ibid., 361.
6 Ibid., 370.
7 Gaustad, *The Religious History of America*, 17.
8 Ibid.
9 Ibid., 25.
10 Calloway, *One Vast Winter Count*, 27.
11 Diamond, *Guns, Germs, and Steel*, 266.
12 Nabokov, *Native American Testimony*, 13.
13 Berkhofer, Jr., *The White Man's Indian*, 6, 7.
14 Ibid., 9, 10.
15 Nabokov, *Native American Testimony*, 91.
16 Kelton, *Cherokee Medicine, Colonial Germs*, 29.
17 Fenn, *Encounters at the Heart of the World*, 29; Prem, "Disease Outbreaks in Central Mexico during the Sixteenth Century," 20-48.
18 Thornton, *Africa and Africans in Making the Atlantic World: 1400-1800*.
19 Stark, *How the West Won*, 228.
20 Butzer, "The Americas Before and After 1492," 345-368; Jahoda, *Trail of Tears*.
21 Stark, *How the West Won*, 27.
22 Ibid., 30, 229, 231.
23 Nichols, *American Indians in U.S. History*, 30.
24 Ibid., 31.
25 Beebe, *Junipero Serra*.
26 Mann, *1491*, 15.
27 Stark, *How the West Won*; Arkus, *The Archaeology of Warfare*; Chacon, *North American Indigenous Warfare*.
28 Gaustad, *The Religious History of America*, 19.
29 Butzer, "The Americas Before and After 1492," 348.
30 Calloway, *One Vast Winter Count*, 120.
31 Mann, *1491*, 146.
32 Gaustad, *The Religious History of America*, 18.
33 Fenn, *Encounters at the Heart of the World*, 29.
34 Calloway, *One Vast Winter Count*, 222.

CHAPTER 4 – CREATE HUMANITY AND CONQUER NATURE: THE BRITISH INVASION
(PAGES 47-62)

1. Berkhofer, Jr., *The White Man's Indian,* 115.
2. Gaustad, *The Religious History of America,* 33.
3. Meacham, *American Gospel,* 41.
4. Ibid., 46.
5. Gaustad, *The Religious History of America,* 37.
6. Ibid., 38.
7. Whitaker, *Good News from Virginia,* 14-17.
8. Gaustad, *The Religious History of America,* 38.
9. Richter, *Facing East from Indian Country,* 75.
10. Berkhofer, Jr., *The White Man's Indian,* 27.
11. Gaskill, *Between Two Worlds.*
12. Nichols, *American Indians in U.S. History,* 47.
13. Gaustad, *The Religious History of America,* 10.
14. Ibid., 11.
15. Meacham, *American Gospel,* 51.
16. Nichols, *American Indians in U.S. History,* 48.
17. Mann, *1491,* 47.
18. Ibid., 390.
19. Ibid.
20. Nabokov, *Native American Testimony,* 69.
21. Gaustad, *The Religious History of America,* 12.
22. Ibid., 113.
23. Mann, *1491,* 63.
24. Ibid., 69.
25. Nichols, *American Indians in U.S. History,* 51.
26. Gaustad, *The Religious History of America,* 43.
27. Nichols, *American Indians in U.S. History,* 63, 64. See also Hoefnagel and Close, "Eleazar Wheelock's Two Schools," in *Dartmouth College Library Bulletin,* November 1999.
28. Ibid., 51.
29. Ibid., 52.
30. Mann, *1491,* 61.
31. Calloway, *One Vast Winter Count,* 315.
32. Nichols, *American Indians in U.S. History,* 66.
33. Kelton, *Cherokee Medicine, Colonial Germs,* 45, 46.
34. Innis, *The Fur Trade in Canada,* 43-115; Fenn, *Encounters at the Heart of the World,* 84.
35. Nichols, *American Indians in U.S. History,* 67.
36. Calloway, *One Vast Winter Count,* 346.
37. Nichols, *American Indians in U.S. History,* 75.
38. Knox, *American State Papers,* 13-14.
39. Anderson, *Ethnic Cleansing and the Indian,* 107.

40 Calloway, *One Vast Winter Count*, 373.
41 Ibid.
42 Stark, *How the West Won*, 357; Trench, *The Road to Khartoum*.
43 Engerman, "Factor of Endowments, Institutions, and Differential Paths of Growth Among the New World Economies," 254; Ferguson, *Empire*.
44 Gray, *The Soul of the Marionette*.

CHAPTER 5 – AMERICAN EXODUS: SURVIVAL ON THE PLAINS (PAGES 63-77)

1 Calloway, *One Vast Winter Count*, 244.
2 Bass, *The Arapaho Way*, 73.
3 Calloway, *One Vast Winter Count*, 271.
4 Ibid., 2.
5 McDonnell, *Masters of Empire*.
6 mappinghistory/uoregon.edu/English/US/US05-00.html.
7 Erdoes, *American Indian Myths and Legends*, 500; Rydford, *Indian Place-Names*.
8 Fenn, *Encounters at the Heart of the World*, 18.
9 Erdoes, *American Indian Myths and Legends*, 502.
10 Calloway, *One Vast Winter Count*, 241.
11 Erdoes, *American Indian Myths and Legends*, 517.
12 Anderson, "Early Dakota Migration and Intertribal War. A Revision," 24.
13 Calloway, *One Vast Winter Count*, 240.
14 Fenn, *Encounters at the Heart of the World*, 34.
15 Ibid., 8.
16 Ibid.
17 Ibid., xiv.
18 Williams, *The Horse*.
19 Secoy, *Changing Military Patterns*, 105.
20 Calloway, *One Vast Winter Count*, 267.
21 Ibid., 268-270.
22 Flores, *American Serengeti*, 70.
23 Calloway, *One Vast Winter Count*, 270.
24 Ibid., 272.
25 Ibid., 298.
26 Ibid., 304.
27 Fenn, *Encounters at the Heart of the World*, 7.
28 Gopnick, *The Gardener and the Carpenter*.
29 Utley, *The Lance and The Shield*, 11, 15.
30 Fenn, *Encounters at the Heart of the World*, 108-109; Bowers, *Mandan Social and Ceremonial Organization*, 94-95; Lowie, *Notes on the Social Organizations & Customs of the Mandan, Hidatsa, & Crow Indians*.
31 Linderman, *American*, 55.

32 Linderman, *Red Mother*, 130.
33 Fenn, *Encounters at the Heart of the World*, 112.
32 Ibid., 12.

CHAPTER 6 – THE BLIND HEALING THE BLIND: WHITE MEDICINE MEN (PAGES 79-98)

1 Bliss, *William Osler*.
2 Black, *War Against the Weak*.
3 Mappinghistory/uoregon.edu/English/US/US05-00.html.
4 CDC stats reported by Achenback, *The Washington Post*, "To Your Health," 4/20/16.
5 *AMA Morning Rounds*, reported May 4, 2016.
6 Thesunmagazine.org/issues/481, "The Miracle in Front of You" by Janice Lynch Schuster, January 2016, Issue 48.
7 Franco-Paredes, "The Spanish Royal Philanthropic Expedition to bring Smallpox Vaccination to the New World and Asia in the 19th Century," 1285-1289.
8 Fisher, *Edward Jenner 1749-1823*.
9 Brown, *Penicillin Man*.
10 Kelton, *Cherokee Medicine, Colonial Germs*, 62.
11 Garrison, *History of Medicine*.
12 Ibid., 97.
13 Adams, *The Genuine Works of Hippocrates*, 17.
14 Siegel, *Galen on the Affected Parts*.
15 Brock, *Greek Medicine*, 207.
16 Ibid.
17 Nutton, *Ancient Medicine*, 226-227.
18 See Paracelsus: German-Swiss Physician at www.Britannica.com.
19 Paracelsus, "Letter From Paracelsus to Erasmus," 142.
20 Pagel, *Paracelsus*, 19.
21 Ibid.
22 Webster, *Paracelsus*.
23 Lemesurier, *Nostradamus*, 48-49.
24 Wilson, *Nostradamus*.
25 Lemesurier, *Nostradamus*, 150-152.
26 Gregory, *Harvey's Heart*.
27 Aldersey-Williams, *In Search of Sir Thomas Browne*.
28 Siraisi, "Medicine, 1450-1620, and the History of Science," 491-514.
29 Hinrichs, *Chinese Medicine and Healing*.
30 Jackson, *The Oxford Handbook of the History of Medicine*.
31 Magner, *A History of Medicine*, 91.
32 Warner, *The Therapeutic Perspective*, 179.
33 Marchant, *Cure*.
34 Willey, *Health of the Seventh Cavalry*, 45.

35 Ibid., 74.
36 Trostle, "Early Works in Anthropology and Epidemiology: From Social Medicine to the Germ Theory, 1840-1920," 39; Bollet, *Civil War Medicine*, 64-70.
37 Randall, *The King and Queen of Malibu*.
38 Wiley, *Health of the Seventh Cavalry*, 73.
39 Barnes, *The Medical and Surgical History of the War of the Rebellion, 1861-1865*, 887.
40 Wiley, *Health of the Seventh Cavalry*, 47; Barnes, *The Medical and Surgical History of the War of the Rebellion, 1861-1865*.
41 Williams, *The Age of Miracles*, 71.
42 Wiley, *Health of the Seventh Cavalry*, 52.
43 Robson, *The Engines of Hippocrates*.
44 Crelin, *Herbal Medicine Past and Present*.
45 Nunn, *Ancient Egyptian Medicine*.
46 Vickers, "Herbal Medicine," 1050-1053.
47 De la Rosa, *Fruit and Vegetable Phytochemicals*.
48 Headrick, *The Tools of Empire*, 71.
49 NYBG.com.
50 Glasser, Matthew F., et al., "A Multi-Modal parcellation of Human Cerebral Cortex," *Nature*, July 20, 2016, http://dx.doi.org/10.1038/nature18933.
51 Nichols, *American Indians in U.S. History*, 29.
52 Bynum, *Spitting Blood*.
53 Ibid.
54 Dowdle, "Influenza Pandemic Periodicity, Virus Recycling, and the Art of Risk Assessment," 34-39.
55 Henige, *Numbers from Nowhere*.
56 Ellenberg, *How Not to Be Wrong*.
57 Archives.gov, under American Indians in the Federal Decennial Census, 1790-1930.
58 Kelton, *Cherokee Medicine, Colonial Germs*, 212.
59 Dippie, *The Vanishing American*, xvii.
60 Crosby, *The Columbian Exchange*.
61 Jennings, *The Invasion of America*.
62 Dippie, *The Vanishing American*, xv.

CHAPTER 7 – WEAPONS OF MASS DESTRUCTION: INFECTIOUS DISEASE
(PAGES 99-124)

1 Mann, *1491*, 112.
2 Ibid., 370.
3 Kelton, *Cherokee Medicine, Colonial Germs*, 39.
4 Ibid., 46.
5 Mann, *1491*, 117.
6 Kelton, *Cherokee Medicine, Colonial Germs*, 18.
7 Nichols, *American Indians in U.S. History*, 40.

8. Crosby, "Virgin Soil Epidemics as a Factor in Aboriginal Depopulation in America," 289-299; Crosby, *Ecological Imperialism*.
9. Diamond, *Guns, Germs, and Steel*, 207.
10. Mann, *1491*, 100.
11. Kelton, *Cherokee Medicine, Colonial Germs*, 27.
12. Mann, *1491*, 100.
13. Francisco de Aguilar, "Eight Jornada," in Schwartz, ed., *Victors and Vanquished*, 198.
14. Kelton, *Cherokee Medicine, Colonial Germs*, 5; Winthrop to D'Ewes, July 21, 1634, in *Winthrop Papers*, 3:171-172.
15. Archdale, "A New Description of that Fertile and Pleasant Province of Carolina," in Salley, ed., *Narratives of Early Carolina*, 285.
16. Stark, *How the West Won*, 336.
17. Binnema, *Common and Contested Ground*, 124, 128.
18. Calloway, *One Vast Winter Count*, 422.
19. Kelton, *Cherokee Medicine, Colonial Germs*, 20.
20. Fenn, *Encounters at the Heart of the World*, 56.
21. Ibid., 61; Jackson, *Voyages of the Steamboat Yellow Stone*, 63.
22. Fenn, *Encounters at the Heart of the World*, 324.
23. Pearson, "Lewis Cass and the Politics of Disease," 21.
24. Ibid.
25. Fenn, *Encounters at the Heart of the World*, 426.
26. Linderman, *Red Mother*, 41.
27. Plain, "John James Audubon Out West," 16.
28. Ibid., 18.
29. Kelton, *Cherokee Medicine, Colonial Germs*, 56.
30. Crosby, *Ecological Imperialism*, 196.
31. Diamond, *Guns, Germs, and Steel*, 373-374.
32. Mann, *1491*, 61.
33. Kelton, *Cherokee Medicine, Colonial Germs*, 9.
34. Fenner, *Smallpox and Its Eradication*, 4.
35. Stelwagon, *Treatise on Diseases of the Skin*, 449-463.
36. Fenner, *Smallpox and Its Eradication*, 115-116; Fenn, *Encounters at the Heart of the World*, 154.
37. Martin, *Keepers of the Game*, 53.
38. McLoughlin, *Cherokee Renascence in the New Republic*, 17, 18.
39. Adair, *History of the American Indians*, 252-253.
40. Staudohar, "Food, Rest, and Happiness," 48-57.
41. Amherst to Bouquet, July 7, 1763, in Stevens et al. eds, *Bouquet Papers*, 6:299-300.
42. Bouquet to Amherst, July 13, 1763, in ibid., ser. 21634, 215.
43. Postscript signed J.A., [Amherst to Bouquet, July 16, 1763], in ibid., 6:315.
44. Fenn. "Biological Warfare in Eighteenth-Century North America," 1552-1580, quote 1553.
45. Behbehani, "The Smallpox Story: Life and Death of an Old Disease." 405-509.
46. Henderson, *Smallpox*.
47. Fenn, *Pox Americana*.
48. Coss, *The Fever of 1721*.

49 Riedel, "Edward Jenner and the History of Smallpox and Vaccination," 21-25.
50 Fisher, *Edward Jenner.*
51 Cash, *Dr. Benjamin Waterhouse.*
52 "An Account of the First Festival of the Royal Jennerian Society for the Extermination of the Small-Pox, on Thursday, May 17, 1803," *Gentleman's Magazine,* May 1803, 463.
53 Baron, *Life of Edward Jenner,* 330-331.
54 Kelton, *Cherokee Medicine, Colonial Germs,* 176.
55 Mann, *1491,* 108, 109.
56 Henderson, *Smallpox.*
57 Robbins, *Pathologic Basis of Disease.*
58 Diamond, *Guns, Germs, and Steel,* 357.
59 Reported by Nicole Skinner in *Nature News,* August 20, 2014, "Seals Brought TB to Americas," Nature.com.
60 Rieder, "Tuberculosis among American Indians of the Contiguous United States," 653-657.
61 Brock, *Robert Koch.*
62 Staudohar, "Food, Rest, and Happiness," 48-57.
63 Rutgers Global Tuberculosis Institute, www.njms.rutgers.edu.
64 Erdoes, *American Indian Myths and Legends,* 513.
65 Hempel, *The Strange Case of the Broad Street Pump.*
66 Levinson, *Review of Medical Microbiology and Immunology.*
67 Wain, "Typhoid Fever," 1136-1145.
68 Jedckie, *Scientific American: Great Inventions of the 20th Century.* PBS on September 9, 2014 aired "The Development of Chlorine" on the story of John Leal developing public water chlorination. Available online at pbs.org.
69 Baker, *The Quest for Pure Water,* 336.
70 McKenzie, "Charles McKenzie's Narratives," 270.
71 Henry, *The Journal of Alexander Henry the Younger, 1799-1814,* 233.
72 Atkinson, *Pertussis Epidemiology and Prevention of Vaccine-Preventable Disease,* 215-230.
73 Baker, "Childhood Vaccine Development," 347-356.
74 Cherry, "Pertussis Vaccine Encephalopathy," 1679-1680.
75 Perry, "The Clinical Significance of Measles," 4-16.
76 Griffin, *Measles.*
77 Offit, *Vaccinated.*
78 Fitzpatrick, *Dermatology in General Medicine,* 1678.
79 Ibid.
80 Taleb, *The Black Swan.*
81 Henige, *Numbers from Nowhere.*

CHAPTER 8 – THE WORLD IS NOT ENOUGH: CULTURAL LITERACY FOR RELIGION (PAGES 127-138)

1 Meacham, *Franklin and Winston.*
2 Hannan, *Inventing Freedom.*

3. See "Churchill Still Stands Alone" by Boris Johnson in *The Wall Street Journal*, November 7, 2014.
4. Jenkins, *Churchill*, 664.
5. Wacker, *America's Pastor*.
6. Kruse, *One Nation Under God*; and Ambrose, *Eisenhower*.
7. Kruse, *One Nation Under God*.
8. Stark, *The Triumph of Faith*.
9. Bret Stephens, "In Defense of Christendom," *The Wall Street Journal*, October 19, 2015.
10. Cimino, *Atheist Awakening*. See also "Secular and Proud of It" by Naomi Schaefer Riley in the January 4, 2015, *The Wall Street Journal*.
11. *America's Changing Religious Landscape, Christians Decline Sharply as Share of Population; Unaffiliated and Other Faiths Continue to Grow*. Pew Research Center: Religion & Public Life. Pewforum.org, May 12, 2015.
12. Survey was conducted June 4 through September 30, 2014, of 35,071 adults. See Jones, *The End of White Christian America* for the latest trends of Christianity in America.
13. Cimino, *Athiest Awakening*.
14. Ibid.
15. Sacks, *Not in God's Name*.
16. Prothero, *God is Not One*.
17. Khalidi, *Islamic Historiography*, 279.
18. Hartwell, "Historical Analogism, Public Policy, and Social Science in Eleventh- and Twelfth-Century China," 691.
19. Gandhi, *Gandhi, An Autobiography*.
20. De Bary, *The Buddhist Tradition in India, China & Japan*.
21. Yao, *An Introduction to Confucianism*.
22. Kohn, *Introducing Daoism*.
23. Walsh, *The World of Shamanism*.
24. Cleary, *The Essential Koran*; Esposito, *What Everyone Needs to Know about Islam*.
25. Harney, "How Do Sunni and Shia Islam Differ?"
26. Atwood, *Handbook of Denominations in the United States*.
27. Collins, *The Language of God*, 41.
28. Taleb, *The Black Swan*, 291.

CHAPTER 9 – THE SPIRIT OF THE WEST: NATIVE AMERICAN RELIGION AND ITS CHRONICLERS (PAGES 139-165)

1. Twiss, *One Church, Many Tribes*, 84.
2. Linderman, *American*, 79.
3. Francis, *Ancient Visions*.
4. Flores, *Visions of the Big Sky*, 24.
5. Catlin, *North American Indians*, Vol. I, 102.
6. Peterson, *Charles M. Russell: Photographing the Legend*.

7 Debelius, *The Spirit World*, 14.
8 Eisler, *The Red Man's Bones*, 326.
9 For Catlin works at the Smithsonian see www.americanart.si.edu.
10 Walker, *Lakota Belief and Ritual*, xiii.
11 Ibid.
12 Williams, *The Soul of the Red Man*, 45-46.
13 Ibid., 47-48.
14 Walker, *Lakota Belief and Ritual*, 140, 141.
15 Peterson, *The Call of the Mountains*, 15.
16 Ibid., 16.
17 McClintock, *The Old North Trail*, 168.
18 Ibid., 170.
19 Ibid., 512.
20 Peterson, *The Call of the Mountains*, 18; McClintock, "Blackfoot Warrior Societies."
21 Mails, *The Mystic Warriors of the Plains*, 75, 76.
22 Neihardt, *Black Elk Speaks*.
23 Linden, *John Neihardt and "Black Elk Speaks."* Also, Jackson, *Black Elk*.
24 Holler, *Black Elk Reader*.
25 Debelius, *The Spirit World*, 10.
26 Deloria, Jr., *God is Red*, 78.
27 Mails, *The Mystic Warriors of the Plains*, 90.
28 Deloria, Jr., *God is Red*, 141.
29 Ibid.
30 Momaday, *The Way to Rainy Mountain*, 17.
31 Dorsey, *The Mythology of the Wichita*, 25-29.
32 Grinnell, *Pawnee, Blackfoot, and Cheyenne*, 121-124.
33 Debelius, *The Spirit World*, 19.
34 Ibid.
35 Underhill, *Papago Woman*, 3.
36 Standing Bear, *Land of the Spotted Eagle*, 248.
37 Seton, *The Gospel of the Red Man*, 58, 59.
38 Woodley, *Shalom and the Community of Creation*, 121.
39 Ibid., 124.
40 Debelius, *The Spirit World*, 66.
41 Ibid., 68.
42 Woodley, *Shalom and the Community of Creation*, 77.
43 Twiss, *One Church, Many Tribes*, 99.
44 Treat, *Native and Christian*, 54, 55.
45 Starkloff, *The People of the Center*, 88.
46 Twiss, *One Church, Many Tribes*, 155.
47 Wright, *Stolen Continents*, 207.
48 Malcomson, *One Drop of Blood*, 15.
49 Debelius, *The Spirit World*, 68.
50 Linderman, *American*, 78.

51 Dodge, *Thirty-Three Years Among Our Wild Indians*, 177, 178.
52 Debelius, *The Spirit World*, 11.
53 Deloria, Jr., *God is Red*, biographical information from back cover.
54 Ibid., 171.
55 Armstrong, *I Have Spoken*, 94, 95.
56 Deloria, Jr., *God is Red*, 181.
57 Armstrong, *I Have Spoken*, 49.
58 Twiss, *One Church, Many Tribes*, 85.
59 Cox, *The Secular City*.
60 Deloria, Jr., *God is Red*, 195.
61 Armstrong, *I Have Spoken*, 95.
62 Wilcomb, *The Indian and the White Man*, 209-214.
63 Twiss, *One Church, Many Tribes*, 9.

CHAPTER 10 – SMOKING TO THE SPIRIT OF THE BUFFALO: PLAINS INDIAN CEREMONIES AND RITUALS (PAGES 167-190)

1 Deloria, Jr., *God is Red*, 280.
2 Woodley, *Shalom and the Community of Creation*, 23.
3 Walker, *Lakota Belief and Ritual*, 41.
4 Ibid., 44.
5 Ibid., 45.
6 Ibid., 67.
7 Ibid., 182.
8 Debelius, *The Spirit World*, 160.
9 Ibid., 155.
10 Fenn, *Encounters at the Heart of the World*, 99.
11 Ibid.
12 Debelius, *The Spirit World*, 71.
13 Mails, *The Mystic Warriors of the Plains*, 94.
14 Linderman, *American*, 43.
15 Wildschut, *Crow Indian Medicine Bundles*, 16, 17.
16 Debelius, *The Spirit World*, 125.
17 Utley, *The Lance and The Shield*, 28.
18 Debelius, *The Spirit World*, 124.
19 Walker, *Lakota Belief and Ritual*, 105.
20 Debelius, *The Spirit World*, 16.
21 Utley, *The Lance and The Shield*, 28.
22 Grinnell, *Blackfoot Lodge Tales*.
23 Woodley, *Shalom and the Community of Creation*, 91.
24 Ibid., 90.
25 Walker, *Lakota Belief and Ritual*, 100.

26 Ibid., 46.
27 Debelius, *The Spirit World*, 104.
28 Ibid., 105.
29 Wildschut, *Crow Indian Medicine Bundles*, 143; Densmore, *Teton Sioux Music*, 195, 266.
30 McClintock, *The Old North Trail*, Appendices.
31 Catlin, *North American Indians*, Vol. 1, 39.
32 Walker, *Lakota Belief and Ritual*, 92.
33 Debelius, *The Spirit World*, 135.
34 Ibid., 123.
35 Bowers, *Mandan Social and Ceremonial Organization*, 337.
36 Point, *Wilderness Kingdom, Indian Life in the Rocky Mountains*, 16.
37 Mails, *The Mystic Warriors of the Plains*, 145.
38 Ibid., 146; Greene, *American Carnage*.
39 Gernet, "North American Indigenous Nicotiana Use and Tobacco Shamanism," 179-180.
40 Fenn, *Encounters at the Heart of the World*, 110.
41 Ibid., 111.
42 Walker, *Lakota Belief and Ritual*, 82.
43 Fenn, *Encounters at the Heart of the World*, 37.
44 Twiss, *One Church, Many Tribes*, 133.
45 Ibid., 102.

CHAPTER 11 – THE LANGUAGE OF GOD: INDIAN MYTHS, LEGENDS, AND THEIR CHRONICLERS (PAGES 191-220)

1 Spude, "Writing the West," 2.
2 Peterson, *The Call of the Mountains*, 2-11.
3 Ibid., 3.
4 Ibid., 10.
5 Grinnell, *Blackfoot Lodge Tales*, xi.
6 Ibid., ix.
7 Ibid., x.
8 Ibid., xii.
9 Ibid., 156.
10 Ibid., 81.
11 Ibid., 82.
12 Ibid.
13 Peterson, *Charles M. Russell: Photographing the Legend* and *Charles M. Russell: Legacy*.
14 Peterson, *Charles M. Russell: Photographing the Legend*, 125.
15 Linderman, *Indian Why Stories*.
16 Ibid.
17 Ibid., vii-x.
18 Ibid., 17-23.

19 Linderman, *Indian Old-Man Stories*, vii-viii.
20 Ibid., xii.
21 Ibid., xix-xx.
22 Peterson, *The Call of the Mountains*; Linderman, *American*.
23 Linderman, *Blackfeet Indians*.
24 Linderman, *American*.
25 Ibid.
26 Ibid., 26
27 Peterson, *The Call of the Mountains*.
28 Edmonds, *Voices of the Winds*.
29 Ibid., 204.
30 Ibid., 208, 209.
31 Ibid., 212, 213.
32 Ibid., 216-218.
33 Ibid., 221-222.
34 Ibid., 223, 224; Grinnell, *Blackfoot Lodge Tales*, 125.
35 Edmonds, *Voices of the Winds*, 228-230.
36 Erdoes, *American Indian Myths and Legends*, 470.
37 Ibid., xv.

CHAPTER 12 – THE WAY: HISTORICAL CHRISTIANITY TO THE DARK AGES (PAGES 221-243)

1 Ehrman, *Jesus, Interrupted*, 4.
2 Lewis, *What Went Wrong?*; Taagepera, "Size and Duration of Empire"; Saggs, *Civilization Before Greece and Rome*.
3 Stark, *How the West Won*, 27.
4 Ibid., 24.
5 Cochrane, *Christianity and Classical Culture*, 342, 390, 417.
6 Ehrman, *Lost Christianities*.
7 Ehrman, *Misquoting Jesus*, 19.
8 Rand, *The 613*.
9 Ehrman, *Did Jesus Exist?*
10 Martin, *Seven Last Words*.
11 Ehrman, *Jesus, Interrupted*, 87
12 Ibid., 156.
13 Ibid.
14 Nouwen, *Bread for the Journey*, Sept. 14 entry; for a memoir of Nouwen see Ford, *Wounded Prophet*.
15 Olson, *The Story of Christian Theology*, 37.
16 Mann, *1491*.
17 Ehrman, *Jesus, Interrupted*, 183.

18. Lewis, *The Problem of Pain*, 105; for a biography of Lewis see Wilson, *C. S. Lewis*.
19. Lewis, *The Screwtape Letters*, 34.
20. Ehrman, *Misquoting Jesus*, 42.
21. Hezser, *Literacy in Roman Palestine*.
22. Ehrman, *Misquoting Jesus*.
23. Ehrman, *Did Jesus Exist?*
24. Campbell, *The Masks of God*.
25. Ehrman, *Did Jesus Exist?*
26. Boin, *Coming Out Christian in the Roman World*.
27. Ehrman, *Did Jesus Exist?*
28. Olson, *The Story of Christian Theology*, 54.
29. Ehrman, *Lost Christianities*, 103-108.
30. Olson, *The Story of Christian Theology*, 68-78.
31. Stark, *How the West Won*, 39; Pearcey, *Total Truth*.
32. Olson, *The Story of Christian Theology*, 63.
33. Ibid., 95.
34. Ibid., 96.
35. Ibid., 135.
36. Ibid., 138; O'Donnell, *Pagans*.
37. Stark, *How the West Won*, 55.
38. Olson, *The Story of Christian Theology*, 138.
39. Ibid., 147.
40. Manchester, *A World Lit Only by Fire*, 7.
41. Olson, *The Story of Christian Theology*, 255.
42. Ibid., 274.
43. Stark, *How the West Won*, 120.
44. Olson, *The Story of Christian Theology*, 269.
45. Osborne, *Civilization*, 163.
46. Stark, *How the West Won*, 69.
47. Judson, *The Habsburg Empire*.
48. Wilson, *Heart of Europe*.
49. Stark, *How the West Won*, 292.
50. Olson, *The Story of Christian Theology*, 306.
51. Manchester, *A World Lit Only by Fire*, 21.
52. Ibid., 22.
53. Stark, *How the West Won*, 77; Johnson, *Art*, 190.
54. Stark, *God's Battalions*, 3, 4.
55. Stark, *How the West Won*, 102.
56. Riley-Smith, *The First Crusades, 1095-1131*, 37-38.
57. Stark, *Acts of Faith*.
58. Turner, *Collective Behavior*.
59. Olson, *The Story of Christian Theology*, 331.
60. Ibid., 346.
61. Aberth, *The Black Death*.

62 Ibid.
63 Stark, *How the West Won*, 150.
64 Navigators, *James*, 102.

CHAPTER 13 – THE FAITH OF OUR FATHERS: RELIGION IN AMERICA (PAGES 245-268)

1 Olson, *The Story of Christian Theology*, 348.
2 Manchester, *A World Lit Only by Fire*, 45.
3 Woodley, *Shalom and the Community of Creation*, 105.
4 Berkhofer, Jr., *The White Man's Indian*, 37.
5 Ibid.
6 Ibid., 38.
7 Stark, *The Victory of Reason*.
8 Haskins, *The Rise of Universities*, 3.
9 Stark, *How the West Won*, 163.
10 Ibid., 170.
11 Olson, *The Story of Christian Theology*, 363.
12 Manchester, *A World Lit Only by Fire*, 37.
13 Ibid., 131.
14 Luther, *Works*, 84.
15 Olson, *The Story of Christian Theology*, 370.
16 Monro, *The Paper Trail*.
17 Holborn, "Printing and the Growth of the Protestant Movement in Germany from 1517 to 1524," 129; Edwards, *Printing, Propaganda, and Martin Luther*; Grendler, "The Universities of the Renaissance and Reformation," 19.
18 Stark, *How the West Won*, 275.
19 Olson, *The Story of Christian Theology*, 370.
20 Martin Luther quoted in George, *Theology of the Reformers*, 77.
21 Hendrix, *Martin Luther*; Pettegee, *Brand Luther*.
22 Deloria, Jr., *God is Red*, 191.
23 Pearcey, *Total Truth*, 381.
24 Baylor, *The German Reformation and the Peasants' War*.
25 Stark, *How the West Won*, 277.
26 Greengrass, *Christendom Destroyed*.
27 Olson, *The Story of Christian Theology*, 403.
28 Ibid., 188.
29 Spurgeon, *Spurgeon's Calvinism*.
30 Manchester, *A World Lit Only by Fire*, 190.
31 Ibid., 191.
32 Olson, *The Story of Christian Theology*, 469.
33 Manchester, *A World Lit Only by Fire*, 211-213.

34. Gaustad, *The Religious History of America*, 85.
35. Ibid., 86.
36. Ibid., 88.
37. For an excellent overview of religion in America see *God In America: How Religious Liberty Shaped America* (2010) by PBS as part of their American Experience/Frontline series available on DVD.
38. Gaustad, *The Religious History of America*, 64.
39. Ibid., 65.
40. Ibid., 83.
41. Mar, *Witches in America*.
42. Noll, *The Scandal of the Evangelical Mind*.
43. Gaustad, *The Religious History of America*, 59.
44. Olson, *The Story of Christian Theology*, 506.
45. Gaustad, *The Religious History of America*, 61.
46. Olson, *The Story of Christian Theology*, 464.
47. Pearcey, *Total Truth*, 261.
48. Ibid., 261.
49. Thorsen, *The Wesleyan Quadrilateral*.
50. Pearcey, *Total Truth*, 267; Kidd, *George Whitefield*.
51. Ibid., 268.
52. Ibid.
53. Finke, *The Churching of America, 1776-1990*, 50.
54. Pearcey, *Total Truth*, 268.
55. Prothero, *American Jesus*, 44.
56. See "America's Spiritual Founding Father" by Barton Swaim in *The Wall Street Journal*, February 13, 2015.
57. Pearcey, *Total Truth*, 283.
58. Prothero, *American Jesus*, 3.
59. Pearcey, *Total Truth*, 289.
60. Ibid., 258.
61. Prothero, *American Jesus*, 6.
62. Ibid., 49.
63. Wuthnow, *Rough Country*.
64. Pearcey, *Total Truth*, 263.
65. Finke, *The Churching of America, 1776-1990*, 33.
66. Pearcey, *Total Truth*, 334.
67. Ibid., 335.
68. Ibid.
69. Rotundo, *American Manhood*, 229.
70. Ibid., 229, 254.
71. Pearcey, *Total Truth*, 338.
72. Turner, *Without God, Without Creed*, 75, 76.
73. Stoll, *Inherit the Holy Mountain*.
74. Marty, *The Modern Schism*, 98, 135, 130.

75 Pearcey, *Total Truth*, 322.
76 Marty, *The Modern Schism*, 129, 130.
77 Pearcey, *Total Truth*, 323.
78 Meacham, *American Gospel*, 16.
79 For the full interview with Raymond Barfield see "The Miracle in Front of You: Raymond Barfield on Practicing Medicine with Compassion," by Janice Lynch Schuster in *The Sun*, January 2016, Issue 481, online at: thesunmagazine.org.

CHAPTER 14 – A REVOLUTION: THE ENLIGHTENMENT, SCIENTIFIC REVOLUTION, AND THE ROMANTIC MOVEMENT (PAGES 271-290)

1 Meacham, *Thomas Jefferson*, 259.
2 Ibid., 260.
3 Martin, *Leonardo*.
4 Pearcey, *Total Truth*, 39.
5 Olson, *The Story of Christian Theology*, 523.
6 Rodis-Lewis, *Descartes' Life and the Development of His Philosophy*, 22.
7 Cottingham, *The Philosophical Writings of Descartes*.
8 Blom, *Descartes*.
9 Descartes, *Meditations on First Philosophy*.
10 McCullough, *John Adams*, 96.
11 Olson, *Total Truth*, 525.
12 Zuckert, *The Natural Rights Republic*, 73-85.
13 Wills, *Inventing America*.
14 Waldron, *God, Locke and Equality*.
15 Goodwin, *Benjamin Franklin in London*; Olson, *The Story of Christian Theology*, 529.
16 Olson, *The Story of Christian Theology*, 529.
17 Hefelbower, *The Relation of John Locke to English Deism*, 117.
18 Byrne, *Religion and the Enlightenment*, 5-10.
19 Olson, *The Story of Christian Theology*, 532.
20 Aristotle, *Rhetoric*.
21 Wooten, *The Invention of Science*.
22 Aldersey-Williams, *In Search of Sir Thomas Browne*.
23 See Nancy Pearcey, "The Birth of Modern Science," *Bible-Science Newsletter*, October 1982; Pearcey, "How Christianity Gave Rise to the Modern Scientific Outlook," *Bible-Science Newsletter*, January 1989; Pearcey, *Soul of Science*.
24 Manchester, *A World Lit Only by Fire*, 89.
25 Ibid., 90.
26 Sharatt, *Galileo*, 17, 213.
27 Lanford, *Galileo, Science and the Church*, 56, 57.
28 Finocchiaro, *Defending Copernicus and Galileo*.
29 Manchester, *A World Lit Only by Fire*, 117.

30 Ibid., 117.
31 Rublack, *The Astronomer and the Witch*.
32 Gaukroger, *Francis Bacon and the Transformation of Early-Modern Philosophy*.
33 Pearcey, *Total Truth*, 298.
34 Whitney, *Francis Bacon and Modernity*.
35 Pearcey, *Total Truth*, 299.
36 Urbach, *Francis Bacon's Philosophy of Science*.
37 Meacham, *Thomas Jefferson*, 260.
38 Grant, *The Foundations of Modern Science in the Middle Ages*.
39 Christianson, *Isaac Newton and the Scientific Revolution*.
40 See "Christianity and the Rise of Western Science" by Peter Harrison in *Religion and Ethics*, May 8, 2012, at www.abc.net.au.
41 Stark, *How the West Won*, 305.
42 Ibid., 309.
43 Westfall, *Isaac Newton*.
44 Ibid.
45 Brewster, *The Life of Isaac Newton;* see also "Isaac Newton was a Genius, but Even He Lost Millions in the Stock Market" by Elena Holodny in *Business Insider,* January 21, 2016, at www.businessinsider.com.au.
46 Westfall, *Isaac Newton*.
47 Ibid.
48 See www.westminster-abbey.org and search Sir Isaac Newton.
49 Pearcey, *Total Truth*, 330.
50 Ibid., 332.
51 Ibid., 102.
52 Ferber, *Romanticism*.
53 Rousseau, *On the Social Contract, with the Geneva Manuscript and Political Economy,* 78.
54 Ellingson, *The Myth of the Noble Savage*.
55 Johansen, *Forgotten Founders*.
56 Moore, "Reappraising Dickens' Noble Savage," 236-243.
57 Damrosch, *Jean-Jacques Rousseau*.
58 Durant, *Rousseau and Revolution*.

CHAPTER 15 – ALL MEN ARE CREATED EQUAL: THOMAS JEFFERSON AND HIS LEGACY (PAGES 291-312)

1 Bordewich, *The First Congress*.
2 Jefferson, *The Jefferson Bible,* 27. Essay by Harry R. Rubenstein and Barbara Clark Smith.
3 Prothero, *American Jesus,* 21.
4 Onuf, *The Mind of Thomas Jefferson*.
5 Prothero, *American Jesus,* 22.
6 Adams, *Jefferson's Extracts from the Gospels,* 333, 345, 347.

7 Jefferson, *The Jefferson Bible*, 25. Essay by Harry R. Rubenstein and Barbara Clark Smith.
8 Adams, *Jefferson's Extracts from the Gospels*, 369.
9 Prothero, *American Jesus*, 25.
10 Adams, *Jefferson's Extracts from the Gospels*, 12.
11 Jefferson, *The Jefferson Bible*, 31. Essay by Harry R. Rubenstein and Barbara Clark Smith.
12 Adams, *Jefferson's Extracts from the Gospels*, 17.
13 Jefferson, *The Jefferson Bible*, 13. Essay by Harry R. Rubenstein and Barbara Clark Smith.
14 Adams, *Jefferson's Extracts from the Gospels*, 385, 406.
15 Jefferson, *The Jefferson Bible*, 6. Essay by Harry R. Rubenstein and Barbara Clark Smith.
16 Prothero, *American Jesus*, 32, 33.
17 Ibid., 42.
18 Meacham, *Thomas Jefferson*, xxi.
19 Ibid., xix.
20 Prothero, *American Jesus*, 19
21 Ibid.
22 Ibid., 20.
23 Adams, *Jefferson's Extracts from the Gospels*, 360.
24 Gordon-Reed, *The Hemingses of Monticello*.
25 Ambrose, *To America*, 14.
26 Ibid., 8; Malone, *Jefferson the Virginian*.
27 Wills, *Lincoln at Gettysburg*.
28 McCullough, *John Adams*, 112.
29 Ibid., 115.
30 Meacham, *Thomas Jefferson*, 48.
31 Ibid., 48.
32 Davis, *The Problem of Slavery in the Age of Revolution, 1770-1823*.
33 Meacham, *Thomas Jefferson*, 102.
34 Ibid., 104.
35 McCullough, *John Adams*, 121.
36 Meacham, *American Gospel*, 29.
37 Meacham, *Thomas Jefferson*, 102.
38 Ibid., 107.
39 Ibid., 108.
40 Berkhofer, Jr., *The White Man's Indian*, 29.
41 Meacham, *Thomas Jefferson*, 111.
42 Ibid., 123.
43 Ibid., 7.
44 Jefferson, *The Jefferson Bible*, 15. Essay by Harry R. Rubenstein and Barbara Clark Smith.
45 Ibid., 20.
46 Baptist, *The Half Has Never Been Told*.
47 Hertzke, ed., *Religious Freedom in America*, 58.
48 Ibid., 59.
49 Wiencek, *An Imperfect God*.
50 Fraser, *The Washingtons*; Ellis, *His Excellency*.

51 Meacham, *Thomas Jefferson*, 124.
52 Guyatt, *Bind Us Apart*.
53 Meacham, *Thomas Jefferson*, 100.
54 Prothero, *American Jesus*, 20.
55 McCullough, *John Adams*, 321.
56 Nabokov, *Native American Testimony*, 119.
57 Other important documents were *The Federalist* papers that were published in 1787 and 1788 authored by Alexander Hamilton, James Madison, and John Jay. They were an authoritative defense of our Constitution. See Levinson, *An Argument Open to All*.
58 Gordon-Reed, *"Most Blessed of the Patriarchs."*
59 Meacham, *Thomas Jefferson*, 218.
60 Guyatt, *Bind Us Apart*.
61 Prothero, *American Jesus*, 21.
62 Meacham, *Thomas Jefferson*, 368.
63 Anderson, *Ethnic Cleansing and the Indian*, 113.
64 Ibid., 117.
65 Ibid., 120.
66 Meacham, *Thomas Jefferson*, 371.
67 Ibid.

CHAPTER 16 – FATHER OF THE AMERICAN WEST: THOMAS JEFFERSON AND THE CORPS OF DISCOVERY (PAGES 313-330)

1 Roberts, *Napoleon*.
2 Bell, *Napoleon*.
3 Gueniffey, *Bonaparte*.
4 Meacham, *Thomas Jefferson*, 387.
5 Ibid., 386.
6 Ibid., 384.
7 Ibid., 387.
8 Sehat, *The Jefferson Rule;* Burstein, *Democracy's Muse*.
9 Bothwell, *Your Country, My Country*.
10 Meacham, *Thomas Jefferson*, 388.
11 Ibid., 392.
12 Ambrose, *Undaunted Courage;* Ronda, *Lewis & Clark among the Indians*.
13 Ambrose, *Undaunted Courage*, 33.
14 Jackson, *Letters of the Lewis and Clark Expedition*, 587, 588.
15 Ambrose, *Undaunted Courage*, 51.
16 Jordan, *White over Black*, 27, 453.
17 Ambrose, *Undaunted Courage*, 59.
18 Ibid., 88.
19 Ibid., 89.

20 Jackson, *Letters of the Lewis and Clark Expedition*, Vol. I, 50.
21 Taylor, *American Colonies*, 33.
22 Ronda, *Lewis & Clark among the Indians*, 3.
23 "The American Indian: Descended from the Ten Lost Tribes?" Part II, Dr. Yitzchok Levine, www.Jewishpress.com.
24 Jackson, *Letters of the Lewis and Clark Expedition*, Vol. I, 54.
25 Ambrose, *Undaunted Courage*, 95.
26 Ibid., 98.
27 Foley, *Wilderness Journey*.
28 Buckley, *William Clark*.
29 Brandt, *The Journals of Lewis and Clark*.
30 Ambrose, *Undaunted Courage*, 157.
31 Ibid., 163.
32 Ibid., 206.
33 Strong, *Seeking Western Waters*; Gilman, *Lewis and Clark Across the Divide*.
34 Cutright, *Lewis and Clark*, 423, 447.
35 Ambrose, *Undaunted Courage*, 484.
36 Ibid., 475.
37 Dippie, *The Vanishing American*, 5.
38 Ibid., 6.
39 Sugden, *Tecumseh*.
40 Miller, *Native America, Discovered and Conquered*, 57.
41 Dippie, *The Vanishing American*, 6.
42 Ibid., 7.
43 Ibid., 8.
44 Meacham, *Thomas Jefferson*, 454.
45 Ibid., 468.
46 Ibid., 469.
47 Hertzke, ed., *Religious Freedom in America*, 63.
48 Meacham, *Thomas Jefferson*, 473.
49 Ibid., 475.
50 Ibid., 486.
51 McCullough, *John Adams*, 645.
52 Ibid., 646.
53 Ibid., 647.
54 Ibid., 648.
55 Gordon-Reed, *"Most Blessed of the Patriarchs."*
56 McCullough, *John Adams*, 648.
57 Singer, *Churchill Style*.
58 Lough, *No More Champagne*.
59 McCullough, *John Adams*, 649.
60 Gaustad, *The Religious History of America*, 198.
61 Ibid.
62 Ibid., 199.
63 Burstein, *Democracy's Muse*.

CHAPTER 17 – FATHER OF THE REMOVAL POLICY: THOMAS JEFFERSON AND THE DOCTRINE OF DISCOVERY (PAGES 331-347)

1. Miller, *Native America, Discovered and Conquered*, 60.
2. See also Miller, *Discovering Indigenous Lands*. I would like to thank Robert Miller for his interest in this book and our phone discussion on July 12, 2016, where I learned even more about the Doctrine of Discovery. His enthusiasm and brilliance is much appreciated. I would also like to thank my good friend Federal Judge Riley Atkins, of Portland, Oregon, for introducing me to Robert Miller.
3. Ibid., 1.
4. Greenberg, *Manifest Destiny and American Territorial Expansion*, 43.
5. Miller, *Native America, Discovered and Conquered*, 1.
6. Rosebrook, "The Boundless West," 58.
7. Fenster, *Jefferson's America*.
8. Miller, "The Doctrine of Discovery in American Indian Law," 21-75.
9. Miller, *Native America, Discovered and Conquered*, 12; Baldwin, *The Origin of the Idea of Crusade*, 155-156.
10. Miller, *Native America, Discovered and Conquered*, 12.
11. Pagden, *Lords of All the World*.
12. Miller, *Native America, Discovered and Conquered*, 18.
13. Ibid., 26.
14. Ibid., 41.
15. Ibid., 44.
16. Miller, "Economic Development in Indian Country: Will Capitalism or Socialism Succeed?" 808, 809.
17. Miller, *Native America, Discovered and Conquered*, 46.
18. Berkhofer, Jr., *The White Man's Indian*, 148.
19. Ibid.
20. Miller, *Native America, Discovered and Conquered*, 3-5.
21. Watson, *Buying America from the Indians*.
22. Miller, *Native America, Discovered and Conquered*, 9.
23. Ibid.
24. Ibid., 10.
25. Ibid., 11.
26. Ibid., 63, 64.
27. Ibid., 71.
28. Richardson, *A Compilation of Messages and Papers of the Presidents*, 360, 363-365, 421, 422, 426.
29. Cohen, "Original Indian Title," 28, 35.
30. Jackson, *Letters of the Lewis and Clark Expedition*, Vol. I, 61-65, 165.
31. Onuf, *Jefferson's Empire*, 15.
32. Ronda, *Lewis & Clark among the Indians*, 62.
33. Miller, *Native America, Discovered and Conquered*, 80.
34. Ibid., 85.

35 Ibid., 85, 86.
36 Greenberg, *Manifest Destiny and American Territorial Expansion*, 56.
37 Ronda, *Lewis & Clark among the Indians*, xiv.
38 Greenberg, *Manifest Destiny and American Territorial Expansion*, 51.
39 Miller, *Native America, Discovered and Conquered*, 88.
40 Ibid., 87.
41 Berkhofer, Jr., *The White Man's Indian*, 146.
42 Miller, *Native America, Discovered and Conquered*, 89.
43 Ibid., 91.
44 Ibid., 93.
45 Ibid., 105.
46 Berkhofer, Jr., *The White Man's Indian*, 145.
47 Miller, *Native America, Discovered and Conquered*, 106.
48 Moulton, *The Definitive Journals of Lewis & Clark*, Vol. 6, 429-431.
49 Malloy, *"Boston Men" on the Coast*, 53, 169.

CHAPTER 18 – MANIFEST DESTINY: IF GOD IS FOR US, THEN WHO COULD EVER STOP US? (PAGES 349-370)

1 Blum, *The National Experience*, 162.
2 Traub, *John Quincy Adams;* Blum, *The National Experience*, 181; Edel, *Nation Builder;* Kaplan, *John Quincy Adams.*
3 Edel, *Nation Builder.*
4 Daley, *Great Inaugural Addresses*, 37.
5 Nabokov, *Native American Testimony*, 71.
6 Blum, *The National Experience*, 191.
7 Ibid.
8 Ibid., 193; Peterson, *John Fery*, 28.
9 Brands, *Andrew Jackson;* Meacham, *American Lion.*
10 Blum, *The National Experience*, 222.
11 Dippie, *The Vanishing American*, 60.
12 Ibid., 61.
13 Ibid., 64.
14 Ibid., 65.
15 Ibid., 67.
16 Ibid.
17 Ibid., 68.
18 Ibid., 70.
19 Ibid., 70.
20 Ibid., 71.
21 Nabokov, *Native American Testimony*, 153.
22 Greenberg, *Manifest Destiny and American Territorial Expansion*, 60.

23 Ibid., 64-66.
24 Nichols, *American Indians in U.S. History*, 107.
25 Nabokov, *Native American Testimony*, 149.
26 Ibid.
27 Greenberg, *Manifest Destiny and American Territorial Expansion*, 68, 69.
28 Ibid., 73.
29 Ibid., 79.
30 Ibid., 98.
31 Ibid., 15.
32 Miller, *Native America, Discovered and Conquered*, 120.
33 Ibid.
34 Blum, *The National Experience*, 260.
35 Ibid., 261.
36 Borneman, *Polk*.
37 Blum, *The National Experience*, 273.
38 Greenberg, *Manifest Destiny and American Territorial Expansion*, 102.
39 Dippie, *The Vanishing American*, 73.
40 Ibid., 73.
41 Ibid., 76.
42 Ibid., 77.
43 Blum, *The National Experience*, 292.
44 Peterson, *John Fery*, 16.
45 Bankston, *Immigration in U.S. History*.
46 Blum, *The National Experience*, 493.

CHAPTER 19 – CLEANSING THE WEST: RELIGION, STEEL, AND ROMANCE (PAGES 371-399)

1 Blum, *The National Experience*, 20.
2 Dippie, *The Vanishing American*, xii.
3 Pierce, *Making the White Man's West*.
4 Pearcey, *Total Truth*, 297.
5 Ibid., 298.
6 Meacham, *American Gospel*, 110.
7 Blum, *The National Experience*, 248.
8 Ibid.
9 Gaustad, *The Religious History of America*, 144.
10 Ibid., 162.
11 Ibid., 181.
12 Ibid., 163.
13 Stark, *How the West Won*, 367.
14 Berkhofer, Jr., *The White Man's Indian*, 151.

15 Ibid., 151.
16 Ibid., 121.
17 Nichols, *American Indians in U.S. History,* 101.
18 Dippie, *The Vanishing American,* 52.
19 Gaustad, *The Religious History of America,* 164.
20 Peterson, *Sacred Encounters;* Jeffrey, *Converting the West.*
21 Bonnie C. Harvey, "The West That Wasn't Won," *Christianity Today,* April 1, 2000, online at www.christianitytoday.com/ch2000/issue66/9.36html.
22 Ibid.
23 Greenberg, *Manifest Destiny and American Expansion,* 70.
24 McCullough, *Brave Companions,* 46.
25 Beebe, *Junípero Serra,* 59, 60.
26 Ibid., 133, 224.
27 See "Junípero Serra" on pbs.org under *New Perspectives of the West,* 2001, The West Film Project and WETA.
28 Beebe, *Junípero Serra,* 364.
29 Ibid., 345.
30 Paxson, *E. S. Paxson,* 71; Lambert, *Montana's State Capitol,* 53-61; Peterson, *Charles M. Russell: Photographing the Legend,* 119-121.
31 Gaustad, *The Religious History of America,* 170.
32 Peterson, *Sacred Encounters,* 97.
33 Ibid., 98.
34 Gaustad, *The Religious History of America,* 170.
35 Ibid.
36 Dippie, *The Vanishing American,* 10.
37 Deloria, Jr., *Custer Died for Your Sins,* 106-109.
38 Twiss, *One Church, Many Tribes,* 55.
39 Hunter, *A History of Industrial Power in the United States, 1730-1930.*
40 Allen, *The British Industrial Revolution in Global Perspective,* 14.
41 Blum, *The National Experience,* 205.
42 Ferguson, *Oliver Evans.*
43 Miller, *Native America, Discovered and Conquered,* 117.
44 O'Brien, *Railways and the Economic Development of Western Europe, 1830-1914.*
45 Young, *The Dutiful Son,* 77.
46 Flores, *American Serengeti.*
47 For an excellent review see Spangenberger, "22 Guns That Won the West," 73-87.
48 Wilson, *Colt;* Wilson, *Winchester;* Zwoll, *America's Great Gunmakers;* Rattenbury, *A Legacy in Arms;* Rattenbury, *The Art of American Arms Makers.*
49 Jones, *Epiphany in the Wilderness.*
50 Haag, *The Gunning of America.*
51 Spangenberger, "22 Guns That Won the West," 74.
52 Rattenbury, *Hunting the American West.*
53 Nabokov, *Native American Testimony,* 174.
54 Rattenbury, *A Legacy in Arms.*

55 Ridley, *The Evolution of Everything*.
56 Peterson, *John Fery*, 31.
57 Jennings, *Paradise Now*.
58 See Edward Rothstein, "The Critique of Reason: Romantic Art, 1760-1860" in *The Wall Street Journal*, April 29, 2015.
59 Berkhofer, Jr., *The White Man's Indian*, 89.
60 Novotny, *Painting and Sculpture in Europe, 1780-1880*.
61 Warrell, *J. M. W. Turner*.
62 Prown, *Discovered Lands, Invented Pasts*, 73.
63 Howat, *American Paradise*.
64 Preston, *Spectacular Yellowstone and Grand Teton National Parks*.
65 Peterson, *L. A. Huffman*; Peterson, *Charles M. Russell: Photographing the Legend*.
66 Anderson, *Albert Bierstadt*, 23.
67 Anderson, *Thomas Moran*.
68 Ibid.
69 Peterson, *Charles M. Russell: Photographing the Legend*.
70 Blum, *The National Experience*, 285-289.
71 Berkhofer, Jr., *The White Man's Indian*, 93.
72 Dippie, *The Vanishing American*, 25.
73 Ibid., 25.
74 Ibid., 34.
75 Ibid., 27.
76 Ibid., 28.
77 Blum, *The National Experience*, 286.
78 Whitman, *Leaves of Grass*.
79 Berkhofer, Jr., *The White Man's Indian*, 92.

CHAPTER 20 – THE DESCENT OF MAN: SCIENTIFIC RACISM (PAGES 401-417)

1 Spiro, *Defending the Master Race*.
2 Ibid., 43-51.
3 "The Colored Citizen," in *African American* newspaper from Pensacola, Florida, February 9, 1923, 2.
4 Peterson, *Charles M. Russell: Photographing the Legend*, 74.
5 Newkirk, *Spectacle*; Brinkley, *The Wilderness Warrior*, 657.
6 Newkirk, *Spectacle*.
7 Peterson, *L. A. Huffman*, 50.
8 Ibid.
9 Flores, *American Serengeti*, 133.
10 Connif, *House of Lost Worlds*.
11 Bradford, *Ota Benga*, 177.
12 "The Scandal at the Zoo" by Mitch Keller, *The New York Times*, August 6, 2006.

13 Ibid.
14 Jay Maeder, "The Little Man in the Zoo," 23.
15 "African Pygmy's Fate is Still Undecided," *The New York Times,* September 16, 1906, 9.
16 Ibid.
17 Bradford, *Ota Benga,* 220.
18 Mesler, *A Brief History of Creation.*
19 Isaac, *The Invention of Racism in Classical Antiquity.*
20 Davidson, *Voltaire.*
21 Ibid.
22 Kidd, *The Forging of Races.*
23 Dobson, *John Hunter.*
24 Berkhofer, Jr., *The White Man's Indian,* 42.
25 Rush, *Essays, Literary, Moral and Philosophical.*
26 Isaac, *The Invention of Racism in Classical Antiquity,* 150.
27 Harris, *The Rise of Anthropological Theory,* 87.
28 Hudnut, "Samuel Stanhope Smith," 540-552.
29 Jackson, *Race, Racism, and Science,* 41, 42.
30 Parsons, *The British Imperial Century, 1815-1914,* 3.
31 Jackson, *Race, Racism, and Science,* 52-54.
32 Livingstone, *Adam's Ancestors,* 112.
33 Jackson, *Race, Racism, and Science,* 45.
34 Thomas, *Skull Wars,* 38-41.
35 Morton, *Some Observations on the Ethnography and Archaeology of the American Aborigines (1846).*
36 Harding, *The "Racial" Economy of Science,* 100.
37 Redman, *Bone Rooms.*
38 Boas, *Franz Boas, 1858-1942.*
39 Horsman, *Josiah Nott of Mobile.*
40 Berkhofer, Jr., *The White Man's Indian,* 59.
41 Dippie, *The Vanishing American,* 7.
42 Lurie, "Louis Agassiz and the Races of Man," 232.
43 Dippie, *The Vanishing American,* 84.
44 Ibid.
45 Berkhofer, Jr., *The White Man's Indian,* 96.
46 Dippie, *The Vanishing American,* 85.
47 Ibid.
48 Ibid., 87.
49 Ibid., 87.
50 Ibid., 93.

CHAPTER 21 – SURVIVAL OF THE FITTEST: CHARLES DARWIN EXPLAINS EVOLUTION (PAGES 419-440)

1. Wulf, *The Invention of Nature*.
2. McCullough, *Brave Companions*, 5.
3. Wulf, *The Invention of Nature*.
4. McCullough, *Brave Companions*, 19.
5. Brinkley, *The Wilderness Warrior*.
6. Canfield, *Theodore Roosevelt in the Field*.
7. Brinkley, *The Wilderness Warrior*, 275.
8. Peterson, *Philip R. Goodwin*.
9. Brinkley, *The Wilderness Warrior*, 812.
10. Ibid.
11. Desmond, *Darwin's Sacred Cause*; Desmond, *Darwin*.
12. Burkhardt, *The Correspondence of Charles Darwin*, 139.
13. Desmond, *Darwin*.
14. Neve, *Charles Darwin, Autobiographies*, 49.
15. Browne, *Charles Darwin*.
16. Thomson, *Private Doubt, Public Dilemma*, 74.
17. Smith, *Engineering Eden*.
18. Flores, *American Serengeti*, 3.
19. Colp, *Darwin's Illness*.
20. Neve, *Charles Darwin, Autobiographies*, 55.
21. Ibid., 50.
22. Ibid.
23. Darwin, *On the Origin of Species by Means of Natural Selection, or the Preservation of Favoured Races in the Struggle for Life*, 126, 127.
24. Thomson, *Private Doubt, Public Dilemma*, 90.
25. For a reprint see Darwin, *Origin of Species*; Fuller, *The Book That Changed America*. There were 1,200 copies of *Origin of Species* first printed in 1859. Many consider it the greatest book of the nineteenth century. One of the original first editions is worth well over $100,000.
26. Secord, *Visions of Science*.
27. Thomson, *Private Doubt, Public Dilemma*, 91.
28. Ibid., 94.
29. Jahoda, *Images of Savages*, 82.
30. Darwin, *The Descent of Man, and Selection in Relation to Sex*, "On the Affinities and Genealogy of Man," 200-201.
31. Thomson, *Private Doubt, Public Dilemma*, 104.
32. Wulf, *The Invention of Nature*.
33. Agassiz, *An Essay on Classification*, 205.
34. McCullough, *Brave Companions*, 30.
35. Wayman, *Edward Sylvester Morse*, 120.

36 Thomson, *Private Doubt, Public Dilemma*, 113.
37 Ward, *A New History of Life*.
38 Ibid.; McCullough, *Brave Companions*, 34.
39 Temple, "A Sermon Preached before the University of Oxford, on Act Sunday, July 1st, 1860," 244.
40 Morris, *The Rise of Theodore Roosevelt*; Morris, *Theodore Rex*; Morris, *Colonel Roosevelt*.
41 Morrison, "Hart, Albert Bushnell." Many of Bushnell's books are available in reprints.
42 Roosevelt, *The Works of Theodore Roosevelt*, Volume 8, xiv.
43 Ibid., 7.
44 Ibid., 15, 16.
45 Ibid., 139, 140.
46 Holloway, *Hamlin Garland*.
47 Roosevelt, *The Works of Theodore Roosevelt*, Volume 8, xxvii-xxviii.
48 Roosevelt, *The Works of Theodore Roosevelt*, Volume 9, 56, 57.
49 Homans, "Putnam, George Haven."
50 Roosevelt, *The Works of Theodore Roosevelt*, Volume 9, x.
51 Ibid., xvi.
52 Cohen, *Imbeciles*.
53 Ibid.
54 Leonard, *Illiberal Reformers*.
55 David Reynolds, "Worse Than 'Dred Scott,'" *The Wall Street Journal*, August 7, 2015.

CHAPTER 22 – THE BETTER ANGELS OF OUR NATURE: CUSTER AND THE FIGHT TO MAKE THE UNION WHOLE (PAGES 443-470)

1 Blum, *The National Experience*, 402.
2 Ward, *The Civil War*, 186.
3 Ibid., 272.
4 Ibid., 307.
5 Ibid., 317.
6 Goodwin, *Team of Rivals*.
7 Meacham, *American Gospel*, 112.
8 Stiles, *Custer's Trials*, 199.
9 Ibid.
10 Custer, *Tenting on the Plains*, 245, 246, 284.
11 Stiles, *Custer's Trials*, 10.
12 Ibid., 12.
13 Ibid., 13.
14 Wert, *Custer*, 31.
15 Crary, *Dear Belle*, 42, 43, 214, 215.
16 Ibid., 42-44.
17 Ibid., 215.

18. Wert, *Custer*, 34, 35.
19. "Custer Agonistes" by Randall Fuller, *The Wall Street Journal*, November 20, 2015.
20. Stiles, *Custer's Trials*, 26.
21. Ambrose, *Eisenhower*, 21; Manchester, *Winston Spencer Churchill: The Last Lion*.
22. Ambrose, *Eisenhower*, 25.
23. Ibid., 26.
24. Ambrose, *Crazy Horse and Custer*, 115.
25. Sublette, *The American Slave Coast*.
26. Emerson, *Divided by Faith*, 23.
27. Ibid., 26.
28. Jacoby, *Strange Gods*.
29. Sinha, *The Slave's Cause*.
30. Bryant, *Dark Places of the Earth*.
31. Ibid.
32. Baptist, *The Half Has Never Been Told*.
33. Sublette, *The American Slave Coast*.
34. Baptist, *The Half Has Never Been Told*.
35. Meacham, *American Gospel*, 116.
36. Wood, *Arrogance of Faith*, 40.
37. Ibid., 309.
38. Emerson, *Divided by Faith*, 35.
39. Wood, *Arrogance of Faith*, 276.
40. Gaustad, *The Religious History of America*, 184.
41. Ibid., 189, 190.
42. Ibid., 191.
43. Ibid., 196.
44. Ibid., 199.
45. Ibid., 199.
46. Ibid., 202.
47. Jaher, *The Witch of Lime Street*.
48. Brookhiser, *Founder's Son*.
49. Goodwin, *Team of Rivals*, 91.
50. Ibid.
51. Ibid., 206.
52. Ibid., 370.
53. Ibid., 406.
54. Ibid., 674.
55. Ibid., 407.
56. Ibid., 466.
57. Doyle, *The Cause of All Nations*.
58. Ibid.
59. Lewis, *Washington*.
60. Davis, *Crucible of Command*.
61. Ibid.

62 Ward, *The Civil War*, 63.
63 Ibid., 68.
64 Ibid., 71.
65 Ibid., 103.
66 Ibid., 104.
67 Ibid., 105.
68 Brands, *The Man Who Saved the Union*, 191.
69 Ward, *The Civil War*, 324.
70 Ibid., 126.
71 Ibid., 324.
72 Ibid., 135.
73 Ibid., 136.
74 Ibid., 158.
75 Ambrose, *To America*, 61.
76 Ward, *The Civil War*, 218.
77 Ibid., 158.
78 Ibid., 173.
79 Brands, *The Man Who Saved the Union*, 229.
80 Ibid., 256.
81 Ibid., 254.
82 Ward, *The Civil War*, 192.
83 Ibid., 194.
84 Ibid., 204.
85 Brands, *The Man Who Saved the Union*, 288.
86 Ward, *The Civil War*, 211.
87 Brands, *The Man Who Saved the Union*, 55.
88 Ibid., 87.
89 Ibid., 88.
90 Ibid., 90.
91 Ward, *The Civil War*, 243.
92 Brands, *The Man Who Saved the Union*, 121.
93 Ibid., 230.
94 Ward, *The Civil War*, 263.
95 Rubin, *Through the Heart of Dixie*.
96 Ibid.
97 McDonough, *William Tecumseh Sherman*; O'Connell, *Fierce Patriot*.
98 Ward, *The Civil War*, 280.
99 Ibid., 280.
100 Ibid., 291.
101 Ibid.
102 Hodes, *Mourning Lincoln*.
103 Ibid.; Fox, *Lincoln's Body*.
104 Brands, *The Man Who Saved the Union*, 393.

CHAPTER 23 – A CIVIL WAR LEGEND UNLEASHED: CUSTER REVEALED
(PAGES 471-488)

[1] Ambrose, *Crazy Horse and Custer*, 168.
[2] McClellan, *McClellan's Own Story*.
[3] Stiles, *Custer's Trials*, 6.
[4] Sears, *To the Gates of Richmond*, 21; Sears, *The Civil War Papers of George B. McClellan*, 105, 106, 110, 111, 137.
[5] Sears, *The Civil War Papers of George B. McClellan*, 103, 134, 176, 177, 188.
[6] Sears, *To the Gates of Richmond*, 21.
[7] Sears, *The Civil War Papers of George B. McClellan*, 127, 128.
[8] McPherson, *Battle Cry of Freedom*, 471.
[9] Stiles, *Custer's Trials*, 62.
[10] Ibid.
[11] McClellan, *McClellan's Own Story*, 487-489.
[12] Stiles, *Custer's Trials*, 73.
[13] Peterson, *Charles M. Russell: Photographing the Legend*, 3.
[14] Wilson, *Mathew Brady*.
[15] Stiles, *Custer's Trials*, 135.
[16] Ibid.
[17] Stiles, *Custer's Trials*, 28.
[18] Hutton, "America's Longest War," 29.
[19] Lowen, *Narcissism*, 26, 27.
[20] Masterson, *The Search for the Real Self*, 91.
[21] Steinke, *Congregational Leadership in Anxious Times*, 169; Masterson, *The Search for the Real Self*, 103.
[22] Stiles, *Custer's Trials*, 36.
[23] Steinke, *Congregational Leadership in Anxious Times*, 165, 175.
[24] Caldwell, *American Narcissism*.
[25] Stiles, *Custer's Trials*, 77.
[26] Ambrose, *Crazy Horse and Custer*, 97.
[27] Leckie, *Elizabeth Bacon Custer and the Making of a Myth*.
[28] Stiles, *Custer's Trials*, 87.
[29] Ibid., 89.
[30] Ibid., 93.
[31] Agassiz, *Meade's Headquarters, 1863-1865*, 14.
[32] *Monroe Commercial*, July 2, 1863.
[33] *Monroe Commercial*, July 23, 1863.
[34] Stiles, *Custer's Trials*, 112.
[35] Ibid., 115.
[36] Ibid., 143.
[37] Ibid., 108.
[38] Ibid.

39 Merington, *The Custer Story*, 79.
40 Stiles, *Custer's Trials*, 140.
41 Merington, *The Custer Story*.
42 Ibid., 93.
43 Ibid., 95.
44 Ibid., 97.
45 Ibid., 98.
46 Stiles, *Custer's Trials*, 111.
47 Steinke, *Congregational Leadership in Anxious Times*, 168.
48 Stiles, *Custer's Trials*, 143.
49 Merington, *The Custer Story*, 101.
50 Ibid., 102.
51 Ibid.
52 Ibid., 103.
53 Ibid., 106.
54 Ibid., 111.
55 Ibid., 113.
56 Ibid., 115.
57 Ibid., 118.
58 Ibid., 122.
59 Ibid., 123.
60 Ibid., 124.
61 Ibid., 141.
62 Ibid., 142.
63 Stiles, *Custer's Trials*, 143.
64 Monaghan, *Custer*, 220.
65 Ambrose, *Crazy Horse and Custer*, 199.
66 Stiles, *Custer's Trials*.
67 Ibid., 126.
68 Ward, *The Civil War*, 215.
69 Ibid., 216.
70 Ibid., 237.

CHAPTER 24 – AMERICAN IDOLS: GRANT AND CUSTER AFTER THE CIVIL WAR (PAGES 489-510)

1 Brands, *The Man Who Saved the Union*, 376; White, *American Ulysses*.
2 Brands, *The Man Who Saved the Union*, 38.
3 Ibid., 394.
4 Purnell, *Clementine*.
5 Stiles, "The Horse Thief," 51-55.
6 Stiles, *Custer's Trials*, 214.

7 Ibid., 224.
8 Ibid., 226.
9 *Des Moines State Register,* July 24, 1868.
10 Stiles, *Custer's Trials,* 233.
11 Custer, *Tenting on the Plains,* 245, 246, 248.
12 Stiles, *Custer's Trials,* 232.
13 Ibid., 236.
14 Foner, *Reconstruction,* 216, 219.
15 Stiles, *Custer's Trials,* 238.
16 Ibid., 241.
17 Ibid., 243.
18 Ibid.
19 Ibid., 245.
20 Simon, *The Papers of Ulysses S. Grant,* 276n, 277n.
21 *Monroe Commercial,* September 20, 1866.
22 Brands, *The Man Who Saved the Union,* 411.
23 Ibid., 412.
24 Ibid., 413.
25 Ibid., 414.
26 Ibid.
27 Ibid., 415.
28 Ibid., 425.
29 Ibid.
30 Ibid., 500.
31 Nabokov, *Native American Testimony,* 192.
32 Berkhofer, Jr., *The White Man's Indian,* 169.
33 Nabokov, *Native American Testimony,* 192.
34 Lossing, "Our Barbarian Brethren," 796.
35 "Our Indian Tribes," *Boston Review,* II, September, 1862, 517-523.
36 Dippie, *The Vanishing Indian,* 131.
37 Ibid., 144.
38 Ellis, *General Pope and U.S. Indian Policy,* 204.
39 Brands, *The Man Who Saved the Union,* 502.
40 Ibid., 502.
41 Ibid., 502, 503.
42 Ibid., 504.
43 Ibid.
44 Ibid., 506.
45 Ibid., 507.
46 Ibid., 561.
47 Twain, *The Noble Red Man.*
48 Ibid.
49 Krause, *Prelude to Glory,* 11. Original appeared in the *Bismarck* (D.T.) *Tribune,* June 17, 1874.

50 Brands, *The Man Who Saved the Union*, 563.
51 Ibid., 564.
52 Ibid.
53 Ibid., 565.
54 Ibid., 565.
55 Ibid., 565, 566.
56 Ibid., 566.
57 Dippie, *The Vanishing American*, 126.
58 Ibid.
59 Gibbon, "Our Indian Question," 102, 106, 107.
60 Dippie, *The Vanishing American*, 130.
61 Brands, *The Man Who Saved the Union*, 588.
62 Ibid., 623.
63 Huberman, *The Quotable Atheist*, 303, 304.
64 Powers, *Mark Twain*, 99.
65 Ibid., 503.
66 Ibid., 504.
67 Ibid., 513.
68 Brands, *The Man Who Saved the Union*, 636.

CHAPTER 25 – SON OF THE AMERICAN WEST: CUSTER, O FALLEN STAR (PAGES 511-545)

1 Nabokov, *Native American Testimony*, 189; Cozzens, *The Earth is Weeping*.
2 Magid, *The Gray Fox*.
3 Magid, *George Crook*.
4 Ibid.
5 Hutton, "The Severed Heads Campaign," 28; Hutton, *The Apache Wars*, 187-191.
6 Hutton, "The Severed Heads Campaign," 32; Hutton, *The Apache Wars*, 190.
7 Hutton, "The Severed Heads Campaign," 32.
8 Ibid., 32.
9 Ibid., 32.
10 Hutton, *The Apache Wars*.
11 Schmitt, *General George Crook, His Autobiography*.
12 Dippie, *The Vanishing American*, 130.
13 Schultz, *Over the Earth I Come*; Konstantin, *This Day in North American Indian History*.
14 Greene, *American Carnage*.
15 Ibid.
16 Brown, *Bury My Heart at Wounded Knee*, 86, 87; Hoig, *The Sand Creek Massacre*.
17 Sides, *Blood and Thunder*, 154, 155; Boggs, "Trail of Tragedy," 48-53.
18 Jackson, *A Century of Dishonor*, 344.
19 Wylie, *Blood on the Marias*; Graybill, *The Red and the White*.
20 Deloria, Jr., *Custer Died for Your Sins*, 148.

21 Shelton, *Cross & Covenant*, 66.
22 Horne, *Hubris*.
23 Fraser, *Forts of the West*.
24 Ibid.
25 Ibid.
26 Stiles, *Custer's Trials*, 265.
27 Chalfant, *Hancock's War*, 76, 77.
28 Jordan, *Winfield Scott Hancock*, 200, 201.
29 Custer, *Tenting on the Plains*, 572-574; Leckie, *Buffalo Soldiers*, 96.
30 Leckie, *Buffalo Soldiers*, 96, 97.
31 Stiles, *Custer's Trials*, 281.
32 Custer, *Tenting on the Plains*, 576-579.
33 Stiles, *Custer's Trials*, 284.
34 Ibid., 290.
35 Frost, *The Court-Martial of General George Armstrong Custer*, 120, 134-136.
36 Custer, *Tenting on the Plains*, 503, 504, 508.
37 Stiles, *Custer's Trials*, 292.
38 Ibid., 293.
39 Simon, *The Papers of Ulysses S. Grant*, Vol. 17, 370-372; Frost, *The Court-Martial of General George Armstrong Custer*, 245, 246.
40 Stiles, *Custer's Trials*, 298; Utley, *Life in Custer's Cavalry*, 128, 130, 131.
41 *The New York Times*, December 7, 1867.
42 Simon, *The Papers of Ulysses S. Grant*, Vol. 18, 373. Wert, *Custer*, 265.
43 Greene, *Washita*, 71, 72; Hutton, *Phil Sheridan and His Army*, 52, 53.
44 Greene, *Washita*, 119-129.
45 Stiles, *Custer's Trials*, 323.
46 Anderson, *Ethnic Cleansing and the Indian*, 262.
47 Stiles, *Custer's Trials*, 324.
48 Ibid., 325.
49 Ibid., 335, 336.
50 Ibid., 351.
51 Tebbel, *The Magazine in America 1741-1900*, 60, 61.
52 Stiles, *Custer's Trials*, 367.
53 Custer, *My Life on the Plains*, 12.
54 Ibid., 13-15.
55 Ibid., 16.
56 Ibid., 17.
57 Ibid., 18.
58 Ibid., 19.
59 Ibid., 21.
60 Ibid., 23.
61 Ibid., 26.
62 Ibid., 33.
63 Ibid., 30.
64 Stiles, *Custer's Trials*, 368.

65 *Independent,* January 4, 1872; *San Francisco Chronicle,* January 30, 1872.
66 Stiles, *Custer's Trials,* 370.
67 Ibid., 375.
68 Connell, *Son of the Morning Star,* 184.
69 Stiles, *Custer's Trials,* 400.
70 Leckie, *Elizabeth Bacon Custer and the Making of a Myth,* 158, 159.
71 Stiles, *Custer's Trials,* 401.
72 Cecil, *Herbicidal Warfare.*
73 Stiles, *Custer's Trials,* 408.
74 *Chicago Inter-Ocean,* September 1, 1874.
75 Merington, *The Custer Story,* 176, 177.
76 Stiles, *Custer's Trials,* 431.
77 Ibid., 435.
78 Ibid., 439.
79 Ibid., 437.
80 Ibid.
81 Ibid., 439.
82 Ibid.
83 Hedren, *Powder River.*
84 Welch, *Killing Custer,* 49.
85 Ibid., 51.
86 Ibid.
87 Stiles, *Custer's Trials,* 440.
88 Michno, *Lakota Noon;* Philbrick, *The Last Stand;* Rankin, *Legacy.*
89 Ambrose, *Crazy Horse and Custer,* 444, 445.
90 Ibid., 447.
91 Utley, *The Lance and The Shield.*
92 Utley, "Custer and Me," 60.
93 Linderman, *Red Mother,* 235.
94 Greene, "The Great Sioux War," 24-26; Hedren, *Powder River.*
95 Greene, "The Great Sioux War," 26.
96 Rogers, *L. Frank Baum, Creator of Oz,* 259.
97 Ibid.
98 Horne, *Hubris.*
99 "Custer Agonistes" by Randall Fuller, *The Wall Street Journal,* November 20, 2015.

CHAPTER 26 – THE CHILDREN OF MANIFEST DESTINY AND SHIFTING SHADOWS: EDUCATION TO KILL THE INDIAN (PAGES 547-580)

1 Miller, *Pop Warner.*
2 Wheeler, *Jim Thorpe.*
3 "Indian Thorpe in Olympiad: Redskin from Carlisle Will Strive for Place on American Team," *The New York Times,* April 28, 1912.

4. Nichols, *American Indians in U.S. History*, 154.
5. Churchill, *Kill the Indian, Save the Man*, 21.
6. Welsh, *Four Weeks Among Some of the Sioux Tribes of Dakota and Nebraska*; Pancoast, *Impressions of the Sioux Tribes in 1882 with Some First Principles in the Indian Question*.
7. Welsh, "The Indian Question Past and Present," 264.
8. Adams, *Education for Extinction*, 15.
9. *Annual Report of the Commissioner of Indian Affairs*, 1879, 124; 1884, 182.
10. *Annual Report of the Commissioner of Indian Affairs*, 1880, 163; 1885, 438; 1905, 2; 1886, 447.
11. Schurtz, "Present Aspects of the Indian Problems," 16, 17.
12. Morgan, "A Plea for the Papoose," 249.
13. *Annual Report of the Commissioner of Indian Affairs*, 1885, 108; 1886, 221, 222.
14. Adams, *Education for Extinction*, 23.
15. Ibid., 27.
16. Ibid.
17. *Annual Report of the Commissioner of Indian Affairs*, 1878, 649; 1879, 112.
18. Adams, *Education for Extinction*, 31.
19. *Annual Report of the Commissioner of Indian Affairs*, 1883, 67.
21. Adams, *Education for Extinction*, 37.
21. Pratt, *Battlefield and Classroom*, 121, 175.
22. Ibid., 158.
23. Eastman, *Pratt*.
24. Nabokov, *Native American Testimony*, 216.
25. Ibid., 217.
26. Pratt, "The Advantage of Mingling Indians with Whites," 56.
27. Whalen, *Native Students at Work*.
28. Pratt, *Battlefield and Classroom*, 283.
29. McKinney, "History of the Albuquerque Indian School," 116.
30. Standing Bear, *My People, the Sioux*, 187.
31. Standing Bear, *Land of the Spotted Eagle*, 68, 69, 230, 231.
32. *Annual Report of the Commissioner of Indian Affairs*, 1886, 417.
33. Garland, "The Red Man's Present Needs," 479.
34. McGillycuddy, *McGillycuddy, Agent*, 205, 206.
35. Flesche, *The Middle Five*, 75.
36. Standing Bear, *My People, the Sioux*, 137.
37. McBeth, *Ethnic Identity and the Boarding School Experience of West-Central Oklahoma American Indians*, 105.
38. Churchill, *Kill the Indian, Save the Man*, 55, 56.
39. *Annual Report of the Commissioner of Indian Affairs*, 1886, 220; 1895, 205; 1899, 159.
40. Nabokov, *Native American Testimony*, 220, 221.
41. Churchill, *Kill the Indian, Save the Man*, 29.
42. Adams, *Education for Extinction*, 131.
43. Ibid.
44. Standing Bear, *Land of the Spotted Eagle*, 16-18.
45. *Annual Report of the Commissioner of Indian Affairs*, 1884, 242.

46 Scudder, *A History of the United States of America,* 18, 21, 93, 94, 95, 418.
47 *Annual Report of the Commissioner of Indian Affairs,* 1881, 243; 1887, 352.
48 Office of Indian Affairs, *Course of Study for the Indian Schools,* 143.
49 *Southern Workman,* February 1885, 20.
50 *Red Man,* March-April 1893, 4.
51 Churchill, *Kill the Indian, Save the Man,* 48.
52 Kneale, *Indian Agent,* 171.
53 Hampton Institute, *Twenty-Two Years' Work of the Hampton Normal and Agricultural Institute at Hampton, Virginia,* 427, 428.
54 Adams, *Education for Extinction,* 279.
55 *Red Man,* July-August 1893, 1.
56 Churchill, *Kill the Indian, Save the Man,* 21.
57 *Red Man,* March 1890, 5.
58 Anderson, *Ethnic Cleansing and the Indian,* 333.
59 Dippie, *The Vanishing American,* 172.
60 Anderson, *Ethnic Cleansing and the Indian,* 335.
61 Nichols, *American Indians in U.S. History,* 160.
62 Nabokov, *Native American Testimony,* 258.
63 Dippie, *The Vanishing American,* 180.
64 Ibid., 189.
65 Wood, "The Evils of the Reservation System," 166.
66 Grinnell, "Tenure of Land among the Indians," 6-8.
67 Dippie, *The Vanishing American,* 181.
68 *Report of Hon. Theodore Roosevelt Made to the United States Civil Service Commission, upon a Visit to Certain Indian Reservations and Indian Schools in South Dakota, Nebraska, and Kansas* [October 5, 1892] (Philadelphia, Penn., 1893): 13-15.
69 Dippie, *The Vanishing American,* 185.
70 Peairs, "United States Indian Schools," 415-417.
71 Nichols, *American Indians in U.S. History,* 167.
72 Adams, *Education for Extinction,* 168.
73 Ibid.
74 Sekaquaptewa, *Me and Mine,* 129.
75 Bogue, *Frederick Jackson Turner.*
76 Turner, *Significance of Sections in American History.*
77 Adams, *Education for Extinction,* 183.
78 Ibid., 181-186.
79 Robertson, *American Myth, American Reality,* 256.
80 Reprinted in *Red Man,* November 1896, 6.
81 Reprinted in *Red Man,* December 1898, 5.
82 Reprinted in *Red Man,* November 1896, 6.
83 Ibid., 4.
84 *Red Man,* September-October 1895, 6.
85 Guiliano, *Indian Spectacle.*
86 Ibid.

87 Adams, *Education for Extinction*, 90.
88 Ibid., 285.
89 Blackmar, "Indian Education," 831.
90 Adams, *Education for Extinction*, 307.
91 Ibid., 310.
92 Garland, "The Red Man's Present Needs," 483, 484; Lummis, "A New Indian Policy," 463.
93 Adams, *Education for Extinction*, 317.
94 Ibid., 320.
95 Ibid., 336, 337.
96 Dippie, *The Vanishing American*, 197.

CHAPTER 27 – LAMENTATIONS OF THE FALL: GENOCIDE, ETHNIC CLEANSING, AND POST-TRAUMATIC STRESS DISORDER (PAGES 581-600)

1 "Sweat Lodge Prayer" by Trevor Persaud in *Christianity Today*, April 2011.
2 Madley, *An American Genocide*.
3 Twiss, *One Church, Many Tribes*, 39.
4 Niea.org.
5 Nativevillage.org.
6 Ibid.
7 Niea.org; for an informative description of life on the reservation today, see Colton, *Counting Coup*.
8 Nativevillage.org.
9 Marmot, *The Health Gap*.
10 Anderson, *Ethnic Cleansing and the Indian*, 8; Woolford, *Colonial Genocide in Indigenous North America*.
11 Benson, *Wallace Stegner*.
12 Stark, *How the West Won*, 2.
13 Cook, *Born to Die*, 214; Royal, *1492 and All That*, 62, 63.
14 Anderson, *Ethnic Cleansing and the Indian*, 4.
15 Ibid., 13.
16 Ibid., 11, 12.
17 Stiles, *Custer's Trials*, 407.
18 Anderson, *Ethnic Cleansing and the Indian*, 21; Anderson, "The Native Peoples of the American West: Genocide or Ethnic Cleansing," 407-433; Hixson, *American Settler Colonialism*; Jacobs, *White Mother to a Dark Race*; Jacobs, "Genocide or Ethnic Cleansing? Are These Our Only Choices?" 444-448. Hixson and Jacobs suggest a more general term than genocide or ethnic cleansing. They prefer settler colonialism, which includes genocide, ethnic cleansing, rape, enslavement, allotment, child removal, termination, relocation, and forced sterilization. The Winter 2016 *The Western Historical Quarterly* has a discussion on ethnic cleansing, genocide, and settler colonialism by these distinguished historians.

19. Ridley, *The Evolution of Everything*.
20. Lindsay, "Ethnic Cleansing and the Indian," 101, 102.
21. Ellis, "Ethnic Cleansing and the Indian," 85, 86.
22. Power, "A Problem from Hell," 29.
23. For full text see hrweb.org.
24. Sands, *East West Street*.
25. Peterson, *Charles M. Russell: Photographing the Legend*, 32, 33; Collins, *The Story of Kodak*, 55.
26. Ben Zimmer, "How 'Genocide' Was Coined," *The Wall Street Journal*, October 24, 2014.
27. Lemkin, *Axis Rule in Occupied Europe*, 79.
28. Davis, *The Genocide Machine in Canada*, 19, 20.
29. Ibid., 20.
30. Ibid.
31. Church, *Kill the Indian, Save the Man*, 7.
32. Ibid., 10.
33. Anderson, *Ethnic Cleansing and the Indian*, 5.
34. Power, "A Problem from Hell," 4.
35. "How the Original Geneva Convention Created Rules for War" by Amanda Foreman, *The Wall Street Journal*, December 12, 2014; Westerman, *Hitler's Ostkrieg and the Indian Wars*.
36. Evans, *The Third Reich in History and Memory*.
37. Bloxham, *The Final Solution*.
38. Blass, *The Man Who Shocked the World*.
39. Kristeva, *Hannah Arendt*.
40. Stargardt, *The German War*.
41. Metaxis, *Bonhoeffer*, 531, 532.
42. Snyder, *Black Earth*.
43. Swaan, *The Killing Compartments*.
44. Ibid.
45. Junger, *Tribe*.
46. Volpe, J. S., "Traumatic Stress: An Overview," http://www.aaets.org/article1.htm.
47. Jones, *Shell Shock to PTSD*.
48. Gersons, "Post-Traumatic Stress Disorder: The History of a Recent Concept," 742-748; Meichenbaum, *A Clinical Handbook/Practical Therapist Manual for Assessing and Treating Adults with Post-Traumatic Stress Disorder*.
49. See Rose, "Post-Traumatic Stress Disorder," 68-115, for an excellent review of the entire subject.
50. Gradus, J. L., "Epidemiology of PTSD," http://www.ptsd.va.gov/professional/PTSD-overview/epidemiological-facts-ptsd.asp.
51. Maguen, "Moral Injury in Veterans of War," 1-6.
52. Peristan, "An Investigation of Potential Holocaust-Related Secondary Trauma in the Third Generation," 95-106.
53. Braga, "Transgenerational Transmission of Trauma and Resilience," 134; Yehuda, "Maternal, Not Paternal, PTSD is Related to Increased Risk for PTSD in Offspring of Holocaust Survivors," 1104-1111.

54. Australian Centre for Posttraumatic Mental Health, "Guidelines for the Treatment of Adults with Acute Stress Disorder and Posttraumatic Stress Disorder." http://www.nhmrc.gov.au/guidelines-publications/mh13-mh14-mh15-mh16.
55. Copeland, "Traumatic Events and Posttraumatic Stress in Childhood," 577-584.
56. Australian Centre for Posttraumatic Mental Health, "Guidelines for the Treatment of Adults with Acute Stress Disorder and Posttraumatic Stress Disorder." http://www.nhmrc.gov.au/guidelines-publications/mh13-mh14-mh15-mh16.
57. Worthen, "Anger Problems and Posttraumatic Stress Disorder in Male and Female National Guard and Reserve Service Members," 52-58.
58. Taft, C., U.S. Department of Veterans Affairs, "Anger, Aggression and PTSD," http://www.ptsd.va.gov/professional/continuing_ed/anger_aggression.asp.
59. Ibid.
60. Hejmanowski, "Alone in a Crowded Room: The Continuum of Post-Traumatic Stress," 15-22.
61. U.S. Department of Veterans Affairs, Department of Defense, "Clinical Practice Guideline for Management of Post-Traumatic Stress," http://www.healthquality.va.gov/guidelines/MH/ptsd/cpg_PTSD-FULL-201011612.pdf.
62. Ibid.
63. Kaplan, A., "Can A Suicide Scale Predict the Unpredictable?" http://www.psychiatriccrimes.com/suicide/can-suicide-scale-predict-unpredictable.
64. Evans, *Third Reich in History and Memory*.

Bibliography

Aberth, John. *The Black Death: The Great Mystery Mortality of 1348-1350. A Brief History with Documents.* Boston and New York: Bedford/St. Martin's, 2005.

Adair, James. *The History of the American Indians.* Edited by Kathryn Holland Braund. Tuscaloosa, University of Alabama Press, 2005.

Adams, David Wallace. *Education for Extinction: American Indians and the Boarding School Experience 1875-1928.* Lawrence: University Press of Kansas, 1995.

———. *Three Roads to Magdalena: Coming of Age in a Southwest Borderland, 1890-1990.* Lawrence: University of Kansas Press, 2016.

Adams, Dickinson W., ed. *Jefferson's Extracts from the Gospels.* Princeton: Princeton University Press, 1983.

Adams, Francis. *The Genuine Works of Hippocrates.* New York: William Wood and Company, 1891.

Agassiz, George R., ed. *Meade's Headquarters, 1863-1865: Letters of Colonel Theodore Lyman, from the Wilderness to Appomattox.* Boston: Atlantic Monthly Press, 1922.

Agassiz, Louis. *An Essay of Classification.* London: Longmans, Green, 1859.

Aldersey-Williams, Hugh. *In Search of Sir Thomas Browne: The Life and Afterlife of the Seventeenth Century's Most Intriguing Mind.* New York: W.W. Norton & Company, 2015.

Allen, Gene, Bev Allen. *The Collotypes of L. A. Huffman: Montana Frontier Photographer.* Helena, MT: Riverbend, 2014.

Allen, Robert C. *The British Industrial Revolution in Global Perspective.* Cambridge, England: Cambridge University Press, 2009.

Ambrose, Stephen E. *Crazy Horse and Custer: Parallel Lives of Two American Warriors.* New York: Anchors Books Doubleday, 1996.

———. *Eisenhower: Soldier and President.* New York: Simon & Schuster, 1991.

———. *To America: Personal Reflections of an Historian.* New York: Simon & Schuster, 2002.

———. *Undaunted Courage: Meriwether Lewis, Thomas Jefferson, and the Opening of the American West.* New York: Simon & Schuster, 1996.

Anderson, Gary Clayton. "Early Dakota Migration and Intertribal War. A Revision." *Western Historical Quarterly* 11 (January 1980): 24.

———. *Ethnic Cleansing and the Indian: The Crime That Should Haunt America.* Norman: University of Oklahoma Press, 2014.

———. "The Native Peoples of the American West: Genocide or Ethnic Cleansing." *Western Historical Quarterly* 47, no. 4 (Winter 2016): 407-433.

Anderson, Nancy K., Linda S. Ferber. *Albert Bierstadt: Art & Enterprise.* New York: The Brooklyn Museum, 1990.

———. *Thomas Moran*. New Haven: Yale University Press, 1997.
Apanius, V. "The Nature of Selection on the Major Histocompatibility Complex," *Critical Reviews in Immunology* 17, no. 2 (1997): 179-224.
Aristotle, *Rhetoric*. Mineola, NY: Dover Publications, 2004.
Arkelian, Marjorie Dakin, George W. Neubert. *Thomas Hill: The Grand View*. Marietta, PA: Mullen Books, 1980.
Arkus, Elizabeth N., Mark W. Allen, eds. *The Archaeology of Warfare: Prehistories of Raiding and Conquest*. Gainesville: University of Florida Press, 2008.
Armstrong, Virginia. *I Have Spoken*. Chicago: Swallow Press, 1971.
Ash, Patricia, David J. Robinson. *The Emergence of Humans: An Exploration of the Evolutionary Timeline*. Hoboken: John Wiley & Sons, 2011.
Atkinson, William. *Pertussis Epidemiology and Prevention of Vaccine-Preventable Diseases*. Washington, D.C.: Public Health Foundation, 2012.
Atwood, Craig. *Handbook of Denominations in the United States*. Nashville: Abingdon Press, 2010.
Audubon, John James. *Ornithological Biography*. Memphis: General Books, 2012.
Bailey, Kenneth E. *Jesus Through Middle Eastern Eyes: Cultural Studies in the Gospels*. Downers Grove, IL: IVP Academic, 2008.
Baker, J. P. "Childhood Vaccine Development: An Overview." *Pediatric Research* 55, no. 2 (2004): 347-356.
Baker, Moses N. *The Quest for Pure Water: The History of Water Purification from the Earliest Records to the Twentieth Century*. Denver: American Water Works Association, 1981.
Baldwin, Marshall W., Walter Goffart. *The Origin of the Idea of Crusade*. Princeton: Princeton University Press, 1977.
Bankston, Carl III, Danielle Hidalgo. *Immigration in U.S. History*. Hackensack: Salem Press, 2006.
Baptist, Edward E. *The Half Has Never Been Told: Slavery and the Making of American Capitalism*. New York: Basic Books, 2014.
Barnes, Joseph K. *The Medical and Surgical History of the War of the Rebellion, 1861-1865*, Part I, Volumes 1 and 2, Medical History. Washington, D.C.: Government Printing Office, 1870.
Baron, John, ed. *The Life of Edward Jenner: With Illustrations of His Doctrines, and Selections from His Correspondence*. London: H. Colburn, 1827-1838.
Bass, Althea. *The Arapaho Way: A Memoir of an Indian Boyhood*. New York: Clarkson N. Potter, 1966.
Baylor, Michael G. *The German Reformation and the Peasants' War: A Brief History with Documents*. Boston and New York: Bedford/St. Martin's, 2012.
Beebe, Rose Marie, Robert M. Senkewicz. *Junípero Serra: California, Indians, and the Transformation of a Missionary*. Norman: University of Oklahoma Press, 2015.
Behbehani, Abbas M. "The Smallpox Story: Life and Death of an Old Disease." *Microbiological Reviews* 9, no. 4 (1983): 455-468.
Bell, David A. *Napoleon: A Concise Biography*. New York: Oxford University Press, 2015.
Benson, Jackson J. *Wallace Stegner: His Life and Work*. New York: Penguin Books, 1996.
Berkhofer, Jr., Robert F. *The White Man's Indian: Images of the American From Columbus to the Present*. New York: Vintage Books, 1978.
Binnema, Theodore. *Common and Contested Ground: A Human and Environmental History of the Northwestern Plains*. Norman: University of Oklahoma Press, 2001.

Black, Edwin. *War Against the Weak: Eugenics and America's Campaign to Create a Master Race*. Westport, CT: Dialog Press, 2012.

Blackmar, Frank. "Indian Education." *Annals of the American Academy of Political and Social Science* 2 (May 1892): 831.

Blainey, Geoffrey. *A Short History of the World*. Chicago: Ivan R. Dee, 2003.

Blass, Thomas. *The Man Who Shocked the World: The Life and Legacy of Stanley Milgram*. New York: Basic Books, 2009.

Bliss, Michael. *William Osler: A Life in Medicine*. New York: Oxford University Press, 2007.

Blitz, John H. "Adoption of the Bow in Prehistoric North America," *North American Archaeologist* 9 (1988): 123-145.

Blom, John J. *Descartes: His Moral Philosophy and Psychology*. New York: New York University Press, 1978.

Bloxham, Donald. *The Final Solution: A Genocide*. Cambridge, England: Cambridge University Press, 1999.

Blum, John M. *The National Experience: A History of the United States*. New York: Harcourt, Brace, Jovanovic, 1973.

Boas, Norman F. *Franz Boas, 1858-1942: An Illustrated Biography*. Mystic, CT: Seaport Autographs Press, 2004.

Boggs, Johnny D. "Trail of Tragedy." *True West Magazine* 61 (November 2014): 48-53.

Bogue, Allan G. *Frederick Jackson Turner: Strange Going Down*. Norman: University of Oklahoma Press, 1998.

Boin, Douglas Ryan. *Coming Out Christian in the Roman World: How the Followers of Jesus Made a Place in Caesar's Empire*. London: Bloomsbury, 2015.

Bollet, Alfred Jay. *Civil War Medicine: Challenges and Triumphs*. Tucson: Galen Press, 2002.

Bordewich, Fergus M. *The First Congress: How James Madison, George Washington, and a Group of Extraordinary Men Invented the Government*. New York: Simon & Schuster, 2016.

Borneman, Walter R. *Polk: The Man Who Transformed the Presidency and America*. New York: Random House, 2009.

Bothwell, Robert. *Your Country, My Country: A United History of the United States and Canada*. New York: Oxford University Press, 2015.

Bottomly-O'looney, Jennifer, Kirby Lambert. *Montana's Charlie Russell: Art in the Collection of the Montana Historical Society*. Helena: Montana Historical Society Press, 2014.

Bowers, Alfred W. *Mandan Social and Ceremonial Organization*. Lincoln: Bison Books, 2004.

Bowman, Sheridan. *Radiocarbon Dating*. London: British Museum Press, 1995.

Bradford, Phillip Verner, Harvey Blume. *Ota Benga: The Pygmy in the Zoo*. New York: St. Martin's Press, 1992.

Braga, Luciana Lorens, Marcelo F. Mello. "Transgenerational Transmission of Trauma and Resilience." *BMC Psychiatry* 12 (2012): 134.

Brahic, Catherine. "Humanity's Forgotten Pioneers." *New Scientist* 2981 (August 9, 2014).

Brands, H. W. *Andrew Jackson: His Life and Times*. New York: Anchor Books, 2006.

———. *T. R.: The Last Romantic*. New York: Basic Books, 1997.

———. *The Man Who Saved the Union: Ulysses Grant in War and Peace*. New York: Anchor Books, 2012.

Brandt, Anthony, abridged by. *The Journals of Lewis and Clark*. Washington, D.C.: National Geographic Adventure Classics, 2002.

Brewster, Sir David. *Life of Isaac Newton.* Charleston, SC: Nabu Press, 2012.
Brinkley, Douglas. *The Wilderness Warrior: Theodore Roosevelt and the Crusade for America.* New York: HarperCollins Publisher, 2009.
Brock, Arthur John. *Greek Medicine.* London: J. M. Dent and Sons, Ltd., 1929.
Brock, Thomas D. *Robert Koch: A Life in Medicine and Bacteriology.* Washington, D.C.: American Society for Microbiology, 1999.
Brookhiser, Richard. *Founder's Son: A Life of Abraham Lincoln.* New York: Basic Books, 2014.
Brown, Dee. *Bury My Heart at Wounded Knee: An Indian History of the American West.* New York: Henry Holt and Company, 1970.
Brown, Kevin. *Penicillin Man: Alexander Fleming and the Antibiotic Revolution.* Stroud, England: The History Press, 2005.
Browne, Janet E. *Charles Darwin: Vol. 1, Voyaging.* London: Jonathan Cape, 1995.
Brummitt, Stella. *Brother Van.* New York: Methodist Book Concern, 1919.
Bryant, Jonathan M. *Dark Places of the Earth: The Voyage of the Slave Ship Antelope.* New York: Liveright Publishing, 2015.
Buckley, Jay H. *William Clark: Indian Diplomat.* Norman: University of Oklahoma Press, 2008.
Burkhardt, Frederick, Sydney Smith, eds. *The Correspondence of Charles Darwin.* Cambridge, England: Cambridge University Press, 1985.
Burnham, Patricia M. "Lewis and Clark at Ross's Hole: The Story behind Charles M. Russell's 1912 Painting." *We Proceeded On: The Journal of the National Lewis and Clark Trail Heritage Foundation* 26 (2000): 18-25.
_____. "The Paintings." In *Montana's State Capitol: The People's House,* edited by Kirby Lambert, Patricia M. Burnham, and Susan M. Near. Helena: Montana Historical Society Press, 32-75, 2002.
_____. "Russell and the Capitol Mural." *Russell's West* 3, no. 1 (1995): 3-7.
Burstein, Andrew. *Democracy's Muse: How Thomas Jefferson Became an FDR Liberal, a Reagan Republican, and a Tea Party Fanatic, All the While Being Dead.* Charlottesville: University of Virginia Press, 2015.
Butzer, Karl W. "The Americas Before and After 1492: An Introduction to Current Geographical Research." *Annals of the Association of American Geographers* 82 (1992): 345-368.
Bynum, Helen. *Spitting Blood: The History of Tuberculosis.* Cambridge, England: Oxford University Press, 2015.
Byrne, James M. *Religion and the Enlightenment: From Descartes to Kant.* Louisville: Westminster John Knox Press, 1996.
Caldwell, Wilber W. *American Narcissism: The Myth of National Superiority.* New York: Algora Publishing, 2006.
Callaway, Ewen. "Ancient Genome Stirs Ethics Debate," *Nature* 506 (February 13, 2014): 162-163.
Calloway, Colin G. *One Vast Winter Count: The Native American West before Lewis and Clark.* Lincoln: University of Nebraska Press, 2003.
_____. *The Victory with No Name: The Native American Defeat of the First American Army.* New York: Oxford University Press, 2014.
Campbell, Joseph. *The Masks of God: Creative Mythology.* New York: Viking Press, 1968.
Canfield, Michael R. *Theodore Roosevelt in the Field.* Chicago: University of Chicago Press, 2015.

Cardozo, Christopher, ed. *Sacred Legacy: Edward S. Curtis and the North American Indian.* New York: Simon & Schuster, 2000.

Cash, Philip. *Dr. Benjamin Waterhouse: A Life in Medicine and Public Service (1754-1846).* Boston: Boston Medical Library & Science Publications, 2006.

Catlin, George. *Letters and Notes on the Manners, Customs, and Condition of the North American Indians* (Vol. 1 and 2). Minneapolis: Ross & Haines, 1965.

Cecil, Paul Frederick. *Herbicidal Warfare: The Ranch Hand Project in Vietnam.* Westport, CT: Praeger Publishers, 1986.

Chacon, Richard J., Ruben G. Mendoza, eds. *North American Indigenous Warfare and Ritual Violence.* Tucson: University of Arizona Press, 2007.

Chalfant, William Y. *Hancock's War: Conflict on the Southern Plains.* Norman: University of Oklahoma Press, 2010.

Cherry, James D. "Pertussis Vaccine Encephalopathy: It's Time to Recognize It as the Myth That It Is." *Journal of the American Medical Association* 263, no. 12 (1990): 1679-1680.

Christianson, Gale E. *Isaac Newton and the Scientific Revolution.* New York: Oxford University Press, 1996.

Churchill, Ward. *Kill the Indian, Save the Man: The Genocidal Impact of American Indian Residential Schools.* San Francisco: City Light Books, 2004.

Cimino, Richard, Christopher Smith. *Atheist Awakening: Secular Activism and Community in America.* New York: Oxford University Press, 2014.

Cleary, Thomas F. *The Essential Koran: The Heart of Islam: An Introductory Selection of Readings from the Qur'an.* San Francisco: HarperSanFrancisco, 1993.

Cochrane, Charles Norris. *Christianity and Classical Culture: A Study of Thought and Action from Augustus to Augustine.* New York: Oxford University Press, 1957.

Cohen, Adam. *Imbeciles: The Supreme Court, American Eugenics, and the Sterilization of Carrie Buck.* New York: Penguin Press, 2016.

Cohen, Felix S. "Original Indian Title." *Minnesota Law Review* 32 (1947): 28, 35.

Collins, Douglas. *The Story of Kodak.* New York: Harry N. Abrams, Inc., 1990.

Collins, Francis S. *The Language of God: A Scientist Presents Evidence for Belief.* New York: Free Press, 2006.

Colp, Ralph, Jr. *Darwin's Illness.* Gainesville: University of Florida Press, 2008.

Colton, Larry. *Counting Coup: A True Story of Basketball and Honor on the Little Big Horn.* New York: Warner Books, 2000.

Connell, Evan S. *Son of the Morning Star: Custer and the Little Bighorn.* New York: HarperPerennial, 1984.

Conniff, Richard. *House of Lost Worlds: Dinosaurs, Dynasties, and the Story of Life on Earth.* New Haven: Yale University Press, 2016.

Cook, Nobel David. *Born to Die: Disease and the New World Conquest, 1492-1650.* Cambridge, England: Cambridge University Press, 1998.

Cooper, Walter. *A Most Desperate Situation: Frontier Adventures of a Young Scout, 1858-1864.* Edited by Rick Newby, with introduction and afterword by Larry Len Peterson. Helena, MT: Falcon Publishing, 2000, 2001.

Copeland, W. E., G. Keeler, A. Angold, E. J. Costello. "Traumatic Events and Posttraumatic Stress in Childhood." *Archives of General Psychiatry* 64 (2007): 577-584.

Coss, Stephen. *The Fever of 1721: The Epidemic That Revolutionized Medicine and American Politics.* New York: Simon & Schuster, 2016.

Cottingham, J., et al. *The Philosophical Writings of Descartes.* Cambridge, England: Cambridge University Press, 1988.

Cox, Harvey. *The Secular City.* New York: Macmillan, 1965.

Cozzens, Peter. *The Earth is Weeping: The Epic Story of the Indian Wars for the American West.* New York: Knopf, 2016.

Crary, Catherine S., ed. *Dear Belle: Letters from a Cadet and Officer to His Sweetheart, 1858-1865.* Middletown, CT: Wesleyan University Press, 1965.

Crelin, J. K., et al. *Herbal Medicine Past and Present: A Reference Guide to Medicinal Plants.* Durham, NC: Duke University Press, 1990.

Crosby, Alfred. *Ecological Imperialism: The Biological Expansion of Europe, 900-1900.* Cambridge, England: Cambridge University Press, 1986.

———. *The Columbian Exchange: Biological and Cultural Consequences of 1492.* Westport, CT: Greenwood Press, 1972.

———. "Virgin Soil Epidemics as a Factor in the Aboriginal Depopulation in America." *William and Mary Quarterly,* 3rd ser., 33 (April 1976): 289-299.

Cunfer, Geoff, Bill Waiser. *Bison and People on the North American Great Plains: A Deep Environmental History.* College Station: Texas A&M University Press, 2016.

Custer, Elizabeth Bacon. *"Boots and Saddles," or Life in Dakota with General Custer.* New York: Harper and Brothers, 1885.

———. *Following the Guidon.* New York: Harper and Brothers, 1890.

———. *Tenting on the Plains, or General Custer in Kansas and Texas.* New York: Harper and Brothers, 1887.

Custer, George Armstrong. *My Life on the Plains.* San Bernardino, CA: History in Words and Pictures Series by John W. Cirignani, 2015.

Cutright, Paul Russell. *Lewis and Clark: Pioneering Naturalists.* Urbana: University of Illinois Press, 1969.

Daley, James, ed. *Great Inaugural Addresses.* Mineola, NY: Dover Publications, Inc., 2010.

Damrosch, Leo. *Jean-Jacques Rousseau: Restless Genius.* New York: Houghton Mifflin, 2005.

Darwin, Charles. *The Descent of Man, and Selection in Relation to Sex.* London: John Murray, 1871.

———. *On the Origin of Species by Means of Natural Selection, or the Preservation of Favoured Races in the Struggle for Life.* London: John Murray, 1859.

———. *Origin of Species.* New York: Bantam Classics, 1999.

Davidson, Ian. *Voltaire: A Life.* New York: Pegasus, 2012.

Davies, D. W., W. W. Davies. *The Codes of Hammurabi and Moses with Copious Comments, Index, and Bible References.* Bel Air, CA: Book Jungle, 2007.

Davis, Daniel M. *The Compatibility Gene.* New York: Penguin Books, 2014.

Davis, David Brion. *The Problem of Slavery in the Age of Revolution, 1770-1823.* New York: Oxford University Press, 1999.

Davis, Robert, Mark Zannis. *The Genocide Machine in Canada: The Pacification of the North.* Montreal, Canada: Black Rose Books, 1973.

Davis, William C. *Crucible of Command: Ulysses S. Grant and Robert E. Lee—The War They Fought, the Peace They Forged.* Boston: Da Capo, 2015.

Day, Michael, "Fossil Reanalysis Pushes Back Origin of *Homo sapiens.*" *Scientific American* (February 17, 2005).

de Bary, William Theodore. *The Buddhist Tradition in India, China & Japan*. New York: Modern Library, 1969.

de la Rosa, L. A., E. Alvarez-Parilla, G. A. Gonzalez-Aguilar. *Fruit and Vegetable Phytochemicals: Chemistry, Nutritional Value and Stability*. New York: Wiley-Blackwell, 2010.

Debelius, Maggie. *The Spirit World*. Henry Woodhead, ed. Alexandria, VA: Time-Life Books, 1992.

Deloria, Vine, Jr. *Custer Died for Your Sins: An Indian Manifesto*. Norman: University of Oklahoma Press, 1988.

_____. *God is Red: A Native View of Religion*. Golden, CO: Fulcrum Publishing, 2003.

Densmore, Frances. *Teton Sioux Music*. Washington, D.C.: Smithsonian Institution Bureau of American Ethnology, Bulletin 61, 1918.

Descartes, Rene. *Meditations on First Philosophy*. New York: Oxford University Press, 2008.

Desmond, Adrian, James Moore. *Darwin*. London: Penguin Group, 1991.

_____. *Darwin's Sacred Cause: Race, Slavery and the Quest for Human Origins*. London: Allen Lane, 2009.

Diamond, Jared. *Guns, Germs, and Steel: The Fates of Human Societies*. New York: W.W. Norton & Company, 1999.

Diettert, Gerald A. *Grinnell's Glacier: George Bird Grinnell and Glacier National Park*. Missoula, MT: Mountain Press Publishing, 1992.

Dippie, Brian W. *Catlin and His Contemporaries: The Politics of Patronage*. Lincoln: University of Nebraska Press, 1990.

_____. *Custer's Last Stand: The Anatomy of an American Myth*. Lincoln: University of Nebraska Press, 1994.

_____. *The Vanishing American: White Attitudes & U.S. Indian Policy*. Lawrence: University Press of Kansas, 1982.

Dobson, Jessie. *John Hunter*. London: E & S Livingstone, 1969.

Dodd, Brian J. *The Problem with Paul*. Downers Grove, IL: IVP Academic, 1996.

Dodge, Richard Irving. *The Hunting Grounds of the Great West: The Plains of the Great West and Their Inhabitants, Being a Description of the Plains, Game, Indians, etc. of the Great North American Desert*. London: Chatto & Windus, 1877.

_____. *Thirty-Three Years Among Our Wild Indians*. New York: Archer House, 1959.

Donovan, James. *A Terrible Glory: Custer and the Little Bighorn—the Last Great Battle of the American West*. New York: Little, Brown and Company, 2008.

Dorsey, George A. *The Mythology of the Wichita*. 1924: reprint, Norman, University of Oklahoma Press, 1995.

Dowdle, W. R. "Influenza Pandemic Periodicity, Virus Recycling, and the Art of Risk Assessment." *Emerging Infectious Diseases* 12, no. 1 (January 2006): 34-39.

Doyle, Don H. *The Cause of All Nations: An International History of the American Civil War*. New York: Basic Books, 2014.

Durant, Will. *Rousseau and Revolution: A History of Civilization in France, England, and Germany from 1756, and in the Remainder of Europe from 1715-1789*. New York: Simon & Schuster, 1967.

Eastman, Elaine Goodale. *Pratt: The Red Man's Moses*. Norman: University of Oklahoma Press, 1935.

Edel, Charles N. *Nation Builder: John Quincy Adams and the Grand Strategy of the Republic.* Cambridge, MA: Harvard University Press, 2014.

Edmonds, Margot, Ella E. Clark. *Voices of the Winds: Native American Legends.* New York: Castle Books, 1989.

Edwards, Mark U., Jr. *Printing, Propaganda, and Martin Luther.* Minneapolis: Fortress Press, 1994.

Egan, Timothy. *Short Nights of the Shadow Catcher: The Epic Life and Immortal Photographs of Edward Curtis.* Boston: Houghton Mifflin Harcourt, 2012.

Ehrman, Bart D. *Did Jesus Exist? The Historical Argument for Jesus of Nazareth.* New York: HarperOne, 2012.

_____. *Forged: Writing in the Name of God—Why the Bible Authors Are Not Who We Think They Are.* New York: HarperOne, 2011.

_____. *Jesus, Interrupted: Revealing the Hidden Contradictions in the Bible (and Why We Don't Know About Them).* New York: HarperOne, 2009.

_____. *Lost Christianities: The Battles for Scripture and the Faiths We Never Knew.* New York: Oxford University Press, 2003.

_____. *Misquoting Jesus: The Story Behind Who Changed the Bible and Why.* San Francisco: HarperSanFrancisco, 2005.

Eisler, Benita. *The Red Man's Bones: George Catlin, Artist and Showman.* New York: W.W. Norton & Company, 2013.

Ellenberg, Jordan. *How Not to Be Wrong: The Power of Mathematical Thinking.* New York: Penguin Press, 2015.

Ellingson, Ter. *The Myth of the Noble Savage.* Berkeley: University of California Press, 2001.

Ellis, Clyde. "Ethnic Cleansing and the Indian: The Crime That Should Haunt America," book review. *Montana The Magazine of Western History* 65 (Spring 2015): 85, 86.

Ellis, Joseph J. *His Excellency: George Washington.* New York: Knopf, 2003.

Ellis, Richard N. *General Pope and U.S. Indian Policy.* Albuquerque: University of New Mexico Press, 1973.

Emerson, Michael O., Christian Smith. *Divided by Faith: Evangelical Religion and the Problem of Race in America.* New York: Oxford University Press, 2000.

Engerman, Stanley L., Kenneth L. Sokoloff. "Factor of Endowments, Institutions, and Differential Paths of Growth Among the New World Economies" In *How Latin America Fell Behind,* Stephen Haber, ed. Stanford: Stanford University Press, 1997, 260-304.

Erdoes Richard, Alfonso Ortiz, eds. *American Indian Myths and Legends.* New York: Pantheon Books, 1984.

Esposito, John. *What Everyone Needs to Know about Islam.* New York: Oxford University Press, 2002.

Evans, Richard J. *The Third Reich in History and Memory.* New York: Oxford University Press, 2015.

Fenn, Elizabeth A. "Biological Warfare in Eighteenth-Century North America: Beyond Jeffrey Amherst." *Journal of American History* 86 (March 2000): 1552-1580.

_____. *Encounters at the Heart of the World: A History of the Mandan People.* New York: Hill and Wang, 2014.

_____. *Pox Americana: The Great Smallpox Epidemic of 1775-82.* New York: Hill and Wang, 2002.

Fenner, F. *Smallpox and Its Eradication.* Geneva, Switzerland: World Health Organization, 1988.

Fenster, Julie. *Jefferson's America: The President, the Purchase, and the Explorers Who Transformed a Nation.* New York: Crown Publishing Group, 2016.

Ferber, Michael. *Romanticism: A Very Short Introduction.* New York: Oxford University Press, 2010.

Ferguson, Eugene S. *Oliver Evans: Inventive Genius of the American Industrial Revolution.* Wilmington, DE: Eleutherian Mills-Haley Foundation, 1980.

Ferguson, Niall. *Empire: The Rise and Demise of the British World Order and the Lessons for Global Power.* New York: Basic Books, 2004.

Finke, Roger, Rodney Stark. *The Churching of America, 1776-1990: Winners and Losers in Our Religious Economy.* New Brunswick, NJ: Rutgers University, 1992.

Finocchiaro, Maurice. *Defending Copernicus and Galileo: Critical Reasoning in the Two Affairs.* New York: Springer, 2010.

Fisher, Richard B. *Edward Jenner 1749-1823.* London: Andre Deutsch, 1991.

Fitzpatrick, Thomas B., et al. *Dermatology in General Medicine.* New York: McGraw-Hill Company, 1979.

Fleagle, John G., et al. "Paleoanthropology of the Kibish Formation, Southern Ethiopia: Introduction." *Journal of Human Evolution* 55, no. 3 (September 2008): 360-363.

Flesche, Francis La. *The Middle Five: Indian Schoolboys of the Omaha Tribe.* Lincoln: University of Nebraska Press, 1963.

Flores, Dan. *American Serengeti: The Last Big Animals of the Great Plains.* Lawrence: University Press of Kansas, 2016.

———. *Coyote America: A Natural and Supernatural History.* New York: Basic Books, 2016.

———. *Visions of the Big Sky: Painting and Photographing the Northern Rocky Mountain West.* Norman: University of Oklahoma Press, 2010.

Foley, William E. *Wilderness Journey: The Life of William Clark.* Columbia: University of Missouri Press, 2004.

Foner, Eric. *Reconstruction: America's Unfinished Revolution, 1863-1877.* New York: Harper and Row, 1988.

Ford, Michael. *Wounded Prophet: A Portrait of Henri J.M. Nouwen.* New York: Image Books Doubleday, 2002.

Fox, Richard Wightman. *Lincoln's Body: A Cultural History.* New York: W.W. Norton and Company, 2015.

Francis, Julie, Larry Loendorf. *Ancient Visions: Petroglyphs and Pictographs from the Wind River and Bighorn Country, Wyoming and Montana.* Salt Lake City: University of Utah Press, 2002.

Franco-Paredes, Carlos, Lorena Lammoglia, Jose Ignacio-Preciado. "The Spanish Royal Philanthropic Expedition to bring Smallpox Vaccination to the New World and Asia in the 19th Century." *Clinical Infectious Diseases* (Oxford Journals) 41, no. 9 (2005): 1285-1289.

Fraser, Flora. *The Washingtons: George and Martha, "Join'd by Friendship, Crown'd by Love."* New York: Knopf, 2015.

Fraser, Robert W. *Forts of the West: Military Forts and Presidios and Posts Commonly Called Forts West of the Mississippi River to 1898.* Norman: University of Oklahoma Press, 1977.

Frost, Lawrence A. *The Custer Album: A Pictorial Biography of General George A. Custer.* Seattle: Superior Publishing Company, 1964.

_____. *The Court-Martial of General George Armstrong Custer.* Norman: University of Oklahoma Press, 1968.

Fuller, Randall. *The Book That Changed America: How Darwin's Theory of Evolution Ignited a Nation.* New York: Viking Press, 2017.

Gandhi, Mahatma. *Gandhi, An Autobiography: The Story of My Experiments with Truth.* Boston: Beacon, 1993.

Garland, Hamlin. "The Red Man's Present Needs." *North American Review* 174 (April 1902): 479.

Garrison, Fielding H. *History of Medicine.* Philadelphia: W.B. Saunders Company, 1966.

Gaskill, Malcolm. *Between Two Worlds: How the English Became Americans.* New York: Basic Books, 2014.

Gaukroger, Stephen. *Francis Bacon and the Transformation of Early-Modern Philosophy.* Cambridge, England: Cambridge University Press, 2001.

Gaustad, Edwin, Leigh Schmidt. *The Religious History of America: The Heart of the American Story from Colonial Times to Today.* New York: HarperOne, 2004.

George, Timothy. *Theology of the Reformers.* Nashville: Broadman, 1988.

Gernet, Alexander von. "North American Indigenous Nicotiana Use and Tobacco Shamanism: The Early Documentary Record, 1520-1660." In *Tobacco Use by Native North Americans: Sacred Smoke and Silent Killer,* Joseph C. Winter, ed. Norman: University of Oklahoma Press, 2000.

Gersons, B. P., I. V. Carlier. "Post-Traumatic Stress Disorder: The History of a Recent Concept. *British Journal of Psychiatry* 161 (1992): 742-748.

Gibbon, John. "Our Indian Question." *Journal of Military Service U.S.* II (1881), 102, 106, 107.

Gilman, Carolyn. *Lewis and Clark Across the Divide.* Washington, D.C.: Smithsonian Books, 2003.

Glassner, David. "Crisis of 1873." In *Business and Cycles and Depressions: An Encyclopedia.* New York: Garland Publishing, 1997.

Goebel, T., et al. "The Late Pleistocene Dispersal of Modern Humans in the Americas." *Science* 319 (February 5, 2010): 1497-1502.

Goldberger, Joseph. "Beans for Prevention of Pellagra." *Journal of the American Medical Association* 63 (October 1914): 1314.

Goodwin, Doris Kearns. *Team of Rivals: The Political Genius of Abraham Lincoln.* New York: Simon & Schuster, 2005.

Goodwin, George. *Benjamin Franklin in London: The British Life of America's Founding Father.* New Haven: Yale University Press, 2016.

Gopnick, Alison. *The Gardener and the Carpenter: What the New Science of Childhood Development Tells Us About the Relationship Between Parents and Children.* New York: Farrar, Strauss and Giroux, 2016.

Gordon-Reed, Annette. *The Hemingses of Monticello: An American Family.* New York: W. W. Norton & Company, 2009.

_____, Peter Onuf. *"Most Blessed of the Patriarchs": Thomas Jefferson and the Empire of the Imagination.* New York: Liveright Publishing, 2016.

Gottfried, Robert S. *The Black Death.* New York: The Free Press, 1985.
Gould, Stephan J. *Wonderful Life: The Burgess Shale and the Nature of History.* New York: W.W. Norton & Company, 1990.
Grant, E. *The Foundations of Modern Science in the Middle Ages: Their Religious, Institutional, and Intellectual Contexts.* Cambridge, England: Cambridge University Press, 1996.
Gray, John. *The Soul of the Marionette: A Short Inquiry into Human Freedom.* New York: Farrar, Strauss and Giroux, 2016.
Graybill, Andrew R. *The Red and the White: A Family Saga of the American West.* New York: Liveright Publishing, 2013.
Green, James. *The Herbal Medicine Maker's Handbook.* White River Junction, VT: Chelsea Green Publishing, 2000.
Greenberg, Amy S. *Manifest Destiny and American Territorial Expansion: A Brief History with Documents.* New York: Bedford/St. Martin's, 2012.
Greene, Jerome A. *American Carnage: Wounded Knee 1890.* Norman: University of Oklahoma Press, 2014.
_____. *Battles and Skirmishes of the Great Sioux War, 1876-1877.* Norman: University of Oklahoma Press, 1993.
_____. *Finding Sand Creek: History, Archeology, and the 1864 Massacre Site.* Norman: University of Oklahoma Press, 2006.
_____. *Lakota and Cheyenne: Indian Views of the Great Sioux War, 1876-1877.* Norman: University of Oklahoma Press, 1994.
_____. "The Great Sioux War." *True West Magazine* 48 (May/June 2001): 24-26.
_____. *Washita: The U.S. Army and the Southern Cheyennes, 1867-1869.* Norman: University of Oklahoma Press, 2008.
Greengrass, Mark. *Christendom Destroyed: Europe 1517-1648.* New York: Penguin Books, 2015.
Gregory, Andrew. *Harvey's Heart: The Discovery of Blood Circulation.* Cambridge, England: Icon Books, 2001.
Grendler, Paul F. "The Universities of the Renaissance and Reformation." *Renaissance Quarterly* 57 (Spring 2004): 1-42.
Griffin, Diane. *Measles: History and Basic Biology.* New York: Springer, 2008.
Grinnell, George Bird. *Pawnee, Blackfoot, and Cheyenne: History and Folklore of the Plains from the Writings of George Bird Grinnell.* New York: Charles Scribner's Sons, 1961.
_____. *Blackfoot Lodge Tales: The Story of a Prairie People.* New York: Charles Scribner's Sons, 1892.
_____. "Tenure of Land among the Indians." *American Anthropology* N.S. IX (January-March 1907): 6-8.
Gueniffey, Patrice. *Bonaparte: 1769-1802.* Cambridge, MA: Harvard University Press, 2015.
Guiliano, Jennifer. *Indian Spectacle: College Mascots and the Anxiety of Modern America.* New Brunswick, NJ: Rutgers University Press, 2015.
Gutierrez, Edward A. *Doughboys on the Great War: How American Soldiers Viewed Their Military Experience.* Lawrence: University Press of Kansas, 2014.
Guyatt, Nicholas. *Bind Us Apart: How Enlightened Americans Invented Racial Segregation.* New York: Basic Books, 2016.

Haag, Pamela. *The Gunning of America: Business and the Making of American Gun Culture.* New York: Basic Books, 2016.

Hally, David J. "Chiefdom of Coosa." In *The Forgotten Centuries: Indians and Europeans in the American South, 1521-1574,* edited by Charles Hudson and Carmen Chaves Tesser, 227-253. Athens, GA: University of Georgia, 1994.

Hampton Institute. *Twenty-Two Years' Work of the Hampton Normal and Agricultural Institute at Hampton, Virginia.* Hampton, VA: Hampton Normal School Press, 1893.

Hannan, Daniel. *Inventing Freedom: How the English-Speaking Peoples Made the Modern World.* New York: HarperCollins, 2014.

Harari, Yuval Noah. *Sapiens: A Brief History of Humankind.* New York: HarperCollins, 2015.

Harbarger, Molly. "Decrepit Fish Camps Built on Broken Promises." *Oregonian,* March 11, 2016.

Harding, Sandra. *The "Racial" Economy of Science: Toward a Democratic Future.* Bloomington: Indiana University Press, 1993.

Harney, John. "How Do Sunni and Shia Islam Differ?" *The New York Times,* January 3, 2016.

Harris, Marvin. *The Rise of Anthropological Theory: A History of Theories of Culture.* Lanham, MD: AltaMira Press, 2001.

Hart, D. G. *Calvinism: A History.* New Haven: Yale University Press, 2013.

Hartwell, Robert. "Historical Analogism, Public Policy, and Social Science in Eleventh- and Twelfth-Century China." *American Historical Review* 76 (1971): 690-727.

Haskins, Charles Homer. [1923] *The Rise of Universities.* New Brunswick, NJ: Transaction, 2002.

Haviland, William A., Dana Walrath, Harald E. L. Prins, Carol Ann McBride. *Evolution and Prehistory: The Human Challenge.* Belmont, CA: Wadsworth Publishing, 2007.

Headrick, Daniel R. *The Tools of Empire: Technology and European Imperialism in the Nineteenth Century.* New York: Oxford University Press, 1981.

Hedren, Paul L. *Powder River: Disastrous Opening of the Great Sioux War.* Norman: University of Oklahoma Press, 2016.

Hefelbower, G. *The Relation of John Locke to English Deism.* Chicago, IL: University of Chicago Press, 1918.

Hejmanowski, T. S., S. P. Cuffe. "Alone in a Crowded Room: The Continuum of Post-Traumatic Stress." *Northeast Florida Medicine* 62 (2011): 15-22.

Hempel, Sandra. *The Strange Case of the Broad Street Pump: John Snow and the Mystery of Cholera.* Berkeley: University of California Press, 2007.

Henderson, Donald. *Smallpox: The Death of a Disease.* New York: Prometheus Books, 2009.

Hendrix, Scott H. *Martin Luther: Visionary Reformer.* New Haven: Yale University Press, 2015.

Henige, David. *Numbers from Nowhere: The American Indian Contact Population Debate.* Norman: University of Oklahoma Press, 1998.

Henry, Alexander. *The Journal of Alexander Henry the Younger, 1799-1814.* Barry M. Gough, ed. Toronto, Canada: Champlain Society, 1988.

Hershkovitz, Israel "Levantine Cranium from Manot Cave (Israel) Foreshadows the First European Modern Humans," *Nature* 520 (April 9, 2015): 216-219.

Hertzke, Allen D., ed. *Religious Freedom in America: Constitutional Roots and Contemporary Challenges.* Norman: University of Oklahoma Press, 2015.

Hezser, Catherine. *Literacy in Roman Palestine.* Tubingen, Germany: Mohr Siebeck, 2001.

Hidy, Ralph W., Muriel E. Hidy, Roy V. Scott, Don L. Hofsommer. *The Great Northern Railway: A History.* Minneapolis: University of Minnesota Press, 1988.
Hinrichs, T. J. Linda L. Barnes, et al. *Chinese Medicine and Healing: An Illustrated History.* Cambridge, MA: Harvard University Press, 2012.
Hixson, Walter L. *American Settler Colonialism.* New York: Palgrave MacMillan, 2015.
Hodes, Martha. *Mourning Lincoln.* New Haven: Yale University Press, 2015.
Hoffecker, John F., Scott A. Elias. *Human Ecology of Beringia.* New York: Columbia University Press, 2007.
Hoffman, Charles. *The Depression of the Nineties: An Economic History.* Westport, CT: Greenwood Publishing, 1970.
Hoig, Stan. *The Sand Creek Massacre.* Norman: University of Oklahoma Press, 2005.
Holborn, Louise W. "Printing and the Growth of the Protestant Movement in Germany from 1517 to 1524." *Church History* 11 (1942): 123-137.
Holler, Clyde, ed. *Black Elk Reader.* Syracuse, NY: Syracuse University Press, 2000.
Holloway, Jean. *Hamlin Garland: A Biography.* Austin: University of Texas, 2014.
Homans, James E. "Putnam, George Haven." *The Cyclopedia of American Biography.* New York: The Press Association Compilers, Inc., 1918.
Honour, Hugh. *The European Vision of America.* Cleveland: The Cleveland Museum of Art, 1975.
Horne, Alistair. *Hubris: The Tragedy of War in the Twentieth Century.* New York: Harper, 2015.
Horsman, Reginald. *Josiah Nott of Mobile: Southerner, Physician, and Racial Theorist.* Baton Rouge: Louisiana State University Press, 1987.
Houldcroft, Charlotte J., Simon J. Underdown. "Neanderthal Genomics Suggests a Pleistocene Time Frame for the First Epidemiologic Transition." *American Journal of Physical Anthropology* 160, no. 3 (July 2016): 379-388.
Howat, John. *American Paradise: The World of the Hudson River School.* New York: Metropolitan Museum of Art, Harry N. Abrams, 1987.
Huberman, Jack. *The Quotable Atheist.* New York: Nation Books, 2007.
Hudnut, William H., III. "Samuel Stanhope Smith: Enlightened Conservative." *Journal of the History of Ideas* 17, no. 4 (1956): 540-552.
Huerta-Sanchez, Emilia, Rasmus Nielsen, et al. "Altitude Adaption in Tibetans Caused by Introgression in Denisovan-like DNA," *Nature* 512 (August 14, 2014): 194-197.
Hunt, Lynn. *Writing History in the Global Era.* New York: W.W. Norton & Company, 2015.
Hunter, Louis C. *A History of Industrial Power in the United States, 1730-1930.* Vol. 2: Steam Power. Charlottesville: University of Virginia Press, 1985.
Hutton, Paul Andrew. "America's Longest War." *True West Magazine* 63 (May 2016): 28-29.
_____. *Phil Sheridan and His Army.* Norman: University of Oklahoma Press, 1999.
_____. *Soldiers West: Biographies from the Military Frontier.* Norman: University of Oklahoma Press, 2009.
_____. *The Apache Wars: The Hunt for Geronimo, the Apache Kid, and the Captive Boy Who Started the Longest War in American History.* New York: Crown Publishing Group, 2016.
_____. *The Custer Reader.* Lincoln: University of Nebraska, 1992.
_____. "The Severed Heads Campaign." *True West Magazine* 62 (March 2015): 28-33.
Innis, Harold A. *The Fur Trade in Canada: An Introduction to Canadian Economic History.* Rev. ed. Toronto, Canada: University of Toronto Press, 1970.

Irmscher, Christoph, ed. *Audubon: Writings and Drawings*. New York: The Library of America, 1999.

Isaac, Benjamin. *The Invention of Racism in Classical Antiquity*. Princeton: Princeton University Press, 2006.

Jackson, Donald, ed. *Letters of the Lewis and Clark Expedition, with Related Documents: 1783-1854*, Vol. I & II. Urbana: University of Illinois Press, 1978.

———. *Voyages of the Steamboat Yellow Stone*. New York: Houghton, Mifflin, 1985.

Jackson, Helen. *A Century of Dishonor: A Sketch of the United States Government's Dealings with Some of the Indian Tribes*. Norman: University of Oklahoma Press, 1995.

Jackson, Joe. *Black Elk: The Life of an American Visionary*. New York: Farrar, Strauss and Giroux, 2016.

Jackson, John P., Nadine M. Weidman. *Race, Racism, and Science: Social Impact and Interaction*. New Brunswick, NJ: Rutgers University Press, 2005.

Jackson, Mark, ed. *The Oxford Handbook of the History of Medicine*. New York: Oxford University Press, 2011.

Jacobs, Margaret D. "Genocide or Ethnic Cleansing? Are These Our Only Choices?" *Western Historical Quarterly* 47, no. 4 (Winter 2016): 444-448.

———. *White Mother to a Dark Race: Settler Colonialism, Maternalism, and the Removal of Indigenous Children in the American West and Australia, 1880-1940*. Lincoln: University of Nebraska Press, 2009.

Jacoby, Susan. *Strange Gods: A Secular History of Conversion*. Austin, TX: River Grove Books, 2016.

Jaher, David. *The Witch of Lime Street: Séance, Seduction, and Houdini in the Spirit World*. New York: Crown Publishing Group, 2015.

Jahoda, Gloria. *Trail of Tears*. New York: Rinehart and Wilson, 1975.

Jahoda, Gustav. *Images of Savages: Ancients Roots of Modern Prejudice in Western Culture*. New York: Routledge, 1998.

Jedicke, Peter. *Great Inventions of the 20th Century*. New York: Scientific American, 2007.

Jefferson, Thomas. *The Jefferson Bible: The Life and Morals of Jesus of Nazareth Extracted Textually from the Gospels in Greek, Latin, French & English*. Smithsonian Edition with Essays by Harry R. Rubenstein, Barbara Clark Smith & Janice Stagnitto Ellis. Washington, D.C.: Smithsonian Books, 2011.

Jeffrey, Julie Roy. *Converting the West: A Biography of Narcissa Whitman*. Norman: University of Oklahoma Press, 1994.

Jenkins, Roy. *Churchill: A Biography*. New York: Farrar, Strauss and Giroux, 2001.

Jenner, Greg. *A Million Years in a Day: A Curious History of Everyday Life from the Stone Age to the Phone Age*. New York: Thomas Dunne Books, 2016.

Jennings, Chris. *Paradise Now: The Story of American Utopianism*. New York: Random House, 2016.

Jennings, Francis. *The Founders of America: How Indians Discovered the Land, Pioneered in It, and Created Great Classical Civilizations*. New York: W. W. Norton & Co, Inc., 1993.

———. *The Invasion of America: Indians, Colonialism, and the Cant of Conquest*. New York: W.W. Norton & Company, 1976.

Johansen, Bruce F. *Forgotten Founders: Benjamin Franklin, the Iroquois, and the Rationale for the American Revolution*. Boston: Harvard Common Press, 1982.

Johnson, Paul. *Art: A New History*. New York: HarperCollins, 2003.

Johnston, Jeremy. "A Wilderness Hunter in the White House: Theodore Roosevelt, the Western Sportsman." *Colorado Heritage* (Autumn 2005): 2-13.

Johnston, Patricia Condon. "Louis W. Hill, Sr.: Artist, Woodsman, Booster . . . The Greatest Press Agent in the Country." *Encounters* 8 (July/August 1985).

Jones, Edgar, Simon Wessely. *Shell Shock to PTSD: Military Psychiatry from 1900 to the Gulf War.* New York: Psychology Press, 2006.

Jones, Karen R. *Epiphany in the Wilderness: Hunting, Nature, and Performance in the Nineteenth-Century American West.* Boulder: University Press of Colorado, 2015.

Jones, Robert P. *The End of White Christian America.* New York: Simon & Schuster, 2016.

Jordan, David M. *Winfield Scott Hancock: A Soldier's Life.* Bloomington: Indiana University Press, 1988.

Jordan, Winthrop D. *White over Black: American Attitudes Toward the Negro, 1550-1812.* Chapel Hill: University of North Carolina Press, 1968.

Judson, Pieter M. *The Habsburg Empire: A New History.* Cambridge, MA: Belknap Press, 2016.

Junger, Sebastian. *Tribe: On Homecoming and Belonging.* New York: Twelve, 2012.

Kaplan, Fred. *John Quincy Adams: American Visionary.* New York: Harper, 2014.

Kelton, Paul. *Cherokee Medicine, Colonial Germs: An Indigenous Nation's Fight against Smallpox, 1518-1824.* Norman: University of Oklahoma Press, 2015.

Khalidi, Tarif. *Islamic Historiography.* Albany: State University of New York, 1975.

Kidd, Colin. *The Forging of Races: Race and Scripture in the Protestant Atlantic World, 1600-2000.* Cambridge, England: Cambridge University Press, 2006.

Kidd, Thomas S. *George Whitefield: America's Spiritual Founding Father.* New Haven: Yale University Press, 2014.

Kinsey, John Louis. *Thomas Moran and the Surveying of the American West.* Washington, D.C.: Smithsonian Press, 1992.

Kissinger, Henry. *World Order.* New York: Penguin Books, 2015.

Kneale, Albert H. *Indian Agent.* Caldwell, ID: Caxton Publishers, 1950.

Knox, Henry. *American State Papers: Indian Affairs,* 2 vols. Washington, D.C.: Gales and Seaton, 1832-1834.

Kohn, Livia. *Introducing Daoism.* New York: Routledge, 2009.

Konstantin, Phil. *This Day in North American Indian History: Important Dates in the History of North America's Native Peoples for Every Calendar Day.* Cambridge, MA: Da Capo Press, 2002.

Krause, Herbert, Gary D. Olson. *Prelude to Glory: A Newspaper Accounting of Custer's 1874 Expedition to the Black Hills.* Sioux Falls, SD: Brevet Press, 1974.

Krause, Johannes, et al. "The Complete Mitochondrial DNA Genome of an Unknown Hominin from Southern Siberia," *Nature* 464 (2010): 894-897.

Kristeva, Julia. *Hannah Arendt: Life is a Narrative.* Toronto, Canada: University of Toronto Press, 2001.

Kruse, Kevin M. *One Nation Under God: How Corporate America Invented Christian America.* New York: Basic Books, 2016.

LaDow, Beth. *The Medicine Line: Life and Death on a North American Borderland.* New York: Routledge, 2001.

Lambert, Kirby, Patricia M. Burnham, and Susan M. Near. *Montana's State Capitol: The People's House.* Helena: Montana Historical Society Press, 2002.

Langford, Jerome K. *Galileo, Science and the Church.* South Bend, IN: St. Augustine Press, 1998.

Laveille, E. *The Life of Father De Smet, S.J. (1801-1873): Apostle of the Rocky Mountains.* Charlotte, NC: Tan Books and Publishers, 2000.

Leakey, Richard, Alan Walker. "Homo Erectus Unearthed." *National Geographic* 168, no. 5 (November 1985): 624-629.

Leckie, Shirley A. *Elizabeth Bacon Custer and the Making of a Myth.* Norman: University of Oklahoma Press, 1998.

Leckie, William H. *Buffalo Soldiers: A Narrative of the Negro Cavalry in the West.* Norman: University of Oklahoma Press, 1999.

Lemesurier, Peter. *Nostradamus, Bibliomancer: The Man, the Myth, the Truth.* Wayne, NJ: Career Press Inc., 2010.

Lemkin, Raphael. *Axis Rule in Occupied Europe: Laws of Occupation, Analysis of Government, Proposals for Redress.* Washington, D.C.: Carnegie Endowment for International Peace, 1944.

Leonard, Thomas C. *Illiberal Reformers: Race, Eugenics, and American Economics in the Progressive Era.* Princeton, NJ: Princeton University Press, 2016.

Levinson, Sanford. *An Argument Open to All: Reading The Federalist in the 21st Century.* New Haven: Yale University Press, 2015.

Levinson, Warren. *Review of Medical Microbiology and Immunology.* New York: McGraw Hill, 2010.

Lewis, Bernard. *What Went Wrong.* New York: Oxford University Press, 2002.

Lewis, C. S. *The Problem of Pain.* New York: A Touchstone Book, 1996.

———. *The Screwtape Letters.* San Francisco: HarperSanFrancisco, 2001.

Lewis, Stephanie. *War for the Plains.* Alexandria, VA: Time-Life Books, 1994.

Lewis, Tom. *Washington: A History of Our National City.* New York: Basic Books, 2015.

Lind, Robert W. *Brother Van: Montana Circuit Rider.* Las Vegas: self-published, 1992.

Linden, George. *John Neihardt and "Black Elk Speaks."* Syracuse, NY: Syracuse University Press, 2000.

Linderman, Frank B. *American: The Life Story of a Great Indian.* New York: John Day Company, 1930.

———. *Blackfeet Indians: Pictures by Winold Reiss.* St. Paul, MN: Great Northern Railway, 1935.

———. *Indian Old-Man Stories: More Sparks From War Eagle's Lodge-Fire.* New York: Charles Scribner's Sons, 1920.

———. *Indian Why Stories: Sparks From War Eagle's Lodge-Fire.* New York: Charles Scribner's Sons, 1915.

———. *Kootenai Why Stories.* New York: Charles Scribner's Sons, 1926.

———. *Montana Adventure: The Recollections of Frank B. Linderman.* Edited by H. G. Merriam. Lincoln: University of Nebraska Press, 1968.

———. *Old Man Coyote (Crow).* New York: The Junior Literary Guild, 1931.

———. *On a Passing Frontier: Sketches from the Northwest.* New York: Charles Scribner's Sons, 1920.

———. *Recollections of Charley Russell.* Edited and with an introduction by H. G. Merriam. Norman: University of Oklahoma Press, 1963.

———. *Red Mother.* New York: John Day Company, 1932.

Lindsay, Brendan. "Ethnic Cleansing and the Indian: The Crime That Should Haunt America," book review. *Western Historical Quarterly* XLVI (Spring 2015): 101, 102.
Livingstone, David N. *Adam's Ancestors: Race, Religion, and the Politics of Human Origins.* Baltimore: Johns Hopkins University Press, 2008.
Lossing, Benson J. "Our Barbarian Brethren." *Harper's Magazine* XL (May 1870): 796.
Lough, David. *No More Champagne: Churchill and His Money.* New York: Picador, 2015.
Lowen, Alexander. *Narcissism: Denial of the True Self.* New York: Macmillan, 1983.
Lowie, Robert Harry. *Notes on the Social Organizations & Customs of the Mandan, Hidatsa, & Crow Indians.* New York: AMS Press, 1976.
Lummis, Charles F. "A New Indian Policy." *Land of the Sunshine* 15 (December 1901): 463.
Lurie, Edward. "Louis Agassiz and the Races of Man." *Isis* 45, no. 3 (September 1954): 232.
Luther, Martin. [1520] *Works,* Vol. 2. Philadelphia: Muhlenberg Press, 1915.
Madley, Benjamin. *An American Genocide: The United States and the California Indian Catastrophe, 1846-1873.* New Haven: Yale University Press, 2016.
Maeder, Jay. "The Little Man in the Zoo." In *Big Town, Big Time: A New York Epic, 1898-1998.* New York: *New York Daily News,* 1999.
Magid, Paul. *George Crook: From the Redwoods to Appomattox.* Norman: University of Oklahoma Press, 2011.
———. *The Gray Fox: George Crook and the Indian Wars.* Norman: University of Oklahoma Press, 2015.
Magner, Lois N. *A History of Medicine.* Boca Raton, FL: CRC Press, 1992.
Maguen, S., B. Litz. "Moral Injury in Veterans of War." *PTSD Research Quarterly* 23 (2012): 1-6.
Mails, Thomas E. *The Mystic Warriors of the Plains.* New York: Marlowe & Company, 1995.
Makari, George. *Soul Machine: The Invention of the Modern Mind.* New York: W.W. Norton & Company, 2015.
Malcomson, Scott I. *One Drop of Blood: American Misadventure of Race.* Darby, PA: Diane Publishing Company, 2000.
Malloy, Mary. *"Boston Men" on the Coast: The American Maritime Fur Trade 1788-1844.* Kingston, Ontario, Canada: Limestone Press, 1998.
Malone, Dumas. *Jefferson the Virginian (Jefferson & His Time).* Charlottesville: University of Virginia Press, 2006.
Malone, Michael P., Richard B. Roeder, and William L. Lang. *Montana: A History of Two Centuries.* Revised ed. Seattle: University of Washington Press, 2003.
———, ed. *Montana Century: 100 Years in Pictures and Words.* Helena, MT: Falcon Publishing Inc., 1999.
Manchester, William. *A World Lit Only by Fire: The Medieval Mind and the Renaissance, Portrait of an Age.* New York: Little, Brown and Company, 1992.
———. *The Last Lion, Winston Spencer Churchill, Visions of Glory: 1874-1932.* Boston: Little, Brown and Company, 1983.
Mann, Charles C. *1491: New Revelations of the Americas Before Columbus.* New York: Vintage Books, 2011.
———. *1493: Uncovering the New World Columbus Created.* New York: Vintage Books, 2012.
Mar, Alex. *Witches in America.* New York: Sarah Crichton Books, 2015.

Marchant, Jo. *Cure: A Journey into the Science of Mind Over Body.* New York: Crown Publishing Group, 2016.

Marmot, Michael. *The Health Gap: The Challenge of an Unequal World.* New York: Bloomsbury Press, 2015.

Martin, Calvin. *Keepers of the Game: Indian-Animal Relationships and the Fur Trade.* Berkeley: University of California Press, 1978.

_____. *The Way of the Human Being.* New Haven: Yale University Press, 1999.

Martin, James. *Seven Last Words: An Invitation to a Deeper Friendship with Jesus.* New York: HarperOne, 2016.

Martin, Marty Kemp. *Leonardo.* New York: Oxford University Press, 2004.

Marty, Martin. *The Modern Schism: Three Paths to the Secular.* New York: Harper & Row, 1969.

Marzio, Peter C. *The Democratic Art: An Exhibition on the History of Chromolithography in America, 1840-1900.* Fort Worth: Amon Carter Museum, 1979.

Masterson, James F. *The Search for the Real Self: Unmasking the Personality of Our Age.* New York: Free Press, 1988.

McBeth, Sally J. *Ethnic Identity and the Boarding School Experience of West-Central Oklahoma American Indians.* Washington, D.C.: University Press of America, 1983.

McClellan, George Brinton. *McClellan's Own Story.* New York: Charles L. Webster and Co., 1887.

McClintock, Walter. "Blackfoot Warrior Societies." *Southwest Museum Leaflets* no. 8 (1937).

_____. *The Old North Trail, or Life, Legends and Religion of the Blackfeet Indians.* London: MacMillan and Co., 1910.

McCracken, Harold. *George Catlin and the Old Frontier.* New York: The Dial Press, 1959.

McCullough, David. *Brave Companions: Portraits in History.* New York: Simon & Schuster, 1992.

_____. *John Adams.* New York: Simon & Schuster, 2001.

_____. *1776.* New York: Simon & Schuster, 2005.

McDonnell, Michael. *Masters of Empire: Great Lakes Indians and the Making of America.* New York: Hill and Wang, 2015.

McDonough, James Les. *William Tecumseh Sherman: In the Service of My Country: A Life.* New York: W.W. Norton & Company, 2016.

McGillycuddy, Julie B. *McGillycuddy, Agent: A Biography of Dr. Valentine T. McGillycuddy.* Stanford: Stanford University Press, 1941.

McKenzie, Charles. "Charles McKenzie's Narratives." In *Early Fur Trade on the Northern Plains: Canadian Traders among the Mandan and Hidatsa Indians, 1738-1818, the Narratives of John Macdonell, David Thompson, Francois-Antoine Larocque, and Charles McKenzie,* W. Raymond Wood and Thomas Thiessen, eds. Norman: University of Oklahoma Press, 1985.

McKinney, Lillie G. "History of the Albuquerque Indian School." *New Mexico Historical Quarterly* 20 (April 1945): 116.

McLoughlin, William. *Cherokee Renascence in the New Republic.* Princeton: Princeton University Press, 1986.

McMurtry, Larry. *Custer.* New York: Simon & Schuster, 2012.

McPherson, James M. *Battle Cry of Freedom: the Civil War Era.* New York: Oxford University Press, 2003.

Meacham, Jon. *American Gospel: God, The Founding Fathers, and the Making of a Nation.* New York: Random House Trade Paperbacks, 2007.

_____. *American Lion: Andrew Jackson in the White House.* New York: Random House, 2009.

_____. *Franklin and Winston: An Intimate Portrait of an Epic Friendship.* New York: Random House Trade Paperbacks, 2004.

_____. *Thomas Jefferson: The Art of Power.* New York: Random House Trade Paperbacks, 2013.

Meichenbaum, D. *A Clinical Handbook/Practical Therapist Manual for Assessing and Treating Adults with Post-Traumatic Stress Disorder.* Waterloo, Ontario, Canada: Institute Press, 1994.

Meltzer, David J. *First Peoples in a New World.* Berkeley: University of California Press, 2009.

Merington, Marguerite, ed. *The Custer Story: The Life and Letters of General George A. Custer and His Wife Elizabeth* [original published in 1950]. New York: Barnes & Noble Books, 1994.

Mesler, Bill, H. James Cleaves II. *A Brief History of Creation: Science and the Search for the Origin of Life.* New York: W.W. Norton & Company, 2015.

Metaxis, Eric. *Bonhoeffer: Pastor, Martyr, Prophet, Spy.* Nashville: Thomas Nelson, 2010.

Michno, Gregory F. *Lakota Noon: The Indian Narrative of Custer's Defeat.* Missoula, MT: Mountain Press Publishing, 1997.

Miller, David R., Dennis J. Smith, Joseph R. McGeshick, James Shanley, Caleb Shields. *The History of the Fort Peck Assiniboine and Sioux Tribes, 1800-2000.* Poplar and Helena, MT: Fort Peck Community College, 2008.

Miller, Jeffrey J. *Pop Warner: A Life on the Gridiron.* Jefferson, NC: McFarland, 2015.

Miller, Robert J., Jacinta Ruru, Larissa Behrendt, Tracey Lindberg. *Discovering Indigenous Lands: The Doctrine of Discovery in the English Colonies.* New York: Oxford University Press, 2010.

_____. "Economic Development in Indian Country: Will Capitalism or Socialism Succeed?" *Oregon Law Review* 80, no. 757 (2002): 808, 809.

_____. *Native America, Discovered and Conquered: Thomas Jefferson, Lewis and Clark, and Manifest Destiny.* Lincoln: University of Nebraska Press, 2008.

_____. *Reservation "Capitalism:" Economic Development in Indian Country.* Westport, CT: Praeger Publishers, 2012.

_____. "The Doctrine of Discovery in American Indian Law." *Idaho Legal Review* 42, no. 1 (2006): 21-75.

Momaday, N. Scott. *The Way to Rainy Mountain.* Albuquerque: University of New Mexico Press, 1969.

Monaghan, Jay. *Custer: The Life of General George Armstrong Custer.* Lincoln: University of Nebraska Press, 1959.

Monro, Alexander. *The Paper Trail: An Unexpected History of a Revolutionary Invention.* New York: Knopf, 2016.

Moore, Grace. "Reappraising Dickens's 'Noble Savage'." *The Dickensian* 98: 458 (2002).

Morgan, "A Plea for the Papoose." In *Americanizing the American Indian: Writings by the "Friends of the Indian" 1880-1900,* Paul Prucha, ed. Cambridge, MA: Harvard University Press, 1973.

Morris, Edmund. *Colonel Roosevelt.* New York: Random House, 2010.

_____. *Theodore Rex.* New York: Random House, 2001.
_____. *The Rise of Theodore Roosevelt.* New York: Random House Trade Paperbacks, 2001.
Morris, Ian. *Foragers, Farmers, and Fossil Fuels: How Human Values Evolve.* Princeton: Princeton University Press, 2015.
Morris, Pam. *Realism.* London: Routledge, 2003.
Morrison, Samuel E. "Hart, Albert Bushnell." *Dictionary of American Biography.* Supplement Three 1941-1945. New York: Charles Scribner's Sons, 1973.
Morton, Samuel George. *Some Observations on the Ethnography and Archaeology of the American Aborigines (1848).* Whitefish, MT: Kessinger Publishing, 2010.
Moulton, Gary E., ed. *The Definitive Journals of Lewis & Clark.* Lincoln and London: University of Nebraska Press, 1987.
Nabokov, Peter. *Native American Testimony.* New York: Penguin Group, 1991.
Navigators, The. *James: A Life-Changing Encounter with God's Word from the Book of James.* Colorado Springs: NavPress, 1988.
Neihardt, John G. *Black Elk Speaks: Being the Life Story of a Holy Man of the Oglala Sioux.* New York: MJF Books, 1996.
Neve, Michael, ed. *Charles Darwin, Autobiographies.* London: Penguin, 1905.
Newkirk, Pamela. *Spectacle: The Astonishing Life of Ota Benga.* New York: Amistad, 2015.
Nichols, Roger L. *American Indians in U.S. History.* Norman: University of Oklahoma, 2003.
Noll, Mark. *The Scandal of the Evangelical Mind.* Grand Rapids, MI: Wm. B. Eerdmans Publishing Co., 1994.
Nouwen, Henri J. *Bread for the Journey: A Daybook of Wisdom and Faith.* San Francisco: HarperSanFrancisco, 1997.
Novotny, Fritz. *Painting and Sculpture in Europe, 1780-1880.* New Haven: Yale University Press, 1971.
Nunn, John. *Ancient Egyptian Medicine.* Norman: University of Oklahoma Press, 2002.
Nutton, Vivian. *Ancient Medicine.* Abingdon-on-Thames, England: Routledge, 2012.
Nye, Bill. *Undeniable: Evolution and the Science of Creation.* New York: St. Martin's Griffin, 2015.
O'Brien, Patrick. *Railways and the Economic Development of Western Europe, 1830-1914.* New York: St. Martin's Press, 1983.
O'Connell, Robert L. *Fierce Patriot: The Tangled Lives of William Tecumseh Sherman.* New York: Random House Trade Paperbacks, 2015.
O'Donnell, James J. *Pagans: The End of Traditional Religion and the Rise of Christianity.* New York: Ecco, 2016.
Office of Indian Affairs. *Course of Study for the Indian Schools.* Washington, D.C.: Government Printing Office, 1901.
Offit, Paul A. *Bad Faith: When Religious Belief Undermines Modern Medicine.* New York: Basic Books, 2015.
_____. *Vaccinated: One Man's Quest to Defeat the World's Deadliest Diseases.* Washington, D.C.: Smithsonian, 2007.
O'Keefe, Michael. *Custer, the Seventh Cavalry, and the Little Big Horn.* Norman, OK: The Arthur H. Clark Company, 2012.
Olson, Roger E. *The Story of Christian Theology: Twenty Centuries of Tradition & Reform.* Downers Grove, IL: IVP Academic, 1999.

Onuf, Peter S. *Jefferson's Empire: The Language of American Nationhood.* Charlottesville: University of Virginia Press, 2000.

———. *The Mind of Thomas Jefferson.* Charlottesville: University of Virginia Press, 2007.

Osborne, Roger. *Civilization: A New History of the Western World.* New York: Pegasus Books, 2006.

Owsley, Douglas, David Hunt. "Clovis and Early Archaic Crania from the Anzick Site (24PA506)." *Plains Anthropologist* (May 2001).

Pääbo, Svante. *Neanderthal Man: In Search of Lost Genomes.* New York: Basic Books, 2014.

Pagden, Anthony. *Lords of All the World: Ideologies of Empire in Spain, Britain and France c. 1500-c 1800.* New Haven: Yale University Press, 1995.

Pagel, Walter. *Paracelsus: An Introduction to Philosophical Medicine in the Era of the Renaissance.* Basel, Switzerland: Karger Publishers, 1982.

Palmer, Alan. *Twilight of the Habsburgs: The Life and Times of Emperor Francis Joseph.* New York: Weidenfeld and Nicolson, 1995.

Pancoast, Henry. *Impressions of the Sioux Tribes in 1882 with Some First Principles in the Indian Question.* Philadelphia: Franklin Printing House, 1883.

Panzer, Mary. *Mathew Brady and the Image of History.* Washington, D.C.: Smithsonian Books, 2004.

Paracelsus. "Letter From Paracelsus to Erasmus." *Provincial Medical Journal and Retrospect of the Medical Sciences* 7, no. 164 (November 18, 1843): 142.

Park, Susie J. *Gentlemen Bankers: The World of J. P. Morgan.* Cambridge, MA: Harvard University Press, 2013.

Parkman, Francis, Jr. *The Oregon Trail.* 1849; reprint, edited, and with an introduction by David Levin. New York: Penguin Books, 1982.

Parsons, Timothy H. *The British Imperial Century, 1815-1914: A History Perspective.* Washington, D.C.: Rowman & Littlefield, 2009.

Patterson, Daniel, ed. *The Missouri River Journals of John James Audubon.* Lincoln: University of Nebraska Press, 2016.

Paxson, William Edgar, Jr. *E.S. Paxson: Frontier Artist.* Boulder, CO: Pruett Publishing Company, 1984.

Peairs, H. B. "United States Indian Schools." *Red Man* VI (June 1914): 414-417.

Pearce, Roy H. *Savagism and Civilization: A Study of the Indian and the American Mind.* Baltimore: John Hopkins University Press, 1965.

Pearcey, Nancy. *Finding Truth: 5 Principles for Unmasking Atheism, Secularism, and Other God Substitutes.* Elgin, IL: David C. Cook, 2015.

———. *Saving Leonardo: A Call to Resist the Secular Assault on Mind, Morals, and Meaning.* Nashville: B & H Books, 2010.

———. *The Soul of Science: Christian Faith and Natural Philosophy.* Wheaton, IL: Crossway Books, 1994.

———. *Total Truth: Liberating Christianity from Its Cultural Captivity.* Wheaton, IL: Crossway Books, 2004.

Pearson, Diane J. "Lewis Cass and the Politics of Disease: The Indian Vaccination Act of 1832." *Wicazo Sa Review* 18 (Fall 2003): 15.

Peristan, P., R. W. Motta. "An Investigation of Potential Holocaust-Related Secondary Trauma in the Third Generation." *Traumatology* 19 (2013): 95-106.

Perry, R. T., N. A. Halsey. "The Clinical Significance of Measles: A Review." *Journal of Infectious Disease* 189, no. 1 (May 1, 2004): 4-16.

Peterson, Jacqueline. *Sacred Encounters: Father De Smet and the Indians of the Rocky Mountain West.* Norman: University of Oklahoma Press, 1993.

Peterson, Larry Len. *The Call of the Mountains: The Artists of Glacier National Park.* Tucson: Settlers West Galleries, 2002.

———. "The Call of the Mountains: Louis Hill and Glacier National Park." *Russell's West* 9, no. 1 (2002): 3-9.

———. "Charles M. Russell, Illustrator of the West." *Russell's West* 7, no. 1 (1999): 13-16.

———. *Charles M. Russell: Legacy.* Helena, MT: Falcon Publishing/C. M. Russell Museum, 1999.

———. *Charles M. Russell: Photographing the Legend, A Biography in Words and Pictures.* Norman: University of Oklahoma Press, 2014.

———. *John Fery: Artist of Glacier National Park and the American West.* Hayden, ID: The Coeur d'Alene Art Auction, with Settlers West Galleries, 2015.

———. *L. A. Huffman: Photographer of the American West.* Tucson: Settlers West Galleries, 2003.

———. *L. A. Huffman: Photographer of the American West.* 2nd ed. Missoula, MT: Mountain Press Publishing, 2005.

———. *L. A. Huffman: Photographer of the American West.* Revised ed. Missoula, MT: Mountain Press Publishing, 2013.

———. *Philip R. Goodwin: America's Sporting & Wildlife Artist.* Hayden, ID: Coeur d'Alene Art Auction, with Settlers West Galleries, 2001.

———. *Philip R. Goodwin, America's Sporting & Wildlife Artist.* Missoula, MT: Mountain Press Publishing, 2007.

———, Michael R. McClung, Kathy Ricert-Boe, and Robert D. Kohler. "Decreased Human Erythrocyte Diphosphoglycerate Mutase (DPGM) Concentrations in Hypothyroidism." In *Thyroid Research VIII,* J. R. Stockigt and S. Nagataki, eds. Canberra, Australia: Australian Academy of Science, 1980.

———. "Red Cell Diphosphoglycerate Mutase, Immunochemical Studies in Vertebrate Red Cells, Including a Human Variant Lacking 2, 3-DPG." *Blood* 52, no. 5 (November 1978): 953-958.

Peterson, Theodore. *Magazines of the 20th Century.* Urbana: University of Illinois Press, 1956.

Pettegee, Andrew. *Brand Luther: How an Unheralded Monk Turned His Small Town Into a Center of Publishing, Made Himself the Most Famous Man in Europe—and Started the Protestant Reformation.* New York: Penguin, 2015.

Pew Research Center: Religion & Public Life. *America's Changing Religious Landscape: Christians Decline Sharply as Share of Population; Unaffiliated and Other Faiths Continue to Grow.* Pewforum.org, May 12, 2015.

Philbrick, Nathaniel. *The Last Stand: Custer, Sitting Bull, and the Battle of the Little Bighorn.* New York: Viking Press, 2010.

Pielou, E. C. *After the Ice Age: The Return of Life to Glaciated North America.* Chicago: University of Chicago Press, 2008.

Pierce, Jason E. *Making the White Man's West: Whiteness and the Creation of the American West.* Boulder: University Press of Colorado, 2016.

Pitblado, B. L. "A Tale of Two Migrations: Reconciling Recent Biological and Archaeological Evidence for the Pleistocene Peopling of Americas." *Journal of Archaeological Research* 9, no. 4 (March 3, 2011): 327-375.

Plain, Nancy. "John James Audubon Out West: The Last Great Adventure." *Western Writers of America Roundup Magazine* XXIII, no. 4 (2016): 19.

Point, Nicolas. *Wilderness Kingdom, Indian Life in the Rocky Mountains: 1840-1847.* New York: Holt, Rinehart and Winston, 1967.

Pollard, Elizabeth. *Worlds Together, Worlds Apart: A History of the World: From the Beginnings of Humankind to the Present.* New York: W.W. Norton & Company, 2014.

Power, Samantha. *"A Problem from Hell": America and the Age of Genocide.* New York: Basic Books, 2002.

Powers, Ron. *Mark Twain: A Life.* New York: Free Press, 2006.

Pratt, Henry Richard. *Battlefield and Classroom: Four Decades with the American Indian 1867-1904.* Robert M. Utley, ed. New Haven: Yale University Press, 1964.

_____. "The Advantages of Mingling Indians with Whites." *Proceedings of the National Conference of Charities and Corrections,* 1892.

Prem, Hans J. "Disease Outbreaks in Central Mexico during the Sixteenth Century." In *Secret Judgment of God: Old World Disease in Colonial Spanish America,* eds. Noble David Cook and W. George Lovell. Norman: University of Oklahoma Press, 1992.

Preston, Charles, Jim Robbins. *Spectacular Yellowstone and Grand Teton National Parks.* New York: Universe, 2008.

Prothero, Stephen. *American Jesus: How the Son of God Became a National Icon.* New York: Farrar, Strauss, and Giroux, 2003.

_____. *God is Not One: The Eight Rival Religions That Run the World.* New York: HarperOne, 2011.

Prown, Jules David, Nancy K. Anderson, William Cronon, Brian W. Dippie, Martha A. Sandweiss, Susan P. Schoelwer, Howard R. Lamar. *Discovered Lands, Invented Pasts: Transforming Visions of the American West.* New Haven: Yale University Press, 1992.

Purnell, Sonia. *Clementine: The Life of Mrs. Winston Churchill.* New York: Viking, 2015.

Raff, Jennifer, Deborah Bolnick. "Palaeogenomics: Genetic Roots of the First Americans." *Nature* 506 (February 13, 2014): 162-163.

Rand, Archie. *The 613.* New York: Blue Rider Press, 2015.

Randall, David K. *The King and Queen of Malibu: The True Story of the Battle of Paradise.* New York: W.W. Norton & Company, 2016.

Rankin, Charles E., ed. *Legacy: New Perspectives on the Battle of the Little Bighorn.* Helena: Montana Historical Society Press, 1996.

Rattenbury, Richard C. *A Legacy in Arms: American Firearm Manufacture, Design, and Artistry, 1800-1900.* Norman: University of Oklahoma Press, 2014.

_____. *The Art of American Arms Makers: Marketing Guns, Ammunition and Western Adventure During the Golden Age of Illustration.* Oklahoma City: National Cowboy & Western Heritage Museum, 2004.

_____. *Hunting the American West: The Pursuit of Big Game for Life, Profit, and Sport.* Missoula, MT: Boone and Crockett Club, 2008.

Redman, Samuel J. *Bone Rooms: From Scientific Racism to Human Prehistory in Museums.* Cambridge, MA: Harvard University Press, 2016.

Reed, Ollie, Jr. "Writing About Buffalo: But Look them in the Eye, Too." *Western Writers of America Roundup Magazine* XXII, no. 4: (April 2015): 11-16.

Reeves, Richard. *Infamy: The Shocking Story of the Japanese American Internment in World War II.* New York: Picador, 2016.

Reich, Richard, et al. "The Genetic History of Ice Age Europe." *Nature* 534 (June 9, 2016): 200-205.

Reiger, John F. *American Sportsmen and the Origins of Conservation.* Revised ed. Norman: University of Oklahoma Press, 1986.

Renz, Louis Tuck. *The History of the Northern Pacific Railroad.* Fairfield, WA: Ye Galleon Press, 1980.

Rewald, John. *The History of Impressionism.* New York: The Museum of Modern Art, 1973.

Richardson, James D., ed. *A Compilation of Messages and Papers of the Presidents,* Vol. 1. Washington, D.C.: Bureau of National Literature, 1913.

Richter, Daniel. *Facing East from Indian Country; A Native History of Early America.* Cambridge, MA: Harvard University Press, 2001.

Ridley, Matt. *The Evolution of Everything: How New Ideas Emerge.* New York: Harper, 2015.

Riedel, Stefan. "Edward Jenner and the History of Smallpox and Vaccination." *Baylor University Medical Center Proceedings* 18, no. 1 (January 2005): 21-25.

Rieder, H. L. "Tuberculosis among American Indians of the Contiguous United States." *Public Health Reports* 104, no. 6 (November-December 1989): 653-657.

Riley-Smith, Jonathan. *The First Crusades, 1095-1131.* Cambridge, England: Cambridge University Press, 1997.

Robbins, Stanley L. *Pathologic Basis of Disease.* Philadelphia: W.B. Saunders Company, 1977.

Roberts, Andrew. *Napoleon: A Life.* New York: Penguin, 2015.

Robertson, James Oliver. *American Myth, American Reality.* New York: Hill and Wang, 1980.

Robson, Barry, O. K. Baek. *The Engines of Hippocrates: From the Dawn of Medicine to Medical and Pharmaceutical Informatics.* New York: John Wiley & Sons, 2009.

Rodis-Lewis, Genevieve. "Descartes' Life and the Development of His Philosophy." In *The Cambridge Companion to Descartes,* John Cottingham. Cambridge, England: Cambridge University Press, 1992.

Roe, Frank Gilbert. *The North American Buffalo: A Critical Study of the Species in Its Wild State.* Toronto, Canada: University of Toronto Press, 1970.

Rogers, Katherine. *L. Frank Baum, Creator of Oz: A Biography.* New York: St. Martin's Press, 2002.

Rogin, Michael P. *Fathers and Children: Andrew Jackson and the Subjugation of the American Indian.* New York: Alfred A. Knopf, 1975.

Ronda, James P. *Lewis & Clark among the Indians.* Lincoln: University of Nebraska Press, 1988.

_____, ed. *Voyage of Discovery: Essays on the Lewis and Clark Expedition.* Helena: Montana Historical Society Press, 1998.

Roosevelt, Theodore. *Hunting Trips of a Ranchman: Sketches of Sport on the Northern Cattle Plains.* New York: Putnam, 1885.

_____. *Ranch Life and the Hunting Trail.* New York: Century, 1888.

_____. *The Wilderness Hunter: An Account of the Big Game of the United States and Its Chase with Horse, Hound, and Rifle.* New York: Putnam, 1893.

_____. *The Works of Theodore Roosevelt.* National Edition. New York: Charles Scribner's Sons, 1926.
Rose, Jeffrey. "New Light on Human Prehistory in the Arabo-Persian Gulf Oasis." *Current Anthropology* 51 (2010): 849-883.
Rose, Mark. "Post-Traumatic Stress Disorder." *NetCE* 141 (2015): 68-115.
Rosebrook, Stuart. "The Boundless West." *True West Magazine* 63, no. 8 (August 2016): 58, 59.
Rosenfeld, Gavriel. *Hi Hitler!: How the Nazi Past is Being Normalized in Contemporary Culture.* Cambridge, England: Cambridge University Press, 2015.
Rotundo, Anthony E. *American Manhood: Transformations in Masculinity from the Revolution to the Modern Era.* New York: Basic Books, 1993.
Rousseau, Jean-Jacques. *On the Social Contract, with the Geneva Manuscript and Political Economy,* Roger Masters, ed. New York: St. Martin's Press, 1978.
Royal, Robert. *1492 and All That.* Washington, D.C.: Ethics and Public Policy Center, 1992.
Rubin, Anne Sarah. *Through the Heart of Dixie: Sherman's March and American Memory.* Chapel Hill: University of North Carolina Press, 2014.
Rublack, Ulinka. *The Astronomer and the Witch; Johanne's Kepler's Fight for His Mother.* New York: Oxford University Press, 2015.
Rush, Benjamin. *Essays, Literary, Moral and Philosophical.* London: Forgotten Books, 2015.
Rydford, John. *Indian Place-Names: Their Origin, Evolution, and Meanings, Collected in Kansas from the Siouan, Algonquin, Shoshonean, Caddoan, Iroquoian, and other Tongues.* Norman: University of Oklahoma Press, 1968.
Sacks, Jonathan. *Not in God's Name: Confronting Religious Violence.* New York: Schocken Books, 2015.
Saggs, H. W. F. *Civilization Before Greece and Rome.* New Haven: Yale University Press, 1989.
Salley, Alexander, S., ed. *Narratives of Early Carolina, 1650-1708.* New York: Charles Scribner's Sons, 1911.
Sands, Philippe. *East West Street: On the Origins of "Genocide" and "Crimes Against Humanity."* New York: Knopf, 2016.
Sandweiss, Martha A. *Print the Legend: Photography and the American West.* New Haven: Yale University Press, 2002.
Sawyer, Susanna. "Nuclear and Mitochondrial DNA Sequences from Two Denisovan Individuals." *Proceedings of the National Academy of Sciences* 112, no. 51 (2015): 15696-15700.
Schmitt, Martin F. *General George Crook, His Autobiography.* Norman: University of Oklahoma Press, 1986.
Schultz, Duane. *Custer: Lessons in Leadership.* New York: Palgrave Macmillan, 2010.
_____. *Over the Earth I Come: The Great Sioux Uprising of 1862.* New York: St. Martin's Press, 1992.
Schultz, James W. *Blackfeet Tales of Glacier National Park.* New York: Houghton Mifflin Company, 1916.
_____. *My Life as an Indian: The Story of a Red Woman and a White Man in the Lodges of the Blackfeet.* New York: Houghton Mifflin Company, 1914.
_____. *With the Indians in the Rockies.* New York: Houghton Mifflin Company, 1911.

Schurtz, Carl. "Present Aspects of the Indian Problem." *North American Review* 133 (July 1881).

Schwartz, Stuart B., ed. *Victors and Vanquished: Spanish and Nahua Views of the Conquest.* New York: Macmillan, 2000.

Scioli, Anthony. *Hope in the Age of Anxiety.* New York: Oxford University Press, 2009.

———. *The Power of Hope: Overcoming Your Most Daunting Life Difficulties—No Matter What.* Deerfield Beach, FL: Health Communications Inc., 2010.

Scudder, Horace E. *A History of the United States of America.* Philadelphia: J.W. Butler, 1884.

Sears, Stephen W., ed. *The Civil War Papers of George B. McClellan: Selected Correspondence, 1860-1865.* New York: Da Capo Press, 1992.

———. *To the Gates of Richmond: The Peninsula Campaign.* Boston: Houghton Mifflin, 2001.

Secord, James A. *Visions of Science: Books and Readers at the Dawn of the Victorian Age.* Chicago: University of Chicago Press, 2015.

Secoy, Frank Raymond. *Changing Military Patterns of the Great Plains Indians (17th Century Through Early 19th Century).* Lincoln: University of Nebraska Press, 1992.

Sehat, David. *The Jefferson Rule: How the Founding Fathers Became Infallible and Our Politics Inflexible.* New York: Simon & Schuster, 2016.

Sekaquaptewa, Helen. *Me and Mine: The Life Story of Helen Sekaquaptewa.* Tucson: University of Arizona Press, 1969.

Seton, Ernest Thompson. *The Gospel of the Red Man.* New York: Doubleday Doran, 1936.

Sharratt, Michael. *Galileo: Decisive Innovator.* Cambridge, England: Cambridge University Press, 1994.

Sheehan, Bernard. *Seeds of Extinction: Jeffersonian Philosophy and the American Indian.* Chapel Hill: University of North Carolina Press, 1973.

Shelton, R. Larry. *Cross & Covenant: Interpreting the Atonement for 21st Century Mission.* Tyrone, GA: Paternoster, 2006.

Shermer, Michael. *The Moral Arc: How Science Makes Us Better People.* New York: Henry Holt and Company, 2015.

Shipman, Pat. *The Invaders: How Humans and Their Dogs Drove Neanderthals to Extinction.* Cambridge, MA: Harvard, 2015.

Sides, Hampton. *Blood and Thunder: The Epic Story of Kit Carson and the Conquest of the American West.* New York: Anchor, 2007.

Siedentop, Larry. *Inventing the Individual: The Origins of Western Liberalism.* Cambridge, MA: Belknap Press, 2014.

Siegel, Rudolph E. *Galen on the Affected Parts: Translation from the Greek Text with Explanatory Notes.* Basel, Switzerland: Karger Publishers, 1976.

Simon, John Y., ed. *The Papers of Ulysses S. Grant.* Carbondale: Southern Illinois University Press, 1988.

Singer, Barry. *Churchill Style: The Art of Being Winston Churchill.* New York: Abram Image, 2012.

Singer, Charles. "Galen on Anatomical Procedures." *Proceedings of the Royal Society of Medicine* 49, no. 10 (1956): 833.

Sinha, Manisha. *The Slave's Cause: A History of Abolition.* New Haven: Yale University Press, 2016.

Siraisi, Nancy G. "Medicine, 1450-1620, and the History of Science." *Isis* 103, no. 3 (2012): 491-514.

Smith, Gary Scott. *Religion in the Oval Office: The Religious Lives of American Presidents.* New York: Oxford University Press, 2015.

Smith, Jordan Fisher. *Engineering Eden: The True Story of a Violent Death, a Trial, and the Fight over Controlling Nature.* New York: Crown Publishing Group, 2016.

Snyder, Timothy. *Black Earth: The Holocaust as History and Warning.* New York: Tim Dugan Books, 2015.

Spangenberger, Phil. "22 Guns That Won the West." *True West Magazine* 62, no. 11 (November 2015): 72-87.

Spiro, Jonathan Peter. *Defending the Master Race: Conservation, Eugenics, and the Legacy of Madison Grant.* Burlington: University of Vermont, 2008.

Spude, Catherine Holder. "Writing the West: What's Truth Got to Do With It." *Roundup Magazine: Western Writers of America* XXIII, no. I (October 2014): 2.

Spurgeon, Charles, Stephen McCaskell, eds. *Spurgeon's Calvinism.* Magnolia, TX: Lucid Books, 2014.

Standing Bear, Luther. *Land of the Spotted Eagle.* Boston: Houghton Mifflin, 1933; reprint, Lincoln: University of Nebraska Press, 1978.

_____. *My People, The Sioux.* 1928; reprint, Lincoln: University of Nebraska Press, 1975.

Stanford, D. J., B. A. Bradley. *Across Atlantic Ice: The Origin of America's Clovis Culture.* Berkeley: University of California Press, 2012.

Stargardt, Nicholas. *The German War: A Nation Under Arms, 1939-1945.* New York: Basic Books, 2015.

Stark, Rodney. *For the Glory of God: How Monotheism Led to Reformation, Science, Witch Hunts, and the End of Slavery.* Princeton: Princeton University Press, 2003.

_____. *God's Battalions: The Case for the Crusades.* San Francisco: HarperOne, 2003.

_____. *How the West Won: The Neglected Story of the Triumph of Modernity.* Wilmington, DE: ISI Books, 2014.

_____. *The Triumph of Faith: Why the World is More Religious Than Ever.* New York: ISI Books, 2015.

_____. *The Victory of Reason: How Christianity Led to Freedom, Capitalism, and Western Success.* New York: Random House, 2005.

_____, Roger Finke. *Acts of Faith: Explaining the Human Side of Religions.* Berkeley: University of California Press, 2000.

Starkloff, Carl. *The People of the Center: American Indian Religion and Christianity.* New York: Seabury Press, 1974.

Staudohar, Connie. "Food, Rest, and Happiness: Limitations and Possibilities in the Early Treatment of Tuberculosis in Montana Part I." *Montana: The Magazine of Western History* 47 (Winter 1997): 48-57.

Steinke, Peter L. *Congregational Leadership in Anxious Times: Being Calm and Courageous No Matter What.* Herndon, VA: 2006.

Stelwagon, Henry W. *Treatise on Diseases of the Skin For the Use of Advanced Students and Practitioners.* Philadelphia: W.B. Saunders & Company, 1902.

Stevens, Sylvester, et al., eds. *The Papers of Colonel Henry Bouquet.* Vol. 18. Harrisburg: Pennsylvania Historical and Museum Commission, 1940-1943.

Stiles, T. J. *Custer's Trials: A Life on the Frontier of a New America.* New York: Knopf, 2015.

———. "The Horse Thief." *Smithsonian* 46 (November 2015): 51-55.

Stoll, Mark. *Inherit the Holy Mountain: Religion and the Rise of American Environmentalism.* New York: Oxford University Press, 2015.

Strong, Emory, Ruth Strong. *Seeking Western Waters: The Lewis and Clark Trail from the Rockies to the Pacific.* Portland: Oregon Historical Society Press, 1995.

Sublette, Ned, Constance Sublette. *The American Slave Coast: A History of the Slave-Breeding Industry.* Chicago: Chicago Review Press, 2015.

Sugden, John. *Tecumseh: A Life.* New York: Holt Paperbacks, 1999.

Swaan, Abram de. *The Killing Compartments: The Mentality of Mass Murder.* New Haven: Yale University Press, 2015.

Swaim, Barton. *The Speechwriter: A Brief Education in Politics.* New York: Simon & Schuster, 2016.

Taagepera, Rein. "Size and Duration of Empires: Growth and Decline Curves, 3000 to 6000 B.C." *Social Science Research* 7 (1978): 180-196.

Taleb, Nassim Nicholas. *The Black Swan: The Impact of the Highly Improbable.* New York: Random House Trade Paperbacks, 2010.

Taubenberger, Jeffrey, David Morens. "1918 Influenza: The Mother of All Pandemics." *Rev Biomed* 17 (2006): 69-79.

Taylor, Alan. *American Colonies: The Settling of North America.* New York: Penguin Press, 2003.

Tebbel, John, Mary Ellen Zuckerman. *The Magazine in America 1741-1900.* New York: Oxford University Press, 1991.

Temple, Frederick. "A Sermon Preached before the University of Oxford, on Act Sunday, July 1st, 1860," quoted in "Oxford British Association Discussion as Related to Spiritual Question." *Christian Remembrance* 40 (1861): 244.

Thomas, David Hurst. *Skull Wars: Kennewick Man, Archaeology, and the Battle for Native American Identity.* New York: Basic Books, 2001.

Thomson, Keith. *Private Doubt, Public Dilemma: Religion and Science Since Jefferson and Darwin.* New Haven: Yale University Press, 2015.

Thornton, John. *Africa and Africans in Making the Atlantic World: 1400-1800.* New York: Cambridge University Press, 1998.

Thorsen, Donald A. *The Wesleyan Quadrilateral: Scripture, Tradition, Reason and Experience as a Model of Evangelical Theology.* Grand Rapids, MI: Zondervan, 1990.

Traub, James. *John Quincy Adams: Militant Spirit.* New York: Basic Books, 2016.

Treat, James. *Native and Christian: Indigenous Voices on Religious Identity in the United States and Canada.* New York: Routledge, 1996.

Trench, Charles Chenevix. *The Road to Khartoum: A Life of General Charles Gordon.* New York: Dorset Press, 1979.

Trostle, James A. "Early Works in Anthropology and Epidemiology: From Social Medicine to the Germ Theory, 1840-1920." In *Anthropology and Epidemiology,* C. Janes, R. Stall, and S. Gifford, eds. Dordrecht, Netherlands: Reidel Publishing Company, 1986, 35-57.

Turner, Frederick Jackson. *Significance of Sections in American History.* Gloucester, MA: Peter Smith Publishers, 1975.

Turner, James. *Without God, Without Creed: The Origins of Unbelief in America.* Baltimore: John Hopkins University Press, 1985.

Turner, Ralph H., Lewis H. Killian. *Collective Behavior.* 3rd ed. Englewood Cliff, NJ: Prentice-Hall, 1987.
Twain, Mark. *The Noble Red Man.* New York: Galaxy, 1870.
Twiss, Richard. *One Church, Many Tribes: Following Jesus the Way God Made You.* Ventura, CA: Regal Books, 2000.
Underhill, Ruth M. *Papago Woman.* Prospect Heights, IL: Waveland Press, 1979.
Urbach, Peter. *Francis Bacon's Philosophy of Science: An Account and a Reappraisal.* La Salle, IL: Open Court Publishing Co., 1987.
Utley, Robert M. "Custer and Me." *True West Magazine* 48 (May/June 2001): 59-64.
_____. *Custer: Cavalier in Buckskin.* Norman: University of Oklahoma Press, 2001.
_____. *Frontier Regulars: The United States Army and the Indian, 1866-1891.* Lincoln: University of Nebraska Bison Books, 1984.
_____. *Frontiersmen in Blue: The United States Army and the Indian, 1846-1865.* New York: Macmillan, 1967.
_____. *Indian Wars.* Boston: Mariner Books, 2002.
_____. *The Lance and The Shield: The Life and Times of Sitting Bull.* New York: Henry Holt and Company, 1993.
_____. *Last Days of the Sioux Nation.* New Haven: Yale University Press, 1963.
_____, ed. *Life in Custer's Cavalry: Diaries and Letters of Albert and Jennie Barnitz, 1867-1868.* Lincoln: University of Nebraska Press, 1977.
_____. *The Indian Frontier of the American West, 1846-1890.* Albuquerque: University of New Mexico Press, 1984.
Vickers, A., C. Zollman. "Herbal Medicine." *British Medical Journal* 319 (October 16, 1999): 1050-1053.
Wacker, Grant. *America's Pastor: Billy Graham and the Shaping of a Nation.* Cambridge, MA: Belknap Press, 2014.
Wain, J., et al. "Typhoid Fever." *Lancet* 385 (March 2015): 1136-1145.
Wakeman, Geoffrey. *Victorian Book Illustration: The Technical Revolution.* Detroit: Gale Research Co., 1973.
Waldron, Jeremy. *God, Locke and Equality.* Cambridge, England: Cambridge University Press, 2002.
Walker, James R., Raymond J. DeMallie, Elaine A. Jahner, eds. *Lakota Belief and Ritual.* Lincoln: University of Nebraska Press, 1991.
Wallach, Alan. "Rethinking 'Luminism:' Taste, Class, and Aestheticizing Tendencies in Mid-Nineteenth-Century American Landscape Painting," 115-147. In *The Cultured Canvas: New Perspective on American Landscape Painting,* Nancy Siegel, ed. Dartmouth, NH: University of New England Press, 2011.
Walsh, Chris. *Cowardice: A Brief History.* Princeton: Princeton University Press, 2014.
Walsh, Roger. *The World of Shamanism: New Views of an Ancient Tradition.* St. Paul, MN: Llewellyn Publications, 2007.
Ward, Geoffrey, Ric Burns, Ken Burns. *The Civil War.* New York: Vintage Books, 1994.
Ward, Peter, Joe Kirschvink. *A New History of Life: The Radical New Discoveries about the Origins and Evolution on Earth.* New York: Bloomsbury Press, 2015.
Warner, John Harley. *The Therapeutic Perspective: Medical Practice, Knowledge, and Identity in America, 1820-1885.* Princeton: Princeton University Press, 1997.
Warrell, Ian, Franklin Kelly. *J. M. W. Turner.* Mustang, OK: Tate, 2007.

Watson, Blake A. *Buying America from the Indians: Johnson vs McIntosh and the History of Native Land Rights*. Norman: University of Oklahoma Press, 2012.

Wayman, Dorothy. *Edward Sylvester Morse*. London, England; Cambridge, MA: Harvard University Press, 1942.

Webster, Charles. *Paracelsus: Medicine, Magic and Mission at the End of Time*. New Haven: Yale University Press, 2008.

Weiss, Robin A., José Esparza. "The Prevention and Eradication of Smallpox: A Commentary on Sloane (1755) 'An Account of Inoculation.'" *Philosophical Transactions of the Royal Society* B 370 (2015): 1-11.

Welch, James. *Killing Custer: The Battle of the Little Bighorn and the Fate of the Plains Indians*. New York: Penguin Books, 1994.

Wells, Spencer, Mark Read. *The Journey of Man: A Genetic Odyssey*. New York: Random House, 2002.

Welsh, Herbert. "The Indian Question Past and Present." *New England Magazine* 3 (October 1890): 264.

_____. *Four Weeks Among Some of the Sioux Tribes of Dakota and Nebraska, Together with a Brief Consideration of the Indian Problem*. Philadelphia: Horace F. McMann, 1882.

Wert, Jeffry D. *Custer: The Controversial Life of George Armstrong Custer*. New York: Simon & Schuster, 1996.

Westerman, Edward B. *Hitler's Ostkrieg and the Indian Wars: Comparing Genocide and Conquest*. Norman: University of Oklahoma Press, 2016.

Westfall, Richard. *Isaac Newton*. Cambridge, England: Cambridge University Press, 2007.

Whalen, Kevin. *Native Students at Work: American Indian Labor and Sherman Institute's Outing Program 1900-1945*. Seattle: University of Washington Press, 2016.

Wheeler, Robert W. *Jim Thorpe: World's Greatest Athlete*. Norman: University of Oklahoma Press, 1981.

Whitaker, Alexander. *Good News from Virginia*. London: Felix Kyngston and William Welby, 1613.

White, Ronald C. *American Ulysses: A Life of U. S. Grant*. New York: Random House, 2016.

Whitly, David S. *The Art of the Shaman: Rock Art of California*. Salt Lake City: University of Utah Press, 2000.

Whitman, Walt. *Leaves of Grass: The First (1855) Edition*. New York: Penguin Classics, 1981.

Whitney, Charles. *Francis Bacon and Modernity*. New Haven: Yale University Press, 1986.

Wiencek, Henry. *An Imperfect God: George Washington, His Slaves, and the Creation of America*. New York: Farrar, Strauss and Giroux, 2004.

Wiesenthal, Simon. *The Sunflower: On the Possibilities and Limits of Forgiveness*. New York: Schocken Books, 1997.

Wignall, Paul B. *The Worst of Times: How Life on Earth Survived Eighty Million Years of Extinction*. Princeton: Princeton University Press, 2015.

Wilcomb, Washburn. *The Indian and the White Man*. Garden City, NY: Doubleday, 1964.

Wilder, Laura Ingalls. *Pioneer Girl: The Annotated Autobiography*. Pierre: South Dakota Historical Society Press, 2014.

Wildschut, William. *Crow Indian Medicine Bundles*. New York: Museum of the American Indian, Heye Foundation, 1960.

Willerslev, Eske, et al. "The Ancestry and Affiliations of Kennewick Man," *Nature* 523 (July 23, 2015): 455-458.

———. "Upper Palaeolithic Siberian Genome Reveals Dual Ancestry of Native Americans," *Nature* 505 (January 2, 2014): 87-91.
Willey, P., Douglas D. Scott, eds. *Health of the Seventh Cavalry: A Medical History.* Norman: University of Oklahoma Press, 2015.
Williams, Guy. *The Age of Miracles: Medicine and Surgery in the Nineteenth Century.* London: Constable and Company, 1981.
Williams, Thomas Benton. *The Soul of the Red Man.* New York: Thomas Benton Williams Publisher, 1937.
Williams, Wendy. *The Horse: The Epic History of Our Noble Companion.* New York: Scientific American/Farrar, Strauss and Giroux, 2015.
Wills, Garry. *Lincoln at Gettysburg: The Words that Remade America.* New York: Simon & Schuster, 2006.
Wilson, A. N. *C. S. Lewis: A Biography.* New York: Fawcett Columbine, 1990.
Wilson, Ian. *Nostradamus: The Evidence.* London: Orion Books Limited, 2003.
Wilson, Peter H. *Heart of Europe: A History of the Holy Roman Empire.* Cambridge, MA: Belknap Press, 2016.
Wilson, R. L. *Colt: An American Legend.* New York: Artabras, 1985.
———. *Winchester: An American Legend.* Edison, NJ: Chartwell Books, 1991.
Wilson, Robert. *Mathew Brady: Portraits of a Nation.* New York: Bloomsbury, 2013.
Wood, Forrest. *Arrogance of Faith.* New York: Knopf, 1991.
Wood, Frank. "The Evils of the Reservation System." *Outlook* LXXV (September 1903).
Woodley, Randy S. *Shalom and the Community of Creation: An Indigenous Vision.* Grand Rapids, MI: William B. Eerdmans Publishing, 2012.
Woolford, Andrew, Jeff Benvenuto, Alexander Laban Hinton, eds. *Colonial Genocide in Indigenous North America.* Durham, NC: Duke University Press, 2014.
Wooten, David. *The Invention of Science: A New History of the Scientific Revolution.* New York: Harper, 2015.
Worswick, Clark. *Edward Sheriff Curtis: The Master Prints.* Santa Fe, NM: Arena Editions, 2001.
Worthen, M., S. D. Rathod, G. Cohen, et al. "Anger Problems and Posttraumatic Stress Disorder in Male and Female National Guard and Reserve Service Members." *Journal of Psychiatric Research* 55 (2014): 52-58.
Wright, N. T. *What Saint Paul Really Said: Was Paul of Tarsus the Real Founder of Christianity.* Grand Rapids, MI: William B. Freedman Publishing Company, 1997.
Wright, Ronald. *Stolen Continents: Five Hundred Years of Conquest and Resistance in the Americas.* New York: Houghton Mifflin, 1992.
Wulf, Andrea. *The Invention of Nature: Alexander von Humboldt's New World.* New York: Knopf, 2015.
Wuthnow, Robert. *Rough Country: How Texas Became America's Most Popular Bible-Belt State.* Princeton: Princeton University Press, 2016.
Wylie, Paul R. *Blood on the Marias: The Baker Massacre.* Norman: University of Oklahoma Press, 2016.
Yao, Xinzhong. *An Introduction to Confucianism.* Cambridge, England: Cambridge University Press, 2000.
Yehuda, R., A. Bell, L. M. Bierer, J. Schmeidler. "Maternal, Not Paternal, PTSD is Related to Increased Risk for PTSD in Offspring of Holocaust Survivors." *Journal of Psychiatric Research* 42 (2008): 1104-1111.

Yenne, Bill. *Sitting Bull.* Yardley, PA: Westholme Publishing, 2008.
Young, Biloine W., Eileen R. McCormack. *The Dutiful Son: Louis W. Hill, Life in the Shadow of the Empire Builder, James J. Hill.* St. Paul, MN: Ramsey County Historical Society, 2010.
Zuckert, Michael. *The Natural Rights Republic.* South Bend, IN: Notre Dame University Press, 1996.
Zwoll, Wayne Van. *America's Great Gunmakers.* South Hackensack: Stoeger Publishing Company, 1992.

A closing thought:

God is in charge of history. He asks us to work, to try, to pour ourselves out to make things better. But he is an actor in history also. He chastises and rescues, he intervenes in ways seen and unseen. Or chooses not to.

PEGGY NOONAN,
THE WALL STREET JOURNAL, NOVEMBER 4, 2016

Index

A

abolitionism, 388, 450–451, 455
Abraham (biblical character), 135, 223–224, 454
Adam (biblical character), 135
Adams, David Wallace, 572, 577, 579
Adams, John, 110, 271–272, 301, 302, 328
Adams, John Quincy, 328, 350–351, 355, 451
Agassiz, Louis, 411, 430–432
Age of Enlightenment (*See* Enlightenment)
Agricultural Revolution, 9, 21–22, 240
alcohol: Indians and, 143, 360, 383, 398, 549, 583–584, 597; laws concerning, 346; preachers on, 550; whites and, 461, 467, 516
Algonquin Indians, 28, 44, 66, 199
Allotment Act, 159, 229, 568–571
Ambrose, Stephen, 298, 317, 449, 462, 478, 540
America as concept, xvii, xxiii, xxiv, xxvi; Custer representing, 488, 516–517, 525, 534–535, 542; God's chosen land, 303, 341, 416; industrialization in, 285; in Jefferson's vision, 292, 296, 309, 321, 341; in John Q. Adams's vision, 350–351; Manifest Destiny contributing to, 363–370, 372; new Israel in, 36, 256, 318–319, 392, 532–533; religions and, 128–129, 153, 220, 243, 254, 257–268, 310, 332–333; scientific racism and, 32–33
American Horse, 145, 170–171, 541
American Revolution, 261, 263, 272, 289, 373 (*See also* Revolutionary War)

Anderson, Gary Clayton, 69, 585–587
anesthesia, 90, 119
Anglican Church, 51–52, 129, 250, 254, 255, 256, 258, 284, 292, 293, 304, 422, 423 (*See also* Episcopalian Church)
animals (*See also* bear; *also* bison; *also* buffalo; *also* coyotes; *also* horses); as disease carriers, 100, 102, 117; domesticated, 25; game, 25, 29, 101; humans, relationship with, 224, 265–266; Indians, importance to, 157, 173–176, 178; prehistoric, 8–9, 18, 71
"Animals, Arts, and the Environment" (Symposium), 601n3
antibiotics, 83, 117
Anzick child (skeleton), 5, 6, 20
Apache Indians, 26, 28, 69, 71–72, 175, 403, 513–514, 559, 576 (*See also* Geronimo)
Aquinas, Thomas, 40, 223, 237, 241–242, 247, 268
Arapaho Indians, 65–66, 69, 170, 172, 214–215, 515
Archaic Era, 22, 26
Arikara Indians: ceremonies of, 170, 189; Custer and, 389, 535, 540; horses and, 72; legends of, 154, 209; migration of, 68; occupations of, 22, 28; smallpox among, 105–106
Aristotle, 223–224
Arius of Alexandria, 236
Arminianism (*See* free will)
Arminius, Jacob, 253
artists, landscape, 394–395
assimilation, xxvii; as failure, 578, 587; as opposed to other actions, 369, 468;

reasons for lack of, 568, 570, 597; viewed as positive, 148, 219–220, 416, 421, 435, 500–502, 551, 553–555, 566, 579
Assiniboine Indians, 68, 71–72, 105–106, 170, 321–322
astrology, 86, 87, 279
Audubon, John James, xvii–xviii, 107–108, 192–193
Augustine of Hippo, Saint, 223, 236–237, 241–242, 408
Aztec Indians, 103–104

B

Bacon, Francis, xxii, 272, 273, 281–283, 284
Baker Massacre, 515–516
Balmis, Francisco Javier de, 82
baptism, 236–237, 250, 254, 256, 259
Baptists: beliefs and practices of, 254, 255–256; educating Indian children, 550; in evangelical movement, 262–263; as revival movement supporters, 261–262; simple style of, 264–265; slavery issue tearing apart, 455; spreading Christianity, 378–379, 550; treatment of, 258, 304; West appealing to, 376
barbarian stereotype, 36, 38, 55–56, 346, 552, 553, 565
Barfield, Raymond, 81, 620n79
Bates, Edward, 457, 458
Battle of the Little Bighorn, xxvi; Arikara Indians in, 389; Custer in, 540–541; in education, 444, 564; football comparison, 575; Grinnell avoiding, 193–194; Sherman on, 506–507; significance of, 512, 516–518, 542, 544–545; survivors of, 151; weapons in, 389
battles: Antietam, 462, 474; Bull Run, 460; ceremonies for, 175; Chancellorsville, 463; Chattanooga, 465–466; Fallen Timbers, 320; Gettysburg, 464; Rosebud, 539; San Jacinto, 365; Seven Days Battles, 473; Shiloh, 460–461; Vicksburg, 464; Wolf Mountains, 542; Yorktown, 306
Baum, L. Frank, 543–544
bear, xx; as game animal, 69; in Indian medicine, 146, 175, 180, 184, 186; in legends, 201; prehistoric, 18; as sacred animals, 155, 157–158, 175, 208
Beebe, Rose Marie, 382–383
Beecher, Lyman, 376, 380–381
beheadings, 513–514
Belknap, William, 503, 537–538
Benga, Ota, 401–407
Benteen, Frederick, xxvi, 528, 540
Bering Land Bridge, xix, 6, 18
Berkhofer, Jr., Robert F., 52, 303, 399
Bible, xxii, xxiii; as art subject, 383–384; Bacon and, 281–282; Darwin on, 423; during Enlightenment, 277, 408; Golden Rule in, 136–137; Indians and, 178, 346, 357; Jefferson and, 326, 327; Jesus in, 226; King James version of, 254; Lincoln and, 457; literal interpretation of, 173, 279, 346, 573–574; Locke and, 275; Luther and, 249; material world in, 157, 222; Newton and, 284; in off-reservation schools, 555, 564; Puritans and, 57; racism, justification for, 411, 431, 453; slavery, justification for, 450, 453–455; variations in copies of, 232; whites and, 128, 142, 221–222 (See also Gospels; Jefferson Bible; New Testament; Old Testament)
Bierstadt, Albert, 393, 395, 396, 404
Bill of Rights, 305, 308
birds, 150, 153, 175–176, 198–199, 217
bison, xvii, xviii, xx, 23–24 (See also buffalo); ceremonies involving, 170–172, 174; as game animal, 24, 25, 28–29, 67, 68, 69–70, 72, 193, 388, 536; in legends, 155; population fluctuations of, 33, 72, 96, 100, 187; prehistoric, 18, 22; as sacred animal, 176; as symbol of the West, 404
Black Death, 95, 100, 238, 242
Black Elk, 149–152, 172, 180
Black Hawk, 36, 360–361
Black Hills, 505–506, 536–537
Black Kettle, 527–528
Black Robes (See Jesuits)
black soldiers, 306, 495, 519, 524

Blackfeet Indians: animals important to, 72–73, 176; ceremonies of, 539; legends of, 196–198, 215–216; McClintock and, 147–149; medicine of, 184; in off-reservation schools, 561–562; religion and spirituality of, 154, 155, 160, 199–200, 202; smallpox among, 106; tribal relationships of, 28, 67, 384–385; writings on, 194–196, 207
Blackfoot Indians, 66–67, 74, 101, 170
blacks, xix, 468–469; attaining citizenship, 490; attitudes toward, 306, 449–450, 468, 493; conversion of, 264–265, 450; former slaves, 457, 459, 465; Lincoln, attitude of toward, 469–470; Muslim heritage of, 136; tuberculosis and, 115 (*See also* slavery)
Blind-dance, 204–205
bloodletting, 85, 86, 87, 89
Bloody Knife, 389, 540
Board of Indian Commissioners, 497–498, 556
boarding schools (*See* off-reservation schools)
Boas, Franz, 288, 403, 412
Boleyn, Anne, 48, 253
Bonaparte, Napoleon, 61, 313–315
bones: in science, 404, 411–412; in tools, 10, 20, 23, 35, 172, 185
Boone and Crockett Club, 194, 402, 404
Booth, John Wilkes, 469, 490
Bradford, William, 53, 56–57
Brady, Mathew, 474–475
Brands, H.W., 445, 467, 510
British people: as colonists, 31–32, 47–52, 55, 104; Indians and, 50–51, 55–58; as missionaries, 376; in pre-colonial America, 46–48; property rights important to, 285 (*See also* Great Britain)
Browne, Thomas, 88
bubonic plague (See Black Death)
Buddhism, 132–133, 137
buffalo (*See also* bison); as sacred animal, 155–156, 176, 183, 198–199, 212–216; as symbol of the West, 24
buffalo jumps, 24, 29, 215–216
buffalo soldiers (*See* black soldiers)

Bull Walking Upright (legendary person), 212–214
Bureau of Indian Affairs, 355, 568, 580, 583
Burns, Ken, xviii, 444–445
Burns, Ric, xv, 445
Byington, Cyrus, 379

C

Caddoan Indians, 70, 100, 218–219
Cahokia society, 26, 27
California, 365–366, 382
California Trail, 118, 366, 519
Calloway, Colin G., 66
Calvin, John, 51, 236, 247, 252, 279, 282
Calvinism, 251–254, 261, 289, 500
Cambrian explosion, 7, 8
Carlisle Indian School, xxvii; football at, 574–576; philosophy of, 571; Pratt and, 219–220, 556–557, 574, 579; staff on, 569; students on, 558, 560–561; Thorpe at, 547–548, 550; treatment of students in, 559–561 (*See also* off-reservation schools)
catastrophism, 431–432
Catherine of Aragon, 48, 253–254
Catholic Church: Beecher and, 380–381; Columbus and, 34–35; conversion efforts by, 241; decline in numbers of, 129–130, 369; Doctrine of Discovery and, 334–335, 347; in Europe, 48, 86, 239, 242, 248–250, 253–254, 314; history of, 236, 238, 243, 248; humanitarian efforts of, 113, 240; Indians and, 43–46, 564; Manifest Destiny and, 379–380; missionaries of, 104, 376, 378, 381–386, 550; science and, 273–274; slavery and, 40; Smet and, 383–385; teachings of, 222
Catlin, George, 76, 143–144, 174, 184, 288, 393, 398
censuses, 96–97, 582
Centennial Exposition, 507, 573
Champlain, Samuel de, 36, 44, 45
Chekhov, Anton, 601n1
Cherokee Indians: as allies of British, 303, 345; converted to Christianity, 356; education of, 550; forced removal of, 40,

307, 354, 361–362; in Indian Territory, 379; lack of materialism among, 159–160; land and, 311, 345, 357, 361–362, 433; medicine of, 181–182; religion and spirituality of, 158, 181–182; as slave owners, 40; smallpox among, 97, 105, 110, 113–114

Cherokee Propitiation and Cementation Ceremony, 168

Cheyenne Indians: ceremonies of, 170, 173; clans in, 157–158; in conflicts, 515, 538–539, 542; Custer and, 527–528, 534, 540; disease among, 69, 101; legends of, 198–199; migrations of, 69; in off-reservation schools, 554–555, 577–578; as traders, 321–322; writings on, 200

Chickasaw Indians, 324, 354, 356, 378, 379

Chinese, 91, 93, 132–133, 369–370

Chippewa Indians, 6, 66, 67, 145, 175, 200–202, 569

Chivington, John Milton, 162, 515–516

chlorination, 120–121, 611n68

Choctaw Indians, 311–312, 354, 356–357, 379, 413

cholera, 71, 83, 118–119

Christianity, xxi, xxiii–xxiv; abolitionism and, 455; conversion to, 374; declining membership of, 129–130; early years of, 234; gender differences among followers, 265; Greek influence on, 222–223, 246; Indians and, 131, 153–154, 163–165, 199, 550–551, 553, 555–556, 567–568, 582; after Jesus Christ, 231–233; Manifest Destiny and, 364–365; nationalism in, 128–129; in Roman Empire, 235–236; schisms in, 248–249; science and, 278–284; slavery and, 455–456; Twain's view on, 509 (*See also* religion)

Christianization (*See* conversion)

Church, Frederic Edwin, 394, 420–421

church and state, separation of, 254, 274, 276, 304–305, 311, 376–377

Church of England (*See* Anglican Church)

Churchill, Ward, 584, 590

Churchill, Winston, 127, 328–329, 448–449, 490–491

circles in Indian life, 155–156, 158–159, 160, 163, 223, 564

Civil Rights Bill (1866), 494

Civil War, xxv–xxvi; battles in, 460, 462–466, 474; beginning of, 458; beliefs bolstered by, 444; Custer in, 444–445, 446, 477–478; diseases causing death during, 121, 462; European views of, 458–459, 462; Grant in, 459, 464, 465–466, 467, 468; Indian affairs affected by, 369; Lee in, 459–460, 462, 469; Lincoln and, 456–457; McClellan and, 460; medicine during, 90–91, 462; North affected by, 490; photography in, 474; saving union as issue in, 461; Sherman in, 460–461, 468; significance of, 306, 488; slavery as issue in, 381–382; South affected by, 453, 489; Union generals, 463; weapons used in, 389, 462–463; West Point and, 448

Clark, William, xxiii; claiming land, 333, 334, 346–347; on Corps of Discovery expedition, 4–5, 81, 289, 312, 322; Indians and, 317, 321–322, 388; Lewis and, 320–321; post-expedition careers of, 321; smallpox and, 105

Clay, Henry, 325, 366, 457

Clemens, Samuel (*See* Twain, Mark)

Cleveland, Grover, 147, 266, 465, 514

Clovis people, 20

Cody, William F. "Buffalo Bill," 389–390

Cognitive Revolution, 9–10

College of William and Mary, 57, 299

colleges and universities, 43, 57, 62, 247, 256, 375

Collins, Francis, 7–8, 136

colonies in America, 55, 335–339

Colt, Sam, 389, 390

Columbia River, 4–5, 368

Columbian Exchange, 33

Columbus, Christopher, 8, 34–37, 116, 123, 318

Colville Indians, 6

Comanche Indians, 69, 389, 576

Common Sense Realism, 281, 373–374
competition in white culture, 128, 285, 372
Confucianism, 132–133, 137
Congregationalists, 51–52, 255–257, 258, 263, 277, 379
Constantine, 235
Constitution, 308, 336, 341, 342, 374, 456, 494
contradictions, religious, 142, 163–164
conversion, xxvii; of blacks, 264–265, 449–450; of Custer, 445–446; in Europe, 237; evangelical, 262–263, 264; Indians and, 43–44, 56–57, 157, 220, 230, 356, 357, 373–379, 500–501, 553, 571–574; Manifest Destiny justifying, 364; McClintock on, 148–149; misrepresented, 383–384; motives of converted for, 102, 110, 231, 241; as opposed to extinction, 386, 434; of Roman Empire, 235; timing of, 337–338, 385–386
Cooke, Jay, 396, 504
Cooper, James Fenimore, 397–398, 531–532
Copernicus, Nicolaus, 249, 278–279
corn and maize, 25, 26, 27, 33, 116, 150, 154, 209
Corps of Discovery, xxiii, 81, 289, 312, 320–323, 347
Cortés, Hernando, 39, 42, 64, 71–72, 103–104
Council of Trent, 250, 280
court cases, 338, 439, 452
cowpox, xxi, 82, 105, 112–113
coyotes, 156, 173–174, 197, 199, 218–219
Cozzens, Peter, xv
craniometry, 408, 411–412, 413
Crazy Horse, 68, 179, 496, 506, 535, 540, 542, 582
creation stories, 154–155
Cree Indians, 67, 200–201
Creek Indians, 345–346, 354, 357
Crook, George R., 512–515, 538–539, 541–542
Crosby, Alfred, 108
Crow Indians: background of, 69–70; bear and, 208; Custer and, 535, 541; land and, 156; marriages in, 75–76; religion and spirituality of, 140–141, 154, 160, 176–178, 185; smallpox among, 101, 105, 106, 107; Sun Dance and, 170, 171, 177; tobacco and, 188; whites, alliance with, 207; writings on, 206–207
Crusades, 103, 240
Custer, George Armstrong, xxv, xxv–xxvii; Andrew Johnson and, 493–494; assassination attempts, rumors of, 492; background of, 445–447, 480; in Battle of the Little Bighorn, 506–507, 512, 540–541; being photographed, 475; characteristics of, 471, 478, 479, 518–519, 545; in Civil War, 464, 471, 474; conversion of, 445–446, 480; court-martial of, 524–526; Darwin and, 530; as deserter, 523; dislike for, 492; financial troubles of, 475, 529, 536–537; Grant and, 495, 506–507, 525; Grinnell and, 193–194; incomplete accounts about, 444–445; Indians and, 534–535; letters to and from, 481–487, 493; marriage of, 481, 520, 521–522, 523, 524, 535; McClellan and, 471–472, 473; mental state of, 475–477, 522; newspapers on, 479–480; post-Civil War years of, 490–495, 505–506, 520–521, 522–523, 526–530, 537–538; as racist, 444, 492–493; stolen horse and, 491, 494–495; in Washita Massacre, 527–528; at West Point, 447–448; women and, 448, 478–479, 494, 528; as writer, 530–534
Custer, Libbie: after husband's death, 476, 542; letters to and from, 481–487, 521, 529, 535; before marriage, 446, 478, 480; marriage of, 480–481, 520, 522–524, 536–537, 540; as racist, 492
Cuvier, Georges, 410, 430, 431

D

Dakota Indians, 68, 210–214, 515
Dana, Charles, 463, 467
Daoism, 133–134
Dark Ages (*See* Middle Ages)
Darwin, Charles, xxiv–xxv, 279; *Beagle*

voyage of, 419, 423–424; influence and legacy of, 432–440, 530, 532–533, 573; influences on, 419–420, 427–428; personal life of, 424–425; religion and, 422–423, 425, 429–430, 432; theories of, 6–9, 425–426; writings of, xxiv–xxv, 10, 402, 416, 421–422, 426–428, 430, 530, 631n25 (*See also* social Darwinism)

Davis, Jefferson, 368, 448, 453, 462

Dawes Act (*See* Allotment Act)

death, 133, 160–163, 218–219, 225–226, 462

Declaration of Independence, xxiii, 256, 274, 275, 281, 297, 299, 300, 301–303, 304–305, 451, 458

degeneration theory, 247, 250

Deism, 261, 274, 275–277, 298–299, 312, 314

Delaware Indians, 56, 255, 309

Deloria, Vine, 162, 164, 167, 516–517, 540–541

Descartes, René, 273–274

deserters, military, 463, 492, 523, 525, 592

"The Development of Chlorine" (PBS), 611n68

Diamond, Jared, 29, 108

Dickens, Charles, 288–289

Dippie, Brian, 98, 324–325, 369, 373, 398, 414, 507–508, 579–580

Discovery rule (*See* Doctrine of Discovery)

diseases, infectious (*See* infectious diseases)

DNA, 5–6, 9–14, 17, 22, 116, 421

Doctrine of Discovery, xxiii; Christianity and, 226, 335, 337–338; European nations honoring, 339, 382; evidence of occupation by, 346–347; land acquisition justified by, 331–335, 336–337, 338–339, 343; as Manifest Destiny basis, 363; presidents and, 339–341, 343, 345, 500

Douglass, Frederick, 415, 458

dreams, 36, 152–153, 155, 160, 171, 176–180, 184, 207, 539

dualism, 130, 228, 274, 277–278, 346, 398, 500

ducks, in legends, 203–205

Dull Knife, 69, 542

Dutch, in America, 46

E

Earth: geological age of, 7–9, 424, 426, 427, 429; Indian concepts of, 42, 150, 155, 161, 210–211, 213, 564; place of, in universe, 279–280, 564

East and Eastern attitudes, 391, 394, 504, 553, 566, 594

education: assimilation as goal of, 551–553, 555–556; Beecher on, 380–381; Christianity's emphasis on, 240, 256, 266, 375, 498–499; of Indians by whites, 57, 207, 351–352, 354, 378, 498–499, 554, 557, 561–562, 578; Jefferson and, 305, 326, 329; money saving objectives of, 552; public, 375; shortcomings of, for Indians, 570; Stowe on, 556 (*See also* Carlisle Indian School; off-reservation schools)

Edwards, Jonathan, 107, 255, 257–258, 260, 274

Ehrman, Bart D., 227

Eisenhower, Dwight D., 128–129, 449, 548

Elliott, Joel, 523, 527, 528

Emancipation Proclamation, 458, 462, 474

Enlightenment, xviii, xx, xxii–xxiii; American Revolution, influence on, 303–304; Aquinas and, 241; Christianity and, 226, 234–235; elitism and, 80, 289–290; Franklin and, 387–388; Indians and, 179; Jefferson and, 296, 304; philosophy of, 272–278; racism justified by, 32, 307, 342; Romantic Movement and, 286, 392; science and, 88–89, 98, 112, 249, 282–283, 293, 408; slavery and, 284

environment versus heredity, 578, 586

epidemics, xx; in America, 59, 95, 104–105; in Europe, 95; off-reservation, 562; smallpox, 57, 67, 85, 100–101, 106, 110, 112–113, 598–599; social and economic significance of, 102; typhus, 120; whooping cough, 121

Episcopalian Church, 254, 263, 411 (*See also* Anglican Church)

ethnic cleansing, xviii, xxvii; defined, 590–591; genocide compared to, 584–587, 594, 599; off-reservation schools and, 565–566; positive views of, 586; religion and, 32, 140, 226 (*See also* genocide)
ethnography, 247, 411
eugenics, xx, xxv, 80, 404, 406–407, 439–440, 578
Europe and Europeans, 33–38, 55–56, 73–74
Eva of Naharon, 4
evangelism: in America, 128–129, 258–259; in Bible, 231; Common Sense Realism and, 373–374; conversion by, 241, 264, 265; Edwards and, 257; history of, 262–263, 266, 267; slavery and, 450–451, 454; style of, 260; women and, 265
Everett, Edward, 355, 376
evolution, 6–9, 265–266, 279, 416, 421–422, 427, 429–430, 431, 530
exceptionalism, 80, 128, 246, 299, 364, 371–372, 542
expansionism, xxiii, 62, 242, 341, 345, 357, 362–364, 519–520, 573
extermination: advocates for, 345–346, 428, 468, 504, 505, 544; negative views of, 356; positive views of, 52, 358, 413, 534; removal compared to, 354 (*See also* genocide)
extinctions, xx; animal, 8, 22, 23; early hominid, 6, 11, 12, 13; Indian, actual, 582; Indian, potential, 71, 324–325, 336, 354, 356, 386, 500–501, 505, 508, 550–553, 585

F

farming: early, 21–22; by Indians, 25–26, 29–30, 33, 70, 345, 364; by whites, 55, 466
Fenn, Elizabeth A., 71, 111
Fetterman Massacre, 535
Fifteenth Amendment, 529
firearms (*See* guns)
First Amendment, 296, 297, 305, 308
First Charter of Virginia, 49
First Continental Congress, 301
First Federal Congress, 337
First Great Awakening, 130, 257–261, 304, 450
First Peoples (PBS), 602n1
First Reich, 238, 246
Five Nations of the Iroquois Confederacy (*See* Iroquois Indians)
Flathead Indians, 201, 383–385
Flores, Dan, 24, 174, 601n3
Florida, 40–41, 43–44, 99–100, 350
flu (*See* influenza)
food source destruction, 535–536, 582
Foote, Shelby, 488
Fort Laramie Treaty, 70, 385, 534, 536, 539
forts: Abraham Lincoln, 514, 534, 537–538, 539–540; Clatsop, 347; Cottonwood, 520; Hays, 520; Leavenworth, 519; McPherson, 520; Riley, 519, 520; Sill, 520; Wallace, 520
Fourteenth Amendment, 305, 470, 490, 495
Fox Indians, 360
France and French people, 43–47, 58–59, 61–62, 64–65, 67–68, 313–315, 335, 339–340
Franciscans, 43, 100, 104, 240, 365–366, 382
Franklin, Benjamin, 112, 260, 287–288, 308
free will, 236–237, 242, 249–250
French and Indian War, 59, 335

G

Galen, 85
Galileo, 249, 279–280
Garland, Hamlin, 436, 559, 578
Garnet, Henry Highland, 415–416
Gaustad, Edwin, xiv
General Allotment Act (*See* Allotment Act)
genes, archaic, 14–15
Geneva Convention, 591
genocide, 226, 439, 503, 584–585, 587–591, 591–595, 643n18 (*See also* ethnic cleansing; extermination)
geological epochs, 424
Geronimo, 405, 475, 514 (*See also* Apache Indians)

Ghost Dance, 151, 187–188, 567, 569, 571
Gibbon, John, 507, 508, 540, 541–542
Gliddon, George, 411, 412–413
Gnosticism, 228–229
Goes-ahead, 75–76
gold, 39, 389, 505, 506, 519, 536
Golden Rule, xxii, 136–137
Goodwin, Doris Kearns, 445
Gospels, 228–229, 234, 277, 295
  (*See also* Bible)
Grant, Ulysses S., xxiv, 496–498; assassination plan for, 490; background of, 459, 466; in Civil War, 460–461, 463–464, 466–469; Crook and, 513; Custer and, 491, 492, 494–495, 506–507, 525, 526–527, 529, 537–538; final years of, 508–509; Indians and, 255, 498–503, 510; in presidential election, 497; scandals surrounding, 503–504; on Sherman, 508
Great Britain: America and, 128, 367–368; imperialism of, 62, 410–411; Indians and, 324–325; in Revolutionary War, 307; Scientific Revolution in, 284; Treaty of Amiens and, 313; in various wars, 58–60; Western medicine and, 87–89, 112–113, 119 (*See also* British people)
Great Commission, 231, 258, 376, 385
Great Plains, xvii, xx, 23–24, 27–28, 68, 72, 108, 345, 388, 519–520
Great Sioux War, 514, 538–545
greed as virtue, 55, 230, 285, 338
Greenberg, Amy S., 364
Greene, Jerome A., 515, 542
Grinnell, George Bird, 181, 192–196, 200, 219 220, 570
Gros Ventre Indians, 67, 69, 72, 160, 170
guns, 45, 58, 67–68, 72, 321, 388–390

H
Habsburg Empire, 238
Hakluyt, Richard, the Younger, 48–49
Halleck, Henry W., 461, 463
Hamilton, Alexander, 271–272, 274, 623n57
Hammurabi, 19–20
Hancock, Winfield Scott, 521, 525–526, 534

Hancock Expedition, 520–521, 534
Harrison, William Henry, 309, 315, 344
Hart, Albert Bushnell, 433–434
Harvard University, 57, 256, 413–414
harvest ceremonies, 175
Harvey, William, 87–88
Hayes, Rutherford, 508, 568
heleocentrism, 279–280
Hemings, Sally, 297, 298, 309–310, 325–326, 328
Henry, Alexander, 76, 121, 188
Henry VIII, 48, 250, 253–254
herbalism, 91–95, 184
heredity versus environment, 578, 586
Hickok, Wild Bill, 521
Hidatsa Indians, 67, 69, 74–75, 105–107, 121
Hill, Thomas, 391
Hinduism, 132, 137
Hippocrates, 84–85, 115, 408
historians, role of, 599–600
Hixson, Walter L., 643n18
HLA (human leukocyte antigen) genes, 14–15
Hohokam culture, 25–26
holism, 277–278
Holmes, Champlain, 486–487
Holmes, Oliver Wendell, 89–90, 411, 413–414, 439
Holodny, Elena, 621n45
Holy Roman Empire, 238, 246
Homo erectus, 12–13
Homo sapiens, 9–10, 12–13, 14
Hopewell culture, 26
Hornaday, William T., 405–406
horses, xvii, 24, 29, 71–73, 170, 388, 491, 495
hubris, xxvii, 476, 545
Hudson River School, 394
Hudson's Bay Company, 67, 72, 368
humanism, 247, 283
humanities, 247, 286
humans, archaic, 9–10
Humboldt, Alexander von, 419–420
humors, 85, 86, 89–90
Hundred Years War, 242

Hunter, John, 89, 409
hunter-gatherers, xix, 9, 13, 14, 15, 73
hunting: by Indians, xx, 4–5, 20, 21, 23–24, 28–29, 67–72, 160, 170, 174–176, 193, 198–199, 214, 414, 539; by whites, xvii, 24, 194, 388–390, 414, 536
Huron Indians, 44–45
Hutchinson, Anne, 53–54
Hutton, Paul Andrew, 475, 512, 513, 514, 536
Huxley, Thomas Henry, 280, 421

I

idealism, 62, 286
ideologies, 19, 48, 364, 390, 392, 444, 519
Ignatius, of Loyola, 44, 240
illiteracy, 232
Immigration Act, 369–370
Indian agents, 60, 255, 344–345, 496, 497, 498, 499, 513, 568
Indian Bureau, 368, 496, 579
Indian Commission, 497–498
Indian Removal Act, 331, 345, 355–356
Indian Territory, 97, 379, 501, 520
Indian Trade and Intercourse Act, 60, 61, 311, 356
Indian Wars, xxv, 207, 403, 444, 488, 497–498, 513
Indians, xvii–xviii, xx, xxi, xxvi; American government and, 60–62, 309, 325, 336–338, 498–503; in art, 383–384, 393; attitudes toward, 317, 346, 449–450, 504–505; British settlers and, 47, 49, 50–52; Catlin on, 143–144; child-rearing by, 54–55; citizenship issues of, 490, 579–580; clans within tribes of, 157–158; Columbus's arrival, at time of, 27–30, 35–38; conversion of, to Christianity, 571–574; diseases and, 98–102, 116, 118–120, 122, 123; education (*See* Carlisle Indian School; education; off-reservation schools); Edwards among, 257; European explorers and settlers and, 41–46, 53–58, 64–66; Grinnell on, 194–200; Kennewick Man's meaning to, 3–6; land and, 156–157, 343–344; Linderman on, 200–208; in literature, 397–398; as Lost Tribes of Israel, 318–319; McClintock on, 147–149; medicine of, 80, 83–84, 91; Neihardt on, 149–152; population counts, 97, 507–508, 582–583; presidents on, 297, 298, 303, 421, 434–435, 436–437; PTSD among, 593–599; pushed westward, 315–316, 354–355, 368, 519–520; religion and spirituality of, 140–142, 152–156, 160–165, 173–176, 277; scientific racism used against, 409–410, 411–416; sharing nature of, 55, 76, 159–160, 229; as slaves, 39–41; smallpox and, 102–108, 110–111, 114; sports and, 576–577; statistics about, 582–584; time concept of, 158–159; values of, 73–77; Walker on, 144–147; whites and, 38–40, 57–58, 303, 323–325, 496 (*See also names of various tribes*)
individualism, 128, 133, 246, 265, 299, 304, 573
indulgences, 248
Industrial Age, 284, 290, 504
Industrial Revolution, 284–285, 289–290, 387–390
infectious diseases, xvii, xx–xxi; in animals, 24, 99–100; during Civil War, 462; in colonies, 50; dense populations causing, 21; gene pools and, 101; in Indians, 11–12, 33, 39, 56–57, 95, 99, 114, 303, 345, 533, 562–563; isolation preventing spread of, 84, 104, 110; lack of immunity for, 11, 101, 102, 108; non-scientific ideas about, 45, 56–57, 101–102, 104, 182, 242; in prehistoric times, 11–12; in slaves, 39–40, 102; statistics about, 95–98; venereal, 89 (*See also* Black Death; smallpox; tuberculosis)
influenza, 95, 100, 102, 562
Inka Indians, 29
Inquisition, 136, 280
Intercourse Act (*See* Trade and Intercourse Act)
Iroquois Indians, 28, 36, 44, 45, 60, 175
Isaac (biblical character), 135, 224

Ishmael (biblical character), 135, 224
Islam, 40, 130, 132, 134–136, 240
Israel, 225, 256, 318
Israel, new, 36, 256, 318–319, 392, 532–533

J

Jackson, Andrew: background of, 353; Indian removal policy of, 345, 354–355, 357–361; in military, 350; as president, 353–354; religion and, 374, 445; as slave owner, 354, 453; as smallpox victim, 107
Jacobs, Margaret D., 643n18
Jamestown, VA, 50, 52, 120
Jay, John, 623n57
Jefferson, Martha Wayles Skelton, 107, 300, 308
Jefferson, Thomas, xxii–xxiii; background of, 296, 299, 316; blacks and, 317; book collection of, 272; Corps of Discovery and, 81, 320, 334; Declaration of Independence and, 274, 301–303; as Deist, 261–262, 277, 298–299; Doctrine of Discovery and, 339–347; final years of, 327–328; grave of, 329; Hemings and, 309–310, 325–326; Humboldt and, 420; as idealist, 291–292; inaugural address, 342–343; Indians and, 303, 310–312, 317, 323, 336, 341–343, 345–346, 398, 552; influences on, 271–272, 282; interests of, 296–297; marriage and family of, 300, 308; non-political careers of, 300, 332; opinions about, 297–298; political career of, 300, 308, 310–312; religion and, 226, 234–235, 292–296, 298–299, 302, 304–305, 308, 326, 373, 386; during Revolutionary War, 307–308; as Secretary of State, 339; as segregationist, 307, 309, 321; slavery and, 300–301, 306–307, 309–310, 328; smallpox and, 113–114; spending habits of, 308; youth of, 300
Jefferson Bible, 292–296
Jenner, Edward, xxi, 81, 82–83, 112–113, 114
Jesuits, 44–45, 56, 89, 102, 104, 240, 376, 383–386

Jesus Christ: as apocalyptic Jew, 226–228; divinity of, 234–235; Great Commission of, 231; historical setting of, 225–226, 232–233; Indians and, 200, 567; in Jefferson's view, 293–294; in Paine's view, 305; as prophet, 135; in Puritan theology, 259; role of, in America, 262; salvation and, 230, 236; slavery, lack of teachings on, 454; teachings of, 137, 159, 187, 229–230; in Unitarians' view, 423
Jews: Christians and, 135, 226–227, 233; hatred toward, 32; Indians compared to, 318–319, 532–533; Muslims compared to, 135; Napoleon and, 314; in Nazi Germany, 593–594, 599–600; written word and, 223–225
Johnson, Andrew, 470, 490, 493–494, 495, 496–497, 521, 526, 529
Jolliet, Louis, 45–46
Joseph, Chief, 162, 164
Josephus, Flavius, 232, 233

K

Kelton, Paul, 97, 108
Kennewick Man, 3–6, 20
Kepler, Johannes, 279–280, 283
"kill the Indian to save the man" philosophy, xxvii, 98, 131, 557, 571, 582
Kiowa Indians, 154–155, 172, 176
Knox, Henry, 60, 271, 336
Koch, Robert, 83, 117
Ku Klux Klan, 529, 537

L

La Salle, Robert Cavelier, 33, 46, 72, 100
lactase persistence, 22
Lake Mohonk Conference, 551, 553
Lakota Indians: animals and, 23–24, 72; background of, 68, 69; medicine of, 182–183; Neihardt on, 151–152; in off-reservation schools, 558; Parkman on, 414; Sun Dance, 152, 169, 170–171; Walker on, 144–147 (*See also* Sioux Indians)
Lame Deer, John, 152–153, 172, 542

Larrabee, Charles, 513
Las Casas, Bartholomew, 41–42
"law of vices and virtues," 398
Léal, John L., 121, 611n68
Lee, Robert E., 445, 459–460, 462, 463, 464, 469, 487
Lemkin, Raphael, 587–591
Leonardo da Vinci, 86, 272–273
Lewis, C.S., 230, 231, 580
Lewis, Meriwether, xxiii; background of, 316, 320; claiming land, 333, 334, 340–341, 346–347; Clark and, 320; on Corps of Discovery expedition, 4–5, 81, 289, 312, 318, 319–320; death of, 323; Indians and, 318, 321–322, 346–347; Jefferson and, 310, 315, 317, 322–323; smallpox and, 105
Lewis and Clark Expedition (*See* Corps of Discovery)
life expectancy, 80–81
Lincoln, Abraham, xxiv, 601n1; Civil War and, 459–460, 461–465, 467–469, 474, 479; death of, 469–470, 490, 512; deserters and, 463; family of, 120, 456; Indians and, 515; Lincoln-Douglas debate, 456–457; McClellan and, 472, 473; as president, 448, 452, 453, 458–459; religion and, 137, 329–330, 453, 455, 456, 462; slavery question and, 456–458, 461–462; as smallpox victim, 107; Stowe and, 381–382
Linderman, Frank Bird, 75–76, 107, 140–141, 160, 200–203, 205–208
liquor (*See* alcohol)
Little Wound, 145, 169, 170–171
Locke, John, xxii, 272, 273, 274–275, 282, 284
Louisiana Territory: American purchase of, xxiii, 62, 289, 309, 314–315, 339–341; Corps of Discovery and, 320–321; Doctrine of Discovery and, 333, 339–341; Indians in, 346; slavery and statehood issues in, 309, 327; transfers of, among nations, 59, 61, 332; westward expansion and, 315–316
Loyola, Ignatious (*See* Ignatius, of Loyola)

Ludlow, William, 193
Luther, Martin, 48, 86, 248–250, 252, 253, 279
Lyell, Charles, 424

M

Madison, James, 238, 274, 292, 304, 305, 307, 311, 324, 623n57
Mails, Thomas E., xv
maize (*See* corn and maize)
Manchester, William, 248, 252, 601n1
Mandan Indians, xvii–xviii; ceremonies of, 172–173, 174; disease among, 71, 105–107, 121, 186; early history of, 70; as farmers, 70–71; legends of, 154; societies within tribe of, 74–75; tobacco and, 186; as traders, 28, 67, 70–71
Manifest Destiny, xviii, xxi, xxiii–xxiv, xxv; as art subject, 383–384, 391, 393–394; background of, 363–365; Civil War bolstering, 444, 473; Custer and, 542; Grant on, 502–503; Jefferson on, 357–359; in land annexations, 231, 242, 364–369; in Mexican-American relations, 366–367; in off-reservation education, 564; as predestination, 242, 349–350, 351, 355, 364, 367, 386; in racism, 33, 140, 413–414, 432; religion in, 130, 140, 226, 230, 267, 370, 377, 379–381, 435; slavery question and, 372, 452–453, 454–455; Winthrop on, 367–368
Mann, Charles, 108
Marquette, Jacques, 45–46
Marshall, John, 338, 361, 451
masculinity, 265–266, 576
mass production, 387, 389
Massachusetts Bay Company, 53, 54
Massacre of 1622, 51
massacres, xx, 434, 515, 544, 585 (*See also* Baker Massacre; Fetterman Massacre; Sand Creek Massacre; Wounded Knee Massacre)
Mather, Cotton, xxii, 55, 111–112, 246, 256, 318, 449–450
McClellan, George B., xxv, 405, 460, 462, 467, 471–474, 478–479

McClintock, Walter, 146–149, 184
Meacham, Jon, 268, 297, 456
measles, 122–123
medicine, Indian: bear medicine in, 180, 184; herbal, 91–95, 183–184; medicine bundles in, 171, 176–178, 182; Western medicine comparison, 80, 83–84, 110, 184 (*See also* medicine men)
medicine, Western, xix, xx; advances in, 90; of Corps of Discovery adviser, 317–318; disbursed to world, 89; early British, 87–91; early European, 85–87; early Greek, 84–85; racism justified by, 33, 407
Medicine Lodge Ceremony, 74
medicine men: bears and, 175; Black Elk, 151; buffalo jumps and, 29; European diseases and, 110, 596; knowledge of, 145, 181–184; in legends, 214–215, 219; methods of, 91; missionaries and, 186–187; role of, 180–181; shamans and, 83–84, 180–181; Sitting Bull, 543
Methodists: appeal of the West to, 376, 379–380; blacks and, 265; Custer and, 445–446; as evangelicals, 264, 374; history of, 255, 258, 259–260, 263; slavery question and, 455
Mexico, 365–367
Michel de Nostredame (*See* Nostradamus)
Middle Ages, xviii; Copernicus's beliefs and, 279; Crusades during, 136; Jews during, 32, 224; life during, 158, 238, 239–240, 246; medicine during, 85; Plato's influence during, 222, 246; religion during, 238–239, 241, 243, 250; universities as product of, 247
migrations, xix–xx; from Africa, 12–13, 39; within Africa, 9–10; to America, 51–52, 319; within America, 28, 66, 69–70, 311, 519; animal, 18, 22, 71, 100; over Bering Land Bridge, 5–6, 17–18, 20–21; Eurasian, 12; from Europe, 368–369, 385
Miles, Nelson A., 514, 529, 541–542, 544
Miller, Robert J., 332, 337, 339–340
"The Miracle in Front of You" (Schuster) *The Sun,* 620n79

miscegenation, 15, 310, 410, 452
missionaries: Catholic, 379–380, 382–386; intent of, 376–377; Protestant, 378–381; on reservations, 386
Mississippian Period and culture, 26–27, 116
Missouri Compromise, 327
Mohammed, 134–135, 137
monogenism, 408
monotheism, 132, 234
Monroe, James, 307, 315, 327, 351–352, 378, 451
Monroe Doctrine, 352
morality and profit-making, 452
Moran, Thomas, 394, 395–396
Morgan, Thomas J., 550, 552
Morning Star (Cheyenne chief) (*See* Dull Knife)
Morning-Star (god), 152, 216–218
Morton, Samuel George, 411
Moses (biblical character), 135, 223
Muir, John, 266
Muskogean culture, 28
mutations, 10, 15, 22, 25, 103, 426
myths and legends, 36, 66, 155, 191–192, 219 (*See also* under various Indian tribes)

N

Nabokov, Peter, 361, 512
narcissism, 475–477
nationalism, 128–129, 454, 488
Native Americans (*See* Indians)
natural selection, 5, 421, 422, 424–425, 425–431
Navajo Indians, 28, 71, 155, 569, 578
Nazism, xviii, xx, 406–407, 439, 487–488, 584, 592–593
Neanderthals, 10–12, 13, 14, 421
Neihardt, John G., 151–152
Neoclassicism, 392–393
Neolithic Revolution (*See* Agricultural Revolution)
New Orleans, LA, 46, 62, 314–315
New Testament, 227, 228–229, 235, 247, 261–262, 292–296 (*See also* Bible; Old Testament)
New York Botanical Garden, 92

New York Zoological Society, 402, 404
Newton, Isaac, xxii, 272, 273, 275, 282–284, 621n45
Nicene Creed, 236, 254
Nichols, Roger L., xiv
Noble Savage concept, 41, 169, 287–289, 317, 319, 397–398
North and Northern attitudes, xxv, 444, 450–451, 455, 457–458, 471, 473, 490, 493
Northwest Indian War, 320
Northwest Ordinance, 61, 308–309, 337
Northwest Territory, 61, 332
Nostradamus, 87
Nott, Josiah Clark, 411, 412–413
Nuremberg Trials, 587–588

O

off-reservation schools: ethnic cleansing at, 554–558; failure of, 73, 586; food at, 562; graduates of, 566–568; illness in, 562–563; intent of, 550–552, 565–566; parents' dislike of, 558; punishment in, 561–562; as segregated from whites, 557; subjects in, 563, 564–565 (*See also* Carlisle Indian School)
Oglala Indians (*See* Lakota Indians)
Ojibwe Indians (*See* Chippewa Indians)
Okipa ceremony, 70, 172–173
Old Testament, 137, 224, 231, 423, 517 (*See also* Bible; New Testament)
Olson, Roger E., 236, 241, 253, 258, 273
Olympics, 548–549
Omaha Indians, 106, 163, 174
Omo 1 (skeleton), 9
oral traditions, 36, 74, 85, 141, 155, 165, 180, 191–192, 232
Ordinance of 1784, 309
Oregon country, 339, 367–368
Oregon Trail, 118, 366, 414, 519
Ottoman Empire, 135, 251

P

Pacific Northwest, 25, 33, 333, 334
paganism, 222–223, 232–233, 235, 239
Paine, Thomas, 276, 305, 373, 456

Paleo-Indians, xix, 18, 20
pandemics, 95, 118, 123–124, 238
Pan-Indianism, 32, 557
Paracelsus, 85–87
Parkman, Francis, 404, 414, 438
Pasteur, Louis, 83, 113
patriotism, 306, 550
Paul, the Apostle, 229, 230, 234, 241, 454
Pawnee Indians, 28, 67, 70, 72, 106, 118, 181, 189, 193, 352
Pawnee Killer, 522–523
Paxson, Edgar, 383–384
Peace of Augsburg, 251
Peace of Paris, 59
peace policy (Quaker) (*See* Quaker policy)
Pearcey, Nancy, 259, 281
Pelagius, 237
penicillin, 83, 124
Penn, William, 254–255, 318–319
Pennsylvania, 255
"Peopling Of The Americas: Eva de Naharon, A 13,600 Year Old Skeleton Found Near Tulum, Mexico" (Anthropology.net), 602n1
pertussis, 71, 121–122
petroglyphs, 141–142, 159
Philadelphia, PA, 255, 573
philosophy, 274, 275, 392–393
photography, 394–395, 474, 475
physicians, xx, 80, 81, 84–91, 106, 112, 117
pictographs, 141–142
Piegan Indians, 67, 106, 207, 216–218, 515–516
Pilgrims, 31–32, 52–58
pioneers, 60, 321, 375–376, 437
pipes, smoking, 151–152, 176, 188, 189, 204, 212–214
Pitt, William, 58, 89
placebo effect, 87, 89, 183
Plains Indian Wars, 90
Plains Indians, 65–66, 66–71, 71–73, 76, 143
Plato, 222–223, 239, 278
Pleistocene epoch, 6, 18, 424
Plenty Coups, 140, 160, 176–177, 207–208
Plenty Kill (*See* Standing Bear, Luther)

Pliny the Younger, 232–233
pluralism, 128, 386, 413
Plymouth, MA, 52–53, 104
Pocahontas, 51
Poe, Edgar Allan, 397
Polk, James, 118, 366
polygenism, 12, 408, 409–410, 411, 428, 430–431
Ponce de León, Juan, 39, 40–41, 44
Pontiac's Rebellion, 59–60, 110–111
Portugal, 34, 39, 335, 367
post-traumatic stress disorder, 593–594
Powhatan Confederacy, 36, 51
Pratt, Richard Henry, xxvii, 219–220, 515, 554–557, 561, 566, 568, 571, 574–575, 578, 579, 586
predestination, xxiv; in Calvinism, 252–253; free will and, 236–237, 239, 249–250; in Indian question, 500, 584; in Jefferson's view, 293, 341; Manifest Destiny and, 242, 349–350, 351, 355, 364, 367, 386; as slavery justification, 452
Presbyterians, 51–52, 255–256, 281–282
Pretty-Shield (Crow woman), 75–76, 107
Priestley, Joseph, 293
priests, Indian (*See* shamans and shamanism)
private ownership, 568
profit-making and morality, 452
Protestantism, 249–250, 276, 379–380
Prothero, Stephen, 296, 297
psychopaths, 592
PTSD, 593–594
Pueblo Revolt, 72
Puebloans, 26, 28
Puritans, 48, 51–52, 256–257, 259, 285, 386
pygmies, 401–402, 403

Q

quackery, 90
Quaker policy, 385, 498–499, 505, 510
Quakers, 57, 254–255, 292, 361, 450, 498–499, 566
Qur'an, 134–135

R

"race educators," 514–515
racism, xviii, xxiv, xxvii; factors in, 15, 79–80, 124; Jefferson and, 297 on; justifications for, 32, 140; Manifest Destiny and, 231, 473; narcissism indicating, 475; physical attributes as factor, 408; religion bolstering, 130; at St. Louis World's Fair, 402–403
racism, scientific (*See* scientific racism)
Radical Reformation, 254–255
radiocarbon dating, 4, 6–7
railways, 387–388, 396, 504, 519
Raleigh, Sir Walter, 48–49
Realism, 281, 288, 350, 396
Reconstruction, 495, 497, 500, 504, 521, 526
Red Cloud, 68, 146–147, 495–496, 497, 501, 506, 514, 517, 542
religion, xviii–xix, xix, xxi; beginnings of, 131; Darwin and, 429–430; Doctrine of Discovery and, 337–338; Jefferson and, 296; as justification, 19, 32, 104, 124, 130–131, 139–140, 142; mixed consequences of, 130, 132, 136, 268; PTSD and, 596; on reservations, 386; science and, 564; technology and, 249; West and, 373–375; world-wide, 132–136 (*See also* Christianity)
Removal Act (*See* Indian Removal Act)
Renaissance, 88, 246–247, 303–304
Reno, Marcus, xxvi, 540
Requerimiento, 42
reservations, xxiv, 290, 369, 370, 386, 396, 498–499, 501, 513, 542, 570
Revolutionary War, 60–62, 300 (*See also* American Revolution)
Rhodes, Elisha, 464, 467
Ridley, Matt, 586
risk and gamble, 518–519
Rocky Boy Indians, 200–201
Rolfe, John, 50, 51
Roman Empire, 235–238
Romans, 85, 225
Romanticism, xxiv; in art, 391–396; in literature, 397–399; in Manifest Destiny, 363; science and, 286–290
Ronda, James, 341, 343

Roosevelt, Franklin Delano, 5, 127
Roosevelt, Theodore, xxv, 145, 147, 266, 298, 406–407, 413–414, 421–422, 432–438, 570–571
Round Dance, 187
Rousseau, Jean-Jacques, 41, 286–287, 289
Rubenstein, Harry R., xv
Rush, Benjamin, 114, 293, 307, 317–318, 319–320, 409
Russell, Charles M., 143, 200–201, 396

S
Sacajawea, 322
Salish Indians, 201, 383–385
Sand Creek Massacre, 162, 515–516, 521
Santa Anna, General, 365, 366
scandals, 503–504, 537–538, 548–549
Schmidt, Leigh, xiv
Schultz, James Willard, 194
Schuster, Janice Lynch, 620n79
scientific racism, xix, xx, xxiv, xxv; Benga and, 401–407; Civil War bolstering, 444; Custer and, 542; Darwin and, 428, 438–439; degeneration theory and, 247; Indians and, 578; polygenism and, 12; slavery and, 454; Western medicine bolstering, 80
Scientific Revolution, xx; Christianity compatible with, 278, 281–282, 283–284; Industrial Revolution and, 284–285; literature and humanities and, 280–281; self-interest in, 285; significance of, 9; Western medicine and, 80
Seattle, Chief, 156–157, 163
Second Great Awakening, xxiii, 130, 259, 261–263, 363, 372, 374, 380, 392
segregationist ideas, 307, 557
Seminole Indians, 350, 354, 357
Senkewicz, Robert M., 382–383
Serra, Junípero, 382–383
Seven Days Battles, 473
7th Cavalry, 506–507, 539–540
"The Severed Heads Campaign," 512–515
Seward, William, 490, 494
shamans and shamanism: in ceremonies, 169–171; Jesuits and, 102; petroglyphs created by, 141–142; role of, 26, 83–84, 91, 146, 180–181, 183–187; shamanism as religious form, 134; smallpox ruining, 110; in whites' view, 54
Sheridan, Phil, xxv; Custer and, 445, 482, 487, 491, 492, 526–527, 528–529, 538; Indians and, 289, 505–506, 536; in Johnson administration, 521; in wars, 466, 468, 537–538
Sherman, William Tecumseh, xxv; blacks and, 465, 468; Custer and, 468, 506, 522, 523, 526, 538, 540; Grant and, 460–461, 463, 466, 467; Indians and, 496–497, 500–501, 521, 523; memoirs of, 508–509; in wars, 460–461, 466, 467–469, 538; Westward expansion and, 536
Shoshone Indians, 69, 322
signing table incident, 445, 487
Sioux Indians: Black Hills and, 536; Clark on, 321; Custer and, 522–523; in Great Sioux War, 539–542; legends of, 176; medicine of, 184; as Plains Indians, 28; relationships with other tribes, 68–69; Teton Sioux, 322; treaties and, 517, 534; whites and, 505–506 (*See also* Lakota Indians)
Sitting Bull: death of, 569; Jesuits and, 385; as medicine man, 181; as smallpox victim, 107; Sun Dance vision of, 539; in wars, 68, 540, 542; whites and, 506, 537; writings on, 73, 543–544
slavery: beginnings of, 39, 40; Christianity and, 240, 449–451, 453–454, 455–456; Custer and, 446–447; disease and, 102; economics of, 452, 453, 454; of Indians, 58; Jefferson and, 292, 300, 306–307, 312, 328; John Quincy Adams and, 350–351; justifications for, 412, 415, 452–455; legality of, 451–452; Locke and, 275; Muslims and, 135; Newton and, 284; pre-Columbian, 40; statehood issues and, 309, 327; Washington and, 306 (*See also* blacks)
smallpox, xvii–xviii, xx–xxi, xxvii, 102–103; Cherokee Indians and, 97, 113–114;

children and, 105; Chippewa Indians and, 145; conversion encouraged by, 110; Cree Indians and, 67; description of, 108–110; Edwards dying from, 257–258; epidemics and outbreaks, 105, 106, 112, 114; Indians and, 57, 59, 95, 100–101, 105–108, 345, 533; in legends, 216–218; Mandan Indians and, 71, 186; mortality rates of, 96; non-medical outcomes of, 39, 45, 101, 110–111; in North American colonies, 104; Pratt and, 556; suicides following, 598–599; transmittal to New World, 103–104; treatments for, 81–83, 85, 106–107, 110–115
Smet, Jeane-Pierre De, 383–385
Smith, Barbara Clark, xv
Smith, Captain John, 50, 51
Smithsonian Institution, 366, 412
Snow, John, 119
social Darwinism, xix, xxiv–xxv; Christianity justifying, 224, 230; Civil War bolstering, 444; Custer and, 518, 542; eugenics and, 406–407; genocide and, 593; Grinnell's opposition to, 200; Indians, effect on, 33, 169, 266, 290, 370; industrial capitalism and, 285; T. Roosevelt believing in, 421, 435–437
societies, within tribes, 74–75, 157, 188
Society of Friends (*See* Quakers)
Society of Jesus (*See* Jesuits)
Soto, Hernando de, 33, 39, 41, 99–100
South and Southern attitudes, 451, 452–454, 488–489, 529
Spain and Spaniards, 34, 38–39, 41–43, 61, 82–83, 335, 350
spontaneous generation, 407–408, 431
sports, 76, 574–576
Spotted Tail, Chief, 163–164, 502, 506, 542
squatters sovereignty, 332, 353
St. Louis World's Fair, 402–403
Standing Bear, Luther, 161, 180, 558, 560–561, 563, 564
Standing Soldier, Mary, 157–158
Stanton, Edwin, 463, 468, 495, 496, 526
Stark, Rodney, 41, 62, 237, 247, 584–585
steam power, 387

sterilization, involuntary, 407, 439
Stiles, T.J., 445, 475, 476–477, 478, 479, 480, 488, 528–529, 530, 585–586
storytelling, 173–176
Stowe, Harriet Beecher, 381–382, 455–456, 556
suicide, 104, 598–599
Sun Dance, xxi, 75, 144, 147, 152, 168–173, 190, 218, 539, 542, 557
Sun Pole, 171–172
Sunrise (legendary person), 213
survival of the fittest, 421, 426, 428–429, 575
Swaan, Abram de, 591–592, 593–594
sweat lodges, 179, 182–183, 216–218
Sword, George, 144–145, 184–185, 189
syphilis, 83, 87, 102, 103, 123–124

T

tabula rasa, xiv, xxvii, 416
Tacitus, 232–233
Taleb, Nassim Nicholas, 124, 136
Taoism, 137
Tecumseh, 310, 324
Ten Lost Tribes of Israel, 318–319, 532–533
Terry, Alfred Howe, 506–507, 538, 540, 541–542
Texas, 263–264, 350, 364, 365, 366, 491–492
Third Great Schism, 248–249
Thirteenth Amendment, 469, 490
Thomson, Keith, xv
Thorpe, Jim, 547–550, 574, 577
time, evolutionary, 7–8
time concepts, 158–159
Tindal, Matthew, 275–276
tinkering, 390
tobacco, 26, 50, 188–190
Tocqueville, Alexis de, 128, 264, 267, 353, 372, 415
Torah, 223–224
Trade and Intercourse Act, 60, 61, 311, 356
trading: among Indians, 26, 28, 35, 66–67, 72; between whites and Indians, 33, 44–45, 58–59, 67–68, 321–322, 346, 496

trading posts, 46, 311, 336, 344, 503
Trail of Tears, 40, 361
transcendentalist writers, 399
Transcontinental Treaty, 350
transformation, cultural, 56, 62
transgenerational trauma, 597
transmutation, 424–425
travois, 24, 68, 72
treaties: 1797, with Tripoli, 262; Amiens, 313; Dancing Rabbit Creek, 356–357; Doctrine of Discovery and, 336, 339; establishing boundaries, 60; Fort Laramie Treaty, 70, 385, 534, 536, 539; Guadalupe Hidalgo, 366–367; Indians and, 309, 323, 360–362, 497, 500; Louisiana Territory and, 314–315, 340; New Echota, 361; Paris, 60; Sioux Treaty, 517; T. Roosevelt on, 436–437; Tordesillas, 39; Transcontinental Treaty, 350; Utrecht, 59; Westphalia, 251
Trinity (Christian), 234–235, 236, 277, 293
tuberculosis, 83, 95, 101–102, 110, 115–117, 145, 562–563
Turner, Frederick Jackson, 80, 573
Turner, Joseph Mallord William, 394
Twain, Mark, 504–505, 508–510, 530
Twiss, Richard, 139–140
typhoid fever, 120–121
typhus, 119–120

U

Underground Railroad, 455
uniformitarianism, 431
Unitarians, 259, 277, 295, 326, 422–423
United Nations, 114, 589–590
U.S. Supreme Court, 262, 361, 451–452
Ute Indians, 28, 71–72
Utley, Robert, 73, 76–77, 178–179, 181, 540–541

V

vaccinations, 81, 105–107, 111–115, 122
variola (See smallpox)
variolization, 111–112, 113, 257–258
Verner, Samuel P., 402–404, 405, 406
Vespucci, Amerigo, 37–38
Vietnam War, 129, 536
virgin soil epidemic, 102, 108
Virginia and Virginians, 49–51, 300, 303, 304–305
Virginia Statute for Religious Freedom, 304
viruses, 124
visions and vision quests (See dreams)
vitamin D, 22
Voltaire, 81, 273, 274, 281, 408–409

W

Wakan Tanka, 73, 146, 147, 154, 161, 178, 185, 539
Walker, James R., 144–147, 168–169, 183
war crimes, 590–591
War Eagle (literary character), 201
War of 1812, 323–325
War of Independence (See Revolutionary War)
Ward, Geoffrey, 445
Warner, Glenn Scobey "Pop," 547, 574, 576, 577
Washington, George, 101, 107, 271–272, 275, 305–306, 316, 336
Washington, Martha, 306
Washita Massacre, 516, 527–528
Wesley, John, 258, 259–260
West (American) and Western attitudes: Christianity in, 263–268, 373–376; Custer representing, 488, 530; Eastern attitudes compared to, 504, 512, 573; Jefferson as father of, 289, 312; missionaries in, 376–386; Romantic art in, 390–396; Romantic literature in, 397–399; romanticized in magazines, 530; T. Roosevelt representing, 421, 432; technology in, 388–390; West as America's Eden, 324, 347, 372, 573–574
West Point, 310, 380–381, 446–448
Whipple, Henry, 515, 555
White Calf, 147
Whitefield, George, 258, 259–260, 261, 450
whites: conflicts with other whites, 58–60; as disease carriers, 116; Indians and, xviii, xx, 36, 38–40, 57–58, 69–70, 303; land, attitude toward, 76; as settlers, 435; white superiority belief and, 52, 407, 431

Whittredge, Worthington, 394
whooping cough, 71, 121–122
Wichita Indians, 28
Wiesenthal, Simon, 599–600
wilderness, xxvi, 518
Willerslev, Eske, 5, 6, 14
Williams, Roger, 55, 246–247
Wilson, Jack (*See* Wovoka)
Wind Demon, 210–211
Winthrop, John, 53–54, 55, 104, 332–333, 377–378
Wissler, Clark, 168–169
Witherspoon, John, 256, 373
Woodley, Randy S., 182
World Health Organization, 115, 117, 123, 124
World's Columbian Exposition, 572–573
Wounded Knee Massacre, xx, 39, 151, 187, 515, 571
Wovoka, 187–188

Y
Yellowstone region, 193, 396, 501
Yosemite region, 391, 396

Z
Zwingli, Ulrich, 251–252

 Dr. Peterson is the recipient of the 2016 C. M. Russell Heritage Award, which recognizes significant contributions in interpreting and documenting the legacy, culture, life, and country of Charles M. Russell's West. He is an award winning scientist, physician, cultural historian, and author. Above all, he is a searcher. Peterson grew up in Plentywood on the Great Plains of northeastern Montana north of Fort Union and next to the Fort Peck Indian Reservation.

He graduated from the Oregon Health and Sciences University (OHSU) in Portland and completed an internal medicine internship, a residency in the visual field of dermatology, and a NIH research fellowship. He has published in numerous scientific and medical periodicals, including the prestigious *The Proceedings of the National Academy of Sciences, Molecular and Cellular Biology*, and *The Journal of Clinical Investigation*. Peterson is the recipient of The Henry W. Stelwagon Award (College of Physicians of Philadelphia) and The Sommers Research Award (OHSU) for outstanding scientific research, among many others.

His distinguished biographies include *Philip R. Goodwin: America's Sporting and Wildlife Artist; The Call of the Mountains: The Artists of Glacier National Park; L. A. Huffman: Photographer of the American West; Charles M. Russell: Photographing the Legend, A Biography in Words and Pictures;* and *John Fery: Artist of Glacier National Park & The American West*. He is a member of the Western Writers of America, Western History Association, and Little Big Horn Associates.

He is the recipient of two Western Heritage Awards, the Scriver Award, The High Plains Book Award, and the Will Rogers Gold Medallion Award. Stuart Rosebrook, in *True West* magazine, selected Dr. Peterson and his *Charles M. Russell: Photographing the Legend, A Biography in Words and Pictures* in his top five authors and books for 2014 and the best photographic and graphic art book.

Dr. Peterson lives with his wife, LeAnne; two Vizsla dogs, Beau and Abby; and two horses, Big Sky and Sunny, on their Spirit of Winter Ranch near Sisters, Oregon, in the shadow of the Three Sisters Mountains—Faith, Hope, and Charity. The aroma of sweetgrass makes him homesick.